Treasures

A Reading/Language Arts Program

Macmillan/McGraw-Hill

Contributors

Time Magazine, The Writers' Express, Accelerated Reader

TIME
FOR KIDS

The Writers' Express
Immediate Impact. Lasting Transformation.   wex.org

RFB&D
learning through listening

Accelerated
Reader

Students with print disabilities may be eligible to obtain an accessible, audio version of the pupil edition of this textbook. Please call Recording for the Blind & Dyslexic at 1-800-221-4792 for complete information.

B

The McGraw-Hill Companies

 **Macmillan/McGraw-Hill**

Published by Macmillan/McGraw-Hill, of McGraw-Hill Education, a division of The McGraw-Hill Companies, Inc., Two Penn Plaza, New York, New York 10121.

Printed in the United States of America

3 4 5 6 7 8 9 10 WEB 15 14 13 12 11

Treasures

A Reading/Language Arts Program

Program Authors

Dr. Diane August
Senior Research Scientist, Center for
   Applied Linguistics
Washington, D.C.

Dr. Donald R. Bear
University of Nevada, Reno
Reno, Nevada

Dr. Janice A. Dole
University of Utah
Salt Lake City, Utah

Dr. Jana Echevarria
California State University, Long Beach
Long Beach, California

Dr. Douglas Fisher
San Diego State University
San Diego, California

Dr. David J. Francis
University of Houston
Houston, Texas

Dr. Vicki L. Gibson
Educational Consultant, Gibson Hasbrouck
   and Associates, Massachusetts

Dr. Jan E. Hasbrouck
Educational Consultant – J.H. Consulting
Los Angeles, California

Dr. Scott G. Paris
Center for Research and Practice,
National Institute of Education
Singapore

Dr. Timothy Shanahan
University of Illinois at Chicago
Chicago, Illinois

Dr. Josefina V. Tinajero
University of Texas at El Paso
El Paso, Texas

 Macmillan/McGraw-Hill

Program Authors

Dr. Diane August

Center for Applied Linguistics, Washington, D.C.

- Principal Investigator, Developing Literacy in Second-Language Learners: Report of the National Literacy Panel on Language-Minority Children and Youth
- Member of the New Standards Literacy Project, Grades 4–5

Dr. Donald R. Bear

University of Nevada, Reno

- Author of *Words Their Way* and *Words Their Way with English Learners*
- Director, E.L. Cord Foundation Center for Learning and Literacy

Dr. Janice A. Dole

University of Utah

- Investigator, IES Study on Reading Interventions
- National Academy of Sciences, Committee Member: Teacher Preparation Programs, 2005–2007

Dr. Jana Echevarria

California State University, Long Beach

- Author of *Making Content Comprehensible for English Learners: The SIOP Model*
- Principal Researcher, Center for Research on the Educational Achievement and Teaching of English Language Learners

Dr. Douglas Fisher

San Diego State University

- Co-Director, Center for the Advancement of Reading, California State University
- Author of *Language Arts Workshop: Purposeful Reading and Writing Instruction* and *Reading for Information in Elementary School*

Dr. David J. Francis

University of Houston

- Director of the Center for Research on Educational Achievement and Teaching of English Language Learners (CREATE)
- Director, Texas Institute for Measurement, Evaluation, and Statistics

Dr. Vicki Gibson

Educational Consultant Gibson Hasbrouck and Associates, Massachusetts

- Author of *Differentiated Instruction: Grouping for Success*

Dr. Jan E. Hasbrouck

Educational Consultant JH Consulting, Los Angeles

- Developed Oral Reading Fluency Norms for Grades 1–8
- Author of *The Reading Coach: A How-to Manual for Success*

Dr. Scott G. Paris

Center for Research and Practice, National Institute of Education, Singapore

- Principal Investigator, CIERA, 1997–2004

Dr. Timothy Shanahan

University of Illinois at Chicago

- Member, National Reading Panel
- President, International Reading Association, 2006
- Chair, National Literacy Panel and National Early Literacy Panel

Dr. Josefina V. Tinajero

University of Texas at El Paso

- Past President, NABE and TABE
- Co-Editor of *Teaching All the Children: Strategies for Developing Literacy in an Urban Setting* and *Literacy Assessment of Second Language Learners*

Consulting and Contributing Authors

Dr. Adria F. Klein
Professor Emeritus,
California State University,
San Bernardino

• President, California
  Reading Association, 1995
• Co-Author of *Interactive
  Writing* and *Interactive
  Editing*

Dolores B. Malcolm
St. Louis Public Schools
St. Louis, MO

• Past President, International
  Reading Association
• Member, IRA Urban
  Diversity Initiatives
  Commission
• Member, RIF Advisory
  Board

Dr. Doris Walker-Dalhouse
Minnesota State University,
Moorhead

• Author of articles on
  multicultural literature and
  reading instruction in urban
  schools
• Co-Chair of the Ethnicity, Race,
  and Multilingualism Committee,
  NRC

Dinah Zike
Educational Consultant

• Dinah-Might Activities, Inc.
  San Antonio, TX

Program Consultants

Kathy R. Bumgardner
Language Arts Instructional
Specialist
Gaston County Schools, NC

Elizabeth Jimenez
CEO, GEMAS Consulting
Pomona, CA

Dr. Sharon F. O'Neal
Associate Professor
College of Education
Texas State University
San Marcos, TX

Program Reviewers

Mable Alfred
Reading/Language Arts Administrator
Chicago Public Schools, IL

Suzie Bean
Teacher, Kindergarten
Mary W. French Academy
Decatur, IL

Linda Burch
Teacher, Kindergarten
Public School 184
Brooklyn, NY

Robert J. Dandorph
Principal
John F. Kennedy Elementary School
North Bergen, NJ

Suzanne Delacruz
Principal, Washington Elementary
Evanston, IL

Carol Dockery
Teacher, Grade 3
Mulberry Elementary
Milford, OH

Karryl Ellis
Teacher, Grade 1
Durfee School, Decatur, IL

Christina Fong
Teacher, Grade 3
William Moore Elementary School
Las Vegas, NV

Lenore Furman
Teacher, Kindergarten
Abington Avenue School
Newark, NJ

Sister Miriam Kaeser
Assistant Superintendent
Archdiocese of Cincinnati
Cincinnati, OH

LaVonne Lee
Principal, Rozet Elementary School
Gillette, WY

SuEllen Mackey
Teacher, Grade 5
Washington Elementary School
Decatur, IL

Jan Mayes
Curriculum Coordinator
Kent School District
Kent, WA

Bonnie Nelson
Teacher, Grade 1
Solano School, Phoenix, AZ

Cyndi Nichols
Teacher, Grade K/1
North Ridge Elementary School
Commack, NY

Sharron Norman
Curriculum Director
Lansing School District
Lansing, MI

Renee Ottinger
Literacy Leader, Grades K–5
Coronado Hills Elementary School
Denver, CO

Michael Pragman
Principal, Woodland Elementary School
Lee's Summit, MO

Carol Rose
Teacher, Grade 2
Churchill Elementary School
Muskegon, MI

Laura R. Schmidt-Watson
Director of Academic Services
Parma City School District, OH

Dianne L. Skoy
Literacy Coordinator, Grades K–5
Minneapolis Public Schools
Minneapolis, MN

Charles Staszewski
ESL Teacher, Grades 3–5
John H. William School, No. 5
Rochester, NY

Patricia Synan
New York City Department
of Education

Stephanie Yearian
Teacher, Grade 2
W. J. Zahnow Elementary
Waterloo, IL

Unit 2   The Big Question

How do people make a difference in their communities?

Enduring Understanding and Essential Questions

In this unit, students will listen, read, and write about how people can make a difference in their communities. They will also develop and apply key comprehension skills that good readers use as they read.

Big Idea	Enduring Understanding	Essential Questions
Theme: Making a Difference	Communities or large neighborhoods are shaped by the people living in them.	How do people make a difference in their communities?

Comprehension	Enduring Understanding	Essential Questions
Author's Purpose Week 1 Week 2	Good readers use the literary language and devices an author uses to determine the author's purpose for writing.	How can recognizing literary language and devices help you determine why the author wrote this selection?
Main Idea and Details Week 3	Good readers think about what the sentences in a passage have in common to determine the main idea and maintain meaning.	What do all of the important details in this selection have in common?
Cause and Effect Week 4	Good readers describe the explicit and implicit relationships in texts that use cause and effect as a text structure.	How can recognizing cause and effect as a text structure help you to describe the relationships between ideas in this text?
Sequence Week 5	Good readers place the main events of a plot in sequence and explain their influence on future events.	How can placing the main events of this story in sequence help you to determine future events?

Theme: Making a Difference

Planning the Unit

Unit Opener

Using the Student Book

Main Selections

Wrapping Up the Unit

How-to Article

Additional Resources

Unit Assessment

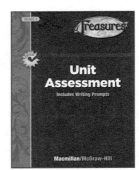

Unit 2 Contents

Unit 2 Planner

Theme Opener, pp xvi–134/135

pp. 140–153

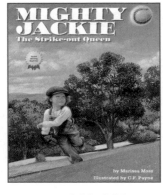

pp. 166–181

	WEEK 1	WEEK 2
ORAL LANGUAGE		
• **Listening Comprehension**	**Theme** Civil Rights	**Theme** Inspiring Women
• **Speaking/Viewing**	**Build Background**	**Build Background**
WORD STUDY		
• **Vocabulary**	✔ **Vocabulary** *unfair, ancestors, numerous, segregation, avoided, injustice* Word Parts: Prefixes and Suffixes	✔ **Vocabulary** *legendary, muttered, gaped, snickering, insult, flinched* Context Clues: Description
• **Phonics/Word Study**	✔ **Phonics** Prefixes	✔ **Phonics** Digraphs
• **Spelling**	✔ **Spelling** Prefixes	✔ **Spelling** Digraphs
READING		
• **Comprehension**	✔ **Comprehension** **Strategy:** Monitor Comprehension **Skill:** Author's Purpose	✔ **Comprehension** **Strategy:** Monitor Comprehension **Skill:** Author's Purpose
• **Fluency**	✔ **Fluency** Repeated Reading: Intonation/Expression	✔ **Fluency** Repeated Reading: Intonation/Expression
• **Leveled Readers**	**Approaching** *Harriet Tubman* **On Level** *Coretta Scott King* **Beyond** *Fighting for Rights* **ELL** *Coretta Scott King*	**Approaching** *Wilma Rudolph* **On Level** *Determined to Win* **Beyond** *Jackie Robinson* **ELL** *Champion Athlete*
LANGUAGE ARTS		
• **Writing**	✔ **Writing** Trait: Ideas	✔ **Writing** Trait: Word Choice
• **Grammar**	✔ **Grammar** Common and Proper Nouns	✔ **Grammar** Singular and Plural Nouns

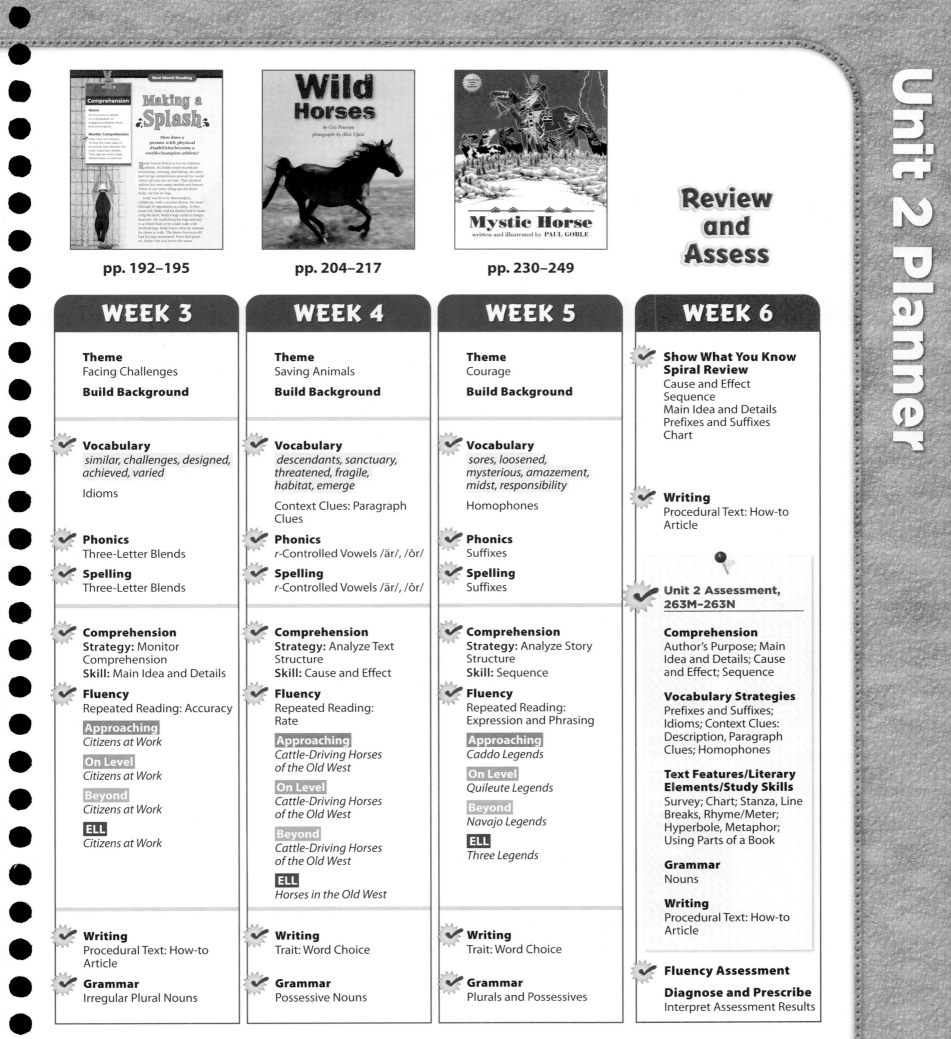

pp. 192–195   pp. 204–217   pp. 230–249

Review and Assess

WEEK 3

Theme
Facing Challenges

Build Background

Vocabulary
similar, challenges, designed, achieved, varied

Idioms

Phonics
Three-Letter Blends

Spelling
Three-Letter Blends

Comprehension
Strategy: Monitor Comprehension
Skill: Main Idea and Details

Fluency
Repeated Reading: Accuracy

Approaching
Citizens at Work

On Level
Citizens at Work

Beyond
Citizens at Work

ELL
Citizens at Work

Writing
Procedural Text: How-to Article

Grammar
Irregular Plural Nouns

WEEK 4

Theme
Saving Animals

Build Background

Vocabulary
descendants, sanctuary, threatened, fragile, habitat, emerge

Context Clues: Paragraph Clues

Phonics
r-Controlled Vowels /är/, /ôr/

Spelling
r-Controlled Vowels /är/, /ôr/

Comprehension
Strategy: Analyze Text Structure
Skill: Cause and Effect

Fluency
Repeated Reading: Rate

Approaching
Cattle-Driving Horses of the Old West

On Level
Cattle-Driving Horses of the Old West

Beyond
Cattle-Driving Horses of the Old West

ELL
Horses in the Old West

Writing
Trait: Word Choice

Grammar
Possessive Nouns

WEEK 5

Theme
Courage

Build Background

Vocabulary
sores, loosened, mysterious, amazement, midst, responsibility

Homophones

Phonics
Suffixes

Spelling
Suffixes

Comprehension
Strategy: Analyze Story Structure
Skill: Sequence

Fluency
Repeated Reading: Expression and Phrasing

Approaching
Caddo Legends

On Level
Quileute Legends

Beyond
Navajo Legends

ELL
Three Legends

Writing
Trait: Word Choice

Grammar
Plurals and Possessives

WEEK 6

Show What You Know Spiral Review
Cause and Effect
Sequence
Main Idea and Details
Prefixes and Suffixes
Chart

Writing
Procedural Text: How-to Article

Unit 2 Assessment, 263M–263N

Comprehension
Author's Purpose; Main Idea and Details; Cause and Effect; Sequence

Vocabulary Strategies
Prefixes and Suffixes; Idioms; Context Clues: Description, Paragraph Clues; Homophones

Text Features/Literary Elements/Study Skills
Survey; Chart; Stanza, Line Breaks, Rhyme/Meter; Hyperbole, Metaphor; Using Parts of a Book

Grammar
Nouns

Writing
Procedural Text: How-to Article

Fluency Assessment

Diagnose and Prescribe
Interpret Assessment Results

Unit 2 Resources

Literature

Student Book

StudentWorks Plus
Online and CD-ROM

Read-Aloud Anthology
Includes Plays for
Readers Theater

**Approaching
Level**

On Level

Beyond Level

ELL

Leveled Readers

Leveled Classroom Library Books (18)

Teaching Support

Teacher's Edition

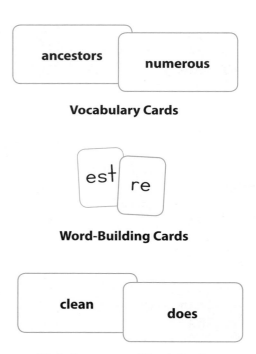

Teacher's Resource Book

Vocabulary Cards

Word-Building Cards

High-Frequency Word Cards

**Sound-Spelling
Cards**

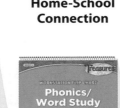

Transparencies
Online and CD-ROM

IWB Interactive White Board Ready

Sound-Spelling WorkBoards

Student Practice

Practice Book

Additional Reproducibles:
Approaching Beyond

Phonics/Spelling Practice Book

Grammar Practice Book

Home-School Connection

Handwriting
• Cursive

Dinah Zike's Foldables®

Reading

Writing

Phonics/ Word Study

Science/ Social Studies

Literacy Workstation Flip Charts

Class Management Tools

Managing Small Groups
A How-to Guide

How-to Guide

Rotation Chart

Rotation Chart
Red
Blue Green
Orange

Weekly Contracts

Weekly Contracts
My To-Do List

Differentiated Resources

English Language Learners

English **L**anguage **L**earner Resource Book

VISUAL VOCABULARY RESOURCES

ELL Resource and Practice Book

Visual Vocabulary Resources

Response to Intervention

Tier 2
• Phonics
• Vocabulary
• Comprehension
• Fluency
• Writing and Grammar

Tier 3

Assessment

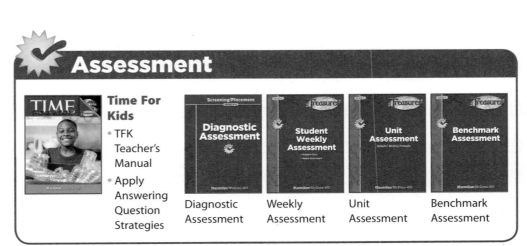

Time For Kids
• TFK Teacher's Manual
• Apply Answering Question Strategies

Diagnostic Assessment

Student Weekly Assessment

Unit Assessment

Benchmark Assessment

Diagnostic Assessment

Weekly Assessment

Unit Assessment

Benchmark Assessment

Digital Solutions

Go to **ConnectED** http://connected.mcgraw-hill.com
Online Center

☑ **Prepare/Plan**

☑ **Teach/Learn**

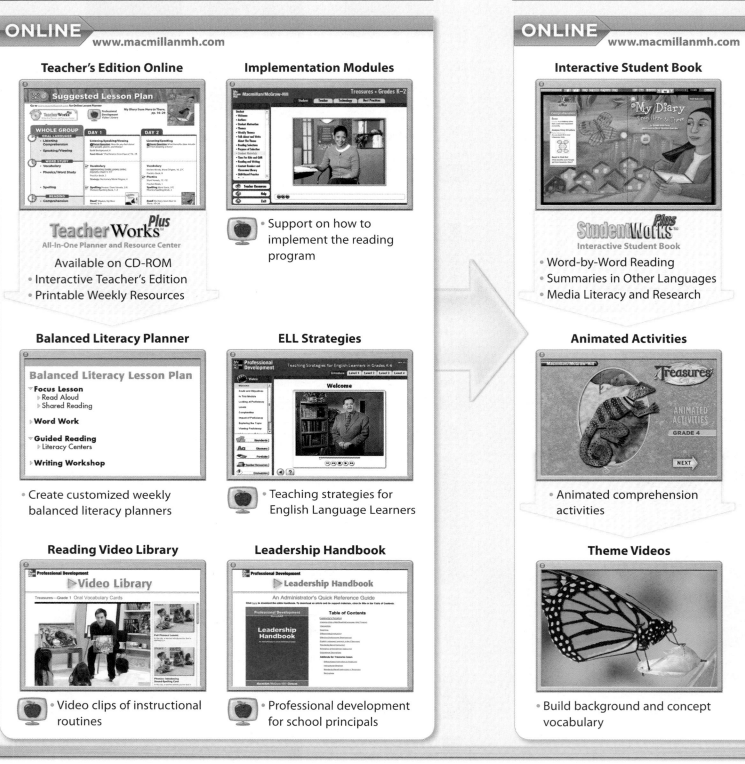

ONLINE www.macmillanmh.com

Teacher's Edition Online

TeacherWorks *Plus*
All-In-One Planner and Resource Center

Available on CD-ROM
• Interactive Teacher's Edition
• Printable Weekly Resources

Implementation Modules

• Support on how to implement the reading program

Balanced Literacy Planner

• Create customized weekly balanced literacy planners

ELL Strategies

• Teaching strategies for English Language Learners

Reading Video Library

• Video clips of instructional routines

Leadership Handbook

• Professional development for school principals

ONLINE www.macmillanmh.com

Interactive Student Book

StudentWorks *Plus*
Interactive Student Book

• Word-by-Word Reading
• Summaries in Other Languages
• Media Literacy and Research

Animated Activities

• Animated comprehension activities

Theme Videos

• Build background and concept vocabulary

Additional Professional Development

• **Instructional Routine Handbook**
• **Writing Professional Development Guide**
• **Managing Small Groups**
• **Leadership Handbook:** *An Administrator's Quick Reference Guide*

Also available
Reading Yes!
Video Workshops on CD-ROM

LOG ON ▶ | VIEW IT | READ IT | LEARN IT | FIND OUT

☑ **Assess**

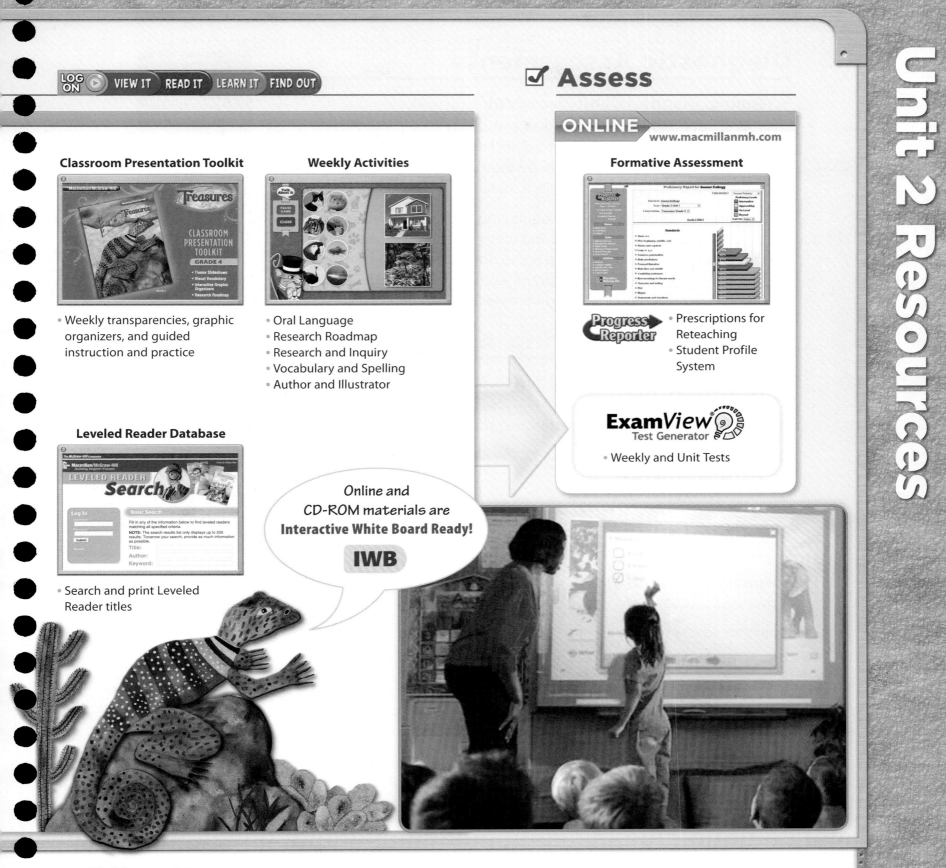

Classroom Presentation Toolkit

CLASSROOM PRESENTATION TOOLKIT GRADE 4

- Weekly transparencies, graphic organizers, and guided instruction and practice

Weekly Activities

- Oral Language
- Research Roadmap
- Research and Inquiry
- Vocabulary and Spelling
- Author and Illustrator

Leveled Reader Database

LEVELED READER Search

- Search and print Leveled Reader titles

Online and CD-ROM materials are **Interactive White Board Ready!**

IWB

ONLINE www.macmillanmh.com

Formative Assessment

Progress Reporter

- Prescriptions for Reteaching
- Student Profile System

ExamView Test Generator

- Weekly and Unit Tests

Available on CD

AUDIO CD
- **Listening Library**
- **Fluency Solutions**
- **Sound Pronunciation**

CD-ROM
StudentWorks Plus
Interactive Student Book
- **Skill Level Up!**
- **Vocabulary PuzzleMaker**

Accelerated Reader
- Accelerated Reader Quizzes

Theme: Making a Difference

Diagnostic Assessments

Screening, Diagnosis, and Placement

Use your state or district screener to identify students at risk. In addition, see tests in our **Diagnostic Assessment** book for information on determining the proficiency of students according to a specific standard or prerequisite skill. The results of the tests will help you place students in the program.

Diagnostics should be given at the beginning of the school year after you have had time to observe students and they have become familiar with classroom routines. Use the diagnostics to determine students in need of intervention or to identify specific prerequisite skill deficiencies that you need to teach during Small Group differentiated instruction time.

Progress Monitoring Assessments

Meeting Grade-Level Expectations

Use the weekly and unit tests (every 6–8 weeks). Multiple questions and next-steps information are provided.

Ongoing Informal Assessments

- Daily Quick Check Observations
- Weekly Tests/Selection Tests; Comprehension Check Questions (Student Book)
- Weekly Fluency Practice Book Passages

Formal Assessments

- Unit Assessments
- Fluency Assessments
- Running Records

Summative Assessments

Links to the State Test

Use the State Assessment and the tests provided in the **Benchmark Assessment**. Give every trimester, midyear, or at the end of the year to determine whether students have mastered the grade-level content standards and to document long-term academic growth.

Digital Assessment

Progress Reporter **Assessment Online**
- Administer the **Weekly** and **Unit Assessment** electronically
- Score all tests electronically
- Prescriptions for Reteaching
- Student Profile System

 **ExamView Test Generator** **Test Generator**
- Available on CD-ROM
- **Weekly** and **Unit Assessments**

Test Alignment

GRADE 4 UNIT 2 ASSESSED SKILLS	TerraNova/ CAT 6	SAT 10	ITBS	NAEP
COMPREHENSION STRATEGIES AND SKILLS				
• Strategies: Monitor comprehension, analyze text structure, analyze story structure	◆	◆	◆	◆
• Skills: Author's purpose, main idea and details, cause and effect, sequence	◆	◆	◆	◆
VOCABULARY STRATEGIES				
• Prefixes and suffixes	◆	◆	◆	
• Context clues: Description, paragraph clues	◆	◆	◆	◆
• Idioms				
• Homophones				
PHONICS/SPELLING				
• Prefixes, suffixes	◆	◆	◆	◆
• Digraphs, three-letter blends				
• *r*-Controlled vowels				
TEXT FEATURES, LITERARY ELEMENTS, AND STUDY SKILLS				
• Survey				
• Lyric poem: Stanza, line breaks, rhyme/meter				
• Using parts of a book	◆	◆	◆	
• Hyperbole, metaphor				
• Chart			◆	◆
GRAMMAR, MECHANICS, USAGE				
• Nouns: Common, proper, singular, plural, irregular plural, possessive	◆	◆	◆	
• Capitalizing proper nouns	◆	◆	◆	
• Using commas in a series	◆	◆	◆	
• Correct plural forms				
• Punctuating titles and letters	◆		◆	

KEY	
TerraNova/CAT 6	TerraNova, The Second Edition
SAT 10	Stanford Early Achievement Test
ITBS	Iowa Tests of Basic Skills
NAEP	National Assessment of Educational Progress

Theme Project

Introduce the Theme Write this theme statement on the board: *Communities, or large neighborhoods, are shaped by the people living in them.* Ask: *If you could choose any community project to research, which one would you choose?*

Help students get ready for their theme projects by brainstorming community projects they may know about or can visit, such as a community mural, a youth center, or a park. Have students pick a specific type of project to pursue. Encourage them to ask open-ended questions, narrow their focus, and create a research plan.

> **LOG ON** ▶ **VIEW IT**
> **Theme Launcher Video**
> www.macmillanmh.com

Research and Inquiry
Self-Selected Theme Project

Step 1 **State the Problem and Identify Needed Information** Tell students that they will research community projects set up by ordinary citizens. Students should start locally by exploring their own communities. They may consult maps, librarians, non-profit organizations, Web sites, and their chamber of commerce.

Step 2 **Research Plan** Have students make a list of all organizations and places they can find information, such as library and media centers, community groups, the Internet, and their local government officials.

Step 3 **Gathering Sources** Have students use the resources that they identified to interview people, visit a community project, and read texts that give information about community projects. Have them use the organizational features of reference sources to help them locate information.

Research Strategies

Using Technology
Make sure Web sites are reliable.

- Take notes in your own words and remember to cite your sources.

- Use a student search engine. Check to see when the Web sites were last updated—especially if the topic is a recent scientific or technological discovery. Make sure that the information comes from a reliable source.

Step 4 **Synthesizing** After students collect their research information, have them sort their notes by topic and subtopic.

See the Unit Closer on pages 263K–263L for **Step 5: Create the Presentation** and **Step 6: Review and Evaluate.**

Minilesson

Collecting Information

Explain We can look for information about a topic in many different places. Along with books and the Internet, surveys, interviews, maps, time lines, graphs, data from experts, and our own personal observations can all be good sources of information. Locating and collecting information is an important part of conducting **research**. When we research a topic or idea, we attempt to find out as much as we can about it. The information we collect is an important part of a good research plan.

Discuss Ask: *What are some other places you might look for information on a research topic?* (You might look at newspapers, magazines, charts, posters, video clips, or encyclopedias.)

Apply Once students have decided on their research topic, have them collect a variety of information, including surveys, interviews, data from experts, reference texts, online searches, and visual sources of information (maps, graphs, etc.).

Minilesson

Consulting an Expert

Explain People with **expert** knowledge about a topic or subject can be wonderful sources of information. Often, a research topic is so large that the amount of information available is unmanageable. **Research librarians** and **local experts** can help you improve the focus of your research. Too much or the wrong kind of information will make your research presentation weak. Experts can help you **evaluate** and **synthesize** the information you have collected and revise your research question to ensure a strong final product.

Discuss Ask: *Why do you think it is important to constantly revisit and evaluate the focus of your research?* (You need to make sure that your research question can be answered with the information you have collected. You may also wish to change your focus if you find an aspect of the topic that especially interests you.)

Apply Have students synthesize and evaluate the information they have collected and consider whether this information will answer their research question. If it will not, encourage students to clarify and revise their question.

LISTENING AND SPEAKING

WORKING IN GROUPS

Remind students to

- respectfully ask questions to obtain or clarify information;

- stay focused on the topic and ask relevant questions;

- give and restate directions in order to make sure that everyone understands them.

See Listening and Speaking Checklists in StudentWorks Plus.

The **Big** Question

How do people make a difference in their communities?

LOG ON ▶ VIEW IT   **Theme Video**
Making a Difference
www.macmillanmh.com

132

133

Introduce Theme Project

MAKING A DIFFERENCE

Review with students what they have learned so far about how people can make a difference.

- Help students point out things in their own communities, however small, that are examples of projects an ordinary person might have initiated (longer after-school programs, the PTA, private tutoring services). Explain how these programs or projects are examples of making a difference.

- Read and discuss the activities on page 134 of the **Student Book**. Help students begin thinking about what community project they might like to research for their theme project.

Connect to Content

Recycling

Recycling is one way in which students can make a difference by helping the environment. Discuss with students ways to recycle at school and at home. Have them decide on a plan for encouraging recycling in their school. Then ask them to write an outline showing the steps they would need to take to put the plan into action.

How do people make a difference in their communities?

Communities, or large neighborhoods, are shaped by the people living in them. If the community needs something, members can make sure the community gets what it needs. For example, if a community wanted to build a playground, community members could do different things like raise money, send letters to their government for help, or build it themselves. They then make a difference in their community by creating a safe, happy place for children of all ages to play. Learning about how people make a difference in their communities can help you do the same in your community.

Research Activities

In this unit, you will collect information about community projects. Choose a project that would be important for your community. Research resources that would help complete this project, such as visiting completed projects and interviewing the people who worked on them.

Keep Track of Ideas

As you read, keep track of all you are learning about how people make a difference in their communities. Use the **Accordion Book Foldable**. In the first panel, write the Unit Theme: *Making a Difference*. On each of the following panels, write the facts you learn each week that will help you in your research and in your understanding of the Unit Theme.

FOLDABLES Study Organizer

Digital Learning

LOG ON ▶ FIND OUT www.macmillanmh.com

StudentWorks *Plus*
Interactive Student Book

- **Research Roadmap**
  Follow a step-by-step guide to complete your research project.

Online Resources
- Topic Finder and Other Research Tools
- Videos and Virtual Field Trips
- Photos and Drawings for Presentations
- Related Articles and Web Resources
- Web Site Links

People and Places

- **Barbara Jordan**
  In 1966, Barbara Jordan became the first African American woman to be elected to the Texas Senate. In 1973, she was elected to the United States House of Representatives. In 1994, she was awarded the Presidential Medal of Freedom.

KEEP TRACK OF IDEAS

Go to page 36 of the Foldables™ book for instructions on how to create the Accordion Book study organizer for this unit. Give students time to create the study organizers.

Read "Keep Track of Ideas" on page 135 of the **Student Book**. Model how students will be using their organizers to keep track of ideas as they read through the stories in the unit. Explain that keeping track of ideas they read about will help them develop ideas for their own theme project.

RESEARCH TOOLS

Tell students that as they read the selections in this unit, they will learn about how people can make a difference. Students will be able to use the Research Tools to help them learn more about making a difference.

LOG ON ▶
StudentWorks *Plus*
Interactive Student Book

Plan, Organize, and Synthesize Activities that will assist students in research planning, organization, and presentation

Listening and Speaking Resources that will help students apply listening and speaking techniques

Week 1 ★ At a Glance

Priority Skills and Concepts

 Comprehension
- **Strategy:** Monitor Comprehension
- **Skill:** Author's Purpose
- **Skill:** Sequence
- **Genre:** Speech, Biography, Expository

 **Robust Vocabulary**
- **Selection Vocabulary:** *unfair, ancestors, numerous, segregation, avoided, injustice*
- **Strategy:** Prefixes and Suffixes

Fluency
- Intonation/Expression

 **Phonics/Spelling**
- **Word Study:** Prefixes, Multisyllabic Words
- **Spelling Words:** *unblock, unload, relearn, rewind, incorrect, overheat, preplan, unborn, unlock, resell, imperfect, illegal, subway, supersize, unchain, recall, rewash, indirect, overact, premix*
- *stone, grown, lower*

 **Grammar/Mechanics**
- Common and Proper Nouns
- Capitalizing Proper Nouns

Writing
- **Trait:** Ideas
- Showing

Key

✔ Tested in program   SPIRAL REVIEW Review Skill

Digital Learning

Digital solutions to help plan and implement instruction

☑ Teacher Resources

LOG ON ▶

ONLINE www.macmillanmh.com

▶ **Teacher's Edition**
  - Lesson Planner and Resources also on CD-ROM

TeacherWorks™ Plus

▶ **Formative Assessment**
  - ExamView® on CD-ROM also available

Progress Reporter

▶ **Instructional Resources**
  - Unit Videos
  - Classroom Presentation Toolkit

VIDEO

▶ **Professional Development**
  - Video Library

Professional Development

☑ Student Resources

LOG ON ▶

ONLINE www.macmillanmh.com

▶ **Interactive Student Book**

StudentWorks™ Plus

▶ **Leveled Reader Database**

▶ **Activities**
  - Research Toolkit
  - Oral Language Activities
  - Vocabulary/Spelling Activities

Listening Library
  - Recordings of Student Books and Leveled Readers

Fluency Solutions
  - Fluency Modeling and Practice

Weekly Literature

Theme: Civil Rights

Student Book

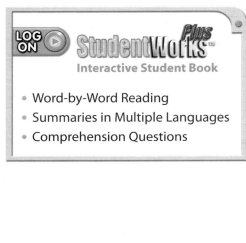

StudentWorks Plus
Interactive Student Book

- Word-by-Word Reading
- Summaries in Multiple Languages
- Comprehension Questions

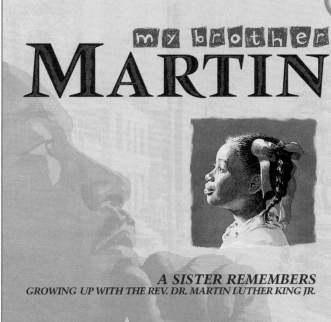

my brother
MARTIN

A SISTER REMEMBERS
GROWING UP WITH THE REV. DR. MARTIN LUTHER KING JR.

BY CHRISTINE KING FARRIS
ILLUSTRATED BY CHRIS SOENTPIET

Main Selection
Genre Biography

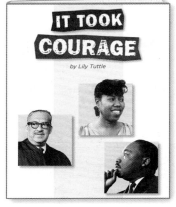

IT TOOK COURAGE
by Lily Tuttle

**Preteach Vocabulary
and Comprehension**
Genre Biography

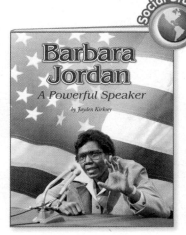

Barbara Jordan
A Powerful Speaker
by Jayden Kirksey

Paired Selection
Genre Expository

Support Literature

INTERACTIVE
Read-Aloud
ANTHOLOGY with PLAYS

**Interactive
Read-Aloud Anthology**
- Listening Comprehension
- Robust Vocabulary
- Readers' Theater Plays for Fluency

Resources for Differentiated Instruction

Leveled Readers: Social Studies

AUDIO CD

Leveled Reader Library

GR Levels N–T

Genre	Biography

- Same Theme
- Same Vocabulary
- Same Comprehension Skills

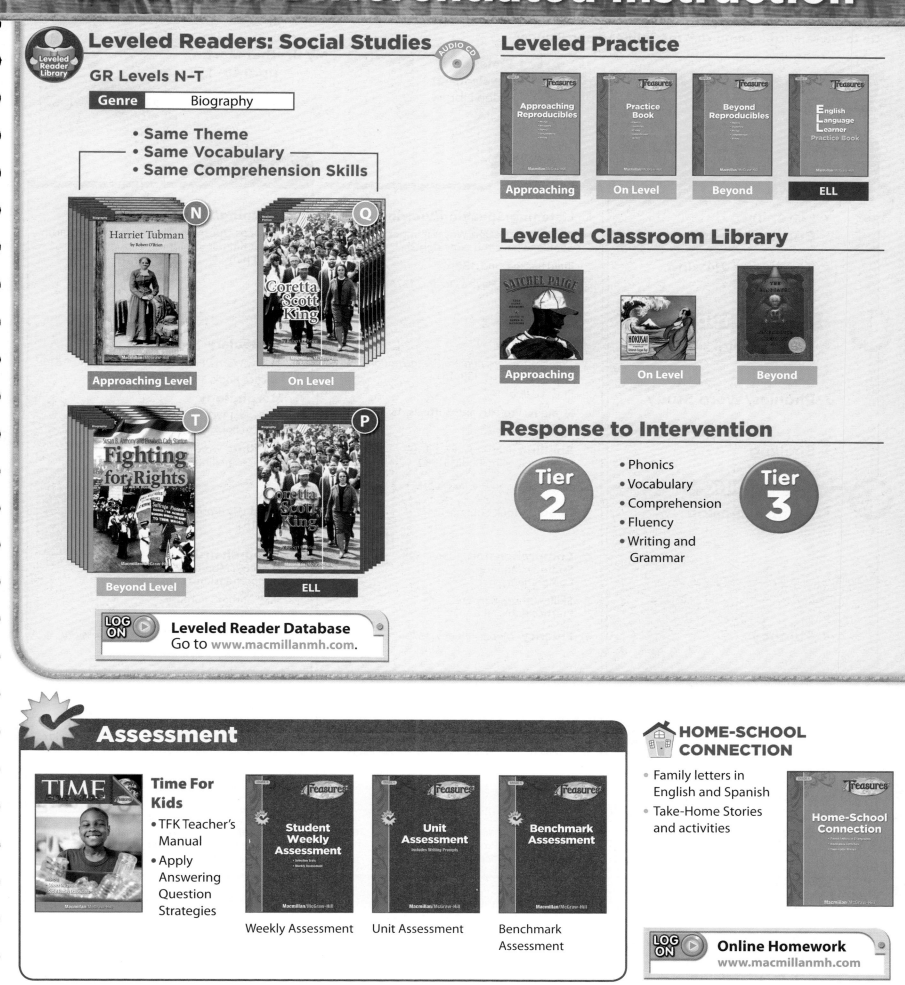

N Harriet Tubman by Robert O'Brien
Approaching Level

Q Coretta Scott King by Robert O'Brien
On Level

T Susan B. Anthony and Elizabeth Cady Stanton *Fighting for Rights*
Beyond Level

P Coretta Scott King
ELL

LOG ON ▶ **Leveled Reader Database**
Go to www.macmillanmh.com.

Leveled Practice

Approaching Reproducibles — **Approaching**

Practice Book — **On Level**

Beyond Reproducibles — **Beyond**

English Language Learner Practice Book — **ELL**

Leveled Classroom Library

Satchel Paige — **Approaching**

Hokusai — **On Level**

The Railroad — **Beyond**

Response to Intervention

Tier 2

- Phonics
- Vocabulary
- Comprehension
- Fluency
- Writing and Grammar

Tier 3

Assessment

TIME For Kids

Time For Kids
- TFK Teacher's Manual
- Apply Answering Question Strategies

Student Weekly Assessment — Weekly Assessment

Unit Assessment — Unit Assessment

Benchmark Assessment — Benchmark Assessment

HOME-SCHOOL CONNECTION

- Family letters in English and Spanish
- Take-Home Stories and activities

Home-School Connection

LOG ON ▶ **Online Homework**
www.macmillanmh.com

Suggested Lesson Plan

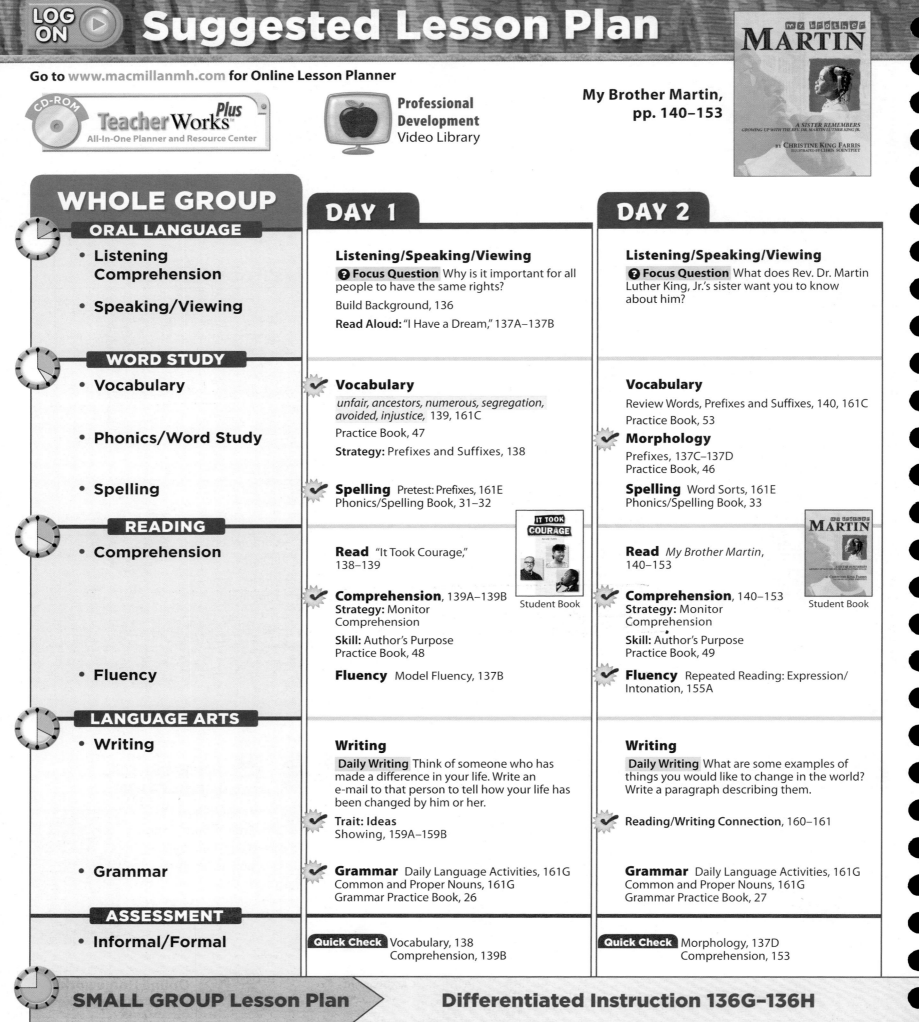

Go to **www.macmillanmh.com** for Online Lesson Planner

CD-ROM
TeacherWorks *Plus*
All-In-One Planner and Resource Center

Professional Development
Video Library

My Brother Martin,
pp. 140–153

MARTIN
A SISTER REMEMBERS
GROWING UP WITH THE REV. DR. MARTIN LUTHER KING JR.
BY CHRISTINE KING FARRIS
ILLUSTRATED BY CHRIS SOENTPIET

WHOLE GROUP

ORAL LANGUAGE
- **Listening Comprehension**
- **Speaking/Viewing**

WORD STUDY
- **Vocabulary**
- **Phonics/Word Study**
- **Spelling**

READING
- **Comprehension**

- **Fluency**

LANGUAGE ARTS
- **Writing**

- **Grammar**

ASSESSMENT
- **Informal/Formal**

DAY 1

Listening/Speaking/Viewing
❓ Focus Question Why is it important for all people to have the same rights?
Build Background, 136
Read Aloud: "I Have a Dream," 137A–137B

Vocabulary
unfair, ancestors, numerous, segregation, avoided, injustice, 139, 161C
Practice Book, 47
Strategy: Prefixes and Suffixes, 138

Spelling Pretest: Prefixes, 161E
Phonics/Spelling Book, 31–32

Read "It Took Courage," 138–139

IT TOOK COURAGE
Student Book

Comprehension, 139A–139B
Strategy: Monitor Comprehension
Skill: Author's Purpose
Practice Book, 48

Fluency Model Fluency, 137B

Writing
Daily Writing Think of someone who has made a difference in your life. Write an e-mail to that person to tell how your life has been changed by him or her.
Trait: Ideas
Showing, 159A–159B

Grammar Daily Language Activities, 161G
Common and Proper Nouns, 161G
Grammar Practice Book, 26

Quick Check Vocabulary, 138
Comprehension, 139B

DAY 2

Listening/Speaking/Viewing
❓ Focus Question What does Rev. Dr. Martin Luther King, Jr.'s sister want you to know about him?

Vocabulary
Review Words, Prefixes and Suffixes, 140, 161C
Practice Book, 53
Morphology
Prefixes, 137C–137D
Practice Book, 46

Spelling Word Sorts, 161E
Phonics/Spelling Book, 33

Read *My Brother Martin,* 140–153

MARTIN
Student Book

Comprehension, 140–153
Strategy: Monitor Comprehension
Skill: Author's Purpose
Practice Book, 49

Fluency Repeated Reading: Expression/Intonation, 155A

Writing
Daily Writing What are some examples of things you would like to change in the world? Write a paragraph describing them.
Reading/Writing Connection, 160–161

Grammar Daily Language Activities, 161G
Common and Proper Nouns, 161G
Grammar Practice Book, 27

Quick Check Morphology, 137D
Comprehension, 153

SMALL GROUP Lesson Plan ▷ **Differentiated Instruction 136G–136H**

Priority Skills

Vocabulary	Comprehension	Writing	Social Studies
Vocabulary Words Prefixes and Suffixes	**Strategy:** Monitor Comprehension **Skill:** Author's Purpose	**Trait:** Ideas Showing	Identify the importance of historical figures such as Barbara Jordan

DAY 3

Listening/Speaking

? Focus Question Compare the experiences of Thurgood Marshall and Dr. Martin Luther King, Jr. How did segregation affect both men?

Summarize, 155

Vocabulary

Review Words, Related Words, 161D

Spelling Word Meanings, 161F
Phonics/Spelling Book, 34

Read *My Brother Martin*, 140–153

Student Book

Comprehension
Comprehension Check, 155

Review Skill: Sequence, 155B
Practice Book, 51

Fluency Repeated Reading: Expression/Intonation, 155A
Practice Book, 50

Writing

Daily Writing Write a short news article describing how volunteers can help in other parts of the world.

Trait: Ideas
Showing, 161A

Grammar Daily Language Activities, 161G
Mechanics and Usage, 161H
Grammar Practice Book, 28

Quick Check Fluency, 155A

DAY 4

Listening/Speaking/Viewing

? Focus Question Think about what you learned from *My Brother Martin* about Martin Luther King, Jr. How are he and Barbara Jordan alike?

Vocabulary

Content Vocabulary: *orator, legacy, opinions,* 156

Review Words, Morphology, 161D

Spelling Proofread, 161F
Phonics/Spelling Book, 35

Read "Barbara Jordan," 156–159

Student Book

Comprehension
Social Studies: Expository

Text Features: Survey, 156
Practice Book, 52

Fluency Repeated Reading: Expression/Intonation, 155A

Time For Kids

Writing

Daily Writing Write a diary entry about a time when you made a difference in someone else's life.

Trait: Word Choice
Descriptive Words and Phrases, 161A

Grammar Daily Language Activities, 161G
Common and Proper Nouns, 161H
Grammar Practice Book, 29

Quick Check Vocabulary, 161D

DAY 5
Review and Assess

Listening/Speaking/Viewing

? Focus Question If you wanted to describe an injustice you saw or heard about, how would you write about it? As an essay? A play? A short story? A letter? Explain your choice.

Vocabulary

Assess Words, Connect to Writing, 161D

Spelling Posttest, 161F
Phonics/Spelling Book, 36

Read Self-Selected Reading, 136K
Practice Book, 54

Comprehension
Connect and Compare, 159

Student Book

Fluency Practice, 136K

Writing

Daily Writing Write a paragraph about a character from a book or movie who made a difference in some way.

Conferencing, 161B

Grammar Daily Language Activities, 161G
Common and Proper Nouns, 161H
Grammar Practice Book, 30

Weekly Assessment, 161II–161JJ

Differentiated Instruction

What do I do in small groups?

Teacher-Led Small Groups

Independent Activities

Focus on Skills

IF... students need additional instruction, practice, or extension based on your **Quick Check** observations for the following priority skills:

✔ **Phonics/Word Study**
Prefixes

✔ **Vocabulary Words**
unfair, ancestors, numerous, segregation, avoided, injustice

✔ **Comprehension**
Strategy: Monitor Comprehension
Skill: Author's Purpose

✔ **Fluency**

THEN...
Approaching ELL	Preteach and Reteach Skills
On Level	Practice
Beyond	Enrich and Accelerate Learning

Suggested Small Group Lesson Plan

CD-ROM TeacherWorks Plus
All-In-One Planner and Resource Center

	DAY 1	DAY 2
Approaching Level Tier 2 • **Preteach/Reteach** **Tier 2 Instruction**	• Prepare to Read, 161I • Academic Language, 161I • Preteach Vocabulary, 161K	• Comprehension, 161M Monitor Comprehension/Author's Purpose **ELL** • Leveled Reader Lesson 1, 161N
On Level • **Practice**	• Vocabulary, 161S • Phonics, 161S Prefixes	• Leveled Reader Lesson 1, 161U
Beyond Level • **Extend/Accelerate** **Gifted and Talented**	• Leveled Reader Lesson 1, 161Y • Analyze Information, 161Y	• Leveled Reader Lesson 2, 161Z • Synthesize Information, 161Z
ELL • **Build English Language Proficiency** • See **ELL** in other levels.	• Prepare to Read, 161AA • Academic Language, 161AA • Preteach Vocabulary, 161BB	• Vocabulary, 161BB • Preteach Main Selection, 161CC

Small Group

Focus on Leveled Readers

Leveled Reader Library

Levels N–T

N — Harriet Tubman by Robert O'Brien — **Approaching**

Q — Coretta Scott King — **On Level**

T — Susan B. Anthony and Elizabeth Cady Stanton — Fighting for Rights — **Beyond**

P — Coretta Scott King — **ELL**

Additional Leveled Readers

LOG ON ▶

Leveled Reader Database
www.macmillanmh.com

Search by

- Comprehension Skill
- Content Area
- Genre
- Text Feature
- Guided Reading Level
- Reading Recovery Level
- Lexile Score
- Benchmark Level

Subscription also available.

Manipulatives

Sound-Spelling WorkBoards

whale
wh — **Sound-Spelling Cards**

about
today — **High-Frequency Word Cards**

VISUAL VOCABULARY RESOURCES — **Visual Vocabulary Resources**

DAY 3

- Phonics Maintenance, 161J
  Prefixes **ELL**
- Leveled Reader Lesson 2, 161O

- Leveled Reader Lesson 2, 161V

- Phonics, 161W
  Prefixes **ELL**

- Vocabulary, 161BB
- Grammar, 161EE

DAY 4

- Reteach Phonics Skill, 161J
  Prefixes **ELL**
- Review Vocabulary, 161L
- Leveled Reader Lesson 3, 161P

- Fluency, 161T

- Vocabulary, 161W
- Write a Survey, 161W
- Fluency, 161X

- Vocabulary, 161BB
- Writing/Spelling, 161FF
- Preteach Paired Selection, 161CC
- Fluency, 161DD
- Leveled Reader, 161GG

DAY 5

- High-Frequency Words, 161L
- Fluency, 161Q
- Self-Selected Independent Reading, 161R
- Book Talk, 161P

- Self-Selected Independent Reading, 161T
- Book Talk, 161V

- Self-Selected Independent Reading, 161X
- Evaluate Information, 161X
- Book Talk, 161Z

- Vocabulary, 161BB
- Leveled Reader, 161GG
- Self-Selected Independent Reading, 161DD
- Book Talk, 161HH

Managing the Class

What do I do with the rest of my class?

- Practice Book and Reproducibles
- ELL Practice Book
- Leveled Reader Activities
- Literacy Workstations
- Online Activities

Classroom Management Tools

Weekly Contract

Name _____ Date _____

My To-Do List

✔ Put a check next to the activities you complete.

Reading
- ☐ Practice fluency
- ☐ Choose a story to read

Phonics/ Word Study
- ☐ Look up word origins
- ☐ Write words with short vowel sounds

Writing
- ☐ Write a letter to the editor
- ☐ Write a radio ad

Science
- ☐ Research two types of rocks
- ☐ Write a chart

Social Studies
- ☐ Create a guide book
- ☐ Role-play an interview

Leveled Readers
- ☐ Write About It!
- ☐ Content Connection

Technology
- ☐ Vocabulary PuzzleMaker
- ☐ Fluency Solutions
- ☐ Listening Library
- ☐ www.macmillanmh.com

Independent Practice
- ☐ Practice Book, 1–8

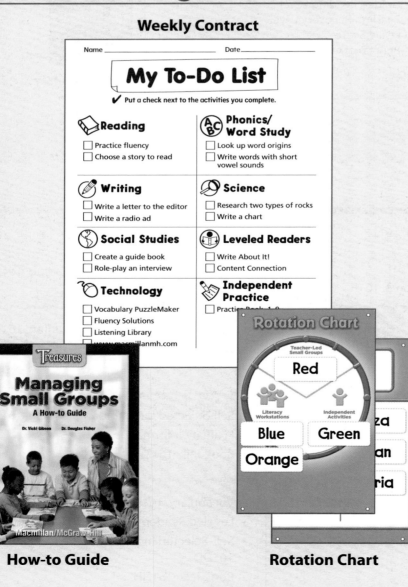

Treasures
Managing Small Groups
A How-to Guide
Dr. Vicki Gibson   Dr. Douglas Fisher

Macmillan/McGraw-Hill

How-to Guide

Rotation Chart

Teacher-Led Small Groups

Red

Literacy Workstations   Independent Activities

Blue   Green

Orange

...za
...an
...ria

Rotation Chart

Digital Learning

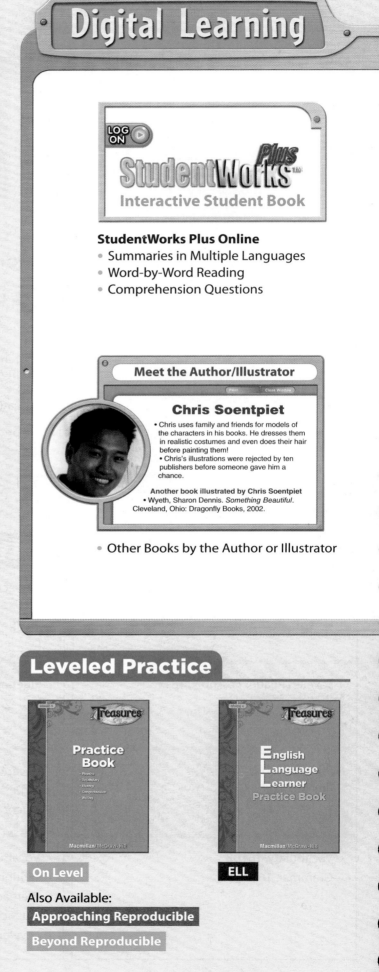

LOG ON ▶

StudentWorks Plus
Interactive Student Book

StudentWorks Plus Online
- Summaries in Multiple Languages
- Word-by-Word Reading
- Comprehension Questions

Meet the Author/Illustrator

Print   Close Window

Chris Soentpiet

- Chris uses family and friends for models of the characters in his books. He dresses them in realistic costumes and even does their hair before painting them!
- Chris's illustrations were rejected by ten publishers before someone gave him a chance.

Another book illustrated by Chris Soentpiet
- Wyeth, Sharon Dennis. *Something Beautiful*. Cleveland, Ohio: Dragonfly Books, 2002.

- Other Books by the Author or Illustrator

Leveled Practice

Treasures
Practice Book
- Practice
- Vocabulary
- Fluency
- Comprehension
- Writing

Macmillan/McGraw-Hill

Treasures
English Language Learner Practice Book

Macmillan/McGraw-Hill

On Level

ELL

Also Available:

Approaching Reproducible

Beyond Reproducible

Independent Activities

LOG ON ▶ ONLINE INSTRUCTION www.macmillanmh.com

Oral Language Activities

- Focus on Vocabulary and Concepts
- English Language Learner Support

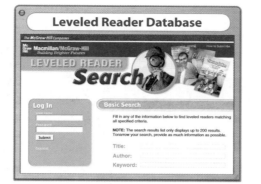

Leveled Reader Database

- Leveled Reader Database
- Search titles by level, skill, content area, and more

Vocabulary/Spelling Activities

Grade 4, Unit 2
Selection 3, Vocabulary

preserve

Look to the sky to find the Answer

to keep from being lost, damaged, or decayed; protect

- Differentiated Lists and Activities

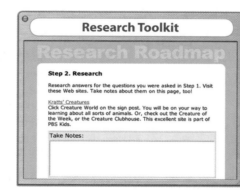

Research Toolkit

Research Roadmap

Step 2. Research

Research answers for the questions you were asked in Step 1. Visit these Web sites. Take notes about them on this page, too!

Kratts' Creatures
Click Creature World on the sign post. You will be on your way to learning about all sorts of animals. Or, check out the Creature of the Week, or the Creature Clubhouse. This excellent site is part of PBS Kids.

Take Notes:

- Research Roadmap
- Research and Presentation Tools
- Theme Launcher Video
- Links to Science and Social Studies

Available on CD

LISTENING LIBRARY
Recordings of selections
- Main Selections
- Paired Selections
- Leveled Readers
- ELL Readers

VOCABULARY PUZZLEMAKER

FLUENCY SOLUTIONS
Recorded passages at two speeds for modeling and practicing fluency

Leveled Reader Activities

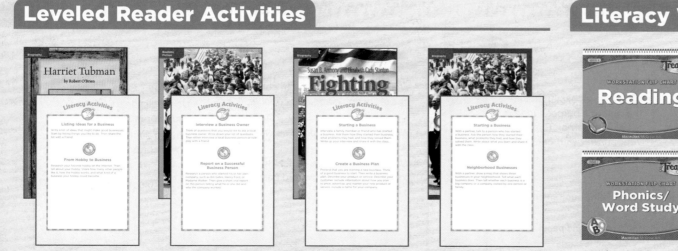

Approaching   **On Level**   **Beyond**   **ELL**

See inside cover of all Leveled Readers.

Literacy Workstations

Reading   Writing
Phonics/Word Study   Science/Social Studies

See lessons on pages 136K–136L.

Teacher-Led Small Groups

Independent Activities

What do I do with the rest of my class?

Reading

Objectives

- Develop fluency through partner reading
- Read independently for a sustained period of time; use **Practice Book** page 54 for Reading Strategies and Reading Log

---

Reading — Fluency — 20 Minutes

- Select a paragraph from the Fluency passage on page 55 of your Practice Book.
- With a partner, take turns reading the paragraph aloud, stressing the most important words in each sentence.

Extension

- Read the paragraph two more times. Each time, emphasize different words.
- Discuss how emphasizing different words changes the meaning of the passage.

Things you need:
- Practice Book

Fluency Solutions
Listening Library

11

Phonics/Word Study

Objectives

- Build and write words with prefixes and suffixes
- Sort words by prefixes
- Use a dictionary to check word meanings

Phonics/Word Study — Prefixes and Suffixes — 20 Minutes

- Create a Three-Tab Foldable®.
- On top tabs, write *Prefix*, *Base Word*, *Suffix*.
- Under each tab, write *un-*, *fair*, *-ly*.
- Say the new word you have formed.
- Use a dictionary to help you write a sentence for the new word.

Extension

- Write additional words with a prefix, base word, and suffix.

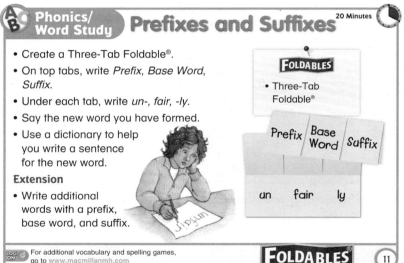

FOLDABLES
- Three-Tab Foldable®

Prefix | Base Word | Suffix

un | fair | ly

For additional vocabulary and spelling games, go to www.macmillanmh.com

FOLDABLES

11

Reading — Independent Reading — 20 Minutes

- Read a book about a person you admire. Think about the author's purpose as you read. Did the author write the book to inform or to entertain? How does the author feel about the person? Does the author try to persuade you to feel the same way about the person? Write your details on note cards.

Extension

- Write an explanation of the author's purpose in your response journal. Support your answer with details from the book.

Things you need:
- book
- pen and paper
- note cards

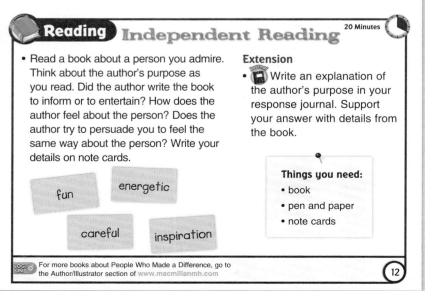

fun

energetic

careful

inspiration

For more books about People Who Made a Difference, go to the Author/Illustrator section of www.macmillanmh.com

12

Phonics/Word Study — PREFIXES — 20 Minutes

- Write these words on note cards: *aware, usual, complete, capable, fair, justice.*
- Write the following prefixes on note cards: *un-* and *in-*.
- Work with a partner. Match the prefix card with the correct word card. Make a list of the words.

Extension

- Use a dictionary to check your words.
- Write a sentence using one of the correct words.

Things you need:
- pen and paper
- note cards
- dictionary

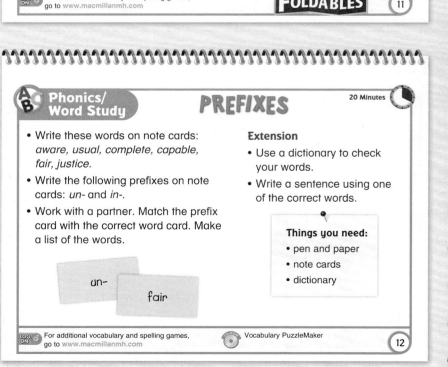

un-

fair

For additional vocabulary and spelling games, go to www.macmillanmh.com

Vocabulary PuzzleMaker

12

Literacy Workstation Flip Charts

Reading · Phonics/Word Study · Writing · Science/Social Studies

Writing

Objectives

- Write a poem about your future
- Practice using strong words
- Write about a person you admire

Content Literacy

Objectives

- Research an African American female scientist
- Research Juneteenth

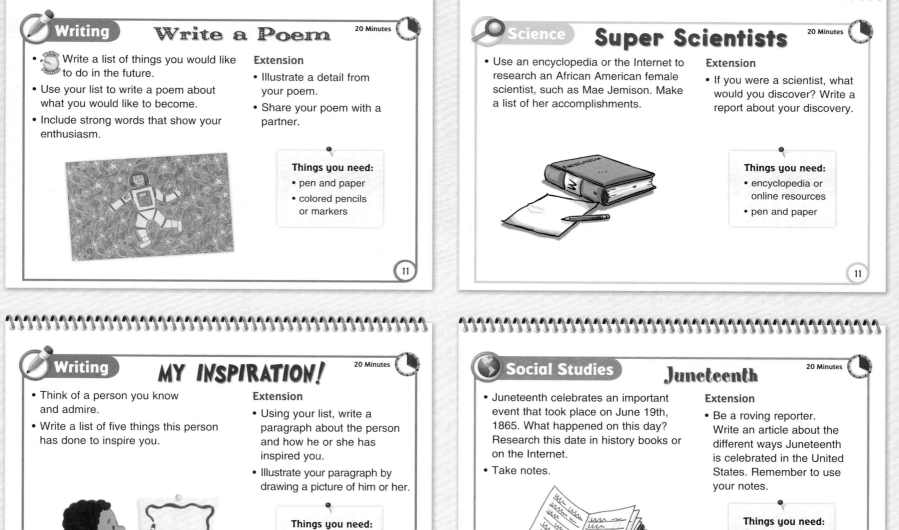

Writing — Write a Poem · 20 Minutes

- Write a list of things you would like to do in the future.
- Use your list to write a poem about what you would like to become.
- Include strong words that show your enthusiasm.

Extension
- Illustrate a detail from your poem.
- Share your poem with a partner.

Things you need:
- pen and paper
- colored pencils or markers

11

Science — Super Scientists · 20 Minutes

- Use an encyclopedia or the Internet to research an African American female scientist, such as Mae Jemison. Make a list of her accomplishments.

Extension
- If you were a scientist, what would you discover? Write a report about your discovery.

Things you need:
- encyclopedia or online resources
- pen and paper

11

Writing — MY INSPIRATION! · 20 Minutes

- Think of a person you know and admire.
- Write a list of five things this person has done to inspire you.

Extension
- Using your list, write a paragraph about the person and how he or she has inspired you.
- Illustrate your paragraph by drawing a picture of him or her.

Things you need:
- pen and paper
- colored pencils or markers

12

Social Studies — Juneteenth · 20 Minutes

- Juneteenth celebrates an important event that took place on June 19th, 1865. What happened on this day? Research this date in history books or on the Internet.
- Take notes.

Extension
- Be a roving reporter. Write an article about the different ways Juneteenth is celebrated in the United States. Remember to use your notes.

Things you need:
- history books or online resources
- pen and paper

LOG ON Internet Research and Inquiry Activity
Students can find more facts at www.macmillanmh.com

12

WHOLE GROUP

ORAL LANGUAGE
- Build Background
- Connect to Theme
- Read Aloud

✓ **PHONICS/WORD STUDY**
- Prefixes

✓ **VOCABULARY**
- Prefixes and Suffixes
- Teach Words

✓ **COMPREHENSION**
- Strategy: Monitor Comprehension
- Skill: Author's Purpose

SMALL GROUP

- Differentiated Instruction, pp. 161I–161HH

Oral Language

Build Background

ACCESS PRIOR KNOWLEDGE

Have students look at the photograph on pages 136–137. Ask them to discuss the photograph. Share the following:

The people in this photograph are on a civil rights march, or organized walk, in 1963. They wanted African Americans to be treated fairly. Notice that the people carry signs. The signs refer to jobs, voting, and schools. Toward the left is Martin Luther King, Jr., the leader who organized the march.

Write the following words on the board and briefly define each one using the **Define/Example/Ask** routine: **civil rights** (the rights all people are entitled

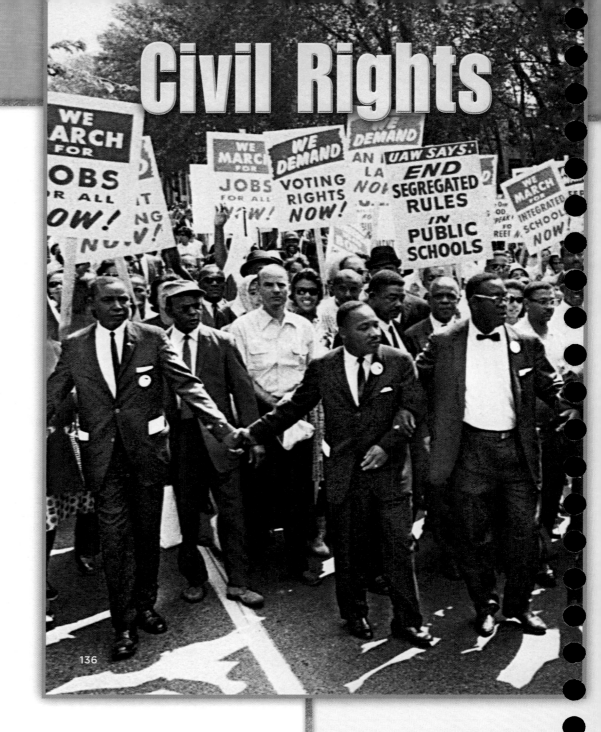

Civil Rights

136

to), **government** (the group that runs a country, state, or city); **signs** (large pieces of paper with messages on them).

FOCUS QUESTION Ask students to read "Talk About It" on **Student Book** page 137, and discuss the following with a partner.

- If you were participating in this march, or group walk, to support a cause, what sign would you carry?

- How are these people making a difference in their community?

Talk About It

Why is it important for all people to have the same rights?

LOG ON ▶ VIEW IT

Oral Language Activities
Civil Rights
www.macmillanmh.com

137

Use the Picture Prompt

BUILD WRITING FLUENCY

Have students write in their Writer's Notebooks what they know about civil rights. Tell students to write as much as they can in eight minutes. Meet with individuals during Writing Conference time to provide feedback and revision assignments. Students should self-correct any errors they find before the conference.

Connect to the Unit Theme

DISCUSS THE BIG IDEA

Early experiences with discrimination affected what Martin Luther King, Jr., would do later in his life to gain civil rights for all people.

Ask what students know about Martin Luther King, Jr., and the fight for civil rights.

- What other leaders have we read about this year? How are they similar?

- Who has made a difference in your community? What did the person do?

USE THEME FOLDABLES

Have students copy the **Big Idea** on their Unit Theme Foldables. Remind them to add details as they complete this week's readings.

Dinah Zike's
FOLDABLES®
Study Organizer

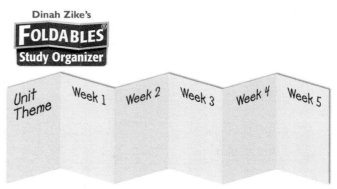

Accordion Book

ELL ENGLISH LANGUAGE LEARNERS

Beginning

Use Visuals Tell students about the photograph. *The people are marching. They are marching for civil rights because they want everyone to have the same rights.* Then ask students to tell you what the people in the photograph are doing. Give students ample time to respond.

Intermediate

Describe Ask students to tell what the people in the photograph are doing. *What do the people want? Why are civil rights important?* Repeat students' responses, correcting for grammar and pronunciation as needed.

Advanced

Explain Ask students to elaborate on civil rights. *What are examples of civil rights? Why are they important?* Ask students to clarify another student's response.

Objectives

- Identify the characteristics of a speech
- Develop vocabulary
- Read sentences fluently, using intonation and expression

Materials

- Read-Aloud Anthology, pp. 51–54.

Read Aloud

Read "I Have a Dream"

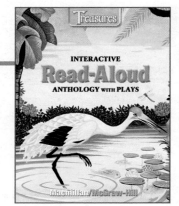

Read Aloud

GENRE: Speech

Share key characteristics of a **speech**:

- A speech is a formal talk about a topic given to a group of people, or audience.

- Some speeches are persuasive. They are written to convince the audience of a particular belief or to support a cause.

Explain that this selection is from a landmark 1963 speech by Martin Luther King, Jr. The speech was addressed to an audience of 200,000 people as a part of the March on Washington for Jobs and Freedom.

FOCUS ON VOCABULARY

Introduce the following words, using the **Define/Example/Ask** routine. Tell students that knowing these words will help them follow the text and understand the author's message as you read.

Vocabulary Routine

Use the routines below to discuss the meaning of each word.

Define: To be **momentous** means to be of great importance.
Example: My grandparents' 50th anniversary was a momentous occasion.
Ask: What is another example of a momentous occasion?

Define: If someone **languished** under difficult conditions, it means he or she lost health and vitality.
Example: The old man languished in the hot, stuffy apartment and fell ill.
Ask: How is languished different from bloomed?

Define: A **prodigious** meal is a very large and magnificent one.
Example: The Queen of England held a prodigious afternoon tea every day.
Ask: How is prodigious different from wealthy?

LISTENING FOR A PURPOSE

Ask students to listen carefully as you read "I Have a Dream" on **Read-Aloud Anthology** pages 51–54. Use the Think Aloud prompts provided. Have students listen to how Dr. King used language to present information to influence what his audience thinks or does.

ELL Interactive Reading Build students' oral language skills by engaging them in discussion about the speech's basic meaning.

- Point to the picture of Dr. King, the monuments, and audience members. Name each and have students repeat. Describe them.

- After the first paragraph, say: *Turn to your partner and discuss why this demonstration was important.*

- After the second paragraph, say: *A beacon light is very bright. Tell how a bright light would affect you if you were sitting in the dark.*

- After the last paragraph, say: *Tell your partner what this section means. Why will people be singing, "Free at last!"?*

Think/Pair/Share Use **Copying Master 2**, "I made a connection when …," to help students summarize and draw conclusions about what they learned about the conditions under which African Americans lived in the 1960s. When they complete it, have students turn to a partner to summarize the speech, identify persuasive language or techniques, and draw conclusions about its message.

RESPOND TO THE SPEECH

Ask students the Think and Respond questions on page 54. Then have them identify ways that people still receive unequal treatment today.

Model Fluency

Reread the speech. Tell students that this time you want them to focus on two aspects of how you read the story—your **expression** and your **intonation**.

Point out that you emphasize sections of the text that are exciting to add drama to your reading. For example, you give special emphasis to exclamations. You also use expression to keep tricky figurative language clear and comprehensible. Model an example.

Think Aloud Listen as I read the second paragraph, where Dr. King discusses the past. Listen to how I emphasize the words "symbolic" and "shadow." Listen to how I say "Emancipation Proclamation" with strength in my voice. Did you notice how much figurative language he uses? I try to convey the image of "seared in the flames of withering injustice" by giving it a lot of expression. Now you try. Repeat after me, using the same intonation.

Establish Fluency Focus Remind students that you will be listening for these same qualities in their reading throughout the week. You will help them improve their reading by varying their expression to add drama and for clarity and using intonation to indicate emphasis.

Point out that good readers show their understanding of a story by reading it in these expressive ways. It shows that the reader is decoding and comprehending at the same time. That is one hallmark of a skilled, fluent reader.

Readers Theater

BUILDING LISTENING AND SPEAKING SKILLS
Distribute copies of "Nat Love, Western Hero," **Read-Aloud Anthology** pages 167–181. Assign parts. Have students practice them throughout the unit. Have students present the play or perform a dramatic reading at the end of the unit.

ELL

Discuss Genre Review speeches with students. Ask: *What do people talk about in speeches? Why do people give speeches? What was Dr. King's speech about? Why do you think it is an important speech?* Correct the meaning of students' responses as needed.

Objective
- Decode multisyllabic words with prefixes

Materials
- Practice Book, p. 46
- Word-Building Cards
- Transparency 6
- Teacher's Resource Book, p. 125

Transfer Skills Some prefixes have similar meanings in English and Spanish. In Spanish, the prefixes *in*, *des*, and *dis* mean "not," and the prefix *re* means "again." Students can use this knowledge as they learn the English prefixes *in*, *dis*, and *re*. Use the Approaching phonics lesson on page 161J for students who need additional practice. See language transfers on pages T16–T31.

HOMEWORK Practice Book, page 46

When added to the beginning of a word, a **prefix** changes the meaning of the word.
The prefixes **un-**, **non-**, and **dis-** mean "not" or "the opposite of."

- **dis** + trust = distrust   to not trust
- **non** + sense = nonsense   something that doesn't make sense
- **un** + covered = uncovered   the opposite of covered

The prefix **mis-** means "badly" or "incorrectly."

- **mis** + spell = misspell   to spell incorrectly

Each of these prefixes has a short vowel sound.

Underline the prefix in the following words. Then write the meaning of the word. **Possible responses provided.**

1. <u>dis</u>obey not obey
2. <u>un</u>sure not sure
3. <u>mis</u>behave behave badly
4. <u>non</u>sense the opposite of sense
5. <u>un</u>happy not happy
6. <u>dis</u>like not like
7. <u>mis</u>understand understand incorrectly
8. <u>dis</u>connect not connect
9. <u>un</u>believable not believable
10. <u>mis</u>calculate calculate incorrectly

Approaching Reproducible, page 46
Beyond Reproducible, page 46

Morphology

 **Prefixes**

EXPLAIN/MODEL

Explain that a prefix is a group of letters that appears at the front of a word. A prefix affects the meaning of the root (base) word to which it is attached. To determine if a group of letters is a prefix, remove them from the word. The letters are a prefix if a known word remains.

Introduce the three most common prefixes. Write each prefix and the sample words on the board. Define the prefix. Then use the prefix's meaning to model determining the meaning of the sample words:

- **un-** usually means "not" but can also mean "do the opposite of."
  I felt <u>un</u>happy when I failed my math test.
  I had to <u>un</u>tie my shoe when a rock slipped in.
- **in-** means "not."
  My work was <u>in</u>complete so I did not get a grade.
  She was <u>in</u>correct when she said the world is flat.
- **re-** means "again."
  Mary had to <u>re</u>apply her makeup after a long day.
  I had to <u>re</u>assure my mother that I was okay after I slipped.

Think Aloud Look at the first word I wrote: *unhappy*. I see the prefix *un-* at the beginning. That means "not." The rest of the word is *happy*. So this word means "not happy."

PRACTICE/APPLY Display **Transparency 6**. Help students underline the prefix, define it, and then use its meaning to determine the meaning of the whole word.

Point out nonexamples, such as *uncle*, *realistic*, and *invent*. The letter clusters in these words are not in fact prefixes, and when they are removed what remains is not a complete word.

reaction	inconvenient	uncomfortable
revisited	indignity	unsettle
returned	inseparable	unable
reattach	incorrect	unafraid

Phonics Transparency 6

✓ Read Multisyllabic Words

TRANSITION TO LONGER WORDS Display the prefixes and the words below. Have students chorally read the prefixes in the first column. Then ask students to underline the prefix in the longer word in the second column. Model how to read the word and determine its meaning. Point out the additional prefixes *im-*, *dis-*, and *ir-*, all meaning "not."

un	undress	un	unaware
in	incapable	in	indefinite
re	reteach	re	redraw
im	impossible	im	imperfect
dis	disable	dis	disagree
ir	irregular	ir	irrational

Phonics Transparency 6

BUILD WORDS Use **Word-Building Cards** *un, re, in, expect, cover, lease, connect, capable, attach, pay, correct, ed*. Display the cards. Have students use the word parts to build as many words with prefixes as possible. These and other words can be formed: *unexpected, uncover, recover, recovered, release, reconnect, reattached, repay, incorrect*.

APPLY DECODING STRATEGY Guide students to use the Decoding Strategy to decode the following words: *revision, irresponsible, impolite, disrespected, undecided, irresistible, unfavorable, indistinct*. Write each word on the board. Remind students to look for common word parts, such as prefixes, in step 1 of the Decoding Strategy procedure. Conclude by discussing the meaning of each word.

Build Fluency

SPEED DRILL Distribute copies of the **Prefix Speed Drill** on **Teacher's Resource Book** page 125. Use the Speed Drill routine to help students become fluent reading words with common prefixes.

Quick Check

Can students read words with prefixes?

During **Small Group Instruction**

Tier 2

If No → **Approaching Level** Reteach the skill using the lesson on p. 161J.

If Yes → **On Level** Consolidate the learning using p. 161S.

Beyond Level Extend the learning using p. 161W.

DAILY Syllable Fluency

Use Word-Building Cards 51–60. Display one card at a time. Have students chorally read each common syllable. Repeat at varying speeds and in random order. Have students work with partners during independent time to write as many words as they can containing each syllable.

Decoding Strategy

Decoding Strategy Chart

Step 1	Look for word parts (prefixes) at the beginning of the word.
Step 2	Look for word parts (suffixes) at the end of the word.
Step 3	In the base word, look for familiar spelling patterns. Think about the six syllable-spelling patterns you have learned.
Step 4	Sound out and blend together the word parts.
Step 5	Say the word parts fast. Adjust your pronunciation as needed. Ask yourself: "Is this a word I have heard before?" Then read the word in the sentence and ask: "Does it make sense in this sentence?"

© Macmillan/McGraw-Hill

Vocabulary

STRATEGY
WORD PARTS

Prefixes and Suffixes Discuss the definitions of prefixes and suffixes on the bookmark on **Student Book** page 138. Point out that prefixes and suffixes often come from Latin, Greek, or other languages. Explain that learning the meanings of prefixes and suffixes can help students figure out the meanings of words with those word parts. Model the strategy using the word *unfair*.

Think Aloud I see the word *unfair* in the first paragraph. Since I know that *fair* means "right and just" and that *un-* means "not," I can figure out the meaning of the whole word. *Unfair* must mean "not fair" or "not right and just." Yes, that meaning makes sense in the sentence.

Write other words beginning with *un-* on the board (*unusual, unlikely, unhappy, unreal*). Remind students that not every word that begins with *un-* is a base with a prefix—for example, *union*.

Review the suffix *-ful* in the same manner. Familiar prefixes, suffixes, and examples can also be displayed visually around the classroom. Tell students to keep a list of prefixes, suffixes, and meanings in their Writer's Notebooks.

Read "It Took Courage"

As you read "It Took Courage" with students, ask them to identify clues that reveal the meanings of the highlighted words. Tell students they will read these words again in *My Brother Martin*.

Vocabulary

unfair	segregation
ancestors	avoided
numerous	injustice

Word Parts

Prefixes are added to the beginnings of words to change their meanings. The prefix *un-* means "not."
unfair = "not fair"
Suffixes are added to the ends of words. The suffix *-ful* means "full of."
peaceful = "full of peace"

138

IT TOOK COURAGE

by Lily Tuttle

CIVIL RIGHTS are equal opportunities for all citizens regardless of race, religion, or gender. At one time, **unfair** laws gave some people more opportunities than others. Several brave people took a stand against this and made a difference.

Thurgood Marshall

Thurgood Marshall's family had come a long way from the time when their **ancestors** were slaves. But when he wanted to attend the University of Maryland Law School, the school rejected him because he was black. Marshall had to go to a different law school.

Later, in one of his first court cases, Marshall helped a young African American student sue the University of Maryland. The school had denied him admission, too.

Marshall worked hard to win **numerous** cases. One of his best-known trials was *Brown v. Board of Education* in 1954. In this case the Supreme Court decided to end **segregation** in schools. The Court made it illegal for black students and white students to be sent to separate locations.

Quick Check

Can students identify word meanings?

During **Small Group Instruction**

Tier 2

If No → **Approaching Level** Reteach the words using the Vocabulary lesson, pp. 161K–161L.

If Yes → **On Level** Consolidate the learning using p. 161S.

Beyond Level Extend the learning using p. 161W.

Ruby Bridges

In 1960 six-year-old Ruby Bridges was the first black child to go to an all-white school in the South. Ruby was young and unsuspecting. She didn't realize how brave she was to do this. White parents decided to take their children out of school. For a whole year Ruby and her teacher were the only people there. Eventually some white children returned. The following year more black children came. Ruby Bridges made a difference.

Dr. Martin Luther King, Jr.

Dr. Martin Luther King, Jr., was a leader in the 1950s and 1960s. He **avoided** violence and asked others to fight in peaceful ways to end **injustice**.

King organized a march on Washington, D.C. There he and thousands of others demanded equal rights for all people. He gave a famous speech that day. He said, "I have a dream." King's dream was that all people would be treated fairly and equally.

Reread for **Comprehension**

Monitor Comprehension

Author's Purpose One way to monitor comprehension is to identify the author's purpose. The reason an author writes a story is the author's purpose. An author writes to entertain, give information, or persuade. Thinking about how and why an author presents events and other information can help you identify the author's purpose. Reread the selection and fill in the Author's Purpose Map.

Clue	Clue	Clue
↓	↓	↓

Author's Purpose

LOG ON ▶ **LEARN IT** Comprehension
www.macmillanmh.com

139

HOMEWORK **Practice Book,** page 47

injustice	ancestors	unfair
numerous	segregation	avoided

Use the clues below to complete the vocabulary word puzzle.

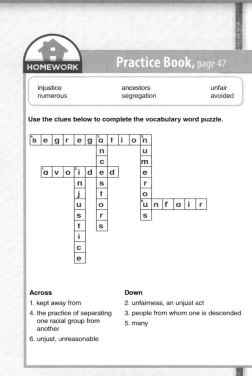

Across
1. kept away from
4. the practice of separating one racial group from another
6. unjust, unreasonable

Down
2. unfairness, an unjust act
3. people from whom one is descended
5. many

Approaching Reproducible, page 47

Beyond Reproducible, page 47

Vocabulary

TEACH WORDS

Introduce each word using the **Define/Example/Ask** routine. Model reading each word using the syllable-scoop technique.

Vocabulary Routine

Define: Something that is **unfair** is not right or just.
Example: It was unfair to deny Native Americans citizenship for centuries.
Ask: What situations have you heard about that are unfair? EXAMPLE

- Your **ancestors** are people who were members of your family before the present generation. *Sean's ancestors came from Ireland.* What do you know about your ancestors? DESCRIPTION

- A group of people or things is **numerous** if there are many of them. *After numerous tries, Sally finally made the soccer team.* What is a synonym for the word *numerous*? SYNONYM

- **Segregation** is the separation of people or things. *In the United States, segregation meant separating people by skin color, making one group use different schools, restaurants, etc.* What adjectives could describe segregation? EXPLANATION

- If you **avoided** something, you stayed away from it. *Jama avoided busy streets when riding her bike.* Describe a time when you avoided something. DESCRIPTION

- If an **injustice** takes place, something unfair has been done. *Not allowing women to vote until 1920 was an injustice to women.* What is an antonym for the word *injustice*? ANTONYM

Objectives

- Monitor comprehension
- Identify the author's purpose
- Recognize how authors present the major events in a person's life
- Use academic language: *monitor comprehension, author's purpose*

Materials

- Transparencies 6a, 6b, 9
- Practice Book, p. 48

Skills Trace

Author's Purpose

Introduce	139A–139B
Practice/ Apply	140–155; Practice Book, 48–49
Reteach/ Review	161M–161Z, 165A–165B, 166–183, 187M–187Z; Practice Book, 57–58
Assess	Weekly Tests; Units 2, 4 Tests
Maintain	195B, 465A–465B, 466–469, 473Q–473DD, 605B

ELL

Academic Language
Preteach the following academic language words to **ELL** and **Approaching Level** students during Small Group time: *monitor comprehension, author's purpose*. See pages 161AA and 161I.

Reread for
Comprehension

STRATEGY
MONITOR COMPREHENSION

What Is It? Explain to students that when they **monitor comprehension**, they check and adjust their understanding of the text using self-correction techniques. This includes stopping and asking questions, rereading aloud, paraphrasing, and reading ahead.

Why Is It Important? Point out that choosing the right self-correction techniques can help students become successful, independent readers.

SKILL
AUTHOR'S PURPOSE

What Is It? The **author's purpose** is the main reason an author has for writing. Authors write to entertain, inform, or persuade.

Why Is It Important? Understanding why the author wrote about a subject can help a reader fully comprehend the text. Some selections, such as biographies, can be written for more than one purpose. Recognizing how authors present the major events in a person's life, and the language they use, can help readers determine the author's purpose.

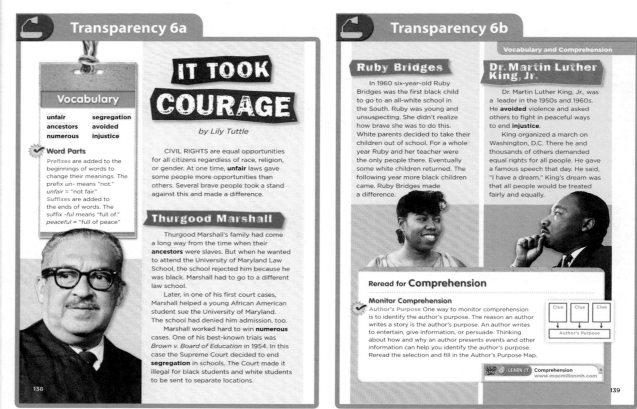

Student Book pages 138–139 available on Comprehension Transparencies 6a and 6b

Point out that if a selection includes humor or exaggeration, the author's purpose is probably to entertain. If the author gives a lot of information, the purpose is probably to inform. Authors whose purpose is to persuade try to convince readers of their opinions.

When reading a biography, students can determine the author's purpose by looking at how the author presents the major events of a person's life. Students should look at the details the author includes and the literary language and devices used. Students should ask themselves questions, such as *Why did the author choose to include these events? Does the author only want to inform readers, or persuade them to accept a certain point of view?*

MODEL

How Do I Use It? Have students reread the first paragraph of "It Took Courage" on **Student Book** page 138.

Think Aloud After the author gives a brief definition of "civil rights," she states that some brave individuals have fought to make sure that all people receive equal opportunities. I will probably learn facts about these people, but when the author uses the word *brave*, she may be stating an opinion. This may be a clue to the author's purpose. As I read, I will look for more clues.

GUIDED PRACTICE

Begin by having students recall the questions they should ask themselves as they read. Then display **Transparency 9**. Help students first look for any evidence that the author's purpose is to entertain. Have them fill in the first clue box on the Author's Purpose Map.

APPLY

Have students complete the Author's Purpose Map. They should look for any evidence that the author's purpose is to inform or to persuade and then decide on the purpose and fill in the bottom box. Ask students to identify the clues in the text that helped them decide.

Quick Check

Can students identify the author's main purpose?

During **Small Group Instruction**

Tier 2

If No → **Approaching Level** Reteach the skill using the Comprehension lesson, pp. 161M–161P.

If Yes → **On Level** Consolidate the learning using pp. 161U–161V.

Beyond Level Extend the learning using pp. 161Y–161Z.

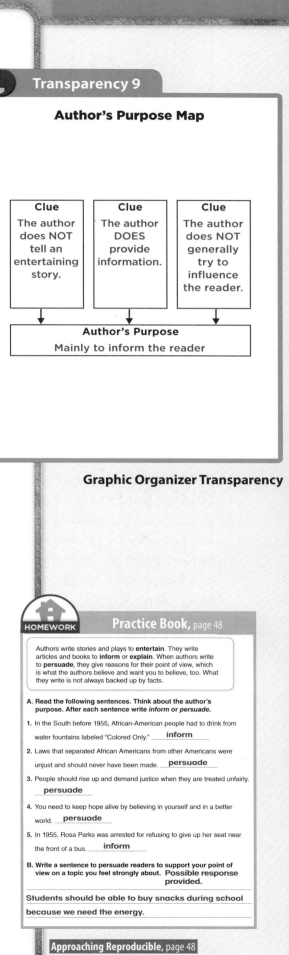

Transparency 9

Author's Purpose Map

Clue	Clue	Clue
The author does NOT tell an entertaining story.	The author DOES provide information.	The author does NOT generally try to influence the reader.

Author's Purpose
Mainly to inform the reader

Graphic Organizer Transparency

Practice Book, page 48

Authors write stories and plays to **entertain**. They write articles and books to **inform** or **explain**. When authors write to **persuade**, they give reasons for their point of view, which is what the authors believe and want you to believe, too. What they write is not always backed up by facts.

A. Read the following sentences. Think about the author's purpose. After each sentence write *inform* or *persuade*.

1. In the South before 1955, African-American people had to drink from water fountains labeled "Colored Only." ___**inform**___

2. Laws that separated African Americans from other Americans were unjust and should never have been made. ___**persuade**___

3. People should rise up and demand justice when they are treated unfairly. ___**persuade**___

4. You need to keep hope alive by believing in yourself and in a better world. ___**persuade**___

5. In 1955, Rosa Parks was arrested for refusing to give up her seat near the front of a bus. ___**inform**___

B. Write a sentence to persuade readers to support your point of view on a topic you feel strongly about. Possible response provided.

Students should be able to buy snacks during school because we need the energy.

Approaching Reproducible, page 48

Beyond Reproducible, page 48

Read

WHOLE GROUP

✓ **MAIN SELECTION**
- *My Brother Martin*
- Skill: Author's Purpose

✓ **PAIRED SELECTION**
- Nonfiction: "Barbara Jordan"
- Text Feature: Surveys

SMALL GROUP

- Differentiated Instruction, pp. 161I–161HH

Main Selection

GENRE: Literary Nonfiction/Biography

Read the definition of Biography on **Student Book** page 140. Students should look for important facts about a real person's life as written by another person. Point out that the events in a biography are usually organized in chronological order.

STRATEGY
MONITOR COMPREHENSION

Remind students to monitor their comprehension as they read. If the text is unclear, students can reread, ask questions, or read ahead to clarify.

SKILL
AUTHOR'S PURPOSE

An author's purpose may be to entertain, persuade, or inform. Thinking about the author's word choice and how the author presents the events in a person's life can help readers identify the author's purpose.

Comprehension

Genre

A **Biography** is a story about the life of a real person written by someone else.

Monitor Comprehension

✓ **Author's Purpose**

As you read, fill in your Author's Purpose Map.

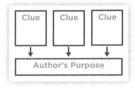

Read to Find Out

What does Rev. Dr. Martin Luther King, Jr.'s sister want you to know about him?

140

Vocabulary

Vocabulary Words Review the tested words while reading: **unfair, ancestors, injustice, avoided, segregation**, and **numerous**.

Additional Selection Words Students may be unfamiliar with these words. Pronounce the words, give student-friendly explanations as needed, and help students use the previously taught vocabulary strategies: word origins, synonyms, antonyms.

waning (p. 144): becoming smaller or fewer in number

streetcar (p. 146): a vehicle that holds many passengers and runs on rails through city streets

indignity (p. 146): something that insults a person's self-respect

bigotry (p. 150): hatred or intolerance toward an entire group of people; prejudice

my brother MARTIN

Award Winning Illustrator

A SISTER REMEMBERS
GROWING UP WITH THE REV. DR. MARTIN LUTHER KING JR.

BY CHRISTINE KING FARRIS
ILLUSTRATED BY CHRIS SOENTPIET

141

Read the Main Selection

Preteach	Read Together	Read Independently
Have Approaching Level students and English Language Learners listen to the selection on **StudentWorks Plus**, the interactive e-Book, before reading with the class.	Use the prompts to guide comprehension and model how to complete the graphic organizer. Have students use **Think/Pair/Share** to discuss the selection.	If students can read the selection independently, have them read and complete the graphic organizer. Suggest that they use their purposes to choose their reading strategies.

LOG ON ▶ StudentWorks Plus
Interactive Student Book

Preview and Predict

QUICK WRITE Ask students to read the title, preview the illustrations, and think about the genre. They should write their predictions about the kinds of information they will find in the text.

Set Purposes

FOCUS QUESTION Discuss the "Read to Find Out" question on **Student Book** page 140. Have students look for the answer as they read. Also have students set their own reading purposes.

Point out the Author's Purpose Map in the Student Book and on **Practice Book** page 49. Tell students they will fill it in as they read.

Read *My Brother Martin*

Use the questions and Think Alouds to support instruction about the comprehension strategy and skill.

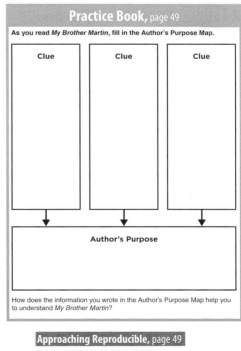

Practice Book, page 49

As you read *My Brother Martin*, fill in the Author's Purpose Map.

Clue	Clue	Clue

Author's Purpose

How does the information you wrote in the Author's Purpose Map help you to understand *My Brother Martin*?

Approaching Reproducible, page 49
Beyond Reproducible, page 49

Develop Comprehension

1 STRATEGY
MONITOR COMPREHENSION

Teacher Think Aloud The author does not directly state her purpose for writing at the beginning of this selection. Knowing the author's purpose can help me choose a reading strategy, so I will monitor my comprehension as I read to help me determine the author's purpose. I will look at how the author has presented the information and events so far. Rereading the title page, I know this selection will be about Martin Luther King, Jr. The subtitle is "A Sister Remembers," so the author is writing about her famous brother when he was born and when he was a child. I know some things about Martin Luther King, Jr., as an adult, but I don't know much about his childhood. Now his sister will tell me about his growing-up years. I notice that she begins right from when they are born and writes in the first person.

1 We were born in the same room, my brother Martin and I. I was an early baby, born sooner than expected. Mother Dear and Daddy placed me in the chifforobe drawer that stood in the corner of their upstairs bedroom. I got a crib a few days afterward. A year and a half later, Martin spent his first night in that hand-me-down crib in the very same room.

The house where we were born belonged to Mother Dear's parents, our grandparents, the Reverend and

142

Monitor Comprehension

Monitor and Clarify: *Read Ahead*

Explain Tell students that if something seems unexplained in a story, they can read ahead for more information. Learning more can be the key to understanding important background.

Discuss Have students infer why the extended King family all live together. (Students might read ahead to page 144 to find out that the King parents were away from home a lot, so someone else needed to be there to watch their children.)

Apply After they read the selection, have students tell how reading ahead helped them understand the selection better.

Mrs. A. D. Williams. We lived there with them and our Aunt Ida, our grandmother's sister.

And not long after my brother Martin—who we called M. L. because he and Daddy had the same name—our baby brother was born. His name was Alfred Daniel, but we called him A. D., after our grandfather.

2

143

Develop Comprehension

2 MONITOR AND CLARIFY: READ AHEAD

Can you tell from the text so far if the three King siblings all got along? (No.) What strategy can you use to get this information? (You can read ahead to see how the three siblings developed and how they got along later in life.)

PHONICS/WORD STUDY

APPLY DECODING SKILLS While reading, point out words with the sound/spelling patterns, syllable types, and word parts students have recently learned. Help students blend these words. You may wish to review selection words with prefixes such as *unsuspecting, indignity,* and *recall.*

ELL ENGLISH LANGUAGE LEARNERS

Beginning

Use Visuals Preteach story content, build language, and develop meaning using the Interactive Question-Response Guide in the **ELL Resource Book**, pages 58–65. Give ample time for students to respond. They may point or use words or short phrases to respond.

Intermediate

Describe Preteach story content, build language, and develop meaning using the Interactive Question-Response Guide in the ELL Resource Book, pages 58–65. Have students respond in complete sentences. Repeat students' responses, correcting pronunciation or grammar as needed.

Advanced

Explain Complete the Intermediate task with students. Elicit details from students for their responses.

Develop Comprehension

3 SKILL
AUTHOR'S PURPOSE

✓ When she says, "And being normal young children, we were almost *always* up to something," what is the **author's purpose** in presenting her childhood in this way? (By stressing the word *always*, she shows enthusiasm and fondness. As she recalls the fun times, you can "hear" her smile. She is entertaining us.)

4 SEQUENCE

 Reread the paragraph about the prank with the piece of fur. What specific details about **sequence** does the author include to help you understand how the children played the prank? Why are these details important? (She says that they only played the prank "once in a while" and did it when evening was approaching. These sequence details are important because they help explain why the prank was successful. If the children had tried the prank more often or at a time of day when it was easier to see, the passersby would not have been as likely to be fooled.)

They called me Christine, and like three peas in one pod, we grew together. Our days and rooms were filled with adventure stories and Tinkertoys, with dolls and Monopoly and Chinese checkers.

And although Daddy, who was an important minister, and Mother Dear, who was known far and wide as a musician, often had work that took them away from home, our grandmother was always there to take care of us. I remember days sitting at her feet, as she and Aunt Ida filled us with grand memories of their childhood and read to us about all the wonderful places in the world.

3 And of course, my brothers and I had each other. We three stuck together like the pages in a brand-new book. And being normal young children, we were almost *always* up to something.

Our best prank involved a fur piece that belonged to our grandmother. It looked almost alive, with its tiny feet and little head and gleaming glass eyes. So, every once in a while, in the waning light of evening, we'd tie that fur piece to a stick, and, hiding behind the hedge in front of our house, we would dangle it in front of unsuspecting passersby. Boy! You could hear **4** the screams of fright all across the neighborhood!

Then there was the time Mother Dear decided that her children should all learn to play piano. I didn't mind too much, but M. L. and A. D. preferred being outside to being stuck inside with our piano teacher, Mr. Mann, who would rap your knuckles with a ruler just for playing the wrong notes. Well, one morning, M. L. and A. D. decided to loosen the legs on the piano bench so we wouldn't have to practice. We didn't tell Mr. Mann, and when he sat . . . *CRASH!* down he went.

144

Text Evidence

Author's Purpose

Reread Question 3. Remind students that to determine the author's purpose in this section, they must find evidence in the text, such as literary language and the literary devices an author uses, and make connections between them.

Then ask, *What simile does the author use to describe her relationship with her brothers? Point to the simile when you find it.* (The author writes in the third paragraph that she and her brothers were stuck together like pages in a brand-new book.) *How does this literary device provide evidence for the author's purpose?* (An author's purpose is to inform, entertain, or persuade. This simile is an exaggeration, so it provides evidence that the author's purpose here is to entertain.)

But mostly we were good, obedient children, and M. L. did learn to play a few songs on the piano. He even went off to sing with our mother a time or two. Given his love for singing and music, I'm sure he could have become as good a musician as our mother had his life not called him down a different path.

But that's just what his life did.

5

> ✓ Author's Purpose
> Why does the author tell so much about Martin's childhood?

6

145

Develop Comprehension

5 MAKE INFERENCES

Did M. L., Christine, and A. D. enjoy their childhood? Give details from the text to support your **inference**. (Yes, they seem to have had a lively, fun childhood. The author says they played a lot of games and pranks and were always together.)

6 SKILL
AUTHOR'S PURPOSE

✓ Think about the **author's purpose** here. What events does the author include? Why does the author tell so much about Martin's childhood? (The events described on these two pages are things experienced by typical, energetic, and playful children. The author wants us to know that, when they were children, M. L. and his siblings played pranks and did other things that most children do.) Add this information to your Author's Purpose Map.

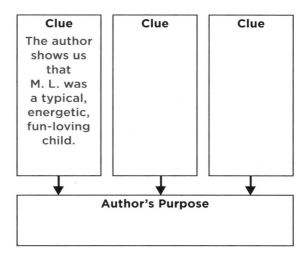

Clue	Clue	Clue
The author shows us that M. L. was a typical, energetic, fun-loving child.		

Author's Purpose

Vocabulary

Word Structure Clues: *Suffixes*

Explain/Model Explain that suffixes are word parts that are added to the end of a base word. Suffixes change a word's meaning and often change its part of speech. Point out the suffix *-ian* can mean "a person who is expert in" and comes from Latin. Write *mathematician*.

Think Aloud When I remove the suffix *-ian*, I see the base word *mathematic*. I know that *-ian* can mean "an expert in." When I put the meaning of the suffix and the base word together, I get "an expert in mathematics."

Practice/Apply Write *electrician*. Have students identify the suffix and say what the word means. Then have them find a word with *-ian* on page 145 and say what it means. (*musician*: an expert in music) Discuss how adding *-ian* to these base words changes the pronunciation of the final *c* so that the letters *ci* spell the sound /sh/.

Develop Comprehension

7 GENRE: Literary Nonfiction/Biography

In a **biography**, the author usually gives information about the time period and places in which the subject lived. How did the laws in Atlanta at the time affect M. L.'s family? (M. L.'s family avoided the unfairness of Atlanta's laws as much as possible by staying close to home. Daddy avoided using the streetcars, and they rarely went to the movies or to Grant Park.) Why does the author include this historical information? (It lets us know the reasons that M. L.'s family chose to live the way they did. It shows that the prejudice they experienced was actually part of the legal system and not just the author's opinion about the way people behaved.)

8 STRATEGY
WORD PARTS

How does knowing the meaning of the **prefix** *re-* help you find the meaning of *recall*? (The prefix *re-* means "again" or "back." For example, *review* means "look at again." So, *recall* means "call again" or "call back." In this context, the author is thinking about the past, so it must mean "call back a memory" or "remember.")

My brothers and I grew up a long time ago. Back in a time when certain places in our country had **unfair** laws that said it was right to keep black people separate because our skin was darker and our **ancestors** had been captured in far-off Africa and brought to America as slaves.

7 Atlanta, Georgia, the city in which we were growing up, had those laws. Because of those laws, my family rarely went to the picture shows or visited Grant Park with its famous Cyclorama. In fact, to this very day I don't recall ever seeing my father on a streetcar.

8 Because of those laws, and the indignity that went with them, Daddy preferred keeping M. L., A. D., and me close to home, where we'd be protected.

We lived in a neighborhood in Atlanta that's now called Sweet Auburn. It was named for Auburn Avenue, the street that ran in front of our house. On our side of the street stood two-story frame houses similar to the one we lived in. Across it crouched a line of one-story row houses and a store owned by a white family.

When we were young all the children along Auburn Avenue played together, even the two boys whose parents owned the store.

146

And since our house was a favorite gathering place, those boys played with us in our backyard and ran with M. L. and A. D. to the firehouse on the corner where they watched the engines and the firemen. **9**

The thought of *not* playing with those kids because they were different, because they were white and we were black, never entered our minds. **10** **11**

147

Develop Comprehension

9 **DRAW CONCLUSIONS**

Do you think M. L. and his siblings understood the laws that kept black people separate in Atlanta? Use information from the selection to explain your **conclusion**. (Daddy protected the children as much as he could, so they may not have felt the effects of the laws. They played with their white neighbors, so the fact that black people were kept separate may not have been obvious to them yet.)

10 **SKILL**
AUTHOR'S PURPOSE

 Why does the author emphasize the word *not*? Use the text to support your answer. (She wants to show that the children had not yet learned to judge or think differently about someone because of skin color. She writes that the thought never entered their minds.)

11 **SELF-SELECTED STRATEGY USE**

What strategies have you used so far to help you understand the selection? Where did you use them? Why? How did they help?

RETURN TO PREDICTIONS AND PURPOSES

Have students respond to the selection by confirming or revising their predictions and purposes for reading. Encourage them to revise or write additional questions to help focus their attention as they continue to read the selection.

Stop here if you wish to read this selection over two days.

Extra Support

Author's Purpose

If students are having difficulty identifying the purpose of this biography, help them answer questions such as the following:

- Is a biography fiction or nonfiction?

- Did the author personally know the subject of this biography? If so, how?

- What part of the subject's life is the author writing about?

- What does the author want you to know about this part of the subject's life?

- How is the subject like other people? How is he different?

Develop Comprehension

12 STRATEGY
MONITOR COMPREHENSION

Teacher Think Aloud I know that the author of a biography has a purpose in choosing which parts of the subject's life to include or leave out. I can monitor my comprehension by paraphrasing the events so far. Using her memories, this author has been telling us about the happy, normal childhood that M. L. and his siblings had. Why did the author include the sad story about losing their friends?

PARTNERS Prompt students to apply the strategy in a Think Aloud by asking them to read ahead to learn more about what this experience meant to M.L.

Student Think Aloud I will read ahead to see if I can find the answer. On page 149, I find that this was the first time the children were treated unjustly. I know that Martin Luther King, Jr., later led the fight against racism and prejudice. The author is showing why this childhood event became important to him. I can add this to my Author's Purpose Map.

Clue	Clue	Clue
The author shows us that M. L. was a typical, energetic, fun-loving child.	The author tells us how M. L. first experiences prejudice in action.	

↓ ↓ ↓

Author's Purpose

Well, one day, M. L. and A. D. went to get their playmates from across the street just as they had done a hundred times before. But they came home alone. The boys had told my brothers that they couldn't play together anymore because A. D. and M. L. were Negroes.

And that was it. Shortly afterward the family sold the store and moved away. We never saw or heard from **12** them again.

148

Looking back, I realize that it was only a matter of time before the generations of cruelty and **injustice** that Daddy and Mother Dear and Mama and Aunt Ida had been shielding us from finally broke through. But back then it was a crushing blow that seemed to come out of nowhere. **13**

"Why do white people treat colored people so mean?" M. L. asked Mother Dear afterward. And with me and M. L. and A. D. standing in front of her trying our best to understand, Mother Dear gave the reason behind it all. **14** **15**

149

Develop Comprehension

13 MAKE JUDGMENTS

How might Martin and his brother be treated differently from their former neighbors as they grow up? Give details from the text to support your answer. (Martin and A. D. might have to live with the pain of feeling discriminated against because of the color of their skin, just as Daddy, Mother Dear, Mama, and Aunt Ida had.)

14 SEQUENCE

SPIRAL REVIEW How would you restate the **sequence** of Martin's childhood as the author describes it so far? (Martin grew up in the South in a close, loving family. Martin, his older sister Christine, and his younger brother A. D. enjoyed their childhood. At first they were sheltered from prejudice. Then an event involving their white friends showed them what prejudice was like, and their understanding of the world changed forever.)

15 AUTHOR'S PERSPECTIVE

How has the **author's perspective** on the King children's childhood changed? (At first, she talks about the enjoyable times and the love the family shared. Now she is discussing the unfair laws and bigotry that they experienced. She uses words such as *cruelty, injustice, crushing*, and *mean* to show that not all of M. L.'s early life was joyful.)

Comprehension

Author's Perspective

Explain The author's point of view about her material is called **author's perspective**. Considering what they know about the author and looking for words that express opinions will help students to figure out the author's viewpoint on her subject.

Discuss Ask students to consider the identity of the author of this biography. What is her perspective on Martin Luther King, Jr.? (The author's perspective is that of a loving sister.)

Apply As they consider the author's perspective on page 149, suggest that students look back over the selection for words that express opinions or persuasive language. What opinion words help them understand the author's perspective on page 144? (Positive words such as *important minister, grand memories*, and *wonderful places* show the Kings' childhood as a mainly pleasant experience.)

Develop Comprehension

16 **SKILL**

AUTHOR'S PURPOSE

What literary device does the author use to describe M. L.'s reaction when his mother explained prejudice to the children? (The author uses dialogue.) Why does the author include this? (By recalling that Martin said he would turn the world upside down, the author identifies the moment when he decided he would take action.) **Add this information to your Author's Purpose Map.**

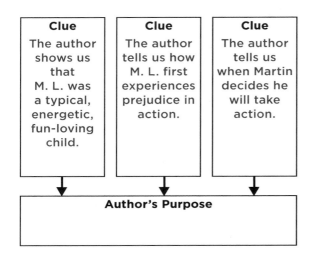

Clue	**Clue**	**Clue**
The author shows us that M. L. was a typical, energetic, fun-loving child.	The author tells us how M. L. first experiences prejudice in action.	The author tells us when Martin decides he will take action.

Author's Purpose

17 **MAKE INFERENCES**

Why does Daddy share with his children his experiences with prejudice and bigotry? Give details from the text to support your answer. (He wants them to know what they might have to face. The author says "Daddy practiced what he preached." Daddy shows them how to stand up for themselves.)

Her words explained the streetcars our family **avoided** and the WHITES ONLY sign that kept us off the elevator at City Hall. Her words told why there were parks and museums that black people could not visit and why some restaurants refused to serve us and why hotels wouldn't give us rooms and why theaters would only allow us to watch their picture shows from the balcony.

But her words also gave us hope.

She answered simply: "Because they just don't understand that everyone is the same, but someday, it will be better."

And my brother M. L. looked up into our mother's face and said the words I remember to this day.

16 He said, "Mother Dear, one day I'm going to turn this world upside down."

In the coming years there would be other reminders of the cruel system called **segregation** that sought to keep black people down. But it was Daddy who showed M. L. and A. D. and me how to speak out against hatred and bigotry and stand up for what's right.

Daddy was the minister at Ebenezer Baptist Church. And after losing our playmates, when M. L., A. D., and I heard our father speak from his pulpit, his words held new meaning.

And Daddy practiced what he preached. He always stood up for himself when confronted with hatred and bigotry, and each day he shared his encounters at the dinner table.

17 When a shoe salesman told Daddy and M. L. that he'd only serve them in the back of the store because they were black, Daddy took M. L. somewhere else to buy new shoes.

150

ELL **ENGLISH LANGUAGE LEARNERS**

STRATEGIES FOR EXTRA SUPPORT

Question 16 AUTHOR'S PURPOSE
Explain the word *reaction*. Ask students to restate the meaning of the word. Correct the meaning of students' responses as needed. Next ask: *What was M. L.'s reaction to Mother Dear's explanation? What does M. L.'s reaction tell us about him? Why does the author tell us so much about his reaction?* Elicit details and information from the text to support students' responses.

Another time, a police officer pulled Daddy over and called him "boy." Daddy pointed to M. L. sitting next to him in the car and said, "This is a boy. I am a man, and until you call me one, I will not listen to you."

These stories were as nourishing as the food that was set before us.

18

19

151

Develop Comprehension

18 PROBLEM AND SOLUTION

How did Reverend King solve his **problems** with the shoe salesman and the police officer? (He left the shoe store, and he refused to listen to the police officer.) What do his actions tell you about his character? (He was a proud man who would not be disrespected.)

19 FIGURATIVE LANGUAGE

What does the author mean when she uses the **simile** that the "stories were as nourishing as the food that was set before us"? (She means that learning about the importance of standing up for one's rights helped the children grow just as much as their food did.) How does the author's use of this simile help you to understand the selection? (It is a vivid way to tell how important it was for the children to hear the stories. We can tell that they listened carefully to the stories and were strongly influenced by them.)

Develop Comprehension

20 STRATEGY
MONITOR COMPREHENSION

How can monitoring your comprehension help you to determine the author's purpose for writing?

Student Think Aloud I will go back and reread when Martin first faced prejudice and reread his father's experiences. Martin lost his friends because of prejudice. His father always stood up for himself and was a great speaker. The author wants to show that these experiences shaped Martin's adult life.

21 SKILL
AUTHOR'S PURPOSE

Why does the author echo Martin's words, "I'm going to turn this world upside down"? (This biography describes events leading up to the time when King realized he wanted to turn the world upside down. The author mentions all the speeches, marches, and prizes that came about because of his desire to change the world, so we realize that what he once said to his mother came true.) Use this information to complete your Author's Purpose Map.

Clue	Clue	Clue
The author shows us that M. L. was a typical, energetic, fun-loving child.	The author tells us how M. L. first experiences prejudice in action.	The author tells us when Martin decides he will take action.

Author's Purpose
To give information about how Martin decided he wanted to change the world.

20 Years would pass, and many new lessons would be learned. There would be **numerous** speeches and marches and prizes. But my brother never forgot the example of our father, or the promise he had made to our mother on the day his friends turned him away.

152

And when he was much older, my brother
M. L. dreamed a dream . . . that turned the
world upside down. **21**

> ✓ **Author's Purpose**
> Why does the author echo Martin's words,
> "I'm going to turn this world upside down"?

153

Quick Check

Can students identify the author's purpose for writing this biography?

During **Small Group Instruction**

If No → **Approaching Level** Reteach the skill and have students apply it to a simpler text. Use Leveled Reader lessons, pp. 161N–161P.

If Yes → **On Level** Have students apply the skill to a new text to consolidate learning. Use Leveled Reader lessons, pp. 161U–161V.

Beyond Level Have students apply the skill to a more complex text to extend learning. Use Leveled Reader lessons, pp. 161Y–161Z.

Develop Comprehension

RETURN TO PREDICTIONS AND PURPOSES

Review students' **predictions** and **purposes** for reading. What did they find out about Dr. King? (Dr. King had a loving family who taught him to take a stand against bigotry and prejudice.) How did knowing that this selection is a biography help students predict what they would read about? (In a biography you can expect to learn facts about a real person's life.)

REVIEW READING STRATEGIES

- **Monitor Comprehension** In what ways did monitoring your comprehension help you understand the selection?

- **Monitor and Clarify: Read Ahead** Do you understand the strategy of reading ahead when you cannot find answers to your questions on the page you are currently reading? When might you use it again?

- **Decoding** What difficult words did you encounter? How did the Reading Multisyllabic Words strategy help you sound out these words?

- **Self-Selected Strategy Use** What strategies did you use to make sense of what you read? Where? How were these strategies helpful?

 PERSONAL RESPONSE

Ask students to write a personal response to this selection. What did they find most surprising or inspiring? Have them support their answers with details from the text.

Author and Illustrator

THE STORIES OF CHRISTINE AND CHRIS

Have students read the biographies of the author and the illustrator. Ask:

- Why is Christine King Farris an especially qualified person to write about Martin Luther King, Jr.?

- What are different ways an author's life and times might be reflected in a text?

- Why is it important for Chris Soentpiet and other illustrators to be accurate when illustrating historical stories?

WRITE ABOUT IT

Author's Craft: Biography
Remind students that not all biographies cover a person's entire life. Have them write a biography of their eighth year.

Author's Purpose

Remind students that an author's personal experiences and relationships often affect his or her writing. Ask students to check their Author's Purpose Maps for clues that tell if Christine King Farris was trying mostly to persuade, inform, or entertain the reader.

The Stories of Christine and Chris

Christine King Farris wrote this story to show children that her famous brother was once a kid just like them. She saw how young Martin laughed, played, and dreamed of a better world. As Christine says, "Dreams are based on imagination. All leaders dream big dreams that are larger than life."

Chris Soentpiet does a lot of research when he illustrates historical stories like this one. He goes to the library to study what clothes people wore and how they lived. Sometimes he even visits the actual locations where story events took place. That is why it often takes Chris up to a year to illustrate a book.

Other books illustrated by Chris Soentpiet

LOG ON ▶ FIND OUT
Author Christine King Farris
Illustrator Chris Soentpiet
www.macmillanmh.com

✔ Author's Purpose

Why did Christine King Farris write *My Brother Martin*? How did the author's relationship with her brother influence this story?

154

Author's Craft

Biography

A biography is the story of someone's life, told by another person.

- For this selection, Christine King Farris focuses on one part of Dr. King's life: his childhood. She deals with a few key childhood events.

- Have students skim the selection to identify and discuss key examples of Christine King Farris's focus, such as "When we were young all the children along Auburn Avenue played together, even the two boys whose parents owned the store." (p. 146)

- Make sure students understand the author's views on ethnicity as well as the historical period described in the text.

- Discuss other biographies students may have read. Do they tell about the person's entire life or focus on one particular time?

Comprehension Check

Summarize

To summarize *My Brother Martin* use the most important details from the story. Information from your Author's Purpose Map may help you.

Clue	Clue	Clue

↓ ↓ ↓

Author's Purpose

Think and Compare

1. In what city did Christine and her brothers grow up? Details

2. What happened after Mother Dear said, "Because they just don't understand that everyone is the same, but someday, it will be better"? Sequence

3. How did Martin feel about **injustice**? Explain using details from the story to support your answer. Make Inferences

4. Identify the simile used in the first paragraph on page 144. How does the author's use of simile help the reader understand the relationship between Christine and her two brothers? Monitor Comprehension: Author's Purpose

5. Read "It Took Courage" on pages 138–139. Compare the experiences of Thurgood Marshall and Dr. Martin Luther King, Jr. How did segregation affect both men? Use details from both selections to explain. Reading/Writing Across Texts

155

Make Connections

Text-to-Self Have students respond to the following question to make connections to their own lives. Use the Think Aloud to model a response. *Suppose you had met Rev. Dr. Martin Luther King, Jr., when he was a child. What character traits would you have in common?*

Think Aloud: In this selection, I read about what Dr. Martin Luther King, Jr., was like as a child. He played pranks and liked to play. He also wanted to change things that he felt were not right. I will compare these traits to traits that I have and see how we are alike.

Text-to-World Have students respond to the following question to make connections to the world. Use the Think Aloud to model a response. *Why is it important to correct injustice?*

Think Aloud: I read that Dr. King and his family were treated differently because of the color of their skin. As Mother Dear says, everyone is the same. All people should be treated equally.

Comprehension Check

SUMMARIZE

Have partners summarize *My Brother Martin* in their own words. Remind students to use their Author's Purpose Maps to help them organize their ideas.

THINK AND COMPARE
Text Evidence

1. **Details** <u>Answer stated in text</u> Christine and her brothers grew up in Atlanta, Georgia. LOCATE

2. **Sequence** <u>Answer stated in text</u> M. L. looked up at his mother and said that one day he would turn the world upside down. This was the moment he decided he would take action against prejudice. COMBINE

3. **Make Inferences** <u>Answer</u> M. L. did not understand injustice. <u>Evidence</u> Students should examine the details in the text, think about their own experiences connected to the text, then make inferences. Martin asked his mother why some people were mean to them. People ask questions when they do not understand something. CONNECT

4. **Author's Purpose** <u>Answer</u> The author writes that she and her brothers were like three peas in a pod. The author's purpose is to show that she and her brothers were very close. <u>Evidence</u> Peas inside a pea pod are very close together. ANALYZE

5. **Text-to-Text** Thurgood Marshall could not go to a certain school, and Martin was not allowed in certain public places in his hometown. They both worked to make sure that African Americans had equal rights. COMPARE TEXT

Objectives

- Read accurately with appropriate intonation and expression
- Rate: 84–104 WCPM

Materials

- Transparency 6
- Practice Book, p. 50
- Fluency Solutions Audio CD

ELL

Develop Comprehension
Break the passage into smaller phrase units, and discuss each paragraph so that students understand what they will read. Use gestures and board sketches to convey meaning. Then read each phrase aloud and have students repeat. Ask students to describe the main idea of the passage in phrases or sentences.

Practice Book, page 50

As I read, I will pay attention to intonation and expression.

	Coretta Scott King never planned on being a civil rights
10	leader. She thought she would become a teacher or a singer.
21	Instead, she became a leader in the fight for equal rights.
32	Coretta Scott was born in 1927 in a small town in
42	Alabama. She walked three miles to get to school each
52	morning. And she walked three miles back each afternoon.
61	Every day she watched school buses drive white children to
71	their school.
73	In those days **segregation** was the law in the South.
83	African Americans could not go to certain restaurants.
91	They could not drink from certain water fountains. They
100	had to sit in the back of public buses. Black children and
112	white children went to separate schools.
118	Coretta's father Obadiah (oh-buh-DIGH-uh) was the
123	first African American in his county to own his own truck.
134	Some white truckers felt that he was taking away their
144	business. One day the Scotts came home from church to
154	find that their home had burned down. 161

Comprehension Check

1. What is the author's purpose? **Author's Purpose** The author's purpose is to inform us about the difficulties Coretta Scott faced as a child.
2. Why do you think the Scotts' house was burned down? **Cause and Effect** The people who thought that Coretta's father was taking business away from white truckers might have had something to do with the fire.

	Words Read	–	Number of Errors	=	Words Correct Score
First Read		–		=	
Second Read		–		=	

Approaching Reproducible, page 50

Beyond Reproducible, page 50

Fluency

Repeated Reading: Intonation/Expression

EXPLAIN/MODEL Point out that part of reading with good expression is using the correct intonation. Explain that paying close attention to punctuation will help students read with proper intonation. Contrast intonation for questions and statements as you model the passage on **Transparency 6**. Also have students notice how you read expressively.

Transparency 6

"Why do white people treat colored people so mean?" M. L. asked Mother Dear afterward. And with me and M. L. and A. D. standing in front of her trying our best to understand, Mother Dear gave the reason behind it all.

Her words explained the streetcars our family avoided and the WHITES ONLY sign that kept us off the elevator at City Hall. Her words told why there were parks and museums that black people could not visit and why some restaurants refused to serve us and why hotels wouldn't give us rooms and why theaters would only allow us to watch their picture shows from the balcony.

But her words also gave us hope.

Fluency (from *My Brother Martin*, pp. 149–150)

PRACTICE/APPLY Divide students into two groups. The first group reads the passage a sentence at a time. The second group echo-reads. Then groups switch roles. Make sure they pay attention to reading the dialogue with expression and to using the proper intonation for different types of sentences.

DAILY FLUENCY Students will practice fluency using **Practice Book** page 50 or the **Fluency Solutions Audio CD**. The passage is recorded at a slow practice speed and a faster fluent speed.

Quick Check

Can students read accurately with appropriate intonation and expression?

During **Small Group Instruction**

If No → **Approaching Level** Use the Fluency lesson and model, p. 161Q.

If Yes → **On Level** See Fluency, p. 161T.

Beyond Level See Fluency, p. 161X.

 Comprehension

REVIEW SKILL
SEQUENCE

EXPLAIN/MODEL

- Remind students that the **sequence** of events is the time-order action of a story or narrative. Sequence, or chronological order, is often indicated by signal words such as *first, next, then, lastly*, and *afterward*. Dates and times also indicate sequence.

- Identifying sequence is important for understanding both fiction and nonfiction texts. Biographies and other informational texts about historical events are usually organized in sequence order.

Read the second and third paragraphs of "It Took Courage" aloud. Point to the word *Later* at the beginning of the third paragraph. Explain that this is a signal word that tells the time-order relationship between two events in Thurgood Marshall's life. Say: *First, he was rejected from the University of Maryland. "Later" tells me that some time after that, he helped a student sue the university.* Help students to identify other signal words for sequence in the selection. (*at one time, when, 1954, 1960, for a whole year, eventually, that day*)

PRACTICE/APPLY

Review *My Brother Martin*. Discuss how certain experiences and events influenced Dr. King as he became a leader for change. Have partners use these questions to make a sequential list of the events.

- What do you learn about the laws in Atlanta when Martin Luther King, Jr., was a child? When was this? (*A long time ago the laws kept people separated by the color of their skin.*)

- How did M.L. and A.D. feel when their white friends said they were not allowed to play with them anymore? Why? (*They felt sad and confused because it was the first time they were treated unfairly because of their skin color.*)

- How did the streetcar and shoe store incidents affect Martin? How old was he then? (*He learned how to stand up for himself when confronted with hatred. He was still a boy.*)

Have students share their lists of the experiences and events that influenced Martin Luther King, Jr., later in life. To extend the activity, have partners generate a research plan for gathering information on Dr. King using encyclopedias or interviews. Then have students collaborate on a time line showing the major events of his life.

PRACTICE BOOK See **Practice Book** page 51 for Persuasive Language.

Objectives

- Identify sequence of events in biographies
- Identify language that signals sequence

Skills Trace

Sequence

Introduce	107A–107B
Practice/ Apply	108–121; Practice Book, 39–40
Reteach/ Review	125M–125Z, 229A–229B, 230–251, 257M–257Z; Practice Book, 84–85
Assess	Weekly Tests; Units 1, 2, 5 Tests
Maintain	155B, 285B, 641A–641B, 642–659, 663M–663Z, 697B

Test Practice

Answering Questions

To apply **answering questions strategies** to content-area reading, see pages 45–52 in *Time For Kids*.

Paired Selection

GENRE: Informational Text/Expository

Read the bookmark on **Student Book** page 156. Explain that expository writing explains, describes, or gives information. Examples include newspaper and magazine articles, research reports, and instructions.

Point out that an expository article

- is nonfiction writing that informs the reader;

- tells who someone is, what something is, how something works, or why something is important;

- may have headings and subheadings that summarize the main ideas and help readers locate information.

✴ Text Feature: Surveys

Point out the **survey** on page 159. Explain that this survey is designed to find out how students feel about different school issues.

- A survey is a series of questions that can often be answered with a "yes," "no," or "undecided."

- A survey is a way of gathering information from people.

- The results of a survey can help leaders know how people feel about certain matters.

Have students identify the purpose of this survey. (to find out which school issues are important to students) Discuss how students can use surveys themselves to gather information. Explain that students will conduct their own surveys after reading this article.

Social Studies

Genre

Expository selections give information and facts about people, places, or things.

✔ Text Feature

Surveys gather information by asking people for their opinions about specific topics.

Content Vocabulary

orators   opinions

legacy

Barbara Jordan
A Powerful Speaker
by Jayden Kirksey

Barbara Jordan was one of the greatest **orators** of our time. Her speeches helped many people understand the importance of equal rights.

Barbara Jordan was born in Houston, Texas, in 1936. Her father was a clerk and a former minister. Her grandfather, who lived with the family, was also a former minister. They taught Barbara how powerful and important words could be. As a child, she also learned the value of a school education. She studied how to write and deliver speeches in debates. This experience helped her to become a successful lawyer later in life.

1

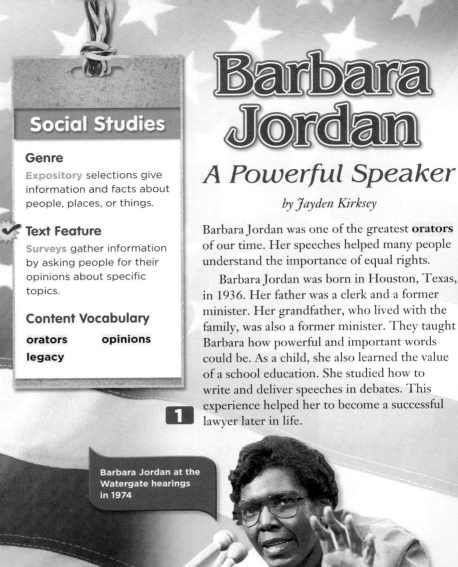

Barbara Jordan at the Watergate hearings in 1974

156

Content Vocabulary

Explain the words using the **Define/Example/Ask** routine. Definitions are provided for this activity.

- **Orators** are public speakers. What skills might orators have in common?

- If you have a **legacy**, what you do remains important for a long time. Who is someone that has left a legacy?

- If you have **opinions**, you have certain beliefs or views. On what topic do you have very strong opinions?

Jimmy Carter and Barbara Jordan at the 1976 Democratic Convention

Working for Change

At the time, many rules discriminated against African Americans. Barbara wanted people to be treated fairly under the law. She ran for political office in 1966 and became the first African American woman ever elected to the Texas Senate. She was later elected to office in the U.S. House of Representatives in 1972. Presidents, such as Lyndon B. Johnson and Jimmy Carter, depended on Barbara's skills and knowledge. She became a powerful voice for **2** justice and equality in our nation's government.

Barbara left politics due to health reasons. Even when she relied on a wheelchair to get around, she continued to write and speak. She became a teacher to help prepare others to carry on her message. Thirty-one schools and universities awarded her honorary degrees to call attention to her achievements. Many of our nation's greatest orators today continue to honor her **legacy**. **3**

157

Social Studies
Connect to Content

SPEECH

Tell students that in 1976, Barbara Jordan became the first African American woman to deliver a keynote address at the Democratic National Convention. Have students use the Internet to locate information about the speech Barbara Jordan delivered at the 1976 convention. Students should write a brief report summarizing the speech and the impact it had on the Democratic party.

Paired Selection

Read "Barbara Jordan: A Powerful Speaker"

As students read, remind them to apply what they have learned about surveys. Also have them identify clues to the meanings of highlighted words.

1 MAIN IDEA AND DETAILS

What details tell you about Barbara Jordan as an orator? What main idea do you learn from these details? (Details: She helped people understand the importance of equal rights; she learned how powerful and important words could be; she studied how to write and deliver speeches. Main idea: Barbara Jordan was a very effective orator.)

2 MAKE INFERENCES

What inferences can you make about Barbara Jordan's accomplishments from the first paragraph on page 157? (Barbara Jordan worked toward helping people achieve justice and equality. She also helped open the door for other African Americans and women to work in government.)

3 ANALYZE TEXT STRUCTURE

What text structure does the author use to organize information on pages 156–157? How can you tell? (The author uses a sequence text structure. Clues include dates such as 1936.)

Use the Interactive Question-Response Guide in the **ELL Resource Book**, pages 66–67, to help students gain access to the paired selection content.

Paired Selection

4 TEXT FEATURE: SURVEYS

Do surveys mainly help you find out facts or opinions? Explain your answer. (Opinions. When people fill out surveys they are not telling you facts that can be proven, but rather their thoughts, feelings, or beliefs.)

5 TEXT FEATURE: SURVEYS

How could you interpret the results of the survey on page 159? (You would tally the responses to each question. The questions with the most "yes" answers are the issues which students are most concerned about. A candidate for class president would want to convince voters that he or she is going to work toward those goals students care about most.)

Conducting a Survey

Barbara Jordan cared about people and she wanted to know if people thought they were being treated unfairly. Surveys help people like Barbara Jordan and other politicians to know what the people they represent are thinking about and what might help them most.

Surveys are useful tools for finding out more about something. They can help us to discover **opinions** on important topics. Unlike facts which can be verified, or proven true, opinions are what somebody thinks, feels, or believes. Surveys play an important role in our government. **4** You could even say that voting is a kind of survey.

If you were running for class president, you might conduct a survey in your school to find out how students feel about a particular issue such as raising money to buy books for the library or starting an online school newspaper. In order to get the best results possible, you should interview a large number of students. Ask them simple direct questions that can be answered with "Yes," "No," or "Undecided." These kinds of questions will make it easier for you to record their answers.

Barbara Jordan gave the keynote address at the 1992 Democratic National Convention.

158

ON YOUR OWN

Practice Book, page 52

A **survey** can help you collect information from a large group of people. Begin by considering what you want to learn. Then write questions for people to answer. The questions should be about your topic and should be answered with "Yes," "No," or "Undecided." To understand the results of the survey, tally the answers to see how most of the people feel about the topic.

Read the following survey and answer the questions.

Survey for Student Council			
Question	Yes	No	Undecided
1. Do you think our playground equipment needs to be replaced?	☐	☐	☐
2. Do you think students should help raise money for new equipment?	☐	☐	☐
3. Do you think the school should have a walk-a-thon to raise money?	☐	☐	☐
4. Do you think the school should hold a bake sale to raise money?	☐	☐	☐

1. Why are all of the questions answered with "Yes," "No," or "Undecided"?
   They are easy to tally.

2. What two ways for raising money are given in this survey?
   walk-a-thon and bake sale

3. Why do you think these two ways of raising money are given?
   So the students can see which way is most popular.

4. What survey topics can you conduct at your school?
   Answers will vary.

Approaching Reproducible, page 52
Beyond Reproducible, page 52

ELL

Content Vocabulary Write the words *orator, legacy,* and *opinion* on the board. Explain the meaning of each word and provide examples using the words in sentences. Brainstorm with students for synonyms or words related to the content vocabulary. List the words on the board. Have students use them in phrases or complete sentences to describe Martin Luther King, Jr., or Barbara Jordan. Give students ample time to respond.

Class President's Survey

Flora Aiken wants to run for president of her class. She created the following survey to help her prepare a speech about why she would make a good class president.

QUESTION	YES	NO	UNDECIDED
1. Do you think we should raise money to buy books for our library?	☐	☐	☐
2. Would you like to see more computers in the library?	☐	☐	☐
3. Do you think we should have more class field trips?	☐	☐	☐
4. Should we serve more fruit in our cafeteria?	☐	☐	☐

5

Connect and Compare

1. Will Flora find out facts or opinions from the questions on her survey? Explain your answer. **Conducting a Survey**

2. Is it a fact that Barbara Jordan was elected to the Texas Senate? How would you prove it? **Apply**

3. Think about what you learned from *My Brother Martin* about Martin Luther King, Jr. How are he and Barbara Jordan alike? **Reading/Writing Across Texts**

Social Studies Activity

Create a survey that would help you to write an article about how to improve something in your school. Explain what you hope to learn from each question. Conduct the survey and report what you find to the class.

LOG ON ▶ FIND OUT **Barbara Jordan**
www.macmillanmh.com

159

Connect to Content

RESEARCH AND INQUIRY

Make a Presidential Time Line Tell students that, like Barbara Jordan, many leaders in the national government have come from Texas, including three Presidents.

Have students conduct research to learn facts about a President from Texas. They can choose from Lyndon Johnson, George H. W. Bush, and George W. Bush. To which political party did the President belong? How did his life in Texas impact his presidency? What legacy did the President leave?

After gathering significant facts about their selected President, students should organize their findings in a time line, and present their completed work to the class.

Paired Selection

Connect and Compare

1. Flora will find out the opinions of students. Her questions ask for students' thoughts on certain issues, rather than for facts that can be proven. CONDUCTING A SURVEY

2. It is a fact that Barbara Jordan was elected to the Texas Senate. You could prove it by looking at Senate records, or by looking at sources such as history books, reliable Internet sites, or newspaper articles from that time period. APPLY

3. **FOCUS QUESTION** Both Barbara Jordan and Martin Luther King, Jr. grew up in the South. Jordan grew up in Houston, Texas. King grew up in Atlanta, Georgia. Their fathers and grandfathers were both ministers. They were both influential African American leaders who spoke about and fought for equal rights. READING/WRITING ACROSS TEXTS

Social Studies Activity

Remind students to pose questions that can be answered with "yes," "no," or "undecided." Students can distribute their surveys to students in the class, the grade, or the school.

Write

WHOLE GROUP

✓ **WRITING WORKSHOP**
- Developing Procedural Writing
- Trait: Ideas
- Showing

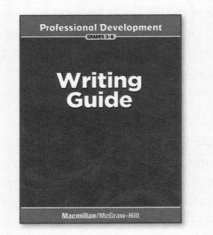

Professional Development
GRADES 3–6

Writing Guide

Macmillan/McGraw-Hill

Trait: Ideas

Strong Sentences: Showing

TEACH/MODEL Remind students that writers add details to tell more about a moment, object, or setting. Tell them that showing is when a writer uses **descriptive details** to give readers a clear image of an idea or experience. Readers can better connect with and understand a writer's ideas or experiences when they can create mental pictures.

Have students imagine that they receive a letter from a friend describing a room decorated for a birthday party. Write the following sentences on the board, and read it aloud:

> I went to a birthday party. The party room looked great.

Teacher Think Aloud This sentence tells me about the room. It tells me that the room looked great. It does not use details to show me what the room looked like, though, so it is hard for me to picture the room in my mind. After I read the sentence, I wonder what made the room look great. I know that I can write a more interesting description of the room by adding details.

Write the following description of the room on the board.

> I walked into the room and saw tons of colorful balloons. Red, yellow, orange, green, blue, and purple balloons were bobbing up and down on all of the walls. A rainbow of crepe paper stretched across the ceiling, from corner to corner. A string of letters hung across the door that spelled H-A-P-P-Y B-I-R-T-H-D-A-Y.

Read the description aloud. Discuss the differences between just saying that the room looked great and using strong sentences with details. Point out the descriptive details, such as *colorful balloons, a rainbow of crepe paper*, and *a string of letters*. Explain that the writer also used **spatial words**, or words that tell location, to show where these objects were in the room. Discuss how this gives readers a clear image of how the room looked.

Teacher Write Aloud

PRACTICE/APPLY Further explore with students the use of descriptive details to show an experience instead of tell. Tell students to imagine that they went to the birthday party in the decorated room. Instead of birthday cake, they ate ice cream sundaes. Write the following sentence about the ice cream sundae on the board. Then complete the Teacher Think Aloud.

> The ice cream sundae looked delicious.

Teacher Think Aloud This sentence tells me that the ice cream sundae looked delicious, but that does not help me picture it in my mind. Let's write a more interesting description of it. We will use descriptive details that will show readers what the sundae looked like and help them create a picture of it in their minds.

Prewrite Ask students to imagine the perfect ice cream sundae. Have them brainstorm details to show what it looks like. List the details on the board. To complete the Teacher Think Aloud, use the details to write a paragraph like the one below. Stop after each sentence to discuss how the details help students picture the sundae in their minds.

> My sundae had mounds of creamy vanilla ice cream on the bottom. Then there was the warm, gooey chocolate sauce dripping down the sides of the ice cream. On top of that was a huge, puffy cloud of whipped cream. Next, there was a sprinkling of chopped walnuts. Then, of course, the sundae had a bright red, juicy cherry on top!

Draft Display the Writing Prompt on **Writing Transparency 18**. Remind students to use descriptive details that show the meal so readers can create mental pictures of it. Circulate and provide Over-the-Shoulder Conferences as students work.

Objective
• Write details that show

Materials
• Writer's Notebooks
• Writing Transparency 18

Daily Journal Prompts

Focus on Showing

Use these and other prompts for independent daily journal writing.

✎ Write about a moment when you tasted something and hated it.

✎ Write about a moment when you tasted something and thought it was delicious.

✎ Write about a moment from your favorite vacation or from a visit to a favorite place.

✎ Write about a moment when you felt very cold.

Transparency 18

Describe the best meal you have ever tasted. Be sure to use words that show what the meal looked like and how it tasted.

Writing Transparency

Reading and Writing Connection

Trait: Ideas

SHOWING

Remind students that showing is when a writer uses details to help readers create images in their minds. Adding descriptive details gives more information to the reader and creates stronger sentences.

Read the Passage

Use the example from *My Brother Martin* as a model of the author's skilled use of showing.

- Have students read the bookmark. Remind them that details give information about people, objects, settings, or actions to help readers create a mental picture.

    Ask: *Have you ever played a trick on someone? Has someone ever played a trick on you?*

- Have students chorally read the excerpt from *My Brother Martin*. Direct their attention to the callout. Have students discuss details that help show them the prank.

    Ask: *Which detail helps you most clearly imagine the prank? Why do you think the author wanted readers to have a clear picture of this moment in their heads?*

Writing

✔ **Trait: Ideas**

Writers include **details** in their writing that show readers a strong image of what they are writing about.

Reading and Writing Connection

Read the passage below. Notice how the author Christine King Farris shows a moment in her story.

An excerpt from
My Brother Martin

The author shows us the prank. The details work together to make a clear picture in our minds about the children's funny trick.

Our best prank involved a fur piece that belonged to our grandmother. It looked almost alive, with its tiny feet and little head and gleaming glass eyes. So, every once in a while, in the waning light of evening, we'd tie that fur piece to a stick, and, hiding behind the hedge in front of our house, we would dangle it in front of unsuspecting passersby. Boy! You could hear the screams of fright all across the neighborhood!

160

Respond to the Selection

Have students write a response to the selection.

✔ **Engagement** Help students deepen their connection to the text and discover their own perspective on it. *Focus on a moment when you saw something happen that you thought was unfair.*

✔ **Response** Help students explore more deeply their reactions to particular passages in the reading. *Focus on a moment in the story when you thought something was unfair. Use text evidence in your writing.*

✔ **Literary Analysis** Help students deepen their connection to the text and discover their own perspective on it. *Focus on a place in the story where the author wanted you to picture what was happening. Use text evidence in your writing.*

Read and Find

Read Damon's writing below. What did he do to show you the moment? Use the checklist below to help you.

Read about Damon's move.

Muscle Man
by Damon L.

The boxes were only about the size of a loaf of bread, but they each weighed as much as a big dictionary. I stacked up five. I could feel my arm muscles straining, but I stuck with it. When I reached the second flight of stairs, I could feel my knees turn to jelly. My arms felt like too-tight rubber bands. Finally, I staggered into our apartment, dropped the boxes, and collapsed on the couch.

Writer's Checklist

✓ Does the writer describe exactly what he sees and feels?

✓ Does the writer include **details** about size, shape, weight, or other features?

☐ Can you picture what it was like for Damon in that moment?

161

Read the Student Model

Have students chorally read the student model at the top of **Student Book** page 161. Discuss what this student writer did to show a moment. Use the Writer's Checklist.

Journal Prompt

Draft Write the following prompt on the board. Have students write a response to the prompt.

> *Think about a moment when something unfair happened to you. Write three to five sentences to show what happened during that moment.*

Tell students that you will be reading and commenting on their writing during Writing Conference time.

Model how to use the Writer's Checklist so students can write and revise their work. Then ask:

- *What is the moment you chose?*

- *What details did you use to show what the moment was like? Will readers be able to clearly picture that moment? If not, what details could you add?*

ELL ENGLISH LANGUAGE LEARNERS

Beginning	Intermediate	Advanced
Write Sentences Provide model sentences based on the Journal Prompt: *It was unfair when I had to ____. I could not ____. I stayed home and ____.* Help students add words to complete the sentences. Guide them in including details that show what happened in the moment.	**Describe** Ask students to write three sentences based on the Journal Prompt. Have them picture the moment in their minds. Then have them use details to describe the moment. Provide a model if necessary. As you read their sentences, correct grammar and spelling as needed.	**Narrate** Ask students to respond to the Journal Prompt. Have them use details that will give readers a clear picture of the moment.

Write

Objectives
- Write showing sentences
- Write strong sentences

Materials
- Writer's Notebooks
- Teacher's Resource Book, p. 183

ELL

Sentence Comprehension
Review the meaning of each sentence. Define, illustrate, or act out terms like *sunset*, *fiery strokes*, *brightened*, and *eyes widened*. Then have students restate each sentence in their own words.

Minilessons

Minilesson 1 Ideas/Showing Sentences

TEACH/MODEL

Remind students that they have been focusing on showing, or using details that help readers picture one moment. Today they will practice recognizing and writing showing sentences. Have students use **Teacher's Resource Book** page 183. Write the following sentences on the board and have students read them.

> Mary Beth shivered and zipped up her coat.
> Martin was scared to open the closet.

Ask students which sentence is a showing sentence and why.

PRACTICE/APPLY

Have students work independently to write two sentences with details that show that Martin was scared to open the closet. Ask students to share their completed work during Sharing Circle.

Minilesson 2 Word Choice/Descriptive Words and Phrases

TEACH/MODEL

Remind students that writers include details in their writing to help their readers create mental images. Tell students that writers use descriptive words and phrases to give more information about each detail. Write the following sentences on the board, and read them aloud. Then ask students which sentences show and which tell. Discuss how showing makes stronger sentences. Have students identify the descriptive words and phrases in the showing sentences.

> The sunset was pretty last night.
> Fiery strokes of red brightened up the sky.
> I liked the sunset.
> My *eyes widened* as I watched the sunset.

PRACTICE/APPLY

In their Writer's Notebooks, have students think of a sunset that they have experienced. Have students write three showing sentences about the sunset. Remind students to use descriptive words and phrases so readers can picture the scene.

Conferencing Routine

Dynamic Feedback System

Step 1 Read and appreciate the writing.

Step 2 Notice how the student uses the targeted skill. (for example, showing: Ask: *Does the writer show rather than tell?*)

Step 3 Write comments that show how the writing has an impact on you. Direct your comments to those places in the piece where the student has used the targeted skill.

Step 4 Meet with and give the student a revision assignment.

Write Effective Comments

Ideas At least one of your comments should highlight the way the student uses the skill of **showing**. Here are some sample comments.

- I like the way you used strong sentences to show. It helps me create a picture in my mind.

- How could you show me this moment rather than tell me about it?

- What descriptive details could you use to help this moment come alive?

Revision Assignments

Ideas Here are some examples of effective revision assignments for showing.

Revise ■ *Reread your entry. Choose one sentence that shows a moment in time. Now rewrite this sentence, adding at least two sentences that include descriptive details that show.*

Revise ■ **[Underline a section.]** Mark a specific section of a student's writing and then ask the student to revise it in a specific way.

Revise ■ **[Underline a section.]** *Read the part that I underlined. I want to be able to imagine this moment in more detail. Write three sentences using descriptive words and phrases to show this moment.*

Teacher-to-Teacher

Over-the-Shoulder Conferences

Use these quick, focused opportunities to comment while students are writing.

- **Step 1** Quietly move close enough to a student that you can read the journal entry he or she is writing.

- **Step 2** Read part of what you see. You don't need to start from the beginning or read the entire piece.

- **Step 3** Show the student a spot in the writing where he or she is using a particular skill or describing something that piques your interest.

- **Step 4** Whisper a sentence or two about why you noticed that spot in the writing, and ask a question that will nudge the student to add details and descriptive words and phrases to show rather than tell.

- **Step 5** Move on to the next student. Select students strategically. You should see 12–15 students in a 15-minute period.

Research Proven Writing Approach

The Writers' Express
Immediate Impact. Lasting Transformation.   wex.org

ON YOUR OWN

Practice Book, page 53

> The prefix **un-** means "not."
> The prefix **re-** means "again."
> The suffix **-able** means "capable of."
>
> **Unfair** means "not fair."
> **Retell** means "tell again."
> **Teachable** means "capable of being taught."

A. Circle the phrases in the story that would sound better using the prefixes un- or re-. Then write the new words below.

"It's terribly (not fair,) Grandmother!" Cordelia exclaimed. "Wilson School is just three blocks away. Why can't I just keep attending my classes there?"

Cordelia's grandmother looked at the bowl of cold, (not eaten) soup and left Cordelia's question (not answered.) "Let me (warm again) that pea soup for you, honey. You'll feel better after you have had your dinner."

"I know you do not like this, Grandmother. Even though you're not saying anything, I know you're terribly (not happy) with the new laws. So, why can't you admit that (scheduling again) our classes miles away is (not acceptable)?"

Marion looked over her glasses at her granddaughter. "No use talking about it around our kitchen table, child. But there will be talk all over this great land of ours. And mark my words, Cordelia; these (not fortunate) days will not go (not noticed)."

unfair	uneaten	unanswered
rewarm	unhappy	rescheduling
unacceptable	unfortunate	unnoticed

B. Find the word with the suffix -able in the story. Write the word and its meaning on the line provided.

acceptable; capable of being accepted

Approaching Reproducible, page 53

Beyond Reproducible, page 53

Build Robust Vocabulary

Day 1 Teach/Practice

CONNECT TO WORDS

■ Practice this week's vocabulary words using the following prompts:

1. Why might something that is *unfair* make you angry?

2. What facts do you know about your *ancestors*?

3. Why might a gathering of *numerous* people be persuasive?

4. Which situation would be worse: *segregation* or emancipation? Why?

5. What kind of behavior is to be *avoided* at a formal event? Why?

6. Does *injustice* mean the same as *unfairness* or the opposite?

ACADEMIC VOCABULARY

■ Review the important academic vocabulary words for the week. These words include: *prefixes, suffixes, author's purpose, monitor comprehension, sequence, survey, intonation, expression*.

■ Write each word on the board. Define each using student-friendly language, and ask students to select the word you are defining. Then point to words in random order for students to define.

Day 2 Review

CONNECT TO WORDS

■ Review the definitions of this week's vocabulary words using **Student Book** pages 138–139. Then discuss each word using these prompts:

1. What event in your life has seemed *unfair*?

2. Would your *ancestors* be interesting people to meet? Why?

3. If *numerous* people support an idea, is the idea popular? Why?

4. What does *segregation* mean to you? Explain.

5. Why might people have *avoided* driving in 1911?

6. What type of person would be likely to speak out about social *injustice*? Why?

PREFIXES AND SUFFIXES

■ Review: Often an unfamiliar word can be decoded by identifying and defining prefixes and suffixes. A prefix is a word part that comes before the root or base. A suffix is a word part that comes after the root or base. The suffix *-able* means "capable of." It comes from Latin.

■ 📄 Display **Transparency 11**. Read the first sentence. Model how to define the underlined word by identifying and defining its word parts.

■ Have students find and define the prefixes and suffixes in the remaining words. Help students use both the prefix and suffix in *inseparable* to decode the word.

Day 3 Reinforce

CONNECT TO WORDS

- Ask students to create Word Squares for each word in their Writer's Notebooks.

- In the first square, students write the word. (Example: *numerous*)

- In the second square, students write their own definition of the word and any related words, such as synonyms. (Example: *many, lots, a great number*)

- In the third square, students draw a simple illustration that will help them remember the word. (Example: *a group of people*)

- In the fourth square, students write nonexamples, including antonyms for the word. (Example: *few, none, a small number*)

RELATED WORDS

- Help students generate words related to *injustice*.

- Point out that *injustice* contains the root or base word *just*, derived from the Latin *justus*, meaning "fair and right."

- Have students brainstorm other words that contain this root or base, and have them record the words in a word web with *just* in the center. Add words not included, such as *justice, unjust, justly, justify, justification*, and *justifiable*.

- Students can check the meanings of each word, as needed, using a dictionary or glossary.

Day 4 Extend

CONNECT TO WORDS

- Review this week's vocabulary using the following True/False sentences. Have students orally answer each.

1. Unfair events make you happy. (F)

2. Your ancestors are people in your family who lived before you were born. (T)

3. Numerous people cannot fit into a typical closet. (T)

4. Segregation means bringing people together. (F)

5. Poisonous snakes should not be avoided. (F)

6. A false arrest is an example of an injustice. (T)

MORPHOLOGY

- Use the additional selection vocabulary word *indignity* as a springboard for students to learn other words.

- Write *indignity* on the board. Explain that the prefix *in-* here means "without." *Dignity* comes from the Latin *dignitas*, meaning "worthiness." So *indignity* refers to a situation where someone is "treated without worthiness."

- Write the words *dignify* and *undignified* on the board. Use word parts to define each word. Remind students that *un-* means "not" and *-fy* means "make." So *dignify* means "make worthy" and *undignified* means "having been made not worthy."

Day 5 Assess and Reteach

POSTTEST

- Display **Transparency 12**. Have students complete the cloze sentences using one of this week's vocabulary words.

- Note how quickly and accurately students can complete this task. Work with students who make errors or require too much time to complete this task during Small Group time.

CONNECT TO WRITING

- Have students write sentences in their Writer's Notebooks using this week's vocabulary. Tell students to write sentences that provide information they learned from this week's readings.

- **ELL** Provide sentence stems for students needing extra support.

Go to pages T14–T15 for **Differentiated Spelling Lists**.

✔ Prefixes

Spelling Words

unblock	unborn	unchain
unload	unlock	recall
relearn	resell	rewash
rewind	imperfect	indirect
incorrect	illegal	overact
overheat	subway	premix
preplan	supersize	

Review stone, grown, lower
Challenge interact, transmit

Dictation Sentences

1. Will you unblock the drain?
2. I will unload the dishwasher.
3. I have to relearn all the math.
4. Don't **rewind** the videotape.
5. The bad behavior was incorrect.
6. Don't overheat the coffee.
7. Let's preplan where to meet.
8. The **unborn** whale was huge.
9. We unlock our bikes in the day.
10. Resell your used books.
11. Fix your imperfect makeup.
12 Breaking the law is illegal.
13. The subway was hot in August.
14. Supersize means a huge portion.
15. Unchain the old dog.
16. There was a recall on baby food.
17. We had to rewash the clothes.
18. She gave him an indirect smile with her eyes.
19. Watching her overact was torture.
20. We had to **premix** the ingredients.

Review/Challenge Words

1. The pot is made of stone.
2. I have grown over the last year.
3. My score was lower than yours.
4. We used to interact at lunchtime.
5. The telegraph will transmit the message.

Words in **bold** are from the main selection.

Day 1 Pretest

ASSESS PRIOR KNOWLEDGE

- Model for students how to spell the word *unlock*. Segment the word syllable by syllable, then attach a spelling to each syllable. Point out that *un-* is a prefix meaning *not*.

- Use the Dictation Sentences. Say the underlined word, read the sentence, and repeat the word. Have students write the words.

- Have students self-correct their tests. Point out that prefixes never appear at the ends of words.

Have students cut apart the **Spelling Word Cards BLM** on **Teacher's Resource Book** page 49 and figure out a way to sort them. Have them save the cards for use throughout the week.

Day 2 Word Sorts and Review

SPIRAL REVIEW

Review the long *o* sound in *stone, grown, lower*. Have students find words in this week's readings with the same sounds.

WORD SORTS

- Have students take turns sorting spelling words and explaining how they sorted them. When students have finished the sort, discuss any questions they might have.

- Review the spelling words, pointing out the prefixes. Use the cards on the Spelling Word Cards BLM. Write the key words *relearn, indirect*, and *premix* on the board. Model how to sort words by prefixes. Place one or two cards beneath the correct key words.

ON YOUR OWN — **Phonics/Spelling,** pages 31–32

Fold back the paper along the dotted line. Use the blanks to write each word as it is read aloud. When you finish the test, unfold the paper. Use the list at the right to correct any spelling mistakes.

1. _____	1. unblock
2. _____	2. unload
3. _____	3. relearn
4. _____	4. rewind
5. _____	5. incorrect
6. _____	6. overheat
7. _____	7. preplan
8. _____	8. unborn
9. _____	9. unlock
10. _____	10. resell
11. _____	11. imperfect
12. _____	12. illegal
13. _____	13. subway
14. _____	14. supersize
15. _____	15. unchain
16. _____	16. recall
17. _____	17. rewash
18. _____	18. indirect
19. _____	19. overact
20. _____	20. premix
Review Words 21. _____	21. stone
22. _____	22. grown
23. _____	23. lower
Challenge Words 24. _____	24. interact
25. _____	25. transmit

HOMEWORK — **Phonics/Spelling,** page 33

unblock	overact	rewind	imperfect	preplan
supersize	unborn	unchain	unload	resell
rewash	relearn	premix	illegal	unlock
indirect	subway	recall	overheat	incorrect

Prefix Power
Write the spelling words that contain the prefixes below.

un-
1. unblock
2. unborn
3. unchain
4. unload
5. unlock

re-
6. recall
7. relearn
8. resell
9. rewash
10. rewind

im-
11. imperfect

in-
12. indirect
13. incorrect

il-
14. illegal

over-
15. overact
16. overheat

sub-
17. subway

pre-
18. premix
19. preplan

super-
20. supersize

Day 3 Word Meanings

CATEGORIES

Have students copy the words below into their Writer's Notebooks. Say the pairs of words aloud and ask students to fill in the missing blanks with a spelling word.

1. unblock, unload, _____ (*unchain*)
2. resell, rewash, _____ (*rewind*)
3. imperfect, indirect, _____ (*illegal*)

Challenge students to come up with other word groups to which they can add spelling words, review words, or challenge words.

Have students do a word hunt for the words in weekly reading or other materials. They should identify the definition of the spelling word being used in context.

Day 4 Proofread

PROOFREAD AND WRITE

Write these sentences on the board. Have students circle and correct each misspelled word.

1. The subweigh overheeted in August. (*subway, overheated*)
2. She wanted to unlok the ilegle mystery. (*unlock, illegal*)
3. We had to premicks the sauce to avoid a recawl. (*premix, recall*)
4. Don't overheet or unlode the liquid gasoline. (*overheat, unload*)

Error Correction Remind students that prefixes can never be repeated within a word.

Day 5 Assess and Reteach

POSTTEST

Use the Dictation Sentences on page 161E for the Posttest.

If students have difficulty with any words in the lesson, have them place the words on a list called *Spelling Words I Want to Remember* in their Writer's Notebooks. Look for students' use of these words in their writings.

Challenge students to find words for each prefix they studied this week.

EXTEND

To extend the lesson, review how to spell words with other prefixes, such as *dis-* and *mis-*. Write *displease* and *misfit* on the board. Have students underline each prefix and discuss the words' meaning. Have students brainstorm and spell other words with these prefixes.

HOMEWORK — Phonics/Spelling, page 34

unblock	overact	rewind	imperfect	preplan
supersize	unborn	unchain	unload	resell
rewash	relearn	premix	illegal	unlock
indirect	subway	recall	overheat	incorrect

A. Words in Sentences
Write a spelling word to complete each sentence.

1. Do you ___recall___ learning about civil rights?
2. It can be helpful to ___relearn___ some of the facts each year.
3. It is ___illegal___ to take away a person's civil rights.
4. Civil rights laws ___unblock___ people's road to success.
5. The laws ___unlock___ doors that lead to good jobs.
6. They help make ___imperfect___ situations better.
7. I'm glad we can't ___rewind___ history to a time without civil rights.
8. It would be ___incorrect___ to think that all civil rights issues have been solved.

B. What Does It Mean?
Write the spelling word that matches each meaning.

9. not born ___unborn___
10. plan ahead of time ___preplan___
11. heat too much ___overheat___
12. underground train ___subway___
13. sell again ___resell___
14. mix before ___premix___
15. make too big ___supersize___
16. not direct ___indirect___
17. opposite of load ___unload___
18. wash again ___rewash___
19. take the chain off ___unchain___
20. act too much ___overact___

ON YOUR OWN — Phonics/Spelling, page 35

A. Proofreading
There are six spelling mistakes in the story below. Circle the misspelled words. Write the words correctly on the lines below.

"It's so hot I think I'm going to overheet," Elena said to Keisha. "Let's take the subbway instead of walking." "It will be my first time," Keisha said. "You'll have to show me what to do."

"It's easy," Elena said. "First we buy tickets. Then we need to make sure we get on the right train so we don't go to the incorrect place. When the train arrives, the doors will unlock. We have to wait for the people who were riding to unlode. Then we can get on."

When the girls were on the train, Keisha gave her seat to a man with a hurt leg. She had sprained her ankle a few months ago and could recal how painful it was to stand. Elena smiled at her friend. "It looks like you already know the most important part—treating others with kindness and respect," she said.

1. ___overheat___   3. ___incorrect___   5. ___unload___
2. ___subway___   4. ___unlock___   6. ___recall___

B. Writing Activity
Write a story about a time when you treated someone else with kindness. Use at least three spelling words in your paragraph. **Answers will vary.**

HOMEWORK — Phonics/Spelling, page 36

Look at the words in each set below. One word in each set is spelled correctly. Use a pencil to fill in the circle next to the correct word. Before you begin, look at the sample set of words. Sample A has been done for you. Do Sample B by yourself. When you are sure you know what to do, you may go on with the rest of the page.

Sample A:
- Ⓐ retry
- Ⓑ ritry
- Ⓒ rietry
- Ⓓ retrie

Sample B:
- Ⓔ priepay
- Ⓕ preepay
- Ⓖ prepay
- Ⓗ preapay

1.
- Ⓐ subbway
- Ⓑ subway
- Ⓒ subeway
- Ⓓ subwaye

2.
- Ⓔ uhnblock
- Ⓕ unbloc
- Ⓖ unblock
- Ⓗ uhnbloc

3.
- Ⓐ ilegal
- Ⓑ ilegle
- Ⓒ illegle
- Ⓓ illegal

4.
- Ⓔ resell
- Ⓕ ricell
- Ⓖ riesell
- Ⓗ risell

5.
- Ⓐ imperfect
- Ⓑ imperfict
- Ⓒ inperfect
- Ⓓ inperfict

6.
- Ⓔ unchane
- Ⓕ unchayn
- Ⓖ unchan
- Ⓗ unchain

7.
- Ⓐ priplan
- Ⓑ perplan
- Ⓒ preplan
- Ⓓ preeplan

8.
- Ⓔ indurect
- Ⓕ indirect
- Ⓖ indireckt
- Ⓗ indrect

9.
- Ⓐ riwach
- Ⓑ rewaush
- Ⓒ riwash
- Ⓓ rewash

10.
- Ⓔ unlock
- Ⓕ uhnlock
- Ⓖ uhnlok
- Ⓗ inlok

11.
- Ⓐ overack
- Ⓑ overackt
- Ⓒ overact
- Ⓓ ovirackt

12.
- Ⓔ ricall
- Ⓕ recal
- Ⓖ riecall
- Ⓗ recall

13.
- Ⓐ unbron
- Ⓑ unborn
- Ⓒ unborne
- Ⓓ unbon

14.
- Ⓔ rewind
- Ⓕ rewinde
- Ⓖ riwind
- Ⓗ riwhind

15.
- Ⓐ suprasize
- Ⓑ superize
- Ⓒ superseyes
- Ⓓ supersize

16.
- Ⓔ ohverheat
- Ⓕ overheat
- Ⓖ overhete
- Ⓗ ovirheat

17.
- Ⓐ premix
- Ⓑ premicks
- Ⓒ permix
- Ⓓ permicks

18.
- Ⓔ imcorrekt
- Ⓕ incorect
- Ⓖ incorrect
- Ⓗ imcorrect

19.
- Ⓐ unlode
- Ⓑ unloade
- Ⓒ unlod
- Ⓓ unload

20.
- Ⓔ rilearn
- Ⓕ relearn
- Ⓖ ruhlearn
- Ⓗ relern

Daily Language Activities

Write the sentences on the board.

DAY 1

When I got to school this morning I was really tired. Last night a noise woke me up, after I had gone to sleep. (1: morning,; 2: up after)

DAY 2

A girl named Lily sat in the bleachers next to me, do you know her. She is tall, but she is not taller than jack. (1: me. Do; 2: her?; 3: Jack.)

DAY 3

A Boy named roger is the best batter at school. His Sister is almost as good. (1: boy; 2: Roger; 3: sister)

DAY 4

The new Coach is Ms. Dowell. Have you herd of her. she has been hear since thursday. (1: coach; 2: heard; 3: her? She; 4: here; 5: Thursday.)

DAY 5

Next week is thanksgiving don't you love the Holidays. When we have four days off we can play so mutch baseball. (1: Thanksgiving. Don't; 3: holidays?; 4: off,; 5: much)

ELL

Proper Nouns Speakers of languages, such as Cantonese and Korean, that do not use alphabets may not be familiar with capitalizing proper nouns. On chart paper have students draw pictures and write or dictate the names of people and places that are special to them. Have them use capital letters. Then elicit from students when they would use capital letters.

✔ Common and Proper Nouns

Day 1 | Introduce the Concept

INTRODUCE COMMON AND PROPER NOUNS

Present the following:

- A **noun** is a word that names a person, a place, or a thing.

- A **common noun** names any person, place, or thing: *sister, museum, house*.

- A **proper noun** is the name or title of a specific person, place, or organization: *Aunt Ida, Brazil, House of Representatives*.

- Proper nouns always begin with capital letters. If a proper noun has more than one word, each important word begins with a capital letter.

See Grammar Transparency 26 for modeling and guided practice.

HOMEWORK — Grammar, page 26

- A **noun** names a person, place, or thing.
- A **common noun** names any person, place, or thing.
  Examples: teacher   city   dog
- A **common noun** does *not* begin with a capital letter.
- A **common noun** does *not* name a particular person, place, or thing. These words are not common nouns: Mr. Smith, Chicago, Spot.

Underline the common nouns in each sentence.

1. <u>Baseball</u> is my favorite <u>sport</u>.
2. The <u>pitcher</u> is named Jackie.
3. My <u>father</u> says the New York Yankees are a great <u>team</u>.
4. Listen to the <u>noise</u> of the <u>crowd</u> sitting in the <u>bleachers</u>.
5. Alissa said the <u>umpire</u> was wrong.
6. Alex and Daniel play <u>baseball</u> in the <u>backyard</u>.
7. My <u>sister</u> uses a wooden <u>bat</u>.
8. Don't throw the <u>ball</u> in the <u>house</u>!
9. The <u>batter</u> has two <u>strikes</u>.
10. John lost his <u>mitt</u>.
11. Your <u>foot</u> has to touch the <u>base</u>.
12. Let's watch the <u>game</u> together.
13. That <u>ball</u> is a <u>foul</u>.
14. Did you bring your <u>cleats</u>?

Day 2 | Teach the Concept

REVIEW COMMON AND PROPER NOUNS

Discuss with students how to recognize common and proper nouns.

INTRODUCE NOUNS THAT NAME PEOPLE, PLACES, DAYS, AND MONTHS

- Common nouns can name people: *girl, man*, and *doctor*. Proper nouns can also name people: *Mary, Mr. Boyd*, and *Dr. Steel*.

- Common nouns can name places: *state, city*, and *park*. Proper nouns can also name places: *Florida, Dallas*, and *Central Park*.

- Words such as *day, month*, and *holiday* are common nouns. Words such as *Monday, June*, and *Labor Day* are proper nouns.

See Grammar Transparency 27 for modeling and guided practice.

ON YOUR OWN — Grammar, page 27

- A **proper noun** names a particular person, place, or thing
  Examples: Ms. Brown   San Francisco   Atlantic Ocean
- A **proper noun** begins with a capital letter.
- Some proper nouns contain more than one word. Each important word begins with a capital letter.
  Examples: Statue of Liberty   Boston Red Sox
- The name of a day, month, or holiday begins with a capital letter.

Read the list of nouns below. Decide whether each noun is common or proper and write it in the correct column. Capitalize the nouns in the Proper column.

independence day	summer	uniform	new york
hank aaron	stadium	ebbets field	july
home plate	jackie robinson	coach	world series
diamond	game	shortstop	ohio

COMMON	PROPER
summer	Independence Day
uniform	New York
stadium	Hank Aaron
home plate	Ebbets Field
coach	July
diamond	Jackie Robinson
game	World Series
shortstop	Ohio

Day 3 Review and Practice

REVIEW NOUNS THAT NAME

Review how to identify common nouns and proper nouns that name people, places, days, and months.

MECHANICS AND USAGE: CAPITALIZING PROPER NOUNS

- Each important word in a proper noun should be capitalized.

- Capitalize proper nouns that name magazines, books, essays, stories, or artworks: *Time For Kids, Ramona, Common Sense, Cinderella, Guernica.*

- Capitalize proper nouns that name historical events and documents, languages, races, or nationalities, and the first word in quotations: *War of 1812, Magna Carta, Spanish, "To be, or not to be …"*

- Capitalize proper nouns for specific days and months: *Friday, March.*

 See Grammar Transparency 28 for modeling and guided practice.

Day 4 Review and Proofread

REVIEW COMMON AND PROPER NOUNS

Ask students to explain the differences between common nouns and proper nouns. Review the rules for capitalizing that students learned yesterday.

PROOFREAD

Have students correct errors in the following sentences.

1. My favorite Day of the year is halloween. (1: day; 2: Halloween)

2. My favorite baseball Player is babe Ruth. (1: player; 2: Babe)

3. Does canada have baseball. (1: Canada; 2: baseball?)

4. July was the Month we played the most games this Year. (1: month; 2: year.)

See Grammar Transparency 29 for modeling and guided practice.

Day 5 Assess and Reteach

ASSESS

Use the Daily Language Activity and **Grammar Practice Book** page 30 for assessment.

RETEACH

Use Grammar Practice Book page 30 and selected pages from the **Grammar and Writing Handbook** for additional reteaching. Remind students that it is important to use nouns correctly as they speak and write. Review the rules for capitalization, including historical events and documents, titles, languages, races, and nationalities.

Check students' writing for use of the skill and listen for it in their speaking. Assign Grammar Revision Assignments in their Writer's Notebooks as needed.

See Grammar Transparency 30 for modeling and guided practice.

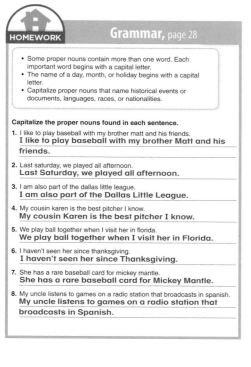

HOMEWORK **Grammar,** page 28

- Some proper nouns contain more than one word. Each important word begins with a capital letter.
- The name of a day, month, or holiday begins with a capital letter.
- Capitalize proper nouns that name historical events or documents, languages, races, or nationalities.

Capitalize the proper nouns found in each sentence.

1. I like to play baseball with my brother matt and his friends.
   I like to play baseball with my brother Matt and his friends.

2. Last saturday, we played all afternoon.
   Last Saturday, we played all afternoon.

3. I am also part of the dallas little league.
   I am also part of the Dallas Little League.

4. My cousin karen is the best pitcher I know.
   My cousin Karen is the best pitcher I know.

5. We play ball together when I visit her in florida.
   We play ball together when I visit her in Florida.

6. I haven't seen her since thanksgiving.
   I haven't seen her since Thanksgiving.

7. She has a rare baseball card for mickey mantle.
   She has a rare baseball card for Mickey Mantle.

8. My uncle listens to games on a radio station that broadcasts in spanish.
   My uncle listens to games on a radio station that broadcasts in Spanish.

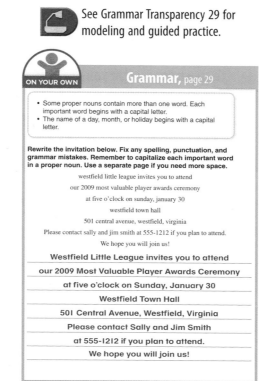

ON YOUR OWN **Grammar,** page 29

- Some proper nouns contain more than one word. Each important word begins with a capital letter.
- The name of a day, month, or holiday begins with a capital letter.

Rewrite the invitation below. Fix any spelling, punctuation, and grammar mistakes. Remember to capitalize each important word in a proper noun. Use a separate page if you need more space.

westfield little league invites you to attend
our 2009 most valuable player awards ceremony
at five o'clock on sunday, january 30
westfield town hall
501 central avenue, westfield, virginia
Please contact sally and jim smith at 555-1212 if you plan to attend.
We hope you will join us!

Westfield Little League invites you to attend
our 2009 Most Valuable Player Awards Ceremony
at five o'clock on Sunday, January 30
Westfield Town Hall
501 Central Avenue, Westfield, Virginia
Please contact Sally and Jim Smith
at 555-1212 if you plan to attend.
We hope you will join us!

HOMEWORK **Grammar,** page 30

A. Find the two nouns in each sentence and write them on the lines.

1. Yogi Berra is a famous coach. _Yogi Berra_ _coach_
2. My uniform is in the dryer. _uniform_ _dryer_
3. The ball landed in Lake Superior. _ball_ _Lake Superior_
4. Dr. Zed talked to my mom. _Dr. Zed_ _mom_
5. This bat is made of aluminum. _bat_ _aluminum_
6. I pitched the ball to the batter. _ball_ _batter_
7. Stretch your legs while in your sweatpants. _legs_ _sweatpants_
8. Write down the score of the game. _score_ _game_

B. Use the nouns in the box to complete each sentence in a way that makes sense. Don't forget to capitalize any proper nouns.

| jill | dog | february | idaho |
| autograph | bleachers | mitt | |

9. We drove from Nebraska to _Idaho_
10. My _dog_ plays catch with me.
11. I asked for the pitcher's _autograph_
12. I've been practicing since _February_
13. Ask _Jill_ to play with us.
14. We sat in the _bleachers_
15. Where is my _mitt_ ?

Daily Planner

DAY 1	• Prepare to Read • Academic Language • Vocabulary (Preteach)
DAY 2	• Comprehension • Leveled Reader Lesson 1
DAY 3	• Phonics/Decoding • Leveled Reader Lesson 2
DAY 4	• Phonics/Decoding • Vocabulary (Review) • Leveled Reader Lesson 3
DAY 5	• High-Frequency Words • Fluency • Self-Selected Reading

Interactive Student Book

If you wish to preteach the main selection, use StudentWorks Plus for:

- Vocabulary Preteaching
- Word-by-Word Highlighting
- Think Aloud Prompts

Academic Language

Academic words include those harder Tier 2 words that appear in much of students' reading materials as well as the language of instruction. The words chosen for instruction were selected from the **Living Word Vocabulary** list and Avril Coxhead's list of **High-Incidence Academic Words**.

Approaching Level

Prepare to Read

Objective Preview *My Brother Martin*
Materials • **StudentWorks Plus** • self-stick notes

PREVIEW THE MAIN SELECTION

■ Have students preview *My Brother Martin* using **StudentWorks Plus**. This version of the selection contains oral summaries in multiple languages, story recording, word-by-word highlighting, Think Aloud prompts, and comprehension-monitoring questions.

■ Remind students that listening carefully to and following along with the word-by-word reading will help them prepare for the reading of the selection with the class. Ask students to place self-stick notes on any challenging words or places that confuse them. Discuss the confusing items with students prior to the reading of the selection with the rest of the class.

■ Ask students to write three or four sentences in their Writer's Notebooks telling what they learned about Martin Luther King, Jr., and his sister as children.

Academic Language

Objective Teach academic language
Materials • none

PRETEACH LANGUAGE OF INSTRUCTION

Tell students that there are many important lesson words you will be using this week. You want them to become familiar with these words *before* the lessons. These words also appear in the directions of the tests they will be taking this year.

Preteach the following academic words: *monitor comprehension, author's purpose, sequence, biography*, and *prefixes*.

■ Define each word using student-friendly language. Tell students that to *monitor comprehension* is to check their understanding of the text and the author's purpose for writing.

■ In addition, relate each word to known words. Connect, for example, *author's purpose* to the *reason* or *why* the story is being told, *sequence* to *order of events*, and *biography* to *real-life story*.

■ Highlight these words when used throughout the week, and reinforce their meanings.

Approaching Level

Phonics/Decoding

Objective   Decode words with prefixes

Materials   • **Approaching Reproducible,** p. 46
• **Sound-Spelling WorkBoards**   • **Word-Building Cards**

PHONICS MAINTENANCE

Tier 2

- Distribute a **WorkBoard** to each student. Say a sound previously taught, including short vowels and long vowels *a, e, i,* and *o*. Have students find the **Sound-Spelling Card** on the board for each sound.

- Review the spelling(s) for each sound and for prefixes by providing a sample word containing those spellings. Guide students to write the word on the board. Model how to segment the word and write the spelling for each sound, as needed. In addition, point out spelling hints, such as many prefixes have a short-vowel sound, as in *dis-, non-,* and *un-*.

- Dictate the following words for students to spell: *rush, spend, float, wide, stray, unable, remind.* Write each word on the board, and have students self-correct their work.

Sound-Spelling WorkBoard

RETEACH SKILL

Prefixes Point to the prefixes **Word-Building Cards** and review the spellings for each prefix. State each spelling and provide a sample word.

- Write the words below on the board. Model how to decode the first word in each row, then guide students as they decode the remaining words. For the multisyllabic words, divide the words into syllables using the syllable-scoop technique to help students read one syllable at a time.

- When completed, point to the words in random order for students to chorally read. Repeat several times.

lock	unlock	view	review	start	restart
precook	prepaid	preschool	pretest	preview	previewed
refresh	remove	repack	rerun	retell	return
undress	unfair	unlike	unlock	unreal	unlocked
dislike	distrust	imperfect	improper	illegal	illegally
indirect	incorrect	overdo	overuse	overheat	overact

Approaching Reproducible, page 46

A **prefix** is a word part that can be added to the beginning of a base word and changes the base word's meaning. The prefixes **dis-, non-,** and **un-** mean "the opposite of" or "without." The prefix **mis-** means "badly" or "incorrectly."

disrespect = without respect   *unhappy* = opposite of happy
nonstop = without a stop   *misbehave* = behave badly

Answer each question with a word from the box that has the same meaning as the underlined words.

uncovered	disappeared	unbelievable
nonfiction	misjudge	disagree

1. What is the most <u>opposite of believable</u> thing someone has told you about dinosaurs? __unbelievable__

2. What should you do if you <u>do not agree</u> with something you have read? __disagree__

3. What kind of <u>not fiction book</u> do you like to read? __nonfiction__

4. What would you do if you <u>opposite of covered</u> a fossil in your yard? __uncovered__

5. Why do you think the dinosaurs <u>opposite of appeared</u>? __disappeared__

6. What might happen if you <u>incorrectly judge</u> your location? __misjudge__

Approaching Level

Vocabulary

Objective Preteach selection vocabulary

Materials
- **Visual Vocabulary Resources**
- **Approaching Reproducible,** p. 47
- **Vocabulary Cards**

✓ **PRETEACH KEY VOCABULARY**

Tier 2

Introduce the Words Use the **Visual Vocabulary Resources** to preteach the key selection words *unfair, ancestors, numerous, segregation, avoided,* and *injustice.* Use the following routine that appears in detail on the cards:

- Define the word in English, and provide the example given.

- Define the word in Spanish, if appropriate, and indicate if the word is a cognate.

- Display the picture, and explain how it illustrates or demonstrates the words.

- Then engage students in structured partner-talk about the image, using the key word.

- Ask students to chorally say the word three times.

- Point out any known sound-spellings or focus on a key aspect of phonemic awareness related to the word.

- You may wish also to distribute copies of the Vocabulary Glossary in the **ELL Resource Book**.

REVIEW PREVIOUSLY TAUGHT VOCABULARY

Display the **Vocabulary Cards** from the previous week: *peculiar, positive, aware, selecting, consisted, advanced.* Remind students that they can look up the pronunciation, syllabication, and meaning of a word in a dictionary or glossary. Have students look up the meanings of the words in the glossary of the **Student Book**. Ask students to write true or false statements using the words, and then exchange papers with a partner and guess the correct answer. For example, *If a person is positive about something, they are unsure.* (false)

Context Clues Remind students that context clues are clues within the text that help a reader figure out what a word means. Have students write a sentence that contains a context clue for each previously taught vocabulary word. For example, *It was peculiar that the man was wearing a winter coat in July.*

Approaching Reproducible, page 47

| injustice | ancestors | unfair |
| numerous | segregation | avoided |

A. Read each clue. Then find the vocabulary word in the row of letters and circle it.

1. Not giving someone a turn to play a game:
   i x z m n o u r t (unfair) q p l k j y a s d f

2. Our great-great-great-great grandparents:
   r q c b (ancestors) w z p o r t j k

3. Unfairness:
   s p x (injustice) m y n r t o o q e l

4. Many:
   t j x (numerous) o e m y s j o p q z x g h o a r z x q o o g

5. Keeping one race of people separate from another:
   w i j g o h u m q c p (segregation) w i p l j b n m x

6. Kept away from:
   w q a z s e r t (avoided) p y r g h u b n a d

B. Write three sentences using one of these vocabulary words in each. Possible responses provided.

7. My *ancestors* came from Iceland.

8. I *avoided* a scolding by telling the truth.

9. Luke thought that his weekend homework assignment was *unfair.*

Approaching Level

Vocabulary

Objective Review vocabulary and high-frequency words

Materials • **Vocabulary Cards** • **High-Frequency Word Cards**

REVIEW VOCABULARY

Review Words Display the **Vocabulary Cards** for *unfair, ancestors, numerous, segregation, avoided, injustice*. Point to each word, read it aloud, and have students chorally repeat.

Then ask the following Yes/No questions. Allow other students to respond.

- Would it be unfair if I gave each of you the same number of marbles?
- Are your ancestors still alive?
- Have you ever tried to do something numerous times?
- Is it a good idea to segregate smelly foods from other foods in the refrigerator?
- Have you ever avoided doing your chores?
- Would giving you a test today without warning be an injustice?

HIGH-FREQUENCY WORDS

Tier 2

Top 250 Words The ability to read accurately and effortlessly the most frequently used words in written English will help students develop reading fluency. Display **High-Frequency Word Cards** 41–50. Then do the following:

- Display one card at a time, and ask students to chorally state each word.
- Have students spell each word aloud.
- Ask students to write each word in their Writer's Notebooks as they state aloud each letter. Then have them read the word again.
- When completed, quickly flip through the Word Card set as students chorally read the words.
- Provide opportunities for students to use the words in speaking and writing; for example, provide sentence starters, such as *I want to drink* <u>some (cold)</u> _____ *water* for oral and written practice. Or point to a Word Card and ask a question, such as *What word means the opposite of clean?* (when pointing to the *dirty* Word Card)
- Continue the routine throughout the week.

ELL

Practice Vocabulary Pair students of different proficiency. Orally model the vocabulary in sentences. For example: *I practiced numerous times to learn the new dance.* On the board, provide sentence frames for pairs to copy and complete using the vocabulary. For example: *My grandparents and other _____ are from _____.* (ancestors; Mexico)

Word Webs

Have students create word webs in their Writer's Notebooks for each vocabulary word. Write the related words provided, and ask students to add other words, phrases, and illustrations.

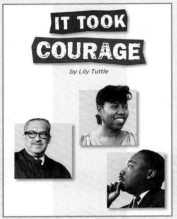

Student Book

Corrective Feedback

Read each paragraph with students. Ask: *What is the author's purpose?* Underline the clues that tell the purpose. Review that an author writes to entertain, inform, or persuade. Nonfiction pieces usually inform.

Approaching Level

Comprehension

Objective   Reteach monitor comprehension and author's purpose
Materials   • **Student Book:** "It Took Courage"

✔ **RETEACH STRATEGY: MONITOR COMPREHENSION**

Tier 2

- **Define** Tell students that monitoring their comprehension means checking their understanding. Students can monitor their comprehension by pausing in their reading to ask themselves questions, slowing down their reading, or rereading passages.

- **Relate to Real Life** Ask students to imagine that a friend is telling them how to play a new game. If they do not understand, they might say, *Wait a minute, I didn't understand that part. What do you mean? Slow down and tell me again.* They would be monitoring their comprehension, or checking their understanding.

- **Set Purposes** Remind students that good readers monitor their comprehension while they read. To make sure they understand what they are reading, they pause to ask themselves questions, slow down their reading rate, or reread parts they do not understand. Determining the author's purpose in writing about a subject is one way for readers to monitor their comprehension.

✔ **RETEACH SKILL: AUTHOR'S PURPOSE**

- **Define** Remind students that the author's purpose is the main reason the author wrote the story or book. Authors may write to entertain, inform, or persuade. In a biography, identifying the literary language and devices the author uses to present the events of a person's life can help students figure out the author's purpose.

- **Relate to Real Life** Ask students to remember why they write book reports. Ask: *Do you write them to entertain your readers or to give your readers information about the book?*

- **Set Purposes** Remind students that good readers search for the author's purpose as they read. Students should look carefully at the author's language to help them identify the author's purpose. This practice helps the reader better understand the text.

- **Apply** Work with students to monitor their comprehension as they read "It Took Courage." Help them find clues that reveal the author's purpose. Students will apply this strategy and skill as they read *Harriet Tubman.*

Approaching Level

Leveled Reader Lesson 1

Objective   Read to apply skills and strategies

Materials   • **Leveled Reader:** *Harriet Tubman*

Leveled Reader

BEFORE READING

Preview and Predict Have students read the title and preview the first chapter. Ask students to make predictions about the author's purpose in writing this section of the book. Students should note any questions they have before they read.

 Review the Vocabulary Words Have students read the vocabulary words on the inside front cover. Briefly define each and ask students to state related words they have learned. Have student identify any prefixes or suffixes.

Set a Purpose for Reading *Let's read to find out more about Harriet Tubman.*

DURING READING

 STRATEGY
MONITOR COMPREHENSION

Remind students that monitoring their comprehension means to stop and check their understanding before continuing to read.

SKILL
AUTHOR'S PURPOSE

Remind students to think about the most important information they are learning as they read. Read Chapter 1 with students. Help students complete the Author's Purpose Map.

As you read, help students decode unknown words. In addition, ask open-ended questions to facilitate rich discussion, such as *How does the author present the events in Harriet Tubman's life?* Build on students' responses to help them develop a deeper understanding of the text.

Stop after every two pages to invite students to ask questions about the text in order to monitor their comprehension before continuing to read. Help struggling students reread difficult pages or passages. Then model identifying language in the text that gives clues to the author's purpose.

AFTER READING

Ask students to compare Harriet Tubman to someone in their own lives. *How are they the same? How are they different?*

Leveled Reader

Approaching Level

Leveled Reader Lesson 2

Objective Reread to apply skills and strategies and develop fluency

Materials
- **Leveled Reader:** *Harriet Tubman*
- **Approaching Reproducible,** p. 50

BEFORE READING

 Review the Strategy and Skill Review students' completed Author's Purpose Maps from the first read. Remind students that to monitor their comprehension means to stop and check their understanding. The author's purpose is the reason an author writes. The author's purpose may be to entertain, inform, or persuade.

Review the Vocabulary Words Have students search the book for each vocabulary word. Ask students to read aloud the sentence containing the word and state the word's definition or provide related words. Point out any prefixes or suffixes.

Set a Purpose for Reading *Let's reread to check our understanding of the information in the book and to work on our reading fluency.*

DURING READING

Reread *Harriet Tubman* with students. Have them read silently two pages at a time, or read aloud to a partner. Stop and have students monitor their comprehension before they read the next two pages. Model asking questions or paraphrasing, as needed.

AFTER READING

Check Comprehension Have partners complete the Comprehension Check on page 16. Review students' answers. Help students find evidence for their answers in the text.

MODEL FLUENCY

Model reading the fluency passage on **Approaching Reproducible** page 50. Tell students to pay close attention to your expression and intonation as you read. Then read one sentence at a time, and have students echo-read the sentences, copying your expression and intonation.

During independent reading time, have students work with a partner using the fluency passage. One student reads aloud while the other repeats each sentence back. If students need additional support, have them listen to the "practice speed" version of the passage on the **Fluency Solutions Audio CD**.

Approaching Reproducible, page 50

As I read, I will pay attention to intonation and expression.

	Harriet Tubman was a small woman. She never went to
10	school. She was forced to work hard jobs as a young child.
22	She suffered blackouts from a head injury. Yet some
31	people thought she was so dangerous that they offered a
41	$40,000 reward for her capture.
46	Harriet Tubman ran away from slavery. But she never
55	ran from the chance to help others. She helped hundreds of
66	other enslaved people. She returned to the South
74	**numerous** times to free other captives.
80	When war broke out, she became a nurse. She used
90	healing tips from her ancestors to cure sick soldiers. Then
100	she became a spy for the Northern Army. After the war,
111	Harriet Tubman worked to make life less **unfair** for
120	women and poor people. 124

Comprehension Check
1. What is the author's purpose? **Author's Purpose**
   The author wrote this to inform readers about the life of Harriet Tubman.
2. What do you learn about Harriet Tubman as a person? **Main Idea and Details** Harriet Tubman spent her life helping others in various ways.

	Words Read	−	Number of Errors	=	Words Correct Score
First Read		−		=	
Second Read		−		=	

Approaching Level

Leveled Reader Lesson 3

Objective   Build fluency

Materials   • **Leveled Reader:** *Harriet Tubman*

✔ FOCUS ON FLUENCY

Timed Reading Tell students that they will be doing a final timed reading of the fluency passage from *Harriet Tubman* that they have been practicing. With each student, follow these directions:

- Place the passage facedown.

- When you say "Go," the student begins reading the passage aloud.

- When you say "Stop," the student stops reading the passage.

As they read, note words students mispronounce and their overall expression and intonation. Stop after one minute. Help students record and graph the number of words they read correctly.

REREAD PREVIOUSLY READ BOOKS

- Distribute copies of the past six **Leveled Readers**. Have students select two to reread. Tell students that rereading these books will help them develop their skills. The more times they read the same words, the quicker they will learn these words. This practice will make the reading of other books easier.

- Circulate and listen in as students read. Stop students periodically and ask them how they are figuring out difficult words and how they are monitoring their comprehension. Note students who need additional work with specific decoding or comprehension skills.

- Encourage students to read other previously read Leveled Readers during independent reading time or for homework.

Leveled Reader

Meet Grade-Level Expectations

As an alternative to this day's lesson, guide students through a reading of the On Level Leveled Reader. See page 161U. Since both books contain the same vocabulary, phonics, and comprehension skills, the scaffolding you provided will help most students gain access to this more challenging text.

Book Talk

Bringing Groups Together Students will work with peers of various language and reading abilities to discuss this week's Leveled Readers. Refer to page 160 in the **Teacher's Resource Book** for more about how to conduct a Book Talk.

Student Book

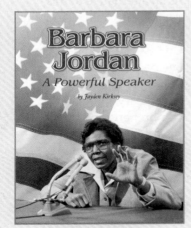

Student Book

Decodable Text

Use the decodable stories in the **Teacher's Resource Book** to help students build fluency with basic decoding patterns.

Approaching Level

Fluency

Objectives	Reread selections to develop fluency; develop speaking skills
Materials	• **Student Book:** *My Brother Martin*, "Barbara Jordan"

✔ REREAD FOR FLUENCY

- Have students reread a portion of *My Brother Martin*. Suggest that they focus on two to four of their favorite pages from the selection. Work with students to read the pages with the appropriate expression and intonation.

- Provide time for students to read their sections of text to you. Comment on their expression and intonation, and provide corrective feedback by modeling proper fluency.

DEVELOP SPEAKING/LISTENING SKILLS

- Have students practice reading a paragraph from the selection "Barbara Jordan."

- Work with students to read with appropriate expression and intonation. Model reading a few sentences at a time. Emphasize the important words with your intonation. Have students repeat.

- Provide time for students to read aloud the passage to partners. Ask students to name ways in which their partner expressed emotion or interest with their voice.

- Have students share with the class the most interesting facts they learned about Barbara Jordan. Instruct students to express an opinion about Barbara Jordan, and use facts from the text to support their opinion. Remind students to employ eye contact, speaking rate, volume, and enunciation effectively.

Approaching Level

Self-Selected Reading

Objective   Read independently to monitor comprehension and identify author's purpose

Materials   • **Leveled Classroom Library**   • other informational books

APPLY SKILLS AND STRATEGIES TO INDEPENDENT READING

- **Read Independently** Have students choose an informational book for sustained silent reading. (See the **Theme Bibliography** on pages T8–T9 for book suggestions.) Remind them that monitoring their comprehension means checking their understanding as they read. By monitoring their comprehension, they can find important clues to the author's purpose. The author's purpose is the author's reason for writing the text. Have students read their books and record their clues on an Author's Purpose Map.

- **Show Evidence of Reading** While reading, students may generate a reading log or journal. After reading, ask students to use their Author's Purpose Maps to paraphrase what the reading was about, maintaining meaning and logical order. Allow students to share their summaries and comment on their reactions to the book while participating in Book Talks. Ask: *Would you recommend this book to a classmate? Why or why not?*

Approaching

Leveled Classroom Library
See Leveled Classroom
Library lessons on pages T2–T7.

Daily Planner

DAY 1	• Vocabulary • Phonics
DAY 2	• Leveled Reader Lesson 1
DAY 3	• Leveled Reader Lesson 2
DAY 4	• Fluency
DAY 5	• Self-Selected Reading

ELL

Practice Vocabulary Pair ELL students with native speakers. On the board, provide sentence frames for pairs to copy and complete using the vocabulary and additional words when necessary. For example: *The surprise test is _____ because we are not _____.* (*unfair; prepared*)

Sound-Spelling WorkBoard

On Level

Vocabulary

Objective	Review vocabulary
Materials	• **Vocabulary Cards**

REVIEW PREVIOUSLY TAUGHT WORDS

Review the Words Display the **Vocabulary Cards** for *unfair, ancestors, numerous, segregation, avoided, injustice.* Point to each word, read it aloud, and have students chorally repeat.

Then provide the following word sets. Ask students to name the word in each set that is not related to the other words.

- unfair, unjust, one-sided, equal
- ancestors, great-aunts, forefathers, sons
- numerous, many, none, plentiful
- segregation, together, separation, isolation
- avoided, dodged, escaped, found
- injustice, justice, crime, abuse

Phonics/Word Study

Objective	Decode multisyllabic words with prefixes
Materials	• **Word-Building Cards** • **Sound-Spelling WorkBoards**

RETEACH SKILL

- **Prefixes** Point to the prefixes **Word-Building Cards**, and review the spellings for each prefix. State each spelling and provide a sample word.

- Write the words below on the board. If necessary, divide the words into syllables using the syllable-scoop technique to help students read one syllable at a time. When completed, point to the words in random order for students to chorally read.

refried	reviewed	previewing	overview	disorderly
precook	prepaid	impatient	imperfect	incorrectly
overdo	undoing	unkindly	supermarket	superpower

- **Spelling** Dictate the following words for students to spell on their **WorkBoards**: *unlucky, replay, rearrange, disagree, incomplete.* Guide students to use the **Sound-Spelling Cards**, and model how to segment words, such as by spelling a word syllable by syllable.

On Level

Fluency

Objectives Reread selections to develop fluency; develop speaking skills

Materials • **Student Book:** *My Brother Martin*, "Barbara Jordan"

REREAD FOR FLUENCY

- Have students reread *My Brother Martin*. Work with students to read with the appropriate expression and intonation. Model as needed.

- Have students read a section of text to you. Comment on their expression and intonation and provide corrective feedback.

DEVELOP SPEAKING/LISTENING SKILLS

- Have students practice reading a paragraph from the selection "Barbara Jordan."

- Work with students to read with appropriate expression and intonation. Model reading a few sentences at a time. Emphasize the important words with your intonation. Have students repeat.

- Have students read aloud the passage to partners. Ask students to point to parts where their partner used expression or intonation.

- Have students share an opinion about Barbara Jordan supported by accurate information from the text. Remind students to employ eye contact, speaking rate, volume, and enunciation effectively.

Self-Selected Reading

Objective Read independently to monitor comprehension and identify author's purpose

Materials • **Leveled Classroom Library** • other informational books

APPLY SKILLS AND STRATEGIES TO INDEPENDENT READING

- **Read Independently** Have students choose an informational book for sustained silent reading. (See the **Theme Bibliography** on pages T8–T9 for book suggestions.) Remind them to monitor their comprehension as they read their books. Have students record clues to the author's purpose on an Author's Purpose Chart.

- **Show Evidence of Reading** While reading, students may generate a reading log or journal. After reading, ask students to use their Author's Purpose Chart to paraphrase what the reading was about, maintaining meaning and logical order. Allow students to share their summaries and comment on their reactions while participating in Book Talks. Ask: *Would you recommend this book to a classmate? Why or why not? What are you basing your recommendation on?*

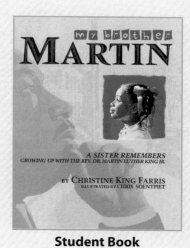

Student Book

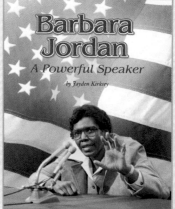

Student Book

On Level

Leveled Classroom Library
See Leveled Classroom
Library lessons on pages T2–T7.

Leveled Reader

On Level

Leveled Reader Lesson 1

| **Objective** | Read to apply strategies and skills |
| **Materials** | • **Leveled Reader:** *Coretta Scott King* |

BEFORE READING

Preview and Predict Have students read the title and preview the book by reading the chapter titles and looking at the photographs. Ask students to predict what this book is about and the types of information they might learn.

 Review the Vocabulary Words Have students read the vocabulary words on the inside front cover. Ask students to state related words they have learned. Review definitions, as needed.

Set a Purpose for Reading *Let's read to find out more about Coretta Scott King.*

DURING READING

 STRATEGY
MONITOR COMPREHENSION

Remind students that monitoring their comprehension means to stop and check their understanding before continuing to read.

SKILL
AUTHOR'S PURPOSE

Remind students that the author's purpose in a selection is the reason the author wrote the story. An author writes to entertain, inform, or persuade. Considering the literary language and devices the author uses can help students identify the author's purpose.

Read Chapter 1 with students. Ask open-ended questions to facilitate rich discussion, such as *What is the author telling us about Coretta Scott King? How does the author present the major events of her life?* Build on students' responses to help them develop a deeper understanding of the text. Have students fill in the first section of the Author's Purpose Chart, then continue reading. They should complete the chart as they read.

Prefixes and Suffixes As they read, have students point out this week's new vocabulary words and any words with prefixes or suffixes.

AFTER READING

Ask students to compare Coretta Scott King to someone they know or have read about. *How are they the same? How are they different? Whom do you like better? Why?*

Leveled Reader Lesson 2

Objective Reread to apply skills and strategies and develop fluency

Materials
- **Leveled Reader:** *Coretta Scott King*
- **Practice Book,** p. 50

Leveled Reader

BEFORE READING

Review the Strategy and Skill Review students' completed Author's Purpose Charts from the first read. Remind students that to monitor their comprehension they should stop and check their understanding as they read and use self-correction strategies.

Remind the group that the author's purpose is the author's reason for writing the book. If students' understanding of author's purpose is incomplete, provide a model or use a student's and revise it as a group.

Set a Purpose for Reading *Let's reread to check our understanding of the information in the book and to work on our reading fluency.*

DURING READING

Reread *Coretta Scott King* with students. Have them read silently two pages at a time, or read aloud to a partner. Stop and have students monitor their comprehension of what they have read before they read the next two pages. Model stopping and asking questions or paraphrasing, as needed.

AFTER READING

Check Comprehension Have partners complete the Comprehension Check on page 20. Review students' answers. Help students find evidence for their answers in the text.

MODEL FLUENCY

Model reading the fluency passage on **Practice Book** page 50. Tell students to pay close attention to your expression and intonation as you read. Then read one sentence at a time, and have students echo-read the sentences, copying your expression and intonation.

During independent reading time, have students work with a partner using the fluency passage. One student reads aloud while the other repeats each sentence back. If students need additional support, have them listen to the "practice speed" version of the passage on the **Fluency Solutions Audio CD**.

Book Talk

Bringing Groups Together Students will work with peers of various language and reading abilities to discuss this week's **Leveled Readers**. Refer to page 160 in the **Teacher's Resource Book** for more about how to conduct a Book Talk.

Practice Book, page 50

As I read, I will pay attention to intonation and expression.

	Coretta Scott King never planned on being a civil rights
10	leader. She thought she would become a teacher or a singer.
21	Instead, she became a leader in the fight for equal rights.
32	Coretta Scott was born in 1927 in a small town in
42	Alabama. She walked three miles to get to school each
52	morning. And she walked three miles back each afternoon.
61	Every day she watched school buses drive white children to
71	their school.
73	In those days **segregation** was the law in the South.
83	African Americans could not go to certain restaurants.
91	They could not drink from certain water fountains. They
100	had to sit in the back of public buses. Black children and
112	white children went to separate schools.
118	Coretta's father Obadiah (oh-buh-DIGH-uh) was the
123	first African American in his county to own his own truck.
134	Some white truckers felt that he was taking away their
144	business. One day the Scotts came home from church to
154	find that their home had burned down. 161

Comprehension Check

1. What is the author's purpose? **Author's Purpose** The author's purpose is to inform us about the difficulties Coretta Scott faced as a child.
2. Why do you think the Scotts' house was burned down? **Cause and Effect** The people who thought that Coretta's father was taking business away from white truckers might have had something to do with the fire.

	Words Read	−	Number of Errors	=	Words Correct Score
First Read		−		=	
Second Read		−		=	

Daily Planner

DAY 1	• Leveled Reader Lesson 1
DAY 2	• Leveled Reader Lesson 2
DAY 3	• Phonics
DAY 4	• Vocabulary • Fluency
DAY 5	• Self-Selected Reading

ELL

Self-Monitor Vocabulary
Have student pairs of different proficiency identify and define unfamiliar words from the main selection using a dictionary. Challenge students to use the new words in sentences. Monitor students as they complete the activity.

Beyond Level

Phonics/Word Study

Objective Decode multisyllabic words with prefixes
Materials • none

EXTEND/ACCELERATE

■ **Read Multisyllabic Words with Prefixes** Write the words below on the board. Challenge students to read the words, using known word parts. When completed, point to the words in random order for students to chorally read.

undecided	inequality	imperfection	unfamiliar
superpower	disappear	prearrange	predestined
overcooking	reconnect	overactive	replacement

■ **Define the Words** Ask students to use their knowledge of word parts to figure out the meanings of the above words. Then have partners find the words in a dictionary and confirm or revise the meanings. Challenge students to use these words in this week's writing assignments.

■ **Spell Words with Prefixes** Dictate the following words for students to spell: *unpainted, unselfishly, indefinite, disappointment, rethink, preheated*. Write the words for students to self-correct.

Vocabulary

Objectives Review procedural texts; conduct a survey
Materials • none

ENRICH VOCABULARY

■ **Review Surveys** Remind students that a survey is a poll, or a list of questions, given to a sample group of people in order to collect data or information about an issue. Discuss common types of surveys, such as those conducted by newspapers before elections.

■ **Write a Survey** Ask students to brainstorm school or community issues that people might have an opinion about. Challenge students to write a list of open-ended questions they would ask on the issue and develop a research plan for gathering the information through a survey. Encourage students to use the vocabulary words they have learned this week as they write their questions. Provide time for students to poll other students using their list of questions and to report the results to the class.

Gifted & Talented

Beyond Level

Fluency

Objectives Reread selections to develop fluency; develop speaking skills
Materials • **Student Book:** *My Brother Martin*, "Barbara Jordan"

REREAD FOR FLUENCY

- Have students reread a portion of *My Brother Martin*. Work with students to read with appropriate expression and intonation.
- Have students read a section of text to you. Comment on their expression and intonation and provide corrective feedback.

DEVELOP SPEAKING/LISTENING SKILLS

- Have students practice reading a paragraph from "Barbara Jordan."
- Work with students to read with appropriate expression and intonation. Model reading a few sentences at a time. Emphasize the important words with your intonation. Have students repeat.
- Have students read aloud the passage to partners. Ask students to point to parts where their partner used expression or intonation.
- Have students share an opinion about Barbara Jordan supported by accurate information from the text. Remind students to employ eye contact, speaking rate, volume, and enunciation effectively.

Self-Selected Reading

Objective Read independently to monitor comprehension of the author's purpose
Materials • **Leveled Classroom Library** • other informational books

APPLY SKILLS AND STRATEGIES TO INDEPENDENT READING

- **Read Independently** Have students choose an informational book for sustained silent reading. (See the **Theme Bibliography** on pages T8–T9 for book suggestions.) Remind them to monitor their comprehension as they read. Then have students record clues to the author's purpose on an Author's Purpose Map.
- **Show Evidence of Reading** While reading, students may generate a reading log or journal. After reading, ask students to use their Author's Purpose Map to paraphrase what the reading was about, maintaining meaning and logical order. Allow students to share their summaries and comment on their reactions to the book while participating in Book Talks. Ask: *Would you recommend this book to a classmate? Why or why not?*
- **Evaluate** Have students evaluate the accuracy of the information provided in their self-selected book. Ask: *Is this a reliable source of information? Why or why not?* Have partners share responses and brainstorm other sources they can use to check the information.

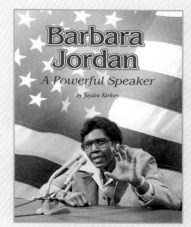

Student Book

Student Book

Beyond

Leveled Classroom Library
See Leveled Classroom Library lessons on pages T2–T7.

Leveled Reader

Beyond Level

Leveled Reader Lesson 1

Objective   Read to apply strategies and skills
Materials   • **Leveled Reader:** *Susan B. Anthony and Elizabeth Cady Stanton: Fighting for Rights*

BEFORE READING

Preview and Predict Have students preview the book by reading the title and chapter titles and looking at the photographs. Ask students to predict what this book is about and the types of information they might learn.

Review the Vocabulary Words Have students read the vocabulary words on the inside front cover. Ask students to state each definition and any related words they have learned.

Set a Purpose for Reading *Let's read to find out more about fighting for basic civil rights.*

DURING READING

STRATEGY
MONITOR COMPREHENSION

Have students define *monitor comprehension*. Remind them that monitoring their comprehension means stopping to check their understanding and using self-correction strategies as needed.

SKILL
AUTHOR'S PURPOSE

Ask students to define the term *author's purpose*. Remind students that the author's purpose is the reason the author wrote the text.

Read the book with students. Ask open-ended questions to facilitate rich discussion, such as *What is the author telling us about women's rights? How does the author present the major events in the lives of Susan B. Anthony and Elizabeth Cady Stanton?* Build on students' responses to help them develop a deeper understanding. Have students fill in an Author's Purpose Map independently as they read.

AFTER READING

Text Structure Remind students authors often organize text by cause and effect, sequence, or compare and contrast. Have students identify the text structure. Ask: *Why did the author choose this text structure?* Then have students create a Venn Diagram comparing the character traits of the two women.

Analyze Have partners analyze how each woman's traits contributed to their fight for women's suffrage.

Gifted & Talented

Beyond Level

Leveled Reader Lesson 2

Objective Reread to apply skills and strategies and develop fluency

Materials
- **Leveled Reader:** *Susan B. Anthony and Elizabeth Cady Stanton: Fighting for Rights*
- **Beyond Reproducible,** p. 50

BEFORE READING

Review the Strategy and Skill Review students' completed Author's Purpose Maps from the first read.

Remind students that the author's purpose is the reason the author wrote the book. If students' Author's Purpose Maps are incomplete, provide a model or use a student's and revise it as a group.

Set a Purpose for Reading *Let's reread to check our understanding of the information in the book and work on our reading fluency.*

DURING READING

Have students reread *Susan B. Anthony and Elizabeth Cady Stanton: Fighting for Rights* silently or with a partner. If they are reading in pairs, prompt students to monitor their comprehension by asking their partner probing questions.

AFTER READING

Check Comprehension Have students independently complete the Comprehension Check. Review students' answers. Help students find evidence for their answers in the text.

Synthesize Ask students to compare these women to people they know or have read about. *How are they the same? How are they different? Whom do you prefer and why?* Have students use their Venn Diagram from Leveled Reader Lesson 1 to help them. Then have students develop questions about civil rights that they would like to research during independent time.

MODEL FLUENCY

Model reading the fluency passage on **Beyond Reproducible** page 50. Tell students to pay close attention to your expression and intonation as you read. Read one sentence at a time, and have them echo-read the sentences, copying your expression and intonation.

During independent reading time, have students work with a partner using the fluency passage. One student reads aloud while the other repeats each sentence back. Students can check their fluency by reading along with the "expert speed" version of the passage on the **Fluency Solutions Audio CD**.

Leveled Reader

Book Talk

Bringing Groups Together Students will work with peers of various language and reading abilities to discuss this week's **Leveled Readers**. Refer to page 160 in the **Teacher's Resource Book** for more about how to conduct a Book Talk.

Beyond Reproducible, page 50

As I read, I will pay attention to intonation and expression.

	In the early 1800s women in the United States had few
11	rights. Women could only hold a few types of jobs. They
22	could teach or work in factories. They couldn't be doctors
32	or lawyers. A woman made less money than a man who
43	had the same type of job. And most important of all,
54	women couldn't vote.
57	When a woman married, all her property became her
66	husband's. Wives had to ask their husbands for spending
75	money. If a woman divorced, her children stayed with her
85	husband. A husband owned everything.
90	By the mid-1800s some people decided it was time to
100	change the way women were treated. Two of those people
110	were Susan B. Anthony and Elizabeth Cady Stanton. They
119	both thought women should be able to vote and have the
130	same rights as men. They worked hard to change the laws
141	and the way people thought.
146	Elizabeth Cady Stanton was born in 1815. Her mother's
154	ancestors were wealthy and well known. Her father worked
163	hard. He studied law and worked in politics. 171

Comprehension Check

1. Why do you think the author wrote about Susan B. Anthony and Elizabeth Cady Stanton? **Author's Purpose The author wrote this to inform readers about what these women did to gain more rights for women in the United States.**

2. Why did these women want to change the laws? **Cause and Effect Susan and Elizabeth wanted women to have the same rights as men.**

	Words Read	–	Number of Errors	=	Words Correct Score
First Read		–		=	
Second Read		–		=	

Daily Planner

DAY 1	• Build Background Knowledge • Vocabulary
DAY 2	• Vocabulary • Access to Core Content *My Brother Martin*
DAY 3	• Vocabulary • Grammar • Access to Core Content *My Brother Martin*
DAY 4	• Vocabulary • Writing/Spelling • Access to Core Content "Barbara Jordan" • Leveled Reader *Coretta Scott King*
DAY 5	• Vocabulary • Leveled Reader *Coretta Scott King* • Self-Selected Reading

StudentWorks Plus
Interactive Student Book

Use StudentWorks Plus for:
• Vocabulary Preteaching
• Word-by-Word Highlighting
• Think Aloud Prompts

Cognates

Help students identify similarities and differences in pronunciation and spelling between English and Spanish cognates.

signs	*signos*
ancestors	*ancestros*
numerous	*numeroso*
segregation	*segregación*
injustice	*injusticia*
evaluate	*evaluar*
author	*autor*
suffix	*sufijo*
prefix	*prefijo*

ELL ENGLISH LANGUAGE LEARNERS

Prepare to Read

Content Objective Explore people who make a difference in civil rights
Language Objective Use key words to discuss the life of Martin Luther King, Jr.
Materials • **StudentWorks Plus**

BUILD BACKGROUND KNOWLEDGE

All Language Levels

■ Have students preview *My Brother Martin* using **StudentWorks Plus**, which contains oral summaries in multiple languages, online multilingual glossaries, word-by-word highlighting, and questions that assess and build comprehension.

■ Students can build their word-reading fluency by reading along as the text is read or by listening during the first reading and, at the end of each paragraph, returning to the beginning of the paragraph and reading along.

■ Students can build their comprehension by reviewing the definitions of key words in the online glossary and by answering the comprehension questions. When appropriate, the text required to answer the question is highlighted to provide students with additional support and scaffolding.

■ After reading, ask students to respond to these questions: *Do you know someone who has experienced prejudice? How did he or she deal with it?*

Academic Language

Language Objective Use academic language in classroom conversations

All Language Levels

■ This week's academic words are **boldfaced** throughout the lesson. Define the word in context and provide a clear example from the selection. Then ask students to generate an example or a word with a similar meaning.

Academic Language Used in Whole Group Instruction

Theme Words	Key Selection Words	Strategy and Skill Words
civil rights **government** **signs**	**unfair** **ancestors** **numerous** **segregation** **avoided** **injustice**	**monitor comprehension** **author's purpose** **suffixes** **prefixes** **common nouns** **proper nouns**

ELL ENGLISH LANGUAGE LEARNERS

Vocabulary

Language Objective Demonstrate understanding and use of key words by describing people who made a difference in civil rights

Materials • **Visual Vocabulary Resources**
• **ELL Resource Book**

Visual Vocabulary Resources

PRETEACH KEY VOCABULARY

Use the **Visual Vocabulary Resources** to preteach the key selection words *unfair, ancestors, numerous, segregation, avoided*, and *injustice*. Focus on two words per day. Use the detailed routine on the cards.

Beginning/Intermediate

■ Point out any known sound-spellings, or focus on a key aspect of phonemic awareness related to the word.

All Language Levels

■ Define the word in English, and provide the example given.

■ Define the word in Spanish, if appropriate, and indicate if the word is a cognate.

■ Display the picture and explain how it demonstrates the word. Engage students in structured activity about the image.

■ Ask students to chorally say the word three times.

■ Distribute copies of the Vocabulary Glossary on **ELL Resource Book**, page 68.

PRETEACH FUNCTION WORDS AND PHRASES

All Language Levels

Use the Visual Vocabulary Resources to preteach the function words and phrases *hand-me down, three peas in one pod, keep someone down*, and *stand up for*. Focus on one word per day. Use the routine on the cards.

■ Define the word in English and, if appropriate, in Spanish. Point out if the word is a cognate.

■ Refer to the picture, and engage students in talk about the word. For example, students will partner-talk using sentence frames.

■ Ask students to chorally repeat the word three times.

TEACH BASIC WORDS

Beginning/Intermediate

Use the Visual Vocabulary Resources to teach the basic words *piano bench, crib, hedge* (noun), *streetcar, frame house*, and *backyard*. Teach these "household/neighborhood items" words using the routine provided on the card.

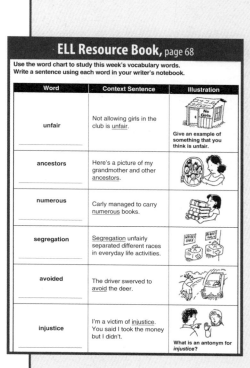

ELL Resource Book, page 68

Use the word chart to study this week's vocabulary words.
Write a sentence using each word in your writer's notebook.

Word	Context Sentence	Illustration
unfair	Not allowing girls in the club is <u>unfair</u>.	Give an example of something that you think is unfair.
ancestors	Here's a picture of my grandmother and other <u>ancestors</u>.	
numerous	Carly managed to carry <u>numerous</u> books.	
segregation	<u>Segregation</u> unfairly separated different races in everyday life activities.	
avoided	The driver swerved to <u>avoid</u> the deer.	
injustice	I'm a victim of <u>injustice</u>. You said I took the money but I didn't.	What is an antonym for *injustice*?

ELL Resource Book

ELL ENGLISH LANGUAGE LEARNERS

Access to Core Content

Content Objective Read grade-level text

Language Objective Discuss text using key words and sentence frames

Materials • **ELL Resource Book,** pp. 58–67

PRETEACH MAIN SELECTION (PAGES 140–153)

All Language Levels

Use the Interactive Question-Response Guide on **ELL Resource Book** pages 58–65 to introduce students to *My Brother Martin*. Preteach half of the selection on Day 2 and half on Day 3.

- Use the prompts provided in the guide to develop meaning and vocabulary. Use the partner-talk and whole-class responses to engage students and increase student talk.

- When completed, have partners reread the story.

PRETEACH PAIRED SELECTION (PAGES 156–159)

All Language Levels

Use the Interactive Question-Response Guide on ELL Resource Book pages 66–67 to preview the paired selection "Barbara Jordan." Preteach the selection on Day 4.

Beginning	Intermediate	Advanced
Use Visuals During the Interactive Reading, select several illustrations. Describe them and have students summarize what you said. Then work with students to identify author's purpose.	**Describe** During the Interactive Reading, select a few lines of text. After you have read and explained it, have students summarize the text. Then ask them to identify the author's purpose for the text.	**Discuss** During the Interactive Reading, select a passage. After you have read and explain it, have students summarize the text. Then have students describe the author's purpose for the text using specific examples.

ELL ENGLISH LANGUAGE LEARNERS

Fluency

Content Objectives Reread selections to develop fluency; develop speaking skills
Language Objective Tell a partner what a selection is about
Materials • **Student Book:** *My Brother Martin*, "Barbara Jordan"
            • **Teacher's Resource Book**

✓ REREAD FOR FLUENCY

Beginning

- Have students read the decodable passages in the **Teacher's Resource Book**, page 10.

Intermediate/Advanced

- Have students reread two to four of their favorite pages of *My Brother Martin*, based on their levels. Help students read the pages with accuracy and the appropriate expression and intonation. For example, read each sentence of the first paragraph and have students echo. Then have students chorally read additional paragraphs. Remind students to add emotion to their voices if necessary when the characters speak.

- Provide time for students to read their sections of text to you. Comment on their expression and intonation, and provide corrective feedback by modeling proper fluency.

DEVELOP SPEAKING/LISTENING SKILLS

All Language Levels

- Have students practice reading "Barbara Jordan." Help students read with accuracy and appropriate expression and intonation.

- Have students read aloud a portion of the article to a partner. Ask students to tell their partner one fact they learned about Barbara Jordan. Provide this sentence frame: *I learned that ____.*

Self-Selected Reading

Content Objective Read independently
Language Objective Orally retell information learned
Materials • **Leveled Classroom Library** • other biographies

APPLY SKILLS AND STRATEGIES TO INDEPENDENT READING

All Language Levels

- Have students choose a biography for independent reading. (See the **Theme Bibliography** on pages T8–T9 for book suggestions.)

- Ask students to orally summarize the book and share their reactions with classmates.

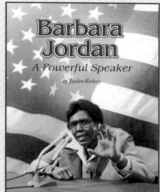

Student Book

Leveled Classroom Library
See Leveled Classroom
Library lessons on pages T2–T7.

ELL ENGLISH LANGUAGE LEARNERS

Transfer Skills

Capitalization In Spanish, not all proper nouns begin with a capital letter as they do in English. Spanish-speaking students may write the days of the week or the months of the year without capitalization. Show students a calendar. Point to these words and explain that in English they always begin with a capital letter. Write several sentences containing dates for students' additional practice. Have students circle the capital letter at the beginning of each proper noun.

Grammar

Content Objective Identify common and proper nouns
Language Objective Speak in complete sentences, using sentence frames

NOUNS

Beginning/Intermediate

- Review nouns. Remind students that a noun is a word that names any person, place, or thing. Write the following on the board: *My brother is a hero.* Underline the nouns. (*brother, hero*) Review pronouns. Write: *Martin Luther King, Jr., grew up in Atlanta, Georgia.* Underline the proper nouns. (*Martin Luther King, Jr.; Atlanta, Georgia*) Explain that these are proper nouns.

All Language Levels

- Review common and proper nouns. Point out that proper nouns begin with a capital letter and name specific people and places. Proper nouns also name specific days, months, holidays, and titles of magazines, newspapers, works of art, musical compositions, and organizations. Write the sentences below on the board. Have students underline the nouns in each sentence. Have them say: ____ is a common noun. ____ is a proper noun.

    Christine King Farris wrote about her brother.
    Julio read an article about Rosa Parks in The New York Times.
    My cousin's Little League game is on Saturday.

PEER DISCUSSION STARTERS

All Language Levels

- Write the following sentences on the board:

    ____ *made a difference by* ____.   *I should treat others* ____.

- Pair students and have them complete each sentence frame. Ask them to expand on their sentences by providing as many details as they can from this week's readings. Circulate, listen in, and take note of each student's language use and proficiency.

Corrective Feedback

During Whole Group grammar lessons, follow the routine on the **Grammar Transparencies** to provide students with extra support. This routine includes completing the items with English Language Learners while other students work independently, having students reread the sentences with partners to build fluency, and providing a generative task, such as writing a new sentence using the skill.

Beginning	**Intermediate**	**Advanced**
Use Visuals Describe the illustrations in *My Brother Martin* to students. Ask: *What do you see?* Help them point out and name common and proper nouns.	**Describe** Ask students to describe the illustrations in *My Brother Martin* using common and proper nouns in their descriptions. Have them use complete sentences. Model sentences if needed.	**Discuss** Ask students to discuss the illustrations in *My Brother Martin* using common and proper nouns in their descriptions. Have them use complete sentences with detailed descriptions.

ELL ENGLISH LANGUAGE LEARNERS

Writing/Spelling

Content Objective Spell words correctly

Language Objective Write in complete sentences, using sentence frames

All Language Levels

- Write the key vocabulary words on the board: *unfair, ancestors, numerous, segregation, avoided, injustice*. Have students copy each word on their **WorkBoards**. Help them say each word and then write a sentence for it. Provide sentence starters, such as:

  Segregation is unfair because ____.

  What interests me most about my ancestors is ____.

  The people are too numerous to count at ____.

  Segregation in the South meant that ____.

  He avoided the other boy because ____.

  Rosa Parks fought injustice by ____.

Beginning/Intermediate

- Help students spell words using their growing knowledge of English sound-spelling relationships. Model how to segment the word students are trying to spell, and attach a spelling to each sound (or spellings to each syllable if a multisyllabic word). Use the **Sound-Spelling Cards** to reinforce the spellings for each English sound.

Advanced

- Dictate the following words for students to spell: *unlock, precook, rerun, overuse, pretest, dislike, unkind*. Use the Sound-Spelling Cards to guide students as they spell each word.

- When completed, review the meanings of words that can be easily demonstrated or explained. Use actions, gestures, and available pictures.

Sound-Spelling WorkBoard

Phonics/Word Study

For English Language Learners who need more practice with this week's phonics/spelling skill, see the Approaching Level lesson on page 161J. Focus on minimal contrasts, articulation, and those sounds that do not transfer from the student's first language to English. For a complete listing of transfer sounds, see pages T16–T31.

Leveled Reader

Vocabulary

Preteach Vocabulary Use the routine in the **Visual Vocabulary Resources**, pages 387–390, to preteach the ELL Vocabulary listed in the inside front cover of the Leveled Reader.

ELL ENGLISH LANGUAGE LEARNERS

Leveled Reader

Content Objective Read to apply skills and strategies

Language Objective Retell information, using complete sentences

Materials • **Leveled Reader:** *Coretta Scott King*
• **ELL Resource Book,** p. 69
• **Visual Vocabulary Resources,** pp. 387–390

BEFORE READING

All Language Levels

- **Preview** Read the title. Ask: *What's the title? Say it again.* Repeat with the author's name. Then page through the book. Use simple language to tell about each page. Immediately follow up with questions, such as *Is this Coretta Scott King? Who was she married to? Why are these people walking?*

- **Review Skills** Use the inside front cover to review the comprehension skill and vocabulary words.

- **Set a Purpose** Say: *Let's read to find out about how Coretta Scott King fought for civil rights.*

DURING READING

All Language Levels

- Have students read each page aloud using the differentiated suggestions. Provide corrective feedback, such as modeling how to blend a decodable word or clarifying meaning by using techniques from the Interactive Question-Response Guide.

- **Retell** After every two pages, ask students to state the main ideas they have learned so far. Help them to complete the Author's Purpose Map. Restate students' comments when they have difficulty using story-specific words. Provide differentiated sentence frames to support students' responses and engage students in partner-talk where appropriate.

Beginning	Intermediate	Advanced
Echo-Read Have students echo-read after you.	**Choral-Read** Have students chorally read with you.	**Choral-Read** Have students chorally read.
Check Comprehension Point to pictures and ask questions, such as *Do you see a picture of [Rosa Parks] on this page? Show it to me.*	**Check Comprehension** Ask questions/prompts, such as *Why does the author show us these pictures? What does the author want us to know?*	**Check Comprehension** Ask: *Why was the bus boycott important? How did it change things for African Americans?*

ELL ENGLISH LANGUAGE LEARNERS

AFTER READING

Use the chart below and Think and Compare questions in the **Leveled Reader** to determine students' progress.

ELL Resource Book

Think and Compare	Beginning	Intermediate	Advanced
1 Review Chapter 1. How do you think the writer feels about segregation? Why do you think this? *(Evaluate Author's Purpose)*	Possible responses: Nonverbal response. Bad. Not like. Unfair. Write about segregation.	Possible responses: The writer feels segregation is unfair. The author told about segregation.	Possible responses: The writer feels that segregation is unfair because he described how segregation affected how people lived.
2 What do you do when you want to learn about an injustice? Do you want to do something about it? Why or why not? *(Synthesize)*	Possible responses: Nonverbal response. Tell people. Want to help.	Possible responses: I tell my parents or my teachers. I want to help.	Possible responses: I tell my parents or my teachers because I want to help to change the injustice.
3 One person working for justice can cause big changes in history. What do you think the history books of the future will say about Coretta Scott King? *(Analyze)*	Possible responses: Nonverbal response. Great woman.	Possible responses: She is a great person.	Possible responses: The history books will say that Coretta Scott King is a great person.

BOOK TALK

Develop Listening and Speaking Skills Distribute copies of **ELL Resource Book** page 69 and form small groups. Help students determine the leader for to discuss the Book Talk questions. Tell students to remember the following while engaged in the activity:

- Distinguish between formal and informal English and know when to use each one. Remind students to note whether the selection is written in formal or informal English. Ask: *Why do you think it is written in this way?* Remind students that they may use informal English when speaking with their classmates, but they should use formal language when they talk to teachers or write essays.

- Express opinions, ideas, and feelings on a variety of social and academic topics. Ask: *What do you think about the characters in the story?*

Book Talk

Bringing Groups Together Students will work with peers of varying language abilities to discuss the Book Talk questions. Form groups so that students who read the Beyond Level, On Level, Approaching Level, and ELL Leveled Readers are in the same group for the activity.

Progress Monitoring

Weekly Assessment

ASSESSED SKILLS

- Vocabulary: Vocabulary Words, Prefixes and Suffixes
- Comprehension: Author's Purpose
- Grammar: Common and Proper Nouns
- Phonics/Spelling: Prefixes

Selection Test for My Brother Martin Also Available

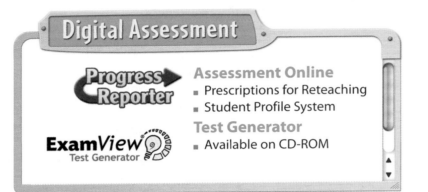

Digital Assessment

Progress Reporter

Assessment Online
- Prescriptions for Reteaching
- Student Profile System

ExamView Test Generator

Test Generator
- Available on CD-ROM

**Weekly Assessment
Unit 2 Week 1**

Fluency Assessment

Assess fluency for one group of students per week. Use the Oral Fluency Record Sheet to track the number of words read correctly. Fluency goal for all students: **84–104 words correct per minute (WCPM).**

Approaching Level	Weeks 1, 3, 5
On Level	Weeks 2, 4
Beyond Level	Week 6

Fluency Assessment

Diagnose		Prescribe
Review the assessment answers with students. Have them correct their errors. Then provide additional instruction as needed.		
	IF...	**THEN...**
VOCABULARY WORDS VOCABULARY STRATEGY Prefixes and Suffixes	0–2 items correct …	See **Vocabulary Intervention Teacher's Edition.** **LOG ON** Online Practice: Go to **www.macmillanmh.com.** **CD-ROM** Vocabulary PuzzleMaker
COMPREHENSION Skill: Author's Purpose	0–3 items correct …	See **Comprehension Intervention Teacher's Edition.** **SPIRAL REVIEW** See Author's Purpose lesson in Unit 2 Week 2, pages 165A–165B.
GRAMMAR Common and Proper Nouns	0–1 items correct …	See **Writing and Grammar Intervention Teacher's Edition.**
PHONICS AND SPELLING Prefixes	0–1 items correct …	**LOG ON** Online Practice: Go to **www.macmillanmh.com.** See **Phonics Intervention Teacher's Edition.**
FLUENCY	79–83 WCPM	**AUDIO CD** Fluency Solutions Audio CD
	0–78 WCPM	See **Fluency Intervention Teacher's Edition.**

Response to Intervention

To place students in Tier 2 or Tier 3 Intervention use the *Diagnostic Assessment*.

- Phonics
- Vocabulary
- Comprehension
- Fluency
- Writing and Grammar

Week 2 ★ At a Glance

Priority Skills and Concepts

Comprehension
- **Strategy:** Monitor Comprehension
- **Skill:** Author's Purpose
- **Skill:** Compare and Contrast
- **Genre:** Poetry, Biography

Robust Vocabulary
- **Selection Vocabulary:** *legendary, muttered, gaped, snickering, insult, flinched*
- **Strategy:** Context Clues: Description

Fluency
- **Intonation/Expression**

Phonics/Spelling
- **Word Study:** Digraphs, Multisyllabic Words
- **Spelling Words:** *choose, kitchen, touch, chance, sketched, ketchup, snatch, stretching, pitcher, chef, rush, thirty, northern, graph, photo, whole, fifth, headphone, whirl, width*
- *unload, relearn, subway*

Grammar/Mechanics
- **Singular and Plural Nouns**
- **Commas in a Series**

Writing
- **Trait: Word Choice**
- Show Actions

Key

 Tested in program    Review Skill

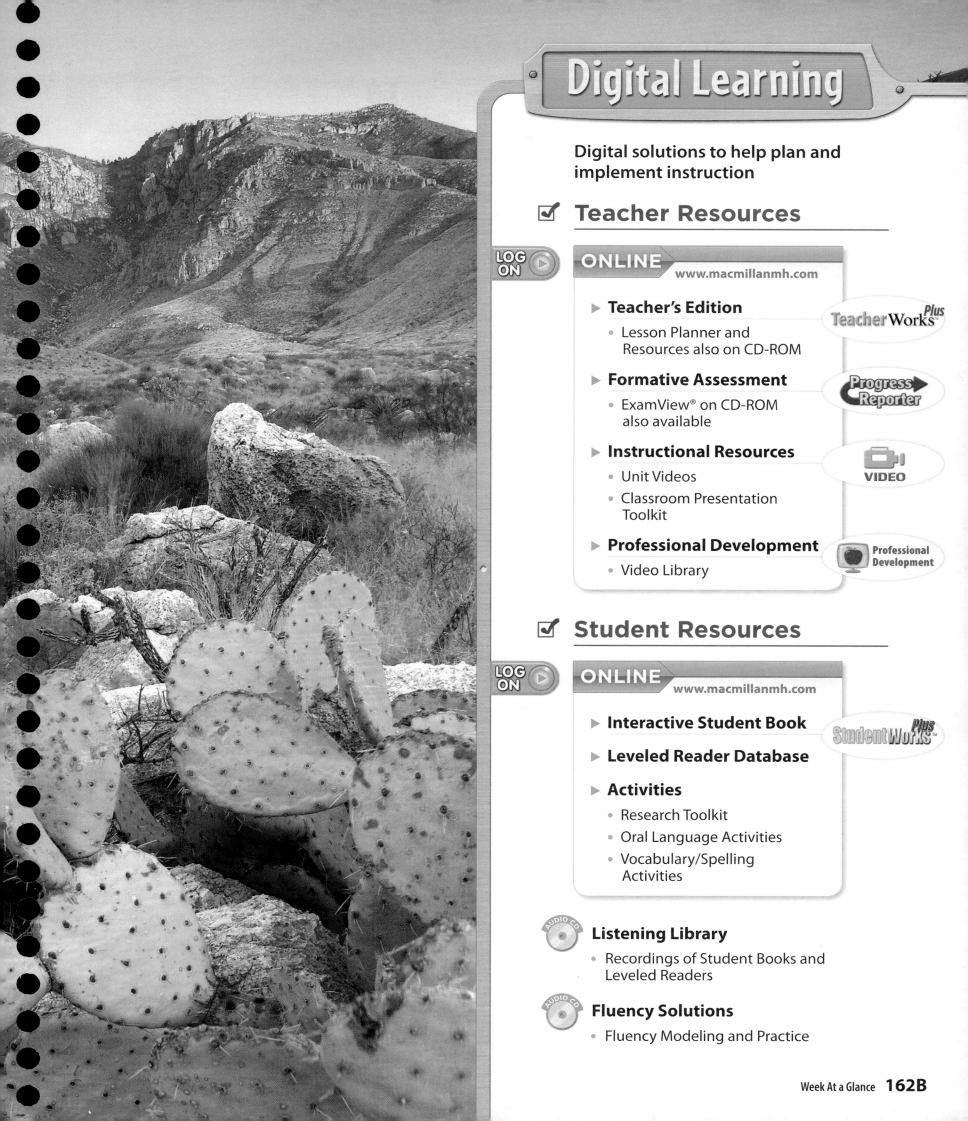

Digital Learning

Digital solutions to help plan and implement instruction

☑ Teacher Resources

LOG ON ▶

ONLINE   www.macmillanmh.com

▶ **Teacher's Edition**
  - Lesson Planner and Resources also on CD-ROM

  TeacherWorks Plus

▶ **Formative Assessment**
  - ExamView® on CD-ROM also available

  Progress Reporter

▶ **Instructional Resources**
  - Unit Videos
  - Classroom Presentation Toolkit

  VIDEO

▶ **Professional Development**
  - Video Library

  Professional Development

☑ Student Resources

LOG ON ▶

ONLINE   www.macmillanmh.com

▶ **Interactive Student Book**

  StudentWorks Plus

▶ **Leveled Reader Database**

▶ **Activities**
  - Research Toolkit
  - Oral Language Activities
  - Vocabulary/Spelling Activities

AUDIO CD

Listening Library
  - Recordings of Student Books and Leveled Readers

AUDIO CD

Fluency Solutions
  - Fluency Modeling and Practice

Weekly Literature

Theme: Inspiring Women

Interactive Student Book
- Word-by-Word Reading
- Summaries in Multiple Languages
- Comprehension Questions

Main Selection

Genre | Biography

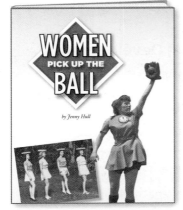

Preteach Vocabulary and Comprehension

Genre | Fiction

Paired Selection

Genre | Poetry

Support Literature

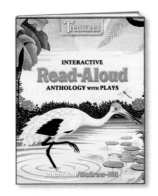

Interactive Read-Aloud Anthology
- Listening Comprehension
- Robust Vocabulary
- Readers' Theater Plays for Fluency

Leveled Readers

Leveled Reader Library

GR Levels O–S

Genre | Biography

- Same Theme
- Same Vocabulary
- Same Comprehension Skills

O
Wilma Rudolph: A True Winner
by Terre Lintner
Macmillan/McGraw-Hill

Approaching Level

Q
Determined to Win: Babe Didrikson Zaharias
by Terre Lintner
Macmillan/McGraw-Hill

On Level

S
Jackie Robinson
A Man Who Stood So Tall
by Sarah Glasscock
Macmillan/McGraw-Hill

Beyond Level

O
Champion Athlete: Babe Didrikson Zaharias
by Terre Lintner
Macmillan/McGraw-Hill

ELL

LOG ON ▶ Leveled Reader Database
Go to www.macmillanmh.com.

Leveled Practice

Treasures
Approaching Reproducibles
Macmillan/McGraw-Hill

Approaching

Treasures
Practice Book
Macmillan/McGraw-Hill

On Level

Treasures
Beyond Reproducibles
Macmillan/McGraw-Hill

Beyond

Treasures
English Language Learner Practice Book
Macmillan/McGraw-Hill

ELL

Leveled Classroom Library

SATCHEL PAIGE

Approaching

HOKUSAI

On Level

Beyond

Response to Intervention

Tier 2

- Phonics
- Vocabulary
- Comprehension
- Fluency
- Writing and Grammar

Tier 3

Assessment

TIME
Time For Kids

- TFK Teacher's Manual
- Apply Answering Question Strategies

Macmillan/McGraw-Hill

Treasures
Student Weekly Assessment
• Selection Tests
• Weekly Assessment
Macmillan/McGraw-Hill

Weekly Assessment

Treasures
Unit Assessment
Includes Writing Prompts
Macmillan/McGraw-Hill

Unit Assessment

Treasures
Benchmark Assessment
Macmillan/McGraw-Hill

Benchmark Assessment

HOME-SCHOOL CONNECTION

- Family letters in English and Spanish
- Take-Home Stories and activities

Treasures
Home-School Connection
Macmillan/McGraw-Hill

LOG ON ▶ Online Homework
www.macmillanmh.com

Go to **www.macmillanmh.com** for Online Lesson Planner

CD-ROM
TeacherWorks™ Plus
All-In-One Planner and Resource Center

Professional Development Video Library

Mighty Jackie: The Strike-out Queen, pp. 166–181

MIGHTY JACKIE
The Strike-out Queen

by Marissa Moss
Illustrated by C.F. Payne

WHOLE GROUP

⏱ ORAL LANGUAGE

- **Listening Comprehension**
- **Speaking/Viewing**

⏱ WORD STUDY

- **Vocabulary**
- **Phonics/Word Study**
- **Spelling**

⏱ READING

- **Comprehension**
- **Fluency**

⏱ LANGUAGE ARTS

- **Writing**
- **Grammar**

⏱ ASSESSMENT

- **Informal/Formal**

DAY 1

Listening/Speaking/Viewing

❓ **Focus Question** How have women's roles in sports changed over time?

Build Background, 162

Read Aloud: "Take Me Out to the Ball Game," 163A–163B

✔ **Vocabulary**
legendary, muttered, gaped, snickering, insult, flinched, 165, 187C
Practice Book, 56
Strategy: Context Clues: Description, 164

✔ **Spelling** Pretest: Digraphs, 187E
Phonics/Spelling Book, 37–38

Read "Women Pick Up the Ball," 164–165

WOMEN PICK UP THE BALL
by Jenna Hall

✔ **Comprehension**, 165A–165B
Strategy: Monitor Comprehension
Skill: Author's Purpose
Practice Book, 57

Student Book

Fluency Model Fluency, 163B

Writing

Daily Writing Would you want to be a baseball player? Write a paragraph explaining why or why not.

✔ **Trait: Word Choice**
Show Actions, 185A–185B

✔ **Grammar** Daily Language Activities, 187G
Singular and Plural Nouns, 187G
Grammar Practice Book, 31

Quick Check Vocabulary, 164
Comprehension, 165B

DAY 2

Listening/Speaking/Viewing

❓ **Focus Question** What made Jackie mighty?

Vocabulary
Review Vocabulary, Context Clues, 166, 187C
Practice Book, 62

✔ **Phonics**
Digraphs, 163C–163D
Practice Book, 55

Spelling Word Sorts, 187E
Phonics/Spelling Book, 39

Read *Mighty Jackie: The Strike-out Queen,* 166–181

MIGHTY JACKIE
The Strike-out Queen

✔ **Comprehension**, 166–181
Strategy: Monitor Comprehension
Skill: Author's Purpose
Practice Book, 58

Student Book

✔ **Fluency** Repeated Reading: Intonation/Expression, 183A

Writing

Daily Writing Write a paragraph describing the similarities and differences between baseball and football.

✔ **Reading/Writing Connection**, 186–187

Grammar Daily Language Activities, 187G
Singular and Plural Nouns, 187G
Grammar Practice Book, 32

Quick Check Phonics, 163D
Comprehension, 181

⏱ **SMALL GROUP Lesson Plan** ▶ **Differentiated Instruction 162G–162H**

Priority Skills

Vocabulary	Comprehension	Writing	
Vocabulary Words	**Strategy:** Monitor Comprehension	**Trait:** Word Choice	
Context Clues: Descriptions	**Skill:** Author's Purpose	Show Actions	

DAY 3

Listening/Speaking

? Focus Question If Jackie had been in the girls' league, do you think the crowds would have treated her differently? Use details from both selections in your answer.

Summarize, 183

Vocabulary

Review Words, Related Words, 187D

Spelling Word Meanings, 187F
Phonics/Spelling Book, 40

Read *Mighty Jackie: The Strike-out Queen*, 166–181

Student Book

Comprehension
Comprehension Check, 183

Review Skill: Compare and Contrast, 183B
Practice Book, 60

Fluency Repeated Reading: Intonation/Expression, 183A
Practice Book, 59

Writing

Daily Writing Sporting events are fun to watch. Write a letter asking your friends to go to a game with you.

Trait: Word Choice
Describe Actions, 187A

Grammar Daily Language Activities, 187G
Mechanics and Usage, 187H
Grammar Practice Book, 33

Quick Check Fluency, 183A

DAY 4

Listening/Speaking/Viewing

? Focus Question Compare Jackie in *Mighty Jackie* to the girl in this poem. What is similar about their situations?

Vocabulary

Review Words, Morphology, 187D

Spelling Proofread, 187F
Phonics/Spelling Book, 41

Read "The New Kid," 184–185

Student Book

Comprehension
Genre: Poetry

Literary Elements: Stanzas, Line Breaks, Rhyme, Meter, 184
Practice Book, 61

Fluency Repeated Reading: Intonation/Expression, 183A

Time For Kids

Writing

Daily Writing Suppose you could interview a famous baseball player. What three questions would you ask?

Trait: Ideas
Steps in an Activity, 187A

Grammar Daily Language Activities, 187G
Singular and Plural Nouns, 187H
Grammar Practice Book, 34

Quick Check Vocabulary, 187D

DAY 5
Review and Assess

Listening/Speaking/Viewing

? Focus Question What kinds of physical and mental preparation do you need to do before playing a professional sport? How might this preparation be different for men and women?

Vocabulary

Assess Words, Connect to Writing, 187D

Spelling Posttest, 187F
Phonics/Spelling Book, 42

Read Self-Selected Reading, 162K
Practice Book, 63

Student Book

Comprehension
Connect and Compare, 185

Fluency Practice, 162K

Writing

Daily Writing Write a review of your favorite sports movie. Briefly describe it and tell why people should see it.

Conferencing, 187B

Grammar Daily Language Activities, 187G
Singular and Plural Nouns, 187H
Grammar Practice Book, 35

Weekly Assessment, 187II–187JJ

Differentiated Instruction

What do I do in small groups?

Teacher-Led Small Groups

Independent Activities

IF... students need additional instruction, practice, or extension based on your **Quick Check** observations for the following priority skills:

✔ **Phonics/Word Study**
Digraphs

✔ **Vocabulary Words**
legendary, muttered, gaped, snickering, insult, flinched
Strategy: Context Clues: Description

✔ **Comprehension**
Strategy: Monitor Comprehension
Skill: Author's Purpose

✔ **Fluency**

THEN...

Approaching **ELL**	Preteach and Reteach Skills
On Level	Practice
Beyond	Enrich and Accelerate Learning

LOG ON ▶ **Suggested Small Group Lesson Plan**

CD-ROM **TeacherWorks** *Plus*
All-In-One Planner and Resource Center

	DAY 1	DAY 2

Approaching Level
• **Preteach/Reteach**
Tier 2 **Tier 2 Instruction**
	• Prepare to Read, 187I
	• Academic Language, 187I
	• Preteach Vocabulary, 187K
		• Comprehension, 187M
		  Monitor Comprehension/Author's
		  Purpose **ELL**
		• Leveled Reader Lesson 1, 187N

On Level • **Practice**	• Vocabulary, 187S • Phonics, 187S Digraphs **ELL**	• Leveled Reader Lesson 1, 187U
Beyond Level • **Extend/Accelerate** **Gifted and Talented**	• Leveled Reader Lesson 1, 187Y • Analyze Information, 187Y	• Leveled Reader Lesson 2, 187Z • Synthesize Information, 187Z
ELL • **Build English Language Proficiency** • See **ELL** in other levels.	• Prepare to Read, 187AA • Academic Language, 187AA • Preteach Vocabulary, 187BB	• Vocabulary, 187BB • Preteach Main Selection, 187CC

Focus on Leveled Readers

Levels
O–S

Wilma Rudolph: A True Winner by Terrie Lintner
Approaching · O

Determined to Win: Babe Didrikson Zaharias by Terrie Lintner
On Level · Q

Jackie Robinson: A Man Who Stood So Tall by Sarah Glasscock
Beyond · S

Champion Athlete: Babe Didrikson Zaharias by Terrie Lintner
ELL · O

Additional Leveled Readers

LOG ON **Leveled Reader Database**
www.macmillanmh.com

Search by
- Comprehension Skill
- Content Area
- Genre
- Text Feature
- Guided Reading Level
- Reading Recovery Level
- Lexile Score
- Benchmark Level

Subscription also available.

Manipulatives

Sound-Spelling WorkBoards

Sound-Spelling Cards

about
today

High-Frequency Word Cards

VISUAL VOCABULARY RESOURCES

Visual Vocabulary Resources

DAY 3

- Phonics Maintenance, 187J
  Digraphs **ELL**
- Leveled Reader Lesson 2, 187O

- Leveled Reader Lesson 2, 187V

- Phonics, 187W
  Digraphs **ELL**

- Vocabulary, 187BB
- Grammar, 187EE

DAY 4

- Reteach Phonics Skill, 187J
  Digraphs **ELL**
- Review Vocabulary, 187L
- Leveled Reader Lesson 3, 187P

- Fluency, 187T

- Vocabulary, 187W
- Write a Poem, 187W
- Fluency, 187X

- Vocabulary, 187BB
- Writing/Spelling, 187FF
- Preteach Paired Selection, 187CC
- Fluency, 187DD
- Leveled Reader, 187GG

DAY 5

- High-Frequency Words, 187L
- Fluency, 187Q
- Self-Selected Independent Reading, 187R
- Book Talk, 187P

- Self-Selected Independent Reading, 187T
- Book Talk, 187V

- Self-Selected Independent Reading, 187X
- Evaluate Information, 187X
- Book Talk, 187Z

- Vocabulary, 187BB
- Leveled Reader, 187GG
- Self-Selected Independent Reading, 187DD
- Book Talk, 187HH

Managing the Class

What do I do with the rest of my class?

Teacher-Led Small Groups

Independent Activities

- Practice Book and Reproducibles
- ELL Practice Book
- Leveled Reader Activities
- Literacy Workstations
- Online Activities

Classroom Management Tools

Weekly Contract

Name _____ Date _____

My To-Do List

✔ Put a check next to the activities you complete.

📖 **Reading**
- ☐ Practice fluency
- ☐ Choose a story to read

🔤 **Phonics/Word Study**
- ☐ Look up word origins
- ☐ Write words with short vowel sounds

✏️ **Writing**
- ☐ Write a letter to the editor
- ☐ Write a radio ad

🔬 **Science**
- ☐ Research two types of rocks
- ☐ Write a chart

🌎 **Social Studies**
- ☐ Create a guide book
- ☐ Role-play an interview

📖 **Leveled Readers**
- ☐ Write About It!
- ☐ Content Connection

🎧 **Technology**
- ☐ Vocabulary PuzzleMaker
- ☐ Fluency Solutions
- ☐ Listening Library
- ☐ www.macmillanmh.com

🎨 **Independent Practice**
- ☐ Practice Book, 1-9

Treasures

Managing Small Groups
A How-to Guide

Dr. Vicki Gibson Dr. Douglas Fisher

Macmillan/McGraw-Hill

How-to Guide

Rotation Chart

Teacher-Led Small Groups

Red

Literacy Workstations

Independent Activities

Blue   **Green**

Orange

...za
...an
...ria

Rotation Chart

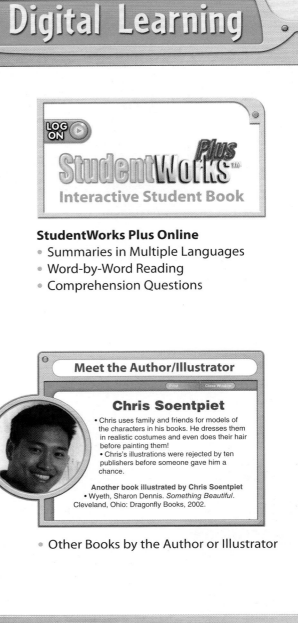

Digital Learning

LOG ON ▶

StudentWorks Plus
Interactive Student Book

StudentWorks Plus Online
- Summaries in Multiple Languages
- Word-by-Word Reading
- Comprehension Questions

Meet the Author/Illustrator

Print   Close Window

Chris Soentpiet

- Chris uses family and friends for models of the characters in his books. He dresses them in realistic costumes and even does their hair before painting them!
- Chris's illustrations were rejected by ten publishers before someone gave him a chance.

Another book illustrated by Chris Soentpiet
- Wyeth, Sharon Dennis. *Something Beautiful.* Cleveland, Ohio: Dragonfly Books, 2002.

- Other Books by the Author or Illustrator

Leveled Practice

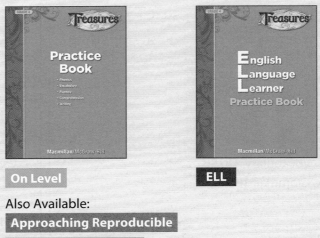

Treasures

Practice Book
- Phonics
- Vocabulary
- Fluency
- Comprehension
- Writing

Macmillan/McGraw-Hill

On Level

Treasures

English Language Learner Practice Book

Macmillan/McGraw-Hill

ELL

Also Available:

Approaching Reproducible

Beyond Reproducible

ONLINE INSTRUCTION   www.macmillanmh.com

Oral Language Activities

- Focus on Vocabulary and Concepts
- English Language Learner Support

Vocabulary/Spelling Activities

Grade 4, Unit 2
Selection 3, Vocabulary

preserve

Look to the sky to find the Answer

to keep from being lost, damaged, or decayed; protect

Answers Found

- Differentiated Lists and Activities

Leveled Reader Database

LEVELED READER
Search

Log In

Basic Search

Fill in any of the information below to find leveled readers matching all specified criteria.

NOTE: The search results list only displays up to 200 results. To narrow your search, provide as much information as possible.

Title:
Author:
Keyword:

- Leveled Reader Database
- Search titles by level, skill, content area, and more

Research Toolkit

Research Roadmap

Step 2. Research

Research answers for the questions you were asked in Step 1. Visit these Web sites. Take notes about them on this page, too!

Kratts' Creatures
Click Creature World on the sign post. You will be on your way to learning about all sorts of animals. Or, check out the Creature of the Week, or the Creature Clubhouse. This excellent site is part of PBS Kids.

Take Notes:

- Research Roadmap
- Research and Presentation Tools
- Theme Launcher Video
- Links to Science and Social Studies

Available on CD

LISTENING LIBRARY
Recordings of selections
- Main Selections
- Paired Selections
- Leveled Readers
- ELL Readers

VOCABULARY PUZZLEMAKER

FLUENCY SOLUTIONS
Recorded passages at two speeds for modeling and practicing fluency

Leveled Reader Activities

Approaching

On Level

Beyond

ELL

See inside cover of all Leveled Readers.

Literacy Workstations

Reading

Writing

Phonics/Word Study

Science/Social Studies

See lessons on pages 162K–162L.

Managing the Class

Teacher-Led Small Groups • *Independent Activities*

What do I do with the rest of my class?

Reading

Objectives

- Develop fluency through partner-reading
- Read independently for a sustained period of time; keep a reading log, **Practice Book** page 63

Phonics/Word Study

Objectives

- Use a dictionary to determine word meanings
- Use context clues to find or clarify a word's meaning
- Build and write words with digraphs

Reading — Fluency
20 Minutes

- Select a paragraph from the Fluency passage on page 65 of your Practice Book.
- With a partner, take turns practicing reading the dialogue aloud. Make words sound as natural as you can.

Extension

- Organize a Readers Theater.
- Find a story with a lot of dialogue. Assign parts, including a narrator. Present your reading to the class.

> **Things you need:**
> - Practice Book

Readers Theater

Fluency Solutions
Listening Library

13

Phonics/Word Study — Sportscaster
20 Minutes

- Look up the following words in the dictionary: *exhibition, flinched, fluke, gaped, insult, legendary, major league, muttered, pitcher,* and *snickering.*
- Use each word in a sentence. Use context clues to help readers figure out the meaning of the words.

Extension

- Give a partner context clues from one of your sentences.
- Have him or her try to guess the correct word by listening to the context clues.

> Pitcher
> On the mound stood the pitcher, ready to throw the ball.

> **Things you need:**
> - dictionary
> - pen and paper

For additional vocabulary and spelling games, go to www.macmillanmh.com — Vocabulary PuzzleMaker

13

Reading — Independent Reading
20 Minutes

- Choose a nonfiction article to read.
- As you read, think about why the author wrote this article. Did the author write to inform, to entertain, or to make a point?
- What do you think the author's purpose is? Write it in your response journal.

Author's Purpose

Extension

- Write a paragraph that explains how you decided the author's purpose. Use details from the article to support your paragraph.

> **Things you need:**
> - nonfiction article
> - pen and paper

For more books about Baseball, go to the Author/Illustrator section of www.macmillanmh.com

14

Phonics/Word Study — Digraphs
20 Minutes

- Create a Table or Chart Foldable®.
- Write *Digraphs* at the top.
- Fold paper into four columns.
- Label each column: *ch, th, sh, wh.*
- Under each digraph, write words with the consonant sounds.

Extension

- Write a story about the first time you tried a new sport. Use as many words from your Foldable as you can.

> **FOLDABLES**
> - Table or Chart Foldable®

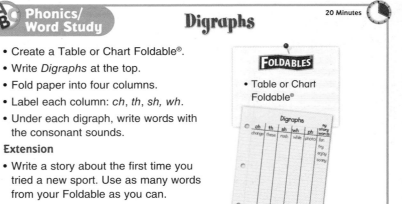

For additional vocabulary and spelling games, go to www.macmillanmh.com — **FOLDABLES**

14

Literacy Workstations

Reading · Phonics/Word Study · Writing · Science/Social Studies

Literacy Workstation Flip Charts

Writing

Objectives

- Write a persuasive letter
- Write a paragraph about team spirit

Content Literacy

Objectives

- Research and write directions for throwing curveballs and sliders
- Create a calendar for a baseball team's schedule

Writing — PLAY BALL! · 20 Minutes

- Choose your favorite sports team.
- Write a letter to a friend telling why your team is a great team. Use reasons that will persuade your friend to agree with you.

Extension

- Share your letter with a partner. Ask your partner if your letter was persuasive enough.
- Add more reasons, if necessary.

Things you need:
- pen and paper

13

Science — Batter Up! · 20 Minutes

- Use the Internet to research how to throw a curve ball or a slider.
- Write the directions in step-by-step order.

Extension

- Predict which ball would float on water: a table tennis ball or baseball. Write down the reasons for your answer. Use the Internet to find out if your prediction was correct.

Things you need:
- online resources
- pen and paper

13

Writing — Team Spirit · 20 Minutes

- Write a paragraph that explains what team spirit means to you.
- Tell why people who work together need team spirit to succeed at a task.

Extension

- Choose a job in which workers need team spirit. Write an advertisement that illustrates why team spirit and cooperation are important in this job.

Let's Work Together

Things you need:
- pencil and paper
- colored pencils or markers

14

Social Studies — Game Time · 20 Minutes

- Use an almanac or the Internet to find out where and when your favorite baseball team is playing.
- Choose one month and write the dates, times, and places where the games will be held.

Extension

- Using the information you found, create a table. For example, you could show how many times your team plays in a certain city or state during the month.

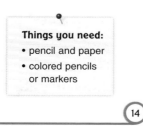

Things you need:
- almanac or online resources
- pencil and paper
- ruler

LOG ON Internet Research and Inquiry Activity
Students can find more facts at www.macmillanmh.com

14

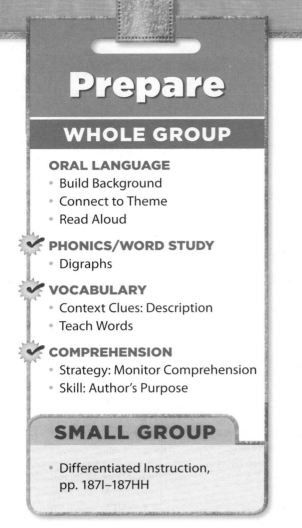

Prepare

WHOLE GROUP

ORAL LANGUAGE
- Build Background
- Connect to Theme
- Read Aloud

✔ **PHONICS/WORD STUDY**
- Digraphs

✔ **VOCABULARY**
- Context Clues: Description
- Teach Words

✔ **COMPREHENSION**
- Strategy: Monitor Comprehension
- Skill: Author's Purpose

SMALL GROUP

- Differentiated Instruction, pp. 187I–187HH

Oral Language

Build Background

ACCESS PRIOR KNOWLEDGE

Share the following information:

The girls in the photo are playing soccer, the world's most popular sport. Their yellow and black uniforms show they are on the same team. The girls are teammates who work together to score goals and to keep the other team from scoring. People of all ages who work together and succeed can inspire others to work hard to reach their goals.

Write the following words on the board and briefly define each using the **Define/Example/Ask** routine: **athlete** (person who plays sports), **influence** (to affect how another person acts or

162

feels), **acceptance** (agreement from others that something is good or true).

FOCUS QUESTION Ask a volunteer to read "Talk About It" on **Student Book** page 163. Then have students turn to a partner and describe the photo. Ask:

- Do the girls seem to be enjoying playing together? How can you tell?

- How can an athlete influence others, or change how they act or feel?

Inspiring Women

Talk About It

How have women's roles in sports changed over time? How can these girls inspire others?

LOG ON ▶ VIEW IT

Oral Language Activities
Inspiring Women
www.macmillanmh.com

163

Use the Picture Prompt

BUILD WRITING FLUENCY

Ask students to write in their Writer's Notebooks what they know about playing on a team. Tell students to write as much as they can for eight minutes without stopping. Meet with individuals during Writing Conference time to provide feedback and revision assignments. Students should self-correct any errors they notice prior to the conference.

Connect to the Unit Theme

DISCUSS THE BIG IDEA

A female baseball player earns acceptance of women in sports by playing against the men and winning.

Ask students what they have learned so far in this unit about making a difference in another person's life.

- Who have we read about who made a difference in another person's life?

- Are people's influences on each other always positive? Why or why not?

USE THEME FOLDABLES

Write the **Big Idea** on the board. Ask students to copy it on their Unit Theme Foldables. Remind them to add details as they complete this week's readings.

Dinah Zike's
FOLDABLES®
Study Organizer

| Unit Theme | Week 1 | Week 2 | Week 3 | Week 4 | Week 5 |

Accordion Book

ELL ENGLISH LANGUAGE LEARNERS

Beginning

Use Visuals Tell students about the photograph. *The girls are playing soccer. They work together to score goals.* Then ask students to tell you what the girls in the photograph are doing. If the answer is correct, repeat it in a louder and slower voice so the rest of the class may hear.

Intermediate

Describe Ask students to tell what the girls in the photograph are doing. *What sport are they playing? What do you think happened? What kinds of things do teammates do?* Repeat students' responses, correcting grammar and pronunciation as needed.

Advanced

Explain Have students elaborate on being a teammate. *How do teammates influence each other?* Revise students' responses for meaning as needed.

Objectives

- Identify the characteristics of a poem
- Develop vocabulary
- Read sentences fluently, focusing on intonation and expression

Materials

- Read Aloud Anthology, pp. 28–30

Read Aloud

Read "Take Me Out to the Ball Game!"

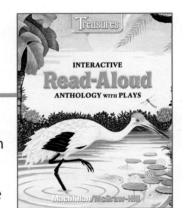

Read Aloud

GENRE: Literary Text/Poetry

Share with students that song lyrics are often considered a form of **poetry**:

- Lyrics are the words that go along with the music of a song.
- Lyrics, like poems, are written in lines and may include rhyme.
- Lyrics often include a refrain, or a set of lines that repeat.

FOCUS ON VOCABULARY

Introduce the following words, using the **Define/Example/Ask** routine. Tell students that knowing these words will help them understand the song lyrics you are reading.

Vocabulary Routine

Use the routine below to discuss the meaning of each word.

Define: To **fret** is to worry.
Example: "Try not to fret about missing the train," said Mrs. Ling to her son.
Ask: What might a baseball player fret about?

Define: To **root** for something is to cheer for it.
Example: Pat stayed for the whole game to root for the players.
Ask: What might a coach root for?

Define: To **pout** is to act disappointed.
Example: Jake started to pout when his mom would not give him a snack before dinner.
Ask: When might you pout?

LISTENING FOR A PURPOSE

Ask students to listen carefully as you read "Take Me Out to the Ball Game!" on **Read-Aloud Anthology** pages 28–30. Use the Think Alouds and Genre Study prompts provided.

ELL **Interactive Reading** Build students' oral language by engaging them in discussion about the passage's basic meaning.

- Point to the picture of the baseball game. Explain that the player with the bat is the batter, the player with the glove is the catcher, and the person standing behind the catcher is the umpire. Have students describe what each person is doing.

- After the first stanza of lyrics, say: *Turn to your partner and discuss why Nelly Kelly would pout.*

- After the second stanza, say: *Show how you might root for something.*

- After the last stanza, say: *Tell your partner what Nelly means when she sings the phrase, "I don't care if I never get back … ," and discuss why she might feel that way.*

Think/Pair/Share Use **Copying Master 2**, "I made a connection when … ," to help students further comprehend what they read. Then have students turn to a partner and orally summarize the lyrics, using their responses to guide them. Finally, have a few students share their summaries with the class.

RESPOND TO THE LYRICS

Ask students the Think and Respond questions on page 30. Then have students discuss why some authors may write lyrics that appeal to only a particular group of people. Have students explain how this might affect the author's popularity.

Model Fluency

Reread the lyrics. Tell students that this time you want them to focus on one aspect of how you read—your **intonation**. Explain that reading with proper intonation is part of reading with good expression.

Point out that as you read your tone of voice changes at times. For example, you stress important words or phrases. Model reading with good intonation for students.

Think Aloud Listen as I read the first part of the refrain. Pay particular attention to how I stress certain words, such as rhyming words or the first word in a line: "Take me out to the ball game,/ Take me out with the crowd./ Buy me some peanuts and Cracker Jack,/ I don't care if I never get back …"
Did you notice how I emphasized certain words in the lyrics? Which words were they? Now you try. Repeat each line after me, using the same intonation that I use.

Establish Fluency Focus Remind students that you will be listening for this same quality in their reading throughout the week. You will help them improve their reading by adjusting their intonation to add emphasis to important words and phrases and to clarify meaning.

ELL

Discuss Genre Review song lyrics with students. *What are lyrics? Do lyrics include rhymes? How are song lyrics like poems?* Ask students to describe the main idea of "Take Me Out to the Ball Game!" Provide ample time for students to respond. Repeat students' responses, correcting for grammar and pronunciation as needed.

Objective

- Decode multisyllabic words with digraphs

Materials

- Sound-Spelling Cards
- Practice Book, p. 55
- Transparency 7
- Word-Building Cards
- Teacher's Resource Book, p. 126

Phonics

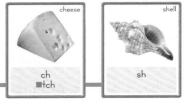

✔ Digraphs

EXPLAIN/MODEL

Display the *Thumb, Shell, Cheese, Whale, Fire*, and *Sing* **Sound-Spelling Cards** for the consonant digraphs. Tell students that sometimes two consonants combined stand for one sound. These spellings are called digraphs.

Point to each digraph spelling on the card and provide a sample word. Remind students that the digraph *th* stands for two sounds, the sound at the beginning of *thumb* and *then*.

- **th** as in *thumb, then*
- **sh** as in *shell*
- **ch, tch** as in *cheese, pitch*
- **wh** as in *whale*
- **ph** as in *phone*
- **ng** as in *sing*

Write the sample words on the board, underline the digraphs, and model blending each one.

Think Aloud Look at the second word I wrote: *t-h-e-n*. I see the *th* making a /th/ sound. Listen and watch as I sound out the word: /then/, *then*. (Run your finger under the word as you sound it out.)

PRACTICE/APPLY

Read the Word List Display **Transparency 7**. The first two lines include words with digraphs that students will encounter in the upcoming selections. Have students underline the digraph in each word. Then have them chorally read the words.

pitcher	while	string	touch
bleach	she	throw	graph
thimble	change	stash	patch
ditch	physical	shiver	slither
phrase	photo	chicken	washing

Phonics Transparency 7

Sort the Words Ask students to sort the words by spelling pattern. Then have them write the word sort in their Writer's Notebooks.

th	sh	wh	ph	ch	tch	ng

Read Multisyllabic Words

TRANSITION TO LONGER WORDS Help students transition from reading one-syllable to multisyllabic words containing digraphs. Have them read a word in the first column, then model how to read the longer word in the second column. Point out the added syllable(s), such as a prefix or suffix. Tell students that in some words, such as *mechanic*, the *ch* digraph stands for the /k/ sound. Provide other examples, such as *chorus* and *chronicle*.

child	childhood	there	therefore
hatch	hatchback	photo	photograph
path	pathway	chip	chipmunk
when	whenever	push	push-up
ship	shipwreck	cheer	cheerleader
patch	patchwork	mechanic	mechanical

Phonics Transparency 7

BUILD WORDS Use **Word-Building Cards** *thick, catch, should, show, thought, shame, bath, thank, ful, er, ing, en*. Display the cards. Have students use the word parts to build as many multisyllabic words with digraphs as possible. These and other words can be formed: *thicker, thicken, thickening, catching, catcher, shoulder, shower, showing, thoughtful, shameful, bathing, thankful, thanking*.

APPLY DECODING STRATEGY Guide students to use the Decoding Strategy to decode: *Philadelphia, whiplash, watchful, photosynthesis, shellfish, channels, whining, wither, therefore, championship*. Write each word on the board. Remind students to look for familiar spellings in step 3 of the Decoding Strategy procedure.

Build Fluency

SPEED DRILL Distribute copies of the **Digraphs Speed Drill, Teacher's Resource Book** page 126. Use the Speed Drill routine to help students become fluent reading words with digraphs.

Quick Check

Can students read words with digraphs?

During **Small Group Instruction**

Tier 2

If No → **Approaching Level** Reteach the skill using the lesson on p. 187J.

If Yes → **On Level** Consolidate the learning using p. 187S.

Beyond Level Extend the learning using p. 187W.

Syllable Fluency

Use Word-Building Cards 61–70. Display one card at a time. Have students chorally read each common syllable. Repeat at varying speeds and in random order. Have students work with partners during independent time to write as many words as they can containing each syllable.

Decoding Strategy

Decoding Strategy Chart

Step 1	Look for word parts (prefixes) at the beginning of the word.
Step 2	Look for word parts (suffixes) at the end of the word.
Step 3	In the base word, look for familiar spelling patterns. Think about the six syllable-spelling patterns you have learned.
Step 4	Sound out and blend together the word parts.
Step 5	Say the word parts fast. Adjust your pronunciation as needed. Ask yourself: "Is this a word I have heard before?" Then read the word in the sentence and ask: "Does it make sense in this sentence?"

© Macmillan/McGraw-Hill

Vocabulary

✓ **STRATEGY**
CONTEXT CLUES

Description Explain to students that if they find an unfamiliar word, they should look for context clues, or clues to the meaning in the nearby words and sentences. Sometimes a description in the same sentence or paragraph might help them understand the unfamiliar word. Point out that such context clues can be helpful for multiple-meaning words as well.

Prompt students to read "Context Clues" in the bookmark on **Student Book** page 164. Then model for students how to use the surrounding words to determine the meaning of the word *snickering*.

Think Aloud I'm not really sure what *snickering* means, but the sentence seems to give some clues. It says, *If people laughed in a mean way, did the girls notice the baseball fans snickering?* The words "laughed in a mean way" seem to describe what snickering people do. So *snickering* probably means "laughing in a mean way."

Read "Women Pick Up the Ball"

As you read "Women Pick Up the Ball" with students, ask them to identify clues that reveal the meanings of the highlighted words. Tell students they will read these words again in *Mighty Jackie*.

Vocabulary

legendary	snickering
muttered	insult
gaped	flinched

✓ **Context Clues**

Descriptions in the text can help you figure out what a word means. Figure out the meaning of *snickering* using descriptions.

WOMEN
PICK UP THE
BALL

by Jenny Hull

Lucy's class was at Cooperstown—site of the **legendary** Baseball Hall of Fame. Lucy wasn't thrilled to be there. "Who cares about the All-American Girls Professional Baseball League?" Lucy **muttered** quietly to herself.

The League's Beginning

The guide explained that in 1942, most young men were being drafted to fight in World War II. Some feared that major-league baseball parks would close. But Philip Wrigley, the owner of the Chicago Cubs, decided to start a girls' league. Some may have stared and **gaped** at the idea, but it soon caught on.

Lucy wondered what it was like for those girls. If people laughed in a mean way, did the girls notice the baseball fans **snickering**?

A woman baseball player makes a leaping catch.

164

Quick Check

Can students identify word meanings?

During **Small Group Instruction**

Tier 2

If No → **Approaching Level** Reteach the words using the Vocabulary lesson, pp. 187K–187L.

If Yes → **On Level** Consolidate the learning using p. 187S.

Gifted Talented

Beyond Level Extend the learning using p. 187W.

The League Succeeds

Girls as young as 15 tried out for the league. The $45- to $85-a-week salaries were a big draw. That might seem like an **insult** today, but back then it was a lot of money.

Players had to follow strict rules of behavior and take classes. They were taught how to dress, act, and take care of themselves.

Female players walked with blocks on their heads for balance and posture.

The success of the league was no fluke. During the war many women worked in factories. This changed the image people had of what women could do.

The League Ends

After the war ended, interest lessened and the league fell apart. One reason was that many people got TVs in the early 1950s. They could watch major-league games without buying a ticket or leaving the house!

Time to Leave

Lucy **flinched** and drew back when her teacher called the class together. She wasn't ready to leave. She wanted to learn more. But Lucy would have to wait until her next visit to learn more about this interesting time in baseball history.

Reread for **Comprehension**

Monitor Comprehension

Author's Purpose One way to monitor comprehension is to identify the author's purpose. An author writes for three purposes, or reasons: to entertain, inform, or persuade. Think about how an author presents events in a person's life. This can help you identify the author's purpose. Reread the selection and fill in the Author's Purpose Map.

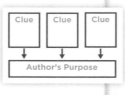

Clue	Clue	Clue

↓ ↓ ↓

Author's Purpose

LOG ON ▶ LEARN IT Comprehension
www.macmillanmh.com

165

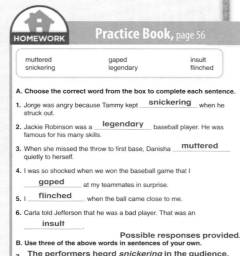

HOMEWORK **Practice Book,** page 56

| muttered | gaped | insult |
| snickering | legendary | flinched |

A. Choose the correct word from the box to complete each sentence.

1. Jorge was angry because Tammy kept _snickering_ when he struck out.

2. Jackie Robinson was a _legendary_ baseball player. He was famous for his many skills.

3. When she missed the throw to first base, Danisha _muttered_ quietly to herself.

4. I was so shocked when we won the baseball game that I _gaped_ at my teammates in surprise.

5. I _flinched_ when the ball came close to me.

6. Carla told Jefferson that he was a bad player. That was an _insult_.

Possible responses provided.
B. Use three of the above words in sentences of your own.

7. The performers heard _snickering_ in the audience.

8. I _muttered_ angrily to myself about the homework.

9. Richard _gaped_ when he saw his 100 on the test.

Approaching Reproducible, page 56

Beyond Reproducible, page 56

Vocabulary

✓ TEACH WORDS

Introduce each word using the **Define/Example/Ask** routine. Model reading each word using the syllable-scoop technique.

Vocabulary Routine

Define: A story that has been handed down for years and has some basis in fact is **legendary**.
Example: Stories about the Vikings are legendary because they are often part fact and part fiction.
Ask: What legendary stories do you know? EXAMPLE

■ **Muttered** means you spoke in a low, unclear tone with your mouth closed. *His mouth was shut, so I didn't hear what he muttered.* How is *muttered* different from *whispered*? COMPARE AND CONTRAST

■ **Gaped** means you stared with your mouth open wide in surprise or wonder. *Sandra gaped as the large shark swam past her.* What surprising things have you gaped at? EXAMPLE

■ People are **snickering** if they are laughing in a disrespectful way. *After Kim slipped on ice, she heard people snickering.* How is snickering different from laughing? COMPARE AND CONTRAST

■ An **insult** is a remark or action that hurts someone's feelings or pride. *When the boys selected Steve last for the team, it was an insult.* How is an insult different from an honor? COMPARE AND CONTRAST

■ If you **flinched**, you reacted to something unpleasant by drawing back quickly. *Jerrod flinched when he saw his mother enter the principal's office.* What is a synonym for *flinched*? SYNONYM

Mighty Jackie **165**

Objectives

- Monitor comprehension
- Identify the author's purpose
- Use academic language: *monitor comprehension, author's purpose*

Materials

- Transparencies 7a, 7b, 9
- Practice Book, p. 57

Skills Trace

Author's Purpose

Introduce	139A–139B
Practice/ Apply	140–155; Practice Book, 48–49
Reteach/ Review	161M–161Z, 165A–165B, 166–183, 187M–187Z; Practice Book, 57–58
Assess	Weekly Tests; Units 2, 4 Tests
Maintain	195B, 465A–465B, 466–469, 473Q–473DD, 605B

ELL

Academic Language
Preteach the following academic language words to **ELL** and **Approaching Level** students during Small Group time: *monitor comprehension, author's purpose, entertain, inform, persuade.* See pages 187AA and 187I.

Reread for Comprehension

STRATEGY
MONITOR COMPREHENSION

What Is It? Explain that **monitoring comprehension** means pausing to check understanding using self-correction techniques. There are many strategies that students can use to monitor and adjust comprehension as they read, including asking themselves questions about the text, summarizing, paraphrasing, and visualizing.

Why Is It Important? Point out to students that monitoring their comprehension can help them clarify text they find confusing and help them ensure that they understand what they have read.

SKILL
AUTHOR'S PURPOSE

What Is It? Remind students that the **author's purpose** is the main reason an author had for writing. The most common purposes are to entertain, inform, and persuade. Point out that an author's purpose may be stated or implied and discuss the difference.

Why Is It Important? Understanding an author's purpose can help readers set a purpose for reading. Are they reading for enjoyment, to be informed, or to decide about an issue?

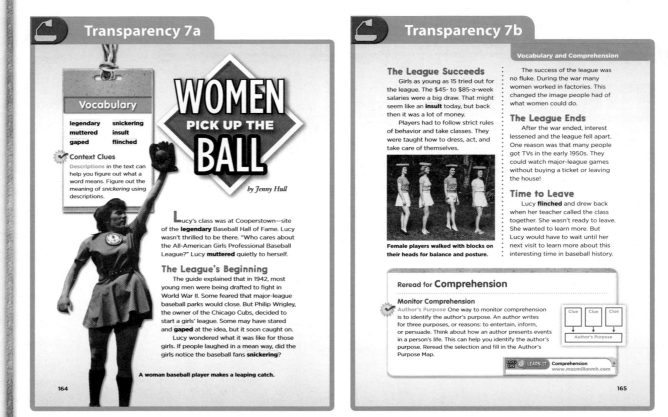

Student Book pages 164–165 available on Comprehension Transparencies 7a and 7b

- As they read, students should look for clues about why the author wrote. If a selection includes humor or exciting action, the author's purpose was likely to **entertain**. If an author provides facts about a topic, the purpose was likely to **inform**. An author who wants to **persuade** uses language to influence how readers think or feel.

- To determine the author's purpose, students should identify important details in the selection and find a connection between those details. When students identify the author's purpose, they need to supply text evidence to support their conclusion.

- The author's purpose shapes the way the text is structured, details given, and words used. In a biography, the author's purpose may affect how he or she presents the major events of a person's life.

MODEL

How Do I Use It? Read aloud the first four paragraphs of "Women Pick Up the Ball" on **Student Book** page 164.

Think Aloud I can see that Lucy is not interested in learning about the All-American Girls Professional Baseball League, but after she learns a few facts, she begins to wonder about how the girls themselves felt. I will keep reading to see if the author presents more facts about the league, including major events in its history.

GUIDED PRACTICE

Have students identify the key facts the author presents in the second paragraph. Use **Transparency 9** to record clues to the author's purpose. Help students decide what to enter into the first clue box on the Author's Purpose Map. (The author includes facts about how the league started.)

APPLY

Help students map additional clues to the author's purpose. Then have students complete the Author's Purpose Map by reaching a conclusion about the author's purpose based on the clues, and writing the purpose in the bottom box. Students should describe how they reached their decision based on text evidence.

Transparency 9

Author's Purpose Map

Clue	Clue	Clue
The author includes facts about how the league started.	The author includes facts about the girls in the league.	The author includes reasons why the league grew, then stopped.

Author's Purpose
To inform the reader about the All-American Girls Professional Baseball League

Graphic Organizer Transparency

HOMEWORK

Practice Book, page 57

Authors write to **entertain**, to **inform**, or to **persuade**.

Read the passages and answer the questions.

Theo sat on the bench and watched as Molly went to bat. She took a big swing at the first pitch and missed. On the next pitch she surprised everyone and bunted the ball. It rolled slowly towards third base, and Molly sprinted to first. She got to first safely. Theo thought to himself, "Wow, that was pretty tricky. The fielders thought that she was going to hit the ball hard, so they weren't ready for that bunt. Maybe I could try that some time."

1. What was the author's purpose in writing this story? **to entertain**
2. What helped you decide on the author's purpose?
   Responses should include the idea that the story is fictional and entertaining.

Jackie Robinson is a member of the Baseball Hall of Fame. Born in 1919 in Cairo, Georgia, Robinson went to college at the University of California in Los Angeles. He played baseball after college and became the first African-American baseball player in the major leagues. He played for the Brooklyn Dodgers for ten years. During that time they won six pennants. Robinson stole home 19 times and was named the Most Valuable Player in 1949.

3. What was the author's purpose in writing the passage? **to inform**
4. What helped you decide on the author's purpose?
   Responses should include that the story includes factual information.

Approaching Reproducible, page 57

Beyond Reproducible, page 57

Quick Check

Can students identify the author's purpose?

During **Small Group Instruction**

Tier 2

If No → **Approaching Level** Reteach the skill using the Comprehension lesson, pp. 187M–187P.

If Yes → **On Level** Consolidate the learning using pp. 187U–187V.

Beyond Level Extend the learning using pp. 187Y–187Z.

Read

WHOLE GROUP

✔ **MAIN SELECTION**
- *Mighty Jackie: The Strike-out Queen*
- Skill: Author's Purpose

✔ **PAIRED SELECTION**
- Poetry: "The New Kid"
- Literary Elements: Stanzas, Line Breaks, Meter, Rhyme

SMALL GROUP

- Differentiated Instruction, pp. 187I–187HH

Main Selection

GENRE: Literary Nonfiction/Biography

Review the definition of Biography on **Student Book** page 166. Students should look for details about the life of a real person as they read.

 STRATEGY
MONITOR COMPREHENSION

Review with students that monitoring comprehension means making sure they understand what they read. Remind students to pause during reading to check their comprehension.

SKILL
AUTHOR'S PURPOSE

Review that an author's purpose for writing usually is to entertain, inform, or persuade. With a biography, thinking about how an author presents major events in a person's life can help you understand why he or she is writing.

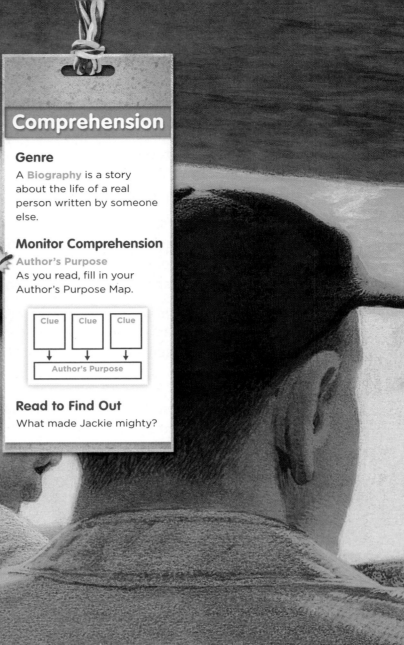

Comprehension

Genre
A **Biography** is a story about the life of a real person written by someone else.

Monitor Comprehension
Author's Purpose
As you read, fill in your Author's Purpose Map.

Clue	Clue	Clue

↓ ↓ ↓

Author's Purpose

Read to Find Out
What made Jackie mighty?

166

Vocabulary

Vocabulary Words Review the tested words while reading: **legendary, insult, muttered, gaped, flinched,** and **snickering**.

Additional Selection Words Students may be unfamiliar with these words. Pronounce the words, give student-friendly explanations as needed, and help students use the previously taught vocabulary strategies: word parts, dictionary, context clues.

exhibition (p. 167): an event for people to watch just for fun

pitcher (p. 168): the member of the baseball team who throws the ball to the batter

major league (p. 168): the highest level in professional baseball

MIGHTY JACKIE
The Strike-out Queen
by Marissa Moss • illustrated by C.F. Payne

Award Winning Illustrator

It was April 2, 1931, and something amazing was about to happen. In Chattanooga, Tennessee, two teams were about to play an exhibition game of baseball.

One was the New York Yankees, a **legendary** team with famous players—Babe Ruth, Lou Gehrig, and Tony Lazzeri.

167

Preview and Predict

QUICK WRITE Ask students to read the title, preview the illustrations, think about the genre, and make predictions about the story. Have any students heard of any players mentioned in the second paragraph?

Set Purposes

FOCUS QUESTION Discuss the "Read to Find Out" question on **Student Book** page 166. Remind students to look for the answer as they read.

Point out the Author's Purpose Map in the Student Book and on **Practice Book** page 58. Explain that students will fill it in as they read.

Read *Mighty Jackie: The Strike-out Queen*

Use the questions and Think Alouds to support instruction about the comprehension strategy and skill.

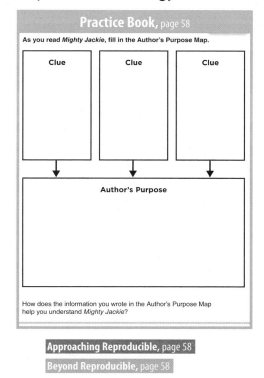

Practice Book, page 58

As you read *Mighty Jackie*, fill in the Author's Purpose Map.

| Clue | Clue | Clue |

↓ ↓ ↓

Author's Purpose

How does the information you wrote in the Author's Purpose Map help you understand *Mighty Jackie*?

Approaching Reproducible, page 58
Beyond Reproducible, page 58

Read the Main Selection

Preteach	Read Together	Read Independently
Have Approaching Level students and English Language Learners listen to the selection on **StudentWorks Plus**, the interactive e-Book, before reading with the class.	Use the prompts to guide comprehension and model how to complete the graphic organizer. Have students use **Think/Pair/Share** to discuss the selection.	If students can read the selection independently, have them read and complete the graphic organizer. Suggest that they use their purposes to choose their reading strategies.

LOG ON StudentWorks Plus
Interactive Student Book

Develop Comprehension

1 STRATEGY
CONTEXT CLUES

Use context clues to help you find the meaning of *sneered*. (First, we read that "everyone knew that girls didn't play major-league baseball, " so we can expect to hear negative comments about Jackie. Next, we read that the newspaper *sneered* that Jackie would "swing 'a mean lipstick' instead of a bat." This is clearly an insult. So if they "sneered" this comment, they must have said it mockingly or insultingly. So *sneered* probably means "mocked" or "insulted.")

2 STRATEGY
MONITOR COMPREHENSION

Teacher Think Aloud I want to make sure I understand what I have read on the first two pages, so I will pause to **monitor comprehension**. One way to monitor comprehension is to summarize what I've read so far. The story takes place in 1931. The New York Yankees are going to play against a team called the Lookouts. The only thing special about the Lookouts is that they have a female pitcher, named Jackie Mitchell. Newspaper reporters make fun of her, saying girls can't play baseball. We will have to see if Jackie is good enough to play against the Yankees.

The other was the Chattanooga Lookouts, a small team, a nothing team, except for the pitcher, Jackie Mitchell.

Jackie was young, only seventeen years old, but that's not what made people sit up and take notice. Jackie was a girl, and everyone knew that girls didn't play major-league baseball.

1 The *New York Daily News* sneered that she would swing "a mean lipstick" instead of a bat. A reporter wrote that you might as well have "a trained seal behind the plate" as have a woman standing there. But Jackie was no trained seal. She was a pitcher, a mighty good one. The question was, was she good enough to play against **3 2** the New York Yankees?

168

Monitor Comprehension

Monitor and Clarify: *Visualize*

Explain Students can better understand what they read if they use their own experiences and details from the text to visualize, or form mental pictures, of the characters, setting, and action.

Discuss Ask students to explain how their own experiences might help them visualize how Jackie might have reacted to being criticized for being a girl and playing baseball. (Students might recall a time when they were criticized for something beyond their control. They may visualize her tensing up or turning red.)

Apply Have students list details on pages 167–168 that help them visualize the characters and setting. Have students apply this strategy as they continue to read.

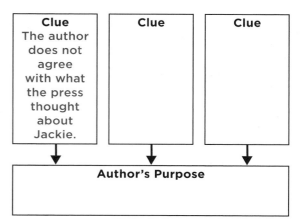

169

Develop Comprehension

3 **SKILL**
AUTHOR'S PURPOSE

Tell whether or not the **author** agrees with what the reporter said about a woman playing baseball. This may be a clue to the **author's purpose** for writing. Then add this information to your Author's Purpose Map. (No, the author does not agree. She says that Jackie was no trained seal and that she was a mighty good pitcher.)

Clue The author does not agree with what the press thought about Jackie.	Clue	Clue

Author's Purpose

PHONICS/WORD STUDY

APPLY DECODING SKILLS While reading, point out words with the sound/ spelling patterns, syllable types, and word parts students have recently learned. Help students blend these words. You may wish to focus on selection words with digraph spelling patterns, such as *she, chance, thousand, threw, they, watched, catcher, flinched, pitch, where*, and *show*.

ELL ENGLISH LANGUAGE LEARNERS

Beginning	**Intermediate**	**Advanced**
Access Content Preteach story content, build language, and develop meaning using the Interactive Question-Response Guide in the **ELL Resource Book**, pages 70–77. Give ample time for students to respond. They may point or use words or short phrases to respond.	**Describe** Preteach story content, build language, and develop meaning using the Interactive Question-Response Guide in the ELL Resource Book, pages 70–77. Have students respond in complete sentences. Repeat students' responses, correcting pronunciation or grammar as needed.	**Explain** Complete the Intermediate task with students. Elicit details from students for their responses.

Develop Comprehension

4 MAKE INFERENCES

What **inference** can you make about how Jackie felt when she heard boys insult each other by saying, "You throw like a girl"? (Jackie knew she could throw well. She was also encouraged by her father and Dazzy Vance. When the boys made their comment, Jackie might have been able to ignore it because she knew it was not true. On the other hand, since it wasn't true, it might have bothered her more. It is also possible that Jackie worked extra hard to prove them wrong.)

5 COMPARE AND CONTRAST

SPIRAL REVIEW

Compare and contrast the reactions of the neighborhood kids, Jackie's father, and Dazzy Vance, to Jackie playing baseball. (The neighborhood kids told Jackie she could not play baseball because she was a girl. Jackie's father and Dazzy Vance told Jackie that she could play baseball and that she was good at it.)

170

Comprehension

Literary Device: *Flashback*

Explain Authors sometimes interrupt the regular time-order of events in a story to take the reader back to a past event. Such an episode, called a *flashback*, shows how the past event affected a current situation and thus contributes to the story's development. Occasionally authors also leap ahead in time, or *flash forward*.

Discuss How does the author signal that the events described on page 171 happened in the past? (She begins with the phrase "As long as she could remember …")

Apply Have students use clues in the text to estimate the number of years covered in the flashback. (10 to 12 years) In what year did Dazzy Vance start to coach Jackie? How do you know? (1922; she was 17 years old in 1931, so 17 years old – 8 years old = 9 years, and 1931 – 9 years = 1922.)

As long as she could remember, Jackie had played ball with her father. She knew girls weren't supposed to. All the kids at school, all the boys in her neighborhood told her that. When one boy yelled at another one, "You throw like a girl!" it was an **insult**—everyone knew girls couldn't throw. Or that's what they thought.

Day after day, in the neighborhood sandlot, Jackie's father told her differently. He said she could throw balls, and she did. She ran bases, she swung the bat. By the time she was eight years old, Dazzy Vance, the star pitcher for the Brooklyn Dodgers, had taught her how to pitch. A real pitcher talking to a little girl was all Jackie needed to start dreaming of playing in the World Series. Her father saw her talent and so did Dazzy. He told her she could be good at whatever she wanted, as long as she worked at it. And Jackie worked at baseball. She worked hard.

She practiced pitching till it was too cold and dark to stay outside. She threw balls until her shoulder ached and her fingers were callused. She pitched until her eyes blurred over and she couldn't see where she was throwing. But it didn't matter, her arm knew. **6**

 Author's Purpose
Why did the author give so much information about Jackie's childhood? **7**

171

Develop Comprehension

6 **STRATEGY**
CONTEXT CLUES

Read the **description** in the last paragraph on the page. Use the context of the sentence to determine the meaning of the phrase *blurred over*. (The author says that Jackie pitched until her eyes "blurred over," and she couldn't see where she was throwing. So, *blurred over* must mean that something happened to her eyes to prevent her from seeing well. Her eyes probably became blurry.)

7 **SKILL**
AUTHOR'S PURPOSE

Think about the **author's purpose** for presenting these details. Why did the author give so much information about Jackie's childhood? (She wants to show how Jackie gained skill and confidence. We also see how learning from a star pitcher encouraged her to have big dreams for her future.) Add this information to your Author's Purpose Map.

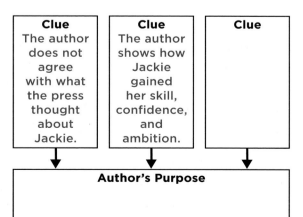

Clue The author does not agree with what the press thought about Jackie.	**Clue** The author shows how Jackie gained her skill, confidence, and ambition.	**Clue**

Author's Purpose

Develop Comprehension

8 SKILL
AUTHOR'S PURPOSE

What is the **author's purpose** in building the suspense at this point, and how does the author use language to create the suspense? (This is Jackie's big chance—the moment she has been preparing for. The author probably wants us to know what it must have felt like for Jackie as she took the mound. The author creates suspense by not having the action start right away. First, we see Jackie looking into the bleachers and the waiting crowd. The repetitions of "They were waiting for her …" and the word *game* in "a man's game, not *her* game" also suggest the tension Jackie was feeling.)

9 GENRE: Literary Nonfiction/Biography

To make a **biography** more vivid, authors sometimes imagine and include what the characters might have been thinking. What information on page 172 could not actually have been seen or heard by anyone while Jackie prepared to pitch? (Although Jackie probably knew what many of the spectators thought would happen, we can never know her or their actual thoughts.)

And now she was finally going to have her chance to play on a *real* baseball team, to pitch to *real* players. The stands were packed. A crowd of four thousand had come to see the strange sight of a woman on the pitcher's mound.

8 She stood tall on the field and looked back at the crowd in the bleachers. They were waiting for her to make a mistake, and she knew it. They were waiting for her to prove that baseball was a man's game, not *her* game.

9 "It *is* my game," she **muttered** to herself and bit her lip. The Yankees were up, top of the first, and the batter was walking up to the plate. Jackie was ready

10 for him, the ball tight in her left hand.

11

172

Text Evidence

Author's Purpose

Reread Question 8. Remind students that looking for evidence in the text helps readers figure out the author's purpose.

Reread the first paragraph on page 172. Ask, *What does the author want to stress here?* (Playing in a professional game was very different from practicing in the neighborhood.) *How does this paragraph help you understand the author's purpose?* (It adds excitement and gives readers a sense of how Jackie must have felt. Such clues help readers form opinions about the author's purpose.)

As students continue to read, encourage them to pay close attention to which events from Jackie Mitchell's life the author includes and does not include. Focusing on such evidence in the text will help them identify and explain the author's purpose.

173

Develop Comprehension

10 SUMMARIZE

How would you **summarize** the story so far? (Seventeen-year-old Jackie Mitchell is about to pitch for the Chattanooga Lookouts in an exhibition game against the New York Yankees. Thousands of people have shown up to see her. Jackie learned to play baseball from her father at a very young age and was coached by a star pitcher named Dazzy Vance. Now, as she takes the mound against the Yankees, Jackie is aware that many people expect her to fail because they believe baseball should only be played by men.)

11 SELF-SELECTED STRATEGY USE

What **strategies** have you used so far to help you understand the selection? Where did you use them? Why? How did they help?

RETURN TO PREDICTIONS AND PURPOSES

Have students respond to the selection by confirming or revising their predictions and purposes for reading. Encourage them to revise or write additional questions to help focus their attention as they continue to read the selection.

Extra Support

Author's Purpose

Help students review the clues about the author's purpose that they added to their Author's Purpose Maps. Ask: *Does the author let us know what she thinks about Jackie? Explain.* (Yes, she disagrees with what the newspapers said about Jackie.) *How do we learn that Jackie got a lot of encouragement as a child?* (The author talks about the coaching she received from her father and Dazzy Vance.) *What do these clues tell you about what the author's purpose might be?* (She wants to inform us about Jackie's life, but probably also wants to explain how Jackie was as good at pitching as any man.)

Stop here if you wish to read this selection over two days. STOP

Develop Comprehension

12 SKILL
AUTHOR'S PURPOSE

The **author** tells us how Babe Ruth felt about women playing baseball. What is her **purpose** for including this information? (The author wants to show what is at stake as Jackie pitches against Babe Ruth. Not only is Jackie pitching to the mighty "Home Run King," but she is working to prove him wrong about women playing the game at all.)

174

Except the batter was Babe Ruth—Babe Ruth, the "Home Run King," a big mountain of a man—and Babe didn't like the idea of a woman pitcher at all. He thought women were "too delicate" for baseball. "They'll never make good," he said. "It would kill them to play ball every day." He walked to the plate and tipped his cap at Jackie. But if she thought he was going to go easy on her, she could forget it! He gripped the bat and got ready to slam the ball out of the ballpark. **12**

Jackie held that ball like it was part of her arm, and when she threw it, she knew exactly where it would go. Right over the plate, right where the Babe wasn't expecting it, right where he watched it speed by and *thwunk* into the catcher's mitt.

"STRRRRIKE ONE!"

13

Babe Ruth **gaped**—he couldn't believe it! The crowd roared. Jackie tried to block them out, to see only the ball, to feel only the ball. But Babe Ruth was facing her down now, determined not to let a girl make a fool out of him. She **flinched** right before the next pitch, and the umpire called a ball.

"Hmmmph," the Babe snorted.

"You can do it!" Jackie told herself. "Girls can throw—show them!"

But the next pitch was another ball. **14**

Now the crowd was hooting and jeering. The Babe was **snickering** with them.

175

Develop Comprehension

13 TEXT FEATURES.

Notice the **text features**. Why do you think the words "STRRRRIKE ONE!" are printed differently from the rest of the text? (The printing imitates the way the umpire sounds when he calls the play. The change in letter size suggests the change in pitch in his voice.)

14 STRATEGY
MONITOR COMPREHENSION

Teacher Think Aloud There is a lot of action on this page. It is confusing to me. I am going to reread a portion aloud to make sure I understand what is going on. What is another way I can monitor my comprehension on this page?

PARTNERS Prompt students to apply the strategy in a Think Aloud by asking them to describe a comprehension monitoring strategy they can use to clarify the events.

Student Think Aloud Since there is a lot of action here, I can visualize. I can picture in my mind what is being described. This will help me get a clearer picture of what is happening at this point in the story.

Act It Out To help students understand the meanings of verbs that describe facial expressions, vocal sounds, and gestures, act out the following words:

• Babe Ruth **gaped** …

• Babe Ruth was **facing her down** …

• "Hmmmph," the Babe **snorted**.

• The crowd was **hooting** and **jeering**.

• The Babe was **snickering** …

Develop Comprehension

15 **MONITOR AND CLARIFY: VISUALIZE**

What details does the author include to help you **visualize** the scene as Jackie prepares to pitch once more to Babe Ruth? (Jackie closes her eyes. Her fingers tingle around the ball. She feels the weight of the ball in her hand. She feels the strength in her shoulders. She hears her father's voice in her mind.)

16 **MAKE INFERENCES**

What is your **inference** about why Jackie's father tells her to pitch to Babe Ruth as though he were an ordinary ballplayer? (If Jackie treats Babe Ruth like an ordinary ballplayer, she will remain calm and be able to pitch her best.)

---

15 Jackie closed her eyes. She felt her fingers tingling around the ball, she felt its heft in her palm, she felt the force of her shoulder muscles as she wound up for the **16** pitch. She remembered what her father had told her: "Go out there and pitch just like you pitch to anybody else."

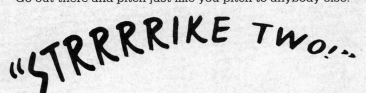

"STRRRRIKE TWO!..."

Now the Babe was mad.

This was serious. The Babe was striking out, and the **17** pitcher was a girl!

Jackie wasn't mad, but she wasn't scared either. She was pitching, really pitching, and it felt like something was happening the way it had always been meant to. She knew the batter would expect the same pitch, close and high, even if the batter was Babe Ruth. So this time she threw the ball straight down the middle with all the speed she could put on it.

"STRRRRIKE THREE!"

Babe Ruth glared at the umpire and threw the bat down in disgust. He told reporters that that would be the last time he'd bat against a woman! The crowd was stunned. A girl had struck out the "Sultan of Swat"! It couldn't be! It was a mistake, a fluke! What would the papers say tomorrow? But wait, here came Lou Gehrig, **18** the "Iron Horse," up to the plate. He'd show her. She couldn't strike him out too.

176

Connect to Content

Social Studies

Social Studies

WOMEN IN STATE HISTORY

Share with students the fact that women who lived during the Great Depression, the time period of this story, found ways to make a difference in society. Behaving in unexpected ways—doing work men most commonly did, or helping charitable causes—enabled women to contribute to society and change how others felt about them.

Tell students to research and write about a famous woman of this time period or earlier from their state who made important contributions to society. Have students share their compositions with the class.

Develop Comprehension

17 COMPARE AND CONTRAST

SPIRAL REVIEW What information does the author provide on page 176 about Jackie's state of mind? **Compare and contrast** her state of mind with Babe Ruth's. Are their states of mind the same or different? Explain. (Jackie is calm and unafraid. She can think clearly and choose the right pitches. Babe Ruth's state of mind is different. He is worried about being struck out by a girl. When he does strike out, his temper shows.)

18 SKILL
AUTHOR'S PURPOSE

In the last paragraph on page 176, the **author** imagines the crowd's reaction after Jackie strikes Babe Ruth out. In what ways does this help the author express her opinion about Jackie? (The author lets us know that the crowd is very surprised. In 1931 no one believes that a girl can strike out a major-league baseball star. Though they have just seen it happen, they think it must be a mistake. The author not only shows that Jackie has great talent, but that it takes courage to do something so unexpected.) Add this information to your Author's Purpose Map.

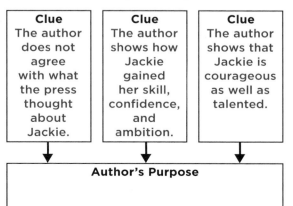

Clue	Clue	Clue
The author does not agree with what the press thought about Jackie.	The author shows how Jackie gained her skill, confidence, and ambition.	The author shows that Jackie is courageous as well as talented.

Author's Purpose

Develop Comprehension

19 MAKE INFERENCES

Lou Gehrig has just seen Jackie strike out his teammate. Why is he "stunned" when he swings and misses Jackie's first pitch? (He does not think that Jackie can strike out two stars in a row. Perhaps he thinks that, having seen Babe Ruth strike out, he is better prepared for the level of Jackie's skill. He may also think he can bat better than Babe Ruth can.)

Vocabulary

Word Structure Clues: *Suffixes*

Explain/Model Remind students that suffixes are word parts added to the end of a base word. Suffixes change a word's meaning and often change its part of speech. Identifying a suffix in a word can help the reader figure out its meaning. The suffix *-y* means "having the quality of," "full of," or "tending to." Write *mighty* on the board.

Think Aloud I see the base word *might* with the suffix *-y*. I know that *-y* can mean "full of." One meaning for *might* is "strength." When I put the meaning of the suffix and the base word together, the entire word means "full of strength."

Practice/Apply Have students find another word with the suffix *-y* on page 179. (*lefty*) Help them use the base word and suffix to figure out what it means. ("having the quality of left" or "left-handed")

Lou Gehrig swung with a mighty grunt, but his bat hit nothing but air.

"STRRRRIKE ONE!" [19]

He looked stunned, then dug in his heels and glared at Jackie.

"STRRRRIKE TWO!..."

Jackie grinned. She was doing what she'd worked so hard and long to do, and nothing could stop her.

She pitched the ball the way she knew best, a lefty pitch with a low dip in it. No one could touch a ball like that when it was thrown right.

"STRRRRIKE THREE!" [20] [21]

179

Develop Comprehension

[20] DRAW CONCLUSIONS

Why does the author describes Gehrig's time at bat more quickly than she described Ruth's time at bat? Explain the reasons for your **conclusion**. (It is not as important to use suspense this time. Jackie is more confident now that she has struck out Ruth.)

[21] THEME

Think about the **theme** of this selection. What message or lesson is the author trying to communicate? (If you work hard and believe in yourself, you can succeed, in spite of other people's lack of faith in you.)

Develop Comprehension

22 STRATEGY
MONITOR COMPREHENSION

How might you check to make sure you understood the ending of the story? If you had trouble comprehending, what would you do?

Student Think Aloud I would try to summarize the story. If I got to a point where I could no longer summarize what happened, I would go back to that point and reread. I would also read that part more slowly, to make sure I was paying attention to what I was reading. It would also help to visualize. If I reread the last page, I would visualize the crowd standing and cheering, and Jackie looking happy and proud.

23 SKILL
AUTHOR'S PURPOSE

Why did Marissa Moss write this story? (She wanted to entertain readers and inform them about how one woman succeeded despite the odds.) Add this information to your Author's Purpose Map.

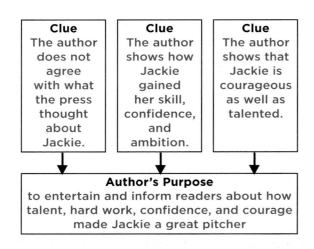

Clue	Clue	Clue
The author does not agree with what the press thought about Jackie.	The author shows how Jackie gained her skill, confidence, and ambition.	The author shows that Jackie is courageous as well as talented.

Author's Purpose
to entertain and inform readers about how talent, hard work, confidence, and courage made Jackie a great pitcher

180

The crowd, so ready to boo her before, rose with a roar, clapping and cheering like crazy. Back to back, Jackie had struck out two of baseball's best batters, Babe Ruth and Lou Gehrig. She'd proven herself and now the fans loved her for it.

But Jackie didn't hear them. She was too proud and too happy. She'd done what she'd always known she could do. She'd shown the world how a girl could throw—as hard and as fast and as far as she wanted.

22

Author's Purpose
Why did Marissa Moss write this story?

23

181

Develop Comprehension

RETURN TO PREDICTIONS AND PURPOSES

Review students' **predictions** and **purposes** for reading. Did they discover how determination can help someone overcome a challenge? (Determination can help people succeed at what they want to do, even when others believe that it is not possible.)

REVIEW READING STRATEGIES

- **Monitor Comprehension** In what ways did monitoring your comprehension and analyzing the author's purpose help you to understand the selection?

- **Monitor and Clarify: Visualize** Do you understand how to use the strategy of visualizing when trying to relate to a character or picture a situation being described? When might you use it again?

- **Decoding** What difficult words did you encounter? How did the Reading Multisyllabic Words strategy help you sound out these words?

- **Self-Selected Strategy Use** What strategies did you use to make sense of what you read? Where? How were these strategies helpful?

PERSONAL RESPONSE

Direct students to write about Jackie from the point of view of Babe Ruth or Lou Gehrig. How might these players have described the events in the story?

Quick Check

Can students identify the author's purpose?

During **Small Group Instruction**

If No → **Approaching Level** Reteach the skill and have students apply it to a simpler text. Use Leveled Reader lessons, pp. 187N–187P.

If Yes → **On Level** Have students apply the skill to a new text to consolidate learning. Use Leveled Reader lessons, pp. 187U–187V.

 Beyond Level Have students apply the skill to a more complex text to extend learning. Use Leveled Reader lessons, pp. 187Y–187Z.

Author and Illustrator

**THE WINNING TEAM:
MARISSA AND C. F.**

Have students read the biographies of the author and the illustrator. Ask:

- Why was Marissa Moss interested in writing about Jackie?

- Analyze the title of this selection. How does it help bring Jackie to life? What would be another appropriate title for this selection? Support your answer with details from the text.

- Why was C. F. Payne a good artist to illustrate this story?

WRITE ABOUT IT

Discuss how Jackie's father encouraged her to be a pitcher. Have students imagine and write a dialogue between Jackie and her father after the game.

Author's Purpose

The narrator is third person. The author probably chose to write in third person to give the reader information Jackie might not have known or written about, such as what people said about her behind her back, what the newspapers wrote about her, or Babe Ruth's comment about women playing baseball.

The Winning Team: Marissa and C.F.

Marissa Moss likes to write about real women like Jackie who have done unusual things. She has also written about a female train engineer and the first woman to fly across the English Channel. Marissa hopes that when kids read her books they will discover things about the past that remind them of their own lives.

Other books by Marissa Moss and C.F. Payne

C.F. Payne has stepped up to the plate to illustrate other baseball stories. C.F. often does caricatures, a kind of art that exaggerates the way people look or act, making them seem larger than life.

LOG ON ▶ **FIND OUT**

Author Marissa Moss
Illustrator C.F. Payne
www.macmillanmh.com

✔ Author's Purpose

Identify whether the narrator of the story is first or third person. Why did the author tell the story from this point of view?

182

Author's Craft

Point of View

Point of view means who is telling the story. The most commonly used points of view are first person and third person omniscient.

- A story with a first-person narrator is told from the point of view of one of the characters, using words like *I* and *me*.

- A third-person omniscient narrator knows everything about all the characters, including what they think and feel. Example: "They were waiting for her to make a mistake, and she knew it." (p. 172) Ask students how this point of view helps readers better understand the story.

- Have students look for and discuss other examples of the point of view, such as "But if she thought he was going to go easy on her, she could forget it!" (p. 175)

 Comprehension Check

Summarize

To summarize *Mighty Jackie* use the most important details from the selection. Information from your Author's Purpose Map may help you.

Clue	Clue	Clue

Author's Purpose

Think and Compare

1. Who taught Jackie how to pitch? Details

2. What happened right after Jackie struck out Babe Ruth and before Lou Gehrig stepped up to the plate? Sequence

3. Why was proving her skill as a pitcher so important to Jackie? Explain using story details. Make Inferences

4. The author states that Ruth and Gehrig were famous baseball players on a **legendary** team. Why does the author say this? Explain using story details. Monitor Comprehension: Author's Purpose

5. Reread "Women Pick Up the Ball" on pages 164–165. Think about *Mighty Jackie*. If Jackie had been in the girls' league, do you think the crowds would have treated her differently? Use details from both selections to explain. Reading/Writing Across Texts

183

Make Connections

Text-to-Self Have students respond to the following question to make connections to their own lives. Use the Think Aloud to model a response. *Have you ever reached a goal that you or other people thought was impossible to achieve?*

Think Aloud: When I read about Jackie striking out Babe Ruth and Lou Gehrig, it reminded me of when I surprised everyone, including myself, by winning first place in the school science fair.

Text-to-World Have students respond to the following question to make connections to their world. Use the Think Aloud to model a response. *How has the role of women in sports changed since the 1930s?*

Think Aloud: In *Mighty Jackie* I learned that in the 1930s it was unacceptable for women to play baseball. In the 1940s, according to "Women Pick Up the Ball," women played professional baseball when men went to fight in World War II. Today, women play professional sports but do not play on men's professional teams.

Comprehension Check

SUMMARIZE

Have partners summarize *Mighty Jackie*. Suggest that they review their Author's Purpose Maps first to help them.

THINK AND COMPARE
Text Evidence

1. **Details** Answer in text Dazzy Vance, a pitcher for the Dodgers, taught Jackie how to pitch. LOCATE

2. **Sequence** Answer in text Babe Ruth glared at the umpire and threw down his bat. COMBINE

3. **Make Inferences** Answer It was important because at that time people thought baseball was only a man's game. Jackie knew this was untrue and wanted to play. Evidence The headlines and people's comments show us what people thought at first. Their cheers at the end prove they were wrong. CONNECT

4. **Monitor Comprehension/Author's Purpose** Answer The author wants to show just how good of a pitcher Jackie was. She was not pitching against just any major league players but against two of the best. Evidence The author helps stress this point by calling Babe Ruth the "Home Run King," and Lou Gehrig the "Iron Horse." COMBINE

5. **Text-to-Text** They probably would have treated her similarly. In both situations the crowds initially scoffed at the idea of women playing baseball. But once they saw that the women played well, they took them seriously. COMPARE TEXT

Objectives

- Read fluently with good intonation and expression
- Rate: 84–104 WCPM

Materials

- Transparency 7
- Practice Book, p. 59
- Fluency Solutions Audio CD

ELL

Phrasing Model reading by breaking the sentences into smaller phrases and have students repeat. Track with your finger under the phrases as you read them aloud. Point out the commas in the sentences and model how to read a sentence that has a comma. Provide ample time for students to repeat after you.

Practice Book, page 59

As I read, I will pay attention to intonation and expression.

	Mildred Ella Didrikson was born on June 26, 1914, in
8	Port Arthur, Texas. Mildred's father built a gym for his
18	children in the backyard. The children played many sports,
27	including baseball. Mildred was a good hitter. So the boys
37	started calling her "Babe," after the **legendary** baseball
45	player Babe Ruth. Ruth was famous for hitting home runs.
55	It was no fluke that Babe Didrikson became a good athlete.
66	Babe's father read newspaper articles about the 1928
73	Olympic Games aloud to his children. Babe was 14 years
82	old at the time. She began to dream about competing in the
94	Olympics someday.
96	Babe attended high school during the late 1920s. She
104	excelled in every sport she tried. At only 5 feet (152 cm)
114	tall and 105 pounds (48 kg), Babe was small. But she was
124	strong. 125

Comprehension Check

1. Why does the author make it a point to explain Mildred Didrikson's nickname? **Author's Purpose** The author wants readers to know that Mildred Didrikson was such a good athlete that boys compared her to Babe Ruth.
2. How did Babe Didrikson's home life help her to become an athlete? **Plot Development** Babe Didrikson's father encouraged physical training by building a gym and reading articles about the Olympics.

	Words Read	–	Number of Errors	=	Words Correct Score
First Read		–		=	
Second Read		–		=	

Approaching Reproducible, page 59

Beyond Reproducible, page 59

Fluency

Repeated Reading: Intonation/Expression

EXPLAIN/MODEL Explain that reading with good intonation helps one read with expression. Model reading **Transparency 7** with good intonation, raising and lowering your voice as needed, and stressing words in italics. Point out that the text has been marked with slashes to indicate stops and pauses. Model grouping words together in appropriate phrases, pausing for punctuation.

> ### Transparency 7
>
> And now she was finally going to have her chance to play on a *real* baseball team,/ to pitch to *real* players.// The stands were packed.// A crowd of four thousand had come to see the strange sight of a woman on the pitcher's mound.//
>
> She stood tall on the field and looked back at the crowd in the bleachers.// They were waiting for her to make a mistake,/ and she knew it.// They were waiting for her to prove that baseball was a man's game,/ not *her* game.//

Fluency (from *Mighty Jackie: The Strike-out Queen*, p. 172)

PRACTICE/APPLY Reread the first two sentences with students. Have them alternate reading sentences with good intonation. Tell them to pay attention to the meaning as they read.

DAILY FLUENCY Students will practice fluency using **Practice Book** page 59 or the **Fluency Solutions Audio CD**. The passage is recorded at a slow practice speed and a faster fluent speed.

Quick Check

Can students read accurately with good intonation?

During **Small Group Instruction**

If No → **Approaching Level** Use the Fluency lesson and model, p. 187Q.

If Yes → **On Level** See Fluency, p. 187T.

Beyond Level See Fluency, p. 187X.

Comprehension

REVIEW SKILL
COMPARE AND CONTRAST

EXPLAIN/MODEL

- A **comparison** tells how two or more things are alike. A **contrast** tells how two or more things are different. Model comparing and contrasting objects in the room.

- When readers compare and contrast facts, events, or ideas in a selection, they consider how each of them are alike and different.

- Sometimes authors structure the text in a way that compares and contrasts facts, events, or ideas. Yet often readers must compare and contrast them on their own, based on information in the text.

Lead a class discussion comparing and contrasting the women in "Women Pick Up the Ball," and Jackie in *Mighty Jackie*. How might some of their experiences have been the same and different?

PRACTICE/APPLY

Have students work in pairs or literature circles to make other comparisons and contrasts involving *Mighty Jackie*.

- Contrast the New York Yankees and the Chattanooga Lookouts. (The Yankees are a legendary team with famous players. The Lookouts are a small team, with no well-known players.)

- Compare the opinions of Babe Ruth, Lou Gehrig, and the crowd, on women baseball players. (They all think girls cannot play baseball and are shocked when they see how well Jackie plays.)

- Contrast the way the crowd reacted to Jackie's pitching at the beginning of the game and at the end of the game. (At first, they were waiting for Jackie to make a mistake. By the end, they were clapping and cheering for her. They realized she was a great player.)

- In an interview, Jackie Mitchell said, "After I threw the second strike, I settled down a little. I figured then that it wasn't going to be so hard for me to get the ball over the plate." Does the story portray how Jackie felt at this point in a similar or different way? (Similarly. After the second strike Jackie was not scared but confident.)

- Imagine that Jackie Mitchell had herself written a fictional story based on these events. How might that story have been different from *Mighty Jackie*? (She may have made the story even more dramatic and may have told it from a first-person point of view.)

PRACTICE BOOK See **Practice Book** page 60 for Compare and Contrast Text Structure.

Objectives

- Compare and contrast facts, events, or ideas in a selection
- Identify similarities and differences in a fictional work and a biography

Skills Trace
Compare and Contrast

Introduce	69A–69B
Practice/ Apply	70–73; Practice Book, 21–22
Reteach/ Review	77Q–77DD, 613A–613B, 614–631, 637M–637Z; Practice Book, 210–211
Assess	Weekly Tests; Units 1, 5 Tests
Maintain	97B, 183B, 659B

Test Practice

Answering Questions

To apply **answering questions strategies** to content-area reading, see pages 53–60 in *Time for Kids*.

Paired Selection

GENRE: Literary Text/Poetry

Have students read the bookmark on **Student Book** page 184. Discuss how lyrical poetry uses literary elements to convey the poet's ideas and emotions.

Explain that a lyric poem

- is about a feeling or a mood;
- usually has end rhymes;
- may sound like a song when read aloud.

✔ Literary Elements: Stanzas, Line Break, Meter, and Rhyme

EXPLAIN/MODEL Point out that a lyric poem has certain literary elements. These elements help the poet emphasize certain parts of the poem.

- Present the definition of **stanzas**. Point out this poem's five stanzas.
- Present the definition of **line break**. Point to *street* in the first stanza. Discuss the first part of the callout.
- Present the definition of **meter**. Read the first stanza aloud, emphasizing the rhythm of the stressed and unstressed syllables. Then discuss the second part of the first callout.
- Present the definition of **rhyme**. Read aloud the first two lines of the fourth stanza and discuss the callout.

APPLY Have students practice reading the second stanza aloud, paying close attention to the meter. Have them tap out the rhythm of the syllables as they read.

Poetry

Lyric Poems express the thoughts and feelings of the poet. They may sometimes sound like a song.

✔ Literary Elements

Stanzas are groups of lines that give the poem its form. A **Line Break** is the place where the line ends.

Meter is the rhythm of stressed and unstressed syllables in a line of poetry.

Words **Rhyme** when their endings sound the same or nearly the same.

The New Kid

by Mike Makley
illustrated by Steve Cieslawski

184

Comprehension/Writing

Poetry: *Lyric Poem*

Explain Poets use lyric poetry to tell a story with a musical quality. They often organize these poems into stanzas with meter and rhyme. These literary elements give the lyric poem its song effect.

Discuss Read aloud the first stanza. Have students identify examples of rhyme, such as *much, Dutch* and *beat, street*. Then have students clap or tap the rhythm of the syllables as they read aloud the first stanza.

Apply Have students write a lyric poem about something they enjoy doing. Remind them to organize the lines of their poem into stanzas with meter and rhyme and to use sensory details. Have students share their poems with the class.

Our baseball team never did very much,
we had me and PeeWee and Earl and Dutch.
And the Oak Street Tigers always got beat
until the new kid moved in on our street.

> Each stanza in this poem has four lines and almost all lines have ten syllables.

The kid moved in with a mitt and a bat
and an official New York Yankee hat.
The new kid plays shortstop or second base
and can outrun us all in any place.

The kid never muffs a grounder or fly
no matter how hard it's hit or how high.
And the new kid always acts quite polite,
never yelling or spitting or starting a fight.

We were playing the league champs just last week;
they were trying to break our winning streak.
In the last inning the score was one-one,
when the new kid swung and hit a home run.

> The words "league," "week," and "streak" all rhyme.

A few of the kids and their parents say
they don't believe that the new kid should play.
But she's good as me, Dutch, PeeWee, or Earl,
so we don't care that the new kid's a girl.

1 **2**

✔ Connect and Compare

1. Read the third stanza of the poem aloud. Is the rhythm of the stressed and unstressed syllables the same in each line? Explain your answer. **Meter**

2. The last line of the poem ends on the word "girl." How does this emphasize the surprise ending? **Line Breaks**

3. Compare Jackie in *Mighty Jackie* to the girl in this poem. What is similar about their situations? **Reading/Writing Across Texts**

4. Think about a sport or hobby that you like to do. Write a poem about it. Form your lines into stanzas and try to use rhyme in your poem. **Apply**

185

---

1 LITERARY ELEMENT: STANZAS

Which stanza describes a game against the league champs? (The fourth stanza describes a game against the league champs.) What happened in that game? (The new kid hit a home run to win the game.)

2 LITERARY ELEMENT: RHYME

Describe the rhyme scheme, or pattern of rhymes, in the poem. (In each stanza, the last words in the first and second lines rhyme, as do the last words in the third and fourth lines.)

Connect and Compare

1. No. The stressed and unstressed syllables are arranged differently in each line, so the rhythm is different. **METER**

2. Throughout the poem, the reader does not suspect that the new kid is a girl. In the last stanza, the author uses the pronoun "she." Then the last word confirms for readers that the new kid is a girl. **LINE BREAKS**

3. **FOCUS QUESTION** Both Jackie and the girl in the poem are the only females on an all-male team. Jackie played professionally as a pitcher. The girl in the poem played shortstop or second base on a neighborhood team. **READING/WRITING ACROSS TEXTS**

4. Check students' poems for stanzas, meter, and rhyme. For additional support, see the Comprehension/Writing minilesson on page 184. **APPLY**

ON YOUR OWN

Practice Book, page 61

A **lyric poem** expresses the poet's feelings in a way that sounds like a song. Lyric poems often use rhyming words and rhythm, or meter. The poem's **meter** is the way the author arranges the accented and unaccented syllables. The author of a lyric poem may use stanzas. A **stanza** is a group of lines. **Line breaks** separate each line in a stanza.

Read the poem and answer the questions.

Mary's Canary

Mary had a pretty bird,
　Feathers bright and yellow,
Slender legs—upon my word
　He was a pretty fellow!

The sweetest note he always sung, ____ **8**
　Which much delighted Mary. ____ **7**
She often, where the cage was hung, ____ **8**
　Sat hearing her canary. ____ **7**

1. How many stanzas are in the poem? ____ **two**

2. How many lines are in the first stanza? ____ **four**

3. What words rhyme in the second stanza? **sung, hung; Mary, canary**

4. Read each line in the second stanza. Count the number of syllables in each line. Write the number on the line.

Approaching Reproducible, page 61
Beyond Reproducible, page 61

Write

WHOLE GROUP

✔ **WRITING WORKSHOP**
- Developing Procedural Writing
- Trait: Word Choice
- Show Actions

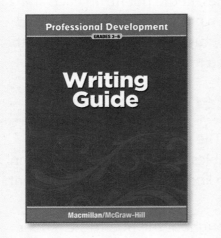

Professional Development
GRADES 3–6

Writing Guide

Macmillan/McGraw-Hill

Trait: Word Choice

Strong Paragraphs: Show Actions

TEACH/MODEL Remind students that showing is when a writer uses descriptive details to help readers form strong images in their minds. Tell students that writers also use descriptive words and phrases to show actions, or how something is done. Explain that each action is made up of a series of small actions. When writers include details about each small action, they help readers create clear mental pictures.

Tell students that writing strong sentences that show actions using descriptive words and phrases will help them write **strong paragraphs** that give readers additional information. Then write the following sentence on the board, and read it aloud:

> Billy jumped into the pool.

Teacher Think Aloud This sentence tells me about an action. It tells me that Billy jumped into the pool, but it does not use descriptive words and phrases to show me the action. That makes it hard for me to picture how Billy jumped into the pool and how he felt about it. After I read the sentence, I wonder if Billy was excited, nervous, or having fun. I know that I can show the action in a more interesting way by adding descriptive words and phrases.

Write the following description of the action, and read it aloud.

> Billy *crossed his arms, bounced up and down,* and *shivered by the side of the pool.* Suddenly, he *gulped down a big breath of air.* He *clenched his fists, closed his eyes tightly,* and *leaped high into the air.* Splash! Billy *catapulted into the pool.* He *plunged deep into the water* and then *popped up again* with a *huge smile on his face.*

Discuss the differences between telling that Billy jumped into the pool and using descriptive words and phrases to show how he jumped into the pool. Point out how using details and spatial words, such as *bounced up and down, gulped down a big breath of air, clenched his fists, catapulted,* and *popped up,* gives readers a clear image that helps them picture Billy jumping into the pool.

Teacher Write Aloud

PRACTICE/APPLY Further explore with students the use of descriptive words and phrases to show actions. Write the following sentences on the board, and read them aloud. Ask students whether the sentences are telling sentences or showing sentences. Then complete the Teacher Think Aloud.

■ Angie runs toward the ball.

■ She kicks the ball.

■ The ball goes into the net.

■ Angie scores a goal.

Teacher Think Aloud These sentences tell me what Angie does. They tell me about an action, but I can't picture this action in my mind. The writer did not use descriptive words and phrases to help show the action. Let's write a more interesting description of the action. We will use details that show a strong image of what Angie does. That will help readers create a mental image of the action.

Ask students to brainstorm descriptive words and phrases that show what people do when they run hard or kick a soccer ball to score a goal. List the descriptions on the board. To complete the Think Aloud, use the list to write a strong paragraph like the one below. Stop after each sentence to discuss how the descriptive words help students picture the action in their minds.

> Angie pumps her arms as she dashes down the field at top speed. She looks as if she's flying! As she approaches the ball, she throws her right leg back and then forward. Whack! The ball flies through the air and sails into the net. Angie jumps up and down and high-fives her teammates. She has just scored the winning goal.

Draft Display the Writing Prompt on **Writing Transparency 19**. Remind students to use descriptive words and phrases that show what they do so readers can create mental pictures. Circulate and provide Over-the-Shoulder Conferences as students work.

Objective
• Write sentences that show actions

Materials
• Writer's Notebooks
• Writing Transparency 19

Daily Journal Prompts

Focus on Showing Actions

Use these and other prompts for independent daily journal writing.

✎ Write about what you do to play your favorite game.

✎ Write about a time when you were surprised.

✎ Write about what you do when your parents say you have to clean your room.

✎ Write about what you do at your favorite outdoor place.

Transparency 19

Describe what you do when you play your favorite sport or watch your favorite team play a game. Use showing to create a picture in the reader's mind.

Writing Transparency

Reading and Writing Connection

✔ Trait: Word Choice

SHOW ACTIONS

Remind students that showing actions rather than telling about them helps readers picture the actions in their minds. Point out that good writers use descriptive words and phrases to write strong paragraphs that show how something is done.

Read the Passage

Use the example from *Mighty Jackie* as a model of the author's skilled use of showing.

- Have students read the bookmark. Remind them that good writers use descriptive words and phrases to show actions. This helps readers create vivid images in their minds as they read.

  Ask: *When have you had to concentrate on something even though there were distractions?*

- Have students read aloud the excerpt from *Mighty Jackie*. Direct their attention to the callout. Have students discuss the descriptive words and phrases that help show the action of Jackie getting ready to pitch the ball.

  Ask: *Which sentence can you imagine the most clearly? Why do you think the author showed us so much about Jackie's hands and arms?*

Reading and Writing Connection

Writing

✔ **Trait: Word Choice**
Writers use **descriptive words and phrases** to show actions.

Read the passage below. Notice how the author Marissa Moss uses descriptive words to show actions.

An excerpt from *Mighty Jackie*

The author shows us what Jackie thinks and feels right before she pitches the ball. The details help us imagine what it was like for Jackie as she pitched.

Now the crowd was hooting and jeering. The Babe was snickering with them.

Jackie closed her eyes. She felt her fingers tingling around the ball, she felt its heft in her palm, she felt the force of her shoulder muscles as she wound up for the pitch. She remembered what her father had told her: "Go out there and pitch just like you pitch to anybody else."

186

Respond to the Selection

Have students write a response to the selection.

☑ **Engagement** Help students deepen their connection to the text and discover their own perspective on it. *Focus on a moment when you made a good move while playing a sport or a game.*

☑ **Response** Help students explore more deeply their reactions to particular passages in the reading. *Focus on a moment in the story when you felt nervous for Jackie or when you felt confident in Jackie. Use text evidence in your writing.*

☑ **Literary Analysis** Help students deepen their connection to the text and discover their own perspective on it. *Focus on a place in the story where the author used showing to help you imagine a moment of action. Use text evidence in your writing.*

Read and Find

Read Rasika's writing below. What words did she use to show actions? Use the checklist below to help you.

Elliot J. Hamster

by Rasika W.

I'd like to introduce you to my best friend (and pet), Elliot J. Hamster. He is covered with soft, butterscotch-colored fur. When he crawls up my arm, his tiny claws scratch a little, but his fur tickles me at the same time. Sometimes he sits up in my hand and looks right at me. I laugh when he does that and wiggles his nose!

Read about Elliot J. Hamster.

Writer's Checklist

✓ Does the writer describe exactly what she sees and feels?

✓ Does the writer include details about size, shape, color, or other features?

☐ Does Rasika use **descriptive words and phrases** to show the actions of her hamster?

187

Write

Read the Student Model

Have students chorally read the student model at the top of **Student Book** page 187. Discuss what this student writer did to show action, and identify any descriptive words and phrases. Use the Writer's Checklist.

Journal Prompt

Draft Write the following prompt on the board. Have students write a response to the prompt.

Think about something you do with your best friend (or pet). Write a paragraph about that action. Use descriptive words and phrases to show what you do.

Tell students that you will be reading and commenting on their writing during Writing Conference time.

Model how to use the Writer's Checklist so students can write and revise their work. Then ask:

- *What action did you choose?*
- *What descriptive words and phrases did you use to show the action? Will readers be able to clearly picture the action? If not, what descriptive words or phrases could you add?*

ELL ENGLISH LANGUAGE LEARNERS

Beginning

Write Sentences Provide model sentences based on the Journal Prompt: *My best friend and I ____ up a mountain. We ____ all the way up. I ____ when I made it to the top.* Guide students to include descriptive words and phrases that show the action.

Intermediate

Describe Ask students to write three sentences based on the Journal Prompt. Have them picture the action in their minds. Then have them list words and phrases to describe what they do. Have them use these words and phrases in their sentences. Provide a model if necessary.

Advanced

Narrate Ask students to respond to the Journal Prompt. Have them use descriptive words and phrases to show what they do and what the action looks like.

Objectives

- Write showing sentences
- Write strong paragraphs

Materials

- Writer's Notebooks
- Teacher's Resource Book, p. 184

ELL

Demonstrate Meaning

Read the first sentence, and have students repeat. Then have them act out what they do when they hurt their finger. Repeat for other sentences.

HOMEWORK **Teacher's Resource Book,** page 184

Please read the following sentences:

Latoya hurt her finger.

Pete drank the entire glass of water in one gulp.

Underline the one that tells instead of shows.

Rewrite the telling sentence so that it shows the reader what is happening. Use descriptive words and phrases to help the reader picture what is happening.

Example: Rushing to put away her laundry, Latoya jammed her finger in her top drawer.

Now, write two more showing sentences about that same moment.

Example: Trying to stop her finger from throbbing, she jumped up and down and shook her hand. Tears welled up in her eyes, and she was wished she hadn't been in such a hurry in the first place.

_____

_____

_____

_____

_____

_____

Extra Practice: Do the same exercise with this sentence:

Steve felt sick.

Minilessons

Minilesson 1 | Word Choice/Describe Actions

TEACH/MODEL

Remind students that they have been using descriptive words and phrases to help readers picture an action. Today they will practice writing showing sentences about an action. Have students use **Teacher's Resource Book** page 184. Ask them to read the two sentences and tell which is a showing sentence and why.

PRACTICE/APPLY

Have students work independently to rewrite the telling sentence to make it a showing sentence. Then have them develop the action into a strong paragraph by writing two more showing sentences. Ask students to share their completed work during Sharing Circle. Discuss the descriptive words and phrases they used.

Minilesson 2 | Ideas/Steps in an Activity

TEACH/MODEL

Remind students that when writers show an action, they use descriptive words and phrases to help readers create a mental image of the action. Point out that sometimes writers use showing to describe steps in an activity. They give details that help readers picture each step in their mind and better understand the activity. Write the following paragraph on the board, and read it aloud. Have students identify the descriptive words and phrases in each step.

> Will you help me blow up balloons for my party? It's not hard. First, stretch out the balloon. Then hold the end of the balloon in front of your lips. Pucker up to make an O with your lips. Now blow. Next pinch the end of the balloon with your finger and your thumb. Finally, tie a knot in the balloon.

PRACTICE/APPLY

Write the following paragraph about how to blow bubbles. In their Writer's Notebooks, have students rewrite the paragraph to show the activity using descriptive words and phrases.

> Take your bubble stick. Put it in the bubble mixture. Hold it up. Blow.

Conferencing Routine

Dynamic Feedback System

Step 1 Read and appreciate the writing.

Step 2 Notice how the student uses the targeted skill. (for example, showing actions: Ask: *Does the writer show rather than tell what someone does?*)

Step 3 Write comments that show how the writing has an impact on you. Direct your comments to those places in the piece where the student has used the targeted skill.

Step 4 Meet with the student and give him or her a revision assignment.

Write Effective Comments

Word Choice At least one of your comments should highlight the way the student **shows actions**. Here are some sample comments.

- I feel as if I am right there watching you (twirl the spaghetti on your fork).

- I'm curious to know more about how you (shot a basketball from the foul line).

- Your details really help me understand how you (made the pizza).

Revision Assignments

Word Choice Here are some examples of effective revision assignments for showing actions.

- **Reread your entry.** *Choose one sentence that shows an action. Now rewrite this sentence, adding at least two sentences that use descriptive words and phrases to show me more about the action.*

Revise
- **[Underline a section.]** Mark a specific section of a student's writing and then ask the student to revise it in a specific way.

Revise
- **[Underline a section.]** *I underlined a section in your entry that I wished I could picture better. Write three sentences that show more about what you did in that moment.*

Teacher-to-Teacher

Over-the-Shoulder Conferences

Use these quick, focused opportunities to comment while students are writing.

- **Step 1** Quietly move close enough to a student that you can read the journal entry he or she is writing.

- **Step 2** Read part of what you see. You don't need to start from the beginning or read the entire piece.

- **Step 3** Show the student a spot in the writing where he or she is using a particular skill or describing something that piques your interest.

- **Step 4** Whisper a sentence or two about why you noticed that spot in the writing, and ask a question that will nudge the student to add descriptive words and phrases to show an action.

- **Step 5** Move on to the next student. Select students strategically. You should see 12–15 students in a 15-minute period.

Research Proven Writing Approach

The Writers' Express
Immediate Impact. Lasting Transformation.   wex.org

Connect Language Arts

WHOLE GROUP

✓ **VOCABULARY**
  • Tested Words

✓ **SPELLING**
  • Digraphs

✓ **GRAMMAR**
  • Singular and Plural Nouns

SMALL GROUP

• Differentiated Instruction, pp. 187I–187HH

Practice Book, page 62

When you come to a word you do not know in a passage, read the entire sentence. Other words in the sentence may give **clues** to the meaning of the unfamiliar word.

A. Circle the clue words in each sentence that help you figure out the meaning of the word in dark type.

1. The crowd was **stupefied** by how (amazingly bad) the team played.

2. The children were afraid of the **cantankerous** old man because he was (angry and always yelled at them).

3. The whole-grain cereal was full of **nutrients** that (keep athletes healthy).

4. Aldo (hit the ball so hard) that no one even saw the ball (fly) **swiftly** through the air.

5. The new stadium was so **colossal** that you could (fit 80,000 people into it) and still have tickets left over.

B. Write your own definitions for three of the words above. First write the word. Then write what it means. Possible responses provided.

6. swiftly: to move quickly

7. stupefied: very surprised or amazed

8. colossal: extremely large

Approaching Reproducible, page 62

Beyond Reproducible, page 62

Build Robust Vocabulary

Day 1 — Teach/Practice

CONNECT TO WORDS

■ Practice this week's vocabulary words using the following prompts:

1. Would you be more likely to recognize the name of a person who is *legendary* or a person who is not?

2. How is *muttering* different from chatting?

3. Why might someone *gape*?

4. When someone *snickers* at another person, is he or she being kind or unkind?

5. If you *insult* someone, what are you doing to him or her?

6. What might cause you to *flinch*?

ACADEMIC VOCABULARY

■ Review the important academic vocabulary words for the week. These words include: *context clues, description, monitor, author's purpose, compare, contrast.*

■ Write each word on the board. Define each using student-friendly language, and ask students to select the word you are defining. Then point to words in random order for students to define.

Day 2 — Review

CONNECT TO WORDS

■ Review the definitions of this week's vocabulary words using **Student Book** pages 164–165. Then discuss each word using the following prompts:

1. What are the names of some *legendary* figures in history?

2. Why might *muttered* words be difficult to understand?

3. When is it inappropriate to *gape*?

4. Why might *snickering* in school get you into trouble?

5. If you were *insulted* by what a friend said, what would you do?

6. If a bird flew down near your head, would you *flinch*?

CONTEXT CLUES

■ Remind students that a description surrounding an unfamiliar word can serve as a clue to help them determine or clarify the meaning of the word.

■  Display **Transparency 13.** Read the first sentence. Model figuring out the meaning of the underlined word using context clues.

■ Have students find clues in the remaining sentences that help define the underlined words and state what they think the words mean.

■ Have students write their own context-rich sentences for this week's vocabulary words in their Writer's Notebooks. Model an example first as needed.

Day 3 Reinforce

- Ask students to create Word Squares for each word in their Writer's Notebooks.

- In the first square, students write the word. (Example: *legendary*)

- In the second square, students write their own definition of the word and any related words, such as synonyms. (Example: *famous, well-known, renowned*)

- In the third square, students draw a simple illustration that will help them remember the word. (Example: drawing of a statue of a person)

- In the fourth square, students write nonexamples, including antonyms for the word. (Example: *infamous, ordinary, unknown*)

RELATED WORDS

- Point out that this week's words, such as *insult* and *legendary*, have clear connotations and may be used for praise or blame. Help students generate words related to compliments or criticism. The classification of antonyms and synonyms can help improve students' vocabularies.

- Draw a T-chart on the board. One column is headed "Kind Words"; the other column is headed "Unkind Words."

- Have students list words they know in each column. Ask students to use a print or online thesaurus. Add words not included, such as (kind) *praise, encouragement, flattering*; (unkind) *rude, cruel, harsh*.

Day 4 Extend

CONNECT TO WORDS

- Review this week's vocabulary using the following sentence stems. Have students orally complete each one.

  1. The woman was legendary for _____.
  2. The student muttered because _____.
  3. Bob gaped when _____.
  4. The children began snickering about _____.
  5. Wesley was insulted by _____.
  6. Patricia flinched when _____.

MORPHOLOGY

- Learning about Greek and Latin roots and affixes can help raise students' word consciousness. Use the word *except* on **Student Book** page 168 as a springboard for students to learn other words.

- Write the word *except* on the board. Underline *ex-*. Explain that *ex-* means "beyond" and that *-cept* means "take" or "grasp." They come from Latin. So *except* means something that is excluded, or beyond being taken.

- Write the words *accept* and *concept* on the board. Have students underline *-cept* in each word.

- Use the word parts to explain the meaning of each word. Explain that *ac-* is a combining form of the prefix *ad-* meaning "to" or "in." Therefore, *accept* means "take in." The prefix *con-* means "with," so a *concept* is an idea you can grasp or take in.

Day 5 Assess and Reteach

POSTTEST

- Display **Transparency 14**. Have students complete the cloze sentences using one of this week's vocabulary words.

- Note how quickly and accurately students can complete this task. Work with students who make errors or require too much time to complete this task during Small Group time.

CONNECT TO WRITING

- Have students write sentences in their Writer's Notebooks using this week's vocabulary. Tell students to write sentences that provide information they learned from this week's readings.

- **ELL** Provide the Day 4 sentence stems for students needing extra support.

5-Day Spelling

Go to pages T14–T15 for **Differentiated Spelling Lists**.

✔ # Digraphs

Spelling Words

choose	stretching	photo
kitchen	pitcher	whole
touch	chef	fifth
chance	rush	headphone
sketched	thirty	whirl
ketchup	northern	width
snatch	graph	

Review unload, relearn, subway
Challenge theater, chemical

Dictation Sentences

1. I choose that red hat.
2. The kitchen smells of baked bread.
3. Do not **touch** that hot pan!
4. She has a **chance** to win the prize.
5. I sketched a picture of my house.
6. I like ketchup on my hamburger.
7. Will the lion snatch the food away?
8. Stretching is good before jogging.
9. The **pitcher** struck out everyone.
10. The chef made a special dessert.
11. We need to rush to the hospital.
12. I have thirty shirts at home.
13. The northern towns are very cold.
14. We made a bar graph in class.
15. That is an old photo of our town.
16. I read the whole book in a day.
17. My sister is in fifth grade.
18. We broke a headphone, so we couldn't listen to our music.
19. The classroom is a whirl of activity.
20. We walked the width of the bridge.

Review/Challenge Words

1. Help me unload the boxes.
2. I need to relearn that song.
3. The subway is fun to ride.
4. The play is at a theater downtown.
5. We used a chemical to clean the rug.

Words in **bold** are from this week's selections.

Day 1 | Pretest

ASSESS PRIOR KNOWLEDGE

- Model for students how to spell *graph*. Segment the word sound by sound, then attach a spelling to each sound. Point out that the *ph* spelling stands for the sound /f/ like an *f*.

- Use the Dictation Sentences. Say the underlined word, read the sentence, and repeat the word. Have students write the words.

- Have students self-correct their tests. Point out that the *wh* spelling can be pronounced in several ways, depending on the word. Also point out that the /sh/ sound in *rush* may be spelled in various ways (for example, *-sion, -tion, -cian*).

- Have students cut apart the **Spelling Word Cards BLM** on **Teacher's Resource Book** page 50 and figure out a way to sort them. Have them save the cards for use throughout the week.

Day 2 | Word Sorts and Review

SPIRAL REVIEW

Review prefixes such as those found in the words *unload, relearn,* and *subway*. Have students find words in this week's readings with the prefixes.

WORD SORTS

- Have students take turns sorting the spelling words and explaining how they sorted them. When students have finished the sort, discuss any words that have unexpected digraph spellings. (*chemical, chef*)

- Review the spelling words, pointing out the digraph spellings. Use the cards on the Spelling Word Cards BLM. Write the key words *photo, whirl, thirty, choose, snatch,* and *rush* on the board. Model how to sort words by digraph spellings. Place one or two cards beneath the correct key words.

ON YOUR OWN — **Phonics/Spelling,** pages 37–38

Fold back the paper along the dotted line. Use the blanks to write each word as it is read aloud. When you finish the test, unfold the paper. Use the list at the right to correct any spelling mistakes.

1. ___	1. choose
2. ___	2. kitchen
3. ___	3. touch
4. ___	4. chance
5. ___	5. sketched
6. ___	6. ketchup
7. ___	7. snatch
8. ___	8. stretching
9. ___	9. pitcher
10. ___	10. chef
11. ___	11. rush
12. ___	12. thirty
13. ___	13. northern
14. ___	14. graph
15. ___	15. photo
16. ___	16. whole
17. ___	17. fifth
18. ___	18. headphone
19. ___	19. whirl
20. ___	20. width
Review Words 21. ___	21. unload
22. ___	22. relearn
Challenge Words 23. ___	23. subway
24. ___	24. theater
25. ___	25. chemical

HOMEWORK — **Phonics/Spelling,** page 39

choose	whole	photo	touch	chance
rush	kitchen	whirl	sketched	ketchup
thirty	northern	fifth	width	headphone
graph	snatch	chef	pitcher	stretching

A. Digraph Power
Write the spelling words that contain the digraphs.

ch
1. choose
2. touch
3. chance
4. chef

tch
5. kitchen
6. sketched
7. ketchup
8. snatch
9. stretching
10. pitcher

sh
11. rush

th
12. thirty
13. northern
14. fifth
15. width

ph
16. graph
17. photo
18. headphone

wh
19. whole
20. whirl

Day 3 — Word Meanings

SYNONYMS

Write the following list of words on the board. Ask students to write other words that have the same meaning as each word on the list.

1. grab (snatch)
2. spin (whirl)
3. hurry (rush)
4. picture (photo)

Instruct students to create analogies using the words on the list and the synonyms they generated. Then challenge students to find five action words in the lists of spelling words, review words, and challenge words. Discuss the words with the class.

Have partners write a sentence for each spelling word, leaving a blank space where the word should go. They can exchange papers and fill in the blanks.

Day 4 — Review and Proofread

PROOFREAD AND WRITE

Write these sentences on the board. Have students circle and correct each misspelled word.

1. What is the size of the hole kichen? (whole, kitchen)
2. That's the fith foto I've seen of your sister. (fifth, photo)
3. Chews a title for the graff. (Choose, graph)
4. Thurty dogs appeared suddenly by shanse. (thirty, chance)
5. Some nothren cities are full of people who always seem to ruch around. (northern, rush)

Error Correction Remind students that the sound /ch/ can be spelled *tch* as well as *ch*. The *tch* spelling never occurs at the beginning of a word or syllable.

Day 5 — Assess and Reteach

POSTTEST

Use the Dictation Sentences on page 187E for the Posttest.

If students have difficulty with any words in the lesson, have them place the words on a list called *Spelling Words I Want to Remember* in their Writer's Notebooks. Look for students' use of these words in their writings.

Challenge students to find words for each digraph spelling and write them in their Writer's Notebooks.

EXTEND

Review alternative spellings of the digraph *sh*. Write *lush, tension, nation,* and *musician* on the board. Help students underline the letters that stand for the /sh/ sound in each word. (*sh, si, ti, ci*) Brainstorm other words with the /sh/ sound spelled in various ways.

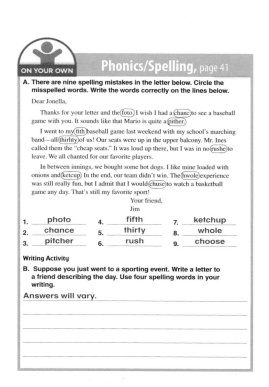

HOMEWORK — Phonics/Spelling, page 40

choose	whole	photo	touch	chance
rush	kitchen	whirl	sketched	ketchup
thirty	northern	fifth	width	headphone
graph	snatch	chef	pitcher	stretching

A. It Takes Three

Write the spelling word that belongs with the other two words.

1. bedroom, den, __kitchen__
2. mustard, mayonnaise, __ketchup__
3. waiter, busboy, __chef__
4. ten, twenty, __thirty__
5. southern, eastern, __northern__
6. third, fourth, __fifth__
7. music, radio, __headphone__
8. length, depth, __width__

B. Words in Sentences

Write a spelling word to complete each sentence.

9. My sister and I __choose__ to be athletes.
10. We practice our sports every __chance__ we get.
11. I begin every day by __stretching__ my muscles.
12. Sometimes I bend and __touch__ my toes.
13. I try to stretch all the muscles in my __whole__ body.
14. On weekends, I __rush__ to the track and run laps.
15. My sister is a softball __pitcher__.
16. She likes to __snatch__ the ball up in her glove.
17. Then she will __whirl__ her arm around.
18. I __sketched__ this drawing of her getting ready to pitch.
19. Once she made a __graph__ of all her strikeouts in a game.
20. Here's a __photo__ that shows her winning a trophy.

ON YOUR OWN — Phonics/Spelling, page 41

A. There are nine spelling mistakes in the letter below. Circle the misspelled words. Write the words correctly on the lines below.

Dear Jonella,

Thanks for your letter and the *foto*. I wish I had a *chanc* to see a baseball game with you. It sounds like that Mario is quite a *pither*.

I went to my *fith* baseball game last weekend with my school's marching band—all *thirhty* of us! Our seats were up in the upper balcony. Mr. Ines called them the "cheap seats." It was loud up there, but I was in no *rushe* to leave. We all chanted for our favorite players.

In between innings, we bought some hot dogs. I like mine loaded with onions and *ketcup*! In the end, our team didn't win. The *hwole* experience was still really fun, but I admit that I would *chuse* to watch a basketball game any day. That's still my favorite sport!

Your friend,
Jim

1. __photo__
2. __chance__
3. __pitcher__
4. __fifth__
5. __thirty__
6. __rush__
7. __ketchup__
8. __whole__
9. __choose__

Writing Activity

B. Suppose you just went to a sporting event. Write a letter to a friend describing the day. Use four spelling words in your writing.

Answers will vary.

HOMEWORK — Phonics/Spelling, page 42

Look at the words in each set below. One word in each set is spelled correctly. Use a pencil to fill in the circle next to the correct word. Before you begin, look at the sample set of words. Sample A has been done for you. Do Sample B by yourself. When you are sure you know what to do, you may go on with the rest of the page.

Sample A:
- Ⓐ peche
- Ⓑ peash
- Ⓒ peach
- Ⓓ peshe

Sample B:
- Ⓔ walle
- Ⓕ whale
- Ⓖ whail
- Ⓗ whall

1. Ⓐ shooze / Ⓑ chooze / Ⓒ shoose / Ⓓ choose
2. Ⓔ fifth / Ⓕ fith / Ⓖ fifph / Ⓗ fipth
3. Ⓐ ruch / Ⓑ rusth / Ⓒ rush / Ⓓ rutch
4. Ⓔ graff / Ⓕ graph / Ⓖ grath / Ⓗ grash
5. Ⓐ whirl / Ⓑ wirl / Ⓒ hwirl / Ⓓ hirl
6. Ⓔ kethup / Ⓕ kechup / Ⓖ ketshup / Ⓗ ketchup
7. Ⓐ tuch / Ⓑ touch / Ⓒ tutch / Ⓓ toutch
8. Ⓔ northen / Ⓕ northern / Ⓖ norhern / Ⓗ norten
9. Ⓐ photo / Ⓑ foto / Ⓒ photoe / Ⓓ fotoe
10. Ⓔ wolle / Ⓕ wole / Ⓖ whole / Ⓗ wholle
11. Ⓐ hedphone / Ⓑ headphone / Ⓒ headfone / Ⓓ hedfone
12. Ⓔ kishen / Ⓕ kitshen / Ⓖ kichen / Ⓗ kitchen
13. Ⓐ chance / Ⓑ shance / Ⓒ shanse / Ⓓ chanse
14. Ⓔ thurty / Ⓕ therty / Ⓖ thirty / Ⓗ thearty
15. Ⓐ pitshur / Ⓑ picher / Ⓒ pitsher / Ⓓ pitcher
16. Ⓔ widph / Ⓕ width / Ⓖ whidth / Ⓗ whith
17. Ⓐ sketched / Ⓑ sctched / Ⓒ skeched / Ⓓ sceched
18. Ⓔ sheph / Ⓕ shef / Ⓖ chef / Ⓗ cheph
19. Ⓐ snach / Ⓑ snatch / Ⓒ snatsh / Ⓓ snash
20. Ⓔ streaching / Ⓕ streatching / Ⓖ streching / Ⓗ stretching

5-Day Grammar

✔ Singular and Plural Nouns

Daily Language Activities

Write the sentences on the board.

DAY 1
A Boy named Lim is in my class. His first Language is not english but he is a good student. (1: boy; 2: language; 3: English, but)

DAY 2
A new Student named Carmen speaks five language. All the other studentz admire her. (1: student; 2: languages.; 3: students)

DAY 3
All the classes in our school had partys on the last day. Two boys made dishs from their native countrys. (1: parties; 2: dishes; 3: countries.)

DAY 4
A family moved next door three dayes ago. their dog has puppies. With floppy eares. (1: days; 2: Their; 3: puppies with; 4: ears.)

DAY 5
The girles have special dresses for the Holidays. Gail had to make a few stitchs in the with of hers. (1: girls; 2: holidays.; 3: stitches; 4: width)

ELL

Transfer Skills In some languages, such as Cantonese and Korean, nouns do not change form to show plurality. Have students use singular and plural nouns in sentences. Repeat their sentences, correcting grammar or pronunciation as needed. Reinforce the use of plural nouns during reading and writing activities. See language transfers on pages T16–T31.

Day 1 — Introduce the Concept

INTRODUCE SINGULAR AND PLURAL NOUNS

- A **singular noun** names one person, place, or thing: *student, museum, baseball.*

- A **plural noun** names more than one person, place, or thing: *students, museums, baseballs.*

- Most nouns can be made plural by adding -s to the end of the singular word.

See Grammar Transparency 31 for modeling and guided practice.

HOMEWORK — Grammar, page 31

- A **singular noun** names one person, place, or thing. Examples: teacher, city, dog
- A **plural noun** names more than one person, place, or thing. Examples: teachers, cities, dogs
- Add **-s** to form the plural of most singular nouns.

Decide whether each underlined word is a singular or plural noun. Then write *singular* or *plural* on the line.

1. There are no <u>jobs</u> here. — plural
2. My family is leaving the <u>country</u>. — singular
3. We're going to stay with my <u>grandparents</u> for now. — plural
4. Papa sent us a <u>letter</u>. — singular
5. He is meeting us at the bus <u>station</u>. — singular
6. We're waiting to get our green <u>cards</u>. — plural
7. This <u>trip</u> is taking forever! — singular
8. It's been <u>weeks</u> since I've seen you. — plural
9. The <u>pages</u> of my diary are filling up. — plural
10. I miss the <u>park</u> I used to go to. — singular
11. I had to sell my <u>bike</u>. — singular
12. The <u>apartment</u> is crowded. — singular
13. I kept my two <u>parrots</u>. — plural
14. We bought some new <u>clothes</u>. — plural
15. She received several <u>letters</u>. — plural

Day 2 — Teach the Concept

REVIEW SINGULAR AND PLURAL NOUNS

Review how to recognize singular and plural nouns. Have students explain how singular and plural nouns differ.

INTRODUCE PLURAL NOUNS WITH -ES AND -IES ENDINGS

- Not all plural nouns are formed simply by adding -s.

- When a singular noun ends with the letters *s, sh, ch, x,* or *z*, add -es: *dresses, brushes, branches, boxes,* and *buzzes.*

- When a singular noun ends with a consonant followed by the letter *y*, change *y* to *i* and add -es: *spy/spies*, and *cherry/cherries.*

- When a singular noun ends with a vowel followed by the letter *y*, add *s*: *stray/strays*, and *boy/boys.*

See Grammar Transparency 32 for modeling and guided practice.

ON YOUR OWN — Grammar, page 32

- Add -s to form the plural of most singular nouns.
- Add -es to form the plural of singular nouns that end in s, sh, ch, or x.
- To form the plural of nouns ending in a consonant and y, change y to i and add -es.
- To form the plural of nouns ending in a vowel and y, add -s.

Write the correct plural form of each noun in parentheses.

1. We saw (foxs) **foxes** running across the prairie.
2. Many people from other (countrys) **countries** have come to the United States.
3. (Massies) **Masses** of people traveled to the west in the 1800s.
4. Some travelers keep (diarys) **diaries**.
5. Gather a few (branchs) **branches** so we can build a fire.
6. She caught a rabbit that was hiding in the (bushs) **bushes**.
7. I asked the neighbor's two (boyes) **boys** to help me milk the cow.
8. Some people used the old trail, but a few found new (pathway) **pathways**.
9. That chest has many (scratchs) **scratches**.
10. Please feed the (babys) **babies**.
11. We need more (boxs) **boxes** than that!
12. I will write two more (pagies) **pages** today.

Day 3 — Review and Practice

REVIEW PLURAL NOUNS WITH -*ES* AND -*IES* ENDINGS

Review the rules for words whose plural forms end in -*es* and -*ies*.

MECHANICS AND USAGE: COMMAS IN A SERIES

- If three or more items are listed in a sentence, use a comma after each item in the series.

- If only two items are listed in a sentence, do not use a comma to separate the items.

- Write a conjunction such as *and* or *or* before the last item in the series. Include a comma before the conjunction but not after it: We saw llamas, zebras, *and* monkeys.

- Commas are also used in dates and between a city and state name:
  May 1, 2010   Fresno, California

 See Grammar Transparency 33 for modeling and guided practice.

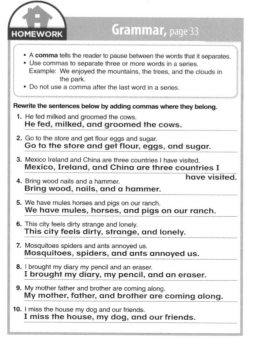

Day 4 — Review and Proofread

REVIEW SINGULAR AND PLURAL NOUNS

Ask students to explain the differences between singular and plural nouns. Ask how to decide to add -*s* or -*es*, or change *y* to *i*.

PROOFREAD

Have students correct errors in the following sentences.

1. We have new girles, boyes and teachers in some classes.
   (1: girls,; 2: boys,)

2. Most come from towns citys and villages. (1: towns,; 2: cities,)

3. The movers packed their books, and toys in boxs. (1: books and; 2: boxes.)

4. The Students from other time zones had to reset their watchs.
   (1: students; 2: watches.)

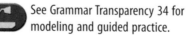 See Grammar Transparency 34 for modeling and guided practice.

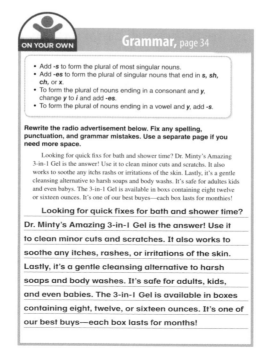

Day 5 — Assess and Reteach

ASSESS

Use the Daily Language Activity and **Grammar Practice Book** page 35 for assessment.

RETEACH

Use Grammar Practice Book page 35 and selected pages from the **Grammar and Writing Handbook** for additional reteaching. Remind students it is important to use nouns correctly as they speak and write.

Check students' writing for use of the skill and listen for it in their speaking. Assign Grammar Revision Assignments in their Writer's Notebooks as needed.

Point out that students will learn more about plural nouns next week, including plurals for nouns that end in -*f*, such as *chief/chiefs* and *leaf/leaves*).

 See Grammar Transparency 35 for modeling and guided practice.

Daily Planner

DAY 1	• Prepare to Read • Academic Language • Vocabulary (Preteach)
DAY 2	• Comprehension • Leveled Reader Lesson 1
DAY 3	• Phonics/Decoding • Leveled Reader Lesson 2
DAY 4	• Phonics/Decoding • Vocabulary (Review) • Leveled Reader Lesson 3
DAY 5	• High-Frequency Words • Fluency • Self-Selected Reading

Interactive Student Book

If you wish to preteach the main selection, use StudentWorks Plus for:

• Vocabulary Preteaching
• Word-by-Word Highlighting
• Think Aloud Prompts

Academic Language

Academic words include those harder Tier 2 words that appear in much of students' reading materials as well as the language of instruction. The words chosen for instruction were selected from the **Living Word Vocabulary** list and Avril Coxhead's list of **High-Incidence Academic Words**.

Approaching Level

Prepare to Read

Objective   Preview *Mighty Jackie: The Strike-out Queen*

Materials   • **StudentWorks Plus**   • self-stick notes

PREVIEW TEXT

- Have students preview *Mighty Jackie: The Strike-out Queen* using **StudentWorks Plus**. This version of the selection contains oral summaries in multiple languages, story recording, word-by-word highlighting, Think Aloud prompts, and comprehension-monitoring questions.

- Remind students that listening carefully to and following along with the word-by-word reading will help them prepare for the reading of the selection with the class. Ask students to place self-stick notes on any challenging words or places that confuse them. Discuss these with students prior to the reading of the selection with the rest of the class.

- Ask students to write three or four sentences in their Writer's Notebooks telling what they learned about Jackie Mitchell.

Academic Language

Objective   Teach academic language

Materials   • none

PRETEACH LANGUAGE OF INSTRUCTION

Tell students that there are many important lesson words you will be using this week. You want them to become familiar with these words *before* the lessons. These words also appear in the directions of the tests they will be taking this year.

Preteach the following academic words: *compare, contrast, monitor comprehension, purpose*, and *description*.

- Define each word using student-friendly language. Tell students that *compare* means to look for what is alike or similar and *contrast* means to look for what is different. Have students compare and contrast themselves with a sibling or friend.

- In addition, relate each word to known words. For example, connect *monitor* to *check, comprehension* to *understanding, purpose* to *reason*, and *description* to *detail*.

- Highlight these words when used throughout the week, and reinforce their meanings.

Approaching Level

Phonics/Decoding

Objective   Decode words with digraphs

Materials
- **Approaching Reproducible,** p. 55
- **Sound-Spelling WorkBoards**

Tier 2

PHONICS MAINTENANCE

- Distribute a **WorkBoard** to each student. Say a sound previously taught, including long and short vowels and digraphs. Have students find the **Sound-Spelling Card** on the board for each sound.

- Review the spelling(s) for each sound and for previously taught prefixes by providing a sample word containing each spelling. Guide students to write the word on the board. Model how to segment the word and write the spelling for each sound, as needed. In addition, point out spelling hints, such as /f/ at the end of a word is usually spelled *f* or *ph*.

- Dictate the following words for students to spell: *thing, unhitch, shoe, disgrace, misplace, whole,* and *graph*. Write each word on the board, and have students self-correct their work.

RETEACH SKILL

Words with Digraphs   Point to the /th/, /sh/, /hw/, /ch/, and /f/ Sound-Spelling Cards on the WorkBoard, and review the spellings for these sounds. State each spelling and provide a sample word.

- Write the words below on the board. Model how to decode the first word in each row, then guide students as they decode the remaining words. For the multisyllabic words, divide the words into syllables using the syllable-scoop technique to help students read one syllable at a time.

- When completed, point to the words in random order for students to chorally read. Repeat several times.

think	bath	throw	earth	math	moth
other	mother	father	bother	either	weather
ship	sheep	ashes	wish	fish	finish
whip	when	white	whale	while	awhile
phase	phrase	phone	graph	graphic	photo
chew	chin	chop	cheese	patch	hatchet

Sound-Spelling WorkBoard

ELL

Minimal Contrasts Focus on articulation. Make the /sh/ sound, and point out your mouth position. Have students repeat. Use the articulation photos on the small Sound-Spelling Cards. Repeat for the /ch/ sound. Then have students say each sound together, noticing the slight difference in mouth position. Continue by having students read minimal contrast word pairs, such as *match/mash, ship/chip, crush/crutch,* and *shoes/choose.*

Approaching Reproducible, page 55

Say the words *shed* and *wish*. You will hear the **sh** sound in each word. The letter pairs **sh, ch, th,** and **ph** are unusual. In each one a consonant pairs with **h** to form a new sound.
- **sh**   <u>sh</u>ed, ru<u>sh</u>
- **ch**   <u>ch</u>op, tou<u>ch</u>
- **th**   <u>th</u>irty, bo<u>th</u>er
- **ph**   <u>ph</u>one, gra<u>ph</u>

The letter pair **wh** sounds about the same as the letter **w** by itself.
wh   <u>wh</u>isk, no<u>wh</u>ere

Add *ch, sh, ph, wh,* or *th* to the blanks below to create words.

1. __th/sh__ anks
2. __ph__ oto
3. tra__sh__
4. bo__th__ er
5. __sh__ out
6. ten__th__
7. __ch/wh/sh__ ip
8. __sh/ch/th__ in
9. por__ch__
10. gra__ph__
11. bru__sh__
12. __th__ ese
13. no__wh__ ere
14. __ch__ eck
15. head__ph__ one
16. wa__sh__ er

Approaching Level

Vocabulary

Objective Preteach selection vocabulary

Materials • **Visual Vocabulary Resources** • **Approaching Reproducible,** p. 56
• **Vocabulary Cards**

PRETEACH KEY VOCABULARY

Tier 2

Introduce the Words Use the **Visual Vocabulary Resources** to preteach the key selection words *legendary, muttered, gaped, snickering, insult*, and *flinched*. Use the following routine that appears in detail on the cards.

- Define the word in English, and provide the example given.

- Define the word in Spanish, if appropriate, and indicate if the word is a cognate.

- Display the picture, and explain how it illustrates or demonstrates the word.

- Then engage students in structured partner-talk about the image, using the key word.

- Ask students to chorally say the word three times.

- Point out any known sound-spellings or focus on a key aspect of phonemic awareness related to the word.

- You may wish to also distribute copies of the Vocabulary Glossary in the **ELL Resource Book**.

REVIEW PREVIOUSLY TAUGHT VOCABULARY

Display the **Vocabulary Cards** from the previous four weeks. Say the meanings of each word, one by one, and have students identify them. Then point to words in random order for students to provide definitions and related words they know.

Context Clues Remind students that context clues are clues within the text that help a reader figure out what a word means. Have students write a context sentence for each vocabulary review word. For example, *Since she had been taking swimming lessons for years, she was able to join the* advanced *swimming group at camp.* Instruct students that when possible, their context sentence should include description. For example, *In the laboratory were rows of test tubes filled with strangely colored liquids with* peculiar *smells.*

Approaching Reproducible, page 56

A. Write the correct word after its meaning.

muttered	gaped	insult
snickering	legendary	flinched

1. shrank away from ____**flinched**____
2. laughing in a way that makes fun of someone ____**snickering**____
3. spoke unclearly in a soft voice ____**muttered**____
4. gazed in surprise with the mouth open ____**gaped**____
5. well-known or famous ____**legendary**____
6. something bad said to a person ____**insult**____

B. Answer each question with a vocabulary word.

7. Which word would you use to describe Babe Ruth?
   ____**legendary**____
8. Which word would you use to describe the way someone talked?
   ____**muttered**____
9. Which word would you use to describe mean people laughing?
   ____**snickering**____

Approaching Level

Vocabulary

Objective   Review vocabulary and high-frequency words

Materials   • **Vocabulary Cards**   • **High-Frequency Word Cards**

✔ **REVIEW VOCABULARY**

Review Words Display the **Vocabulary Cards** for *legendary, muttered, gaped, snickering, insult,* and *flinched.* Point to each word, read it aloud, and have students chorally repeat.

Then ask students to respond to these questions:

- Which person is legendary: Abraham Lincoln or John Doe?

- In which location might you have muttered: the library or the baseball park?

- At which situation might you have gaped: an acrobatic performance or children in the park?

- In which situation might someone be snickering: when that person wants to be nice or wants to be mean.

- Which word is an insult: *stupid* or *intelligent*?

- In which situation might you have flinched: being struck on the arm by a baseball or receiving a hug from a loved one?

HIGH-FREQUENCY WORDS

Top 250 Words The ability to read accurately and effortlessly the most frequently used words in written English will help students develop reading fluency. Display **High-Frequency Word Cards** 61–60. Then do the following:

- Display one card at a time, and ask students to chorally state each word.

- Have students spell each word aloud.

- Ask students to write each word in their Writer's Notebooks as they state aloud each letter. Then have them read the word again.

- When completed, quickly flip through the Word Card set as students chorally read the words.

- Provide opportunities for students to use the words in speaking and writing. For example, provide sentence starters, such as *I don't eat _____,* for oral and written practice. Or point to a Word Card and ask a question, such as *What word means the opposite of this word?* (when pointing to the *done* Word Card).

- Continue the routine throughout the week.

Tier 2

ELL

Practice Vocabulary Pair students of different proficiency. Orally model the vocabulary in sentences. For example: *Hank Aaron was a legendary baseball player.* On the board, provide sentence frames for pairs to copy and complete using the vocabulary. For example: *I _____ when the bug bit me.* (*flinched*)

Word Webs

Have students create word webs in their Writer's Notebooks for the vocabulary words. Write the related words provided, and ask students to add other words, phrases, and illustrations.

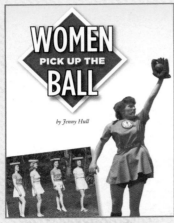

Student Book

Approaching Level

Comprehension

Objective Reteach monitor comprehension and author's purpose

Materials • **Student Book:** "Women Pick Up the Ball"

Tier 2

✔ RETEACH STRATEGY: MONITOR COMPREHENSION

- **Define** Tell students that monitoring their comprehension means pausing in their reading and asking themselves questions or taking other actions to make sure they understand what they have read.

- **Relate to Real Life** Explain that a *baby monitor* is a machine that allows parents to monitor, or check on, their baby while they are in another room. Tell students that when they *monitor* their comprehension, they *check* on their own understanding.

- **Set Purposes** Remind students that good readers stop from time to time as they are reading to monitor their comprehension. If they do not understand what they have read, they might ask themselves questions, reread a passage, or read ahead to see if they can find clues to help them understand what is happening.

✔ RETEACH SKILL: AUTHOR'S PURPOSE

- **Define** Tell students that writers write for various reasons. They may write to inform, entertain, or persuade.

- **Relate to Real Life** Point out that people act for varying reasons, too. A student may take out the trash or clean a room to help his family. Another student may complete a math assignment because she hopes to get a good grade or because she wants to be a scientist one day. Explain that people behave certain ways for different reasons, just as writers write for different reasons.

- **Set Purposes** Remind students that identifying an author's purpose for writing can help them understand the author's other choices regarding structure, word use, and point of view. Identifying an author's purpose can also help students select appropriate reading strategies and skills for that text.

- **Apply** Work with students to find clues about the author's purpose for writing as they read "Women Pick Up the Ball." Point out that an author may have more than one purpose for writing. There may also be different purposes for each paragraph. Students will apply this strategy and skill to simpler text as they read *Wilma Rudolph: A True Winner*.

Corrective Feedback

Throughout the lessons, provide feedback based on students' responses. If the answer is correct, ask another question. If the answer is tentative, restate key information to assist the student. If the answer is wrong, provide corrective feedback such as hints or clues, refer to a visual such as a **Sound-Spelling Card** or story illustration, or probe with questions to help the student clarify any misunderstanding.

Approaching Level

Leveled Reader Lesson 1

Objective Read to apply skills and strategies

Materials • **Leveled Reader:** *Wilma Rudolph: A True Winner*

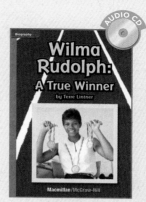

Leveled Reader

BEFORE READING

Preview and Predict Have students read the title and preview the first two chapters. Ask students to make predictions about the author's purpose(s) for writing. Students should note any questions they have before they read.

 Review Vocabulary Words Have students read the vocabulary words on the inside front cover. Briefly define each and ask students to state related words they have learned.

Set a Purpose for Reading *Let's read to find out who Wilma Rudolph was, and what she accomplished.*

DURING READING

STRATEGY
MONITOR COMPREHENSION

Remind students that when you monitor your comprehension, you pause to make sure you understand what you have read.

SKILL
AUTHOR'S PURPOSE

Remind students to think about whether the author is writing to inform, entertain, or persuade. Review that with a biography, analyzing how an author presents events in a person's life can help readers understand why he or she is writing. Read Chapter 1 with students. Help students complete the Author's Purpose Map.

As you read, help students decode unknown words. Ask open-ended questions to facilitate rich discussion, such as *Why does the author include photographs? Why does the author include a time line?* Build on students' responses to develop a deeper understanding of the text.

Stop after every two pages. Ask students if they understand what was read. If not, have them share what they can do to improve their comprehension of the text. Then have them use text evidence to figure out the author's purpose for writing the book.

AFTER READING

Ask students to compare the story of Wilma Rudolph to another real-life story. *Do you know another person who is a winner? How is he or she like Wilma Rudolph? Different?* Have students tell which part of the story they found most inspiring.

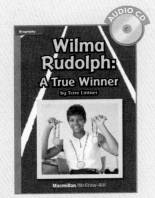

Leveled Reader

Approaching Level

Leveled Reader Lesson 2

Objective Reread to apply skills and strategies and develop fluency

Materials
- **Leveled Reader:** *Wilma Rudolph: A True Winner*
- **Approaching Reproducible,** p. 59

BEFORE READING

Review the Strategy and Skill Review students' completed Author's Purpose Maps from the first read. Review that monitoring their comprehension means pausing to make sure they understand what they have read. Remind students to find text clues to help them figure out the author's purpose(s) for writing the story.

Review Vocabulary Words Have students search the book for each vocabulary word. Ask students to read aloud the sentence containing the word and state the word's definition or provide related words. Point out any context clues provided, such as description.

Set a Purpose for Reading *Let's reread to check our understanding of the information in the book and to work on our reading fluency.*

DURING READING

Reread *Wilma Rudolph: A True Winner* with students. Have them read silently, two pages at a time, or read aloud to partners. Stop and have students summarize what they read before they read the next two pages, to make sure they are comprehending. Model oral summaries, as needed.

AFTER READING

Check Comprehension Have partners complete the Comprehension Check on page 20. Review students' answers. Help students find evidence for their answers in the text.

MODEL FLUENCY

Model reading the fluency passage on **Approaching Reproducible** page 59. Tell students to pay close attention to your intonation, or the rise and fall of your voice, as you read. Then read one sentence at a time, and have students echo-read the sentences, copying your intonation.

During independent reading time, have students work with a partner using the fluency passage. One student reads aloud, while the other repeats each sentence back. If students need additional support, have them listen to the "practice speed" version of the passage on the **Fluency Solutions Audio CD**.

Approaching Reproducible, page 59

As I read, I will pay attention to intonation and expression.

	Wilma Rudolph calmly walked to the starting line.
8	"Wilma!" the crowd yelled. It was 1960. She was running
17	in the Olympics.
20	People were shouting Wilma's name because she was
28	fast. They didn't care that she was African American or
38	poor. Here in Rome, Italy, Wilma was just another athlete
48	— a good one.
51	Wilma Rudolph won three gold medals at the 1960
59	Summer Olympics. That was amazing. Getting there at all
68	was even more amazing. When Wilma was a child, her
78	doctors said she would never walk.
84	Wilma worked hard. If she failed at something, she
93	worked harder. 95

Comprehension Check

1. How does the author want you to feel about Wilma Rudolph? **Author's Purpose** The author wants you to feel inspired by Wilma and how she struggled to become a great athlete despite the many obstacles in her life.

2. How does the setting make Wilma feel calm? **Plot Development** Wilma feels calm because she is at the Olympics and the only thing that matters there is that she is a good athlete.

	Words Read	−	Number of Errors	=	Words Correct Score
First Read		−		=	
Second Read		−		=	

Approaching Level

Leveled Reader Lesson 3

Objective Build fluency

Materials • **Leveled Reader:** *Wilma Rudolph: A True Winner*

FOCUS ON FLUENCY

Timed Reading Tell students that they will be doing a final timed reading of the fluency passage that they have been practicing. With each student, follow these directions:

- Place the passage facedown.

- When you say "Go," the student begins reading the passage aloud.

- When you say "Stop," the student stops reading the passage.

As they read, note words students mispronounce and their overall expression. Stop after one minute. Help students record and graph the number of words they read correctly.

REREAD PREVIOUSLY READ BOOKS

- Distribute copies of the past three **Leveled Readers**. Have students select two to reread. Tell students that rereading these books will help them develop their skills. The more times they read the same words, the quicker they will learn these words. This will make the reading of other books easier.

- Circulate and listen in as students read. Stop students periodically and ask them how they are figuring out difficult words and how they are monitoring their comprehension. Note students who need additional work with specific decoding or comprehension skills.

- Encourage students to read other previously read Leveled Readers during independent reading time or for homework.

Meet Grade-Level Expectations

As an alternative to this day's lesson, guide students through a reading of the On Level Leveled Reader. See page 187U. Since both books contain the same vocabulary, phonics, and comprehension skills, the scaffolding you provided will help most students gain access to this more challenging text.

Book Talk

Bringing Groups Together Students will work with peers of various language and reading abilities to discuss this week's Leveled Readers. Refer to page 160 in the **Teacher's Resource Book** for more about how to conduct a Book Talk.

Student Book

Student Book

Approaching Level

Fluency

Objectives Reread selections to develop fluency; develop speaking skills

Materials • **Student Book:** *Mighty Jackie: The Strike-out Queen*, "The New Kid"

REREAD FOR FLUENCY

- Have students reread a portion of *Mighty Jackie: The Strike-out Queen*. Suggest that they focus on two to four of their favorite pages from the selection. Work with students to read the pages with the appropriate intonation.

- Provide time for students to read their sections of text to you. Comment on their intonation, and provide corrective feedback by modeling proper fluency.

DEVELOP SPEAKING/LISTENING SKILLS

- Have students practice reading "The New Kid."

- Work with students to read with appropriate intonation and good tempo, or rate. Model reading a few lines at a time. Emphasize the meter and rhyme. Have students repeat.

- Provide time for students to read aloud the poem to partners. Students should listen attentively as their partners read. Ask students to name the ways their partners expressed meaning with their voices. Have them mention other positive aspects of their partner's reading.

- Challenge students to memorize and recite one stanza of the poem for the class.

Decodable Text

Use the decodable stories in the **Teacher's Resource Book** to help students build fluency with basic decoding patterns.

Approaching Level

Self-Selected Reading

Objective Read independently to identify author's purpose

Materials • **Leveled Classroom Library** • other biographies or fiction books

APPLY SKILLS AND STRATEGIES TO INDEPENDENT READING

- **Read Independently** Have students choose a book of historical fiction or a biography for sustained silent reading. (See the **Theme Bibliography** on pages T8–T9 for book suggestions.) Remind them that the author's purpose is the author's reason for writing a book. An author might write to inform, to entertain, or to persuade. The organization and the details provide clues to the author's purpose. Have students read their books and record the author's purpose on an Author's Purpose Map.

- **Show Evidence of Reading** While reading, students may generate a reading log or journal. After reading, ask students to use their Author's Purpose Maps and logs to paraphrase the content of the book, maintaining meaning and logical order. They may write or state an oral summary of the book. Ask students to share their summaries and reactions to the books while participating in Book Talks. Ask: *Based on the author's purpose(s) for writing, to whom would you recommend this book and why?*

Approaching

Leveled Classroom Library
See Leveled Classroom
Library lessons on pages T2–T7.

Daily Planner

DAY 1	• Vocabulary • Phonics
DAY 2	• Leveled Reader Lesson 1
DAY 3	• Leveled Reader Lesson 2
DAY 4	• Fluency
DAY 5	• Self-Selected Reading

ELL

Practice Vocabulary Pair ELL students with native speakers. On the board, provide sentence frames for pairs to copy and complete using the vocabulary and additional words when necessary. For example: *The shy girl _____ quietly to herself so people _____ her.* (*muttered; could not hear*)

Sound-Spelling WorkBoard

On Level

Vocabulary

Objective	Review vocabulary
Materials	• **Vocabulary Cards**

REVIEW PREVIOUSLY TAUGHT WORDS

Review the Words Display the **Vocabulary Cards** for *legendary, muttered, gaped, snickering, insult,* and *flinched*. Point to each word, read it aloud, and have students chorally repeat.

Then ask students which vocabulary word they would associate with each of the following actions. Ask students to explain their choices.

- telling stories about Davy Crockett (*legendary*)
- calling someone dumb or lazy (*insult*)
- being startled by a loud noise (*flinched*)
- talking to yourself (*muttered*)
- making a basket from half court (*gaped*)
- laughing at someone's mistake (*snickering*)

Phonics/Word Study

Objective	Decode multisyllabic words with digraphs
Materials	• **Sound-Spelling WorkBoards**

RETEACH SKILL

- **Digraphs** Point to the /th/, /sh/, /ch/, and /f/ **Sound-Spelling Cards** on the **WorkBoard**, and review the spellings for these sounds. State each spelling and provide a sample word.

- Write the words below on the board. If necessary, divide the words into syllables using the syllable-scoop technique to help students read one syllable at a time. When completed, point to the words in random order for students to chorally read.

myth	thread	brother	whether
splashing	friendship	whisper	somewhat
phonics	orphan	phantom	pheasant
sandwich	archway	itchy	blotchy

- **Spelling** Dictate the following words for students to spell on their WorkBoards: *bathtub, wheelbarrow, photograph, hatchet, charity,* and *dishes*. Guide students to use the Sound-Spelling Cards. Model how to segment words, such as spelling a word syllable by syllable.

On Level

Fluency

Objectives Reread selections with fluency; develop speaking skills

Materials • **Student Book:** *Mighty Jackie: The Strike-out Queen*, "The New Kid"

REREAD FOR FLUENCY

- Have students reread *Mighty Jackie: The Strike-out Queen*. Work with students to read with appropriate intonation.

- Provide time for students to read a section of text aloud. Comment on their intonation and provide corrective feedback as needed.

DEVELOP SPEAKING/LISTENING SKILLS

- Have students practice reading from "The New Kid."

- Work with students to read with appropriate intonation and rate or tempo. Model reading a few lines at a time, with attention to rhyme and meter. Have students repeat.

- Have students read aloud the poem to partners. Partners should listen attentively. Ask them to name ways in which the reader expressed emotion or interest with his or her voice. Have them mention other positive aspects of their partner's reading.

- Challenge students to add gestures to their readings.

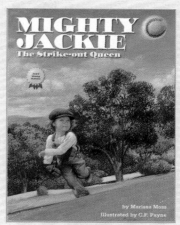

Student Book

Student Book

Self-Selected Reading

Objective Read independently to identify author's purpose

Materials • **Leveled Classroom Library** • other biographies or historical fiction

APPLY SKILLS AND STRATEGIES TO INDEPENDENT READING

- **Read Independently** Have students choose a book of historical fiction or another biography for sustained silent reading. (See the **Theme Bibliography** on pages T8–T9 for book suggestions.) Have students read their books and record the author's purpose on an Author's Purpose Map.

- **Show Evidence of Reading** While reading, students may generate a reading log or journal. After reading, ask students to use their Author's Purpose Maps and logs to paraphrase the content of the book, maintaining meaning and logical order. They may write or state a summary of the book. Have them share their summaries and their reactions to the book while participating in Book Talks. Ask: *Based on the author's purpose for writing, to whom would you recommend this book and why?*

On Level

Leveled Classroom Library
See Leveled Classroom Library lessons on pages T2–T7.

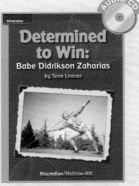

Leveled Reader

On Level

Leveled Reader Lesson 1

Objective   Read to apply strategies and skills
Materials   • **Leveled Reader:** *Determined to Win: Babe Didrikson Zaharias*

BEFORE READING

Preview and Predict Have students read the title and preview the book by reading the chapter titles and looking at the photographs. Ask students to predict what this book is about and the types of information they might learn.

 Review Vocabulary Words Have students read the vocabulary words on the inside front cover. Ask them to state related words they have learned. Review definitions, as needed.

Set a Purpose for Reading *Let's read to find out who Babe Didrikson was, and what she accomplished.*

DURING READING

 **STRATEGY**
MONITOR COMPREHENSION

Remind students that when you monitor your comprehension, you pause to make sure you understand what you have read.

SKILL
AUTHOR'S PURPOSE

Remind students that authors usually write to inform, entertain, or persuade, and sometimes have more than one purpose for writing. With biography, analyzing how an author presents important events in a person's life can help readers understand the author's purpose.

Read Chapter 1 with students. Ask open-ended questions to facilitate rich discussion, such as *What does the author want us to know about Babe Didrikson? What can we tell from the way the major events of her life are presented?* Build on students' responses to help them develop a deeper understanding of the text. Have them fill in the first section of the Author's Purpose Map, then continue reading.

Context Clues As they read, have students point out this week's new vocabulary words and any context clues the author provides, such as descriptions.

AFTER READING

Ask students to compare the story of Babe Didrikson to another real-life story. *Do you know another person who is a winner? How is he or she like Babe Didrikson? How is he or she different?* Have students tell which part of the story they found most inspiring.

On Level

On Level

Leveled Reader Lesson 2

Objective Reread to apply skills and strategies and develop fluency

Materials • **Leveled Reader:** *Determined to Win: Babe Didrikson Zaharias*
• **Practice Book,** p. 59

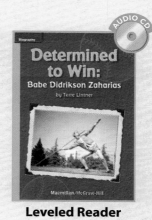

Leveled Reader

BEFORE READING

Review the Strategy and Skill Review students' completed Author's Purpose Maps from the first read. Remind students that while reading they should consider whether the author is writing to inform, entertain, or persuade.

Review with students that monitoring comprehension means pausing in their reading to make sure they understand what they have read so far. Students can use strategies such as asking themselves questions, rereading a portion aloud, paraphrasing, and visualizing to help them check and improve their understanding.

Set a Purpose for Reading *Let's reread to check our understanding of the information in the book and to work on our reading fluency.*

DURING READING

Reread *Determined to Win: Babe Didrikson Zaharias* with students. Have them read silently, two pages at a time, or read aloud to partners. Stop and have students summarize what they read before they read the next two pages, to make sure they are comprehending. Model oral summaries, as needed.

AFTER READING

Check Comprehension Have partners complete the Comprehension Check on page 20. Review students' answers. Help students find evidence for their answers in the text.

MODEL FLUENCY

Model reading the fluency passage on **Practice Book** page 59. Tell students to pay close attention to your intonation, or tone of voice, as you read. Then read one sentence at a time, and have students echo-read the sentences, copying your intonation.

During independent reading time, have students work with a partner using the fluency passage. One student reads aloud, while the other repeats each sentence back. If students need additional support, have them listen to the "practice speed" version of the passage on the **Fluency Solutions Audio CD**.

Book Talk

Bringing Groups Together Students will work with peers of various language and reading abilities to discuss this week's **Leveled Readers**. Refer to page 160 in the **Teacher's Resource Book** for more about how to conduct a Book Talk.

Practice Book, page 59

As I read, I will pay attention to intonation and expression.

	Mildred Ella Didrikson was born on June 26, 1914, in
8	Port Arthur, Texas. Mildred's father built a gym for his
18	children in the backyard. The children played many sports,
27	including baseball. Mildred was a good hitter. So the boys
37	started calling her "Babe," after the **legendary** baseball
45	player Babe Ruth. Ruth was famous for hitting home runs.
55	It was no fluke that Babe Didrikson became a good athlete.
66	Babe's father read newspaper articles about the 1928
73	Olympic Games aloud to his children. Babe was 14 years
82	old at the time. She began to dream about competing in the
94	Olympics someday.
96	Babe attended high school during the late 1920s. She
104	excelled in every sport she tried. At only 5 feet (152 cm)
114	tall and 105 pounds (48 kg), Babe was small. But she was
124	strong. 125

Comprehension Check

1. Why does the author make it a point to explain Mildred Didrikson's nickname? **Author's Purpose** The author wants readers to know that Mildred Didrikson was such a good athlete that boys compared her to Babe Ruth.

2. How did Babe Didrikson's home life help her to become an athlete? **Plot Development** Babe Didrikson's father encouraged physical training by building a gym and reading articles about the Olympics.

	Words Read	−	Number of Errors	=	Words Correct Score
First Read		−		=	
Second Read		−		=	

Beyond Level

Phonics

Daily Planner

DAY 1	• Leveled Reader Lesson 1
DAY 2	• Leveled Reader Lesson 2
DAY 3	• Phonics
DAY 4	• Vocabulary • Fluency
DAY 5	• Self-Selected Reading

Objective   Decode multisyllabic words with digraphs *th, sh, wh, ch, tch*, and *ph*

Materials   • none

EXTEND/ACCELERATE

■ **Read Multisyllabic Words with Digraphs** Write the words below on the board. Challenge students to read the words, using known word parts. When completed, point to the words in random order for students to chorally read.

theater	breathless	thoroughly	healthcare
rhythm	weathering	gathering	northernmost
potash	establish	shambles	shareholder
whiteout	buckwheat	overwhelm	cartwheel
trophy	emphasis	geography	sophomore
charbroil	cheerfully	ratchet	wrenching

■ **Define Words** Ask students to use their knowledge of word parts to figure out the meanings of the words. Then have partners use a dictionary to confirm or revise the meanings. Challenge students to use these words in this week's writing assignments.

■ **Spell Words with Digraphs** Dictate these words for students to spell: *telegraph, fisherman, everywhere, southern, alphabet*. Write the words for students to self-correct. Afterward, challenge students to decode and then spell words with other spellings of /sh/ such as *election, politician*, and *vision*. Review the meanings of the words as well.

Vocabulary

Objectives   Review poetry; write a poem

Materials   • reference books and the Internet

ENRICH VOCABULARY

■ **Review Poetry** Remind students that the author of "The New Kid" tells a story in poetry form. Review that it is a lyric poem, which expresses the thoughts and feelings of the poet. Ask students who the hero of the poem is. What do they know about her?

■ **Write a Poem** Have students think of someone who has excelled in a certain area or has accomplished something important. Challenge students to write a lyric poem about this person using the vocabulary words they have learned in this week's selections.

ELL

Self-Monitor Vocabulary
Have student pairs of different proficiency identify and define unfamiliar words from the main selection using a dictionary. Challenge students to use the new words in sentences. Monitor students as they complete the activity.

Gifted & Talented

Beyond Level

Fluency

Objectives Reread selections to develop intonation; develop speaking skills
Materials • **Student Book:** *Mighty Jackie: The Strike-out Queen*, "The New Kid"

REREAD FOR FLUENCY

- Have students reread a portion of *Mighty Jackie: The Strike-out Queen*. Work with students to read the book with the appropriate intonation.

- Provide time for students to read a section of text to you. Comment on their intonation and provide corrective feedback.

DEVELOP SPEAKING/LISTENING SKILLS

- Have students practice reading the poem "The New Kid."

- Work with students to read with appropriate intonation and good tempo or rate. Model reading a few lines at a time. Emphasize the meter and rhyme. Have students repeat.

- Have students read the poem to the class. Ask others to listen attentively and to tell ways the reader expressed emotion with his or her voice.

- Challenge students to add gestures to their readings.

Self-Selected Reading

Objective Read independently to identify the author's purpose
Materials • **Leveled Classroom Library** • other literary nonfiction or historical fiction books

APPLY SKILLS AND STRATEGIES TO INDEPENDENT READING

- **Read Independently** Have students choose a literary nonfiction or historical fiction book for sustained silent reading. (See the **Theme Bibliography** on page T8–T9 for book suggestions.) Have them read their books and fill out the Author's Purpose Map.

- **Show Evidence of Reading** While reading, students may generate a reading log or journal. After reading, have students use their Author's Purpose Maps and logs to paraphrase the content of the book, maintaining meaning and logical order. They may write or state an oral summary of the book. Ask students to share their summaries and reactions to the book while participating in Book Talks. Ask: *To whom would you recommend this book and why?*

- **Evaluate** Challenge students to discuss how the books they have chosen relate to the theme of this week, Inspiring Women. Ask: *Whom did you read about? Was that person inspiring? Explain.*

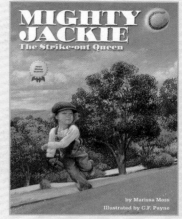

Student Book

Student Book

Beyond

Leveled Classroom Library
See Leveled Classroom Library lessons on pages T2–T7.

Leveled Reader

Beyond Level

Leveled Reader Lesson 1

Objective Read to apply strategies and skills
Materials • **Leveled Reader:** *Jackie Robinson: A Man Who Stood So Tall*

BEFORE READING

Preview and Predict Have students preview the book by reading the title and chapter titles and looking at the photographs. Ask students to predict what this book will be about and the types of information they might learn.

 Review the Vocabulary Words Have students read the vocabulary words on the inside front cover. Ask students to give each definition and name any related words they have learned.

Set a Purpose for Reading *Let's read to find out who Jackie Robinson was and what he accomplished.*

DURING READING

 **STRATEGY**
MONITOR COMPREHENSION

Have students define *monitor comprehension*. Remind them that it means to pause as they read to make sure they are comprehending. They can also paraphrase, adjusting reading rate, and ask questions.

SKILL
AUTHOR'S PURPOSE

Ask students to list the purposes for which authors write. Remind them that an author may write for more than one purpose. With a biography, thinking about how an author presents major events in a person's life can help readers understand why he or she is writing.

Read the book with students. Ask open-ended questions to facilitate rich discussion, such as *What does the author want us to know about Jackie Robinson? What is the author telling us about his accomplishments?* Build on students' responses to develop deeper understanding of the text. Have students fill in the Author's Purpose Map as they read.

AFTER READING

Compare Have students compare and contrast the experiences of Jackie Robinson with those of Jackie Mitchell.

Analyze Discuss how Jackie Robinson might have felt at various points in his career. Have students choose a few of these times and write "diary" entries, expressing Jackie Robinson's thoughts and feelings.

Gifted Talented

Beyond Level

Leveled Reader Lesson 2

Objective Reread to apply skills and strategies and develop fluency

Materials
- **Leveled Reader:** *Jackie Robinson: A Man Who Stood So Tall*
- **Beyond Reproducible,** p. 59

BEFORE READING

Review the Strategy and Skill Review students' completed Author's Purpose Maps from the first read.

Remind students that monitoring comprehension means making sure they understand what they are reading. To check if they are comprehending, students should pause at various points during their reading to see if they can summarize what they have read.

Set a Purpose for Reading *Let's reread to check our understanding of the information in the book and work on our reading fluency.*

DURING READING

Have students reread *Jackie Robinson: A Man Who Stood So Tall* silently or with a partner. If they are reading in pairs, prompt students to stop every two pages and monitor comprehension by asking each other about conclusions they have drawn while reading.

AFTER READING

Check Comprehension Have students independently complete the Comprehension Check on page 24. Review students' answers. Help them find evidence for their answers in the text.

Synthesize How might sportscasters or newscasters have announced Jackie Robinson's acceptance into the major leagues? Have students write a sportscast or newscast announcing this event, and read it to the class.

MODEL FLUENCY

Model reading the fluency passage on **Beyond Reproducible** page 59. Tell students to pay close attention to your intonation, or tone of voice, as you read. Then read one sentence at a time, and have students echo-read the sentences, copying your intonation.

During independent reading time, have students work with a partner using the fluency passage. One student reads aloud, while the other repeats each sentence back. Students can check their fluency by reading along with the "expert speed" version of the passage on the **Fluency Solutions Audio CD**.

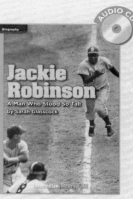

Leveled Reader

Book Talk

Bringing Groups Together Students will work with peers of various language and reading abilities to discuss this week's **Leveled Readers**. Refer to page 160 in the **Teacher's Resource Book** for more about how to conduct a Book Talk.

Beyond Reproducible, page 59

As I read, I will pay attention to intonation and expression.

	Jackie Robinson walked toward home plate, swinging
7	his bat. He was in a slump. He just couldn't seem to hit
20	the ball. He couldn't seem to catch it either. His team was
32	expecting more from him. So were the fans in Ebbets Field.
43	After all, he was the first African-American player in the
54	major league.
56	As Jackie stepped up to the plate, he couldn't believe
66	what he heard. Insults were flying out of the Philadelphia
76	Phillies dugout.
78	He almost put down his bat and quit the game of
89	baseball forever. Then he thought of his wife Rachel sitting
99	in the stands. He thought of all the people who wanted him
111	to succeed.
113	Planting his feet firmly in the ground, Jackie waited
122	for the pitch. The ball shot toward him, and, with a
133	tremendous smack, he sent it into center field. Later, in a
144	daring move, Jackie stole two bases. The fans jumped to
154	their feet. 156

Comprehension Check

1. What lesson do you think the author wants you to take away from this story? **Author's Purpose** The author wants you to learn how to be courageous, even in difficult times.

2. What problem does Jackie Robinson face? How does he overcome it? **Problem and Solution** He faces insults and wants to quit baseball. He overcomes it by deciding not to give up.

	Words Read	−	Number of Errors	=	Words Correct Score
First Read		−		=	
Second Read		−		=	

Daily Planner

DAY 1	• Build Background Knowledge • Vocabulary
DAY 2	• Vocabulary • Access to Core Content *Mighty Jackie*
DAY 3	• Vocabulary • Grammar • Access to Core Content *Mighty Jackie*

DAY 4	• Vocabulary
	• Writing/Spelling
	• Access to Core Content
	  "The New Kid"
	• Leveled Reader
	  Champion Athlete

DAY 5	• Vocabulary • Leveled Reader *Champion Athlete* • Self-Selected Reading

LOG ON ▶ StudentWorks *Plus*

Interactive Student Book

Use StudentWorks Plus for:
• Vocabulary Preteaching
• Word-by-Word Highlighting
• Think Aloud Prompts

Cognates

Help students identify similarities and differences in pronunciation and spelling between English and Spanish cognates.

athlete	*atleta*
influence	*influencia*
acceptance	*aceptación*
legendary	*legendario*
insult	*insulto*
comprehension	*comprensión*
context	*contexto*
description	*descripción*
singular	*singular*
plural	*plural*

ELL ENGLISH LANGUAGE LEARNERS

Prepare to Read

Content Objective Learn about women who made a difference in sports

Language Objective Use key words about women who made a difference in sports

Materials • **StudentWorks Plus**

BUILD BACKGROUND KNOWLEDGE

All Language Levels

■ Have students preview *Mighty Jackie* using **StudentWorks Plus**, which contains oral summaries in multiple languages, online multilingual glossaries, word-by-word highlighting, and questions that assess and build comprehension.

■ Students can build their word-reading fluency by reading along as the text is read or by listening during the first reading and, at the end of each paragraph, returning to the beginning of the paragraph and reading along.

■ Students can build their comprehension by reviewing the definitions of key words in the online glossary and by answering the comprehension questions. When appropriate, the text required to answer the question is highlighted to provide students with additional support and scaffolding.

■ After the reading, ask students to write about a question that links the story to their personal experiences, such as *Have you tried to do something new? How did you feel when you succeeded?*

Academic Language

Language Objective Use academic language in classroom conversations

All Language Levels

■ This week's academic words are **boldfaced** throughout the lesson. Define the word in context, and provide a clear example from the selection. Then ask students to generate an example or a word with a similar meaning.

Academic Language Used in Whole Group Instruction

Theme Words	Key Selection Words	Strategy and Skill Words
athlete **influence** **acceptance**	**legendary** **muttered** **gaped** **snickering** **insult** **flinched**	**monitor comprehension** **author's purpose** **context clues** **description** **singular nouns** **plural nouns**

ELL ENGLISH LANGUAGE LEARNERS

Vocabulary

Language Objective Demonstrate understanding and use of key words by discussing women in sports

Materials
- **Visual Vocabulary Resources**
- **ELL Resource Book**

Visual Vocabulary Resources

✓ PRETEACH KEY VOCABULARY

Use the **Visual Vocabulary Resources** to preteach the key selection words *legendary, muttered, gaped, snickering, insult*, and *flinched*. Focus on two words per day. Use the following routine, which appears in detail on the cards.

Beginning/Intermediate

- Point out any known sound-spellings, or focus on a key aspect of phonemic awareness related to the word.

All Language Levels

- Define the word in English, and provide the example given.
- Define the word in Spanish, if appropriate, and indicate if the word is a cognate.
- Display the picture, and explain how it demonstrates the word. Engage students in structured activity about the image.
- Ask students to chorally say the word three times.
- Distribute copies of the Vocabulary Glossary on **ELL Resource Book**, page 80.

PRETEACH FUNCTION WORDS AND PHRASES

All Language Levels

Use the Visual Vocabulary Resources to preteach the function words and phrases *sit up and take notice, eyes blurred over, face (someone) down*, and *make good*. Focus on one word or phrase per day. Use the detailed routine on the cards.

- Define the word in English and, if appropriate, in Spanish. Point out if the word is a cognate.
- Refer to the picture and engage students in talk about the word. For example, students will partner-talk using sentence frames.
- Ask students to chorally repeat the word three times.

TEACH BASIC WORDS

Beginning/Intermediate

Use the Visual Vocabulary Resources to teach the basic words *exhibition, sandlot, mound, bleachers, wind up*, and *strike out*. Teach these "baseball" words using the routine provided on the card.

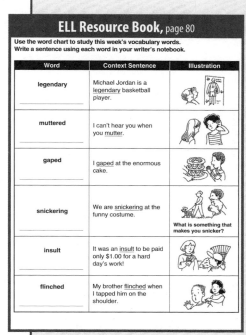

ELL Resource Book, page 80

Use the word chart to study this week's vocabulary words. Write a sentence using each word in your writer's notebook.

Word	Context Sentence	Illustration
legendary	Michael Jordan is a <u>legendary</u> basketball player.	
muttered	I can't hear you when you <u>mutter</u>.	
gaped	I <u>gaped</u> at the enormous cake.	
snickering	We are <u>snickering</u> at the funny costume.	What is something that makes you snicker?
insult	It was an <u>insult</u> to be paid only $1.00 for a hard day's work!	
flinched	My brother <u>flinched</u> when I tapped him on the shoulder.	

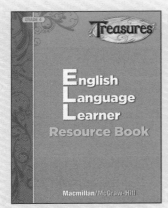

ELL Resource Book

ELL ENGLISH LANGUAGE LEARNERS

Access to Core Content

Content Objective Read grade-level text

Language Objective Discuss text using key words and sentence frames

Materials • **ELL Resource Book**, pp. 70–79

PRETEACH MAIN SELECTION (PAGES 166–181)

All Language Levels

Use the Interactive Question-Response Guide on **ELL Resource Book** pages 70–77 to introduce students to *Mighty Jackie*. Preteach half of the selection on Day 2 and half on Day 3.

- Use the prompts provided in the guide to develop meaning and vocabulary. Use the partner-talk and whole-class responses to engage students and increase student talk.

- When completed, have partners reread the story.

PRETEACH PAIRED SELECTION (PAGES 184–185)

All Language Levels

Use the Interactive Question-Response Guide on ELL Resource Book pages 78–79 to preview the paired selection "The New Kid." Preteach the selection on Day 4.

Beginning	Intermediate	Advanced
Use Visuals During the Interactive Reading, select several illustrations. Describe them and have students summarize what you said. Then work with students to identify author's purpose.	**Describe** During the Interactive Reading, select a few lines of text. After you have read and explained it, have students summarize the text. Then ask them to identify the author's purpose for the text.	**Discuss** During the Interactive Reading, select a passage. After you have read and explained it, have students summarize the text. Then have students describe the author's purpose for the text using specific examples.

ELL ENGLISH LANGUAGE LEARNERS

Fluency

Content Objectives Reread selections to develop fluency; develop speaking skills

Language Objective Tell a partner what a selection is about

Materials • **Student Book:** *Mighty Jackie*, "The New Kid"
 • **Teacher's Resource Book**

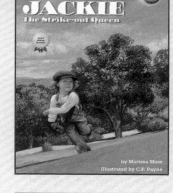

REREAD FOR FLUENCY

Beginning

■ Have students read the decodable passages in the **Teacher's Resource Book**, page 11.

Intermediate/Advanced

■ Have students reread a portion of *Mighty Jackie*. Have them focus on two to four of their favorite pages from the selection, based on their level. Work with them to read the pages with the appropriate intonation. For example, have students read the paragraph that begins, "Jackie held the ball like it was part of her arm …." Have students stop reading at the end of the page. Then have them continue by chorally reading other paragraphs.

■ Provide time for students to read the text. Comment on their intonation. Provide corrective feedback by modeling proper fluency.

Student Book

DEVELOP SPEAKING/LISTENING SKILLS

All Language Levels

■ Have students practice reading "The New Kid." Work with students to read with the appropriate intonation.

■ Provide time for students to read to a partner. Ask students to tell their partner what they admired most about the kid. Provide the sentence frame: *The kid was remarkable because* ____.

Self-Selected Reading

Content Objective Read independently

Language Objective Orally retell information learned

Materials • **Leveled Classroom Library** • other biographies

APPLY SKILLS AND STRATEGIES TO INDEPENDENT READING

All Language Levels

■ Have students choose a biography for silent independent reading. (See the **Theme Bibliography** on pages T8–T9 for suggestions.)

■ Ask students to orally summarize the book. Provide time for students to share their reactions with classmates. Ask: *Would you recommend this book to a classmate? Why or why not?*

Leveled Classroom Library
See Leveled Classroom
Library lessons on pages T2–T7.

Transfer Skills

Plural Nouns In Hmong and Khmer, nouns do not change form to show the plural. Display and name classroom people and objects (*girl/girls, book/books*) to illustrate the singular and plural forms of regular nouns. Have students repeat with multiple classroom objects. Then look for opportunities to point out plural nouns to students as they read the selections.

Corrective Feedback

During Whole Group grammar lessons, follow the routine on the **Grammar Transparencies** to provide students with extra support. This routine includes completing the items with English Language Learners while other students work independently, having students reread the sentences with partners to build fluency, and providing a generative task such as writing a new sentence using the skill.

Grammar

Content Objective Identify singular and plural nouns
Language Objective Speak in complete sentences, using sentence frames

PLURAL NOUNS

Beginning/Intermediate

■ Review with students that a singular noun is a word that names one person, place, or thing and that a plural noun names more than one person, place, or thing. Remind students that we add -*s* or -*es* to most nouns to show "more than one." Write *book* on the board as you say the word and hold up one book. Then write *books* on the board as you say the word, emphasizing and underlining the -*s*, and hold up two books. Repeat with the nouns *pencil/pencils*.

All Language Levels

■ Review singular and plural nouns with students. Write sentences on the board, such as those provided below. Have students underline the plural nouns in each sentence. For each plural noun, have them say: ＿＿ *is a plural noun.*

> *Girls play sports as well as boys.*
>
> *Those boxes are full of wonderful books.*
>
> *There are many stories about female athletes.*
>
> *Some players can hit the ball into the bushes!*

PEER DISCUSSION STARTERS

All Language Levels

■ Write the following sentences on the board.

Jackie Mitchell was ＿＿.   I learned that years ago, women ＿＿.

■ Pair students and have them complete each sentence frame. Ask them to expand on their sentences by providing as many details as they can from this week's readings. Circulate, listen in, and take note of each student's language use and proficiency.

Beginning	Intermediate	Advanced
Use Visuals Describe the illustrations in *Mighty Jackie* to students. Ask: *What do you see?* Help them point and name singular and plural nouns.	**Describe** Ask students to describe the illustrations in *Mighty Jackie* using singular and plural nouns in their descriptions. Have them use complete sentences. Model sentences if needed.	**Discuss** Ask students to discuss the illustrations in *Mighty Jackie* using singular and plural nouns in their descriptions. Challenge them to use complex sentences.

ELL ENGLISH LANGUAGE LEARNERS

Writing/Spelling

Content Objective Spell words correctly

Language Objective Write in complete sentences, using sentence frames

All Language Levels

■ Write the key vocabulary words on the board: *legendary, muttered, gaped, snickering, insult, flinched*. Have students copy each word on their **WorkBoards**. Help them say each word and then write a sentence for it. Provide sentence starters such as:

> *A legendary athlete is someone who ____.*
>
> *She muttered quickly, so I could not ____.*
>
> *My mouth hung open when I gaped at ____.*
>
> *We all started snickering when ____.*
>
> *It is an insult to call someone a ____.*
>
> *I flinched when the ball ____.*

Beginning/Intermediate

■ Help students spell words using their growing knowledge of English sound-spelling relationships. Model how to segment the word students are trying to spell, and attach a spelling to each sound (or spellings to each syllable if a multisyllabic word). Use the **Sound-Spelling Cards** to reinforce the spellings for each English sound.

Advanced

■ Dictate the following words for students to spell: *think, ship, phase, chin, when, bathroom, fish, much, graph, meanwhile*. Use the Sound-Spelling Cards to guide students as they spell each word.

■ When completed, review the meanings of words that can be easily demonstrated or explained. Use actions, gestures, and available pictures.

Sound-Spelling WorkBoard

Phonics/Word Study

For English Language Learners who need more practice with this week's phonics/spelling skill, see the Approaching Level lesson on page 187J. Focus on minimal contrasts, articulation, and those sounds that do not transfer from the student's first language to English. For a complete listing of transfer sounds, see pages T16–T31.

Leveled Reader

Vocabulary

Preteach Vocabulary Use the routine in the **Visual Vocabulary Resources**, pages 391–396, to preteach the ELL Vocabulary listed in the inside front cover of the **Leveled Reader**.

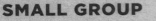

ELL ENGLISH LANGUAGE LEARNERS

Leveled Reader

Content Objective Read to apply skills and strategies

Language Objective Retell information, using complete sentences

Materials
- **Leveled Reader:** *Champion Athlete: Babe Didrikson Zaharias*
- **ELL Resource Book,** p. 81
- **Visual Vocabulary Resources,** pp. 391–396

BEFORE READING

All Language Levels

- **Preview** Read the title *Champion Athlete: Babe Didrikson Zaharias.* Ask: *What is the title? Say it again.* Repeat with the author's name. Then page through the book. Use simple language to tell about each page. Immediately follow up with questions, such as *What is the main idea the author wants readers to understand from this page?*

- **Review Skills** Use the inside front cover to review the comprehension skill and vocabulary words.

- **Set a Purpose** Say: *Let's read to find out why Babe Didrikson Zaharias is an important person in sports history.*

DURING READING

All Language Levels

- Have students read each page aloud using the differentiated suggestions. Provide corrective feedback, such as modeling how to blend a decodable word or clarifying meaning by using techniques from the Interactive Question-Response Guide.

- **Retell** After every two pages, ask students to state the main ideas they have learned so far. Help them to complete the Author's Purpose Map. Restate students' comments when they have difficulty using story-specific words. Provide differentiated sentence frames to support students' responses and engage students in partner-talk where appropriate.

Beginning	Intermediate	Advanced
Echo-Read Have students echo-read after you.	**Choral-Read** Have students chorally read with you.	**Choral-Read** Have students chorally read.
Check Comprehension Point to pictures and ask questions, such as *What is happening in this picture?*	**Check Comprehension** Ask questions or provide prompts, such as *What happened when Babe competed at the 1932 Olympics?*	**Check Comprehension** Ask: *Why do you think the author decided to write about Babe Didrikson Zaharias?*

ELL ENGLISH LANGUAGE LEARNERS

AFTER READING

Use the chart below and Think and Compare questions in the **Leveled Reader** to determine students' progress.

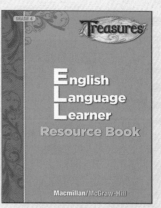

ELL Resource Book

Think and Compare	Beginning	Intermediate	Advanced
1 Reread page 4. How did Babe get her nickname? Why do you think the author put this information in the book? *(Evaluate Author's Purpose)*	Possible responses: Nonverbal response. Baseball player. Inform.	Possible responses: Babe was a good hitter. I think the author's purpose is to inform.	Possible responses: She was a good hitter like the baseball player Babe Ruth. I think the author wants to inform us about Babe.
2 What were some of Babe's qualities? Do you admire them? Explain your answer. *(Analyze)*	Possible responses: Nonverbal response. Do things. Yes, I do.	Possible responses: Babe was brave. Yes, I admire her qualities. She did what she wanted to do.	Possible responses: Babe was brave and outspoken. I admire her qualities because she didn't let anyone stop her from doing what she wanted to do.
3 Do you think Babe Didrikson Zaharias helped girls become interested in sports? Why? *(Evaluate)*	Possible responses: Nonverbal response. Yes. We do everything.	Possible responses: Yes, she helped girls. We can do everything boys do.	Possible responses: Yes, she helped girls get interested in sports because she proved to the world that a woman can do all the sports men do.

BOOK TALK

Develop Listening and Speaking Skills Distribute copies of **ELL Resource Book** page 81, and form small groups. Help students determine the leader to discuss the Book Talk questions. Tell students to remember the following while engaged in the activity:

- Share information in cooperative learning interactions. Remind students to work with their partners to retell the story and complete any activities. Ask: *What happened next in the story?*

- Narrate, describe, and explain with specificity and detail. Ask: *Where did the story take place? Can you describe the setting? What else did you notice?*

- Express opinions, ideas, and feelings on a variety of social and academic topics. Ask: *What do you think about the characters in the story?*

Book Talk

Bringing Groups Together Students will work with peers of varying language abilities to discuss the Book Talk questions. Form groups so that students who read the Beyond Level, On Level, Approaching Level, and English Language Learner Leveled Readers are in the same group for the activity.

Progress Monitoring

Weekly Assessment

ASSESSED SKILLS

- Vocabulary: Vocabulary Words, Context Clues
- Comprehension: Author's Purpose
- Grammar: Singular and Plural Nouns
- Phonics/Spelling: Digraphs

Selection Test for Mighty Jackie *Also Available*

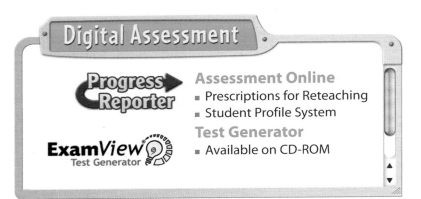

Progress Reporter **Assessment Online**
- Prescriptions for Reteaching
- Student Profile System

ExamView Test Generator **Test Generator**
- Available on CD-ROM

**Weekly Assessment
Unit 2 Week 2**

Fluency Assessment

Assess fluency for one group of students per week.
Use the Oral Fluency Record Sheet to track the number of
words read correctly. Fluency goal for all students:
84–104 words correct per minute (WCPM).

Approaching Level	Weeks 1, 3, 5
On Level	Weeks 2, 4
Beyond Level	Week 6

Fluency Assessment

Diagnose		Prescribe
Review the assessment answers with students. Have them correct their errors. Then provide additional instruction as needed.		
	IF...	**THEN...**
VOCABULARY WORDS VOCABULARY STRATEGY Context Clues: Description	0–2 items correct ...	See **Vocabulary Intervention Teacher's Edition.** **LOG ON ▶** Online Practice: Go to www.macmillanmh.com. **CD-ROM** Vocabulary PuzzleMaker
COMPREHENSION Skill: Author's Purpose	0–3 items correct ...	See **Comprehension Intervention Teacher's Edition.** **SPIRAL REVIEW** See Author's Purpose lesson in Unit 2 Week 3, page 195B.
GRAMMAR Singular and Plural Nouns	0–1 items correct ...	See **Writing and Grammar Intervention Teacher's Edition.**
PHONICS AND SPELLING Digraphs	0–1 items correct ...	**LOG ON ▶** Online Practice: Go to www.macmillanmh.com. See **Phonics Intervention Teacher's Edition.**
FLUENCY	79–83 WCPM	**AUDIO CD** Fluency Solutions Audio CD
	0–78 WCPM	See **Fluency Intervention Teacher's Edition.**

Response to Intervention

To place students in Tier 2 or Tier 3 Intervention use the *Diagnostic Assessment.*

- Phonics
- Vocabulary
- Comprehension
- Fluency
- Writing and Grammar

Week 3 ★ At a Glance

Priority Skills and Concepts

 Comprehension
- **Strategy:** Monitor Comprehension
- **Skill:** Main Idea and Details
- **Skill:** Author's Purpose
- **Genre:** Biography, Expository

 **Robust Vocabulary**
- **Selection Vocabulary:** *similar, challenges, designed, achieved, varied*
- **Strategy:** Idioms

 **Fluency**
- **Accuracy**

 **Phonics/Spelling**
- **Word Study:** Three-Letter Blends, Multisyllabic Words
- **Spelling Words:** *shred, through, sprout, sprawl, split, throb, throat, shrink, screw, shrimp, screech, straighten, sprang, shriek, splashing, straps, strand, script, thrill, throne*
- *choose, photo, whole*

 **Grammar/Mechanics**
- **Irregular Plural Nouns**
- **Correct Plural Forms**

 Writing
- **Writing a How-to Article**

Key

 Tested in program   Review Skill

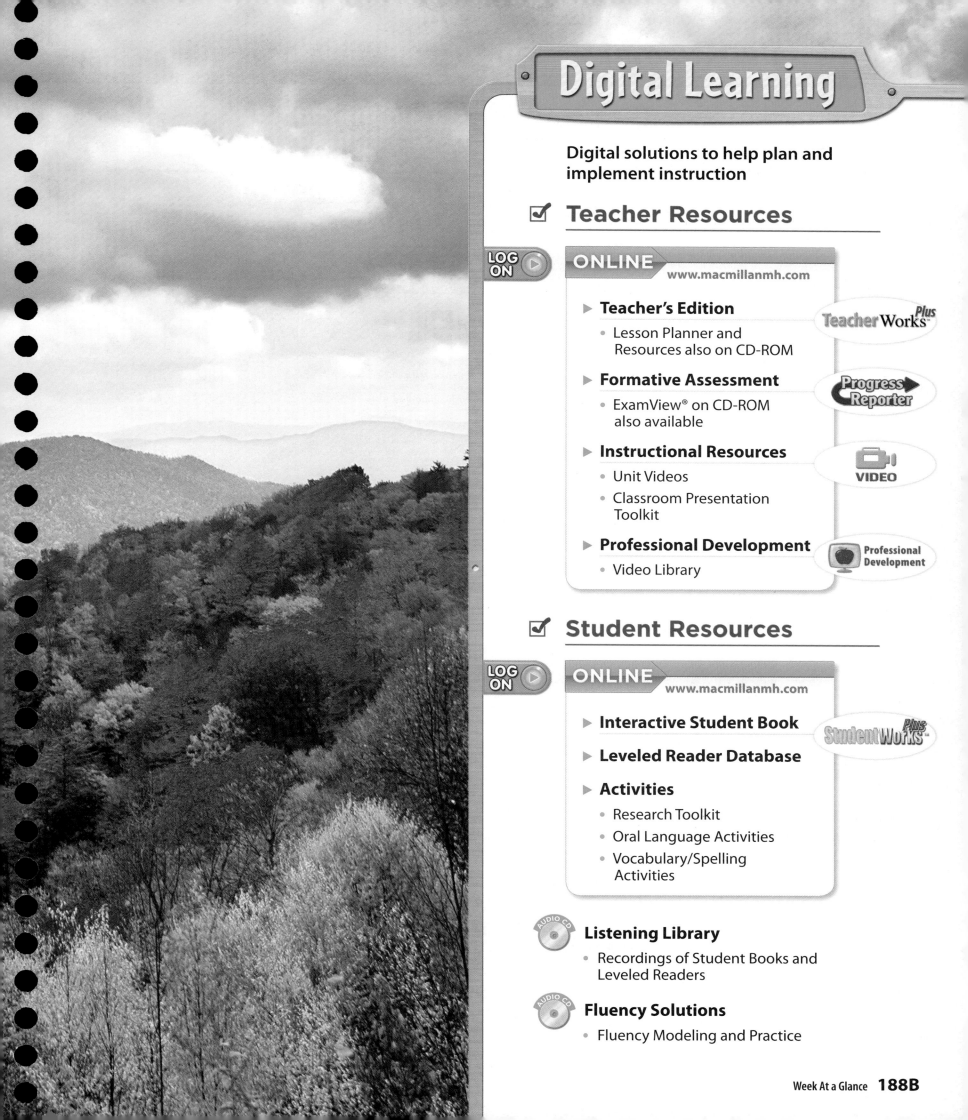

Digital Learning

Digital solutions to help plan and implement instruction

☑ Teacher Resources

LOG ON ▶

ONLINE www.macmillanmh.com

▶ **Teacher's Edition**
- Lesson Planner and Resources also on CD-ROM

TeacherWorks™ Plus

▶ **Formative Assessment**
- ExamView® on CD-ROM also available

Progress Reporter

▶ **Instructional Resources**
- Unit Videos
- Classroom Presentation Toolkit

VIDEO

▶ **Professional Development**
- Video Library

Professional Development

☑ Student Resources

LOG ON ▶

ONLINE www.macmillanmh.com

▶ **Interactive Student Book**

StudentWorks™ Plus

▶ **Leveled Reader Database**

▶ **Activities**
- Research Toolkit
- Oral Language Activities
- Vocabulary/Spelling Activities

AUDIO CD
Listening Library
- Recordings of Student Books and Leveled Readers

AUDIO CD
Fluency Solutions
- Fluency Modeling and Practice

Weekly Literature

Theme: Facing Challenges

LOG ON StudentWorks *Plus*
Interactive Student Book

- Word-by-Word Reading
- Summaries in Multiple Languages
- Comprehension Questions

Real World Reading

Comprehension

Genre
An Expository article in a newspaper or magazine presents facts and information.

Monitor Comprehension
Main Idea and Details
To find the main idea of an article, first identify the most important details. Then decide what these details have in common.

Making a Splash

How does a person with physical disabilities become a world-champion athlete?

Rudy Garcia-Tolson is not an ordinary athlete. He holds world records for swimming, running, and biking. He takes part in top competitions around the world, where all eyes are on him. This talented athlete has won many medals and honors. There is one other thing special about Rudy: He has no legs.

Rudy was born in Bloomington, California, with a serious illness. He went through 15 operations as a baby. At five years old, Rudy and his family had to make a big decision. Rudy's legs could no longer function. He could keep his legs and stay in a wheelchair or he could walk with artificial legs. Rudy knew what he wanted; he chose to walk. The brave five-year-old had his legs amputated. From that point on, Rudy's life was never the same.

Main Selection

Genre Expository

The Paralympics

Preteach Vocabulary and Comprehension

Genre Expository

STANDING TALL

Test Practice

Genre Expository

Treasures
INTERACTIVE
Read-Aloud
ANTHOLOGY WITH PLAYS

Macmillan/McGraw-Hill

Interactive Read-Aloud Anthology

- Listening Comprehension
- Robust Vocabulary
- Readers' Theater Plays for Fluency

Resources for Differentiated Instruction

Leveled Readers: Social Studies

GR Levels O–T

Genre	Expository

- Same Theme
- Same Vocabulary
- Same Comprehension Skills

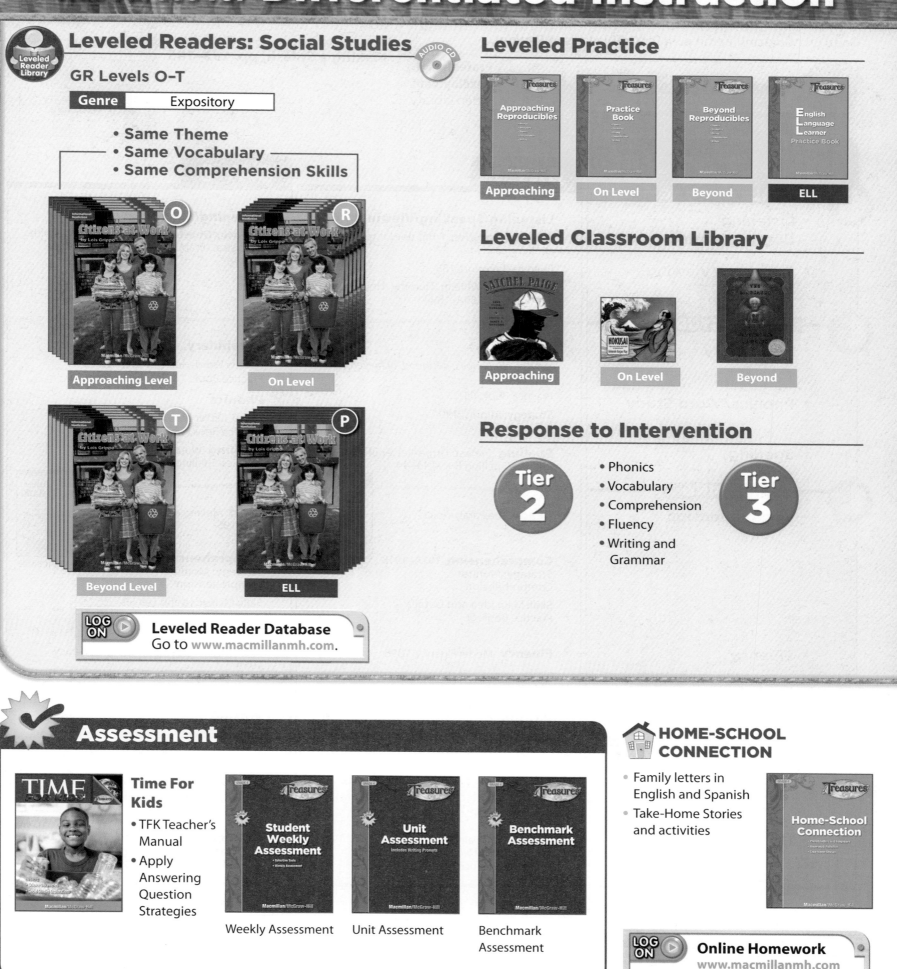

O — Approaching Level

R — On Level

T — Beyond Level

P — ELL

LOG ON **Leveled Reader Database**
Go to www.macmillanmh.com.

Leveled Practice

Approaching Reproducibles — **Approaching**

Practice Book — **On Level**

Beyond Reproducibles — **Beyond**

English Language Learner Practice Book — **ELL**

Leveled Classroom Library

Satchel Paige — **Approaching**

Hokusai — **On Level**

Beyond

Response to Intervention

Tier 2

- Phonics
- Vocabulary
- Comprehension
- Fluency
- Writing and Grammar

Tier 3

Assessment

Time For Kids
- TFK Teacher's Manual
- Apply Answering Question Strategies

Student Weekly Assessment — Weekly Assessment

Unit Assessment — Unit Assessment

Benchmark Assessment — Benchmark Assessment

HOME-SCHOOL CONNECTION

- Family letters in English and Spanish
- Take-Home Stories and activities

Home-School Connection

LOG ON **Online Homework**
www.macmillanmh.com

Suggested Lesson Plan

Go to **www.macmillanmh.com** for Online Lesson Planner

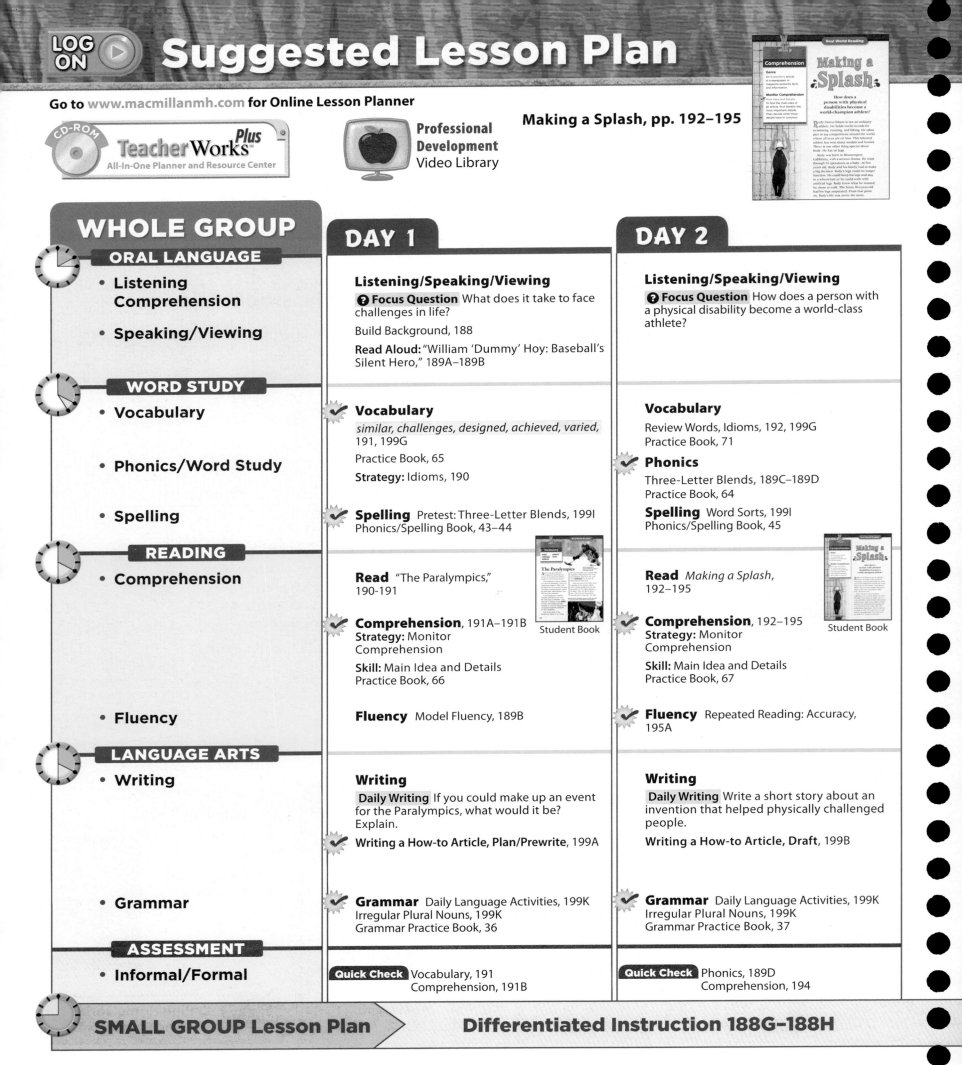

TeacherWorks *Plus*
All-In-One Planner and Resource Center

Professional Development
Video Library

Making a Splash, pp. 192–195

WHOLE GROUP

ORAL LANGUAGE
- **Listening Comprehension**
- **Speaking/Viewing**

WORD STUDY
- **Vocabulary**
- **Phonics/Word Study**
- **Spelling**

READING
- **Comprehension**
- **Fluency**

LANGUAGE ARTS
- **Writing**
- **Grammar**

ASSESSMENT
- **Informal/Formal**

DAY 1

Listening/Speaking/Viewing
❷ Focus Question What does it take to face challenges in life?
Build Background, 188
Read Aloud: "William 'Dummy' Hoy: Baseball's Silent Hero," 189A–189B

Vocabulary
similar, challenges, designed, achieved, varied, 191, 199G
Practice Book, 65
Strategy: Idioms, 190

Spelling Pretest: Three-Letter Blends, 199I
Phonics/Spelling Book, 43–44

Read "The Paralympics," 190-191

Student Book

Comprehension, 191A–191B
Strategy: Monitor Comprehension
Skill: Main Idea and Details
Practice Book, 66

Fluency Model Fluency, 189B

Writing
Daily Writing If you could make up an event for the Paralympics, what would it be? Explain.
Writing a How-to Article, Plan/Prewrite, 199A

Grammar Daily Language Activities, 199K
Irregular Plural Nouns, 199K
Grammar Practice Book, 36

Quick Check Vocabulary, 191
Comprehension, 191B

DAY 2

Listening/Speaking/Viewing
❷ Focus Question How does a person with a physical disability become a world-class athlete?

Vocabulary
Review Words, Idioms, 192, 199G
Practice Book, 71
Phonics
Three-Letter Blends, 189C–189D
Practice Book, 64
Spelling Word Sorts, 199I
Phonics/Spelling Book, 45

Read *Making a Splash*, 192–195

Student Book

Comprehension, 192–195
Strategy: Monitor Comprehension
Skill: Main Idea and Details
Practice Book, 67

Fluency Repeated Reading: Accuracy, 195A

Writing
Daily Writing Write a short story about an invention that helped physically challenged people.
Writing a How-to Article, Draft, 199B

Grammar Daily Language Activities, 199K
Irregular Plural Nouns, 199K
Grammar Practice Book, 37

Quick Check Phonics, 189D
Comprehension, 194

SMALL GROUP Lesson Plan ▷ **Differentiated Instruction 188G–188H**

Priority Skills

Vocabulary	Comprehension	Writing	Science
Vocabulary Words Idioms	**Strategy:** Monitor Comprehension **Skill:** Main Idea and Details	Writing a How-to Article	Evaluate the impact of research on society

DAY 3

Listening/Speaking

? Focus Question What do the athletes in "The Paralympics" and *Making a Splash* have in common?

Vocabulary

Review Words, Related Words, 199H

Spelling Word Meanings, 199J
Phonics/Spelling Book, 46

Read *Making a Splash*, 192–195

Student Book

Comprehension
Comprehension Check, 195

Review Skill: Author's Purpose, 195B
Practice Book, 69

Fluency Repeated Reading: Accuracy, 195A
Practice Book, 68

Writing

Daily Writing You are a physically challenged athlete participating in the Paralympics. Write about your experience.

Writing a How-to Article, Revise and Conferencing, 199C–199E

Grammar Daily Language Activities, 199K
Mechanics and Usage, 199L
Grammar Practice Book, 38

Quick Check Fluency, 195A

DAY 4

Listening/Speaking/Viewing

? Focus Question How would you describe Grayson in "Standing Tall"? Use details from the article to support your answer.

Vocabulary

Review Words, Morphology, 199H

Spelling Proofread, 199J
Phonics/Spelling Book, 47

Read "Standing Tall," 196–197

Test Practice:
Answering Questions

Student Book

Research and Study Skills

Parts of a Book, 195C–195D
Practice Book, 70

Fluency Repeated Reading: Accuracy, 195A

Time For Kids

Writing

Daily Writing Suppose you could interview a famous swimmer. What three questions would you ask?

Writing Prompt, 198–199

Writing a How-to Article, Conferencing Proofread/Edit, 199E–199F

Grammar Daily Language Activities, 199K
Irregular Plural Nouns, 199L
Grammar Practice Book, 39

Quick Check Vocabulary, 199H

DAY 5
Review and Assess

Listening/Speaking/Viewing

? Focus Question Summarize the main points you have learned about disabled athletes and prosthetics. Have you formed any new opinions about disabled people? Explain.

Vocabulary

Assess Words, Connect to Writing, 199H

Spelling Posttest, 199J
Phonics/Spelling Book, 48

Read Self-Selected Reading, 188K
Practice Book, 72

Student Book

Comprehension
Strategy: Monitor Comprehension

Skill: Main Idea and Details

Fluency Practice, 188K

Writing

Daily Writing You have been chosen to interview someone who competed in the Paralympics. What questions will you ask?

Writing a How-to Article, Publish and Share, 199F

Grammar Daily Language Activities, 199K
Irregular Plural Nouns, 199L
Grammar Practice Book, 40

Weekly Assessment, 199MM–199NN

Differentiated Instruction

What do I do in small groups?

Teacher-Led Small Groups

Independent Activities

Focus on Skills

IF... students need additional instruction, practice, or extension based on your **Quick Check** observations for the following priority skills:

✓ **Phonics/Word Study**
Three-Letter Blends

✓ **Vocabulary Words**
similar, challenges, designed, achieved, varied
Strategy: Idioms

✓ **Comprehension**
Strategy: Monitor Comprehension
Skill: Main Idea and Details

✓ **Fluency**

THEN...

Approaching **ELL**	Preteach and Reteach Skills
On Level	Practice
Beyond	Enrich and Accelerate Learning

LOG ON ▶ Suggested Small Group Lesson Plan

TeacherWorks *Plus*
CD-ROM
All-In-One Planner and Resource Center

	DAY 1	DAY 2
Approaching Level **Tier 2** • **Preteach/Reteach** **Tier 2 Instruction**	• Prepare to Read, 199M • Academic Language, 199M • Preteach Vocabulary, 199O	• Comprehension, 199Q Monitor Comprehension/Main Idea and Details **ELL** • Leveled Reader Lesson 1, 199R
On Level • **Practice**	• Vocabulary, 199W • Phonics, 199W Three-Letter Blends **ELL**	• Leveled Reader Lesson 1, 199Y
Beyond Level **Gifted and Talented** • **Extend/Accelerate**	• Leveled Reader Lesson 1, 199CC • Analyze Information, 199CC	• Leveled Reader Lesson 2, 199DD • Synthesize Information, 199DD
ELL • **Build English Language Proficiency** • See **ELL** in other levels.	• Prepare to Read, 199EE • Academic Language, 199EE • Preteach Vocabulary, 199FF	• Vocabulary, 199FF • Preteach Main Selection, 199GG

Focus on Leveled Readers

Leveled Reader Library

**Levels
O–T**

O	R	T	P
Citizens at Work by Lois Grippo	*Citizens at Work* by Lois Grippo	*Citizens at Work* by Lois Grippo	*Citizens at Work* by Lois Grippo
Approaching	**On Level**	**Beyond**	**ELL**

Social Studies

Teacher's Annotated Edition

Identify the importance of historical figures who modeled active participation in the democratic process.

Additional Leveled Readers

LOG ON

Leveled Reader Database
www.macmillanmh.com

Search by

- Comprehension Skill
- Content Area
- Genre
- Text Feature
- Guided Reading Level
- Reading Recovery Level
- Lexile Score
- Benchmark Level

Subscription also available.

Manipulatives

Sound-Spelling WorkBoards

Sound-Spelling Cards

about
today

High-Frequency Word Cards

VISUAL VOCABULARY RESOURCES

Visual Vocabulary Resources

DAY 3

- Phonics Maintenance, 199N
  Three-Letter Blends **ELL**
- Leveled Reader Lesson 2, 199S

- Leveled Reader Lesson 2, 199Z

- Phonics, 199AA
  Three-Letter Blends **ELL**

- Vocabulary, 199FF
- Grammar, 199II

DAY 4

- Reteach Phonics Skill, 199N
  Three-Letter Blends **ELL**
- Review Vocabulary, 199P
- Leveled Reader Lesson 3, 199T

- Fluency, 199X

- Vocabulary, 199AA
- Write an Interview, 199AA
- Fluency, 199BB

- Vocabulary, 199FF
- Writing/Spelling, 199JJ
- Fluency, 199HH
- Leveled Reader, 199KK

DAY 5

- High-Frequency Words, 199P
- Fluency, 199U
- Self-Selected Independent Reading, 199V
- Book Talk, 199T

- Self-Selected Independent Reading, 199X
- Book Talk, 199Z

- Self-Selected Independent Reading, 199BB
- Evaluate Information, 199BB
- Book Talk, 199DD

- Vocabulary, 199FF
- Leveled Reader, 199KK
- Self-Selected Independent Reading, 199HH
- Book Talk, 199LL

Managing the Class

What do I do with the rest of my class?

- Practice Book and Reproducibles
- ELL Practice Book
- Leveled Reader Activities
- Literacy Workstations
- Online Activities

Classroom Management Tools

Weekly Contract

Name _____ Date _____

My To-Do List

✔ Put a check next to the activities you complete.

📖 **Reading**
☐ Practice fluency
☐ Choose a story to read

🔤 **Phonics/ Word Study**
☐ Look up word origins
☐ Write words with short vowel sounds

✏️ **Writing**
☐ Write a letter to the editor
☐ Write a radio ad

🔬 **Science**
☐ Research two types of rocks
☐ Write a chart

🌐 **Social Studies**
☐ Create a guide book
☐ Role-play an interview

🔊 **Leveled Readers**
☐ Write About It!
☐ Content Connection

💻 **Technology**
☐ Vocabulary PuzzleMaker
☐ Fluency Solutions
☐ Listening Library
☐ www.macmillanmh.com

🖌️ **Independent Practice**
☐ Practice Book A–O

Rotation Chart

Teacher-Led Small Groups

Red

Literacy Workstations   Independent Activities

Blue   Green

Orange

...za
...an
...ria

How-to Guide

Treasures
Managing Small Groups
A How-to Guide
Dr. Vicki Gibson   Dr. Douglas Fisher

Macmillan/McGraw-Hill

How-to Guide

Rotation Chart

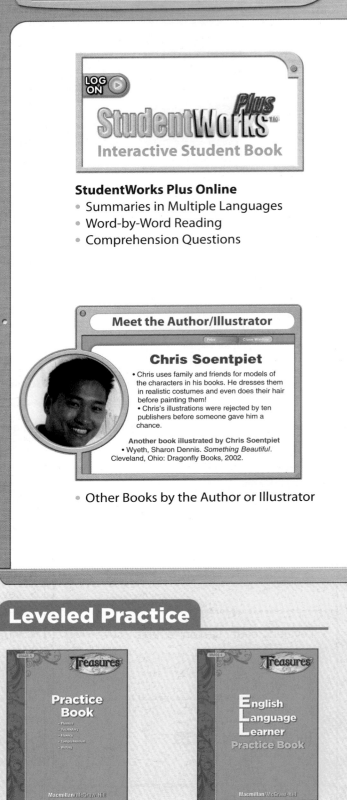

Digital Learning

LOG ON ▶

StudentWorks Plus
Interactive Student Book

StudentWorks Plus Online
- Summaries in Multiple Languages
- Word-by-Word Reading
- Comprehension Questions

Meet the Author/Illustrator

Print   Close Window

Chris Soentpiet

- Chris uses family and friends for models of the characters in his books. He dresses them in realistic costumes and even does their hair before painting them!
- Chris's illustrations were rejected by ten publishers before someone gave him a chance.

Another book illustrated by Chris Soentpiet
- Wyeth, Sharon Dennis. *Something Beautiful*. Cleveland, Ohio: Dragonfly Books, 2002.

- Other Books by the Author or Illustrator

Leveled Practice

Treasures
Practice Book
- Phonics
- Vocabulary
- Fluency
- Comprehension
- Writing

Macmillan/McGraw-Hill

On Level

Treasures
English Language Learner
Practice Book

Macmillan/McGraw-Hill

ELL

Also Available:
Approaching Reproducible
Beyond Reproducible

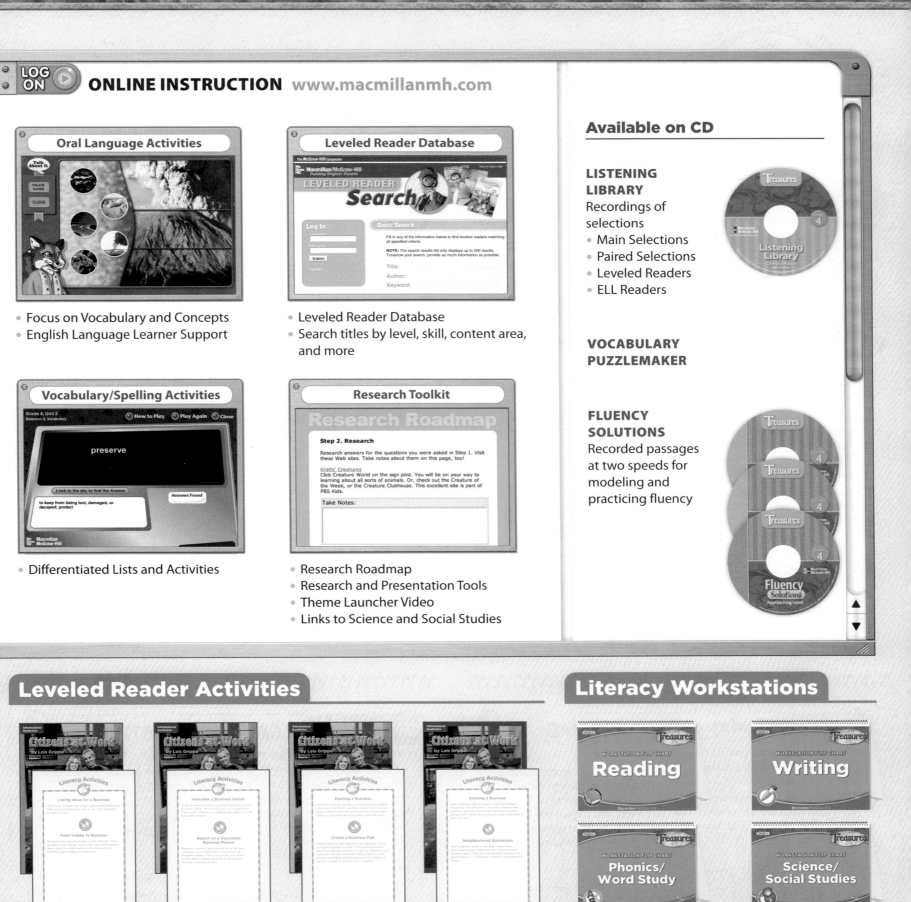

ONLINE INSTRUCTION www.macmillanmh.com

Oral Language Activities

- Focus on Vocabulary and Concepts
- English Language Learner Support

Vocabulary/Spelling Activities

preserve

to keep from being lost, damaged, or decayed; protect

- Differentiated Lists and Activities

Leveled Reader Database

- Leveled Reader Database
- Search titles by level, skill, content area, and more

Research Toolkit

Step 2. Research

Research answers for the questions you were asked in Step 1. Visit these Web sites. Take notes about them on this page, too!

Kratts' Creatures
Click Creature World on the sign post. You will be on your way to learning about all sorts of animals. Or, check out the Creature of the Week, or the Creature Clubhouse. This excellent site is part of PBS Kids.

Take Notes:

- Research Roadmap
- Research and Presentation Tools
- Theme Launcher Video
- Links to Science and Social Studies

Available on CD

LISTENING LIBRARY
Recordings of selections
- Main Selections
- Paired Selections
- Leveled Readers
- ELL Readers

VOCABULARY PUZZLEMAKER

FLUENCY SOLUTIONS
Recorded passages at two speeds for modeling and practicing fluency

Leveled Reader Activities

Approaching

On Level

Beyond

ELL

See inside cover of all Leveled Readers.

Literacy Workstations

Reading

Writing

Phonics/Word Study

Science/Social Studies

See lessons on pages 188K–188L.

Managing the Class

What do I do with the rest of my class?

Reading

Objectives

- Develop fluency through partner-reading
- Read independently for a sustained period of time; use **Practice Book** page 72 for Reading Strategies and Reading Log

---

Reading — Fluency
20 Minutes

- Select a paragraph from the Fluency passage on page x of your Practice Book.
- With a partner, take turns reading the sentences aloud.
- Listen for the pronunciation of unfamiliar or difficult words.

Extension

- Slow down if you come to unfamiliar words and break them into syllables.
- Listen to the Audio CD.

Things you need:
- Practice Book

Fluency Solutions
Listening Library

15

Reading — Independent Reading

- Choose an article to read. Think about the main point the author is trying to make.
- Find examples of persuasive techniques that the author used. List two or three persuasive statements found in the article.

Extension

- In your response journal, write a summary of the author's arguments. Tell which argument you thought was the most persuasive. Explain your choice.

Things you need:
- articles
- pen and paper

For more information on Special Olympics, go to the Author/Illustrator section of www.macmillanmh.com

16

Phonics/Word Study

Objectives

- Define and use idioms
- Sort words with consonant clusters or three-letter blends

Phonics/Word Study — Idioms
20 Minutes

- Write the following idioms on a piece of paper:
  1. Under the weather
  2. Hold your horses
  3. Cat has your tongue
- Write the meaning next to each idiom.

Extension

- Think of another idiom you know. Draw a picture of the idiom.
- Write the idiom and the meaning below the picture.

Things you need:
- pen and paper
- colored pencils or markers

For additional vocabulary and spelling games, go to www.macmillanmh.com

Vocabulary PuzzleMaker

15

Phonics/Word Study — CONSONANT CLUSTERS
20 Minutes

- Write the column headings *str, thr, spr, shr, scr,* and *spl* on a piece of paper.
- Then write these words under the correct column heading: *throat, strand, shrimp, split, splashing, strain, straps, shrink, screw, shred, sprout, throb, sprang, screech, sprawl, script, through, shriek, straighten, thrill, threaten,* and *strictly.*

Extension

- Choose one word from each column.
- Use all six words in one sentence. Repeat this exercise two more times.

Things you need:
- pen and paper

str	thr	spr	shr	scr	spl

For additional vocabulary and spelling games, go to www.macmillanmh.com

16

Literacy Workstations

Reading   Phonics/Word Study   Writing   Science/Social Studies

Literacy Workstation Flip Charts

Writing

Objectives

- Write and illustrate a personal narrative
- Practice writing with vivid words
- Write precise directions and instructions

Writing — The Great Outdoors
20 Minutes

- Write a personal narrative about an outdoor experience, such as a hike or a bicycle ride that you enjoyed.
- Tell about your experience. Use vivid words that express your feelings.

Extension

- Illustrate your narrative. Share it with your classmates.

Things you need:
- pen and paper
- colored pencils

15

Writing — Step-by-Step
20 Minutes

- Think about your favorite activity and write a paragraph that tells how to do this activity. First explain what the activity is. Then describe how to do it in steps.
- Use sequence words such as *first, next, then,* and *finally.*

Extension

- Draw a picture of yourself doing your favorite activity. Write a caption under the picture.

first, next, then, and finally

Things you need:
- pen and paper
- colored pencils or markers

16

Content Literacy

Objectives

- Research inventions that help people with physical challenges
- Research how computers help people with physical challenges

---

Science — Helpful Inventions
20 Minutes

- Use the Internet to find out who invented braille.
- Now research the wheelchair. How has it changed over the years? Record the information you find.

Extension

- What would you invent to help people with physical challenges? Draw your invention and write about how it works.

Things you need:
- online resources
- pen and paper
- colored pencils or markers

15

Social Studies — Computers Today
20 Minutes

- Use the Internet to find out how computers help people with physical disabilities.
- Write a report about your findings. Have a partner check your report for correct grammar, spelling, and punctuation.

Extension

- Write a short paragraph about why computers are so important.

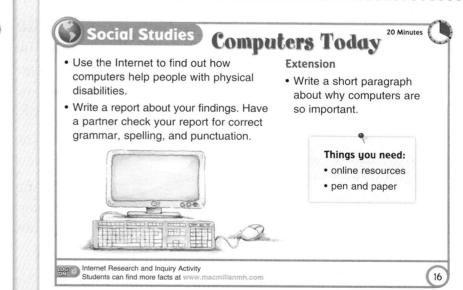

Things you need:
- online resources
- pen and paper

LOG ON Internet Research and Inquiry Activity
Students can find more facts at www.macmillanmh.com

16

Prepare

WHOLE GROUP

ORAL LANGUAGE
- Build Background
- Connect to Theme
- Read Aloud

✔ **PHONICS/WORD STUDY**
- Three-Letter Blends

✔ **VOCABULARY**
- Idioms
- Teach Words

✔ **COMPREHENSION**
- Strategy: Monitor Comprehension
- Skill: Main Idea and Details

SMALL GROUP

- Differentiated Instruction,
  pp. 199M–199LL

Oral Language

Build Background

ACCESS PRIOR KNOWLEDGE

Share the following information: People with physical challenges can enjoy athletic activities and may even compete at a very high level. Many are able to play sports with adapted rules and equipment, such as the special wheelchairs used by the racers in the photograph.

Write these words on the board, and briefly define each one using the **Define/Example/Ask** routine: **adapt** (change based on circumstances), **equipment** (gear used for an activity), **victory** (win). Ask: *What adaptations, or adjustments, can help people with*

Talk About It

What does it take to face challenges in life?

LOG ON ▶ VIEW IT

**Oral Language Activities
Facing Challenges**
www.macmillanmh.com

188

physical challenges take part in sports?

FOCUS QUESTION Ask students to read "Talk About It" on **Student Book** page 188. Then have them turn to a partner and describe the photo. Ask:

- Which racer do you think will achieve a victory, or a win? Why?

- What special equipment, or gear, are these athletes using to help them?

TIME FOR KIDS

Facing Challenges

189

Use the Picture Prompt

BUILD WRITING FLUENCY

Ask students to write in their Writer's Notebooks about facing life challenges. Have them write as much as they can for eight minutes. During Writing Conference time provide feedback and revision assignments. Students should self-correct any errors they notice prior to the conference.

Connect to the Unit Theme

DISCUSS THE BIG IDEA

People can make a difference in the lives of those with physical challenges through advancements in technology or by simply lending a hand.

Ask students what they have learned about ways one can make a difference.

- How have some of the people we have read about made a difference? What challenges have they faced?

- How might people who have faced physical challenges make a difference and inspire others?

USE THEME FOLDABLES

Write the **Big Idea** statement on the board. Ask students to copy it on their Unit Theme Foldables. Remind them to add details as they complete this week's readings.

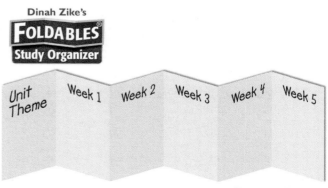

Dinah Zike's
FOLDABLES Study Organizer

Unit Theme | Week 1 | Week 2 | Week 3 | Week 4 | Week 5

Accordion Book

ELL ENGLISH LANGUAGE LEARNERS

Beginning	Intermediate	Advanced
Use Visuals Tell students about the photograph. *The people are in a race. The woman is very happy. She has finished the race.* Then ask students to tell you what the people are doing. Repeat correct answers in a louder and slower voice so the rest of the class may hear.	**Describe** Ask students to tell what the people in the photograph are doing. *What are the people doing? What kind of equipment do they use? How have they met challenges?* Repeat the responses, correcting grammar and pronunciation as needed.	**Discuss** Ask students to discuss how the athletes in the photograph have adapted to meet challenges. Elicit details from students to clarify their responses.

Objectives

- Identify the characteristics of a biography
- Develop vocabulary
- Read sentences fluently, focusing on accuracy

Materials

- Read-Aloud Anthology, pp. 72–76

Read Aloud

Read "William 'Dummy' Hoy: Baseball's Silent Hero"

Read Aloud

GENRE: Literary Nonfiction/Biography

Share with students the following key characteristics of a **biography**:

- A biography is a true story about a person's life written by another person.
- A biography is usually about a person who has made a difference or done something unique or noteworthy.

FOCUS ON VOCABULARY

Introduce the following words, using the **Define/Example/Ask** routine. Tell students that knowing these words will help them better understand the life of William Hoy, the subject of the biography.

Vocabulary Routine

Use the routines below to discuss the meaning of each word.

Define: A **cobbler** is someone who fixes shoes.
Example: When Mom broke the heel on her shoe, the cobbler fixed it.
Ask: Why would a cobbler need to be good with his or her hands?

Define: A **feat** is a noteworthy act that usually requires skill or daring.
Example: Walking a tightrope is a feat.
Ask: Which would more likely be a feat: splashing in a puddle or diving off a high diving board? Why?

Define: Something that is done **en masse** is done by a whole group.
Example: At lunchtime, our class goes to the cafeteria en masse.
Ask: What is something people do en masse during the summertime?

LISTENING FOR A PURPOSE

Ask students to listen carefully as you read "William 'Dummy' Hoy: Baseball's Silent Hero" on **Read-Aloud Anthology** pages 72–76. Use the Think Alouds and Genre Study prompts provided.

ELL **Interactive Reading** Build students' oral language by engaging them in talk about the biography's basic meaning.

- Point to the drawings and identify each player: umpire, batter, catcher. Have students repeat the names.

- After the second paragraph, say: *Turn to your partner and tell why Hoy went deaf.*

- After the fifth paragraph, say: *William Hoy came up with hand signals. Show me a hand signal.*

- After the last paragraph, say: *Tell your partner how Hoy was physically challenged and why baseball owes so much to him.*

Think/Pair/Share Use **Copying Master 6**, "I thought _____ was important in this text because . . . ," to help students summarize what they learned about the important events in William Hoy's life. When completed, have students turn to a partner and orally summarize the selection. Have a few students share their summaries with the class.

RESPOND TO THE BIOGRAPHY

Ask students the Think and Respond questions on page 76. Have students share what is inspiring about William Hoy. Then encourage them to list other athletes they admire and explain why they are inspired by them.

Model Fluency

Reread the biography. Tell students that this time you want them to focus on one aspect of how you read the text—your **accuracy**.

Explain that when you read accurately, you pronounce each word correctly. You do not skip words or sentences, and you do not change the words the author wrote. Model an example.

Think Aloud Listen as I read the part that explains William Hoy's nickname, "Dummy." First I'm going to read this paragraph accurately. Now listen as I read it and skip a word: *William said that his nickname bothered him.*
When I accidentally skip the word *never* in the sentence *William said that his nickname never bothered him,* it completely changes the meaning of the text. It is important to read with accuracy so that you can understand what you read and avoid changing the author's meaning. Now you try. Repeat each sentence after me, with the same accuracy as I read it.

Establish Fluency Focus Remind students that you will be listening for this same quality in their reading throughout the week. You will help them improve their reading by giving them multiple opportunities to read the same text in order to improve their accuracy.

Objective

- Decode multisyllabic words with three-letter blends

Materials

- Practice Book, p. 64
- Word-Building Cards
- Transparency 8
- Teacher's Resource Book, p. 127

ELL

Transfer Sounds Students who speak Asian languages may need extra practice pronouncing words with the three-letter blends *scr, spr,* and *str.* Emphasize the individual sounds in each blend, and model blending the sounds together. Contrast words such as *Spain/sprain,* and *sting/string.* Use the Approaching Level lesson on page 199N to contrast words with digraphs and three-letter blends. See language transfers on pages T16–T31.

Practice Book, page 64

In some **three-letter blends,** you hear the sounds of the three consonants, as in **scrape** and **strain.** Sometimes, a three-letter blend is formed by a digraph and a third consonant, as in **shrug** and **thread.**

A. Circle the three-letter blend at the beginning of each word.

1. (spl)endid
2. (shr)ink
3. (thr)one
4. (str)eam
5. (spl)ash

6. (thr)ead
7. (shr)imp
8. (scr)unch
9. (spl)it
10. (thr)ough

B. Read the paragraph below. Circle six words that begin with a three-letter blend. Then continue the story. Use at least two words that begin with a three-letter blend and circle the words.

It was the first swim meet of the (spring) season. Juan climbed onto the starting block at the edge of the pool. He (shrugged) his shoulders to loosen his muscles, then plunged into the water, hardly making a (splash) As his (strong) arms cut (through) the water, he saw his closest opponent about (three) feet behind him.

Possible response.
Juan was tired, but he (strained) to keep swimming fast.

Water (sprayed) from his kicking feet.

Approaching Reproducible, page 64

Beyond Reproducible, page 64

Phonics

✓ Three-Letter Blends

EXPLAIN/MODEL

Tell students that three consonants at the beginning of a word form a three-letter blend, or a consonant cluster. Some common three-letter blends, or clusters, include *shr, thr, spr, scr, spl,* and *str.* The cluster may begin with a digraph, such as *sh,* or a blend, such as *sp.* The final letter of three-letter blends is often *r* or *l.* To pronounce these clusters, blend the sounds of the consonants together. Write *shred* on the board.

Think Aloud I see that *shred* begins with the digraph *sh. Sh* is pronounced /sh/. Then I must blend the *r* before I get to the final sound—/sh-r-ed/. After I blend each sound slowly, I blend them together more quickly to read the word *shred.* This sounds like a word I know.

PRACTICE/APPLY

Read the Word List Display **Transparency 8**. The first three lines contain words with three-letter blends that students will encounter in the upcoming selections. Have students underline the three-letter blend in each word. Then have them chorally read the words.

strong	street	shrug	spray
through	thrash	scrap	scrub
split	string	splurge	splash
shed	shred	shriek	shrink
spring	spruce	stay	stray
scratch	scream	throw	three

Phonics Transparency 8

Sort the Words Ask students to sort the words by spelling pattern. Then have them write the word sort in their Writer's Notebooks.

shr	thr	spr	scr	spl	str

✓ Read Multisyllabic Words

TRANSITION TO LONGER WORDS Help students transition from reading one-syllable to multisyllabic words with three-letter blends. Have students read the word in the first column. Model reading the longer word in the second column. Point out the added syllable(s), such as a prefix or suffix, to help students gain an awareness of these common word parts.

through	throughout	shrink	shrinking
stretch	stretching	spread	spreading
splat	splatter	scribe	inscribe
scrape	skyscraper	strain	unstrained
splint	splinter	spray	hairspray
throw	throwing	straw	strawberry

Phonics Transparency 8

BUILD WORDS Use **Word-Building Cards** *scr, spl, spr, str, thr, ay, ash, eet, eam, een,* and *ow.* Display the cards. Have students use the word parts to build as many words with three-letter blends as possible. These and other words can be formed: *scream, spleen, thrash, throw.*

APPLY DECODING STRATEGY Help students use the Decoding Strategy to decode: *splendor, thrilled, inscription, threshold, sprinter, stranded.* Write each word on the board. Remind students to look for three-letter blends and to use steps 2 and 3 of the Decoding Strategy procedure to identify prefixes and suffixes.

Build Fluency

SPEED DRILL Distribute copies of the **Three-Letter Blends Speed Drill** on **Teacher's Resource Book** page 127. Use the Speed Drill routine to help students become fluent reading words with three-letter blends.

Quick Check

Can students read words with three-letter blends?

During **Small Group Instruction**

Tier 2

If No → **Approaching Level** Reteach the skill using the lesson on p. 199N.

If Yes → **On Level** Consolidate the learning using p. 199W.

Beyond Level Extend the learning using p. 199AA.

DAILY Syllable Fluency

Use Word-Building Cards 71–80. Display one card at a time. Have students chorally read each common syllable. Repeat at varying speeds and in random order. Have students work with partners during independent time to write as many words as they can containing each syllable.

Decoding Strategy

Decoding Strategy Chart

Step 1	Look for word parts (prefixes) at the beginning of the word.
Step 2	Look for word parts (suffixes) at the end of the word.
Step 3	In the base word, look for familiar spelling patterns. Think about the six syllable-spelling patterns you have learned.
Step 4	Sound out and blend together the word parts.
Step 5	Say the word parts fast. Adjust your pronunciation as needed. Ask yourself: "Is this a word I have heard before?" Then read the word in the sentence and ask: "Does it make sense in this sentence?"

© Macmillan/McGraw-Hill

Vocabulary

STRATEGY
IDIOMS

Tell students that an idiom is a figurative expression whose meaning cannot be determined from the meanings of its individual words. To determine the meaning of an idiom, they must use the surrounding words and phrases and think about how they have heard the expression used before.

Point to the idiom *be held back* in the fourth paragraph on **Student Book** page 190. Then model for students how to use the surrounding words and their prior knowledge to determine the meaning of the expression *be held back*.

Think Aloud To figure out the meaning of *be held back*, I will look for clues in the surrounding sentences. The sentence before this idiom tells me that Paralympians are world-class athletes. I know that Paralympians have physical challenges, so their challenges must not stop them from becoming great athletes. I think *be held back* means "be prevented or stopped." This meaning makes sense. I've heard people say "something held me back" when they have had doubts about doing something.

Read "The Paralympics"

As you read "The Paralympics" with students, ask them to identify clues that reveal the meanings of the highlighted words. Tell students they will read these words again in *Making a Splash*.

Vocabulary

similar	achieved
challenges	varied
designed	

The Paralympics

Mono-skiing lets a paralyzed skier go down a hill while sitting.

A special group of athletes prepare for the Paralympic Games at the same time athletes prepare for the Olympic Games.

The Paralympics are for athletes with physical disabilities. When the Paralympics began in 1960, 400 athletes from 23 countries took part. Time flies. In the Paralympic Games, 44 years later, 3,806 athletes from 136 countries competed.

In the Paralympics, athletes compete with others who have the same type of disability. They take part in athletic events **similar** to those that Olympic athletes compete in. However, Paralympians use special equipment designed for their disabilities.

One of the goals of the Paralympic Games is to change the way the public views people with disabilities. Paralympians are world-class athletes. They don't shy away from **challenges**, nor do they let themselves be held back.

American mono-skier Muffy Davis competes in the women's slalom. At 16, a skiing accident left her legs paralyzed. At first, Muffy refused to ski again. Then, she did an about-face. "The limits we have are the ones we put on ourselves," she says.

Athletes from Germany took part in the opening ceremonies of the 2004 Winter Paralympics.

190

ELL

Preteach Vocabulary See pages 199FF and 199O to preteach the vocabulary words to **ELL** and **Approaching Level** students. Use the **Visual Vocabulary Resources** to demonstrate and discuss each word. To further reinforce concepts, have students complete page 84 in the **ELL Resource Book**.

HOMEWORK **Practice Book,** page 65

similar	challenges	designed
achieved	varied	

A. Write a complete sentence to answer each question below. In your answer, use the vocabulary word in bold type.
Possible answers provided.

1. Why do you think goalball might be **similar** to soccer?
   Goalball might be *similar* to soccer because players try to get a ball into a goal.

2. What is one of the **challenges** that an athlete with physical disabilities might face? One of the *challenges* might be that the person cannot see well.

3. What kind of equipment might be specially **designed** for an athlete in the Paralympics? A wheelchair might be *designed* for an athlete in the Paralympics.

4. What are two of the **varied** games included in the Paralympics? Two of the *varied* games are boccia and ice sledge hockey.

5. What is something that you **achieved** in the past last year? I *achieved* my goal of learning how to play the flute.

B. Now use one of the words above in a sentence of your own.

6. Possible response: My brother and I have similar haircuts.

Approaching Reproducible, page 65
Beyond Reproducible, page 65

The Ride of His Life

California native Alejandro Abor builds handcycles. These bikes are **designed** and made for people who can't use their legs. They are powered by hand pedals.

Alejandro is also a handcycle rider. He lost both of his legs in an accident, but he wanted to continue playing sports. Alejandro learned how to do things without his legs. He taught himself to kayak and to play basketball. He even competed in difficult triathlons.

For years, Alejandro continued training. Today he is a handcycling champion on the U.S. Paralympic Cycling Elite Team. In the 2004 Paralympic Games, he won a silver medal.

Alejandro inspires others to do their best. He talks to people about disabilities and builds handcycles for kids with physical challenges. He also is a great dad to his three children. Through hard work, Alejandro has **achieved** his dreams.

In 2006, Abor won a 267-mile handcycle-wheelchair race.

Good Sports

Football 5-a-side players compete for the ball.

Paralympian sports are **varied**. Many are familiar to most people, such as track and field or skiing. Some sports, like those mentioned below, are just a little different.

Football 5-a-side—In this soccer game, each team has five players who are either blind or vision-impaired. The ball makes a noise when it moves.

Wheelchair Rugby—The goal of this very physical game is for players in wheelchairs to carry a ball over the opponent's goal line.

Ice sledge hockey—Players with lower limb disabilities sit in sleds. They use two short hockey sticks to push themselves around the ice.

191

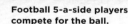

Quick Check

Can students identify word meanings?

During **Small Group Instruction**

Tier 2

If No → **Approaching Level** Reteach the words using the Vocabulary lesson, pp. 199O–199P.

If Yes → **On Level** Consolidate the learning using p. 199W.

Gifted Talented

Beyond Level Extend the learning using p. 199AA.

Vocabulary

TEACH WORDS

Introduce each word using the **Define/Example/Ask** routine. Model reading each word using the syllable-scoop technique.

Vocabulary Routine

Define: When things are **similar**, they are like each other in many ways.
Example: My sister and I look similar because we are both tall with brown hair and brown eyes.
Ask: What are some ways that basketball and soccer are similar? EXPLANATION

- **Challenges** are difficult situations that require a special effort. *High temperatures and a lack of water are some of the challenges of living in a desert.* What are some challenges faced by new students? EXAMPLE

- If you **designed** something, you planned it or created it for a specific purpose. *A sports car is designed to be fast.* Describe the best thing you have ever designed. DESCRIPTION

- If you **achieved** something, you reached your goal. *Luis studied hard and achieved an A on his vocabulary test.* What is the opposite of the word *achieved*? ANTONYM

- Something that is **varied** includes different kinds of that thing. *The grocery store has a varied selection of fruits and vegetables.* What sort of varied collection would you like to have? EXPLANATION

Objectives

- Monitor comprehension
- Identify the main idea and supporting details
- Use academic language: *main idea, details, explicit, implied, monitor comprehension*

Materials

- Transparency 8
- Practice Book, p. 66

Skills Trace

Main Idea and Details

Introduce	191A–191B
Practice/ Apply	192–195; Practice Book, 66–67
Reteach/ Review	199Q–199DD, 545A–545B, 546–563, 569M–569Z; Practice Book, 183–184
Assess	Weekly Tests; Units 2, 5 Tests
Maintain	219B, 601A–601B, 602–605, 609Q–609DD, 631B

ELL

Academic Language
Preteach the following academic language words to **ELL** and **Approaching Level** students during small group time: *main idea, supporting details, explicit, implied*. See pages 199EE and 199M.

Reread for Comprehension

STRATEGY
MONITOR COMPREHENSION

What Is It? When students monitor their comprehension they are making sure they understand what they read. They may pause and ask themselves questions about the text, summarize, or paraphrase.

Why Is It Important? Point out that monitoring comprehension can help students self-correct to make sense of their reading. To improve comprehension one can reread, adjust reading rate, or visualize.

SKILL
MAIN IDEA AND DETAILS

What Is It? The **main idea** is the most important point an author makes, or what a selection is mostly about. To determine the main idea, students examine the details by asking what the sentences in a text tell about or describe. Then they decide what these **details** have in common, or how they are connected.

Why Is It Important? Determining the main idea in a passage or selection can help students summarize what they have read. Summarizing the selection will help students comprehend and clarify the reading.

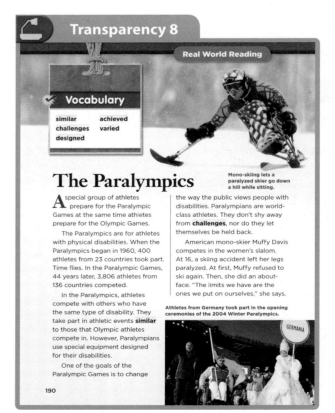

Student Book page 190 available on Comprehension Transparency 8

- The main idea is sometimes **explicit**, or stated in the text. Usually, however, the main idea is **implied**, or not directly stated in the text.

- Whether or not the main idea is directly stated, students must still ask themselves what the sentences in the paragraph or passage have in common, and classify these details to determine the main idea. They can then summarize the main ideas and supporting details in a text in ways that maintain meaning. Point out that this will help students remember the most important information.

MODEL

How Do I Use It? Read aloud the first three paragraphs of "The Paralympics" on **Student Book** page 190.

Think Aloud I see that the Paralympics is the topic of this article. After reading the first three paragraphs, I will ask myself what the sentences in these paragraphs explain or describe, and look for the important details. This will help me find the main idea. Let's see. The Paralympics are held at the same time as the Olympics, and they began in 1960. They are for athletes with physical disabilities. Athletes compete with others who have the same disabilities using special equipment. All these details give information about the Paralympics and what they are. So this is what the passage is mostly about: The Paralympics are like the Olympics except they are for athletes with physical disabilities. This is the main idea.

GUIDED PRACTICE

Help students use this thinking process to determine the main idea of the passage "The Ride of His Life." (This passage is mostly about Alejandro Abor, a handcycle rider who competes on the U.S. Paralympic Cycling Team.)

APPLY

Have students determine the main idea of "Good Sports." (This passage is mostly about the different kinds of Paralympian sports.) Then ask students to write a summary of "Good Sports" that includes the most important details.

Quick Check

Can students identify main ideas and supporting details?

During Small Group Instruction

Tier 2

If No → Approaching Level Reteach the skill using the Comprehension lesson, pp. 199Q–199T.

If Yes → On Level Consolidate the learning using pp. 199Y–199Z.

Beyond Level Extend the learning using pp. 199CC–199DD.

HOMEWORK **Practice Book,** page 66

The **main idea** is what a paragraph is mostly about. A main idea can be **explicit**, or stated at the beginning of the paragraph. A main idea can also be **implied**, meaning that readers must think about how the details in the text are related.

Read the passage. Then answer the questions below.

Beep Baseball is a lot like baseball. It uses a ball. It uses bases. It has two teams. The players use a bat to hit the ball.

Unlike players on baseball teams, the players on Beep Baseball teams are sighted and non-sighted people. The sport is played with a big ball and a big bat. There are only two bases, which look like soft towers.

When a batter hits a ball, one of the bases begins to beep loudly. The batter runs toward the sound. If the batter can reach the base before someone throws a ball to the base, his or her team scores a point.

1. What is the main idea of the first paragraph?
Beep Baseball is a lot like baseball.

2. Is that main idea explicit or implied?
explicit

3. What is a detail that supports that main idea?
Possible response: The players use a bat to hit the ba

4. The main idea of the second paragraph is implied, or not stated. What is the main idea of this paragraph?
Possible response: In some ways, Beep Baseball is different from baseball.

5. Is the main idea of the third paragraph explicit or implied?
implied

6. What would be a good main idea sentence for the third paragraph?
Possible response: This is how Beep Baseball is played.

Approaching Reproducible, page 66
Beyond Reproducible, page 66

Read

WHOLE GROUP

MAIN SELECTION
- *Making a Splash*
- Skill: Main Idea and Details

TEST PRACTICE
- "Standing Tall"
- Answering Questions

SMALL GROUP

- Differentiated Instruction, pp. 199M–199LL

Main Selection

GENRE: Informational Text/Expository

Have a student read the definition of Expository article on **Student Book** page 192. Remind students to pay attention to text features, such as subheadings, photos, and captions.

STRATEGY
MONITOR COMPREHENSION

Remind students to **monitor comprehension** to assess their understanding of what they read. Based on their assessment, they may ask for help, adjust their reading rate, reread for clarification, or take notes.

SKILL
MAIN IDEA AND DETAILS

Remind students that to find the **main idea** they must ask themselves what the sentences in a paragraph or passage have in common, tell about, explain, or describe.

Comprehension

Genre

An **Expository** article in a newspaper or magazine presents facts and information.

Monitor Comprehension

Main Idea and Details
To find the main idea of an article, first identify the most important details. Then decide what these details have in common.

192

Making a Splash

How does a person with physical disabilities become a world-champion athlete?

Rudy Garcia-Tolson is not an ordinary athlete. He holds world records for swimming, running, and biking. He takes part in top competitions around the world, where all eyes are on him. This talented athlete has won many medals and honors. There is one other thing special about Rudy: He has no legs.

Rudy was born in Bloomington, California, with a serious illness. He went through 15 operations as a baby. At five years old, Rudy and his family had to make a big decision. Rudy's legs could no longer function. He could keep his legs and stay in a wheelchair or he could walk with artificial legs. Rudy knew what he wanted; he chose to walk. The brave five-year-old had his legs amputated. From that point on, Rudy's life was never the same.

Vocabulary

Vocabulary Words Review the tested vocabulary words: **similar, challenges, designed, achieved**, and **varied**.

Additional Selection Words Students may be unfamiliar with these words. Pronounce the words, give student-friendly explanations as needed, and help students use the previously taught vocabulary strategies: word parts, context clues, dictionary.

artificial (p. 192): made by humans

amputated (p. 192): removed or cut off, often by surgery

triathlon (p. 193): a three-part athletic event, usually consisting of running, biking, and swimming

flume (p. 194): a channel through which water flows

treadmill (p. 194): an exercise machine used for running in place

Flying in the Water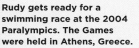

After his operation, Rudy took swimming lessons. He joined a local swim team and soon competed in races. By the time he was eight, Rudy had earned 43 ribbons and 13 medals for swimming. At the age of ten, he completed his first triathlon. Rudy didn't let physical **challenges** get in the way of his dreams. He **achieved** every goal he set. Rudy won many awards for running and biking. "I'm unstoppable," the young Rudy often said.

Now Rudy is a swimmer for the U.S. Paralympic Elite Team. In 2004, Rudy won a gold medal for swimming in the Athens Paralympic Games. In 2006 he finished an Ironman triathlon. Rudy continues to train hard for future Paralympic Games.

Rudy Garcia-Tolson carries the Olympic Flame during the 2002 Salt Lake Olympic Torch Relay in San Francisco, California.

Rudy gets ready for a swimming race at the 2004 Paralympics. The Games were held in Athens, Greece.

193

Read the Main Selection

Preteach	Read Together	Read Independently
Have Approaching Level students and English Language Learners listen to the selection on **StudentWorks Plus**, and use the **ELL Resource Book**, pages 82–83, before reading with the class.	Use the prompts to guide comprehension and model how to complete the graphic organizer. Have students use **Think/Pair/Share** to discuss the selection.	If students can read the selection independently, have them read and complete the graphic organizer. Suggest that they use their purposes to choose their reading strategies.

LOG ON StudentWorks *Plus*
Interactive Student Book

Preview and Predict

QUICK WRITE Ask students to read the title, preview the photographs and subheads, think about the genre, and write predictions about the kind of information the text will contain.

Set Purposes

FOCUS QUESTION Discuss the question under the title of the article on **Student Book** page 192.

Point out the Main Idea Chart on **Practice Book** page 67. Students will use it to help them identify main ideas and supporting details in this article.

Read *Making a Splash*

Use the questions and Think Alouds to support instruction about the comprehension strategy and skill.

1 STRATEGY
MONITOR COMPREHENSION

Teacher Think Aloud While **monitoring** my **comprehension**, I realize I am confused by all the numbers in the first paragraph. I decide to reread the paragraph and take notes, writing down what Rudy accomplished at different ages. Why might taking notes also help me understand the next paragraph?

PARTNERS

Prompt students to apply the strategy in a Think Aloud by considering how taking notes might be helpful.

Student Think Aloud The next paragraph lists a number of Rudy's achievements. It is difficult to keep track of what he did when. Writing down the information will help me follow the sequence of events.

Develop Comprehension

2 SKILL
MAIN IDEA AND DETAILS

How are all the details in "Leg Work" connected? What do they have in common? **(They are all about how Rudy uses different parts of his body. Rudy does not use his artificial legs for surfing and swimming. He uses different feet and legs for running and biking.) Based on this information, what is the main idea of "Leg Work"? (Rudy relies on different body parts for different activities.) Add this information to your Main Idea and Details Chart.**

Detail
Rudy does not use his artificial legs for surfing and swimming but relies on his upper body.
Detail
Rudy chooses his feet and legs depending on the activity.
Detail
Rudy uses different feet and legs for running and biking.
Main Idea
Rudy relies on different body parts for different activities.

3 AUTHOR'S PURPOSE

SPIRAL REVIEW

The author describes a special swimming flume. What is the author's purpose in including this information, and is this purpose stated or implied? **(The author's purpose is to give information about the flume and to tell how the flume helps athletes with their training. It is implied, because the text does not directly state the author's purpose.)**

Leg Work

When Rudy swims or surfs, he doesn't use artificial legs. He relies on his strong upper body in the water. He chooses his feet and legs depending on his activity. He also uses different feet and legs for running and cycling.

2 Rudy rides a bike in a special wind tunnel. It helps him test how well his prosthetic legs work.

Going for the Gold

Rudy lives at the Olympic Training Center in Colorado. The center is **designed** to train Olympic athletes for the Games. Rudy and other swimmers use a state-of-the-art swimming pool. Here, swimmers learn to go the extra mile—literally! Underwater cameras film the athletes as they swim. Athletes and coaches study the film to help the swimmers train better.

Olympic swimmers also train in a swimming flume. The flume is like a swimming treadmill that contains 50,000 gallons of water. The water current can be adjusted for each swimmer. The altitude, or height, of the flume can also be changed. Swimmers can train in **3** conditions **similar** to sea level or to more than a mile above sea level.

This **varied** type of technology helps athletes get better and stronger. Rudy knows he'll be ready to go for the gold at future Games. "A brave heart is a powerful weapon," he says.

194

Working for Others

Rudy's feet are made of carbon fiber, a light material that bends easily. The carbon fiber feet perform like human feet. They bend and help push the body forward. They also absorb shock from walking and running.

People who use artificial legs work with prosthetists. They are doctors who help people choose artificial legs. Rudy and his prosthetist have been working together since he was a child.

The doctor studies new artificial legs and feet. Rudy tests them out during training and racing. Sometimes things go wrong with the legs. They may be uncomfortable. His body may hurt after long races. Rudy and his doctor work together to fix the problems. Over the years, their research has made artificial legs better for all people.

Rudy swam to a world record in the 12th Paralympic Games in Athens.

Think and Compare

1. What did Rudy achieve in 2006?

2. Why are Rudy's artificial feet able to bend?

3. What is this article mainly about? Use details from the text to support your answer.

4. What do the athletes in "The Paralympics" and "Making a Splash" have in common?

195

ELL

The nonfiction writing frames are especially useful for English Language Learners when speaking and writing because they focus on transition words. Suggest all students use these frames when presenting information to the class.

Reproducible, page 173

Description Writing Frame

Summarize "Making a Splash." Use the Description Writing Frame below.

Rudy Garcia-Tolson has become a world-champion athlete.

To be a great swimmer, he _____

_____

_____

_____

He also _____

_____

_____

_____

In addition, his legs and feet _____

_____

_____

_____

All of these things have helped make him an Olympic champion!

Rewrite the completed summary on another sheet of paper. Keep it as a model for writing a summary of an article or selection using this text structure.

Develop Comprehension

TEST PREP

Comprehension Check

SUMMARIZE

Have students summarize the selection using the Nonfiction Text Structure Writing Frame Reproducible on **Teacher's Resource Book** page 173. Have them use their Main Idea Charts to help complete their summaries.

THINK AND COMPARE
Text Evidence

1. **Details** Answer stated in text In 2006 Rudy finished an Ironman triathlon. LOCATE

2. **Cause and Effect** Answer stated in text They are able to bend because they are made of carbon fiber, a light, bendable material. COMBINE

3. **Main Idea and Details** Answer Although Rudy Garcia-Tolson has a physical disability, it does not hold him back. Evidence Rudy has no legs, yet he is a world-class athlete, winning numerous medals in swimming, and competing in triathlons, where he has to swim, run, and bike. CONNECT

4. **Text-to-Text** They have physical disabilities, but they are great athletes. They train hard, may use special equipment, and compete in events similar to those in which athletes without special needs participate. COMPARE TEXT

Objectives
- Read fluently and accurately
- 84–104 WCPM

Materials
- Transparency 8
- Practice Book, p. 68
- Fluency Solutions Audio CD

ELL

Develop Comprehension
Explain that this passage describes a difficult decision Rudy had to make. Explain that when people make a decision, they usually have to choose between two or more options. Point out the conjunction *or* and explain that it indicates the two options. Explain the two options to students. Then have students tell which option Rudy chose. If a student's response is correct, repeat it slowly and clearly for the class to hear.

Practice Book, page 68

As I read, I will focus on reading accurately.

	"Are we there yet?" Jamal asked, crossing his arms
9	across his chest.
12	"Almost, honey," his mom replied. "Look out the
20	window. Isn't it beautiful?"
24	Jamal didn't answer, but he did look. Out his mom's
34	window, all he could see was a rising, rocky cliff. Out his
46	own window, the cliff dropped down, and Jamal could see
56	the road winding below them. Below that were green
65	fields. A few houses and farms were scattered about.
74	The city was a long way away. It felt like they had been
87	driving forever.
89	They were driving up into the mountains to spend a
99	week at a ranch. His mom had lived at this ranch when
111	she was a little girl. "Some vacation," Jamal thought to
121	himself. 122

Comprehension Check

1. How does Jamal feel about his vacation? **Plot Development**
   Jamal is annoyed and feels far from his home in the city.
2. How does Jamal's mom feel about the vacation? **Plot Development**
   She is happy. She says the view is beautiful, and they are going to where she lived as a child.

	Words Read	–	Number of Errors	=	Words Correct Score
First Read		–		=	
Second Read		–		=	

Approaching Reproducible, page 68
Beyond Reproducible, page 68

Fluency

Repeated Reading: Accuracy

EXPLAIN/MODEL Tell students that they will be doing an echo-reading. Model reading **Transparency 8** for them fluently and accurately. Explain that when they read accurately, they read each word correctly and do not change the meaning of the text by skipping words or mispronouncing them.

Transparency 8

Rudy was born in Bloomington, California, with a serious illness. He went through 15 operations as a baby. At five years old, Rudy and his family had to make a big decision. Rudy's legs could no longer function. He could keep his legs and stay in a wheelchair or he could walk with artificial legs. Rudy knew what he wanted; he chose to walk. The brave five-year-old had his legs amputated. From that point on, Rudy's life was never the same.

Fluency (from *Making a Splash*, p. 192)

PRACTICE Model reading aloud the entire passage. Then read one sentence at a time, having students echo-read each sentence back. Finally, have students echo-read with a partner, allowing them to switch roles. Have students write down any mispronounced words.

DAILY FLUENCY Students will practice fluency using **Practice Book** page 68 or the **Fluency Solutions Audio CD**. The passage is recorded at a slow practice speed and a faster fluent speed.

Quick Check

Can students read fluently and accurately?

During **Small Group Instruction**

If No → **Approaching Level** Use the Fluency lesson and model, p. 199U.

If Yes → **On Level** See Fluency, p. 199X.

Beyond Level See Fluency, p. 199BB.

Comprehension

SPIRAL REVIEW

REVIEW SKILL
AUTHOR'S PURPOSE

EXPLAIN/MODEL

Remind students that an **author's purpose** is his or her main reason for writing. Authors usually write to entertain, inform, or persuade. Thinking about the genre of a selection can help readers to determine the author's purpose.

- Authors sometimes create stories for readers' enjoyment, or to **entertain**. Fiction is usually written to entertain.

- Authors present facts and information about a topic when they want to **inform** readers. Nonfiction books and articles are written to inform. Authors may also describe a process or try to teach, as in textbooks, cookbooks, instructions, and manuals.

- Authors may try to **persuade**, or convince, the reader to do something or to think in a certain way. Speeches, letters, advertisements, and editorials are often written to persuade. Texts written to persuade will present the author's opinions, as well as supporting facts, and try to convince readers to agree.

Sometimes the author's purpose is stated in the text. Often, it is only implied, and students must use text evidence to figure it out. Model identifying the purpose of "The Ride of His Life" on **Student Book** page 191. Point out that the text gives dates and provides facts.

PRACTICE/APPLY

Guide students in identifying the author's purpose for writing *Making a Splash* by helping them recognize clues. Have them explain whether the purpose is stated or implied. Ask:

- What is the genre of *Making a Splash*? How do you know? (Expository; it tells facts and teaches about a real person.)

- Does *Making a Splash* have characters and a plot? Does the author try to persuade you to do something? Does the author teach how something is done or how something works? (no)

- What is the author's purpose for writing *Making a Splash*? (The author wants to inform.)

- How does the author feel about Rudy Garcia-Tolson? How can you tell? (The author admires him. The article describes Rudy as "a talented athlete" and "brave," and tells how he achieved his goals.)

PRACTICE BOOK See **Practice Book** page 69 for Author's Stated and Implied Purpose.

Objectives

- Use the parts of a book
- Use text features to gain an overview of the contents of text and find information

Materials

- Transparency 2
- Practice Book, p. 70

Study Skills

✔ Using Parts of a Book

EXPLAIN

Tell students that if they need to find information in a nonfiction book, they can use the **parts of a book** to help them. These organizational features are designed to make the information easier for readers to find quickly.

Discuss common parts of a nonfiction book and how to use them to locate information. Use any reference books available in the classroom to provide examples. Also point out that using the parts of a book will help students decide which book or books to use when having to choose from among possible sources.

- The **title page** is usually the first page and lists the title, author, illustrator, and publisher.

- The second page may be the **copyright page**, which tells when, where, and by whom the book was published. You can use it to check if the information in the book is current. Remember that to credit a source properly you will need to identify its author, title, publisher, and publication year. Open to the title and copyright pages of a book and find the book's author, title, publisher, and publication year.

- The **table of contents** is near the front of the book. It lists the chapter titles or sections of the book and the pages on which they begin. Scan the table of contents to see in which chapter or section you would find information.

- The **glossary** and **index** are at the back of the book. The glossary gives the meanings of important words found in the book and may also give their pronunciations and syllabications. The index lists the subjects covered (names, places, events, and topics) and gives page numbers where information can be found. Both sections are listed in alphabetical order. Use the guide words at the top of each page in a glossary to help you find any terms you are looking for.

- Some reference books may contain other special sections, such as a **preface** (a brief introductory section) or an **appendix** (a section in the back containing extra information, sometimes in the form of charts or diagrams).

- The text itself may contain **headings** and **subheadings**, which tell what each section is about. Scan these as well as any topic and concluding sentences to locate information quickly. Also look for bold or italicized words, which may help you find important terms.

MODEL

Display **Transparency 2**. Model how to use a table of contents and an index to locate information.

Transparency 2

Using Parts of a Book
Table of Contents

Chapter 1................. 5

China at a Glance

Chapter 2 25

History of Chinese Dynasties

Chapter 3 45

Understanding Chinese Culture

Chapter 4................. 80

China's Trade and Economy

Chapter 5 100

The Future of China

Index
M

Mandarin,................. 60

merchants,................ 74, 80–83

Ming Dynasty,.......... 30–33

money,...................... 40, 89

Mongols, ... 10–12

mountains,................ 77

Study Skills Transparency

Think Aloud I want to know if I can find more information about the money that the ancient Chinese used. I will use Transparency 2 to help me find this information. The table of contents of a book called *Ancient China* shows that Chapter 4 is titled "China's Trade and Economy" and begins on page 80. Since the term *economy* refers to money, I might find information about money there. Next, I look in the index to see if *money* is an entry. I see that it is, and it lists page numbers 40 and 89. I'll look on those pages first.

PRACTICE/APPLY

Have students use the transparency to answer the following questions: *In what chapter would you look for information about Chinese culture?* (Chapter 3) *In what chapter would you find information about the Ming Dynasty?* (Chapter 2) *On what pages?* (pages 30–33)

Remind students to keep careful track of the sources they use and discuss how to credit them properly by recording relevant materials on a source list. Have students create a sample citation, including the author, title, publisher, and publication year of the source.

Practice Book, page 70

Looking at the different parts of a book can help you figure out if the book will have the information you need. If you use a book as a source for a report, remember to note the author, title, publisher, and publication year.

title page	table of contents	index
glossary	headings	subheadings
copyright page		

Answer each question below by writing the name of the book part in the space provided.

1. What part of a book tells you the name of the author?
   title page

2. Where could you find the meaning of an unfamiliar word that was used in the book? **glossary**

3. Where would you look to see if a particular topic is in the book?
   index

4. What two book parts tell you what individual sections of a book are about?
   headings and subheadings

5. What part of the book tells you the names of chapters in the book?
   table of contents

6. Choose a book and identify the author, title, publisher, and year of publication.
   Responses will vary.

Approaching Reproducible, page 70

Beyond Reproducible, page 70

Test Practice

Answering Questions

EXPLAIN

Good test takers know how to answer the question that's asked.

- **Read the selection**.
- **Read** the **question** and all the **answers**.
- **Paraphrase** the question. Put it into your own words to make sure you understand what the question is asking.
- **Reread** or **scan** the selection to determine the best answer.
- Some answers are **stated**. An answer stated in one place is **right there**. When an answer is in two places, **think and search** to locate and combine the information.
- Sometimes the answer is **not stated**. **Connect** clues and evidence from the selection or **analyze** the text evidence to determine the answer.

MODEL

Remind students to record their answers on a separate sheet of paper.

Question 1 Read the question and all of the answer choices.

Think Aloud This question is asking for the best title for the web. I see that the web includes the following details: *Artificial leg, Bubble-like plastic, Heat gun,* and *Flesh-colored.* All of these details describe Grayson's invention and how he made it. When I **combine** these details, they tell me

---

Test Practice

Answering Questions

Right There answers are found in one place in the text. **Think and Search** answers are found in more than one place. **Author and Me** answers ask the reader to look for clues.

STANDING TALL

❶ Grayson Rosenberger creates some wild inventions. He once made a go-kart skateboard, but his family didn't think it was safe. However, there was one invention they really liked.

❷ Grayson created a covering for a prosthetic, or artificial leg. Some types of artificial legs are made of metal rods. Grayson used bubble-like plastic wrapping material and tape to cover the metal leg. Then he shaped the leg with a heat gun to make it look real.

❸ Artificial legs that look real are very expensive. Many amputees, people who no longer have their arms or legs, can't pay $1,000 to buy a real-looking leg, so they use metal legs. Grayson's invention costs $15 to make, so more people can afford it.

❹ Grayson's parents run Standing with Hope. This group provides artificial legs to people in Ghana, in Africa. Grayson remembers the story of Daniel, a boy in Ghana who received an artificial metal leg. It didn't have a covering. "He's made fun of in school," says Grayson. Grayson and his family are returning to Ghana, and Grayson's first priority is Daniel.

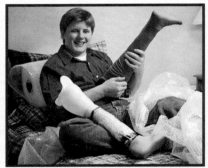

Grayson holds up his invention. One leg is covered only in plastic wrap. The other has a flesh-colored stocking to make it look real. A person who makes prosthetics for a living said, "It surprised me a kid came up with this."

196

Answering Questions

QAR Strategies

A good reader thinks about **question-answer relationships** and different ways to reread a text to answer questions.

Right There: The answer is stated in the text. You can locate the answer in one place.

Think and Search: The reader combines information stated in different parts of the text to find the answer.

Author and Me: The answer is not directly stated. The reader must infer the answer by finding clues in the text.

Use "Standing Tall" to answer questions 1–3.

1 Look at the following web of information from the article.

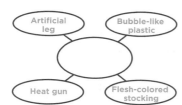

Artificial leg — Bubble-like plastic — Heat gun — Flesh-colored stocking

Which would be the best title for this web?

A Go-Kart Skateboard
B Grayson's Invention
C Standing with Hope
D Daniel in Ghana

2 Artificial legs that look real are —

F made in Africa
G difficult to use
H made of metal
J very expensive

3 Paragraph 4 is mainly about —

A Daniel, a boy in Ghana
B the go-kart skateboard
C Grayson's parents
D how much artificial legs cost

197

Monitor Comprehension

Self-Monitoring for Reading Comprehension

Ask yourself:

- Am I determining my answer by using personal experience instead of real proof from the selection?
- Am I adding information that is not connected to the selection to determine my answer?
- Can I prove my answer with text evidence?
- Is there a logical connection between my answer and the text evidence I am using to prove my answer?

that the best title for this web would be "Grayson's Invention." The best answer is B. **THINK AND SEARCH**

GUIDED PRACTICE

Question 2 Read the question and all of the answer choices. Ask: *How can you rephrase this incomplete sentence to turn it into a question?* (What is true about artificial legs that look real?) *Where in the selection can you **locate** information about artificial legs that look real?* (in the first sentence of the third paragraph) *What does the text say about these artificial legs?* (Artificial legs are very expensive.) *Which is the best answer?* (The best answer is J.) **RIGHT THERE**

APPLY

Have students answer Question 3.

Question 3 After students have determined an answer, ask: *What did this question ask you to do?* (to tell what the fourth paragraph is mainly about) *What evidence did you find to help you determine the main idea of the paragraph?* (Daniel, a boy in Ghana, received an artificial metal leg that did not have a covering. The children at school made fun of him. When Grayson and his family return to Ghana, his first priority will be Daniel.) *How did you **connect** this evidence to the **unstated answer**?* (Each detail tells about Daniel or things that happened to him, so paragraph 4 is mainly about a boy named Daniel who lives in Ghana. The best answer is A.) **AUTHOR AND ME**

Writing Prompt

EXPLAIN

Tell students that often when taking a test, they will be asked to write to a prompt. Explain that a prompt provides the context or **topic** for a specific writing assignment.

An effective composition is one that readers can understand. First you must determine the **purpose** of your writing. Then you can decide which **genre** or writing mode is most appropriate.

- You can write to entertain. (imaginative or personal narrative)

- You can write to explain or inform. (expository or procedural)

- You can write to influence. (persuasive)

MODEL

Determine the Topic and Purpose Read the prompt on page 198 of the **Student Book**. Explain that an expository composition is written to inform others about a topic. Expository writing gives facts, details, and explanations. Ask: *How can you tell what this composition is supposed to be about?* (Point out the words *job* and *skills*. This prompt tells students to write about a job that uses specific skills.) Ask: *What is the purpose of this piece?* (to provide information)

Determine the Genre or Writing Mode Ask: *What is the best way to accomplish this purpose?* (Since the prompt says to write about job skills, an expository composition is most appropriate.)

✎ Write to a Prompt

> Write a composition about a job that requires specific skills.

| Think about the purpose of the composition. | As you write your composition, think about how to clearly express your ideas. |

Below, see how one student begins a response to the prompt above.

The writer listed specific skills.

Explorers need special qualities and skills. They should like danger, traveling, and studying. It's hard to think of a more dangerous job than diving to the bottom of the ocean or digging in a dark chamber. Any problem could result in a serious injury or death. Like the explorer in "Adventures," explorers should probably go to college. They need to study a subject and become experts in their field. This way they can recognize things other people might not notice. A knowledge of their surroundings helps explorers while they are out working. A deep sea explorer should be able to see a fish and figure out if the fish is a threat.

198

Writing Prompt

Respond in writing to the prompt below. Review the hints below before and after you write.

> Write a composition about a job that interests you.

Writing Hints

☑ Remember to write about a job that interests you. Think about genre.

☑ Plan your writing by organizing your ideas.

☑ Include important details to support your ideas.

☑ Check that each sentence you write helps the reader to understand your ideas.

☑ Use correct spelling and punctuation.

☑ Review and edit your writing.

199

PRACTICE

Topic Have students read the writing prompt on **Student Book** page 199 and restate the topic.

Purpose The prompt asks students to write about a job that interests them. Students should write to inform.

Genre or Writing Mode This expository prompt asks students to write an informational piece. They should include facts and details.

APPLY

Writing Prompt Students can practice writing from the prompt, simulating a test-taking situation. Distribute paper for students' responses.

Tell students: *You may use scrap paper to think about and plan your composition before you begin to write. Use the Writing Hints to make sure you have followed all of the necessary steps for responding to the prompt.*

For a guided writing process lesson, see pages 199A–199F.

4-POINT SCORING RUBRIC			
4 Excellent	**3** Good	**2** Fair	**1** Unsatisfactory
Focus and Coherence Sustained focus shows sense of completeness and how ideas are related.	**Focus and Coherence** Focus generally shows sense of completeness and clear relationship between ideas.	**Focus and Coherence** Somewhat focused paragraphs and/or composition has some sense of completeness but may shift quickly from idea to idea.	**Focus and Coherence** Weak connection to prompt and abrupt shifts from idea to idea show lack of focus and little or no sense of completeness.
Organization Logical progression of thought, with meaningful transitions and effective presentation of ideas.	**Organization** Generally logical progression of thought, with mostly meaningful transitions and generally effective organizational strategy.	**Organization** Progression of thought may not be completely logical and requires more meaningful transitions; organizational strategy is not effective.	**Organization** Progression of thought is not logical, and transitions are minimal or lacking; no evidence of organizational strategy.
Development of Ideas Thorough, insightful, and specific development of ideas shows interesting connections and willingness to take compositional risks.	**Development of Ideas** Development of ideas may be thoughtful but shows little evidence of willingness to take compositional risks.	**Development of Ideas** Development of ideas, using lists or brief explanations, is superficial, inconsistent, or contrived.	**Development of Ideas** Development of ideas is general or vague.
Voice Authentic and original writing expresses unique perspective.	**Voice** Mostly authentic and original writing generally expresses unique perspective.	**Voice** Shows some authenticity or originality but has difficulty expressing unique perspective.	**Voice** Shows little or no sense of individual voice.
Conventions Demonstrates consistent command of spelling, capitalization, punctuation, grammar, usage, and sentence structure.	**Conventions** Generally demonstrates good command of spelling, capitalization, punctuation, grammar, usage, and sentence structure.	**Conventions** Demonstrates limited command of spelling, capitalization, punctuation, grammar, usage, and sentence structure.	**Conventions** Demonstrates little or no command of spelling, capitalization, punctuation, grammar, usage, and sentence structure.

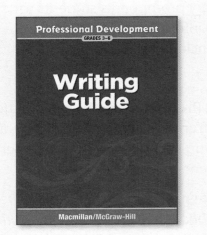

Professional Development
GRADES 3–6

Writing Guide

Macmillan/McGraw-Hill

How-To Article

✓ Plan/Prewrite

TEACH/MODEL

Define the Genre Tell students that a how-to article shows the reader how to do something. It includes steps that explain a process or a task. Discuss features of a how-to article.

Transparency 22

Features of a How-To Article

• A how-to article **explains**, or shows, how to do something.

• It begins with an introduction that identifies the **topic**, or task that will be explained.

• It contains **step-by-step directions**.

• It has specific **details** that show how to complete the steps.

• It uses **time-order** and **spatial words**.

Writing Transparency

Set the Purpose Explain that students are going to select a Writer's Notebook entry about something they enjoy doing and use it as a starting point for writing a how-to article. Remind students that they have been working on many different pieces of writing that show actions. In a few moments they will look at a how-to article that another student wrote. The author started out with a journal entry and revised it to make it a how-to article.

Consider the Audience In a how-to article, a writer describes how to do something in detail. The writer wants readers to be able to picture exactly what steps to follow and in what order. As students read the following how-to article, prompt them to think about the details that help them understand the steps.

DISCUSS THE STUDENT SAMPLE

Student Sample Display **Writing Transparency 23**. Read the journal entry aloud. Then display **Writing Transparencies 20** and **21**. Read the how-to article aloud. Discuss how the writer revised the journal entry to write the how-to article. Point out how the writer used details, ordered the steps, and included time-order and spatial words. Then, on chart paper or the board, write students' ideas about what makes the how-to article strong. Ask the following:

- *What does the writer explain in this article?* (how to make a paper airplane)

- *What is the first step in the process?* (fold your paper in half)

- *What details does the writer give to show you the step?* (the long way; press the paper down; slide your thumb)

- *What are some time-order and spatial words that the writer uses?* (first, after, now, then, next, finally; down, at the top, in the middle, over, half-inch from the point)

Select a Journal Entry Students can select one or two entries from their Writer's Notebooks. See Selecting Journal Entries for guidance on how to help students identify appropriate journal entries to take through the writing process.

Brainstorm Ideas Students can also select a new topic to write about. Have students work in pairs to brainstorm and discuss what they can write a how-to article about. Remind students to review the features of a how-to article to help them choose a topic.

Organize your Ideas Once students have chosen their topics, they can complete a Sequence Chart to record the steps they want to include in their how-to articles. See page 265 in the **Teacher's Resource Book**.

✔ Draft

Have students begin their drafts. Students can work on their selected journal entries by developing steps that teach how to do the activity described in the entry. Prompt them to think about what details will help them show readers how to do the activity and what order the steps should be in.

Students who choose to write about a new activity should review their Sequence Charts. Before they start to write, tell students to think about the entries on their charts as steps to use in their writing. Students should organize the steps into paragraphs. Each paragraph should include details that will explain how to complete the step.

Objectives

- Define genre of how-to article
- Plan/prewrite a draft
- Develop a draft

Materials

- Writer's Notebooks
- Writing Transparencies 20–23
- Teacher's Resource Book, page 265

Selecting Journal Entries

This quick classroom routine encourages students to reread their work with a purpose and make some judgments about their own writing.

1. Read each student's Writer's Notebook, select two of the strongest entries from recent student writing, and flag them with self-stick notes.

2. Explain that you have posted a self-stick note on two pieces that you thought were strong. The student's job is to reread them and choose one of the pieces for you to give an individual Revision Assignment. Give the student a basis for choosing the entry, and post the criteria. For example:

☑ Choose a piece in which you've used descriptive details to tell about an activity you enjoy doing.

☑ Choose a piece that is about something you could teach readers to do.

☑ After deciding on a piece, write a big check mark (√) on the self-stick note attached to the entry that you want me to read.

Objectives
- Check sequence of steps and add time-order words
- Revise a draft

Materials
- Writer's Notebooks
- Writing Transparency 22

ELL

Time-Order Words Write time-order words such as *first, second, next, then, before, after,* and *finally* on word cards. Display and read each word. To show examples of each word's meaning, perform a series of actions, such as sitting in a chair, standing up, and clapping your hands. Then ask: *What did I do first? What did I do next? What did I do after?* Have students use the time-order words in their responses.

Teacher-to-Teacher

Meeting in small groups is a great way to help students add steps to their articles and check the sequence of steps and use of time-order words. It is helpful to meet with students before they complete their articles to get them off to a good start. It is also helpful to highlight places in their journals that need revision if students are having difficulty.

How-To Article

Minilesson 1: Organization

TEACH/MODEL

Set the Purpose Tell students that the steps in their articles should be organized in sequential order. Explain that using time-order words, such as *first, next,* and *last,* helps readers understand the sequence of the steps. Explain that students will practice revising their articles by correcting sequence and adding time-order words.

Add Time-Order Words Remind students that yesterday, they read a how-to article about making a paper airplane. Write these sentences:

> After you fold your paper, make a crease.
> First, fold your paper.
> Then use your thumb to press the paper down.

Ask: *Are these steps in the right order? How do you know?* (No, the steps don't make sense. You can't make a crease until after you have folded your paper. The second step should be first. It also includes the time-order word *first*.) *What is the right order?*

 ### Revise

PRACTICE/APPLY

Review the features of a how-to article on **Writing Transparency 22**. Then explain to students that they are going to revise their own how-to articles to check and correct the sequence of steps and to add time-order words.

Allow students time to work individually on revising their how-to articles. Students should be sure to put the steps in the correct order and to add time-order words. Ask them to share their articles. Point out examples of time-order words, and compliment students on their efforts.

Summarize Learning Point out the following: *When you write a how-to article, you should always present the steps in the correct order. Time-order words help readers understand the steps. What time-order words did you use in your how-to article?*

How-To Article

Minilesson 2: Sentence Fluency

TEACH/MODEL

Set the Purpose Explain to students that good writers use a variety of sentence types in their writing. In how-to articles, some sentences are statements. Many statements are commands that tell the reader what to do. Writers may use questions or exclamations, too. The purpose of the last sentence is wrap up the activity. It can be a concluding statement, question, or exclamation. Display **Writing Transparency 25** and read it aloud.

> **Transparency 25**
>
> Now that you have folded and creased your paper, what do you do? Open the paper up again! You have a sheet of paper with a crease in the middle. Choose one end of your paper. You are going to fold in both corners on that end so the edges touch the center fold. Start at the crease, and fold the first corner in. Then fold the second corner in. Look! You have made a point at the end of the paper.

Writing Transparency

Discuss the different types of sentences. Point out that using different sentence types grabs a reader's attention.

✔ Revise

PRACTICE/APPLY

Tell students that now they will revise their how-to articles to include a variety of sentence types. Display **Writing Transparency 26**.

> **Transparency 26**
>
> 1. Reread your Writer's Notebook entry.
> 2. Underline one statement. Circle one question. Draw a box around one command. Put an X over one exclamation.
> 3. Add at least one more of each type of sentence.

Writing Transparency

Then have students share some of their sentences. Record different types of sentences on **Writing Transparency 27**.

Summarize Learning Discuss the following: *What types of sentences did you use? Remember, different types of sentences make your writing more interesting and grab the reader's attention.*

Objective

- Use a variety of sentence types

Materials

- Writer's Notebooks
- Writing Transparencies 24–27
- Teacher's Resource Book, p. 185

CREATING RUBRICS

Teacher-Developed Rubric

As a follow-up, display **Transparency 24**. Have students refer to **Teacher's Resource Book** page 185. Work with students to fill in the rubric for this week's writing. Tell students that you will use this rubric to evaluate their completed pieces. They should refer to the rubric as they write, revise, and proofread.

ON YOUR OWN Teacher's Resource Book, page 185

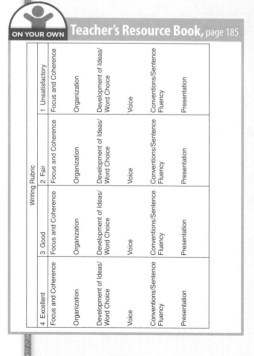

Objective

- Meet with students to discuss writing and give revision assignments

Materials

- Writer's Notebooks

Peer Review

Think, Pair, Share Ask students to read their revised drafts aloud to partners. Suggest that listeners act out the steps. Listeners then point out what they were easily able to do and what steps need more detail or to be in a different order. Encourage writers to use their partners' input when revising their drafts.

Flexible Pairing Option Consider pairing students who do not know each other well or do not regularly work together.

Research Proven Writing Approach

The Writers' Express
Immediate Impact. Lasting Transformation.   wex.org

Conferencing Routine

Dynamic Feedback System

Step 1 Read and appreciate the writing.

Step 2 Notice how the student uses the targeted skill (for example, time-order words: Ask: *What time-order words did you use?*).

Step 3 Write comments that show how the writing has an impact on you. Direct your comments to those places in the piece where the student has used the targeted skill.

Step 4 Meet with and give the student a revision assignment.

Write Effective Comments

How-To Article At least one of your comments should highlight the way the student uses the skills related to the genre. Here are some sample comments. Use these comments to get you started. Once you're comfortable, you can craft your own comments to be more specific to a particular entry.

- I like the way you described each step in the process. I think I could follow these directions easily.

- I'm a little confused about what to do next. Can you fix the sequence of steps by adding time-order words?

- I like your use of commands. Can you add some questions and exclamations?

- Your steps really showed me how to complete the process. Great use of showing!

Revision Assignments

How-To Article Below are examples of effective revision assignments. Use them to get started.

 I'm a little confused about what to do next. Write two more sentences about this step in the process.

 This step is not clear. Rewrite this step using descriptive details and examples. Include time-order words.

How-To Article

✔ Edit/Proofread: Conventions

During the editing process, students should proofread their own work for spelling, grammar, and punctuation. Remind students to

- check for complete sentences with subjects and predicates;

- use singular and plural nouns correctly;

- check for correct spelling of plural nouns, including irregular plurals, such as *leaves* and *children*;

- combine shorter sentences into compound sentences;

- correct any run-on sentences.

Use the Grammar, Mechanics, and Spelling lessons on pages 199I–199L for minilessons on conventions with which students may have difficulty.

Publish and Share

Ask students to type or write, in cursive script or manuscript printing, a final copy of their how-to articles. Remind them to use their best handwriting to correctly form letters. Model for them how to create documents with appropriate spacing between words, sentences, paragraphs, and correct margins.

It is important to post students' work. Post examples of detailed sequenced steps and a variety of sentence types.

Have students publish their how-to articles in a class book. They can draw pictures to illustrate the steps.

Presentations Ask students to present their articles to the class. They can demonstrate the steps during their presentations or have a partner follow directions for the class.

Objectives

- Edit drafts for grammar, mechanics, and spelling
- Publish a written work for a specific purpose

WRITING RUBRICS

Evaluate Students' Writing Use the rubric on page 263G. Review your evaluation with each student. Refer to the rubric you created with students to clearly identify strengths in their writing and areas on which they should focus.

Connect
Language Arts

WHOLE GROUP

✔ **VOCABULARY**
- Tested Words

✔ **SPELLING**
- Three-Letter Blends

✔ **GRAMMAR**
- Irregular Plural Nouns

SMALL GROUP

- Differentiated Instruction, pp. 199M–199LL

Build Robust Vocabulary

Day 1 — Teach/Practice

CONNECT TO WORDS

- Practice this week's vocabulary words using the following prompts:

  1. What are the advantages and disadvantages of being friends with someone who is *similar* to you?

  2. When you face *challenges*, do you feel excited, nervous, or both? Why?

  3. Why are houses *designed* before they are built?

  4. What are some things people receive to show they have *achieved* something?

  5. Are *similar* and *varied* synonyms or antonyms? Explain.

ACADEMIC VOCABULARY

- Review the important academic vocabulary words for the week. These words include: *main idea, details, explicit, implied, author's purpose, idiom.*

- Write each word on the board. Define each using student-friendly language, and ask students to select the word you are defining. Then point to words in random order for students to define.

Day 2 — Review

CONNECT TO WORDS

- Review the definitions of this week's vocabulary words using **Student Book** pages 190–191. Then discuss each word using the following prompts:

  1. What is a synonym for *similar*?

  2. Would you expect a vacation that included outdoor *challenges* to be relaxing or exciting? Why?

  3. If you accidentally created a new recipe by adding the wrong ingredient, would you say you *designed* it? Why or why not?

  4. How do people feel when they have *achieved* something?

  5. Why might people prefer to visit a museum with *varied* exhibits?

IDIOMS

- Remind students that an idiom is an expression whose meaning cannot be determined from the literal meanings of its individual words.

- Display **Transparency 15**. Read the first sentence, and model how to figure out the meaning of the underlined idiom.

- Have students find clues that help define other underlined idioms.

- Help students to brainstorm a list of common idioms. Have them write three in their Writer's Notebooks and illustrate the literal and figurative meanings. Then have them use each idiom in a sentence.

Practice Book, page 71

To understand the meaning of an **idiom**, you need to use the words and phrases around the idiom or think about how you might have heard the expression before.

A. Read the idioms in the box. Find and underline the idioms in the sentences below. Then circle the words in the sentence that help you understand the expression.

has a green thumb	get the hang of it
make a splash	lend a hand

1. I'd be happy to lend a hand and help you paint your room.

2. When you see all her healthy plants, it's easy to figure out that Mrs. Potts has a green thumb.

3. It took me a long time to learn how to download pictures onto my computer, but now that I get the hang of it, I do it all the time.

4. Unlike my friend who always likes to make a vivid impression on people, I don't usually like to make a splash.

B. Read the idioms below. Think about how you have heard them used. Then write a sentence that includes context clues that would help a reader understand each idiom.
Possible responses provided.

5. catching a cold I'm beginning to cough and sneeze, so I think I'm catching a cold.

6. pull my leg I realize that you're trying to trick me, so you can stop trying to pull my leg.

Approaching Reproducible, page 71

Beyond Reproducible, page 71

Day 3 Reinforce

CONNECT TO WORDS

- Have students create Word Squares for each word in their Writer's Notebooks.

- In the first square, students write the word. (Example: *similar*)

- In the second square, students write their own definition of the word and any related words, such as synonyms. (Example: *alike, same, resembling*)

- In the third square, students draw a simple illustration that will help them remember the word. (Example: a drawing of two flowers that look alike but are not exactly the same)

- In the fourth square, students write nonexamples, including antonyms for the word. (Example: *different, dissimilar, unlike*)

RELATED WORDS

- Classifying related words can build word consciousness and improve students' vocabularies. Help them generate words related to *varied*.

- Draw a web and write *varied* in the center.

- Have students brainstorm a list of words that are related to *varied* by origin, such as *vary, variety, variable,* and *variation*. They can use a dictionary to help. Discuss how knowing the meaning of *varied* can help them figure out and remember the meaning of the related words. Have students confirm the meanings of the words in their webs using a dictionary.

Day 4 Extend

CONNECT TO WORDS

- Review this week's vocabulary using the following sentence stems. Have students orally complete each one.

  1. House cats and lions are similar because ____.

  2. You face challenges when you ____.

  3. A classroom is designed for ____.

  4. I felt ____ when I achieved ____.

  5. The varied food at a picnic might include ____.

MORPHOLOGY

- Use the additional selection vocabulary word *triathlon* as a springboard for students to learn other words.

- Write *triathlon* on the board. Underline *tri-*. Explain that *tri-* is a prefix meaning "three" and comes from the Latin and Greek words for *three*. A *triathlon* is an athletic event made up of three sports.

- Write *tricycle* and *triangle* on the board. Have students underline *tri-* in each word.

- Use the word parts to define each word. Explain that *tri-* means "three" and *cycle* means "wheel." Therefore, *tricycle* means "a vehicle that has three wheels." A *triangle* is a shape with three angles and three sides. Direct students to list other words that begin with *tri-*, such as *trimester, triplet,* and *tripod*. As needed, discuss nonexamples, such as *triumph* and *trial*.

Day 5 Assess and Reteach

POSTTEST

- Display **Transparency 16**. Have students complete the cloze sentences using one of this week's vocabulary words.

- Note how quickly and accurately students can complete this task. Work with students who make errors or require too much time to complete this task during Small Group time.

CONNECT TO WRITING

- Have students write sentences in their Writer's Notebooks using this week's vocabulary. Tell students to write sentences that provide information they learned from this week's readings.

- **ELL** Provide the Day 4 sentence stems for students needing extra support.

Go to pages T14–T15 for **Differentiated Spelling Lists**.

✔ Three-Letter Blends

Spelling Words

shred	shrink	splashing
through	screw	straps
sprout	shrimp	strand
sprawl	screech	script
split	straighten	thrill
throb	sprang	throne
throat	shriek	

Review choose, photo, whole
Challenge threaten, strictly

Dictation Sentences

1. Can you <u>shred</u> this paper?
2. Go **through** that first door.
3. Seeds <u>sprout</u> in the spring.
4. I like to <u>sprawl</u> out on the couch.
5. Please <u>split</u> your lunch with me.
6. I felt a <u>throb</u> of pain in my head.
7. I ate ice cream for my sore <u>throat</u>.
8. We can <u>shrink</u> the large picture.
9. A <u>screw</u> will hold the shelf on.
10. We ate <u>shrimp</u> for dinner.
11. The car might <u>screech</u> to a halt.
12. Try to <u>straighten</u> up this mess.
13. I <u>sprang</u> out of bed.
14. Did you hear her <u>shriek</u> with joy?
15. We were **splashing** in the pool.
16. Use the <u>straps</u> to carry the backpack.
17. In class, we studied a <u>strand</u> of hair.
18. I read the <u>script</u> for the play.
19. It was a <u>thrill</u> to win the game.
20. The queen sat on her <u>throne</u>.

Review/Challenge Words

1. Did you <u>choose</u> your project yet?
2. What a great <u>photo</u> of you that is!
3. The <u>whole</u> book has 600 pages.
4. Don't <u>threaten</u> me with extra chores!
5. The rules are <u>strictly</u> kept.

Words in **bold** are from this week's selections.

Day 1 Pretest

ASSESS PRIOR KNOWLEDGE

- Model for students how to spell *shred*. Segment the word sound by sound, and then attach a spelling to each sound. Point out that the consonant cluster *shr* is usually found at the beginning of words.

- Use the Dictation Sentences. Say the underlined word, read the sentence, and repeat the word. Have students write the words.

- Have students self-correct their tests. Point out that the *shr* sound never appears at the end of an English word.

- Have students cut apart the **Spelling Word Cards BLM** on **Teacher's Resource Book** page 51 and figure out a way to sort them. Have them save the cards for use throughout the week.

Day 2 Word Sorts and Review

SPIRAL REVIEW

Review the digraphs in *choose*, *photo*, and *whole*. Have students find words in this week's readings with the same sounds. Remind students of other spellings of the /sh/ sound usually spelled by the digraph *sh*, as in the words *musician*, *action*, and *expression*.

WORD SORTS

- Have students take turns sorting the spelling words and explaining their choices. When students have finished, discuss any words that are giving them problems.

- Review the spelling words, pointing out the three-letter blends *shr*, *thr*, *spr*, *scr*, *str*, and *spl*. Use the cards from the Spelling Word Cards BLM. Write the key words *shred*, *through*, *sprout*, *screw*, *strand*, and *split* on the board. Model how to sort words by placing a card beneath one or two of the correct key words.

ON YOUR OWN — **Phonics/Spelling,** pages 43-44

Fold back the paper along the dotted line. Use the blanks to write each word as it is read aloud. When you finish the test, unfold the paper. Use the list at the right to correct any spelling mistakes.

1. _____	1. shred
2. _____	2. through
3. _____	3. sprout
4. _____	4. sprawl
5. _____	5. split
6. _____	6. throb
7. _____	7. throat
8. _____	8. shrink
9. _____	9. screw
10. _____	10. shrimp
11. _____	11. screech
12. _____	12. straighten
13. _____	13. sprang
14. _____	14. shriek
15. _____	15. splashing
16. _____	16. straps
17. _____	17. strand
18. _____	18. script
19. _____	19. thrill
20. _____	20. throne
Review Words 21. _____	21. choose
22. _____	22. photo
Challenge Words 23. _____	23. whole
24. _____	24. threaten
25. _____	25. strictly

HOMEWORK — **Phonics/Spelling,** page 45

shred	split	screw	sprang	throne
through	throb	shrimp	shriek	strand
sprout	throat	screech	splashing	script
sprawl	shrink	straighten	straps	thrill

A. Pattern Power
Write the spelling words with these spelling patterns.

words beginning with *shr*
1. shred
2. shrink
3. shrimp
4. shriek

words beginning with *thr*
5. through
6. throb
7. throat
8. thrill
9. throne

words beginning in *spr*
10. sprout
11. sprawl
12. sprang

words beginning in *scr*
13. screw
14. screech
15. script

words beginning in *str*
16. straighten
17. straps
18. strand

words beginning in *spl*
19. split
20. splashing

Rhyme Time
Write the spelling word that rhymes with each word.
21. crawl — sprawl
22. creek — shriek
23. mob — throb
24. plane — strain
25. preach — screech
26. pill — thrill

Day 3 Word Meanings

CONTEXT CLUES

Write these sentences on the board. Have students copy them into their Writer's Notebooks. Say the sentences aloud and ask students to fill in the blanks with a spelling word.

1. The tiny plant was now just a little _____ but would soon be a huge flower. (*sprout*)

2. I like to eat _____ better than crab. (*shrimp*)

3. What a _____ it was to ride on the roller coaster! (*thrill*)

Challenge students to come up with other context-clue sentences that use spelling words, review words, or challenge words. Have them note any words that have multiple meanings.

Have students do a word hunt for the words in the weekly reading or other materials. They should define the spelling word being used in context.

Day 4 Proofread

PROOFREAD AND WRITE

Write these sentences on the board. Have students circle and correct each misspelled word.

1. Your throte might thorb if you eat too many spicy peppers. (*throat, throb*)

2. I had to shreek when I read the skript for the school play. (*shriek, script*)

3. She watched with a thrill as her hero ran though the lobby. (*thrill, through*)

Error Correction Some students will leave out one letter of the three-letter blend. Stretch the sounds of the blend and help students segment it, attaching one letter to each sound they hear. In the case of *th*, remind them that this spelling stands for /th/ as in *think*.

Day 5 Assess and Reteach

POSTTEST

Use the Dictation Sentences on page 199I for the Posttest.

If students have difficulty with any words in the lesson, have them place them on a list called *Spelling Words I Want to Remember* in their Writer's Notebooks. Look for students' use of these words in their writings.

Challenge students to look for other words that have the *thr, shr, spr, scr, str,* and *spl* spellings and add them to their Writer's Notebooks.

HOMEWORK — Phonics/Spelling, page 46

shred	split	screw	sprang	throne
through	throb	shrimp	shriek	strand
sprout	throat	screech	splashing	script
sprawl	shrink	straighten	straps	thrill

A. Finish the Word
Write the missing letters to correctly complete the words in the sentences.

Many farmers in the Chinese village raise 1. shr **imp**. They raise them in large, shallow pools of water. Water runs 2. thr **ough** all of them. No weeds are allowed to 3. spr **out**. Sometimes a gull will fly overhead and 4. scr **eech**. Then everyone will run outside to scare the gull away.

It is quite a 5. thr **ill** to watch the farmers harvest the shrimp. They use nets. One walks down the middle of the pool to 6. spl **it** it in half. As the net gets smaller and smaller, the shrimp strain to get out, but they are caught. When the farmers lift the net out of the water, there is much 7. spl **ashing**. The net will 8. thr **ob** with shrimp. The farmers dump their catch in buckets and carry them away with 9. str **aps** over their shoulders.

B. Word Groups
Write the spelling word that belongs in each group.
10. chair, seat, **throne**
11. expand, stretch, **sprawl**
12. tack, nail, **screw**
13. cut, divide, **split**
14. rip, tear, **shred**

ON YOUR OWN — Phonics/Spelling, page 47

A. There are five spelling mistakes in this short story about Lei. Circle the misspelled words. Write the words correctly on the lines below.

Lei jumped rope with the girls at school. She played with her friends after school. She studied hard like her parents told her to. Lei was like other girls in most every way. But Lei had something no one else had—her grandmother's pink pearl necklace. Lei liked to wear the necklace around her (throte) on special days.

Lei received the pearl necklace when she was 11. The pearl was very old and special. It was a pearl that was worn by a princess in the ancient Chinese dynasties. It gave Lei such a (threel) to wear it.

One day, Lei was jumping rope at a party. All of a sudden, the (shrand) of pearls broke. The pearls flew off Lei's neck and scattered on the ground. Lei let out a (shreak) as she (spraing) to the ground to pick up the pearls. Her father saw what happened and helped Lei pick up the pearls. From then on, Lei was more careful with her necklace.

1. **throat**   3. **strand**   5. **sprang**
2. **thrill**   4. **shriek**

B. Writing Activity
Imagine that you are a prince or princess of an ancient Chinese dynasty. You have just received a pearl necklace like Lei's. Write a short story about what you would do with such a special necklace. Use at least four spelling words in your story.

Stories will vary.

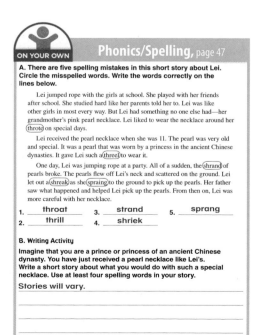

HOMEWORK — Phonics/Spelling, page 48

Look at the words in each set below. One word in each set is spelled correctly. Use a pencil to fill in the circle next to the correct word. Before you begin, look at the sample set of words. Sample A has been done for you. Do Sample B by yourself. When you are sure you know what to do, you may go on with the rest of the page.

Sample A:
- Ⓐ throw ●
- Ⓑ throo
- Ⓒ thro
- Ⓓ throu

Sample B:
- Ⓔ skrach
- Ⓕ skratch
- Ⓖ scratch ●
- Ⓗ scrach

1. Ⓐ schred / Ⓑ shred / Ⓒ shread / Ⓓ schread
2. Ⓔ through / Ⓕ throu / Ⓖ threwe / Ⓗ throughe
3. Ⓐ sprowt / Ⓑ sprout / Ⓒ sprot / Ⓓ spruot
4. Ⓔ sprall / Ⓕ spraul / Ⓖ sprawle / Ⓗ sprawl
5. Ⓐ splitt / Ⓑ splet / Ⓒ splitte / Ⓓ split

6. Ⓔ throbb / Ⓕ throb / Ⓖ throub / Ⓗ throbbe
7. Ⓐ throte / Ⓑ throate / Ⓒ throat / Ⓓ throet
8. Ⓔ shrink / Ⓕ shrinck / Ⓖ shrinke / Ⓗ shrenk
9. Ⓐ scrue / Ⓑ skrew / Ⓒ screw / Ⓓ skroo
10. Ⓔ schrimp / Ⓕ shrimp / Ⓖ shremp / Ⓗ schremp

11. Ⓐ skreach / Ⓑ screche / Ⓒ screech / Ⓓ skreech
12. Ⓔ straiten / Ⓕ straten / Ⓖ straighten / Ⓗ straitin
13. Ⓐ sprange / Ⓑ spraing / Ⓒ sprang / Ⓓ spreang
14. Ⓔ schreik / Ⓕ shreek / Ⓖ schriek / Ⓗ shriek
15. Ⓐ splaching / Ⓑ splasching / Ⓒ splashene / Ⓓ splashing

16. Ⓔ strapps / Ⓕ strapz / Ⓖ straps / Ⓗ strappz
17. Ⓐ throne / Ⓑ throen / Ⓒ throan / Ⓓ thron
18. Ⓔ strande / Ⓕ schtrand / Ⓖ stranned / Ⓗ strand
19. Ⓐ script / Ⓑ skript / Ⓒ schript / Ⓓ scripped
20. Ⓔ trhill / Ⓕ thrill / Ⓖ thrille / Ⓗ thrile

Irregular Plural Nouns

Daily Language Activities

Write the sentences on the board.

DAY 1

I live in Omaha Nebraska? Where do you live! (1: Omaha, Nebraska.; 2: live?)

DAY 2

Those man and their wifes like to play music. They use Drums and tap their foots. sometimes the music is so loud it scares the mouses? (1: men; 2: wives; 3: drums; 4: feet; 5: Sometimes; 6: mice.)

DAY 3

The farmer has two sheeps and one cow. I like to see his childs because they are nice? (1: sheep; 2: children; 3: nice.)

DAY 4

The meltaway Diner has great fishes. They even have a menu for childrens. you can get a banana spilt for dessert. (1: Meltaway; 2: fish.; 3: children.; 4: You; 5: split)

DAY 5

Did you read the skript. There are three elfs in this play. They have to Be small? (1: script?; 2: elves; 3: be small.)

Day 1 — Introduce the Concept

INTRODUCE IRREGULAR PLURAL NOUNS

Present the following:

- Explain that some nouns have **irregular plurals**. They cannot be made plural by adding -s or -es, or by changing a y to an i and adding -es.

- One kind of irregular plural comes from singular words that end in -f or -fe. Many of these words change the f to a v and add -es, such as wolf/wolves.

- Other irregular plurals change their vowel sound from the singular, such as goose/geese, man/men, and foot/feet.

- Some irregular plurals use a different ending to form the plural, such as child/children.

See Grammar Transparency 36 for modeling and guided practice.

HOMEWORK — Grammar, page 36

- Some nouns have special plural forms.

calves	lice	children	feet	geese
gentlemen	leaves	potatoes	knives	halves
mice	wives	thieves	heroes	tomatoes
lives	men	women	oxen	teeth

Look in the above box for the plural form of each singular noun. Write it on the line provided.

1. man — men
2. child — children
3. woman — women
4. life — lives
5. calf — calves
6. thief — thieves
7. potato — potatoes
8. goose — geese
9. ox — oxen
10. wife — wives
11. foot — feet
12. hero — heroes
13. tooth — teeth
14. gentleman — gentlemen
15. knife — knives
16. tomato — tomatoes
17. mouse — mice
18. louse — lice
19. leaf — leaves
20. half — halves

Day 2 — Teach the Concept

REVIEW IRREGULAR PLURAL NOUNS

Review with students examples of irregular plurals. Have them explain how irregular plurals are different from other plurals. Ask them to recall rules that some irregular plurals follow.

INTRODUCE OTHER IRREGULAR PLURALS

Present the following:

- The plural and singular forms of some words are exactly the same. Examples include sheep, deer, and fish.

- Other words change greatly from singular to plural. Examples include person/people and mouse/mice.

See Grammar Transparency 37 for modeling and guided practice.

ON YOUR OWN — Grammar, page 37

- A few nouns have the same plural and singular form.
- To determine whether the noun is singular or plural, look at the rest of the sentence.

Read the sentences below. Then decide whether the underlined noun is singular or plural. Write your answer on the line.

1. There was not one sheep on Papa's farm. — singular
2. A herd of buffalo trampled across the land. — plural
3. Moose live in cold places, like Canada. — plural
4. This species of insect only lives for two days. — singular
5. I ate clams and shrimp at dinner. — plural
6. Be quiet or you might scare that deer away. — singular
7. We caught five fish today. — plural
8. We saw a moose at the zoo. — singular
9. He dipped each shrimp into the cocktail sauce. — singular
10. Sheep produce wool for sweaters. — plural
11. We raked the leaves today. — plural
12. I am not afraid of the mouse. — singular
13. She is getting her teeth cleaned. — plural
14. Several oxen passed the ranch. — plural
15. He wanted a baked potato. — singular

Day 3 — Review and Practice

REVIEW IRREGULAR PLURALS

Review irregular plural nouns and their singular forms. Have students write sentences using irregular plural nouns and check their spelling.

MECHANICS AND USAGE: CORRECT PLURAL FORMS

- Explain that students will need to memorize irregular plurals that are not based on rules, such as *man/men, foot/feet,* and *child/children.*

- Remind students that there is a rule for forming the plural of words that end in *-f* or *-fe,* but not all words follow it: *roof/roofs; handkerchief/ handkerchiefs.*

- Also remind students that some words have the same singular and plural forms (*deer, sheep, moose*).

Day 4 — Review and Proofread

REVIEW CORRECT PLURAL FORMS

Direct students to discuss the different types of irregular plurals. Have them give examples to illustrate each type. Review the correct spellings of the irregular plural nouns as needed.

PROOFREAD

Have students correct the errors in the following sentences.

1. I bought two loafs of bread. (loaves)

2. Keisha lost three tooths last year. (teeth)

3. At the zoo, I saw many wolfs, sheeps, and gooses. (1: wolves; 2: sheep; 3: geese)

4. They say that cats have nine lifes. (lives)

Day 5 — Assess and Reteach

ASSESS

Use the Daily Language Activity and **Grammar Practice Book** page 40 for assessment.

RETEACH

Use Grammar Practice Book page 40 and selected pages from the **Grammar and Writing Handbook** for additional reteaching. Remind students that it is important to use nouns correctly as they speak and write.

Check students' writing for use of the skill and listen for it in their speaking. Assign Grammar Revision Assignments in their Writer's Notebooks as needed.

 See Grammar Transparency 38 for modeling and guided practice.

See Grammar Transparency 39 for modeling and guided practice.

See Grammar Transparency 40 for modeling and guided practice.

Grammar, page 38
HOMEWORK

- Some nouns have special plural forms.
- A few nouns have the same singular and plural forms.

Read each sentence. Draw a line under the word in parentheses that is the correct plural form.

1. Chinese (factoryes, <u>factories</u>) produced lots of paper.
2. Wheelbarrows, invented in China, were compared to wooden [oxes, <u>oxen</u>].
3. Chinese inventors experimented with magnetism by placing iron (<u>fish</u>, fishes) in water.
4. The first kites floated through the air like (leafs, <u>leaves</u>).
5. I wonder who first realized it's a good idea to brush your (tooths, <u>teeth</u>)?
6. Magicians placed pieces of lodestone into the (bellys, <u>bellies</u>) of wooden turtles.
7. A member of the Chinese court invented a machine to predict (<u>earthquakes</u>, earthquaks).
8. I didn't know the Chinese had made (compassies, <u>compasses</u>).
9. I think of inventors as (<u>heroes</u>, heros).
10. What different (speciesee, <u>species</u>) of animals come from China?
11. These inventions have changed many people's (<u>lives</u>, lifes).
12. (<u>Tomatoes</u>, Tomatos) come with the meal.

Grammar, page 39
ON YOUR OWN

- A few nouns have the same plural and singular form.
- To determine whether the noun is singular or plural, look at the rest of the sentence.

Rewrite the narrative below. Fix any spelling, punctuation, and grammar mistakes. Be sure to correct the 11 incorrectly formed plural nouns.

I want to be a chef who invents new, delicious dishs for people to enjoy! I decided this after visiting a new restaurant a few days ago. All of the mens, womans, and childs there watched the chef with great excitement. I watched him handle his long, sharp knifes carefully. Effortlessly, he diced potatos and tomatoeies into halfs and quarters. The shrimpses and fishies sizzled as he cooked them on the hot grill. When our excellent meal arrived, we really sank our toothes into it. That's when I decided cooking must be a fun way to be creative.

I want to be a chef who invents new, delicious dishes for people to enjoy! I decided this after visiting a new restaurant a few days ago. All of the men, women, and children there watched the chef with great excitement. I watched him handle his long, sharp knives carefully. Effortlessly, he diced potatoes and tomatoes into halves and quarters. The shrimp and fish sizzled as he cooked them on the hot grill. When our excellent meal arrived, we really sank our teeth into it. That's when I decided cooking must be a fun way to be creative.

Grammar, page 40
HOMEWORK

A. Write *yes* if the noun below has the same singular and plural forms. Write *no* if the noun does not have the same singular and plural forms.

1. ship ___no___
2. deer ___yes___
3. calf ___no___
4. species ___yes___
5. moose ___yes___
6. ox ___no___
7. half ___no___
8. shrimp ___yes___

B. Complete each sentence with the plural form of the singular noun in parentheses.

9. Two baby (calf) ___calves___ were born last night.
10. Which of the inventors were (woman) ___women___?
11. It is easier for (child) ___children___ to learn a new language than it is for adults to learn one.
12. King Henry VIII had many (wife) ___wives___
13. There were a few (mouse) ___mice___ under the stove in the kitchen.
14. The (thief) ___thieves___ were soon caught.
15. My (foot) ___feet___ are so tired.
16. That dog has plenty of (louse) ___lice___

LOG ON **StudentWorks** Plus
Interactive Student Book

If you wish to preteach the main selection, use StudentWorks Plus for:

• Vocabulary Preteaching
• Word-by-Word Highlighting
• Think Aloud Prompts

Academic Language

Academic words include those harder Tier 2 words that appear in much of students' reading materials as well as the language of instruction. The words chosen for instruction were selected from the **Living Word Vocabulary** list and Avril Coxhead's list of **High-Incidence Academic Words**.

Approaching Level

Prepare to Read

Objective   Preview *Making a Splash*
Materials   • **StudentWorks Plus**   • self-stick notes

PREVIEW THE MAIN SELECTION

- Have students preview *Making a Splash* using **StudentWorks Plus**. This version of the selection contains oral summaries in multiple languages, story recording, word-by-word highlighting, Think Aloud prompts, and comprehension-monitoring questions.

- Remind students that listening carefully to and following along with the word-by-word reading will help them prepare for the reading of the selection with the class. Ask students to place self-stick notes on any challenging words or on places that confuse them. Discuss these with students prior to the reading of the selection with the rest of the class.

- Tell students to write three or four sentences in their Writer's Notebooks telling what they learned about how athletes can overcome physical challenges.

Academic Language

Objective   Teach academic language
Materials   • none

PRETEACH LANGUAGE OF INSTRUCTION

Tell students that there are many important lesson words you will be using this week. You want them to become familiar with these words *before* the lessons. These words also appear in the directions of the tests they will be taking this year.

Preteach the following academic words: *monitor comprehension, main idea, details, explicit, implied, idiom, title page, table of contents, glossary,* and *index.*

- Define each word using student-friendly language. Help students locate the *title page, table of contents, glossary,* and *index* in their **Student Books** or an informational book. Say the name of each book part as students locate it, and then discuss and model the use of each part.

- In addition, relate each word to known words. For example, connect *purpose* to the *reason* or *why* something is done, *explicit* to *directly stated,* and *implied* to *not stated.*

- Highlight these words when used throughout the week, and reinforce their meanings.

Approaching Level

Phonics/Decoding

Sound-Spelling WorkBoard

Objective Decode words with three-letter blends

Materials • **Approaching Reproducible,** p. 64
• **Sound-Spelling WorkBoards**

✓ PHONICS MAINTENANCE

Tier 2

- Distribute a **WorkBoard** to each student. Say a sound previously taught, including consonant digraphs, such as *ch, sh, th, wh,* and *ph*. Have students find the **Sound-Spelling Card** on the WorkBoard for each sound.

- Review the spelling(s) for each sound by providing a sample word containing that spelling. Guide students to write the word on the board. Model how to segment the word and write the spelling for each sound, as needed. In addition, point out spelling hints, such as one-syllable words ending in /ik/ will usually end with the digraph *ck*, as in *sick*. Two-syllable words will usually end in *-ic*, as in *clinic*.

- Dictate the following words for students to spell: *shrink, shred, thrash, throw, scrap, splash, string*. Write the words on the board, and have students self-correct their work.

RETEACH SKILL

Three-Letter Blends Write the blends on the board. For each blend, slide your finger underneath each letter in the blend as you pronounce the individual sound, for example: /s/-/p/-/r/. Then blend them together: /spr/.

- Write the words below on the board. Model how to decode the first word in each row. Then guide students as they decode the remaining words. For the multisyllabic words, divide the words into syllables using the syllable-scoop technique to help students read one syllable at a time.

- When completed, point to the words in random order for students to chorally read. Repeat several times.

strip	stripe	saw	straw	stung	strung
shed	shred	rink	shrink	rug	shrug
rust	thrust	thrift	thrifty	through	throughout
print	sprint	spring	springy	spread	spreading
cream	scream	scrap	scrape	scrub	scrubbing
lash	splash	splint	splinter	spend	splendid

Approaching Reproducible, page 64

Three consonants at the beginning of a word form a **three-letter blend**. Sometimes, you hear the sounds of the three consonants in the blend, as in **scrape** and **strain**. Sometimes, the first two consonants form a digraph and a third consonant is blended with the digraph, as in **shrug** and **thread**.

Circle the three-letter blend at the beginning of each word.

1. (spl)ash   7. (spr)ing
2. (scr)ap   8. (scr)unch
3. (thr)ew   9. (spl)it
4. (str)eet   10. (thr)one
5. (shr)ink   11. (shr)imp
6. (thr)ead   12. (scr)eam

Approaching Level

Vocabulary

Objective   Preteach selection vocabulary

Materials   • **Visual Vocabulary Resources**   • **Approaching Reproducible,** p. 65
                • **Vocabulary Cards**

✔ PRETEACH KEY VOCABULARY

Tier 2

Introduce the Words   Use the **Visual Vocabulary Resources** to preteach the key selection words *similar, challenges, designed, achieved,* and *varied.* Focus on two words per day. Use the following routine, which appears in detail on the cards.

- Define the word in English, and provide the example given.

- Define the word in Spanish, if appropriate, and indicate if the word is a cognate.

- Display the picture, and explain how it illustrates or demonstrates the word.

- Then engage students in structured partner-talk about the image, using the key word.

- Ask students to chorally say the word three times.

- Point out any known sound-spellings, or focus on a key aspect of phonemic awareness related to the word.

- You may wish to also distribute copies of the Vocabulary Glossary in the **ELL Resource Book**.

REVIEW PREVIOUSLY TAUGHT VOCABULARY

Display the **Vocabulary Cards** from the previous four weeks. Say the meanings of the words, one by one, and have students identify them. Then point to words in random order for students to provide definitions and related words they know.

Context Clues   Remind students that context clues are clues within the text that help a reader figure out what a word means. Have students write a context-rich sentence for each vocabulary word. For example, *It was an* insult *when Maria told me she didn't like my haircut.*

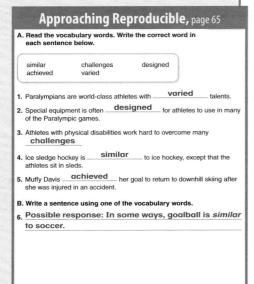

Approaching Reproducible, page 65

A. Read the vocabulary words. Write the correct word in each sentence below.

| similar | challenges | designed |
| achieved | varied | |

1. Paralympians are world-class athletes with _____varied_____ talents.

2. Special equipment is often ___designed___ for athletes to use in many of the Paralympic games.

3. Athletes with physical disabilities work hard to overcome many __challenges__

4. Ice sledge hockey is ___similar___ to ice hockey, except that the athletes sit in sleds.

5. Muffy Davis ___achieved___ her goal to return to downhill skiing after she was injured in an accident.

B. Write a sentence using one of the vocabulary words.

6. Possible response: In some ways, goalball is *similar* to soccer.

Approaching Level

Vocabulary

Objective Review vocabulary and high-frequency words

Materials • **Vocabulary Cards** • **High-Frequency Word Cards**

REVIEW VOCABULARY

Review Words Display the **Vocabulary Cards** for *similar, challenges, designed, achieved,* and *varied.* Point to each word, read it aloud, and have students chorally repeat.

Then provide the following word sets. Ask students to name the word in each set that is not related to the other words.

- similar, different, alike, same
- challenges, difficulties, obstacles, advantages
- designed, created, copied, planned
- achieved, won, accomplished, failed
- varied, similar, different, assorted

HIGH-FREQUENCY WORDS

Tier 2

Top 250 Words The ability to read accurately and effortlessly the most frequently used words in written English will help students develop reading fluency. Display **High-Frequency Word Cards** 61–70. Then do the following:

- Display one card at a time, and ask students to chorally state each word.
- Have students spell each word aloud.
- Ask students to write each word in their Writer's Notebooks as they state aloud each letter. Then have them read the word again.
- When completed, quickly flip through the Word Card set as students chorally read the words.
- Provide opportunities for students to use the words in speaking and writing. For example, provide sentence starters, such as *I would walk to the store, but it is too_____ away.* Or point to the Word Cards and ask questions such as, *What is the first thing you do each morning?* or *What is the best thing you ever found?*
- Continue the routine throughout the week.

Word Webs

Have students create word webs in their Writer's Notebooks for each vocabulary word. Write the related words provided, and ask students to add other words, phrases, and illustrations.

Student Book

Corrective Feedback

Read each paragraph with students. Ask: *What is this paragraph mostly about?* Underline the details in the paragraph and circle the main idea, if stated. If unstated, model how you determine the main idea. Also, explain how each detail relates to the main idea.

Approaching Level

Comprehension

Objective Reteach monitor comprehension and main idea and details

Materials • **Student Book:** "The Paralympics"

RETEACH STRATEGY: MONITOR COMPREHENSION

Tier 2

- **Define** Tell students that monitoring comprehension means checking their understanding of what they are reading. To do this, they may pause while reading to ask themselves questions. If they are not understanding, they may slow down their reading rate or reread passages.

- **Relate to Real Life** Ask students to imagine that a friend is telling them how to play a new video game. If they do not understand, they might say, *Wait a minute. I don't understand that part. What do you mean? Slow down and tell me again*. They are monitoring their comprehension, or checking their understanding.

- **Set Purposes** Remind students that good readers monitor their comprehension while they read to help clarify confusing text and to ensure that they understand what they have read.

RETEACH SKILL: MAIN IDEA AND DETAILS

- **Define** Tell students that the main idea is the most important point an author makes about a topic. To determine the main idea, first examine the details and decide what they have in common, or how they are connected.

- **Relate to Real Life** Tell students that movie trailers show the most important parts of a movie so that people will know what the movie is about. Have students explain the plots of their favorite movies. Remind them that they should only retell the most important events from the movie.

- **Set Purposes** Remind students that good readers search for the main ideas as they read. This process helps the reader better remember the most important events or ideas in a selection. Authors sometimes state the main idea in the first sentence of a paragraph, but more often students will need to infer the main idea based on text clues.

- **Apply** Work with students to determine the main idea in each paragraph in "The Paralympics." Then use the main ideas to state a summary of the entire text. Have students restate your summary in their own words. Students will apply this strategy and skill to a simpler text as they read *Citizens at Work*.

Approaching Level

Leveled Reader Lesson 1

Objective   Read to apply skills and strategies

Materials   • **Leveled Reader:** *Citizens at Work*

Leveled Reader

BEFORE READING

Preview and Predict   Have students read the title and preview the first chapter. Ask them to make predictions about the main idea of this section. Students should note any questions they have before they read.

 Review Vocabulary Words   Have students read the vocabulary words on the inside front cover. Briefly define each, and ask students to state related words they have learned.

Set a Purpose for Reading   *Let's read to find out about what makes a good citizen.*

DURING READING

 **STRATEGY**
MONITOR COMPREHENSION

Remind students that monitoring their comprehension means pausing to check their understanding before they continue reading.

SKILL
MAIN IDEA AND DETAILS

Remind students to think about the most important information they are learning as they read. Read Chapter 1 with students. Help them complete the Main Idea Chart.

As you read, help students decode unknown words. Ask open-ended questions to facilitate rich discussion, such as *What does the author want you to know about people who have helped their communities?* Build on students' responses to develop deeper understanding of the text.

Stop after each two pages, and ask students to summarize the information they read to check their understanding before reading on. If they struggle, help students reread the difficult pages or passage. Then model determining the main idea of the chapter.

AFTER READING

Ask students to compare and contrast the accomplishments of two different people mentioned in the book. Then ask: *Which person contributed more to his or her community? Explain your answer.*

Leveled Reader

Approaching Level

Leveled Reader Lesson 2

Objective Reread to apply skills and strategies and develop fluency

Materials
- **Leveled Reader:** *Citizens at Work*
- **Approaching Reproducible,** p. 68

BEFORE READING

Review the Strategy and Skill Review students' completed Main Idea Charts from the first read. Remind them that the main idea is the most important point an author makes about a topic. A summary includes the main ideas from the book.

Review Vocabulary Words Have students search the book for each vocabulary word. Ask them to read aloud the sentence containing the word and state the word's definition or provide related words. Point out any idioms, and clarify meanings as necessary.

Set a Purpose for Reading *Let's reread to check our understanding of the information in the book and to work on our reading fluency.*

DURING READING

Reread *Citizens at Work* with students. Have them read silently two pages at a time or read aloud to a partner. Stop and have students summarize before reading the next two pages. Model oral summaries, as needed.

AFTER READING

Check Comprehension Have partners complete the Comprehension Check on page 20. Review students' answers. Help students find evidence for their answers in the text.

MODEL FLUENCY

Model reading the fluency passage on **Approaching Reproducible** page 68. Tell students to pay close attention to your accuracy, noting how you read each word correctly and do not skip words or sentences. Read one sentence at a time, and have students echo-read the sentences, focusing on reading each sentence accurately.

During independent reading time, have students work with a partner using the fluency passage. One student reads aloud, and the other repeats each sentence. If students need additional support, have them listen to the "practice speed" version of the passage on the **Fluency Solutions Audio CD**.

Approaching Reproducible, page 68

As I read, I will focus on reading accurately.

	Kathryn was staying with her uncle and aunt in their
10	new house in the Arizona desert. The living room was
20	cluttered with moving boxes. Uncle Abe had found an old
30	book. On the cover it read, "ZYV'H YLLP — PVVK LFG!"
36	"It's written in code," her uncle said.
43	"What's a code?" Kathryn asked.
48	"It's a secret way of writing things," said Uncle Abe.
58	"You can read it, but others can't. You make it by replacing
70	one letter with another. My code works like this." Uncle
80	Abe wrote the code out for Kathryn.
87	Kathryn tried to figure out the cover. "Oh, I get it," she
99	said. "It says 'Abe's Book — Keep Out!'" 106

Comprehension Check

1. How can you tell that Uncle Abe has just moved? **Plot Development**
   You can tell that Uncle Abe has just moved into a new house because he is unpacking moving boxes.

2. What does Kathryn learn from her uncle? **Plot Development**
   Kathryn learns how to read her uncle's old code.

	Words Read	−	Number of Errors	=	Words Correct Score
First Read		−		=	
Second Read		−		=	

Approaching Level

Leveled Reader Lesson 3

Objective Build fluency

Materials
- **Leveled Reader:** *Citizens at Work*
- **Approaching Reproducible,** p. 68

FOCUS ON FLUENCY

Timed Reading Tell students that they will be doing a final timed reading of the fluency passage on **Approaching Reproducible** page 68 that they have been practicing. With each student, follow these directions:

- Place the passage facedown.
- When you say "Go," the student begins reading the passage aloud.
- When you say "Stop," the student stops reading the passage.

As they read, note words students mispronounce and their overall accuracy. Stop after one minute. Help students record and graph the number of words they read correctly.

REREAD PREVIOUSLY READ BOOKS

- Distribute copies of the past six **Leveled Readers**. Have students select two to reread. Tell students that rereading these books will help them develop their skills. The more times they read the same words, the quicker they will learn those words. This will make the reading of other books easier.

- Circulate and listen in as students read. Stop students periodically and ask them how they are figuring out difficult words and how they are monitoring their comprehension. Note students who need additional work with specific decoding or comprehension skills.

- Encourage students to read other previously read Leveled Readers during independent reading time or for homework.

Meet Grade-Level Expectations

As an alternative to this day's lesson, guide students through a reading of the On Level Leveled Reader. See page 199Y. Since both books contain the same vocabulary, phonics, and comprehension skills, the scaffolding you provided will help most students gain access to this more challenging text.

Book Talk

Bringing Groups Together Students will work with peers of various language and reading abilities to discuss this week's Leveled Readers. Refer to page 161 in the **Teacher's Resource Book** for more about how to conduct a Book Talk.

Student Book

Student Book

Approaching Level

Fluency

Objectives Reread selections to develop fluency; deliver an oral summary

Materials • **Student Book:** *Making a Splash*, "Standing Tall"

REREAD FOR FLUENCY

- Have students reread a portion of *Making a Splash*. Suggest that they focus on their two favorite pages from the selection. Work with students to read the pages with accuracy.

- Provide time for students to read their sections of text to you. Comment on their accuracy, and provide corrective feedback by modeling proper fluency.

DEVELOP SPEAKING/LISTENING SKILLS

- Have students deliver an oral summary of "Standing Tall."

- Work with students to determine the main ideas and key supporting details they should include in their summary.

- Provide time for students to practice reading their summaries accurately. Suggest that students write each main idea on a separate note card to help them remember the most important information. Listeners should listen attentively to readers.

- Have students present their summaries to the class.

Approaching Level

Self-Selected Reading

Objective   Read independently to summarize main ideas and supporting details

Materials   • **Leveled Classroom Library**   • other informational books

APPLY SKILLS AND STRATEGIES TO INDEPENDENT READING

- **Read Independently** Have students choose an informational book for sustained silent reading. (See the **Theme Bibliography** on pages T8–T9 for book suggestions.) Remind them that to determine the main idea of a selection they should figure out what the details have in common. Have students read their books and record important details and then the main idea on a Main Idea Chart.

- **Show Evidence of Reading** While reading, students may generate a reading log or journal. After reading, ask students to use their Main Idea Charts and logs to paraphrase the content of the book, maintaining meaning and logical order. They may write or orally state a summary of the book. Provide time for students to share their summaries and their reactions to the book while participating in Book Talks. Ask: *What is the most interesting idea or fact you learned from this book?*

Approaching

Leveled Classroom Library
See Leveled Classroom
Library lessons on pages T2–T7.

Daily Planner

DAY 1	• Vocabulary • Phonics
DAY 2	• Leveled Reader Lesson 1
DAY 3	• Leveled Reader Lesson 2
DAY 4	• Fluency
DAY 5	• Self-Selected Reading

ELL

Practice Vocabulary Pair ELL students with native speakers. On the board, provide sentence frames for pairs to copy and complete using the vocabulary and additional words when necessary. For example: *The new exhibition at the museum had a _____ collection of _____.* (*varied; artifacts*)

Sound-Spelling WorkBoard

On Level

Vocabulary

Objective   Review vocabulary
Materials   • **Vocabulary Cards**

REVIEW PREVIOUSLY TAUGHT WORDS

Review the Words Display the **Vocabulary Cards** for *similar, challenges, designed, achieved*, and *varied*. Point to each word, read it aloud, and have students chorally repeat.

Then provide the following questions. Have students answer each question and explain their response. Allow other students to respond. Use the discussions to determine each student's depth of word knowledge.

- Are jackets and sweaters *similar*? Why or why not?
- Do *challenges* make it easier or harder to be successful? Explain.
- Is something that is *designed* planned or accidental?
- If you *achieved* something, did you fail or succeed?
- Does a *varied* shell collection have one kind of shell or many kinds?

Phonics/Word Study

Objective   Decode multisyllabic words with three-letter blends
Materials   • **Sound-Spelling WorkBoards**

RETEACH SKILL

- **Three-Letter Blends** Write the three-letter blends *shr, thr, spr, scr, spl,* and *str* on the board. Pronounce each blend and then provide the following sample words: *shriek, throw, spread, script, split, stripe.*
- Write the words below on the board. If necessary, divide the words into syllables using the syllable-scoop technique to help students read one syllable at a time. When completed, point to the words in random order for students to chorally read.

shrinking	shrivel	throttle	throughout	throwaway
sprawling	springboard	sprinkler	scramble	scrumptious
splatter	splinter	striking	straightened	stranded

- **Spelling** Dictate the following words for students to spell on their **WorkBoards**: *shredded, threadbare, spreading, scripted, splendid, structure.* Model how to segment words, such as spelling a word syllable by syllable.

On Level

Fluency

Objective Reread selections to develop accuracy and present an oral summary

Materials • **Student Book:** *Making a Splash*, "Standing Tall"

REREAD FOR FLUENCY

- Have students reread *Making a Splash*. Work with them to read fluently and accurately. Model fluent reading as needed.

- Provide time for students to read a section of text to you. Comment on their accuracy, and provide corrective feedback.

DEVELOP SPEAKING/LISTENING SKILLS

- Have students deliver an oral summary of "Standing Tall."

- Have students determine the main ideas and significant details they should include in their summaries.

- Provide time for students to practice reading their summaries accurately. Direct them to write each main idea on a separate note card in order to help them remember the most important information.

- Have students present their summaries to the class. Instruct them to look up from their note cards and make eye contact to engage their audience. Remind the audience to listen attentively.

Self-Selected Reading

Objective Read independently to summarize the main idea and supporting details

Materials • **Leveled Classroom Library** • other informational books

APPLY SKILLS AND STRATEGIES TO INDEPENDENT READING

- **Read Independently** Have students choose an informational book for sustained silent reading, such as a **Leveled Classroom Library** book. (See the **Theme Bibliography** on pages T8–T9 for other book suggestions.) Have students read their books, write down important supporting details, and then determine the main ideas.

- **Show Evidence of Reading** While reading, students may generate a reading log or journal. After reading, have students use their main idea and details lists and logs to paraphrase the content of the book, maintaining meaning and logical order. They may write or state an oral summary of the book. Ask students to share their summaries and reactions to the book while participating in Book Talks. Ask: *What did you learn from reading this book? Would you recommend it to a classmate? Why or why not?*

Student Book

Student Book

On Level

Leveled Classroom Library
See Leveled Classroom
Library lessons on pages T2–T7.

Leveled Reader

On Level

 Leveled Reader Lesson 1

Objective Read to apply strategies and skills
Materials • **Leveled Reader:** *Citizens at Work*

BEFORE READING

Preview and Predict Have students read the title and preview the book by reading the chapter titles and looking at the photographs. Have students predict what this book is about and the types of information they might learn.

 Review Vocabulary Words Have students read the vocabulary words on the inside front cover. Ask them to state related words they have learned. Review definitions as needed.

Set a Purpose for Reading *Let's read to find out how different people helped out their communities.*

DURING READING

 STRATEGY
MONITOR COMPREHENSION

Remind students that monitoring their comprehension means to stop to check their understanding before continuing to read.

SKILL
MAIN IDEA AND DETAILS

Remind students that the main idea is the most important point an author makes about a topic. To determine the main idea, they should examine the details and decide what they have in common, or how they are connected.

Read Chapter 1 with students. Ask open-ended questions to facilitate rich discussion, such as, *What did the author want us to know about people who have contributed to their communities?* Build on students' responses to help them develop a deeper understanding of the text. Have students fill in the first section of the Main Idea Chart, then continue reading.

Idioms As they read, have students point out this week's new vocabulary words and any idioms the author may use. Have students use context to determine the meanings of the idioms.

AFTER READING

Ask students to compare one or two people profiled in *Citizens at Work* with Rudy Garcia-Tolson. Ask: *How are they the same? How are they different?* Have students discuss how Rudy Garcia-Tolson has contributed to his community.

On Level

Leveled Reader Lesson 2

Objective Reread to apply skills and strategies and develop fluency

Materials
- **Leveled Reader:** *Citizens at Work*
- **Practice Book,** p. 68

Leveled Reader

BEFORE READING

Review the Strategy and Skill Review students' completed Main Idea Charts from the first read. Remind them that the main idea is the most important idea in a passage or text.

A summary includes the main ideas from the book in the student's own words. If students' summaries are incomplete, provide a model summary or use a student summary and revise it as a group. Have students copy the revised summary in their Writer's Notebooks.

Set a Purpose for Reading *Let's reread to check our understanding of the information in the book and to work on our reading fluency.*

DURING READING

Reread *Citizens at Work* with students. Have them read silently two pages at a time or read aloud to a partner. Stop and have students summarize before reading the next two pages. Model oral summaries as needed.

AFTER READING

Check Comprehension Have partners complete the Comprehension Check on page 20. Review students' answers. Help students find evidence for their answers in the text.

MODEL FLUENCY

Model reading the fluency passage on **Practice Book** page 68. Tell students to pay close attention to your accuracy as you read. Then read one sentence at a time, and have students echo-read the sentences, focusing on reading each word correctly.

During independent reading time, have students work with a partner using the fluency passage. One student reads aloud, and the other repeats each sentence. If students need additional support, have them listen to the "practice speed" version of the passage on the **Fluency Solutions Audio CD**.

Book Talk

Bringing Groups Together Students will work with peers of various language and reading abilities to discuss this week's **Leveled Readers**. Refer to page 161 in the **Teacher's Resource Book** for more about how to conduct a Book Talk.

Practice Book, page 68

As I read, I will focus on reading accurately.

	"Are we there yet?" Jamal asked, crossing his arms
9	across his chest.
12	"Almost, honey," his mom replied. "Look out the
20	window. Isn't it beautiful?"
24	Jamal didn't answer, but he did look. Out his mom's
34	window, all he could see was a rising, rocky cliff. Out his
46	own window, the cliff dropped down, and Jamal could see
56	the road winding below them. Below that were green
65	fields. A few houses and farms were scattered about.
74	The city was a long way away. It felt like they had been
87	driving forever.
89	They were driving up into the mountains to spend a
99	week at a ranch. His mom had lived at this ranch when
111	she was a little girl. "Some vacation," Jamal thought to
121	himself. 122

Comprehension Check

1. How does Jamal feel about his vacation? **Plot Development**
Jamal is annoyed and feels far from his home in the city.
2. How does Jamal's mom feel about the vacation? **Plot Development**
She is happy. She says the view is beautiful, and they are going to where she lived as a child.

	Words Read	−	Number of Errors	=	Words Correct Score
First Read		−		=	
Second Read		−		=	

Beyond Level

Daily Planner

DAY 1	• Leveled Reader Lesson 1
DAY 2	• Leveled Reader Lesson 2
DAY 3	• Phonics
DAY 4	• Vocabulary • Fluency
DAY 5	• Self-Selected Reading

ELL

Self-Monitor Vocabulary
Have student pairs of different proficiency identify and define unfamiliar words from the main selection using a dictionary. Challenge students to use the new words in sentences. Monitor students as they complete the activity.

Phonics/Word Study

Objective Decode multisyllabic words with three-letter blends
Materials • none

EXTEND/ACCELERATE

■ **Read Multisyllabic Words with Three-Letter Blends** Write the words below on the board. Challenge students to read the words, using known word parts. When completed, point to the words in random order for students to chorally read.

shrinkable	unscripted	unthreatened	restructured
rethreaded	resplendent	sprinkling	shrewdly
inscribed	restraining	scrutinized	thriftiness
spreading	shrubbery	splendidly	springboard

■ **Define Words** Ask students to use their knowledge of word parts to figure out the meanings of the above words. Then have partners find the words in a dictionary and confirm or revise the meanings. Challenge students to use these words in this week's writing assignments.

■ **Spell Words with Three-Letter Blends** Dictate the following words for students to spell: *shriveling, unthreatening, springboard, prescription, splintering, strengthening*. Write the words for students to self-correct.

Vocabulary

Objectives Review main idea; write an interview
Materials • **Student Book:** *Making a Splash*

ENRICH VOCABULARY

■ **Review Main Idea** Remind students that to determine the main idea of *Making a Splash*, they should locate the key details of the selection. Have students list the details and identify what they have in common. Guide students in arriving at the main idea.

■ **Write an Interview** Have students write questions they would like to ask one of the people they have read about. Suggest they include the vocabulary words in their questions. Then have them exchange papers with a partner and answer the questions they receive as if they were the person being interviewed. Tell them to refer to the selection to help them answer the questions.

Beyond Level

Fluency

Objectives Reread selections to develop fluency; deliver an oral summary
Materials • **Student Book:** *Making a Splash*, "Standing Tall"

REREAD FOR FLUENCY

- Have students reread *Making a Splash*. Work with them to read the selection with fluency and accuracy.

- Provide time for students to read a section of text to you. Comment on their accuracy, and provide corrective feedback.

DEVELOP SPEAKING/LISTENING SKILLS

- Students will deliver a first-person oral summary of "Standing Tall."

- Have students determine the main ideas and most significant details they should include in their summary.

- Provide time for students to practice reading their summaries accurately. Instruct them to memorize their summaries, and remind them to use first person.

- Have students present their summaries to the class, and remind them to make eye contact to engage the audience. Direct the audience to listen attentively.

Self-Selected Reading

Objective Read independently to determine the main idea and supporting details
Materials • **Leveled Classroom Library** • other informational books

APPLY SKILLS AND STRATEGIES TO INDEPENDENT READING

- **Read Independently** Have students choose an informational book for sustained silent reading. (See the **Theme Bibliography** on pages T8–T9 for book suggestions.) Have them read their books and write down key details and then the main ideas.

- **Show Evidence of Reading** While reading, students may generate a log or journal. After reading, have students use their main idea and details lists and logs to paraphrase the content of the book, maintaining meaning and logical order. They may write or orally state a summary of the book. Ask students to share their summaries and reactions to the book while participating in Book Talks. Ask: *What did you learn from this book?*

- **Evaluate** Challenge students to discuss how the books they have chosen relate to the theme of Facing Challenges. Ask: *What are different ways people can face challenges?* Have students discuss challenges they have had to face.

Student Book

Student Book

Beyond
Leveled Classroom Library
See Leveled Classroom Library lessons on pages T2–T7.

Leveled Reader

Beyond Level

Leveled Reader Lesson 1

Objective Read to apply strategies and skills

Materials • **Leveled Reader:** *Citizens at Work*

BEFORE READING

Preview and Predict Have students preview the book by reading the title and chapter titles and looking at the photographs. Ask students to predict what this book is about and the types of information they might learn.

 Review Vocabulary Words Have students read the vocabulary words on the inside front cover. Ask them to state each definition and any related words they have learned.

Set a Purpose for Reading *Let's read to find out how different citizens have contributed to their communities.*

DURING READING

 STRATEGY
MONITOR COMPREHENSION

Ask students to define the term *monitor comprehension*. Remind students that *monitoring comprehension* is the same as *checking understanding*.

SKILL
MAIN IDEA AND DETAILS

Ask students to define the term *main idea*. Remind them that the main idea is the most important point an author makes about a topic. To determine the main idea, readers examine the details and decide what they have in common, or how they are connected.

Read the book with students. Ask open-ended questions to facilitate rich discussion, such as *What does the author want you to know about the people mentioned in the book? What does the author want to tell you about good citizens?* Build on students' responses to develop deeper understanding of the text. Have students fill in the graphic organizer for this week as they read.

AFTER READING

Compare As a group, have students compare and contrast the accomplishments of two or more people mentioned in this book.

Analyze Students should discuss ways in which the people profiled in the book helped others. Then have them identify other people who have helped their communities in similar and different ways.

Gifted Talented

Beyond Level

Leveled Reader Lesson 2

Objective   Reread to apply skills and strategies and develop fluency

Materials
- **Leveled Reader:** *Citizens at Work*
- **Beyond Reproducible,** p. 68

Leveled Reader

BEFORE READING

Review the Strategy and Skill   Review students' completed Main Idea Charts from the first read.

Remind students that a summary includes the main ideas from the book. If students' summaries are incomplete, provide a model summary or use a student summary and revise it as a group. Have students copy the revised summary in their Writer's Notebooks.

Set a Purpose for Reading   *Let's reread to check our understanding of the information in the book and work on our reading fluency.*

DURING READING

Have students reread *Citizens at Work* silently or with a partner. If they are reading in pairs, prompt students to stop every two pages and summarize or ask their partner probing questions.

AFTER READING

Check Comprehension   Have students independently complete the Comprehension Check on page 20. Review their answers. Help students find evidence for their answers in the text.

Synthesize   Challenge students to think of ways they can help their community. Working in pairs, students should think of a project they can do to help others. Have them design a flier describing the project and persuading others to participate.

MODEL FLUENCY

Model reading the fluency passage on **Beyond Reproducible** page 68. Tell students to pay close attention to your accuracy as you read. Then read one sentence at a time, and have students echo-read the sentences, focusing on reading fluently and accurately.

During independent reading time, have students work with a partner using the fluency passage. One student reads aloud, and the other repeats each sentence. Students can check their fluency by reading along with the "expert speed" version of the passage on the **Fluency Solutions Audio CD**.

Book Talk

Bringing Groups Together Students will work with peers of various language and reading abilities to discuss this week's **Leveled Readers**. Refer to page 161 in the **Teacher's Resource Book** for more about how to conduct a Book Talk.

Beyond Reproducible, page 68

As I read, I will focus on reading accurately.

Their mother gave them bottles of water and little bags of trail mix.
13 "This way," she called as she headed off.
21 "Slow down!" Nick called out. He wanted to have time to look
33 around. Everything here was so different from the city. The city was
45 cluttered with cars, buildings, people, and loud noises. In the woods,
56 there were nothing but trees and the gentle "ssshhhhh" of the wind.
68 Up ahead Nick could see that Felix had reached the edge of the
81 forest and stopped. Beside him was a woman wearing a green uniform.
93 When Nick caught up, his eyes filled with wonder. They were standing
105 on top of a hill made of sand. Below them was the ocean. The air was
121 filled with the salty smell of the water. All around them were more hills
135 of sand. Some were small. Others, like the one they stood on, were huge.
149 Nick felt a little dizzy as he looked down. 158

Comprehension Check

1. What does Nick find interesting about the place he is exploring?
   Plot Development It is so different from the city where Nick lives. He is also impressed by the view from the top of the sand dune he is standing on.
2. How are Nick and Felix different in their approaches to exploring?
   Plot Development Felix wants to run while Nick wants to walk. Nick wants more time to examine the things he sees. Felix just wants to go as far as he can.

	Words Read	−	Number of Errors	=	Words Correct Score
First Read		−		=	
Second Read		−		=	

Daily Planner

DAY 1	• Build Background Knowledge • Vocabulary
DAY 2	• Vocabulary • Access to Core Content *Making a Splash*
DAY 3	• Vocabulary • Grammar • Access to Core Content *Making a Splash*
DAY 4	• Vocabulary • Writing/Spelling • Access to Core Content *Making a Splash* • Leveled Reader *Citizens at Work*
DAY 5	• Vocabulary • Leveled Reader *Citizens at Work* • Self-Selected Reading

StudentWorks *Plus*

Interactive Student Book

Use StudentWorks Plus for:
- Vocabulary Preteaching
- Word-by-Word Highlighting
- Think Aloud Prompts

Cognates

Help students identify similarities and differences in pronunciation and spelling between English and Spanish cognates.

adapt	*adaptar*
victory	*victoria*
similar	*similar*
designed	*diseñado*
varied	*variado*
comprehension	*comprensión*
idea	*idea*
irregular	*irregular*
plural	*plural*

ELL ENGLISH LANGUAGE LEARNERS

Prepare to Read

Content Objective Explore athletes who overcome physical challenges

Language Objective Use key words to discuss athletes who overcome challenges

Materials • StudentWorks Plus

BUILD BACKGROUND KNOWLEDGE

All Language Levels

- Have students preview *Making a Splash* using **StudentWorks Plus**, which contains oral summaries in multiple languages, online multilingual glossaries, word-by-word highlighting, and questions that assess and build comprehension.

- Students can build their word-reading fluency by reading along as the text is read or by listening during the first reading and, at the end of each paragraph, returning to the beginning of the paragraph and reading along.

- Students can build their comprehension by reviewing the definitions of key words in the online glossary and by answering the comprehension questions. When appropriate, the text required to answer the question is highlighted to provide students with additional support and scaffolding.

- After reading, ask students to respond to questions: *Do you know anyone who is physically challenged? How do they overcome these challenges?*

Academic Language

Language Objective Use academic language in classroom conversations

All Language Levels

- This week's academic words are **boldfaced** throughout the lesson. Define the word in context, and provide a clear example from the selection. Then ask students to generate an example or a word with a similar meaning.

Academic Language Used in Whole Group Instruction

Theme Words	Key Selection Words	Strategy and Skill Words
adapt **equipment** **victory**	**similar** **challenges** **designed** **achieved** **varied**	**monitor comprehension** **main idea** **details** **idioms** **irregular plural nouns**

ELL   ENGLISH LANGUAGE LEARNERS

Vocabulary

Language Objective Demonstrate understanding and use of key words by discussing athletes who overcome physical challenges

Materials • **Visual Vocabulary Resources**
• **ELL Resource Book**

PRETEACH KEY VOCABULARY

Use the **Visual Vocabulary Resources** to preteach the key selection words *similar, challenges, designed, achieved*, and *varied*. Focus on two words per day. Use the below routine, detailed on the cards.

Beginning/Intermediate

■ Point out any known sound-spellings, or focus on a key aspect of phonemic awareness related to the word.

All Language Levels

■ Define the word in English, and provide the example given.

■ Define the word in Spanish, if appropriate, and indicate if the word is a cognate.

■ Display the picture, and explain how it demonstrates the word. Engage students in a structured activity about the image.

■ Ask students to chorally say the word three times.

■ Distribute copies of the Vocabulary Glossary, **ELL Resource Book** page 84.

PRETEACH FUNCTION WORDS AND PHRASES

All Language Levels

Use the Visual Vocabulary Resources to preteach the function words and phrases *the same as, want something bad enough, get better and better*, and *absorb shock*. Focus on one word per day. Use the detailed routine on the cards.

■ Define the word in English and, if appropriate, in Spanish. Point out if the word is a cognate.

■ Use the picture to engage students in talk about the word. For example, students will partner-talk using sentence frames.

■ Ask students to chorally repeat the word three times.

TEACH BASIC WORDS

Beginning/Intermediate

Use the Visual Vocabulary Resources to teach the basic words *athlete, champion, treadmill, swimming, running*, and *biking*. Teach these "sports" words using the routine provided on the card.

Visual Vocabulary Resources

ELL Resource Book, page 84

Use the word chart to study this week's vocabulary words.
Write a sentence using each word in your writer's notebook.

Word	Context Sentence	Illustration
similar	We were dressed nearly alike. Our sweaters were <u>similar</u>.	Name something you have that is similar to a friends'.
challenges	His physical <u>challenges</u> did not keep him from playing.	
designed	The cup is <u>designed</u> so the contents won't spill if the cup tips over.	
achieved	She hoped to get an A on the test, and she <u>achieved</u> it.	What is something you worked for and achieved?
varied	The height of the team members <u>varied</u>.	

ELL Resource Book

ELL ENGLISH LANGUAGE LEARNERS

Access to Core Content

Content Objective Read grade-level text
Language Objective Discuss text using key words and sentence frames
Materials • **ELL Resource Book,** pp. 82–83

PRETEACH MAIN SELECTION (PAGES 192–195)

All Language Levels

Use the Interactive Question-Response Guide on **ELL Resource Book** pages 82–83 to introduce students to *Making a Splash*. Preteach half of the selection on Day 2 and half on Day 3.

■ Use the prompts provided in the guide to develop meaning and vocabulary. Use the partner-talk and whole-class responses to engage students and increase student talk.

■ When completed, have partners reread the story.

Beginning	Intermediate	Advanced
Use Visuals During the Interactive Reading, select several photographs. Describe the main idea of each photograph. Have students point to the photograph and repeat the main idea.	**Describe** During the Interactive Reading, select a few lines of text. After you have read and explained the text, have students describe the main idea of the text.	**Summarize** During the Interactive Reading, select a text passage. After you have read and explained the passage, have students describe the main idea and details of the passage.

ELL ENGLISH LANGUAGE LEARNERS

Fluency

Content Objectives Reread selections to develop fluency; develop speaking skills

Language Objective Tell a partner what a selection is about

Materials • **Student Book:** *Making a Splash*, "Standing Tall"
• **Teacher's Resource Book**

REREAD FOR FLUENCY

Beginning

■ Have students read the decodable passages on page 12 in the **Teacher's Resource Book**.

Intermediate/Advanced

■ Have students reread a portion of *Making a Splash*. Have them focus on one or two pages from the selection, based on their levels. Help students read with accuracy. For example, read each sentence of the first paragraph and have students echo. Then have students continue by choral-reading additional paragraphs.

■ Provide time for students to read their sections. Comment on their accuracy and provide corrective feedback by modeling proper fluency.

DEVELOP SPEAKING/LISTENING SKILLS

All Language Levels

■ Have students practice reading "Standing Tall." Work with students to read with accuracy.

■ Provide time for students to read aloud the article to a partner. Ask students to tell their partner about the article. Provide the sentence frame: *This article is about ____.*

Student Book

Self-Selected Reading

Content Objective Read independently

Language Objective Orally retell information learned

Materials • **Leveled Classroom Library** • other nonfiction books

APPLY SKILLS AND STRATEGIES TO INDEPENDENT READING

All Language Levels

■ Have students choose a nonfiction book, such as a biography, for silent independent reading. (See the **Theme Bibliography** on pages T8–T9 for book suggestions.)

■ After reading, ask students to orally summarize the book and share their comments with classmates. Ask: *Would you recommend this book to a classmate? Why or why not?*

Leveled Classroom Library
See Leveled Classroom
Library lessons on pages T2–T7.

ELL ENGLISH LANGUAGE LEARNERS

Grammar

Content Objective Identify irregular plural nouns

Language Objective Speak in complete sentences, using sentence frames

IRREGULAR PLURAL NOUNS

Beginning/Intermediate

- Review singular and plural nouns. Remind students that we use plural-noun names for more than one person, place, or thing. Demonstrate that we add -s or -es to most nouns to show "more than one." For example: *book/books; beach/beaches*.

All Language Levels

- Review plural nouns and how to form them. Explain that some nouns have irregular plural forms. Provide examples and point out that irregular plural forms are *not* formed by adding -s or -es: *child/children; foot/feet; tooth/teeth; man/men*. Write the sentences below on the board. Have students choose the plural noun to complete each sentence. Have them say: ____ *is an irregular plural noun. Irregular plural nouns do not end with ____.*

    Some (childs/children) have physical challenges.

    My (feet/foots) are too big for my shoes.

    Next year, I will need braces on my (tooths/teeth).

    Get those (mice/mouses) out of the kitchen!

PEER DISCUSSION STARTERS

All Language Levels

- Write the following sentences on the board:

    Rudy doesn't ____.   *I learned that the Paralympics ____.*

- Pair students and have them complete each sentence frame. Have them expand on their sentences by providing as many details as they can from this week's readings. Circulate, listen in, and take note of each student's language use and proficiency.

Beginning	**Intermediate**	**Advanced**
Use Visuals Describe the photographs in *Making a Splash* to students, using singular and plural nouns. Ask: *What do you see?* Help them point and name singular and plural nouns.	**Describe** Ask students to describe the photographs in *Making a Splash* using singular and plural nouns. Have them use complete sentences. Challenge them to identify nouns that have irregular plural forms.	**Describe** Ask students to describe the photographs in *Making a Splash* using singular and plural nouns. Have them identify nouns that have irregular plural forms.

ELL ENGLISH LANGUAGE LEARNERS

Writing/Spelling

Content Objective Spell words correctly

Language Objective Write in complete sentences, using sentence frames

All Language Levels

- Write the key vocabulary words on the board: *similar, challenges, designed, achieved, varied*. Have students copy each word on their **WorkBoards**. Help them say each word and then write a sentence for it. Provide sentence starters, such as:

  One way that an orange is similar to an apple is that _____.

  Some challenges faced by new students are _____.

  A good video game is designed to _____.

  I achieved an A on a _____.

  The grocery store has a varied selection of _____.

Beginning/Intermediate

- Help students spell words using their growing knowledge of English sound-spelling relationships. Model how to segment the word students are trying to spell, and attach a spelling to each sound (or spellings to each syllable if a multisyllabic word). Use the **Sound-Spelling Cards** to reinforce the spellings for each English sound.

Advanced

- Dictate the following words for students to spell: *strip, splash, spring, scrap, spray, scrub, stream, split*. Use the Sound-Spelling Cards to guide students as they spell each word.

- When completed, review the meanings of words that can be easily demonstrated or explained. Use actions, gestures, and available pictures.

Sound-Spelling WorkBoard

Phonics/Word Study

For English Language Learners who need more practice with this week's phonics/spelling skill, see the Approaching Level lesson on page 199N. Focus on minimal contrasts, articulation, and those sounds that do not transfer from the student's first language to English. See language transfers on pages T16–T31.

Leveled Reader

Vocabulary

Preteach Vocabulary Use the routine in the **Visual Vocabulary Resources**, pages 397–402, to preteach the ELL Vocabulary listed in the inside front cover of the **Leveled Reader**.

ELL ENGLISH LANGUAGE LEARNERS

Leveled Reader

Content Objective Read to apply skills and strategies

Language Objective Retell information, using complete sentences

Materials • **Leveled Reader:** *Citizens at Work*
• **ELL Resource Book,** p. 85
• **Visual Vocabulary Resources,** pp. 397–402

BEFORE READING

All Language Levels

- **Preview** Read the title *Citizens at Work*. Ask: *What's the title? Say it again*. Repeat with the author's name. Then page through the book. Use simple language to tell about each page. Immediately follow up with questions, such as *How can citizens help their communities?*

- **Review Skills** Use the inside front cover to review the comprehension skill and vocabulary words.

- **Set a Purpose** Say: *Let's read to find out about different ways citizens help their communities.*

DURING READING

All Language Levels

- Have students read each page aloud using the differentiated suggestions. Provide corrective feedback, such as modeling how to blend a decodable word or clarifying meaning by using techniques from the Interactive Question-Response Guide.

- **Retell** After every two pages, ask students to state the main ideas they have learned so far. Help them to complete the Main Idea and Details Chart. Restate students' comments when they have difficulty using story-specific words. Provide differentiated sentence frames to support students' responses and engage students in partner-talk where appropriate.

Beginning	Intermediate	Advanced
Echo-Read Have students echo-read after you.	**Choral-Read** Have students chorally read with you.	**Choral-Read** Have students chorally read.
Check Comprehension Point to pictures and ask questions, such as *Who is this? What did this person do?*	**Check Comprehension** Ask questions/prompts, such as *Who was Sam Houston? What did he do for his community?*	**Check Comprehension** Ask: *Who was Lyndon B. Johnson? What did he do when he was President of the United States?*

ELL ENGLISH LANGUAGE LEARNERS

AFTER READING

Use the chart below and Think and Compare questions in the **Leveled Reader** to determine students' progress.

ELL Resource Book

Think and Compare	Beginning	Intermediate	Advanced
1 Reread page 10. What sentence tells the main idea? Give two details from the paragraph that support the main idea. *(Main Idea and Details)*	Possible responses: Nonverbal response. First sentence. Pay medical care. Operation Head Start.	Possible responses: Nonverbal response. The first sentence tells the main idea. President Johnson helped families pay for medical care. He started Operation Head Start.	Possible responses: Nonverbal response. The first sentence tells the main idea. President Johnson created a program to help families pay for medical care and he created Operation Head Start to help young children.
2 Which person you read about in this book do you admire the most? Tell why *(Apply)*	Possible responses: Nonverbal response. President Johnson. Helped families and children	Possible responses: I admire President Johnson the most. He helped families and children have better lives.	I admire President Johnson the most because he helped all citizens have better lives. He started a program to make American society great.
3 Leaders such as Al Gore make a difference by speaking out. Why is speaking out a good way to bring about change? Explain. *(Evaluate)*	Possible responses: Nonverbal response. Tell people problem.	Possible responses: Speaking out can help people learn about problems.	Possible responses: Speaking out is a good way because people can learn about problems and find solutions.

BOOK TALK

Develop Listening and Speaking Skills Distribute copies of **ELL Resource Book** page 85 and form small groups. Help students determine the leader to discuss the Book Talk questions. Tell students to remember the following while engaged in the activity:

■ Distinguish between formal and informal English and know when to use each one. Remind students to note whether the selection is written in formal or informal English. Ask: *Why do you think it is written in this way?* Remind students that they may use informal English when speaking with their classmates, but they should use formal language when they talk to teachers or write essays.

■ Use high-frequency English words to describe people, places, and objects.

Book Talk

Bringing Groups Together Students will work with peers of varying language abilities to discuss the Book Talk questions. Form groups so that students who read the Beyond, On Level, Approaching, and ELL Leveled Readers are in the same group for the activity.

Progress Monitoring
Weekly Assessment

ASSESSED SKILLS

- Vocabulary: Vocabulary Words, Idioms
- Comprehension: Main Idea and Details
- Grammar: Irregular Plural Nouns
- Phonics/Spelling: Three-Letter Blends

Selection Test for **Making a Splash** *Also Available*

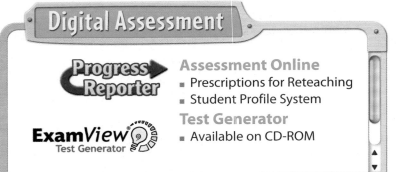

Digital Assessment

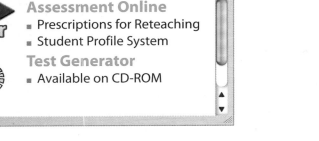

Progress Reporter

Assessment Online
- Prescriptions for Reteaching
- Student Profile System

ExamView Test Generator

Test Generator
- Available on CD-ROM

**Weekly Assessment
Unit 2 Week 3**

Fluency Assessment

Assess fluency for one group of students per week.
Use the Oral Fluency Record Sheet to track the number of
words read correctly. Fluency goal for all students:
84–104 words correct per minute (WCPM).

Approaching Level	Weeks 1, 3, 5
On Level	Weeks 2, 4
Beyond Level	Week 6

Fluency Assessment

Diagnose		Prescribe
Review the assessment answers with students. Have them correct their errors. Then provide additional instruction as needed.		
	IF...	**THEN...**
VOCABULARY WORDS VOCABULARY STRATEGY Idioms	0–2 items correct …	See **Vocabulary Intervention Teacher's Edition.** ⬛LOG ON ▶ Online Practice: Go to www.macmillanmh.com. 💿CD-ROM Vocabulary PuzzleMaker
COMPREHENSION Skill: Main Idea and Details	0–3 items correct …	See **Comprehension Intervention Teacher's Edition.** 🌀SPIRAL REVIEW See Main Idea and Details lesson in Unit 2 Week 4, page 219B.
GRAMMAR Irregular Plural Nouns	0–1 items correct …	See **Writing and Grammar Intervention Teacher's Edition.**
PHONICS AND SPELLING Three-Letter Blends	0–1 items correct …	⬛LOG ON ▶ Online Practice: Go to www.macmillanmh.com. See **Phonics Intervention Teacher's Edition.**
FLUENCY	79–83 WCPM	💿AUDIO CD Fluency Solutions Audio CD
	0–78 WCPM	See **Fluency Intervention Teacher's Edition.**

Response to Intervention

To place students in Tier 2 or Tier 3 Intervention use the *Diagnostic Assessment*.

- Phonics
- Vocabulary
- Comprehension
- Fluency
- Writing and Grammar

Week 4 ★ At a Glance

Priority Skills and Concepts

✔ Comprehension
- **Strategy:** Analyze Text Structure
- **Skill:** Cause and Effect
-  **Skill:** Main Idea and Details
- **Genre:** Fiction, Expository, Folktale

✔ Robust Vocabulary
- **Selection Vocabulary:** *descendants, sanctuary, threatened, fragile, habitat, emerge*
- **Strategy:** Context Clues: Paragraph Clues

✔ Fluency
- **Rate**

✔ Phonics/Spelling
- **Word Study:** *r*-Controlled Vowels /är/ and /ôr/, Multisyllabic Words
- **Spelling Words:** *door, dart, fort, morning, carpet, ford, core, cord, spark, award, smart, charge, worn, argue, stormy, bore, guard, ward, warp, backyard*
- *screech, shrimp, throat*

✔ Grammar/Mechanics
- **Possessive Nouns**
- **Titles**

✔ Writing
- **Trait: Word Choice**
- **Strong Verbs**

Key

 Tested in program   SPIRAL REVIEW Review Skill

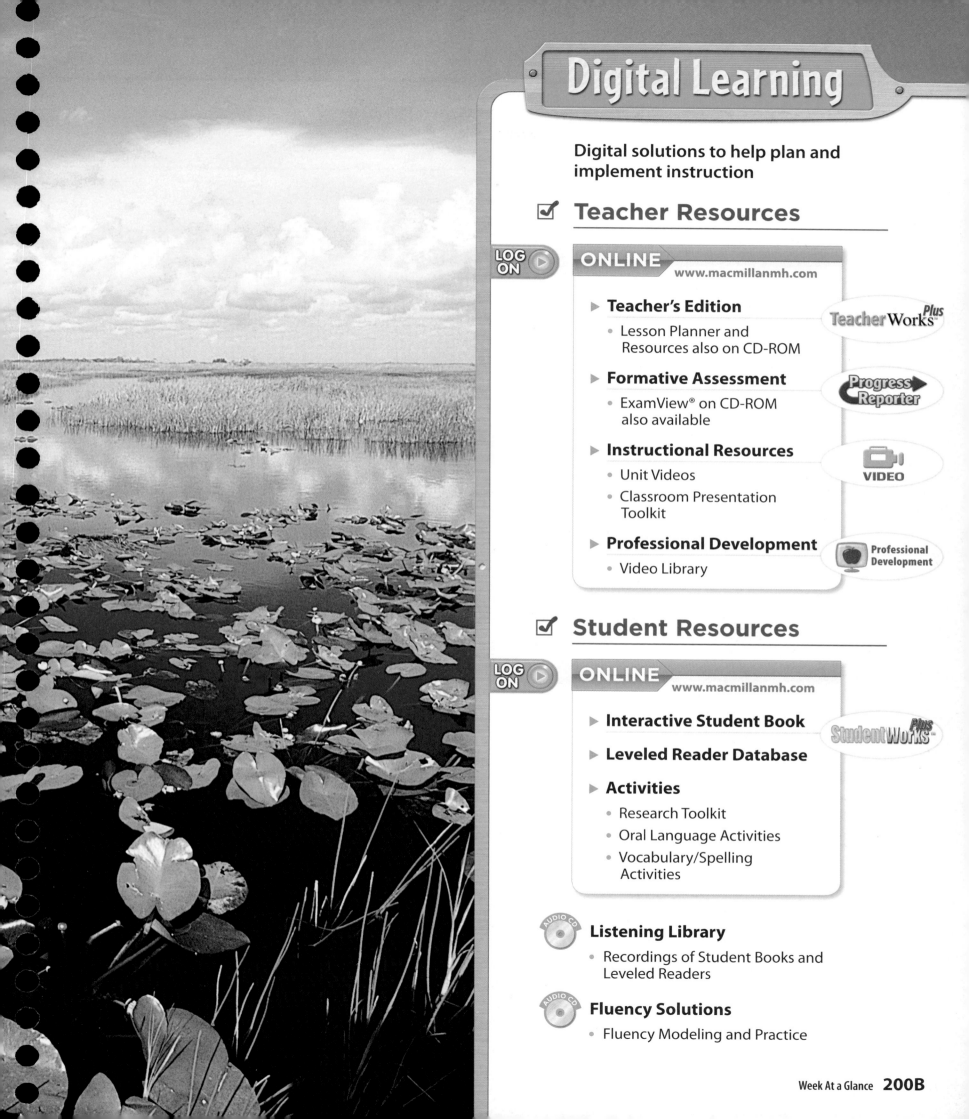

Digital Learning

Digital solutions to help plan and implement instruction

☑ Teacher Resources

LOG ON ▶

ONLINE
www.macmillanmh.com

▶ **Teacher's Edition**
- Lesson Planner and Resources also on CD-ROM

TeacherWorks Plus

▶ **Formative Assessment**
- ExamView® on CD-ROM also available

Progress Reporter

▶ **Instructional Resources**
- Unit Videos
- Classroom Presentation Toolkit

VIDEO

▶ **Professional Development**
- Video Library

Professional Development

☑ Student Resources

LOG ON ▶

ONLINE
www.macmillanmh.com

▶ **Interactive Student Book**

StudentWorks Plus

▶ **Leveled Reader Database**

▶ **Activities**
- Research Toolkit
- Oral Language Activities
- Vocabulary/Spelling Activities

Listening Library
- Recordings of Student Books and Leveled Readers

Fluency Solutions
- Fluency Modeling and Practice

Weekly Literature

Theme: Saving Animals

StudentWorks *Plus*
Interactive Student Book

- Word-by-Word Reading
- Summaries in Multiple Languages
- Comprehension Questions

Wild Horses
by Cris Peterson
photographs by Alvis Upitis

Main Selection

Genre Expository

The **Wild Ponies** of **Chincoteague**
by Gregory Searle

Preteach Vocabulary and Comprehension

Genre Expository

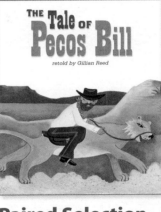

THE Tale OF **Pecos Bill**
retold by Gillian Reed

Paired Selection

Genre Folktale

Support Literature

INTERACTIVE **Read-Aloud** ANTHOLOGY WITH PLAYS

Interactive Read-Aloud Anthology
- Listening Comprehension
- Robust Vocabulary
- Readers' Theater Plays for Fluency

Resources for Differentiated Instruction

Leveled Readers: Social Studies

AUDIO CD

Leveled Reader Library

GR Levels O-T

Genre Expository

- Same Theme
- Same Vocabulary
- Same Comprehension Skills

O
Cattle-Driving Horses of the Old West
by Ann Gadzikowski

Approaching Level

R
Cattle-Driving Horses of the Old West
by Ann Gadzikowski

On Level

T
Cattle-Driving Horses of the Old West
by Ann Gadzikowski

Beyond Level

P
Horses in the Old West
by Ann Gadzikowski

ELL

LOG ON ▶ **Leveled Reader Database**
Go to www.macmillanmh.com.

Leveled Practice

Treasures — Approaching Reproducibles

Treasures — Practice Book

Treasures — Beyond Reproducibles

Treasures — English Language Learner Practice Book

Approaching | **On Level** | **Beyond** | **ELL**

Leveled Classroom Library

SATCHEL PAIGE

HOKUSAI

Approaching | **On Level** | **Beyond**

Response to Intervention

Tier 2
- Phonics
- Vocabulary
- Comprehension
- Fluency
- Writing and Grammar
Tier 3

Assessment

Time For Kids
- TFK Teacher's Manual
- Apply Answering Question Strategies

TIME FOR KIDS

Treasures — Student Weekly Assessment
- Selection Tests
- Weekly Assessment

Treasures — Unit Assessment
Includes Writing Prompts

Treasures — Benchmark Assessment

Weekly Assessment | Unit Assessment | Benchmark Assessment

HOME-SCHOOL CONNECTION

- Family letters in English and Spanish
- Take-Home Stories and activities

Treasures — Home-School Connection

LOG ON ▶ **Online Homework**
www.macmillanmh.com

TeacherWorks *Plus*
All-In-One Planner and Resource Center

Professional Development
Video Library

Wild Horses, pp. 204–217

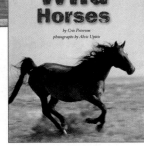
Wild Horses
by Cris Peterson
photographs by Alvis Upitis

WHOLE GROUP

ORAL LANGUAGE

- **Listening Comprehension**
- **Speaking/Viewing**

WORD STUDY

- **Vocabulary**

- **Phonics/Word Study**

- **Spelling**

READING

- **Comprehension**

- **Fluency**

LANGUAGE ARTS

- **Writing**

- **Grammar**

ASSESSMENT

- **Informal/Formal**

DAY 1

Listening/Speaking/Viewing

❓ **Focus Question** The horses on pages 200–201 live in a big marsh in southern France. What do you see that tells you they are wild?

Build Background, 200

Read Aloud: "Misty of Chincoteague," 201A–201B

Vocabulary
descendants, sanctuary, threatened, fragile, habitat, emerge, 203, 225C

Practice Book, 74

Strategy: Context Clues/Paragraph Clues, 202

Spelling Pretest: *r*-Controlled Vowels /är/ and /ôr/, 225E
Phonics/Spelling Book, 49–50

Read "The Wild Ponies of Chincoteague," 202–203

The Wild Ponies of Chincoteague
by Gregory Searle
Student Book

Comprehension, 203A–203B
Strategy: Analyze Text Structure
Skill: Cause and Effect
Practice Book, 75

Fluency Model Fluency, 201B

Writing

Daily Writing Create a poster to convince people to donate money to help a campaign to save wild horses.

Trait: Word Choice
Strong Verbs, 223A–223B

Grammar Daily Language Activities, 225G
Possessive Nouns, 225G
Grammar Practice Book, 41

Quick Check Vocabulary, 202
Comprehension, 203B

DAY 2

Listening/Speaking/Viewing

❓ **Focus Question** What is it that makes a wild horse wild?

Vocabulary
Review Words, Context Clues, 204, 225C
Practice Book, 80

Phonics
r-Controlled Vowels /är/ and /ôr/, 201C–201D
Practice Book, 73

Spelling Word Sorts, 225E
Phonics/Spelling Book, 51

Read *Wild Horses,* 204–217

Wild Horses
Student Book

Comprehension, 204–217
Strategy: Analyze Text Structure
Skill: Cause and Effect
Practice Book, 76

Fluency Repeated Reading: Rate, 219A

Writing

Daily Writing Write a list of ways that wild horses and domestic horses are alike and different.

Reading/Writing Connection, 224–225

Grammar Daily Language Activities, 225G
Possessive Nouns, 225G
Grammar Practice Book, 42

Quick Check Phonics, 201D
Comprehension, 217

SMALL GROUP Lesson Plan ▶ **Differentiated Instruction 200G–200H**

Priority Skills

Vocabulary	Comprehension	Writing	Science
Vocabulary Words	**Strategy:** Analyze Text Structure	Trait: Word Choice	Identify characteristics that allow a species to survive
Context Clues/ Paragraph Clues	**Skill:** Cause and Effect	Strong Verbs	

DAY 3

Listening/Speaking

❓ Focus Question Compare Assateague Island with the Black Hills Wild Horse Sanctuary. How are the two places alike? How are they different?

Summarize, 219

Vocabulary

Review Words, Related Words, 225D

Spelling Word Meanings, 225F
Phonics/Spelling Book, 52

Read *Wild Horses*, 204–217

Student Book

Comprehension
Comprehension Check, 219

Review Skill: Main Idea and Details, 219B

Practice Book, 78

Fluency Repeated Reading: Rate, 219A
Practice Book, 77

Writing

Daily Writing Write an e-mail to a government official explaining why wild horses should be saved from extinction.

Trait: Word Choice
Strong Verbs, 225A

Grammar Daily Language Activities, 225G
Mechanics and Usage, 225H
Grammar Practice Book, 43

Quick Check Fluency, 219A

DAY 4

Listening/Speaking/Viewing

❓ Focus Question Compare Widow-Maker to the mustangs described in *Wild Horses*. How are they similar? How are they different?

Vocabulary

Review Words, Morphology, 225D

Spelling Proofread, 225F
Phonics/Spelling Book, 53

Read "The Tale of Pecos Bill," 220–223

Student Book

Comprehension
Literary Elements: Hyperbole, Metaphor, 220
Practice Book, 79

Time For Kids

Fluency Repeated Reading: Rate, 219A

Writing

Daily Writing Suppose you could adopt a wild horse. Describe in a paragraph its looks and what its name might be.

Trait: Word Choice
Strong Verbs in Steps, 225A

Grammar Daily Language Activities, 225G
Possessive Nouns, 225H
Grammar Practice Book, 44

Quick Check Vocabulary, 225D

DAY 5
Review and Assess

Listening/Speaking/Viewing

❓ Focus Question Based on your readings about wild horses, what kinds of things would cause a community to control an animal's population?

Vocabulary

Assess Words, Connect to Writing, 225D

Spelling Posttest, 225F
Phonics/Spelling Book, 54

Read Self-Selected Reading, 200K
Practice Book, 81

Student Book

Comprehension
Connect and Compare, 223

Fluency Practice, 200K

Writing

Daily Writing If you were a wild horse, where would you want to live and why? Write a description.

Conferencing, 225B

Grammar Daily Language Activities, 225G
Possessive Nouns, 225H
Grammar Practice Book, 45

Weekly Assessment, 225II–225JJ

Differentiated Instruction

What do I do in small groups?

Teacher-Led Small Groups

Independent Activities

Focus on Skills

IF... students need additional instruction, practice, or extension based on your **Quick Check** observations for the following priority skills:

- ✔ **Phonics/Word Study**
  r-Controlled Vowels /är/ and /ôr/

- ✔ **Vocabulary Words**
  descendants, sanctuary, threatened, fragile, habitat, emerge
  Strategy: Context Clues: Paragraph Clues

- ✔ **Comprehension**
  Strategy: Analyze Text Structure
  Skill: Cause and Effect

- ✔ **Fluency**

THEN...

Approaching **ELL**	Preteach and Reteach Skills
On Level	Practice
Beyond	Enrich and Accelerate Learning

LOG ON ▶ **Suggested Small Group Lesson Plan**

CD-ROM **TeacherWorks** *Plus*
All-In-One Planner and Resource Center

	DAY 1	DAY 2
Approaching Level **Tier 2** • **Preteach/Reteach** **Tier 2 Instruction**	• Prepare to Read, 225I • Academic Language, 225I • Preteach Vocabulary, 225K	• Comprehension, 225M Analyze Text Structure/Cause and Effect **ELL** • Leveled Reader Lesson 1, 225N
On Level • **Practice**	• Vocabulary, 225S • Phonics, 225S *r*-Controlled Vowels /är/ and /ôr/ **ELL**	• Leveled Reader Lesson 1, 225U
Beyond Level *Gifted and Talented* • **Extend/Accelerate** **Gifted and Talented**	• Leveled Reader Lesson 1, 225Y • Analyze Information, 225Y	• Leveled Reader Lesson 2, 225Z • Synthesize Information, 225Z
ELL • **Build English Language Proficiency** • See **ELL** in other levels.	• Prepare to Read, 225AA • Academic Language, 225AA • Preteach Vocabulary, 225BB	• Vocabulary, 225BB • Preteach Main Selection, 225CC

Small Group

Focus on Leveled Readers

Leveled Reader Library

Levels O–T

O Cattle-Driving Horses of the Old West by Ann Gadzikowski
Approaching

R Cattle-Driving Horses of the Old West by Ann Gadzikowski
On Level

T Cattle-Driving Horses of the Old West by Ann Gadzikowski
Beyond

P Horses in the Old West by Ann Gadzikowski
ELL

Social Studies

Teacher's Annotated Edition

Explain the growth and development of the cattle industry.

Additional Leveled Readers

LOG ON ▶
Leveled Reader Database
www.macmillanmh.com

Search by
- Comprehension Skill
- Content Area
- Genre
- Text Feature
- Guided Reading Level
- Reading Recovery Level
- Lexile Score
- Benchmark Level

Subscription also available.

Manipulatives

Sound-Spelling WorkBoards

Sound-Spelling Cards

about today
High-Frequency Word Cards

Visual Vocabulary Resources

DAY 3

- Phonics Maintenance, 225J
  r-Controlled Vowels /är/ and /ôr/ **ELL**
- Leveled Reader Lesson 2, 225O

- Leveled Reader Lesson 2, 225V

- Phonics, 225W
  r-Controlled Vowels /är/ and /ôr/ **ELL**

- Vocabulary, 225BB
- Grammar, 225EE

DAY 4

- Reteach Phonics Skill, 225J
  r-Controlled Vowels /är/ and /ôr/ **ELL**
- Review Vocabulary, 225L
- Leveled Reader Lesson 3, 225P

- Fluency, 225T

- Vocabulary, 225W
- Write a Tall Tale, 225W
- Fluency, 225X

- Vocabulary, 225BB
- Writing/Spelling, 225FF
- Preteach Paired Selection, 225CC
- Fluency, 225DD
- Leveled Reader, 225GG

DAY 5

- High-Frequency Words, 225L
- Fluency, 225Q
- Self-Selected Independent Reading, 225R
- Book Talk, 225P

- Self-Selected Independent Reading, 225T
- Book Talk, 225V

- Self-Selected Independent Reading, 225X
- Evaluate Information, 225X
- Book Talk, 225Z

- Vocabulary, 225BB
- Leveled Reader, 225GG
- Self-Selected Independent Reading, 225DD
- Book Talk, 225HH

Managing the Class

What do I do with the rest of my class?

- Practice Book and Reproducibles
- ELL Practice Book
- Leveled Reader Activities
- Literacy Workstations
- Online Activities

Classroom Management Tools

Weekly Contract

Name _____ Date _____

My To-Do List

✔ Put a check next to the activities you complete.

📖 **Reading**
- ☐ Practice fluency
- ☐ Choose a story to read

🔤 **Phonics/ Word Study**
- ☐ Look up word origins
- ☐ Write words with short vowel sounds

✏️ **Writing**
- ☐ Write a letter to the editor
- ☐ Write a radio ad

🔬 **Science**
- ☐ Research two types of rocks
- ☐ Write a chart

🌍 **Social Studies**
- ☐ Create a guide book
- ☐ Role-play an interview

📖 **Leveled Readers**
- ☐ Write About It!
- ☐ Content Connection

💻 **Technology**
- ☐ Vocabulary PuzzleMaker
- ☐ Fluency Solutions
- ☐ Listening Library
- ☐ www.macmillanmh.com

🖌️ **Independent Practice**
- ☐ Practice Book 1-9

Treasures

Managing Small Groups
A How-to Guide

Dr. Vicki Gibson   Dr. Douglas Fisher

Macmillan/McGraw-Hill

How-to Guide

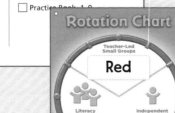

Rotation Chart

Teacher-Led Small Groups

Red

Literacy Workstations   Independent Activities

za

Blue   Green   an

Orange   ria

Rotation Chart

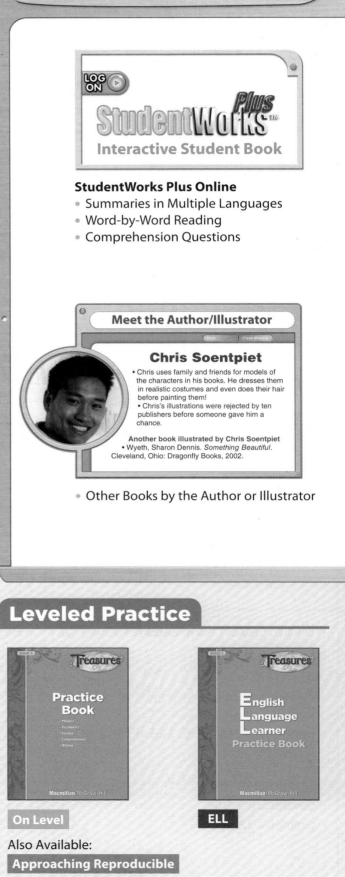

LOG ON ▶

StudentWorks Plus
Interactive Student Book

StudentWorks Plus Online
- Summaries in Multiple Languages
- Word-by-Word Reading
- Comprehension Questions

Meet the Author/Illustrator

Chris Soentpiet
- Chris uses family and friends for models of the characters in his books. He dresses them in realistic costumes and even does their hair before painting them!
- Chris's illustrations were rejected by ten publishers before someone gave him a chance.

Another book illustrated by Chris Soentpiet
- Wyeth, Sharon Dennis. *Something Beautiful.* Cleveland, Ohio: Dragonfly Books, 2002.

- Other Books by the Author or Illustrator

Leveled Practice

Treasures

Practice Book
- Phonics
- Vocabulary
- Fluency
- Comprehension
- Writing

Macmillan/McGraw-Hill

On Level

Treasures

English Language Learner Practice Book

Macmillan/McGraw-Hill

ELL

Also Available:

Approaching Reproducible

Beyond Reproducible

ONLINE INSTRUCTION www.macmillanmh.com

Oral Language Activities

- Focus on Vocabulary and Concepts
- English Language Learner Support

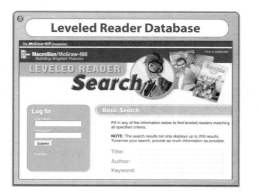

Leveled Reader Database

- Leveled Reader Database
- Search titles by level, skill, content area, and more

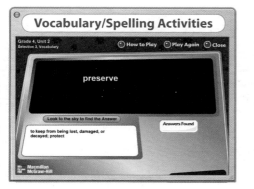

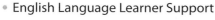

Vocabulary/Spelling Activities

- Differentiated Lists and Activities

Research Toolkit

Step 2. Research

Research answers for the questions you were asked in Step 1. Visit these Web sites. Take notes about them on this page, too!

Kratts' Creatures
Click Creature World on the sign post. You will be on your way to learning about all sorts of animals. Or, check out the Creature of the Week, or the Creature Clubhouse. This excellent site is part of PBS Kids.

Take Notes:

- Research Roadmap
- Research and Presentation Tools
- Theme Launcher Video
- Links to Science and Social Studies

Available on CD

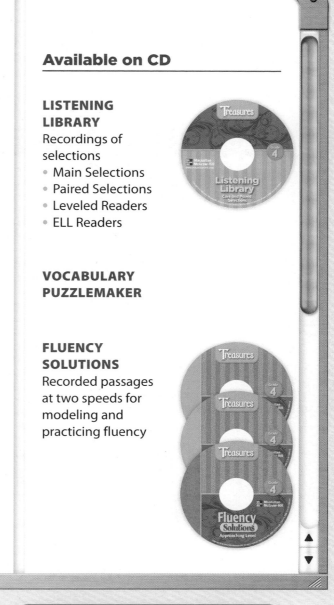

LISTENING LIBRARY
Recordings of selections
- Main Selections
- Paired Selections
- Leveled Readers
- ELL Readers

VOCABULARY PUZZLEMAKER

FLUENCY SOLUTIONS
Recorded passages at two speeds for modeling and practicing fluency

Leveled Reader Activities

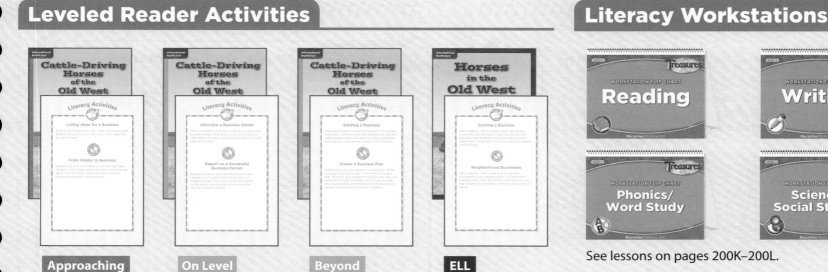

Approaching   **On Level**   **Beyond**   **ELL**

See inside cover of all Leveled Readers.

Literacy Workstations

Reading   **Writing**

Phonics/Word Study   **Science/Social Studies**

See lessons on pages 200K–200L.

Managing the Class

What do I do with the rest of my class?

📖 Reading

Objectives

- Develop fluency through partner-reading
- Read independently for a sustained period of time; keep a reading log, **Practice Book** page 81

Reading   **Fluency**   20 Minutes

- Select a paragraph from the Fluency passage on page 85 of your Practice Book.
- With a partner, take turns reading the sentences aloud. Stop when you come to a period.

Extension

- Reread the paragraph without stopping at the periods. Discuss how the sentences sound when you don't stop at end punctuation.
- Listen to the Audio CD.

> **Things you need:**
> - Practice Book

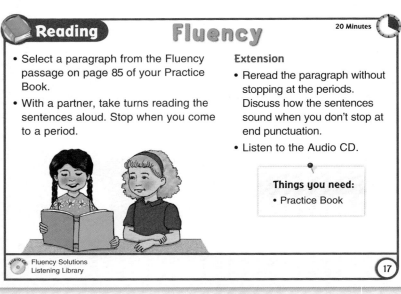

Fluency Solutions
Listening Library   17

Reading   **Independent Reading**   20 Minutes

- Choose a tall tale to read.
- 🎧 As you read, look for examples of cause-and-effect relationships and take notes in your response journal.

Extension

- Using your notes, make a Cause-and-Effect chart.
- In one box, list a cause from the story. In the next box, list the effect.

| Cause | → | Effect |

> **Things you need:**
> - tall tales
> - pen and paper

For more books about Horses, go to the Author/Illustrator section of www.macmillanmh.com   18

🔤 Phonics/Word Study

Objectives

- Write a paragraph using context clues
- Sort words according to spelling patterns

Phonics/Word Study   **Context Clues**   20 Minutes

- Using a dictionary, look up the definition of the following words: *habitat, sanctuary,* and *fragile.*
- Write a paragraph using the words. Use context clues to help readers understand what these words mean.

Extension

- Ask a partner to read your paragraph to see if the clues you used are helpful. Make new clues, if necessary.

> The fragile branch broke easily.

> **Things you need:**
> - dictionary
> - pen and paper

For additional vocabulary and spelling games, go to www.macmillanmh.com   Vocabulary PuzzleMaker   17

Phonics/Word Study   **The /är/ and /ôr/ Sounds**   20 Minutes

- Create a Three-pocket Foldable®.
- On each pocket, write ar, or, ore.
- On note cards, write *dart, fort, core, spark, bore, worn, guard.*
- Sort the cards in the correct pockets.

Extension

- Place cards facedown. Take turns picking cards with a partner. Say a word that rhymes and has the same spelling pattern.

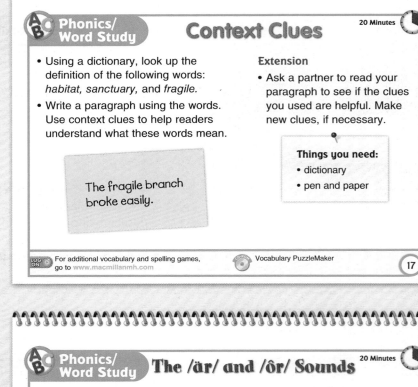

FOLDABLES

- Three-Pocket Foldable®

For additional vocabulary and spelling games, go to www.macmillanmh.com   **FOLDABLES®**   18

Literacy Workstations

Literacy Workstation Flip Charts

Writing

Objectives

- Write a description of a tall tale character
- Research tall tale characters, and write a journal entry from a character's point of view

Content Literacy

Objectives

- Research information about a breed of horse
- Research information about the history of horses
- Take notes to make a time line

Writing — Tall Tale
20 Minutes

- Make up a character who might appear in a tall tale.
- Write a descriptive paragraph about your character. Use vivid words and specific details that will make this character come to life.

Extension

- Add an example of hyperbole, or exaggeration, to your description. For example, you might write that your character has hands as big as frying pans.

Things you need:
- pen and paper

Science — Horses
20 Minutes

- Using the Internet and other reference materials, look up the following information about one breed of horse, such as a Mustang or a Clydesdale.
- Where does this breed live? What physical characteristics help it survive? How is this breed of horse used today?

Extension

- Using the facts you found, write a magazine article about your breed of horse.
- Support your article with illustrations and captions.

Things you need:
- books on horses
- online resources
- pen and paper
- colored pencils or markers

17

Writing — A Day in the Life
20 Minutes

- Research different characters from tall tales.
- Choose a tall tale character and write a journal entry of what a day in the life of the character might be like.

Extension

- With a partner, role-play the tall tale character you chose.

Things you need:
- tall tales
- pen and paper

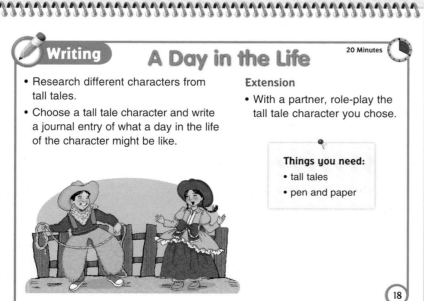

18

Social Studies — Horses of North America
20 Minutes

- Use an encyclopedia or the Internet to find the answers to the following questions about horses.
- When were horses introduced into North America? How were they used? How did they impact transportation and the economy?
- Take notes.

Extension

- Use your notes to help make a time line that shows the history of horses in North America.

Things you need:
- encyclopedia
- online resources
- pen and paper

Internet Research and Inquiry Activity
Students can find more facts at www.macmillanmh.com

18

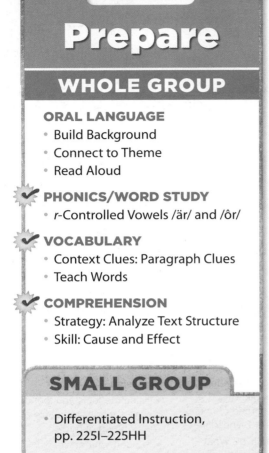

Prepare

WHOLE GROUP

ORAL LANGUAGE
- Build Background
- Connect to Theme
- Read Aloud

PHONICS/WORD STUDY
- *r*-Controlled Vowels /är/ and /ôr/

VOCABULARY
- Context Clues: Paragraph Clues
- Teach Words

COMPREHENSION
- Strategy: Analyze Text Structure
- Skill: Cause and Effect

SMALL GROUP

- Differentiated Instruction, pp. 225I–225HH

Oral Language

Build Background

200

ACCESS PRIOR KNOWLEDGE

Share the following information: This picture shows wild horses in France. Wild horses live on open land and run free. For horses to be truly wild, they must come from families of horses that were always free. There are few true wild horses left in the world. When a type of animal becomes very rare, it is in danger of becoming extinct, or no longer existing.

Write the following words on the board and briefly define each using the **Define/Example/Ask** routine: **tame** (taken from a wild or natural state by humans and made gentle or obedient),

wild (living or growing naturally), **extinct** (no longer existing).

FOCUS QUESTION Ask students to read "Talk About It" on **Student Book** page 201 and describe the photo. Ask:

- Why might the wild horses in this photo need to be saved?

- How important is it for people to save an animal from becoming extinct? Why do you think so?

Talk About It

These wild horses live in a big marsh in southern France. Why is it important to save wild animals?

LOG ON ▶ **VIEW IT**

Oral Language Activities
Saving Animals
www.macmillanmh.com

SAVING ANIMALS

201

Use the Picture Prompt

BUILD WRITING FLUENCY

Ask students to write in their Writer's Notebook what they know about wild horses. Tell students to write as much as they can for eight minutes without stopping. Meet with individuals during Writing Conference time to provide feedback and revision assignments. Students should self-correct any errors they notice prior to the conference.

Connect to the Unit Theme

DISCUSS THE BIG IDEA

One person devotes his time and money to save wild horses from abuse.

Ask students what they learned so far in this unit about making a difference.

- From what you have read so far, what are some ways people have made a difference? In what other ways can people work to make a difference?

- What are the rewards of making a difference in the lives of animals?

USE THEME FOLDABLES

Write the **Big Idea** statement on the board. Ask students to copy it on their Unit Theme Foldables. Remind them to add details as they complete this week's readings.

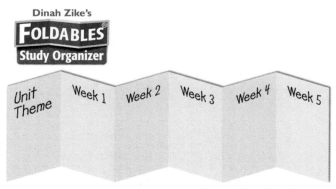

Dinah Zike's
FOLDABLES®
Study Organizer

Unit Theme | Week 1 | Week 2 | Week 3 | Week 4 | Week 5

Accordion Book

ELL ENGLISH LANGUAGE LEARNERS

Beginning	Intermediate	Advanced
Use Visuals Describe the photograph to students. *These horses are wild. They live freely in nature. They are not tame, or trained by humans.* Ask students to tell you about the horses. If the response is correct, repeat it in a louder and slower voice so the class may hear.	**Describe** Ask students to describe the horses in the photograph. *What are these horses doing? Are they wild or tame horses? What do wild horses do?* Repeat students' responses, correcting grammar and pronunciation as needed.	**Compare** Ask students to compare being wild and tame. *How are wild and tame horses alike?* Elaborate on their responses, using examples.

Objectives

- Identify the characteristics of a novel
- Develop vocabulary
- Read sentences fluently, using the appropriate rate

Materials

- Read-Aloud Anthology, pp. 101–104

Read Aloud

Read "Misty of Chincoteague"

Read Aloud

GENRE: Literary Text/Fiction

Share with students these key characteristics of a novel, a book-length work of **fiction**:

- Novels are made-up stories about characters and events. These characters and events can be true to life.

- Novels are usually long and have a detailed plot.

FOCUS ON VOCABULARY

Introduce the following words, using the **Define/Example/Ask** routine. Tell students that knowing these words will help them follow the actions of the characters as you read.

Vocabulary Routine

Use the routine below to discuss the meaning of each word.

Define: A **game warden** is a person in charge of protecting animals in a specific area.
Example: The game warden told us that hunting was not allowed.
Ask: What kinds of jobs might a game warden have?

Define: A **filly** is a young female horse.
Example: The filly followed close behind its mother.
Ask: Where might you find a filly?

Define: A **corral** is a pen or enclosure where horses are kept.
Example: The cowboy led the horses into the corral.
Ask: What is the difference between a corral and a ranch?

LISTENING FOR A PURPOSE

Ask students to listen carefully as you read "Misty of Chincoteague" on **Read-Aloud Anthology** pages 101–104. Use the Think Aloud and Genre Study prompts provided.

ELL **Interactive Reading** Build students' oral language by engaging them in talk about the story's basic meaning.

- Point to the picture of the girl and boy hiding from the horses. Explain in a simple sentence what they are hiding from and why. Have the students repeat.

- After the first paragraph, say: *Turn to your partner and discuss where the girl and boy are and what is happening there.*

- After the last paragraph on page 102, say: *Act out what Paul and Maureen did when they saw the band of ponies coming.*

- After the last paragraph on page 103, say: *What was Paul sure he would be able to do?*

PARTNERS **Think/Pair/Share** Use **Copying Master 5**, "I noticed the author … ," to help students make inferences about the story. When completed, have students turn to a partner and summarize the story. Then have a few students share their summaries with the class.

RESPOND TO THE STORY

Ask students the Think and Respond questions on page 104. Then have them discuss whether or not they think the Phantom was real.

Model Fluency

Reread the novel excerpt. Tell students that this time you want them to focus on one aspect of how you read the story—your rate.

Point out that you speed up in sections of the text that are exciting and slow down at points that are suspenseful to add drama to your reading. Model an example.

Think Aloud In a story, some parts should be read slowly, and others should be read more quickly. It depends on the mood of the story at the time. This story starts out very calmly. Listen as I read the first two sentences. *The girl looked around about her. Everything was still on Assateague Island.* Did you notice how I read this part slowly to set the right mood? Now you try. Repeat each sentence after me, using the same pace that I use. Now let us read the second paragraph. The girl is suddenly frightened. I realize this part should be read at a quicker pace: *"Paul," she asked in a hushed voice, "do you feel like we're trespassing?"* Do you see how reading more quickly fits this part better? Now you try. Repeat each sentence after me, copying my pace.

Establish Fluency Focus Remind students that you will be listening for these same qualities in their reading throughout the week. You will help them improve their reading by adjusting their reading rate to fit the mood of the story.

Readers Theater

BUILDING LISTENING AND SPEAKING SKILLS Distribute copies of "Nat Love, Western Hero," **Read-Aloud Anthology** pages 167–181. Have students practice reading the play throughout the unit. Assign parts. Have students present the play or perform it as a dramatic reading at the end of the unit.

ELL

Discuss Genre Review novels with students. Ask: *What makes this story a novel?* Have students describe the plot of the story. *Are the characters in the story real? Are the events in the story real?* Elicit details from the story to support students' responses.

Objective

- Decode multisyllabic words with *r*-controlled vowels

Materials

- Sound-Spelling Cards
- Practice Book, p. 73
- Transparency 9
- Word-Building Cards
- Teacher's Resource Book, p. 128

ELL

Transfer Sounds The *r*-controlled vowel sounds /ôr/ and /är/ may be difficult for students, such as Korean speakers. Demonstrate how to pronounce words with the /ôr/ and /är/ sounds, saying them slowly and emphasizing the sound in each word. Use the Approaching phonics lesson on page 225J for students who need additional practice. See language transfers on pages T16–T31.

Practice Book, page 73

Sometimes when the letter *r* comes after a vowel, the sound of the short vowel changes. Say the following words aloud and notice the sound of the vowels.

bat   bar   cat   cart   fox   floor

The sounds of these vowels are shown as /**är**/ and /**ôr**/.

Circle the word with /är/ or /ôr/ to complete each sentence. Then write /är/ or /ôr/ on the blank at the end.

1. Please close the _____ when you leave. ___/ōr/___
   dear   (door)   dare

2. The _____ used watercolors to finish his painting. ___/är/___
   roar   rear   (artist)

3. The _____ on the rosebush are sharp. ___/ôr/___
   horns   (thorns)   stars

4. Ben Franklin's inventions _____ still in use today. ___/är/___
   care   core   (are)

5. We are going to have a birthday _____. ___/är/___
   (party)   pat   trap

6. My new _____ is nice and warm. ___/är/___
   (scarf)   calm   pretty

Approaching Reproducible, page 73
Beyond Reproducible, page 73

Phonics

✔ *r*-Controlled Vowels /är/ and /ôr/

EXPLAIN/MODEL

Explain that an *r*-controlled vowel is a vowel followed by the letter *r*. Display the *Star* and *Corn* **Sound-Spelling Cards** for *r*-controlled vowel sounds /är/ and /ôr/. Tell students that /är/ is usually spelled *ar*, and /ôr/ can be spelled different ways. Point to each spelling on the card, and provide a sample word. For example, /ôr/ can be spelled:

- **or** as in *corn*
- **oar** as in *roar*
- **ore** as in *store*

Write the sample words on the board, underline the *r*-controlled vowel spellings, and model blending each one.

Think Aloud Look at the first word I wrote: *c-o-r-n*. I see the *r*-controlled vowel *or*. Listen and watch as I sound out the word: /kôrn/, *corn*. (Run your finger under the word as you sound it out.)

PRACTICE/APPLY

Read the Word List Display **Transparency 9**. The first line includes /är/ and /ôr/ words students will encounter in the upcoming selections. Have students underline the /är/ or /ôr/ spelling in each word. Then have them chorally read the words.

horse	born	swore	barn
charge	chore	yarn	art
short	jar	thorn	soar
barbed	dark	hardly	shore
harsh	torch	farm	force
partner	scarf	sport	marsh

Phonics Transparency 9

Sort the Words Ask students to sort the words by spelling pattern. Then have them write the word sort in their Writer's Notebooks.

ar	or	oar	ore

✔ Read Multisyllabic Words

TRANSITION TO LONGER WORDS Help students transition from reading one-syllable to multisyllabic words with /är/ and /ôr/. Display the words below. Have students read a word in the first column, then model how to read the longer word in the second column. Point out the added syllable(s), to help build awareness of these word parts.

start	start-up	storm	thunderstorm
north	northwest	short	shortened
large	enlarge	port	export
cord	cordless	score	scoring
yard	junkyard	smart	outsmart
bombard	bombardment	park	parking

Phonics Transparency 9

BUILD WORDS Display **Word-Building Cards** *de, im, al, dis, part, ment, yard, back, barn, arm, more, any, ever, plat*. Have students use the word parts to build as many /är/ and /ôr/ words as possible. These and other words can be formed: *depart, backyard, barnyard, alarm*.

CONNECT TO 6 SYLLABLE TYPES Explain that when a vowel is followed by the letter *r*, the vowel and the *r* must appear in the same syllable. They act as a team that cannot be broken up. (m<u>ar</u>/ket)

APPLY DECODING STRATEGY Guide students to use the Decoding Strategy to decode the following words: *apartment, party, enforce, alarming, artwork, starch, absorb, forty, garlic, forgive*. Write each word on the board. Remind students to look for *r*-controlled spellings in step 3 of the Decoding Strategy procedure.

Build Fluency

SPEED DRILL Distribute copies of the *r*-Controlled Vowels Speed Drill, Teacher's Resource Book page 128. Use the Speed Drill routine to help students become fluent reading words with *r*-controlled vowels.

Quick Check

Can students read words with *r*-controlled vowels?

During **Small Group Instruction**

Tier 2

If No → Approaching Level Reteach the skill using the lesson on p. 225J.
If Yes → On Level Consolidate the learning using p. 225S.
Beyond Level Extend the learning using p. 225W.

DAILY Syllable Fluency

Use Word-Building Cards 81–90. Display one card at a time. Have students chorally read each common syllable. Repeat at varying speeds and in random order. Have students work with partners during independent time to write as many words as they can containing each syllable.

Decoding Strategy

Decoding Strategy Chart

Step 1	Look for word parts (prefixes) at the beginning of the word.
Step 2	Look for word parts (suffixes) at the end of the word.
Step 3	In the base word, look for familiar spelling patterns. Think about the six syllable-spelling patterns you have learned.
Step 4	Sound out and blend together the word parts.
Step 5	Say the word parts fast. Adjust your pronunciation as needed. Ask yourself: "Is this a word I have heard before?" Then read the word in the sentence and ask: "Does it make sense in this sentence?"

Vocabulary

✓ **STRATEGY**
CONTEXT CLUES

Paragraph Clues Explain that when they see an unfamiliar word or a word they know used in an unfamiliar way, students can use context clues in the surrounding paragraph to help determine the meaning. The paragraph may contain an antonym, synonym, example, or definition of the word.

Tell students to read "Context Clues" on the bookmark on **Student Book** page 202. Model using context clues to determine the meaning of *habitat*.

Think Aloud The word *habitat* in the last paragraph is unfamiliar to me. The phrase right after it, though, seems like a definition or description. Could a *habitat* be "the area in which an animal or plant naturally lives"? Yes, that meaning makes sense with the rest of the sentence and the paragraph.

Help students identify and use context clues to the meaning of *descendants* in the second paragraph. They should recognize that *descendants* and *ancestors* are antonyms.

Read "The Wild Ponies of Chincoteague"

As you read "The Wild Ponies of Chincoteague" with students, have them identify clues that reveal the meanings of the highlighted words. Tell students they will read these words again in *Wild Horses*.

Vocabulary

- sanctuary
- descendants
- threatened
- emerge
- fragile
- habitat

✓ **Context Clues**

Paragraph Clues are words in a sentence or paragraph that help readers figure out the meaning of unfamiliar words. Use paragraph clues, such as examples or definitions, to figure out what *habitat* means.

The Wild Ponies of Chincoteague
by Gregory Searle

Every year since 1924, a pony swim has taken place between two tiny islands in the Atlantic Ocean. Assateague and Chincoteague islands are located off the coasts of Maryland and Virginia.

The calm, quiet privacy of the islands provides a **sanctuary** for the wild ponies. The ponies are **descendants** of wild horses. How the ancestors of these ponies ended up on an island, no one knows for sure.

202

Quick Check

Can students identify word meanings?

During **Small Group Instruction**

Tier **2**

If No → **Approaching Level** Reteach the words using the Vocabulary lesson, pp. 225K–225L.

If Yes → **On Level** Consolidate the learning using p. 225S.

Beyond Level Extend the learning using p. 225W.

Gifted & Talented

The Pony Swim

In the 1920s several terrible fires broke out on Chincoteague. In response, the Chincoteague Volunteer Fire Department was founded in 1924. In order to raise money to buy equipment for the fire department, the annual pony swim and auction was started.

Every year, thousands of people come to watch the pony swim and the auction. Many watch from boats out on the water.

The firemen "round up" the wild ponies on Assateague Island. At first the ponies feel **threatened** and head back into the trees. After some coaxing, the ponies swim across the channel to **emerge** from the water onto Chincoteague Island.

These ponies are small, but they are not **fragile**. They are very strong and intelligent animals. Many farmers want to buy a Chincoteague pony. Some of the foals are auctioned off to good homes. The rest of the ponies swim back to Assateague Island a few days later. The fire department uses the money that is raised to update their safety equipment.

Protecting the Ponies

The pony swim is important for another reason, too. The number of horses living on Assateague has to be controlled. If too many horses are born, there won't be enough grass for the rest to eat. Keeping the population of ponies under control protects the **habitat**, the area in which an animal or plant naturally lives, and its natural resources for future generations.

Reread for **Comprehension**

Analyze Text Structure

Cause and Effect Text structure is the way an author organizes a selection to present information. Cause and effect is a type of text structure. A cause is why something happens. An effect is what happens. Readers can look for explicit and implicit causes and effects in a selection to help them check their understanding. Reread the selection and fill in your Cause and Effect Chart to help you identify what happens in the selection and why.

Cause → Effect
→
→
→
→

LOG ON **LEARN IT** **Comprehension** www.macmillanmh.com

203

Vocabulary

TEACH WORDS

Introduce each word using the **Define/Example/Ask** routine. Model reading each word using the syllable-scoop technique.

Vocabulary Routine

Define: **Descendants** are those family members who are born after others in a family.
Example: Children are the descendants of their parents and grandparents.
Ask: What is the difference between ancestors and decendants? COMPARE AND CONTRAST

- A **sanctuary** is a place that is safe or protected. *We visited the bird sanctuary on the island.* Why would people set aside land for an animal sanctuary? **EXPLANATION**

- If something is **threatened**, it is in danger. *Many of our rain forests are threatened by logging, mining, and farming.* What else can you think of that is threatened? **EXAMPLE**

- When things **emerge**, they come into view. *Ten people emerged from the kitchen.* What is a synonym for *emerge*? **SYNONYM**

- Anything that is **fragile** can be easily broken. *The china plates were very fragile.* What is an antonym for *fragile*? **ANTONYM**

- An animal's **habitat** is the area where it lives. *Growing cities are one danger to the habitats of many animals because the animals are forced to move to a new location.* Describe one kind of animal habitat. **PRIOR KNOWLEDGE**

ELL

Preteach Vocabulary
See pages 225BB and 225K to preteach the vocabulary words to **ELL** and **Approaching Level** students. Use the **Visual Vocabulary Resources** to demonstrate and discuss each word. To further reinforce concepts, have students complete page 96 in the **ELL Resource Book**.

HOMEWORK **Practice Book,** page 74

| descendants | habitat | threatened |
| emerge | fragile | sanctuary |

Label each statement True or False. If the statement is false, explain why.

1. Something is *fragile* if it is hard to break.
   False; fragile objects break easily.

2. The desert is the whale's natural *habitat*.
   False; its natural habitat is the ocean.

3. When the Sun does not *emerge* from behind the clouds, the day is very bright and sunny.
   False; *emerge* means "to come out from," so the day would be overcast.

4. Children are *descendants* of their grandparents.
   True

5. If you think you are safe from harm, you may feel *threatened*.
   False; you do not feel threatened when you feel safe.

6. A *sanctuary* is a place where wild animals can live safely.
   True

   Possible response provided.
7. Write a sentence that contains two of the above vocabulary words.
   The coral reef is a *fragile habitat*.

Approaching Reproducible, page 74

Beyond Reproducible, page 74

Objectives

- Analyze text structure
- Identify cause and effect
- Use academic language: *analyze, text structure, cause, effect*

Materials

- Transparencies 5, 9a, 9b
- Practice Book, p. 75

Skills Trace

Cause and Effect	
Introduce	203A–203B
Practice/ Apply	204–219; Practice Book, 75–76
Reteach/ Review	225M–225Z, 707A–B, 708–723, 729M–729Z; Practice Book, 237–238
Assess	Weekly Tests; Units 2, 6 Tests
Maintain	251B, 333B, 737B

ELL

Academic Language
Preteach the following academic language words to ELL and Approaching Level students during Small Group time: *analyze text structure, cause, effect*. See pages 225AA and 225I.

Reread for Comprehension

STRATEGY
ANALYZE TEXT STRUCTURE

What Is It? Point out that different texts are organized in different ways. **Analyzing text structure** means looking at the organizational pattern, or how authors have structured the ideas and information they present. Sometimes the relationships among ideas are explicit, or stated. Sometimes the relationships are implicit, or unstated.

Why Is It Important? Analyzing text structure can help students to understand the topic and to identify how the author feels about the topic. It can also help students judge the author's purpose for writing.

SKILL
CAUSE AND EFFECT

What Is It? A **cause** is what makes something happen. The **effect** is what happens as a result.

Why Is It Important? Knowing how and why each event leads to another event or action will deepen students' understanding. Recognizing the explicit and implicit relationships between causes and effects will help students see more clearly why events in a selection happen and why the people act the way they do.

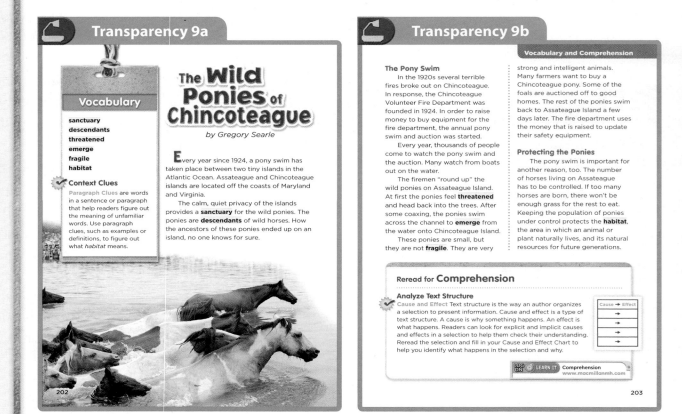

Transparency 9a

Vocabulary

- sanctuary
- descendants
- threatened
- emerge
- fragile
- habitat

Context Clues

Paragraph Clues are words in a sentence or paragraph that help readers figure out the meaning of unfamiliar words. Use paragraph clues, such as examples or definitions, to figure out what *habitat* means.

The Wild Ponies of Chincoteague
by Gregory Searle

Every year since 1924, a pony swim has taken place between two tiny islands in the Atlantic Ocean. Assateague and Chincoteague islands are located off the coasts of Maryland and Virginia.

The calm, quiet privacy of the islands provides a **sanctuary** for the wild ponies. The ponies are **descendants** of wild horses. How the ancestors of these ponies ended up on an island, no one knows for sure.

202

Transparency 9b

Vocabulary and Comprehension

The Pony Swim

In the 1920s several terrible fires broke out on Chincoteague. In response, the Chincoteague Volunteer Fire Department was founded in 1924. In order to raise money to buy equipment for the fire department, the annual pony swim and auction was started.

Every year, thousands of people come to watch the pony swim and the auction. Many watch from boats out on the water.

The firemen "round up" the wild ponies on Assateague Island. At first the ponies feel **threatened** and head back into the trees. After some coaxing, the ponies swim across the channel to **emerge** from the water onto Chincoteague Island.

These ponies are small, but they are not **fragile**. They are very strong and intelligent animals. Many farmers want to buy a Chincoteague pony. Some of the foals are auctioned off to good homes. The rest of the ponies swim back to Assateague Island a few days later. The fire department uses the money that is raised to update their safety equipment.

Protecting the Ponies

The pony swim is important for another reason, too. The number of horses living on Assateague has to be controlled. If too many horses are born, there won't be enough grass for the rest to eat. Keeping the population of ponies under control protects the **habitat**, the area in which an animal or plant naturally lives, and its natural resources for future generations.

Reread for Comprehension

Analyze Text Structure

Cause and Effect Text structure is the way an author organizes a selection to present information. Cause and effect is a type of text structure. A cause is why something happens. An effect is what happens. Readers can look for explicit and implicit causes and effects in a selection to help them check their understanding. Reread the selection and fill in your Cause and Effect Chart to help you identify what happens in the selection and why.

Cause → Effect
→
→
→
→

Comprehension
www.macmillanmh.com

203

Student Book pages 202–203 available on Comprehension Transparencies 9a and 9b

- Cause-and-effect relationships often provide structure for a story or nonfiction work. Students should look for words and phrases that the author uses to signal cause and effect. Examples are *because, due to, as a result, since,* and *therefore.*

- These relationships may not be explicitly stated, however. As they read, students should look for events that cause actions to happen. They might ask, "What happens because of this event?" or "What brought about that action?"

MODEL

How Do I Use It? Read aloud the first two paragraphs of "The Wild Ponies of Chincoteague" on **Student Book** page 202.

Think Aloud On the first page, I learn about a pony swim on two islands off the coasts of Virginia and Maryland. I also learn that the ponies are descendants of wild horses, and that nobody knows how the wild horses got to Chincoteague Island. Even though I do not know the cause of the wild horses getting to the island, I do know the effect. The effect is that because the wild horses once lived on the island, their descendants, the ponies, live on Chincoteague Island today. Another way I can say this is that the cause of the ponies living on Chincoteague Island today is the fact that wild horses came to the island many years ago.

GUIDED PRACTICE

Help students find causes and effects in the first two paragraphs on page 203. Display **Transparency 5** and have students record this information in a Cause and Effect Chart.

APPLY

Direct students to reread the remainder of "The Wild Ponies of Chincoteague." Tell them to make sure they identify explicit and implicit causes and effects as they read, and to add them to their Cause and Effect Chart. Have students identify and explain the most important cause and effect of the pony swim.

Quick Check

Can students identify causes and effects?

During **Small Group Instruction**

Tier 2

If No → **Approaching Level** Reteach the skill using the Comprehension lesson, pp. 225M–225P.

If Yes → **On Level** Consolidate the learning using pp. 225U–225V.

Beyond Level Extend the learning using pp. 225Y–225Z.

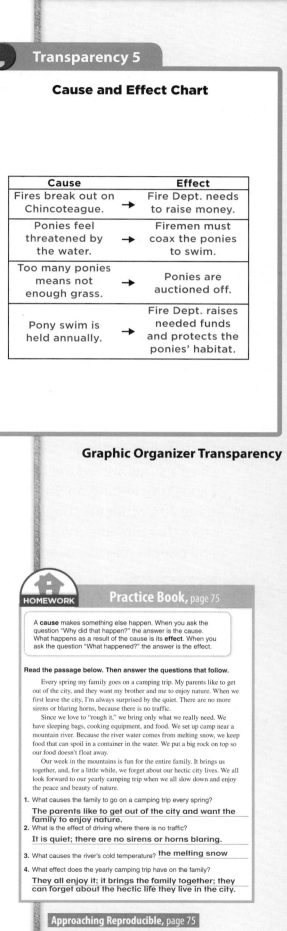

Transparency 5

Cause and Effect Chart

Cause	Effect
Fires break out on Chincoteague. →	Fire Dept. needs to raise money.
Ponies feel threatened by the water. →	Firemen must coax the ponies to swim.
Too many ponies means not enough grass. →	Ponies are auctioned off.
Pony swim is held annually. →	Fire Dept. raises needed funds and protects the ponies' habitat.

Graphic Organizer Transparency

HOMEWORK **Practice Book,** page 75

A **cause** makes something else happen. When you ask the question "Why did that happen?" the answer is the cause. What happens as a result of the cause is its **effect**. When you ask the question "What happened?" the answer is the effect.

Read the passage below. Then answer the questions that follow.

Every spring my family goes on a camping trip. My parents like to get out of the city, and they want my brother and me to enjoy nature. When we first leave the city, I'm always surprised by the quiet. There are no more sirens or blaring horns, because there is no traffic.

Since we love to "rough it," we bring only what we really need. We have sleeping bags, cooking equipment, and food. We set up camp near a mountain river. Because the river water comes from melting snow, we keep food that can spoil in a container in the water. We put a big rock on top so our food doesn't float away.

Our week in the mountains is fun for the entire family. It brings us together, and, for a little while, we forget about our hectic city lives. We all look forward to our yearly camping trip when we all slow down and enjoy the peace and beauty of nature.

1. What causes the family to go on a camping trip every spring?
The parents like to get out of the city and want the family to enjoy nature.

2. What is the effect of driving where there is no traffic?
It is quiet; there are no sirens or horns blaring.

3. What causes the river's cold temperature? the melting snow

4. What effect does the yearly camping trip have on the family?
They all enjoy it; it brings the family together; they can forget about the hectic life they live in the city.

Approaching Reproducible, page 75
Beyond Reproducible, page 75

Read

WHOLE GROUP

✔ **MAIN SELECTION**
- *Wild Horses*
- Skill: Cause and Effect

✔ **PAIRED SELECTION**
- Folktale: "The Tale of Pecos Bill"
- Literary Elements: Hyperbole and Metaphor

SMALL GROUP

- Differentiated Instruction, pp. 225I–225HH

Main Selection

GENRE: Informational Text/Expository

Have a student read the definition of Expository writing on **Student Book** page 204. Students should look for a story that provides information about real people, situations, and events.

✔ **STRATEGY**
ANALYZE TEXT STRUCTURE

Point out that authors of nonfiction can organize their texts in various ways to help readers understand the information they are presenting.

✔ **SKILL**
CAUSE AND EFFECT

Remind students that cause-and-effect relationships often help organize the events of a selection. One event or action will lead directly to another. Authors sometimes state cause-effect relationships directly, but often readers must infer them based on text evidence.

Comprehension

Genre

Expository writing can be an account of actual persons, living things, situations, or events.

Analyze Text Structure

Cause and Effect
As you read, fill in your Cause and Effect Chart.

Cause → Effect
→
→
→
→

Read to Find Out

What is it that makes a wild horse wild?

204

Vocabulary

Vocabulary Words Review the tested words while reading: **descendants, sanctuary, threatened, emerge, fragile**, and **habitat**.

Additional Selection Words Students may be unfamiliar with these words. Pronounce the words, give student-friendly explanations as needed, and help students use previously taught vocabulary strategies: context clues, word parts, using a dictionary.

docile (p. 206): easy to train or handle

adaptability (p. 206): the ability to adapt easily

skitter (p. 213): skip quickly

vigilance (p. 214): watchfulness, caution and care

Wild Horses

by Cris Peterson
photographs by Alvis Upitis

205

Read the Main Selection

Preteach	Read Together	Read Independently
Have Approaching Level students and English Language Learners listen to the selection on **StudentWorks Plus**, the interactive e-Book, before reading with the class.	Use the prompts to guide comprehension and model how to complete the graphic organizer. Have students use **Think/Pair/Share** to discuss the selection.	If students can read the selection independently, have them read and complete the graphic organizer. Suggest that they use their purposes to choose their reading strategies.

StudentWorks Plus
Interactive Student Book

Preview and Predict

QUICK WRITE Ask students to read the title, preview the illustrations, think about the genre, and write predictions about the kind of information they will find in the text. They may include what they already know about wild horses.

Set Purposes

FOCUS QUESTION Discuss the "Read to Find Out" question on **Student Book** page 204. Remind students to look for the answer as they read.

Point out the Cause and Effect Chart in the Student Book and on **Practice Book** page 76. Explain that students will fill it in as they read.

Read *Wild Horses*

Use the questions and Think Alouds to support instruction about the comprehension strategy and skill.

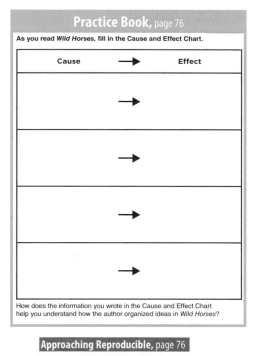

Practice Book, page 76

As you read *Wild Horses,* fill in the Cause and Effect Chart.

Cause	→	Effect

How does the information you wrote in the Cause and Effect Chart help you understand how the author organized ideas in *Wild Horses*?

Approaching Reproducible, page 76
Beyond Reproducible, page 76

Develop Comprehension

ANALYZE TEXT STRUCTURE

Teacher Think Aloud I know that authors of informational texts organize information, or build **text structure**, in different ways. For example, they may use sequence, cause and effect, or compare and contrast. As I read, I see that the author at first uses description to help create the text structure. Her descriptive words help me to picture the setting of the story and the horses themselves. For example, in describing the group of horses going down to the river, the author writes, "Their long tangled manes and tails ruffle in the night breeze." As I continue to read, I will look for other ways in which the author organizes the text.

In the deepest, darkest part of night, when the crickets and tree frogs are almost silent, shadowy shapes **emerge** from the ponderosa pine ridge and tiptoe down to the glassy Cheyenne River below. Their long tangled manes and tails ruffle in the night breeze. Ever alert and watchful for predators, they swiftly drink their fill. Then they turn on their heels and lunge up the rocky hills to safety.

In the misty glow of dawn, one can see these mysterious visitors aren't backyard pasture mares with swishing tails and docile, trusting eyes. These horses are wild—from another century, another era, another world. They are American mustangs, whose freedom, adaptability, **1** and toughness define the western wilderness.

206

Monitor Comprehension

Monitor and Clarify: *Reread to Clarify*

Explain Tell students that when something they have read does not make sense, or if they do not understand it, they can read the passage again. They can also go back to an earlier part of the selection and read that again. They may even want to reread a portion out loud.

Discuss Ask students where the horses are going at night and why they are going there. If they are not sure, they should reread the first paragraph aloud. (They are going to the Cheyenne River to drink.)

Apply As they read the selection, have students self-monitor by going back and rereading to clarify any part that may be confusing.

Some of the mares have names. Medicine Hattie is easy to spot. Her dark ears jut out above her ghostly white face and corn-silk mane. Painted Lady's pure white coat is splashed with brown spots; she always seems to know where the sweetest grasses are.

And there are others. Funny Face has a creamy white blaze that slides down the sides of her face like melting ice cream on a hot day. She loves to stand on the highest rock-strewn spot with her face to the wind. Yuskeya, whose name means freedom in the Sioux language, always stands at the edge of the herd, alert for danger and ready to run. **2**

207

Develop Comprehension

2 FIGURATIVE LANGUAGE

How does the author use **figurative language** and sensory details to describe the horses on page 207? (She describes the colors of the horses with such images as "ghostly white face, splashed with brown spots," and "creamy white blaze." She compares Medicine Hattie's mane to a part of a plant in the metaphor "corn-silk mane." She uses a simile when she says that Funny Face's markings look "like melting ice cream on a hot day." She uses personification when she describes the horses' behavior in human terms: "… she always seems to know …; She loves to stand …."

Phonics/Word Study

APPLY DECODING SKILLS While reading, point out words with the sound/spelling patterns, syllable types, and word parts students have recently learned. Help students blend these words. You may wish to focus on selections words with /ôr/ and /är/ spelling patterns, such as *darkest, backyard, horses, northern, doorstep, smart, barbed*, and *starvation*.

ELL ENGLISH LANGUAGE LEARNERS

Beginning	Intermediate	Advanced
Access Content Preteach story content, build language, and develop meaning using the Interactive Question-Response Guide in the **ELL Resource Book**, pages 86–93. Give ample time for students to respond. They may point or use words or short phrases to respond.	**Describe** Preteach story content, build language, and develop meaning using the Interactive Question-Response Guide in the ELL Resource Book, pages 86–93. Have students respond in complete sentences. Repeat their responses, correcting pronunciation or grammar as needed.	**Explain** Complete the Intermediate task with students. Elicit details from students for their responses.

Develop Comprehension

3 MONITOR AND CLARIFY: REREAD TO CLARIFY

In the first paragraph on page 209, there are many details and descriptions. What is the author trying to say there? (If you want to see the wild horses, you should go to the Black Hills Wild Horse Sanctuary. The author describes the scenery you would see along the way.)

208

To find these horses, cross Cascade Creek where the South Dakota Black Hills meet the prairie, and turn right onto a pothole-strewn gravel road. This is the land of silver sagebrush and cowboy legends. Scraggly buzzards perch on fence posts near the entry gate to the Black Hills Wild Horse **Sanctuary**, home for more than three hundred wild horses and one determined cowboy-conservationist named Dayton Hyde. **3**

Dayton was a gangly, growing thirteen-year-old boy when he met his first horse. It was a dirt-colored pony he found drinking from a puddle of old soapy dishwater behind his family's summer cabin in northern Michigan. He recalls that for a time he thought all horses blew bubbles out of their noses. **4**

Soon after that encounter, word came from Dayton's cattle rancher uncle in Oregon that his cowboys had just captured a band of wild horses. Dayton hopped a westbound train and arrived on his uncle's doorstep, where he grew up as a cowboy learning to love the western range and its wild horses. **5**

Mustangs are **descendants** of the horses brought to America by Spanish explorers nearly five hundred years ago. By 1900, more than two million smart, fast, surefooted wild horses roamed the West.

209

Develop Comprehension

4 GENRE: Informational Text/Expository

What clues tell you that this **expository text** is an informational account? (The author includes information about the South Dakota Black Hills and the Black Hills Wild Horse Sanctuary. These are both real places. She also talks about a real cowboy named Dayton Hyde and provides details about his life. Real places and people usually indicate a work of nonfiction.)

5 SKILL

CAUSE AND EFFECT

Why did Dayton Hyde hop a train to Oregon? (His uncle was a cattle rancher and had just caught a group of wild horses for his ranch. Hyde went to help him with these horses.) How did this move affect Hyde? (Dayton Hyde learned to love the West and the wild horses.) Add this information to your Cause and Effect Chart.

Cause →	Effect
Dayton goes to his uncle and grows up as a cowboy.	Dayton comes to love the western range and its wild horses.

Develop Comprehension

6 STRATEGY
CONTEXT CLUES

Use **paragraph clues** to figure out the meaning of *prohibited*. (The paragraph says an act of Congress "prohibited" killing wild horses, and afterwards, the horse population grew. So, *prohibited* must mean "forbade" or "did not allow.")

7 SKILL
CAUSE AND EFFECT

Why did the mustang population increase during the 1970s? (Congress made it illegal to capture or kill wild horses, so the herds increased.) **What was the result of this?** (Horses were crowded into feedlots.)

Add this information to your Cause and Effect Chart.

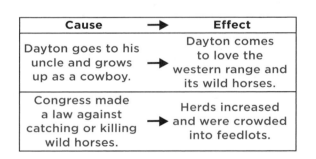

Cause	→	Effect
Dayton goes to his uncle and grows up as a cowboy.	→	Dayton comes to love the western range and its wild horses.
Congress made a law against catching or killing wild horses.	→	Herds increased and were crowded into feedlots.

When newly invented barbed wire fences began crisscrossing the rangelands, the horses lost access to sources of food and water and became a pesky problem for local residents. Thousands of them were slaughtered for fertilizer or pet food. By 1950, less than seventeen thousand survived.

6 After a Congressional act prohibited the capture or slaughter of wild horses in 1971, the wild horse population again grew quickly. Many died of thirst and starvation in the harsh western winters. In an attempt to manage the size of the herds, the United States government gathered up the animals and maintained them in fenced feedlots until they could be adopted.

One day in the early 1980s, Dayton Hyde, who by this time owned his uncle's ranch and had a grown family of his own, drove by one of these feedlots. Shocked and dismayed by the sight of dozens of muddy and dejected horses locked in a corral, he **7** felt he had to do something.

8
9

> **Cause and Effect**
> Why did the mustang population increase during the 1970s?

210

Text Evidence

Cause and Effect

Reread Question 7. Remind students that they should look for events that cause other events or actions to happen. Have students reread the second paragraph on page 210. Guide them in using text evidence to describe implicit cause-and-effect relationships. Ask, *What event happened first in this paragraph? Point to the information when you find it.* (Congress passed a law protecting wild horses.) *What happened as a result of this?* (The population of horses grew so quickly that many died of hunger and thirst.) *What did the United States government do to try and solve this problem?* (They moved the horses into crowded feedlots.)

211

Develop Comprehension

8 MAIN IDEA AND DETAILS

SPIRAL REVIEW How would you summarize the **main ideas** and supporting **details** in this selection so far? (This selection describes the wild horses and tells how they were being killed for food and fertilizer. Although the U.S. government protected them, they locked them in feedlots. A cowboy named Dayton Hyde decided to help the horses.)

9 SELF-SELECTED STRATEGY USE

What strategies have you used so far to help you understand the selection? Where did you use them? Why? How did they help?

RETURN TO PREDICTIONS AND PURPOSES

Have students respond to the selection by confirming or revising their predictions and purposes for reading. Encourage them to revise or write more questions as they continue to read.

Extra Support

Cause and Effect

Guide students who need help locating cause-and-effect relationships. Have them reread the first two paragraphs on page 210, and guide them in answering questions such as the following:

- What kept the horses from finding food? (Much of the land was fenced off, and the horses could not get to food or water sources.)

- Why did people begin to kill the horses? (The horses were becoming a problem for them.)

- What made the horse population quickly grow again? (The government no longer allowed people to kill the horses.)

- What was the result of the growing size of the herds? (In the winter, many horses could not find enough to eat.)

Stop here if you wish to read this selection over two days. STOP

Develop Comprehension

10 SKILL
CAUSE AND EFFECT

What **caused** Dayton Hyde to spend months searching and trying to work with the government? (He was upset by the condition of the horses in the feedlots and wanted to convince the government to create a place for the wild horses to live.) What was the **effect** of his hard work? (Government officials agreed with him, and he acquired eleven thousand acres of land near the Black Hills.) Add this information to your Cause and Effect Chart.

Cause	→	Effect
Dayton goes to his uncle and grows up as a cowboy.	→	Dayton comes to love the western range and its wild horses.
Congress made a law against catching or killing wild horses.	→	Herds increased and were crowded into feedlots.
Hyde wanted a place for the wild horses to live.	→	Hyde acquired eleven thousand acres of land for them.

11 MAIN IDEA AND DETAILS

SPIRAL REVIEW

What **details** can you identify in the first paragraph? (It took Dayton months to find land. He spent many long days convincing government officials to accept his plan. He hoped wild horses that would not be adopted could run free there.) Think about what these details have in common. What is the **main idea** of the paragraph? (Dayton acquired the land and hoped the wild horses would run free on it one day.)

10   After months of searching and many long days spent convincing government officials to accept his plan of creating a special place for wild horses, he acquired eleven thousand acres of rangeland and rimrock near the Black Hills in South Dakota. Here, among yawning canyons and sun-drenched pastures, he hoped wild horses—some too ugly, old, or knobby kneed to be adopted—could run free forever.

11   Before he could ship his wild horse rejects to their new home, Dayton had to build eight miles of fences to ensure they wouldn't wander into his neighbors' wheat fields. He also fenced in a fifty-acre training field where the horses would spend their first few days on the ranch adjusting to their new surroundings.

212

On a miserably cold fall day, huge creaking semi-trailers **12** filled with snorting, stomping steeds finally arrived at the ranch. After hours of coaxing, Dayton succeeded in getting Magnificent Mary to skitter off the trailer. She was a battle-scarred, mean-eyed mare with a nose about twice as long as it should be. The rest of the herd clattered behind her, eyes bulging with fear.

213

Vocabulary

Graphophonic, Syntactic, and Semantic Cues

Explain/Model Point out that when good readers come to a word they do not understand, they look for clues to the word's meaning. The clues may relate to the word's sound or spelling, the way the word functions grammatically, or the context in which the word appears. Model using clues to find the meaning of *steeds* on page 213.

Think Aloud Sometimes when I sound out a word, I realize it's familiar, but that doesn't help this time. From its position in the sentence, I can tell that *steeds* is a plural noun. Since the sentences before talk about the wild horses coming to the ranch, I think *steeds* is another word for *horses*. That makes sense with the photo, too.

Practice/Apply Have students use graphophonic, syntactic, and semantic cues to help them with *coaxing* and *skitter* on page 213.

Develop Comprehension

12 STRATEGY
ANALYZE TEXT STRUCTURE

Teacher Think Aloud As I read, I see many examples of cause and effect. I realize that this is another **text structure** the author is using. I have already identified a cause-and-effect relationship in the first paragraph of page 212. Now I will look in the second paragraph. I see that Dayton builds fences. I ask myself *why*? I read that, without fences, the horses would wander into the neighbors' wheat fields. The cause is that horses would wander into other people's fields. The effect is that Dayton builds fences to stop them from doing this. Now you look for cause-and-effect relationships on page 213.

PARTNERS Prompt students to apply the strategy in a Think Aloud by asking them to identify a cause-and-effect relationship.

Student Think Aloud I read that the horses arrived at the ranch, but they did not want to leave the semi-trailers. Only after hours of coaxing did Magnificent Mary walk off the trailer. The rest of the herd then followed. It seems that without the coaxing, the horses would not have left the trailer. So I found my first cause and effect. Cause: Dayton coaxed the horses to leave. Effect: Magnificent Mary left the trailer. I also notice that when Magnificent Mary left the trailer, the other horses followed her. Cause: Magnificent Mary left the trailer. Effect: The other horses followed her.

Develop Comprehension

13 STRATEGY
CONTEXT CLUES

Use words in the surrounding paragraph, or **paragraph clues**, to help figure out the meaning of *vigilance*. (In order not to frighten the horses, Dayton had to watch them secretly. He sat in his pickup truck and peeked out at the horses through the corner of his eye. He did this for almost a week nonstop. We read that finally, after nearly a week, he swung the gate open. *Vigilance* must mean "watchfulness.")

14 SKILL
CAUSE AND EFFECT

What has been the **effect** of Dayton Hyde's creating a home for the wild horses? (By making a sanctuary for the horses, Dayton Hyde has enabled dozens of new colts to be born every spring. Now the horses won't die off.) Add this information to your Cause and Effect Chart.

Cause	→	Effect
Dayton goes to his uncle and grows up as a cowboy.	→	Dayton comes to love the western range and its wild horses.
Congress made a law against catching or killing wild horses.	→	Herds increased and were crowded into feedlots.
Hyde wanted a place for the wild horses to live.	→	Hyde acquired eleven thousand acres of land for them.
Hyde creates a sanctuary for the wild horses.	→	Dozens of wild horses are now born each spring.

Dayton's worst fear was that the horses would spook and charge through his carefully constructed six-wire fence, scattering across the prairie like dry leaves in a whirlwind. Aware that wild horses often feel **threatened** by being watched, he sat in the cab of his old pickup truck, peeking at them out of a corner of his eye. Finally, after nearly a week of around-the-clock vigilance, he swung open the gate from the training field **13** to his wild horse sanctuary.

Many years have passed since Dayton held his breath and pushed that corral gate open. Every spring, dozens of his wild horses give birth to tottering colts that learn the ways of the back country from their mothers. They share the vast, quiet land with coyotes, mountain lions, and countless deer. Star lilies, bluebells, and prairie roses nod in the wind along with the prairie short grass that feeds **14** the herd.

214

Vocabulary

Figurative Language: *Idioms*

Explain/Model Remind students that in an idiom, a group of words has a meaning that cannot be understood from their usual meaning. For example, "pull someone's leg" means "trick or tease." Model determining the meaning of "held his breath" on page 214.

Think Aloud I know this phrase has a meaning beyond the literal meanings of the words. From the previous sentence, I can tell that Dayton had waited a week before opening the gate. I think "held his breath" meant that he was waiting and hoping for something.

Practice/Apply Have students look for other idioms in the selection, such as "hopped a train" (page 209) and "round-the-clock" (page 214). Then have them describe times they "held their breath," "pulled someone's leg," or "hopped a train."

Thousands of visitors arrive each summer to get a glimpse **15** of wild horses in their natural **habitat**, a habitat that has been preserved through Dayton's careful planning. Throughout the grazing season, he moves the herd from one area of the ranch to another so the horses don't damage the **fragile** rangeland. In the process, he searches for his marker mares: Painted Lady, Medicine Hattie, Funny Face, Yuskeya, Magnificent Mary, and several others. When he spots them all, he knows the whole herd **16** is accounted for.

215

Develop Comprehension

15 **AUTHOR'S CRAFT: WORD CHOICE**

Why do you think the author uses the word *glimpse* to describe how visitors to the sanctuary see the horses? (*Glimpse* is a more specific word than *look*. To glimpse something is to see it only for a moment. Using this word shows how quickly the horses move or how hidden they are in the overall landscape.)

16 **SKILL**
CAUSE AND EFFECT

Describe the **cause-and-effect** relationships in this paragraph. (Cause: The horses' habitat has been preserved; Effect: Thousands of visitors can see the horses each summer. Cause: Dayton moves the herd from one area of the ranch to another; Effect: The rangeland does not get damaged. Cause: Dayton finds his marker mares; Effect: He knows the whole herd is there.)

Develop Comprehension

17 **STRATEGY**
ANALYZE TEXT STRUCTURE

How does the author use cause-and-effect relationships on the last page of the selection?

Student Think Aloud The last page of the story sums up the fact that wild mustangs that were once crowded into a feedlot are now galloping freely across the Cheyenne River. I realize that this is also an example of cause and effect. The cause is that thanks to Dayton, there is a sanctuary for wild horses. The effect is that the wild mustangs now run free.

18 **SKILL**
CAUSE AND EFFECT

How did the horses from the feedlot end up in the Black Hills Wild Horse Sanctuary? (Dayton Hyde saw wild horses crowded into feedlots and was unhappy about it. He wanted to make a home for the horses that were not adopted by ranchers. It took many months, but he finally found land and convinced the government to let him make a sanctuary for the horses. He built fences and a training ground to help them get used to their new home. The sanctuary was a success.)

216

Listening/Speaking

Have selected students share their Response to Literature descriptions. Tell students to give details and examples from the selection to clarify information and to help listeners focus. After students listen to one presenter, say: *Let's make sure we understood. Turn to a partner and summarize the speaker's main ideas and supporting details*. If students can successfully summarize what they heard, they have listened attentively.

Sometimes in the fall while he's checking on the horses, Dayton notices a gaunt, aging mare whose ribs stand out through her ragged coat. He knows this old friend won't survive the winter. As the pale December daylight slips over the rimrock, the old mare lies down and goes to sleep for the last time. After years of running free, the wild mustang returns to the earth and completes the circle of life.

The wild mustangs Dayton Hyde once discovered crowded into a feedlot now gallop across the Cheyenne River free as the prairie wind. They splash through the glistening water and bolt up a ravine. Here in this rugged wilderness, one man's vision of a sanctuary for wild horses has become a reality. **17**

> ✔ **Cause and Effect**
> How did the horses from the feedlot end up in the Black Hills Wild Horse Sanctuary? **18**

217

Quick Check

Can students describe causes-and-effect relationships?

During **Small Group Instruction**

If No → **Approaching Level** Reteach the skill and have students apply it to a simpler text. Use Leveled Reader lessons, pp. 225N–225P.

If Yes → **On Level** Have students apply the skill to a new text to consolidate learning. Use Leveled Reader lessons, pp. 225U–225V.

Beyond Level Have students apply the skill to a more complex text to extend learning. Use Leveled Reader lessons, pp. 225Y–225Z.

Gifted Talented

Develop Comprehension

RETURN TO PREDICTIONS AND PURPOSES

Review students' **predictions** and **purposes**. Were they correct? Did they learn what makes a wild horse wild? (A wild horse is not used by humans for transportation, labor, or food.)

REVIEW READING STRATEGIES

- **Analyze Text Structure** In what ways did analyzing text structure help you understand the selection?

- **Monitor and Clarify: Reread** Do you understand the strategy of rereading when what you read does not make sense to you? When might you use it again?

- **Decoding** What difficult words did you encounter? How did the Reading Multisyllabic Words strategy help you sound out these words?

- **Self-Selected Strategy Use** What strategies did you use to make sense of what you read? Where? How were these strategies helpful?

 ## RESPONSE TO LITERATURE

Provide the following prompt. *Describe what wild horses are like. Use story details to support your answer.*

Remind students to

- show understanding of the selection;

- give examples and details from the selection;

- use correct grammar, spelling, punctuation, and capitalization.

Author and Illustrator

RIDE AWAY WITH CRIS AND ALVIS

Have students read the biographies of the author and the photographer. Ask:

- How might Cris Peterson's life as a farmer have sparked her interest in wild horses?

- How did working together previously affect the relationship between Cris Peterson and Alvis Upitis?

WRITE ABOUT IT

Author's Craft: Alliteration

Remind students how the author uses alliteration within her description. Have students write descriptive paragraphs of their own using alliteration.

Author's Purpose

Remind students that the author uses many descriptive details. Have students think about how these details helped them form a clear picture of the horses in their minds. This will help them figure out that Cris Peterson's main purpose for writing was to inform readers.

Ride Away with Cris and Alvis

Cris Peterson lives on a big dairy farm in Wisconsin. Tending 500 cows keeps Cris pretty busy, but she still finds time to write. Cris writes a lot about farm life and animals. She often uses her own experiences to inspire her books. Cris believes it is very important to give readers a true picture of farms and animals, so she chooses her details carefully.

Alvis Upitis has provided the photographs for many of Cris's books. He is a good partner. When Cris was very busy with farm work and did not think she'd have time to write, Alvis encouraged her to try.

Other books by Cris and Alvis

LOG ON ▶ FIND OUT
Author Cris Peterson
Illustrator Alvis Upitis
www.macmillanmh.com

✔ Author's Purpose

Cris Peterson tried to create a true picture of the animals in her story *Wild Horses*. What does this suggest about her purpose for writing? Explain using story details.

218

Author's Craft

Alliteration

- Explain that alliteration is the repetition of a sound at the beginning of words. It makes descriptions more vivid. For example: "deepest, darkest part of the night" and "shadowy shapes emerge" (page 206).

- Ask students how the writer uses alliteration in the story to enhance the descriptive images. Challenge them to discuss whether or not the author is using alliteration intentionally.

- Have students look for other examples of alliteration. They will find some on pages 212 and 213. For example: "snorting, stomping steeds," "rangeland and rimrock," and "mean-eyed mare."

Comprehension Check

Summarize

To summarize *Wild Horses* use the most important details from the selection. Information from your Cause and Effect Chart may help you.

Cause → Effect
→
→
→
→

Think and Compare

1. By 1950, how many wild horses were left? Details

2. Why did Dayton Hyde want to help the wild horses? Explain your answer. Analyze Text Structure: Cause and Effect

3. Explain how Dayton manages to care for the **fragile** land while allowing the horses free range. Include details from the selection. Summarize

4. How does the author let the reader know how she feels about Dayton Hyde's wild horse sanctuary? Use details from the selection to explain your answer. Author's Purpose

5. Read "The Wild Ponies of Chincoteague" on pages 202–203. Compare Assateague Island with the Black Hills Wild Horse Sanctuary. Use details from both selections to support your answer. Reading/Writing Across Texts

219

Make Connections

Text-to-Self Have students respond to the following question to make connections to their own lives. Use the Think Aloud to model a response. *How would you help an animal in trouble? Explain.*

Think Aloud: If I saw an animal in trouble, I might call a veterinarian to come take a look. Or, I might take the animal to a rescue center or sanctuary. If I could see that the animal was hungry or thirsty, I would bring it some food and water.

Text-to-World Have students respond to the following question to make connections to the world. Use the Think Aloud to model a response. *Why is it important to care for and protect animals?*

Think Aloud: Animals help keep the environment in balance. When the world loses an entire group of animals, it causes problems. I know that it is our responsibility to protect animals that cannot protect themselves.

Comprehension Check

SUMMARIZE

Have partners summarize *Wild Horses* orally in their own words.

THINK AND COMPARE

Text Evidence

1. **Details** Answer stated in text By 1950, less than 17,000 horses were left. LOCATE

2. **Cause and Effect** Answer stated in text When wild horses became a problem for town residents, many of them were slaughtered. Then they were crowded together in feedlots. Hyde cared about the wild horses, so he wanted to help them. He made a sanctuary where they could run free. COMBINE

3. **Summarize** Answer Hyde moves the herd to protect the rangeland. Evidence During grazing season, he moves the horses from one area to another so that they do not damage the rangeland. CONNECT

4. **Author's Purpose** Answer The author lets the reader know she approves of the sanctuary through her descriptions. Evidence She writes of Hyde's careful planning and describes the beauty of the sanctuary he created. These descriptions stand in contrast to the horses' lives before, when they were scraggly and dejected. ANALYZE

5. **Text-to-Text** Both places are home to untamed horses. The Black Hills Sanctuary is in South Dakota and has 300 horses. The islands are on the East Coast, where numbers of ponies swim from one island to the other. COMPARE TEXT

Read
Fluency/Comprehension

Objectives
- Read fluently with appropriate rate
- Rate: 84–104 WCPM

Materials
- Transparency 9
- Practice Book, p. 77
- Fluency Solutions Audio CD

Develop Comprehension
Discuss the passage to ensure understanding. Give simpler synonyms for key words such as *mare, herd,* and *habitat* (*horse, group, home*), and have students use them in sentences. Model reading the entire passage. Track with your finger under sentences as you read. Next, have students repeat as you read again. This time, break sentences into shorter phrases. Provide ample time for students to respond.

Practice Book, page 77

As I read, I will pay attention to my reading rate.

	By the 1800s, huge herds of wild horses were roaming the
10	open range.
12	Picture this: You must catch a wild animal that can run as
24	fast as a train. You must tame that wild animal by riding on its
38	back. You must teach that animal to follow your every command.
49	And you must trust that animal with your life.
58	That is exactly what cowboys did when they caught, tamed,
68	and rode wild mustangs.
72	Capturing a wild mustang was a team effort. One cowboy
82	could not do it alone. Cowboys rode together on tamed horses in
94	order to catch the wild mustangs. The cowboys used their fastest
105	and strongest horses to chase the wild mustangs.
113	When the wild mustangs were exhausted, the cowboys drove
122	them into a fenced corral. The mustangs couldn't see the fence
133	until it was too late. Tired and thirsty from the long chase and
146	glistening with sweat, the mustangs could run no more. 155

Comprehension Check

1. What was the effect that a cowboy obtained by following these steps? **Cause and Effect** He would get a horse that would follow his commands and that he could trust with his life.
2. How were mustangs captured? **Main Idea and Details** Cowboys chased wild horses to make them tired, then drove them into a corral to capture them.

	Words Read	–	Number of Errors	=	Words Correct Score
First Read		–		=	
Second Read		–		=	

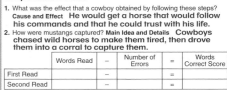

Approaching Reproducible, page 77

Beyond Reproducible, page 77

Fluency
Repeated Reading: Rate

EXPLAIN/MODEL Remind students that reading with a proper rate means reading at an appropriate speed or tempo. Model reading the passage on **Transparency 9**. As you read, slow your rate when you come to the names *Yuskeya* and *Magnificent Mary*. Write *Yuskeya* on the board and tell students that the second syllable is accented.

> ### Transparency 9
>
> Thousands of visitors arrive each summer to get a glimpse of wild horses in their natural habitat, a habitat that has been preserved through Dayton's careful planning. Throughout the grazing season, he moves the herd from one area of the ranch to another so the horses don't damage the fragile rangeland. In the process, he searches for his marker mares: Painted Lady, Medicine Hattie, Funny Face, Yuskeya, Magnificent Mary, and several others. When he spots them all, he knows the whole herd is accounted for.

Fluency (from *Wild Horses*, p. 215)

PRACTICE/APPLY Do a cloze reading of the passage. Have students read along with you chorally at a moderate rate until you come to the names of the mares. Stop and have students say the names slowly and distinctly. Then resume reading together at a moderate rate.

DAILY FLUENCY Students will practice fluency using **Practice Book** page 77 or the **Fluency Solutions Audio CD**. The passage is recorded at a slow practice speed and a faster fluent speed.

Quick Check

Can students read fluently with an appropriate rate?

During **Small Group Instruction**

If No → **Approaching Level** Use the Fluency lesson and model, p. 225Q.

If Yes → **On Level** See Fluency, p. 225T.

Beyond Level See Fluency, p. 225X.

Comprehension

SPIRAL REVIEW

REVIEW SKILL
MAIN IDEA AND DETAILS

EXPLAIN

- The **main idea** is what all of the **details** in a text or passage have in common, or what it is mostly about.

- To determine the main idea, students need to ask themselves what the sentences in a paragraph or passage tell about, explain, or describe. Then they examine and classify the details in these sentences to determine what they have in common.

MODEL

Model for students how to determine the main idea in "The Wild Ponies of Chincoteague."

Think Aloud After rereading this article, I will ask myself what the sentences in the article explain or describe. Then I will think about the details, and determine what they have in common, and how they are connected. This will help me determine the main idea. Let's see. A pony swim has taken place every year since 1924 between two tiny islands in the Atlantic Ocean. The ponies swim from Chincoteague to Assateague Island. The fire department on Chincoteague Island needed money for new equipment, so they started the pony swim and charged people to see the horses. People buy some of the horses, which controls their population, so the pony swim also protects the horses. All these details give information about the ponies and the pony swim. I can then determine the main idea: *Each year since 1924, the wild ponies of Chincoteague take part in a pony swim to raise money for the Chincoteague Fire Department.*

PRACTICE/APPLY

PARTNERS

Have students work in cooperative groups to identify key details in *Wild Horses* and discuss what those details have in common. Caution students to distinguish between significant details and minor ones. Then students should classify and summarize those details in a Main Idea and Details Chart.

Tell students to use their Main Idea and Details Charts to generate written summaries of the selection, maintaining meaning and logical order. Have selected students present their summaries to the class.

PRACTICE BOOK See **Practice Book** page 78 for Paraphrasing Independent Reading.

Objectives

- Identify main idea and details
- Distinguish between stated and implied main ideas and details

Skills Trace

Main Idea	
Introduce	191A–191B
Practice/ Apply	192–195; Practice Book, 66–67
Reteach/ Review	199Q–199DD, 545A–545B, 546–563, 569M–569Z; Practice Book, 183–184
Assess	Weekly Tests; Units 2, 5 Tests
Maintain	219B, 601A–601B, 602–605, 609Q–609DD, 631B

Test Practice

Answering Questions

To apply **answering questions strategies** to content-area reading, see pages 69–76 in *Time For Kids*.

Paired Selection

GENRE: Literary Text/Folktale

Have students read the bookmark on **Student Book** page 220. Explain that tall tales are folktale stories that

- are full of exaggerations;

- have heroes who are clever, brave, and resourceful;

- often include regional dialects.

Point out that legend says Pecos Bill was born in Texas in the 1830s. As they read, help students watch for any language usage that reflects the culture and region of the setting.

Literary Elements:
Hyperbole and Metaphor

EXPLAIN Sensory language, such as hyperboles and metaphors, makes tall tales more exciting and creates imagery that helps the reader visualize the story.

- **Hyperbole** is the use of exaggeration or overstatement. The author does not expect the reader to take the statements literally but uses hyperbole to create humor. Point out the use of hyperbole in this sentence on page 222: "She was riding a catfish the size of a boat and whooping at the top of her lungs."

- A **metaphor** compares two things that are not alike. Point out that the description "Pecos Bill roared at a gold prospector" on page 220 is a metaphor comparing Bill's voice to that of a lion or another wild animal.

APPLY Ask students to create their own hyperboles or metaphors about the tale.

Language Arts

Genre

Tall Tales are stories with events so exaggerated that they are beyond belief. Tall tales are an American form of folklore, or storytelling.

Literary Elements

Hyperbole is the use of exaggeration for emphasis. The author does not expect the reader to believe it. An example is: *I told you a million times to clean your room.*

A **Metaphor** is the comparison of two unlike things without the use of *like* or *as*.

THE Tale OF Pecos Bill

retold by Gillian Reed

Pecos Bill was the best cowboy and toughest man there ever was. He had bounced out of his family's wagon when he was a baby and landed in the Pecos River. He was raised by coyotes, but he didn't talk about that very much.

One day Bill showed up on the Texas range wearing a blue bandanna and a big Stetson hat. "Hey, partner," Pecos Bill roared at a gold prospector, "I'm lookin' for some real cowhands. Got me a ranch in New Mexico — well, to tell the truth, New Mexico is my ranch. I need some tough guys to work for me. I'm looking for the kind of man who can eat a pot of beans in one gulp and pick his teeth with barbed wire."

> Pecos Bill's description of a tough guy is **hyperbole**. It's a humorous exaggeration that the reader is not meant to believe.

220

The prospector said some tough cowhands were camped out 200 miles down the river. Bill and his horse set off in that direction, and before long a mountain lion leaped from a boulder straight down onto Pecos Bill.

Bill's horse didn't wait around to see what happened next. If he had, all he would have seen was a blur of flying fur. He would have heard nothing but hideous snarls and groans. When the fur settled, the big cat was apologizing to Bill.

"How can I make it up to you?" it asked.

"You can't, but I'm putting this saddle on you," said Bill. "You scared off my horse, and I hate walkin'."

So Pecos Bill rode the cat to the tough guys' campsite. Those tough men took one look at Bill on that mountain lion and made him their new boss. Then the whole crew headed out for New Mexico. **1** **2**

221

Paired Selection

Read "The Tale of Pecos Bill"

As you read, remind students to apply what they have learned about tall tales, hyperbole, and metaphors.

1 LITERARY ELEMENTS: HYPERBOLE

Find two examples of hyperbole in the description of Pecos Bill on pages 220–221. (Answers will include: He was raised by coyotes. He fought, saddled, and rode a mountain lion.)

2 CAUSE AND EFFECT

How does Pecos Bill come to be riding on a mountain lion? (A mountain lion frightened away Pecos Bill's horse, and Pecos Bill did not want to walk. So he put a saddle on the mountain lion.)

Use the Interactive Question-Response Guide in the **ELL Resource Book**, pages 94–95, to help English Language Learners gain access to the paired selection content.

Science

Connect to Content

ANIMAL ADAPTATIONS

Have students discuss the similarities and differences between a horse and a mountain lion. Using the Internet, science textbooks, or reference books, students should list how these animals have adapted to their surroundings. Have students create a poster that compares the two animals. Students should include their research on their posters.

Paired Selection

3 LITERARY ELEMENTS: HYPERBOLE

What example of hyperbole do you see in the first paragraph? (The wild black horse had the power of twelve horses.)

4 CAUSE AND EFFECT

Why did Pecos Bill try to stop Slue-Foot Sue from riding Widow-Maker? (He loves his wife and knows that Widow-Maker will throw Sue if she tries to ride him. Widow-Maker is strong and will not let anyone but Bill ride him.) What might happen if Slue-Foot Sue tries to ride Widow-Maker anyway? (Sue might get seriously hurt when Widow-Maker throws her.)

5 COMPARE AND CONTRAST

How are Pecos Bill and Slue-Foot Sue alike? How are they different? (Pecos Bill and Slue-Foot Sue both enjoy adventure and riding wild animals. They are different because Bill can ride Widow-Maker without any trouble, but Sue cannot.)

3

Back on the ranch, Pecos Bill caught a wild black horse for himself and named it Widow-Maker. That crazy horse had the power of twelve horses and wouldn't let anyone but Bill ride him.

Pecos Bill also got himself a spouse. He first spied Slue-Foot Sue on the Rio Grande. She was riding a catfish the size of a boat and whooping at the top of her lungs. Bill admired her fog-horn voice.

The day she married Bill, Slue-Foot Sue wore a dress with one of those old-time bustles. The bustle was a steel-spring contraption that made the back of her dress stick out a mile.

4

After the wedding, Sue wanted to ride Widow-Maker. Now, Pecos Bill loved Slue-Foot Sue, so he attempted to talk her out of this notion.

"Widow-Maker won't let anybody ride him but me. He'd throw you in a second."

222

Practice Book, page 79

A **metaphor** is a comparison of two things that are not alike without the use of *like* or *as*.
Hyperbole is the use of exaggeration for emphasis or to make a point.

Read the following sentences. Put a check in the box for the sentences that contain hyperbole. Underline the hyperbole. Put an X in the box for the sentences that contain metaphors. Circle the two things that are being compared.

1. Suzie is so fast she can run two miles before you've put on your shoes. ☑
2. Timothy is a snail when it comes to making his bed. ☒
3. Jim used a lasso to catch a hundred horses at once. ☑
4. This pillow is a cloud. I love sleeping on it. ☒
5. The emerald eyes of the cat shone in the darkness. ☒
6. My baby sister is an angel. I can't wait to see her. ☒
7. She was so thirsty she drank a lake and said she was still thirsty! ☑

ELL

Understand Exaggeration
Read aloud the first paragraph on page 220, and point out and discuss the exaggerated events. Use the illustration on page 221 of Pecos Bill riding the mountain lion to explain exaggeration. Discuss why an author would use exaggeration in a story. Elaborate on students' responses.

Approaching Reproducible, page 79
Beyond Reproducible, page 79

But Sue insisted, and Bill finally let Sue give it a try. Sue got on Widow-Maker, who bucked and jumped and bucked again. Then he threw Slue-Foot Sue, and she sped into the sky like she'd been shot from a cannon. When Sue finished going up, she plummeted down. And when she hit the ground, she bounced on her steel-spring bustle, a giant pogo stick, that sent her up again, even higher than before. She even hit her head on the moon.

> Sue's bustle is not a pogo stick, but the comparison helps the reader picture what happened. This is an example of **metaphor**.

For days Pecos Bill watched his bouncing bride. Up and down she went. Every time Sue landed, she bounced up higher, until she came down to Earth only once every few weeks.

It took a long time for Pecos Bill to find another bride as accomplished as Slue-Foot Sue. And he never again allowed a wife of his to ride Widow-Maker.

✓ Connect and Compare

1. Find two examples of hyperbole in the descriptions of Slue-Foot Sue and her adventures. Explain why they are examples of hyperbole. **Hyperbole**

2. Identify the metaphor on page 222 and explain what two things are being compared. **Metaphor**

3. Compare Widow-Maker to the mustangs described in *Wild Horses*. How are they similar? How are they different? **Reading/Writing Across Texts**

LOG ON ▶ FIND OUT Language Arts Tall tales
www.macmillanmh.com

Comprehension

Comparing Characters

Explain Point out that that the legendary cowboy Pecos Bill is the subject of many tall tales. The character of Pecos Bill is usually portrayed as being enormously strong, clever, brave, and funny.

Discuss Ask how this tale resembles other tales from classical and traditional literature. Discuss how many folktales feature a hero of superhuman strength or skill; include other colorful characters; and use hyperbole, metaphor, and other literary elements.

Apply Have students compare Pecos Bill with another tall tale hero, such as Paul Bunyan, or another hero known for his strength, such as Hercules. Students should tell how Pecos Bill, the other hero, and their exploits are alike and different.

Paired Selection

Connect and Compare

1. Two examples are the descriptions of Sue riding a catfish the size of a boat and of her bouncing so high that she hit the moon and came down to Earth only once every few weeks. They are examples of hyperbole because these events are exaggerations and could not happen in real life. HYPERBOLE

2. The metaphor is that Slue-Foot Sue's voice is a fog horn. The author is comparing Sue's voice to a fog horn, which means that her voice is very loud. METAPHOR

3. **FOCUS QUESTION** Widow-Maker and the mustangs are similar in that they are all wild horses that live in the West. Some of the mustangs are caught and tamed. Widow-Maker is also caught, but he is not very tame because he allows only Pecos Bill to ride him. They are also different because Widow-Maker is a tall-tale creature, while the mustangs are real.

READING/WRITING ACROSS TEXTS

Write

WHOLE GROUP

✓ **WRITING WORKSHOP**
- Developing Procedural Writing
- Trait: Word Choice
- Strong Verbs

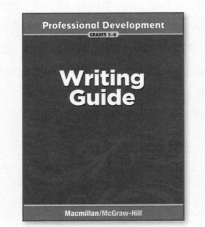

Professional Development
GRADES 3–6

Writing Guide

Macmillan/McGraw-Hill

UNIT 2

Developing Procedural Writing

WEEK 1	**Strong Sentences/Trait: Ideas** Showing
WEEK 2	**Strong Paragraphs/Trait: Word Choice** Show Actions
WEEK 3	**How-To Article**
WEEK 4	**Strong Sentences/Trait: Word Choice** Strong Verbs, 223A–223B
	• Reading/Writing Connection, 224–225
	• Minilessons, 225A Word Choice: Strong Verbs
	• Conferencing Routine, 225B
WEEK 5	**Strong Paragraphs/Trait: Word Choice** Strong Verbs and Descriptive Details
WEEK 6	**How-To Article**

Trait: Word Choice

Strong Sentences: Strong Verbs

TEACH/MODEL Tell students that writers use **strong verbs** to show rather than tell about an action. Strong verbs describe actions in a vivid way so that readers can really picture what's happening.

Point out that adding strong verbs to their writing can help students build **strong sentences** that help readers imagine the action, or "see" it in their minds. Write the following sentence on the board, and read it aloud:

> Maria sat on the chair.

Teacher Think Aloud I know from reading this sentence that Maria sat in a chair. But I do not know *how* she sat in chair. That's because *sat* is an ordinary verb that does not help me form a picture in my mind. *Sat* is not a strong verb.

Write the following sentences, and read them aloud.

> Maria **plopped down** in the chair.
> Maria **perched** on the chair.

Point out that each sentence uses a strong verb. Ask: *What are the strong verbs?* (plopped, perched)

Explain that each strong verb creates a different picture of how Maria sat in the chair. Ask students to show how to plop down in a chair. Then have them show you how to perch in a chair.

Ask: *How does the strong verb in the first sentence help you imagine Maria sitting in the chair?* (she sits down heavily and lazily) *How does the strong verb in the second sentence help you imagine Maria sitting in the chair?* (she sits very straight, at the edge of the chair)

Discuss with students how the strong verbs give more information to the reader and create stronger, more interesting sentences.

Teacher Write Aloud

PRACTICE/APPLY Further explore with students the use of strong verbs to show actions. Write the following sentences on the board. Then complete the Teacher Think Aloud.

> Rex ran into the water park.
> "Yeah! We are finally here," he said.
> Rex ran to his favorite ride, the water slide.
> He walked up the long set of stairs.
> Then he went down the slide.
> At the end, he went into the water.

Teacher Think Aloud These sentences tell me what Rex does at the water park, but they don't show me. That's because they don't use strong verbs. Let's make these sentences stronger. We will use strong verbs that show us what Rex does at the park. The strong verbs will help readers imagine the actions.

Ask students to brainstorm strong verbs that they could substitute for the ordinary verbs in the sentences. List the strong verbs on the board. To complete the Think Aloud, choose strong verbs to create strong sentences as part of a paragraph like the one below. Stop after each sentence to discuss how the strong verbs help students picture the actions.

> Rex dashed into the water park. "Yeah! We are finally here!" he shouted. Then Rex raced to his favorite ride, the water slide. He scrambled up the long set of stairs. Then he zoomed down the slide. At the end, he splashed into the water.

Draft Display the Writing Prompt on **Writing Transparency 28**. Remind students to use strong verbs so readers can imagine the actions. Circulate and provide Over-the-Shoulder Conferences as students work.

Objective
- Write sentences with strong verbs

Materials
- Writer's Notebooks
- Writing Transparency 28

Daily Journal Prompts

Focus on Strong Verbs

Use these and other prompts for independent daily journal writing.

- Write about a moment when you were trying to get somewhere quickly.
- Write about a moment when you very tired but were trying to stay awake.
- Write about a moment when you were waiting for someone or something.
- Write about a moment when you were riding a bike up or down a steep hill.

Transparency 28

Focus on a moment from your morning routine (waking up, brushing your teeth, getting dressed, eating breakfast). Try to include some strong verbs!

Writing Transparency

Reading and Writing Connection

Trait: Word Choice

STRONG VERBS

Remind students that strong verbs help readers create images in their minds. Point out that good writers use strong verbs to describe action in a way that helps readers picture what is happening.

Read the Passage

Use the example from *Wild Horses* as a model of the author's skilled use of strong verbs.

- Have students read the bookmark. Remind them that strong verbs are more descriptive than ordinary verbs. Ask students to quickly call out strong verbs they could use in their writing instead of the ordinary verb *said*.

- **Ask:** *Have you ever been nervous about being in a new place? Where were you?*

- Have students chorally read the excerpt from *Wild Horses*. Direct their attention to the callout. Have students discuss strong verbs that help them picture what the horses did.

- **Ask:** *Which strong verbs from the text make you think of sounds? Which strong verbs help you "see" what the author wants you to see?*

Writing

✔ **Trait: Word Choice**
Writers include **strong verbs** in their writing to help readers see exactly what is happening.

Reading and Writing Connection

Read the passage below. Notice how the author Cris Peterson uses strong verbs in her story.

An excerpt from
Wild Horses

The author uses strong verbs to help us see exactly how the horses moved and looked in this moment. She chose verbs that put specific pictures in our heads so that we can "see" what she wants us to see.

On a miserably cold fall day, huge creaking semi-trailers filled with snorting, stomping steeds finally arrived at the ranch. After hours of coaxing, Dayton succeeded in getting Magnificent Mary to skitter off the trailer. She was a battle-scarred, mean-eyed mare with a nose about twice as long as it should be. The rest of the herd clattered behind her, eyes bulging with fear.

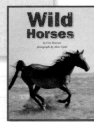

224

Respond to the Selection

Have students write a response to the selection.

- ☑ **Engagement** Help students deepen their connection to the text and discover their own perspective on it. *Focus on a moment when you wanted to help someone.*
- ☑ **Response** Help students explore more deeply their reactions to particular passages in the reading. *Focus on a moment in the story when a strong verb made you think about something other than horses. Use text evidence in your writing.*
- ☑ **Literary Analysis** Help students deepen their connection to the text and discover their own perspective on it. *Focus on a place in the story where you think the author chose an unusual verb. Use text evidence in your writing.*

Read and Find

Read Pat's writing below. How did she use strong verbs to help you picture the moment? Use the checklist below to help you.

Flying to Milwaukee
by Pat S.

I gazed out the plane's tiny window. As the plane's engine roared to life, I clutched the armrests and squeezed my eyes shut. The intercom squawked out a final message from our pilot, and the plane picked up speed. As we zoomed down the runway, I felt like a giant hand was pressing me into my seat. I finally peeked out again, and we were soaring high above the city.

Read about Pat's flight.

Writer's Checklist

☑ Does the writer choose verbs that describe specific actions?

☑ Does the writer use several **strong verbs** instead of the same verb over and over?

☐ Do you get a clear image of the actions as Pat experienced them?

225

ELL ENGLISH LANGUAGE LEARNERS

Beginning	**Intermediate**	**Advanced**
Write Sentences Provide model sentences based on the Journal Prompt: *I saw my friends playing a game. I ____ to them. We ____ for a while. Then I ____.* Help students add words, including strong verbs, that show what they did in the moment.	**Narrate** Ask students to write three sentences based on the Journal Prompt. Have them think about what they did in the moment. Have them use strong verbs to show the action. Provide a model if necessary. As you read their sentences, correct grammar and spelling as needed.	**Describe** Ask students to respond to the Journal Prompt. Have them use strong verbs to describe the actions in that moment. Ask students to use complete sentences.

Write

Read the Student Model

Have students read aloud the student model at the top of **Student Book** page 225. Discuss what this student writer did to help readers picture what was happening, and identify strong verbs. Use the Writer's Checklist.

Journal Prompt

Draft Write the following prompt on the board. Have students write a response to the prompt.

Think about an activity you recently did or sport you recently played. Write three to five sentences about that moment. Use strong verbs.

Tell students that you will be reading and commenting on their writing during Writing Conference time.

Model how to use the Writer's Checklist so students can write and revise their work. Then ask:

- *What is the moment you chose?*
- *What strong verbs did you use to show what happened? Will readers be able to clearly picture that moment? If not, what strong verbs could you add?*

Objectives
- Write strong verbs to complete sentences
- Write strong sentences

Materials
- Writer's Notebooks
- Teacher's Resource Book, p. 186

ELL

Vocabulary Development
Help students brainstorm strong verbs by helping them to use a thesaurus to find synonyms for an ordinary verb. Then act out the strong verbs to show the difference in their meanings.

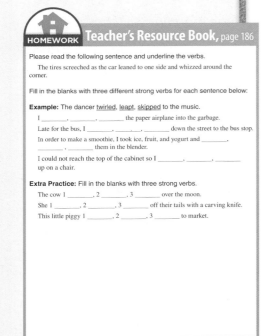

HOMEWORK Teacher's Resource Book, page 186

Please read the following sentence and underline the verbs.
  The tires screeched as the car leaned to one side and whizzed around the corner.

Fill in the blanks with three different strong verbs for each sentence below:

Example: The dancer _twirled_, _leapt_, _skipped_ to the music.

I _____, _____, _____ the paper airplane into the garbage.
Late for the bus, I _____, _____, _____ down the street to the bus stop.
In order to make a smoothie, I took ice, fruit, and yogurt and _____, _____, _____ them in the blender.
I could not reach the top of the cabinet so I _____, _____, _____ up on a chair.

Extra Practice: Fill in the blanks with three strong verbs.
The cow 1 _____, 2 _____, 3 _____ over the moon.
She 1 _____, 2 _____, 3 _____ off their tails with a carving knife.
This little piggy 1 _____, 2 _____, 3 _____ to market.

Minilessons

Minilesson 1 | Word Choice/Strong Verbs

TEACH/MODEL

Remind students that they have been focusing on strong verbs, or verbs that help readers picture the action described. Today they will brainstorm different strong verbs they could use in sentences. Have students use **Teacher's Resource Book** page 186. Ask them to read the sentence at the top of the page and underline the strong verbs.

PRACTICE/APPLY

Have students work independently to complete the sentences with three strong verbs. Ask students to share their completed work during Sharing Circle. Discuss the strong verbs they used and how they help readers picture the actions.

Minilesson 2 | Word Choice/Strong Verbs in Steps

TEACH/MODEL

Tell students that writers use strong verbs in steps to show how to do something. Write the following steps on the board. Read them aloud. Discuss how the strong verbs made the sentences more interesting.

> Scoop peanut butter from the jar.
> Spread it on a slice of bread.
> Plop some jelly on top.
> Now spread the jelly.
> Place another slice of bread on top.
> Gobble up your sandwich.

PRACTICE/APPLY

Write the following sentences on the board. In their Writer's Notebooks, have students replace the ordinary verbs with strong verbs. Then have students think of something they know how to make. Have them explain how to do the activity using strong verbs.

> Put ice cream in a bowl.
> Put chocolate sauce on top of the ice cream.
> Put whipped cream on, too.
> Put a cherry on top.

Conferencing Routine

Dynamic Feedback System

Step 1 Read and appreciate the writing.

Step 2 Notice how the student uses the targeted skill (for example, strong verbs: Ask: *What strong verbs did the writer use?*).

Step 3 Write comments that show how the writing has an impact on you. Direct your comments to those places in the piece where the student has used the targeted skill.

Step 4 Meet with and give the student a revision assignment.

Write Effective Comments

Word Choice At least one of your comments should highlight the way the student uses **strong verbs**. Here are some sample comments.

- Your use of strong verbs really helps me picture the moment.

- Your skilled use of showing is clear from all the strong verbs you used.

- I am eager to know more about this moment. What strong verbs can you add to help me picture it better?

Revision Assignments

Word Choice Here are some examples of effective revision assignments for strong verbs.

 ■ **Reread your entry.** *Choose one sentence that describes an action. Now rewrite this sentence adding strong verbs.*

 ■ **[Underline a section.]** Mark a specific section of a student's writing and then ask the student to revise it in a specific way.

 ■ **[Underline a section.]** *Read the part that I underlined. I'm curious about what other verbs might capture the action you describe here. Rewrite the sentence in three different ways. Use a different strong verb in each sentence.*

Teacher-to-Teacher

Over-the-Shoulder Conferences

Use these quick, focused opportunities to comment while students are writing.

- **Step 1** Quietly move close enough to a student that you can read the journal entry he or she is writing.

- **Step 2** Read part of what you see. You don't need to start from the beginning or read the entire piece.

- **Step 3** Show the student a spot in the writing where he or she is using a particular skill or describing something that piques your interest.

- **Step 4** Whisper a sentence or two about why you noticed that spot in the writing, and ask a question that will nudge the student to add a strong verb.

- **Step 5** Move on to the next student. Select students strategically. You should see 12–15 students in a 15-minute period.

Research Proven Writing Approach

The Writers' Express®
Immediate Impact. Lasting Transformation.   wex.org

Connect
Language Arts

WHOLE GROUP

✓ **VOCABULARY**
   • Tested Words

✓ **SPELLING**
   • *r*-Controlled Vowels /är/ and /ôr/

✓ **GRAMMAR**
   • Possessive Nouns

SMALL GROUP

• Differentiated Instruction, pp. 225I–225HH

Practice Book, page 80

Context clues can help readers determine the meaning of unfamiliar words. Sometimes, the other words and sentences in the paragraph can help you figure out the word's meaning.

A. Read the passage below. Use context clues to help you figure out the meanings of the words in dark type.

We were standing around the **corral**, leaning on the fence and watching the horses. "Midnight's a good mother," I said, as the black mare's **foal** followed closely behind her. Only two days old, it was still getting used to walking on its long, **wobbly** legs.

My aunt sighed. "Sometimes I wonder if they would have been better off in the canyon, living in the **wilderness** instead of around people," she said.

B. Write the definition for each word, along with the context clues that helped you identify the word's meaning.

1. **corral**   definition: a fenced-in area for animals
   context clues: fence; horses

2. **foal**   definition: a baby horse
   context clues: followed mother; only two days old

3. **wobbly**   definition: unsteady
   context clues: getting used to walking; legs

4. **wilderness**   definition: a natural area without people
   context clues: in the canyon; instead of living around people

Approaching Reproducible, page 80
Beyond Reproducible, page 80

Build Robust Vocabulary

Day 1 Teach/Practice

CONNECT TO WORDS

■ Practice this week's vocabulary words using the following prompts:

1. How can *descendants* find out about their ancestors?

2. Why might you bring an animal to a *sanctuary*?

3. What are some animals that have been *threatened* with extinction?

4. When you suddenly *emerge* from a dark room, what happens to your eyesight?

5. What object in your home is *fragile*?

6. If you could live in any kind of *habitat*, what would it be?

ACADEMIC VOCABULARY

■ Review the important academic vocabulary words for the week. These words include: *text structure, cause, effect, expository, hyperbole, metaphor.*

■ Write each word on the board. Define each using student-friendly language, and ask students to select the word you are defining. Then point to words in random order for students to define.

Day 2 Review

CONNECT TO WORDS

■ Review the definitions of this week's vocabulary words using **Student Book** pages 202–203. Then discuss each word using these prompts:

1. Of whom are you a *descendant*?

2. If you went to a bird *sanctuary*, what would you expect to see?

3. Have you ever felt *threatened*? When?

4. If you had a magic box, what would you want to *emerge* from it?

5. Where might you find many *fragile* objects?

6. What animals would you expect to see in a desert *habitat*?

CONTEXT CLUES

■ Remind students that often a writer gives clues about the meaning of unfamiliar words through other words in the same paragraph. Those clues might include definitions, examples, synonyms, or antonyms. Students can also use context clues to determine or clarify the meaning of multiple meaning words.

■ Display **Transparency 17**, and read the first sentence. Model using context clues to figure out the meaning of the underlined word.

■ Have students find the clues in the remaining sentences that help define the underlined words.

■ Have students write their own context-rich sentences for this week's vocabulary words in their Writer's Notebooks.

Day 3 Reinforce

CONNECT TO WORDS

- Have students create Word Squares for each word in their Writer's Notebooks.

- In the first square, students write the word. (Example: *descendants*)

- In the second square, students write their own definition of the word and any related words, such as synonyms. (Example: *children, young, offspring, later generations, family living many years later, great grandchildren*)

- In the third square, students draw a simple illustration that will help them remember the word. (Example: grandparent, parent, and child)

- In the fourth square, students write nonexamples, including antonyms for the word. (Example: *nonrelation, stranger*)

RELATED WORDS

- Help students generate words related to *fragile*.

- Draw a circle on the board. Above it, write *fragile*. Divide the circle into a pie chart with eight sections.

- Have students list related words, and write each one in a pie slice. Tell students to use a print or online thesaurus. Add words they might not have included, such as *delicate, flimsy*, and *brittle*.

Day 4 Extend

CONNECT TO WORDS

- Review this week's vocabulary using the following sentence stems. Have students orally complete each one.

  1. I would like for my descendants to be _____.

  2. I plan to make a cat sanctuary to _____.

  3. The boys felt threatened when _____.

  4. The fragile _____ was destroyed when_____.

  5. Animals such as _____ fill the _____ habitat.

  6. I was shocked when _____ suddenly emerged from _____.

MORPHOLOGY

- Use the additional selection word *adaptability* as a springboard for students to learn other words.

- Write *adaptability* on the board. Circle *adapt*. Explain that *adapt* means "adjust" or "get used to." Draw a line under -*ability*. Explain that *adaptability* means "the ability to adjust, or get used to something." Point out that *adapt* and *ability* both derive from Latin.

- Write *adaptable, adapted*, and *adaptation* on the board. Have students underline *adapt* in each.

- Use the word parts to define each word. Students should see *adaptable* means "able to adapt"; *adapted* means "changed" or "adjusted"; and *adaptation* means "the process or result of changing something."

Day 5 Assess and Reteach

POSTTEST

- Display **Transparency 18**. Have students complete the cloze sentences using one of this week's vocabulary words.

- Note how quickly and accurately students can complete this task. Work with students who make errors or require too much time to complete this task during Small Group time.

CONNECT TO WRITING

- Have students write sentences in their Writer's Notebooks using this week's vocabulary. Tell students to write sentences that provide information they learned from this week's readings.

- ELL Provide the Day 4 sentence stems for students needing extra support.

5-Day Spelling

✔ r-Controlled Vowels /är/ and /ôr/

Go to pages T14–T15 for **Differentiated Spelling Lists**.

Spelling Words

door	cord	stormy
dart	spark	bore
fort	award	guard
morning	smart	ward
carpet	charge	warp
ford	worn	backyard
core	argue	

Review screech, shrimp, throat
Challenge charcoal, forecast

Dictation Sentences

1. Shut the **door** when you leave.
2. He threw a dart at the board.
3. We passed by an old fort.
4. I work best in the morning.
5. The carpet we bought is soft.
6. Please help the horse ford the stream.
7. Is the core of the apple edible?
8. The telephone cord is broken.
9. The fire threw off a spark.
10. He won the attendance award.
11. It was smart to bring a sweater.
12. A battery has an electric **charge**.
13. I was worn out after the game.
14. I won't listen to you argue.
15. If it's stormy outside, we stay in.
16. Please don't bore me with that story again.
17. The guard let us enter the gate.
18. The spray will ward off bugs.
19. Dampness made the door warp.
20. Are the animals in the **backyard**?

Review/Challenge Words

1. I could hear the owl screech.
2. She made shrimp salad.
3. I have a sore throat.
4. We burn charcoal in our grill.
5. Did you hear the weather forecast?

Words in **bold** are from this week's selections.

Day 1 Pretest

ASSESS PRIOR KNOWLEDGE

- Model for students how to spell the words *ward* and *warp*. Segment the words sound by sound. Then attach a spelling to each sound. Point out that even though these words have an *ar* combination, because they follow a *w* they have an /ôr/ pronunciation.

- Use the Dictation Sentences. Say the underlined word, read the sentence, and repeat the word. Have students write the words.

- Have students self-correct their tests. Point out that in the word *guard* there is a silent *u*.

- Have students cut apart the **Spelling Word Cards BLM** on **Teacher's Resource Book** page 52 and figure out a way to sort them. Have them save the cards for use throughout the week.

Day 2 Word Sorts and Review

SPIRAL REVIEW

Review for students how to spell the words *screech, throat,* and *shrimp*. Have students find words in this week's readings with the same sounds.

WORD SORTS

- Have students take turns sorting the spelling words and explaining how they sorted them. When students have finished the sort, discuss any words that have unexpected vowel spellings (*door, award, ward,* and *warp*).

- Review the spelling words, pointing out the /ôr/ and /är/ r-controlled sounds. Use the cards on the Spelling Word Cards BLM. Write the key words *ford* and *dart* on the board. Model how to sort words by r-controlled sounds. Place one or two cards beneath the correct key words.

ON YOUR OWN — Phonics/Spelling, pages 49–50

Fold back the paper along the dotted line. Use the blanks to write each word as it is read aloud. When you finish the test, unfold the paper. Use the list at the right to correct any spelling mistakes.

1. ___	1. door
2. ___	2. dart
3. ___	3. fort
4. ___	4. floor
5. ___	5. carpet
6. ___	6. ford
7. ___	7. core
8. ___	8. cord
9. ___	9. spark
10. ___	10. yard
11. ___	11. smart
12. ___	12. large
13. ___	13. worn
14. ___	14. far
15. ___	15. stormy
16. ___	16. bore
17. ___	17. bark
18. ___	18. warp
19. ___	19. tar
20. ___	20. backyard
Challenge Words 21. ___	21. argue
22. ___	22. morning
Review Words 23. ___	23. screech
24. ___	24. shrimp
25. ___	25. throat

HOMEWORK — Phonics/Spelling, page 51

ford	guard	door	carpet	stormy
spark	smart	bore	cord	ward
charge	worn	dart	fort	backyard
morning	carpet	award	argue	warp

Pattern Power
Write the spelling words with each of these spelling patterns.

words with -or
1. ford
2. morning
3. worn
4. door
5. bore
6. cord
7. fort
8. stormy

words with -ar
9. spark
10. charge
11. guard
12. smart
13. dart
14. award
15. carpet
16. argue
17. ward
18. backyard
19. warp
20. carpet

All in Order
Write the following words in alphabetical order: ward, fort, cord, stormy, backyard, guard, carpet, dart, smart, morning.
21. backyard
22. carpet
23. cord
24. dart
25. fort
26. guard
27. morning
28. smart
29. stormy
30. ward

Day 3 — Word Meanings

ANALOGIES

Remind students that analogies show relationships between two pairs of words. Point out that analogies often use synonym and antonym pairs. Then read each analogy below. Have students copy the analogies into their Writer's Notebooks. Tell them to complete each analogy by writing a spelling word in the blank.

1. *dark* is to *night* as *light* is to _____ (*morning*)

2. *clear skies* are to *calm* as *lightning* is to _____ (*stormy*)

3. *curtains* are to *window* as _____ is to *floor* (*carpet*)

4. *read* is to *library* as *play* is to _____ (*playground*)

Have students create more analogies using spelling words, review words, and challenge words. Suggest they include synonyms and antonyms.

Day 4 — Proofread

PROOFREAD AND WRITE

Write these sentences on the board. Have students circle and correct each misspelled word.

1. I will get the aword at the ceremony in the moorning. (*award, morning*)

2. Don't bor the gard with those jokes. (*bore, guard*)

3. The corpet was stuck under the doar. (*carpet, door*)

4. I was smort to prepare for the sturmy weather. (*smart, stormy*)

5. The library will chorge extra if you worp the pages. (*charge, warp*)

Error Correction Some students will leave off the final *e* in the common *-ore* spelling pattern. Provide *-ore* word lists for students to read, such as *before, store, anymore, evermore*, and *explore*. Have students write multiple sentences using these words.

Day 5 — Assess and Reteach

POSTTEST

Use the Dictation Sentences on page 225E for the Posttest.

If students have difficulty with any words in the lesson, have them place the words on a list called *Spelling Words I Want to Remember* in their Writer's Notebooks. Look for students' use of these words in their writings.

Challenge students to find words that have the same *r*-controlled spelling patterns they studied this week.

HOMEWORK — Phonics/Spelling, page 52

ford	guard	door	carpet	stormy
spark	smart	bore	cord	ward
charge	worn	dart	fort	backyard
morning	carpet	award	argue	warp

What's the Word?
Write the spelling words that match the clues below.

1. rug — **carpet**
2. rope — **cord**
3. to bend — **warp**
4. area behind a house — **backyard**
5. for soldiers — **fort**
6. protects — **guard**
7. dull — **bore**
8. win — **award**
9. fight — **argue**
10. wake up — **morning**
11. static — **spark**
12. on the floor — **carpet**

What's the Word?
Complete each sentence below with a spelling word.

13. You must be very **smart** to be an inventor.
14. I heard a knock on the **door**.
15. Ben Franklin researched electricity on a rainy and **stormy** night.
16. The doctors treat the patients in the hospital **ward**.
17. These shoes are **worn** out.
18. Try to throw the **dart** at the bull's eye.
19. He felt an electric **charge** during the storm.
20. How did he cross the **ford** of the river?

ON YOUR OWN — Phonics/Spelling, page 53

A. There are six spelling mistakes in these paragraphs. Circle the misspelled words. Write the words correctly on the lines below.

Early in the mourning, Ben Franklin had a good feeling. He could tell it was going to be a starmy day and he needed lightning to test his idea. Ben was so excited he didn't even change his clothes. He just wore the same clothes he had warn yesterday.

His idea was that lightning is a large spork like the ones he would get by rubbing his feet on the corpet and touching the doar handle.

That night, he was finally ready. He tied his kite string to a key and then he flew his kite. Up it went into the windy night and soon lightning struck it. To his delight, he saw a spark jump from the key. He knew he had been right.

1. **morning** 3. **worn** 5. **carpet**
2. **stormy** 4. **spark** 6. **door**

Writing Activity

B. If you could interview Ben Franklin, what questions would you ask him? Write your questions on the lines below. Use four spelling words in your interview questions. Answers will vary.

HOMEWORK — Phonics/Spelling, page 54

Look at the words in each set below. One word in each set is spelled correctly. Use a pencil to fill in the circle next to the correct word. Before you begin, look at the sample set of words. Sample A has been done for you. Do Sample B by yourself. When you are sure you know what to do, you may go on with the rest of the page.

Sample A:
- Ⓐ sprout
- Ⓑ sport
- Ⓒ sporet
- Ⓓ spart

Sample B:
- Ⓔ scharks
- Ⓕ sharx
- Ⓖ sharks
- Ⓗ scharcks

1.
- Ⓐ ford
- Ⓑ phord
- Ⓒ phorde
- Ⓓ forde

2.
- Ⓔ spaurk
- Ⓕ sparke
- Ⓖ spark
- Ⓗ spaurke

3.
- Ⓐ charj
- Ⓑ charg
- Ⓒ charge
- Ⓓ charje

4.
- Ⓔ morening
- Ⓕ morning
- Ⓖ morneen
- Ⓗ mowrning

5.
- Ⓐ guard
- Ⓑ gard
- Ⓒ garred
- Ⓓ guarde

6.
- Ⓔ smard
- Ⓕ smart
- Ⓖ smarte
- Ⓗ smardt

7.
- Ⓐ wourn
- Ⓑ worne
- Ⓒ woren
- Ⓓ worn

8.
- Ⓔ core
- Ⓕ caur
- Ⓖ corr
- Ⓗ corre

9.
- Ⓐ dore
- Ⓑ dor
- Ⓒ doore
- Ⓓ door

10.
- Ⓔ bore
- Ⓕ bour
- Ⓖ boore
- Ⓗ borre

11.
- Ⓐ daurt
- Ⓑ darte
- Ⓒ daurte
- Ⓓ dart

12.
- Ⓔ uhward
- Ⓕ aword
- Ⓖ award
- Ⓗ uhword

13.
- Ⓐ carpette
- Ⓑ carpet
- Ⓒ carpit
- Ⓓ caurpet

14.
- Ⓔ coured
- Ⓕ corred
- Ⓖ courd
- Ⓗ cord

15.
- Ⓐ phort
- Ⓑ fortte
- Ⓒ fort
- Ⓓ phorte

16.
- Ⓔ argue
- Ⓕ argew
- Ⓖ argoo
- Ⓗ argou

17.
- Ⓐ stormy
- Ⓑ stormie
- Ⓒ stormee
- Ⓓ stourmy

18.
- Ⓔ warde
- Ⓕ worde
- Ⓖ ward
- Ⓗ wourd

19.
- Ⓐ backyart
- Ⓑ backyard
- Ⓒ bakyard
- Ⓓ backyaurd

20.
- Ⓔ worp
- Ⓕ warp
- Ⓖ waurp
- Ⓗ wourp

Daily Language Activities

Write the sentences on the board.

DAY 1
My classmates gave animal reports these past two dayes. Some topics were wolfs, gooses deer, and sheeps. Mine was about beares. (1: days.; 2: wolves; 3: geese,; 4: sheep; 5: bears)

DAY 2
those are my sisters toys. She got those blocks' from my dads sister. (1: Those; 2: sister's; 3: blocks; 4: dad's)

DAY 3
We discussed ideas for the familys' gifts. The childrens' suggestions were the most good. (1: family's; 2: children's; 3: best)

DAY 4
I read a book about a mans' experiences inventing solutions. It was called How Ben Franklin Stole the Lightning? (1: man's; 2: *How Ben Franklin Stole the Lightning.*)

DAY 5
I reviewed a magazine article called Keep Trying. It was about the authors aword-winning inventions. (1: "Keep Trying."; 2: author's; 3: award-winning)

ELL

Language Transfer
Forming possessive nouns will be challenging for some students, since many languages use phrases rather than endings to indicate possession. To reinforce using possessives, model changing phrases such as *the toys of my sister* to *my sister's toys*. See language transfers on pages T16–T31.

✔ Possessive Nouns

Day 1 · Introduce the Concept

INTRODUCE POSSESSIVE NOUNS

- A **possessive noun** shows ownership.

- When a possessive noun is used before another noun, it shows to what or to whom that noun belongs: *I used Mike's skates. My sister's hat is too big for me.*

- To form the possessive of most singular nouns, add an **apostrophe** and an *-s* to the end of the noun: *baby's bottle, river's current, Jonathan's dinner.*

Day 2 · Teach the Concept

REVIEW SINGULAR POSSESSIVE NOUNS

Review with students how to recognize singular possessive nouns. Ask them to identify the difference between singular and plural (but not possessive) forms of the same nouns.

INTRODUCE PLURAL POSSESSIVE NOUNS

Present the following:

- To form the possessive of a plural noun that ends in *-s*, add only an apostrophe to the end of the noun: *markers' colors.*

- To form the possessive of a plural noun that does not end in *-s*, add an apostrophe and an *-s* to the end of the noun: *children's books.*

See Grammar Transparency 41 for modeling and guided practice.

See Grammar Transparency 42 for modeling and guided practice.

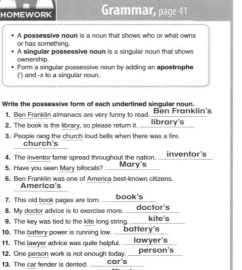

HOMEWORK — **Grammar,** page 41

- A **possessive noun** is a noun that shows who or what owns or has something.
- A **singular possessive noun** is a singular noun that shows ownership.
- Form a singular possessive noun by adding an **apostrophe** (') and *-s* to a singular noun.

Write the possessive form of each underlined singular noun.
1. Ben Franklin almanacs are very funny to read. **Ben Franklin's**
2. The book is the library, so please return it. **library's**
3. People rang the church loud bells when there was a fire. **church's**
4. The inventor fame spread throughout the nation. **inventor's**
5. Have you seen Mary bifocals? **Mary's**
6. Ben Franklin was one of America best-known citizens. **America's**
7. This old book pages are torn. **book's**
8. My doctor advice is to exercise more. **doctor's**
9. The key was tied to the kite long string. **kite's**
10. The battery power is running low. **battery's**
11. The lawyer advice was quite helpful. **lawyer's**
12. One person work is not enough today. **person's**
13. The car fender is dented. **car's**
14. I created the office design. **office's**

ON YOUR OWN — **Grammar,** page 42

- A **plural possessive noun** is a plural noun that shows ownership.
- To form the possessive of a plural that ends in **s**, add an apostrophe.
- To form the possessive of a plural noun that does not end in **s**, add an apostrophe and *-s*. A few nouns have the same plural and singular form.

Write the plural possessive form of each underlined noun.
1. Those experiments purpose was to teach us more about electricity. **experiments'**
2. For the first time, the post office delivered mail directly to people houses. **people's**
3. The mayor honored the firefighters heroism. **firefighters'**
4. Electrical charges effects can be dangerous. **charges'**
5. Ben Franklin won several countries respect. **countries'**
6. The church bells ringing woke me. **bells'**
7. Most limes skins are green, but one kind of lime is yellow. **limes'**
8. The children book was very interesting. **children's**
9. That is the workers break room. **workers'**
10. The bulbs shoots will sprout flowers. **bulbs'**
11. Twelve sinks drains must be cleaned out. **sinks'**
12. The insects habits inspired my work. **insects'**
13. Airplanes tires are fully inflated. **Airplanes'**
14. Those objects tags are missing. **objects'**

Day 3 — Review and Practice

REVIEW POSSESSIVE NOUNS

Review how to use singular possessives and plural possessives.

MECHANICS AND USAGE: TITLES

- Underline or italicize titles of television shows, movies, books, CDs, and names of newspapers and magazines: I read my class newspaper, *The Lincoln Gazette.*

- Use quotation marks around titles of stories, articles, essays, songs, and poems: I wrote a story called "Italy."

- Each word in any title should be capitalized, with a few exceptions: articles (*a, an, the*), conjunctions (*and, or*), and short prepositions (*of, for, to*), unless they are the first or last words in the title: *I read* Jack and the Beanstalk *to my sister.*

 See Grammar Transparency 43 for modeling and guided practice.

HOMEWORK — **Grammar,** page 43

- Capitalize the first and last words and all important words in the titles of books and newspapers.
- Underline titles of books, newspapers, magazines, and TV series.
- Put quotation marks around the titles of short stories, articles, songs, poems, and book chapters.
- Remember to use apostrophes to form possessive nouns.

Rewrite each sentence, making sure the titles are written correctly.

1. One of Ben Franklin's best-known books is titled poor Richard's almanac.
   One of Ben Franklin's best-known books is titled Poor Richard's Almanac.

2. Lewis Latimer wrote a book called incandescent electric lighting in 1890.
   Lewis Latimer wrote a book called Incandescent Electric Lighting in 1890.

3. I learned about Thomas Edison and Lewis Latimer from an article called great american inventors of the past.
   I learned about Thomas Edison and Lewis Latimer from an article called "Great American Inventors of the Past."

4. The article was published in the magazine science for kids.
   The article was published in the magazine Science for Kids.

5. My friend is writing a short story titled the amazing mind of lewis latimer.
   My friend is writing a short story titled "The Amazing Mind of Lewis Latimer."

6. He hopes to get his story published in his local newspaper, the miami herald.
   He hopes to get his story published in his local newspaper, the Miami Herald.

Day 4 — Review and Proofread

REVIEW SINGULAR AND PLURAL POSSESSIVE NOUNS

Review the differences between singular and plural possessives. Ask students how to decide whether to add an apostrophe and -*s*, or only an apostrophe.

PROOFREAD

Have students correct errors in the following sentences.

1. Ellens article was called Paddling up the river. (1: Ellen's; 2: "Paddling up the River.")

2. I read the poem in my parents's study. (parents')

3. This book about womens' inventions won an aword. (1: women's; 2: award)

 See Grammar Transparency 44 for modeling and guided practice.

ON YOUR OWN — **Grammar,** page 44

- A **singular possessive noun** is a singular noun that shows ownership.
- A **plural possessive noun** is a plural noun that shows ownership.

Rewrite the book review below. Fix any spelling, punctuation, and grammar mistakes. Be sure to correct any mistakes in titles or possessive nouns.

I found Akimi Gibsons book, Lewis Howard Latimer: an inventive Mind, very interesting. Latimer, an African-American inventor, was born in the mid-1800s. He made drawings of other inventors creations, which were used to apply for patents. Then Latimers own ideas for inventions began to unfold. He helped improve the lavatories on trains and assisted with Alexander Graham Bells invention of the telephone. While working for the U. S. Electric Lighting Company, he found a way to protect light bulbs' filaments so they would not burn out quickly. This was a great improvement to Thomas Edisons' light bulb. Gibsons biography of Latimer is an informative one.

I found Akimi Gibson's book, Lewis Howard Latimer: An Inventive Mind, very interesting. Latimer, an African-American inventor, was born in the mid-1800s. He made drawings of other inventors' creations, which were used to apply for patents. Then Latimer's own ideas for inventions began to unfold. He helped improve the lavatories on trains and assisted with Alexander Graham Bell's invention of the telephone. While working for the U.S. Electric Lighting Company, he found a way to protect light bulbs' filaments so they would not burn out quickly. This was a great improvement to Thomas Edison's light bulb. Gibson's biography of Latimer is an informative one.

Day 5 — Assess and Reteach

ASSESS

Use the Daily Language Activity and **Grammar Practice Book** page 45 for assessment.

RETEACH

Use Grammar Practice Book page 45 and selected pages from the **Grammar and Writing Handbook** for additional reteaching. While reviewing the rules for punctuating and capitalizing titles, also review other rules for capitalization, including capitalization of historical events and documents, languages, races, and nationalities.

Check students' writing for use of the skill and listen for it in their speaking. Assign Grammar Revision Assignments in their Writer's Notebooks as needed.

See Grammar Transparency 45 for modeling and guided practice.

HOMEWORK — **Grammar,** page 45

A. Choose the correct singular possessive form to complete each sentence.

1. _____ invention changed the world.
   a. Edisons b. Edison' **c. Edison's** d. Edisons'

2. The _____ effect was devastating.
   a. fire' **b. fire's** c. fires' d. fires

3. The _____ temperature is warmer in some places.
   a. oceans b. oceans' c. ocean **d. ocean's**

4. The _____ laughter lasted a long time.
   a. king's b. kings c. kings' d. king'

B. Choose the correct plural possessive form to complete each sentence.

5. These _____ inventions were amazing!
   a. people b. peoples c. peoples' **d. people's**

6. African-American _____ right to take out patents was recognized after the Civil War.
   a. inventors b. inventor's **c. inventors'** d. inventor'

7. The many _____ efforts led to a new creation.
   a. worker **b. workers'** c. workers d. worker's

8. The _____ amazement showed on their faces.
   a. childs' b. childrens' **c. children's** d. childrens

9. All of the _____ covers were torn.
   a. books **b. books'** c. book's d. book

10. These _____ purposes must be made clearer.
    a. experiments b. experiment's c. experiment' **d. experiments'**

Daily Planner

DAY 1	• Prepare to Read • Academic Language • Vocabulary (Preteach)
DAY 2	• Comprehension • Leveled Reader Lesson 1
DAY 3	• Phonics/Decoding • Leveled Reader Lesson 2
DAY 4	• Phonics/Decoding • Vocabulary (Review) • Leveled Reader Lesson 3
DAY 5	• High-Frequency Words • Fluency • Self-Selected Reading

Interactive Student Book

If you wish to preteach the main selection, use StudentWorks Plus for:

• Vocabulary Preteaching
• Word-by-Word Highlighting
• Think Aloud Prompts

Academic Language

Academic words include those harder Tier 2 words that appear in much of students' reading materials as well as the language of instruction. The words chosen for instruction were selected from the **Living Word Vocabulary** list and Avril Coxhead's list of **High-Incidence Academic Words**.

Approaching Level

Prepare to Read

Objective   Preview *Wild Horses*
Materials   • **StudentWorks Plus**   • self-stick notes

PREVIEW THE MAIN SELECTION

- Have students preview *Wild Horses* using **StudentWorks Plus**. This version of the selection contains oral summaries in multiple languages, story recording, word-by-word highlighting, Think Aloud prompts, and comprehension-monitoring questions.

- Remind students that listening carefully to and following along with the word-by-word reading will help them prepare for the reading of the selection with the class. Ask students to place self-stick notes on any challenging words or places that confuse them. Discuss the confusing items with students prior to the reading of the selection with the rest of the class.

- Ask students to write three or four sentences in their Writer's Notebooks telling what they learned about the Black Hills Wild Horse Sanctuary.

Academic Language

Objective   Teach academic language
Materials   • none

PRETEACH LANGUAGE OF INSTRUCTION

Tell students that there are many important lesson words you will be using this week. You want them to become familiar with these words *before* the lessons. These words also appear in the directions of the tests they will be taking this year.

Preteach the following academic words: *analyze text structure, expository, cause and effect, hyperbole,* and *metaphor.*

- Define each word using student-friendly language. Tell students that *analyze* means "study something carefully." A scientist who analyzes a rock asks many questions about it and finds out all that he or she can about it. Point out that students analyze things in their daily lives all the time, even if *analyze* is a new word to them.

- In addition, relate each word to known words. Connect, for example, *expository* to *true* or *facts,* and *cause and effect* to *what happened and why.*

- Highlight these words when used throughout the week, and reinforce their meanings.

Approaching Level

Phonics/Decoding

Objective Decode words with *r*-controlled vowels /är/ and /ôr/

Materials
- **Approaching Reproducible,** p. 73
- **Sound-Spelling WorkBoards**

Sound-Spelling WorkBoard

✔ PHONICS MAINTENANCE

Tier 2

- Distribute a **WorkBoard** to each student. Say a sound previously taught, including letter blends, prefixes, and digraphs. Have students find the **Sound-Spelling Cards** on the board for the sounds you say.

- Review the spelling(s) for each sound by providing a sample word containing that spelling. Guide students to write the word on the board. Model how to segment the word and write the spelling for each sound, as needed. In addition, point out spelling hints, such as the *or, oar*, and *ore* spellings for /ôr/.

- Dictate the following words for students to spell: *cart, short, tore, market, starting, pour*, and *large*. Write the words on the board, and have students self-correct their work.

RETEACH SKILL

r-**Controlled Vowels /är/ and /ôr/** Point to Sound-Spelling Cards for *r*-controlled /är/and /ôr/ on the WorkBoard and review the spellings for these sounds. State each spelling and provide a sample word.

- Write the words below on the board. Model how to decode the first word in each column; then guide students as they decode the remaining words. For the multisyllabic words, divide the words into syllables using the syllable-scoop procedure to help students read one syllable at a time.

- When completed, point to the words in random order for students to chorally read. Repeat several times.

apart	fork	store	roared
smart	torn	before	hoarse
carton	absorb	adore	soaring
barber	former	restore	coarsely
margin	stormy	ashore	aboard
jargon	cornered	galore	boardroom

Approaching Reproducible, page 73

The *ar* in <u>argue</u> and <u>spark</u> stand for the **/är/** sound spelled *ar*. The letters *or* in <u>stormy</u> and <u>fort</u> stand for the **/ôr/** sound and is usually spelled **or**. However, it is sometimes spelled *ar*, as in the word <u>warp</u>.

A. Read the definition. Look at the word next to it. Decide whether the missing letter is an *a* or an *o*. Fill in the missing letter. Then write the whole word.

1. **a.** a place where animals and crops are raised — f <u>a</u> rm — farm

   b. the shape of an object — f <u>o</u> rm — form

2. **a.** a harbor — p <u>o</u> rt — port

   b. a piece of something — p <u>a</u> rt — part

3. **a.** a stiff rectangular piece of paper — c <u>a</u> rd — card

   b. a thin rope made of several strands twisted together — c <u>o</u> rd — cord

B. Circle the correct sound for each word.

4. ward /är/ (/ôr/)
5. start (/är/) /ôr/
6. warm /är/ (/ôr/)
7. door /är/ (/ôr/)
8. carpet (/är/) /ôr/

Approaching Level

Vocabulary

Objective Preteach selection vocabulary
Materials
- **Visual Vocabulary Resources**
- **Approaching Reproducible,** p. 74   • **Vocabulary Cards**

PRETEACH KEY VOCABULARY

Tier **2**

Introduce the Words Display the **Visual Vocabulary Resources** to preteach the key selection words *descendants, sanctuary, threatened, emerge, fragile*, and *habitat*. Use the following routine that appears in detail on the cards.

- Define the word in English, and provide the example given.

- Define the word in Spanish, if appropriate, and indicate if the word is a cognate.

- Display the picture, and explain how it illustrates or demonstrates the word.

- Engage students in structured partner-talk about the image, using the key word.

- Ask students to chorally say the word three times.

- Point out any known sound-spellings or focus on a key aspect of phonemic awareness related to the word.

- You may wish to also distribute copies of the Vocabulary Glossary in the **ELL Resource Book**.

REVIEW PREVIOUSLY TAUGHT VOCABULARY

Display the **Vocabulary Cards** from the previous four weeks. Say the meanings of each word, one by one, and have students identify them. Then point to words in random order for students to provide definitions and related words they know.

Context Clues Remind students that context clues are clues within the text that help a reader figure out what a word means. Have students write a context sentence for each vocabulary word for this week and the previous weeks. For example, *The scared cat would not* emerge *from behind the couch.*

Approaching Reproducible, page 74

A. Read each clue. Then find the vocabulary word in the row of letters that best fits the clue and circle it.

| descendants | habitat | threatened |
| emerge | fragile | sanctuary |

1. grandchildren   lab**descendants**bxer

2. natural living area   fret**habitat**gthbats

3. endangered   **threatened**hterphin

4. safe place   garttipx**sanctuary**

5. come into view   batf**emerge**xingyoup

6. delicate   ecr**fragile**trangeml

B. Read the sentences below. Then edit them by crossing out the words that can be substituted with a vocabulary word. Write that word on the line.

7. I completed our family tree with my parents in the center. First, I filled in the names of their ancestors. Then I filled in the names of their ~~children and grandchildren.~~ __descendants__

8. On safari you can see wildlife in their own ~~natural place where they live.~~ __habitat__

9. I spent the whole afternoon trying to get the cat to ~~come out~~ from her hideout so I could see her. __emerge__

Approaching Level
Vocabulary

Objective Review vocabulary and high-frequency words
Materials • **Vocabulary Cards** • **High-Frequency Word Cards**

REVIEW VOCABULARY

Review Words Display the **Vocabulary Cards** for *descendants, sanctuary, threatened, emerge, fragile,* and *habitat.* Point to each word, read it aloud, and have students chorally repeat.

Then ask the following Yes/No questions. Have other students respond. Judge comprehension based on the discussion.

- Are you *descendants* of your grandparents?
- Do you think that school is a kind of *sanctuary* for children?
- In the springtime, do bears *emerge* from the places where they have been hibernating?
- Are people sometimes *threatened* by wild animals? Are wild animals sometimes *threatened* by people?
- Is your desk a *fragile* object?
- Can a city be a *habitat* for animals as well as for people?

HIGH-FREQUENCY WORDS

Tier 2

Top 250 Words The ability to read accurately and effortlessly the most frequently used words in written English will help students develop reading fluency. Display **High-Frequency Word Cards** 71–80. Then do the following:

- Display one card at a time, and ask students to chorally state each word.
- Have students spell each word aloud.
- Ask students to write each word in their Writer's Notebooks as they state aloud each letter. Then have them read the word again.
- When completed, quickly flip through the Word Card set as students chorally read the words.
- Provide opportunities for students to use the words in speaking and writing. For example, provide sentence starters such as *Please give ____,* for oral and written practice. Or point to a Word Card and ask a question, such as *What is a synonym for this word?* (when pointing to the *good* Word Card)
- Continue the routine throughout the week.

ELL

Practice Vocabulary Pair students of different proficiency. Orally model the vocabulary in sentences. For example: *People feel threatened when they see a bear in a forest.* On the board, provide sentence frames for pairs to copy and complete using the vocabulary. For example: *I am a ____ of my grandparents.* (*descendant*)

Word Webs

Have students create word webs in their Writer's Notebooks for each vocabulary word. Write the related words provided, and ask students to add other words, phrases, and illustrations.

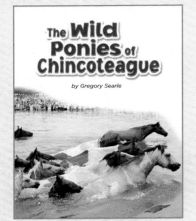

The Wild Ponies of Chincoteague
by Gregory Searle

Student Book

Corrective Feedback

If students have difficulty identifying implicit causes and effects, suggest they try inserting clue words to clarify cause-and-effect relationships. Review cause-and-effect clue words that students can use, such as *because, therefore, as a result, since,* and *due to.* Model an example: *Because* Chincoteague ponies are smart and strong, *therefore* many farmers want to buy them.

Approaching Level

Comprehension

Objective   Reteach analyze text structure and cause and effect
Materials   • **Student Book:** "The Wild Ponies of Chincoteague"

Tier 2

RETEACH STRATEGY: ANALYZE TEXT STRUCTURE

- **Define** Tell students that analyzing text structure means thinking carefully about the way an author organizes the information in a text. An author chooses a text structure that will best communicate what he or she wants to say to you, the reader. If you understand the structure of a text, you should have a better idea about the author's purpose for writing.

- **Relate to Real Life** Ask students to think about how their school building was constructed. Explain that there is a foundation, a frame to create walls and to hold up the ceilings, and a roof on top. Explain that texts are like buildings: It is important to think about how they are structured, or organized.

- **Set Purposes** Remind students that good readers learn to think about how a text is structured, or organized, as they read. Doing so helps them know what to look for as they read. It also helps them understand and remember what they read.

RETEACH SKILL: CAUSE AND EFFECT

- **Define** Remind students that cause and effect is one way to structure a text. An author who chooses this structure wants to tell readers why certain things happened (causes), what happened as a result of an action or event (effects), or both. For example, an author might write about why an animal is endangered (causes) and what might happen if it disappeared (effects).

- **Relate to Real Life** Ask students if they ate breakfast this morning. Ask: *What caused you to want breakfast? As a result, what did you do?*

- **Set Purposes** Remind students that good readers search for causes and effects as they read. Doing so will help them better understand the text's structure.

- **Apply** Work with students to identify causes and effects that give structure to "The Wild Ponies of Chincoteague." Have them summarize the passage highlighting causes and effects. Students will apply this strategy and skill to a simpler text as they read *Cattle-Driving Horses of the Old West.*

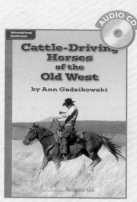

Leveled Reader

Approaching Level

Leveled Reader Lesson 1

Objective   Read to apply skills and strategies
Materials   • **Leveled Reader:** *Cattle-Driving Horses of the Old West*

BEFORE READING

Preview and Predict Have students read the title and preview the first chapter. Ask them to predict what they will learn in this section, including the causes and effects they might come across. They should note any questions they have before they read.

 **Review Vocabulary Words** Have students read the vocabulary words on the inside front cover. Briefly define each and ask students to state related words they have learned.

Set a Purpose for Reading *Let's read to find out how cowboys and wild horses worked together in the Old West.*

DURING READING

STRATEGY
ANALYZE TEXT STRUCTURE

Remind students that analyzing text structure means thinking carefully about the way an author organizes information in a text.

SKILL
CAUSE AND EFFECT

Remind students to think as they read about events from the text and what caused them to happen. Read Chapter 1 with students. Help students complete the Cause and Effect Chart.

As you read, help students decode unknown words. In addition, ask open-ended questions to facilitate rich discussion, such as *What is the author trying to tell you about cowboys and mustangs? Why is the author telling you about cowboys?* Build on students' responses to help them develop a deeper understanding of the text.

Stop after each two pages and ask students to summarize the information they read to check their understanding before reading on. If they struggle, help students reread the difficult pages or passage. Then model analyzing the text structure of the chapter.

AFTER READING

Have students conduct cowboy interviews. Split the class into pairs. One student will be the interviewer. The other will role-play a "cowboy." The interviewer will ask the cowboy about his life and his horses. Have pairs perform their interviews in front of the class.

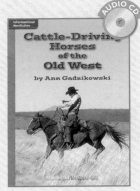

Leveled Reader

Approaching Level

Leveled Reader Lesson 2

Objective Reread to apply skills and strategies and develop fluency

Materials
- **Leveled Reader:** *Cattle-Driving Horses of the Old West*
- **Approaching Reproducible,** p. 77

BEFORE READING

Review the Strategy and Skill Review students' completed Cause and Effect Charts from the first read. Remind students that causes (reasons why something happened) and effects (results of actions or events) can help an author organize information. Thinking carefully about the author's organization—that is, analyzing the text's structure—is part of students' jobs as readers.

Review Vocabulary Words Have students search the book for each vocabulary word. Ask students to read aloud the sentence containing the word and state the word's definition or provide related words. Point out any context clues provided, such as surrounding words.

Set a Purpose for Reading *Let's reread to check our understanding of the information in the book and to work on our reading fluency.*

DURING READING

Reread *Cattle-Driving Horses of the Old West* with students. Have them read silently two pages at a time, or read aloud to a partner. Stop and have students identify at least one cause or effect before they read the next two pages. Model such an analysis, as needed.

AFTER READING

Check Comprehension Have partners complete the Comprehension Check on page 20. Review students' answers. Help students find evidence for their answers in the text.

MODEL FLUENCY

Model reading the fluency passage on **Approaching Reproducible** page 77. Tell students to pay close attention to your rate—that is, the way you speed up or slow down, according to what the author is saying—as you read. Then read one sentence at a time, and have students echo-read the sentences, copying your rate.

During independent reading time, have students work with a partner using the fluency passage. One student reads aloud while the other repeats each sentence back. If students need additional support, have them listen to the "practice speed" version of the passage on the **Fluency Solutions Audio CD**.

Approaching Reproducible, page 77

As I read, I will pay attention to my reading rate.

	Once there were millions of buffalo. The buffalo lived on the
11	Great Plains. Buffalo were a main source of food for the Native
23	Americans of the Plains. Hunting buffalo was an important part of life.
35	Hunting was hard. Hunters had to walk everywhere. It was hard to
47	surprise the buffalo. Buffalo have a good sense of smell. If they smell
60	danger, they run.
63	But there was a way to fool the buffalo. The hunters covered
75	themselves with wolf skins. Then the buffalo did not smell the hunters.
87	They did not feel threatened, so they did not run away.
98	The hunters crept close to the buffalo. When they were very close,
110	they killed the buffalo with arrows and spears.
118	Once horses were brought to the Plains, things changed. Horses
128	meant that the tribes of the Plains could hunt over greater distances.
140	On horseback, hunters could move quickly. 146

Comprehension Check

1. What changed the lives of Plains Indians? What was the effect of that change? **Cause and Effect Horses changed their lives. Hunters could move more quickly and travel farther.**

2. How did people hunt buffalo before horses? **Main Idea and Details People hid under wolf skins and crept toward the buffalo. Then they attacked with arrows and spears.**

	Words Read	−	Number of Errors	=	Words Correct Score
First Read		−		=	
Second Read		−		=	

Approaching Level

Leveled Reader Lesson 3

Objective Build fluency

Materials • **Leveled Reader:** *Cattle-Driving Horses of the Old West*
• **Approaching Reproducible,** p. 77

✓ FOCUS ON FLUENCY

Timed Reading Tell students that they will be doing a final timed reading of the fluency passage on **Approaching Reproducible** page 85 that they have been practicing. With each student, follow these directions:

- Place the passage facedown.

- When you say "Go," the student begins reading the passage aloud.

- When you say "Stop," the student stops reading the passage.

As they read, note words students mispronounce and their overall rate. Stop after one minute. Help students record and graph the number of words they read correctly.

REREAD PREVIOUSLY READ BOOKS

- Distribute copies of the past six **Leveled Readers**. Have students select two to reread. Tell students that rereading these books will help them develop their skills. The more times they read the same words, the quicker they will learn these words. This will make the reading of other books easier.

- Circulate and listen in as students read. Stop students periodically and ask them how they are figuring out difficult words and how they are monitoring their comprehension. Note students who need additional work with specific decoding or comprehension skills.

- Encourage students to read other previously read Leveled Readers during independent reading time or for homework.

Meet Grade-Level Expectations

As an alternative to this day's lesson, guide students through a reading of the On Level Leveled Reader. See page 225U. Since both books contain the same vocabulary, phonics, and comprehension skills, the scaffolding you provided will help most students gain access to this more challenging text.

Book Talk

Bringing Groups Together Students will work with peers of various language and reading abilities to discuss this week's Leveled Readers. Refer to page 162 in the **Teacher's Resource Book** for more about how to conduct a Book Talk.

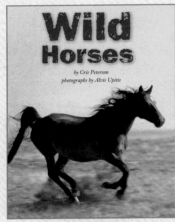

Student Book

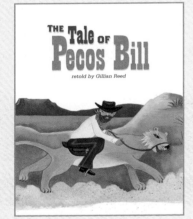

Student Book

Approaching Level

Fluency

Objectives Reread selections to develop fluency; develop speaking skills
Materials • **Student Book:** *Wild Horses*, "The Tale of Pecos Bill"

REREAD FOR FLUENCY

- Have students reread a portion of *Wild Horses*. Suggest that they focus on two to four of their favorite pages from the selection. Work with students to read the pages with the appropriate rate.

- Provide time for students to read their sections of text to you. Comment on their rate, and provide corrective feedback by modeling proper fluency.

DEVELOP SPEAKING/LISTENING SKILLS

- Have students practice reading the first page of "The Tale of Pecos Bill."

- Work with students to read with an appropriate rate and good expression. Model reading a few sentences at a time. Emphasize the way you use your voice to show that the narrator and Pecos Bill are speaking and to emphasize the action of the story. Have students repeat.

- Provide time for students to read aloud the first page of the tale to partners. Ask students to name the ways their partner distinguished the narrator from Pecos Bill and expressed emotion with his or her voice.

- Challenge students to memorize and recite a few paragraphs of the tale for the class.

Approaching Level

Self-Selected Reading

Objective Read independently to analyze text structure and describe cause and effect

Materials • **Leveled Classroom Library** • other informational books

APPLY SKILLS AND STRATEGIES TO INDEPENDENT READING

- **Read Independently** Have students choose an informational book for sustained silent reading. (See the **Theme Bibliography** on pages T8–T9 for book suggestions.) Remind them that causes (reasons why something happened) and effects (results of actions or events) can help an author organize information and give a text its structure. Have students read their books and record the causes and effects on a Cause and Effect Chart.

- **Show Evidence of Reading** While reading, students may generate a reading log or journal. After reading, ask students to use their Cause and Effect Chart and logs to paraphrase the content of the book, maintaining meaning and logical order. They may write a summary of the book or state one orally. Provide time for students to share their summaries and reactions to the book while participating in Book Talks. Ask: *Would you like to read other books on this topic or other books by this same author? Why or why not?*

Approaching

Leveled Classroom Library
See Leveled Classroom
Library lessons on pages T2–T7.

Daily Planner

DAY 1	• Vocabulary • Phonics
DAY 2	• Leveled Reader Lesson 1
DAY 3	• Leveled Reader Lesson 2
DAY 4	• Fluency
DAY 5	• Self-Selected Reading

ELL

Practice Vocabulary Pair ELL students with native speakers. On the board, provide sentence frames for pairs to copy and complete using the vocabulary and additional words when necessary. For example: *This glass bowl is _____, so I need to be _____ when I use it.* (fragile; careful)

Sound-Spelling WorkBoard

On Level

Vocabulary

Objective Review vocabulary

Materials • **Vocabulary Cards**

REVIEW PREVIOUSLY TAUGHT WORDS

Review the Words Display the **Vocabulary Cards** for *descendants, sanctuary, threatened, emerge, fragile*, and *habitat*. Point to each word, read it aloud, and have students chorally repeat.

Then provide the following questions. Ask students to answer each question, justifying their answer. Allow other students to respond. Use the discussions to determine each student's depth of word knowledge.

- Who will be your *descendants*?
- What kind of *sanctuary* might you like to build?
- What is a time when people are *threatened* by bad weather?
- What kind of insect might *emerge* from a cocoon?
- Why should you be careful around *fragile* objects?
- What might happen to an animal that loses its *habitat*?

Phonics/Word Study

Objective Decode multisyllabic words with *r*-controlled /är/ and /ôr/

Materials • **Sound-Spelling WorkBoards**

RETEACH SKILL

- *r*-**Controlled Vowels /är/ and /ôr/** Point to the *r*-controlled /är/ and /ôr/ **Sound-Spelling Cards** *Star* and *Corn* on the **WorkBoard**, and review the spellings for these sounds. State each spelling and give a sample word.

- Write the words below on the board. If necessary, divide the words into syllables using the syllable-scoop technique to help students read one syllable at a time. When completed, point to the words in random order for students to chorally read.

remark	ardent	formal	galore	depart
afford	chorus	parlor	hornet	portal
partner	torture	four	apartment	pouring

- **Spelling** Dictate the following words for students to spell on their WorkBoards: *horses, scarlet, stardom, target, boring*. Guide students to use the Sound-Spelling Cards, and model how to segment words, such as by spelling a word syllable by syllable.

On Level

Fluency

Objectives   Reread selections to develop fluency; develop speaking skills
Materials   • **Student Book:** *Wild Horses*, "The Tale of Pecos Bill"

REREAD FOR FLUENCY

- Have students reread a portion of *Wild Horses*. Suggest that they focus on two to four of their favorite pages from the selection. Work with students to read the pages with the appropriate rate.

- Provide time for students to read their sections of text to you. Comment on their pacing and provide corrective feedback.

DEVELOP SPEAKING/LISTENING SKILLS

- Have students practice reading the first two pages of "The Tale of Pecos Bill."

- Work with students to read with an appropriate rate. Model reading a few sentences at a time. Emphasize the way you use your voice to show that various characters are speaking and to emphasize the action of the story. Have students repeat.

- Provide time for students to read aloud the first two pages of the tale to partners. Ask students to name the ways their partner distinguished characters and expressed emotion with their voice.

- Ask students to memorize and recite a paragraph or two of the tale for the class.

Self-Selected Reading

Objectives   Read independently to analyze text structure and identify cause and effect
Materials   • **Leveled Classroom Library**   • other expository books

APPLY SKILLS AND STRATEGIES TO INDEPENDENT READING

- **Read Independently** Have students choose an expository book for sustained silent reading. (See the **Theme Bibliography** on pages T8–T9 for book suggestions.) Have students read their books and record the causes and effects on a Cause and Effect Chart.

- **Show Evidence of Reading** While reading, students may generate a reading log or journal. After reading, ask students to use their Cause and Effect Chart and logs to paraphrase the content of the book, maintaining meaning and logical order. They may write or orally state a summary of the book. Have students share their summaries and comments on the book through Book Talks. Ask: *Would you recommend this book to a classmate? Why or why not?*

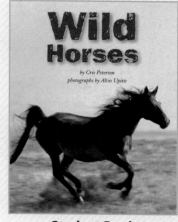

Student Book

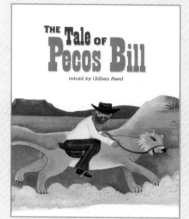

Student Book

On Level

Leveled Classroom Library
See Leveled Classroom
Library lessons on pages T2–T7.

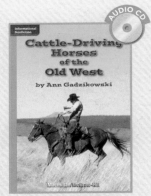

Leveled Reader

On Level

 Leveled Reader Lesson 1

Objectives   Read to apply strategies and skills
Materials   • **Leveled Reader:** *Cattle-Driving Horses of the Old West*

BEFORE READING

Preview and Predict Have students read the title and preview the book by reading the chapter titles and looking at the photographs. Ask students to predict what this book is about and the types of information they might learn.

 Review Vocabulary Words Have students read the vocabulary words on the inside front cover. Ask students to state related words they have learned. Review definitions, as needed.

Set a Purpose for Reading *Let's read to find out how the cowboys and mustangs worked together.*

DURING READING

 STRATEGY
ANALYZE TEXT STRUCTURE

Remind students that analyzing text structure means thinking carefully about the way an author organizes information in a text.

SKILL
CAUSE AND EFFECT

Remind students that an author who chooses cause and effect as a text structure wants to tell readers how or why certain things happened (causes), what happened as a result of an action or event (effects), or both.

Read Chapter 1 with students. Ask open-ended questions to facilitate rich discussion, such as *What is the author trying to tell you about wild mustangs? Why is the author telling you about cowboys?* Build on students' responses to help them develop a deeper understanding of the text. Have students fill in the first section of the Cause and Effect Chart, then continue reading.

Context Clues As they read, have students point out this week's new vocabulary words and any context clues the author provides, such as definitions or nearby words with similar meanings.

AFTER READING

Ask students to give an oral presentation to the class, role-playing cowboys and describing their everyday tasks, responsibilities, and experiences.

On Level

Leveled Reader Lesson 2

Objective   Reread to apply skills and strategies and develop fluency

Materials
- **Leveled Reader:** *Cattle-Driving Horses of the Old West*
- **Practice Book,** p. 77

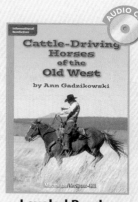

Leveled Reader

BEFORE READING

✓ **Review the Strategy and Skill** Review students' completed Cause and Effect Charts from the first read. Explain that analyzing text structure means understanding how the author organized the text.

Review: Causes (reasons why something happened) and effects (results of actions or events) can help an author organize information in a text. If students' Cause and Effect Charts are incomplete, provide a model chart or use a student chart and revise it as a group. Have students copy the revised chart in their Writer's Notebooks.

Set a Purpose for Reading *Let's reread to check our understanding of life for cowboys and mustangs in the Old West, and to work on our reading fluency.*

DURING READING

Reread *Cattle-Driving Horses of the Old West* with students. Have them read silently two pages at a time, or read aloud to a partner. Stop and have students identify at least one cause or effect before they read the next two pages. Model such an analysis, as needed.

AFTER READING

Check Comprehension Have partners complete the Comprehension Check on page 20. Review students' answers. Help students find evidence for their answers in the text.

MODEL FLUENCY

Model reading the fluency passage on **Practice Book** page 77. Tell students to pay close attention to your rate—that is, the way you speed up or slow down, according to what the author is saying—as you read. Then read one sentence at a time, and have students echo-read the sentences, copying your rate.

During independent reading time, have students work with a partner using the fluency passage. One student reads aloud while the other repeats each sentence back. If students need additional support, have them listen to the "practice speed" version of the passage on the **Fluency Solutions Audio CD**.

Book Talk

Bringing Groups Together Students will work with peers of various language and reading abilities to discuss this week's **Leveled Readers**. Refer to page 162 in the **Teacher's Resource Book** for more about how to conduct a Book Talk.

Practice Book, page 77

As I read, I will pay attention to my reading rate.

10	By the 1800s, huge herds of wild horses were roaming the open range.
12	Picture this: You must catch a wild animal that can run as
24	fast as a train. You must tame that wild animal by riding on its
38	back. You must teach that animal to follow your every command.
49	And you must trust that animal with your life.
58	That is exactly what cowboys did when they caught, tamed,
68	and rode wild mustangs.
72	Capturing a wild mustang was a team effort. One cowboy
82	could not do it alone. Cowboys rode together on tamed horses in
94	order to catch the wild mustangs. The cowboys used their fastest
105	and strongest horses to chase the wild mustangs.
113	When the wild mustangs were exhausted, the cowboys drove
122	them into a fenced corral. The mustangs couldn't see the fence
133	until it was too late. Tired and thirsty from the long chase and
146	glistening with sweat, the mustangs could run no more. 155

Comprehension Check

1. What was the effect that a cowboy obtained by following these steps? **Cause and Effect** He would get a horse that would follow his commands and that he could trust with his life.
2. How were mustangs captured? **Main Idea and Details** Cowboys chased wild horses to make them tired, then drove them into a corral to capture them.

	Words Read	−	Number of Errors	=	Words Correct Score
First Read		−		=	
Second Read		−		=	

Daily Planner

DAY 1	• Leveled Reader Lesson 1
DAY 2	• Leveled Reader Lesson 2
DAY 3	• Phonics
DAY 4	• Vocabulary • Fluency
DAY 5	• Self-Selected Reading

ELL

Self-Monitor Vocabulary
Have student pairs of different proficiency identify and define unfamiliar words from the main selection using a dictionary. Challenge students to use the new words in sentences. Monitor students as they complete the activity.

Beyond Level

Phonics/Word Study

Objective Decode multisyllabic words with *r*-controlled vowels /är/ and /ôr/

Materials • none

EXTEND/ACCELERATE

- **Read Multisyllabic Words with *r*-Controlled Vowels /är/ and /ôr/**
  Write the words below on the board. Challenge students to read the words, using known word parts. When completed, point to the words in random order for students to chorally read.

harvested	smorgasbord	porthole	remarkable
departure	partition	fourteen	partnership
forlorn	participatory	dormitory	torturous
varnished	sordid	cartwheel	glorification

- **Define Words** Ask students to use their knowledge of word parts to figure out the meanings of the above words. Then have partners find the words in a dictionary and confirm or revise the meanings. Challenge students to use these words in this week's writing assignments.

- **Spell *r*-Controlled Vowels /är/ and /ôr/ Words** Dictate the following words for students to spell: *adorable, garnished, affordable, garbled, charter*. Write the words for students to self-correct.

Vocabulary

Objectives Retell a tall tale; write a tall tale

Materials • other tall tales

ENRICH VOCABULARY

- **Retell** Review the tall tale "The Tale of Pecos Bill" with students. Brainstorm a list of the story's main events and memorable details. Then have students take turns using the list to retell the tall tale. Encourage each student to retell the story in his or her own way while still maintaining the meaning and following a logical order.

- **Write a Tall Tale** Prompt students to think about the tall tale genre. Have them read or review other tall tales and consider the tales' structure, character types, and other common features. Then challenge students to write and share their own tall tale about anything they like, using some of the vocabulary words they have learned in this week's selections.

Gifted Talented

Beyond Level

Fluency

Objectives Reread selections to develop fluency; develop speaking skills

Materials • **Student Book:** *Wild Horses*, "The Tale of Pecos Bill"

REREAD FOR FLUENCY

- Have students reread *Wild Horses*. Work with students to read the selection with the appropriate rate.

- Provide time for students to read a section of text to you. Comment on their rate and provide corrective feedback.

DEVELOP SPEAKING/LISTENING SKILLS

- Have students practice reading "The Tale of Pecos Bill." Work with students to read with an appropriate rate and with good expression. Model reading a few lines at a time. Emphasize the way you use your voice to show when the narrator or various other distinct characters are speaking and to emphasize the action.

- Provide time for students to read aloud the tale to the class. Ask students to name ways the reader distinguished characters and expressed emotion with his or her voice. Also discuss how reading this tale aloud differed from reading aloud from *Wild Horses*.

Self-Selected Reading

Objective Read independently to analyze text structure and cause and effect

Materials • **Leveled Classroom Library** • other informational books

APPLY SKILLS AND STRATEGIES TO INDEPENDENT READING

- **Read Independently** Have students choose an informational book for sustained silent reading. (See the **Theme Bibliography** on pages T8–T9 for book suggestions.) Have students read their books and record causes and effects on a Cause and Effect Chart.

- **Show Evidence of Reading** While reading, students may generate a reading log or journal. After reading, ask students to use their Cause and Effect Charts to write a summary of the book, maintaining meaning and logical order. Provide time for students to share their summaries and to comment on their reactions to the book through Book Talks. Ask: *Would you recommend this book to a classmate? Why or why not?*

- **Evaluate** Challenge students to discuss programs or laws that relate to the unit theme, Making a Difference. Ask: *What changes have been made to improve the lives of people in need? How did these changes come about?* Have students discuss the causes and effects of the changes.

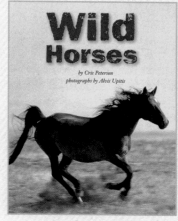

Student Book

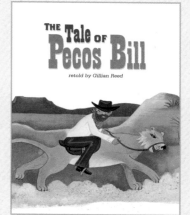

Student Book

Beyond

Leveled Classroom Library
See Leveled Classroom
Library lessons on pages T2–T7.

Leveled Reader

Beyond Level

Leveled Reader Lesson 1

Objective   Read to apply strategies and skills

Materials   • **Leveled Reader:** *Cattle-Driving Horses of the Old West*

BEFORE READING

Preview and Predict Have students preview the book by reading the title and chapter titles and looking at the photographs. Ask students to predict what this book is about and the types of information they might find in it.

Review the Vocabulary Words Have students read the vocabulary words on the inside front cover. Ask students to state each definition and name any related words they have learned.

Set a Purpose for Reading *Let's read to find out how wild mustangs helped cowboys.*

DURING READING

STRATEGY
ANALYZE TEXT STRUCTURE

Ask students to define the terms *analyze* and *text structure*. Remind students that analyzing text structure means thinking carefully about the way an author organizes the information in a text.

SKILL
CAUSE AND EFFECT

Ask students to define the terms *cause* and *effect*. Remind students that an author who chooses this structure wants to tell readers why certain things happened (causes), what happened as a result of an action or event (effects), or both.

Read the book with students. Ask open-ended questions to facilitate rich discussion, such as *What is the author trying to say about the cowboy and mustang partnership?* Build on students' responses to help develop a deeper understanding of the text. Have students fill in their Cause and Effect Charts independently as they read.

AFTER READING

Journal Ask students to create a "cowboy journal." Have students jot down the various daily tasks of a cowboy, as well as some of the hardships. Then have students record this information in a journal format, as if the cowboy wrote it.

Analyze Have students discuss and compare the daily life of a cowboy to their own daily lives. Partners should create a chart of the similarities and differences they discussed.

Gifted Talented

Beyond Level

Leveled Reader Lesson 2

Objective Reread to apply skills and strategies and develop fluency

Materials
- **Leveled Reader:** *Cattle-Driving Horses of the Old West*
- **Beyond Reproducible,** p. 77

BEFORE READING

✔ **Review the Strategy and Skill** Review students' completed Cause and Effect Charts from the first read.

Remind students that causes (reasons why something happened) and effects (results of actions or events) can help an author organize information and structure a text. If students' charts are incomplete, provide a model chart or use a student chart and revise it as a group. Have students copy the revised chart in their Writer's Notebooks.

Set a Purpose for Reading *Let's reread to check our understanding of the information in the book and work on our reading fluency.*

DURING READING

Have students reread *Cattle-Driving Horses of the Old West* silently or with a partner. If they are reading in pairs, prompt students to stop every two pages and identify at least one cause or one effect.

AFTER READING

Check Comprehension Have students independently complete the Comprehension Check on page 20. Review students' answers. Help students find evidence for their answers in the text.

Synthesize Have students imagine that a cowboy from the Old West has joined their class as a new student. Challenge students to think of what they will need to explain to their new classmate, since he is from a different time period.

MODEL FLUENCY

Model reading the fluency passage on **Beyond Reproducible** page 77. Tell students to pay close attention to how you adjust your rate, or speed, according to what the author is saying, as you read. Then read one sentence at a time and have students echo-read the sentences, copying your rate.

During independent reading time, have students work with a partner using the fluency passage. One student reads aloud while the other repeats each sentence back. Students can check their fluency by reading along with the "expert speed" version of the passage on the **Fluency Solutions Audio CD**.

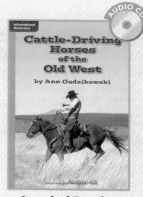

Leveled Reader

Book Talk

Bringing Groups Together Students will work with peers of various language and reading abilities to discuss this week's **Leveled Readers**. Refer to page 162 in the **Teacher's Resource Book** for more about how to conduct a Book Talk.

Beyond Reproducible, page 77

As I read, I will pay attention to my reading rate.

	Somewhere in Kentucky, a thoroughbred horse has just been born.
10	Within hours, the glistening newborn will be on its feet and taking its
23	first wobbly steps. The horse will stay close to its mother for about six
37	months. A horse breeder runs the farm. He has high hopes for this young
51	horse. Its mother and father were both fine racehorses.
60	When a young horse is ready to begin training, it is often sold to a new
76	owner. Some promising yearlings are sold for millions of dollars. The new
88	owner will make sure the horse receives the right training to become a
101	strong racehorse.
103	First, a young racehorse must get used to wearing a bridle. Then the
116	horse must get used to carrying a rider on its back. Trainers teach these
130	new tasks gently and slowly. They don't want the horses to feel frightened
143	or **threatened**.
145	Young horses are not allowed to run fast until their bodies have grown.
158	In an exercise known as "ponying," a riderless horse is led around the track.
172	Trainers must also teach a horse to enter a starting gate. At first, a horse
187	may be afraid of the starting gate. With gentle coaxing, the horse will
200	become used to it. 204

Comprehension Check

1. Why do trainers treat young racehorses so carefully? What do they hope the result will be? **Cause and Effect The horses are very valuable. One day they may be winning racehorses.**

2. What kind of training do young racehorses receive? **Main Idea and Details First they must get used to wearing a bridle and carrying a rider on their backs. They are trained to run around a track and to enter a starting gate.**

	Words Read	–	Number of Errors	=	Words Correct Score
First Read		–		=	
Second Read		–		=	

Daily Planner

DAY 1	• Build Background Knowledge • Vocabulary
DAY 2	• Vocabulary • Access to Core Content *Wild Horses*
DAY 3	• Vocabulary • Grammar • Access to Core Content *Wild Horses*

DAY 4	• Vocabulary
	• Writing/Spelling
	• Access to Core Content
	  "The Tale of Pecos Bill"
	• Leveled Reader
	  Horses in the Old West

DAY 5	• Vocabulary • Leveled Reader *Horses in the Old West* • Self-Selected Reading

StudentWorks Plus
Interactive Student Book

Use StudentWorks Plus for:
- Vocabulary Preteaching
- Word-by-Word Highlighting
- Think Aloud Prompts

Cognates

Help students identify similarities and differences in pronunciation and spelling between English and Spanish cognates.

extinct	*extinto*
descendants	*descendientes*
sanctuary	*santuario*
fragile	*frágil*
habitat	*hábitat*
emerge	*emerger*
analyze	*analizar*
cause	*causa*
effect	*efecto*

Prepare to Read

Content Objective Explore people who made a difference in the lives of animals
Language Objective Use key words to talk about wild horses
Materials • **StudentWorks Plus**

BUILD BACKGROUND KNOWLEDGE

All Language Levels

- Have students preview *Wild Horses* using **StudentWorks Plus**, which contains oral summaries in multiple languages, online multilingual glossaries, word-by-word highlighting, and questions that assess and build comprehension.

- Students can build their word-reading fluency by reading along as the text is read or by listening during the first reading and, at the end of each paragraph, returning to the beginning of the paragraph and reading along.

- Students can build their comprehension by reviewing the definitions of key words in the online glossary and by answering the comprehension questions. When appropriate, the text required to answer the question is highlighted to provide students with additional support and scaffolding.

- Following the reading, ask students to respond in writing to a question that links the story to their personal experiences, such as: *Do you like horses? Have you ever ridden a horse?*

Academic Language

Language Objective Use academic language in classroom conversations

All Language Levels

- This week's academic words are **boldfaced** throughout the lesson. Define the word in context and provide a clear example from the selection. Then ask students to generate an example or a word with a similar meaning.

Academic Language Used in Whole Group Instruction

Theme Words	Key Selection Words	Strategy and Skill Words
tame **wild** **extinct**	**descendants** **sanctuary** **threatened** **fragile** **habitat** **emerge**	**analyze text structure** **cause** **effect** **possessive nouns** **paragraph clues**

ELL ENGLISH LANGUAGE LEARNERS

Vocabulary

Language Objective Demonstrate understanding and use of key words by talking about horses

Materials • **Visual Vocabulary Resources**
• **ELL Resource Book**

PRETEACH KEY VOCABULARY

Use the **Visual Vocabulary Resources** to preteach the key selection words *descendants, sanctuary, threatened, emerge, fragile,* and *habitat.* Focus on two words per day. The below routine is detailed on the cards.

Beginning/Intermediate

■ Point out any known sound-spellings, or focus on a key aspect of phonemic awareness related to the word.

All Language Levels

■ Define the word in English, and provide the example given.

■ Define the word in Spanish, if appropriate, and indicate if the word is a cognate.

■ Display the picture, and explain how it illustrates the key word. Engage students in a structured activity about the image.

■ Ask students to chorally say the word three times.

■ Distribute copies of the Vocabulary Glossary, **ELL Resource Book**, page 96.

PRETEACH FUNCTION WORDS AND PHRASES

All Language Levels

Use the Visual Vocabulary Resources to preteach the phrases *hop a train, peek out of a corner of an eye, spook and charge,* and *bolt up.* Focus on one phrase per day. Use the detailed routine on the cards.

■ Define the phrase in English and, if appropriate, in Spanish. Point out if the word is a cognate.

■ Refer to the picture and engage students in talk about the phrase; for example, students will partner-talk using sentence frames.

■ Ask students to chorally repeat the word three times.

TEACH BASIC WORDS

Beginning/Intermediate

Use the Visual Vocabulary Resources to teach the basic words *mustang, mare, mane, herd, steed,* and *pony.* Teach these "horse" words using the routine provided on the card.

Visual Vocabulary Resources

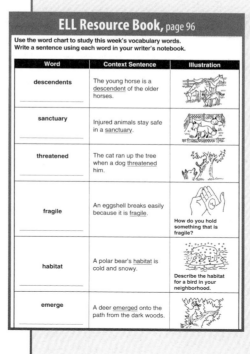

ELL Resource Book, page 96

Use the word chart to study this week's vocabulary words.
Write a sentence using each word in your writer's notebook.

Word	Context Sentence	Illustration
descendents	The young horse is a descendent of the older horses.	
sanctuary	Injured animals stay safe in a sanctuary.	
threatened	The cat ran up the tree when a dog threatened him.	
fragile	An eggshell breaks easily because it is fragile.	How do you hold something that is fragile?
habitat	A polar bear's habitat is cold and snowy.	Describe the habitat for a bird in your neighborhood.
emerge	A deer emerged onto the path from the dark woods.	

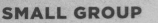

ELL Resource Book

ELL ENGLISH LANGUAGE LEARNERS

Access to Core Content

Content Objective Read grade-level text

Language Objective Discuss text using key words and sentence frames

Materials • **ELL Resource Book,** pp. 86–95

PRETEACH MAIN SELECTION (PAGES 204–217)

All Language Levels

Use the Interactive Question-Response Guide on **ELL Resource Book** pages 86–93 to introduce students to *Wild Horses*. Preteach half of the selection on Day 2 and half on Day 3.

- Use the prompts provided in the guide to develop meaning and vocabulary. Use the partner-talk and whole-class responses to engage students and increase student talk.

- When completed, have partners reread the story.

PRETEACH PAIRED SELECTION (PAGES 220–223)

All Language Levels

Use the Interactive Question-Response Guide on ELL Resource Book pages 94–95 to preview the paired selection "The Tale of Pecos Bill." Preteach the selection on Day 4.

Beginning	Intermediate	Advanced
Use Visuals During the Interactive Reading, select several photographs. Use the photographs to explain a cause and effect. Have students summarize what you said.	**Describe** During the Interactive Reading, select a few lines of text that describe a cause and effect. After you have read and explained it, have students describe the effect based on the text.	**Discuss** During the Interactive Reading, select a text passage that describes a cause and effect. After you have read and explained it, have students discuss the cause and effect based on the passage.

ELL ENGLISH LANGUAGE LEARNERS

Fluency

Content Objectives Reread selections to develop fluency; develop speaking skills

Language Objective Tell a partner what a selection is about

Materials • **Student Book:** *Wild Horses*, "The Tale of Pecos Bill"
  • **Teacher's Resource Book**

REREAD FOR FLUENCY

Beginning

- Have students read the decodable passages on **Teacher's Resource Book** page 13.

Intermediate/Advanced

- Have students reread a portion of *Wild Horses*. Have them focus on two to four of their favorite pages, based on their levels. Help students read the pages with appropriate pacing. For example, read the first paragraph and have students echo. Then have students continue by chorally reading additional paragraphs.

- Provide time for students to read the text to you. Comment on their pacing, and provide corrective feedback by modeling proper fluency.

DEVELOP SPEAKING/LISTENING SKILLS

All Language Levels

- Have students practice reading portions of "The Tale of Pecos Bill." Work with students to read with appropriate pacing.

- Provide time for students to read aloud to a partner. Ask students to tell about their favorite part of the tall tale. Provide the sentence frame: *My favorite part of the tall tale was ____.*

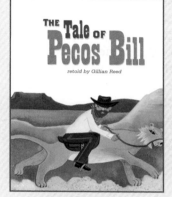

Student Book

Self-Selected Reading

Content Objective Read independently

Language Objective Orally retell information learned

Materials • **Leveled Classroom Library** • other nonfiction books

APPLY SKILLS AND STRATEGIES TO INDEPENDENT READING

All Language Levels

- Have students choose a nonfiction book for silent independent reading. (See the **Theme Bibliography** on pages T8–T9.)

- After reading, ask students to orally summarize the book. Provide time for students to share their reactions to the book with classmates. Ask: *Would you recommend this book to a classmate? Why or why not?*

Leveled Classroom Library
See Leveled Classroom
Library lessons on pages T2–T7.

ELL ENGLISH LANGUAGE LEARNERS

Grammar

Content Objective Identify possessive nouns
Language Objective Speak in complete sentences, using sentence frames

POSSESSIVE NOUNS

Beginning/Intermediate

- Remind students that a noun is a word that names a person, place, or thing. Write on the board *Kim has a sister*. Underline the noun *Kim*. Below that sentence write *Kim's sister is five years old*, and circle the apostrophe -*s*. Review that apostrophe -*s* is used for singular nouns. It shows who or what has something. Repeat for plural possessive nouns with these sentences, using -*s* apostrophe: *My two cats have stripes. My cats' stripes are gray.*

All Language Levels

- Review possessive nouns. Write the below sentences on the board. Have students underline the possessive noun in each sentence. Have them say: ___ *is a possessive noun*.

    Dayton's pony drinks soapy dishwater.

    The mustangs' descendants came to America in the 1500s.

    My favorite horse's spots are brown.

    The children's feet are loose in the stirrups.

PEER DISCUSSION STARTERS

All Language Levels

- Write the following sentences on the board.
    Dayton Hyde wanted ___.
    The mustangs were threatened because ___.

- Pair students and have them complete each sentence frame. Ask them to expand on their sentences by providing as many details as they can from this week's readings. Circulate, listen in, and take note of each student's language use and proficiency.

Transfer Skills

Possessive Nouns Spanish, Hmong, and Khmer avoid the use of apostrophe -*s* (*my sister's arm*) to show possession. Instead, speakers of these languages will exclusively or more commonly use a prepositional phrase (*the arm of my sister*) to show possession. Model correct usage and have students repeat. Look for opportunities to point out the use of apostrophe -*s* and *s*- apostrophe in texts that students read.

Corrective Feedback

During Whole Group grammar lessons, follow the routine on the **Grammar Transparencies** to provide students with extra support. This routine includes completing the items with English Language Learners while other students work independently, having students reread the sentences with partners to build fluency, and providing a generative task such as writing a new sentence using the skill.

Beginning	**Intermediate**	**Advanced**
Use Visuals Describe the photographs in *Wild Horses* to students, using possessive nouns in simple sentences. Ask: *What do you see?* Help them point and repeat the sentences.	**Describe** Ask students to describe the photographs in *Wild Horses* using possessive nouns in their descriptions. Have them use complete sentences.	**Discuss** Ask students to describe the photographs in *Wild Horses* using possessive nouns and plural possessive nouns in their descriptions.

Writing/Spelling

Content Objective Spell words correctly
Language Objective Write in complete sentences, using sentence frames

All Language Levels

■ Write the key vocabulary words on the board: *descendants, sanctuary, threatened, emerge, fragile*, and *habitat*. Have students copy each word on their **WorkBoards**. Help them say each word and then write a sentence for it. Provide sentence starters, such as:

> *My descendants will be ____.*
>
> *I wish someone would provide a sanctuary for ____.*
>
> *When I am threatened, I feel ____.*
>
> *In the morning, I emerge from ____.*
>
> *You have to be careful with fragile things because ____.*
>
> *A whale's natural habitat is ____.*

Beginning/Intermediate

■ Help students spell words using their growing knowledge of English sound-spelling relationships. Model how to segment the word students are trying to spell, and attach a spelling to each sound (or spellings to each syllable if a multisyllabic word). Use the **Sound-Spelling Cards** to reinforce the spellings for each English sound.

Advanced

■ Dictate the following words for students to spell: *cart, form, bark, sport, thorn, smart, large*. Use the Sound-Spelling Cards to guide students as they spell each word.

■ When completed, review the meanings of words that can be easily demonstrated or explained. Use actions, gestures, and available pictures.

Sound-Spelling WorkBoard

Phonics/Word Study

For English Language Learners who need more practice with this week's phonics/spelling skill, see the Approaching Level lesson on page 225J. Focus on minimal contrasts, articulation, and those sounds that do not transfer from the student's first language to English. For a complete listing of transfer sounds, see pages T16–T31.

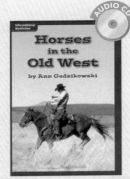

Leveled Reader

ELL ENGLISH LANGUAGE LEARNERS

Leveled Reader

Content Objective Read to apply skills and strategies

Language Objective Retell information using complete sentences

Materials
- **Leveled Reader:** *Horses in the Old West*
- **ELL Resource Book,** p. 97
- **Visual Vocabulary Resources,** pp. 403–408

BEFORE READING

All Language Levels

- **Preview** Read the title *Horses in the Old West*. Ask: *What's the title? Say it again*. Repeat with the author's name. Then page through the book. Use simple language to tell about each page. Immediately follow up with questions, such as *Were there cowboys in the Old West? These horses run very fast. What do you think it might be like to ride one?*

- **Review Skills** Use the inside front cover to review the comprehension skill and vocabulary words.

- **Set a Purpose** Say: *Let's read to find out about horses in the Old West.*

DURING READING

All Language Levels

- Have students read each page aloud using the differentiated suggestions. Provide corrective feedback, such as modeling how to blend a decodable word or clarifying meaning by using techniques from the Interactive Question-Response Guide.

- **Retell** After every two pages, ask students to state the main ideas they have learned so far. Help them to complete the Cause and Effect Chart. Restate students' comments when they have difficulty using story-specific words. Provide differentiated sentence frames to support students' responses and engage students in partner-talk where appropriate.

Vocabulary

Preteach Vocabulary Use the routine in the **Visual Vocabulary Resources**, pages 403–408, to preteach the ELL Vocabulary listed in the inside front cover of the **Leveled Reader**.

Beginning	Intermediate	Advanced
Echo-Read Have students echo-read after you.	**Choral-Read** Have students chorally read with you.	**Choral-Read** Have students chorally read.
Check Comprehension Point to pictures and ask questions, such as *Show me the saddle in this picture.*	**Check Comprehension** Ask questions/prompts, such as *Describe what you see in this photo. What did the author tell us about rodeos?*	**Check Comprehension** Ask: *Tell me what you learned about a cowboy's job in this chapter. Read sentences that tell why a cowboy's life was hard.*

AFTER READING

Use the chart below and Think and Compare questions in the **Leveled Reader** to determine students' progress.

ELL Resource Book

Think and Compare	Beginning	Intermediate	Advanced
1 Review page 17. Describe what happened after the mustangs were almost extinct. *(Cause and Effect)*	Possible responses: Nonverbal response. Law. Protect horses.	Possible responses: A new law protects the mustangs.	Possible responses: A new federal law was passed, so people cannot capture or kill mustangs.
2 What do you think would be the hardest thing about being a cowboy? Why? *(Analyze)*	Possible responses: Nonverbal response. Cattle. Train horses.	Possible responses: The cattle drive is the hardest for a cowboy. He can't lose the cattle.	Possible responses: The cattle drive would be the hardest part of being a cowboy because he has to keep the cattle together and not lose them.
3 What do you think is the best way for people to treat horses? Do you think all horses should be free and wild? Do you think some horses should work for people? *(Evaluate)*	Possible responses: Nonverbal response. Nice. Free. Work for people.	Possible responses: People should care for horses. Some horses should be free. Some horses can work for people.	Possible responses: People should care about the horses. Most horses should be free and wild, but it is important to have some horses work for people.

BOOK TALK

Develop Listening and Speaking Skills Distribute copies of **ELL Resource Book** page 97, and form small groups. Help students determine the leader to discuss the Book Talk questions. Tell students to remember the following while engaged in the activity:

- Narrate, describe, and explain with specificity and detail. Ask: *Where did the story take place? Can you describe the setting? What else did you notice?*

- Express opinions, ideas, and feelings on a variety of social and academic topics. Ask: *What do you think about the characters in the story?*

- Employ self-corrective techniques and monitor their own and other students' language production. Students should ask themselves: *What parts of this passage were confusing to me? Can my classmates help me clarify a word or sentence that I don't understand?*

Book Talk

Bringing Groups Together Students will work with peers of varying language abilities to discuss the Book Talk questions. Form groups so that students who read the Beyond Level, On Level, Approaching Level, and English Language Learner Leveled Readers are in the same group for the activity.

Progress Monitoring
Weekly Assessment

ASSESSED SKILLS

- Vocabulary: Vocabulary Words, Context Clues
- Comprehension: Cause and Effect
- Grammar: Possessive Nouns
- Phonics/Spelling: *r*-Controlled Vowels /är/ and /ôr/

Selection Test for **Wild Horses** *Also Available*

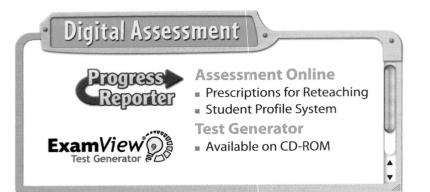

Digital Assessment

Progress Reporter

Assessment Online
- Prescriptions for Reteaching
- Student Profile System

Test Generator
- Available on CD-ROM

ExamView Test Generator

Weekly Assessment
Unit 2 Week 4

Fluency Assessment

Assess fluency for one group of students per week.
Use the Oral Fluency Record Sheet to track the number of
words read correctly. Fluency goal for all students:
84–104 words correct per minute (WCPM).

Approaching Level	Weeks 1, 3, 5
On Level	Weeks 2, 4
Beyond Level	Week 6

Fluency Assessment

Diagnose		Prescribe
Review the assessment answers with students. Have them correct their errors. Then provide additional instruction as needed.		
	IF...	**THEN...**
VOCABULARY WORDS **VOCABULARY STRATEGY** Context Clues: Paragraph Clues	0–2 items correct …	See **Vocabulary Intervention Teacher's Edition.** **LOG ON** ▶ Online Practice: Go to www.macmillanmh.com. Vocabulary PuzzleMaker
COMPREHENSION Skill: Cause and Effect	0–3 items correct …	See **Comprehension Intervention Teacher's Edition.** See Cause and Effect lesson in Unit 2 Week 5, page 251B.
GRAMMAR Possessive Nouns	0–1 items correct …	See **Writing and Grammar Intervention Teacher's Edition.**
PHONICS AND SPELLING *r*-Controlled Vowels / är/ and /ôr/	0–1 items correct …	**LOG ON** ▶ Online Practice: Go to www.macmillanmh.com. See **Phonics Intervention Teacher's Edition.**
FLUENCY	79–83 WCPM	Fluency Solutions Audio CD
	0–78 WCPM	See **Fluency Intervention Teacher's Edition.**

Response to Intervention

To place students in Tier 2 or Tier 3 Intervention use the *Diagnostic Assessment.*

- Phonics
- Vocabulary
- Comprehension
- Fluency
- Writing and Grammar

Week 5 ★ At a Glance

Priority Skills and Concepts

Comprehension

- **Strategy:** Analyze Story Structure
- **Skill:** Sequence
-  **Skill:** Cause and Effect
- **Genre:** Poetry, Legend, Expository

Robust Vocabulary

- **Selection Vocabulary:** *sores, loosened, mysterious, amazement, midst, responsibility*
- **Strategy:** Homophones

Fluency

- **Expression and Phrasing**

Phonics/Spelling

- **Word Study:** Suffixes, Multisyllabic Words
- **Spelling Words:** *sickly, hardly, quickly, slowly, carefully, wonderful, beautiful, graceful, spoonful, darkness, shapeless, ageless, illness, goodness, spotless, painless, weakness, darkest, clearest, thoughtful*
-  *door, smart, argue*

Grammar/Mechanics

- **Plurals and Possessives**
- **Punctuation in Letters**

Writing

- **Trait: Word Choice**
- **Strong Verbs and Descriptive Details**

Key

 Tested in program    Review Skill

Digital Learning

Digital solutions to help plan and implement instruction

☑ Teacher Resources

LOG ON ▶

ONLINE www.macmillanmh.com

▶ **Teacher's Edition**
 • Lesson Planner and Resources also on CD-ROM

TeacherWorks Plus

▶ **Formative Assessment**
 • ExamView® on CD-ROM also available

Progress Reporter

▶ **Instructional Resources**
 • Unit Videos
 • Classroom Presentation Toolkit

VIDEO

▶ **Professional Development**
 • Video Library

Professional Development

☑ Student Resources

LOG ON ▶

ONLINE www.macmillanmh.com

▶ **Interactive Student Book**

StudentWorks Plus

▶ **Leveled Reader Database**

▶ **Activities**
 • Research Toolkit
 • Oral Language Activities
 • Vocabulary/Spelling Activities

AUDIO CD
Listening Library
 • Recordings of Student Books and Leveled Readers

AUDIO CD
Fluency Solutions
 • Fluency Modeling and Practice

Weekly Literature

Theme: Courage

Student Book

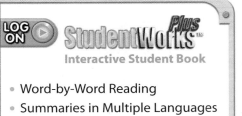

Interactive Student Book

- Word-by-Word Reading
- Summaries in Multiple Languages
- Comprehension Questions

Mystic Horse
written and illustrated by **PAUL GOBLE**

Main Selection

Genre | Legend

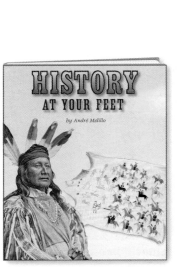

Preteach Vocabulary and Comprehension

Genre | Fiction

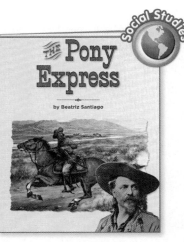

Paired Selection

Genre | Expository

Support Literature

Interactive Read-Aloud Anthology
- Listening Comprehension
- Robust Vocabulary
- Readers' Theater Plays for Fluency

Resources for Differentiated Instruction

Leveled Readers

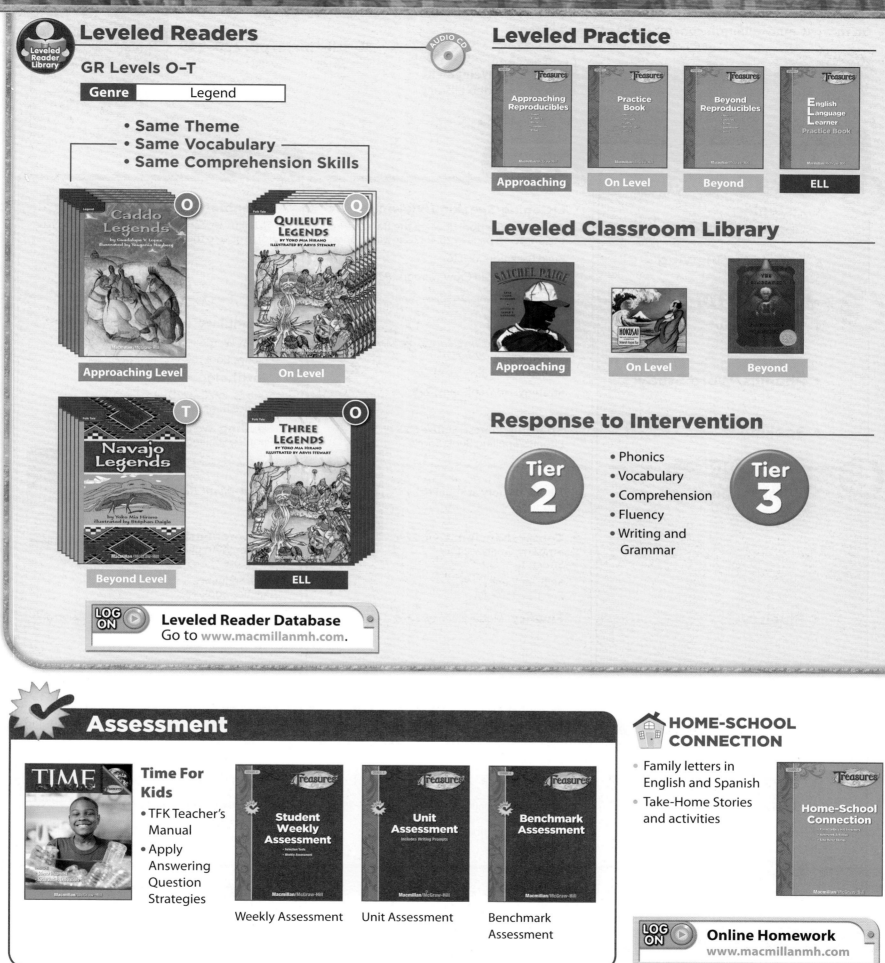

GR Levels O–T

Genre Legend

- Same Theme
- Same Vocabulary
- Same Comprehension Skills

O Caddo Legends
by Guadalupe V. Lopez
illustrated by Yevgenia Nayberg

Approaching Level

Q QUILEUTE LEGENDS
BY YOKO MIA HIRANO
ILLUSTRATED BY ARVIS STEWART

On Level

T Navajo Legends
by Yoko Mia Hirano
illustrated by Stéphan Daigle

Beyond Level

O THREE LEGENDS
BY YOKO MIA HIRANO
ILLUSTRATED BY ARVIS STEWART

ELL

LOG ON ▶ **Leveled Reader Database**
Go to www.macmillanmh.com.

Leveled Practice

Approaching Reproducibles — Approaching
Practice Book — On Level
Beyond Reproducibles — Beyond
English Language Learner Practice Book — ELL

Leveled Classroom Library

Approaching — SATCHEL PAIGE
On Level — HOKUSAI
Beyond

Response to Intervention

Tier 2

- Phonics
- Vocabulary
- Comprehension
- Fluency
- Writing and Grammar

Tier 3

Assessment

Time For Kids
- TFK Teacher's Manual
- Apply Answering Question Strategies

Student Weekly Assessment
- Selection Tests
- Weekly Assessment

Weekly Assessment

Unit Assessment
Includes Writing Prompts

Unit Assessment

Benchmark Assessment

Benchmark Assessment

HOME-SCHOOL CONNECTION

- Family letters in English and Spanish
- Take-Home Stories and activities

Home-School Connection

LOG ON ▶ **Online Homework**
www.macmillanmh.com

Suggested Lesson Plan

Go to www.macmillanmh.com for Online Lesson Planner

 TeacherWorks *Plus*
All-In-One Planner and Resource Center

Professional Development Video Library

Mystic Horse, pp. 230–249

WHOLE GROUP

⏰ ORAL LANGUAGE

- **Listening Comprehension**
- **Speaking/Viewing**

⏰ WORD STUDY

- **Vocabulary**
- **Phonics/Word Study**
- **Spelling**

⏰ READING

- **Comprehension**
- **Fluency**

⏰ LANGUAGE ARTS

- **Writing**
- **Grammar**

ASSESSMENT

- **Informal/Formal**

DAY 1

Listening/Speaking/Viewing
❓ Focus Question How are the travelers in the photo on pages 226–227 showing courage?
Build Background, 226
Read Aloud: "Old Crow Warriors," 227A–227B

✓ **Vocabulary**
sores, loosened, mysterious, amazement, midst, responsibility, 229, 257C
Practice Book, 83
Strategy: Homophones, 228

✓ **Spelling** Pretest: Suffixes, 257E
Phonics/Spelling Book, 55–56

Read "History at Your Feet," 228–229

Student Book

✓ **Comprehension**, 229A–229B
Strategy: Analyze Story Structure
Skill: Sequence
Practice Book, 84

✓ **Fluency** Model Fluency, 227B

Writing
Daily Writing Pretend that you are a Pawnee boy who lived long ago. Write a paragraph about a day in your life.
✓ **Trait: Word Choice**
Strong Verbs and Descriptive Details, 255A–255B

✓ **Grammar** Daily Language Activities, 257G
Plurals and Possessives, 257G
Grammar Practice Book, 46

Quick Check Vocabulary, 228
Comprehension, 229B

DAY 2

Listening/Speaking/Viewing
❓ Focus Question What gift does the mystic horse give to the boy and his tribe?

Vocabulary
Review Words, Homophones, 230, 257C
Practice Book, 89
✓ **Morphology**
Suffixes, 227C–227D
Practice Book, 82

Spelling Word Sorts, 257E
Phonics/Spelling Book, 57

Read *Mystic Horse*, 230–249

Student Book

✓ **Comprehension**, 230–249
Strategy: Analyze Story Structure
Skill: Sequence
Practice Book, 85

✓ **Fluency** Repeated Reading: Expression and Phrasing, 251A

Writing
Daily Writing Write a dialogue between two animals that you think might have something interesting to say if they could talk.
✓ **Reading/Writing Connection**, 256–257

Grammar Daily Language Activities, 257G
Plurals and Possessives, 257G
Grammar Practice Book, 47

Quick Check Morphology, 227D
Comprehension, 249

⏰ **SMALL GROUP Lesson Plan** ▶ **Differentiated Instruction 226G–226H**

| **Vocabulary**
Vocabulary Words
Homophones | **Comprehension**
Strategy: Analyze Story
Structure
Skill: Sequence | **Writing**
Trait: Word Choice
Strong Verbs and
Descriptive Details | **Social Studies**
Explain how
developments in
communication have
influenced the region |

DAY 3

Listening/Speaking

? Focus Question What do *Mystic Horse* and "Who Were the Pawnee?" teach the reader about Pawnee life?

Summarize, 251

Vocabulary

Review Words, Related Words, 257D

Spelling Word Meanings, 257F
Phonics/Spelling Book, 58

Read *Mystic Horse,* 230–249

Student Book

Comprehension
Comprehension Check, 251

Review Skill: Cause and Effect, 251B
Practice Book, 87

Fluency Repeated Reading:
Expression and Phrasing, 251A
Practice Book, 86

Writing

Daily Writing Write a paragraph that tells what you know about horses and how horses have been used in the past.

Trait: Word Choice
Strong Verbs and Descriptive Details, 257A

Grammar Daily Language Activities, 257G
Mechanics and Usage, 257H
Grammar Practice Book, 48

Quick Check Fluency, 251A

DAY 4

Listening/Speaking/Viewing

? Focus Question How were Pony Express riders similar to the grandson in *Mystic Horse*? Use details to support your answer.

Vocabulary

Content Vocabulary: *relays, intervals, frontier, telegraph,* 252

Review Words, Morphology, 257D

Spelling Proofread, 257F
Phonics/Spelling Book, 59

Read "The Pony Express," 252–255

Student Book

Comprehension
Genre: Expository

Text Feature: Chart, 252
Practice Book, 88

Time For Kids

Fluency Repeated Reading:
Expression and Phrasing, 251A

Writing

Daily Writing Write five questions that you would like to ask someone who rode in the Pony Express.

Trait: Sentence Fluency
Combine, 257A

Grammar Daily Language Activities, 257G
Plurals and Possessives, 257H
Grammar Practice Book, 49

Quick Check Vocabulary, 257D

DAY 5
Review and Assess

Listening/Speaking/Viewing

? Focus Question What would be the first thing you did if you went to a powwow or visited a museum about Native Americans?

Vocabulary

Assess Words, Connect to Writing, 257D

Spelling Posttest, 257F
Phonics/Spelling Book, 60

Read Self-Selected Reading, 226K
Practice Book, 90

Student Book

Comprehension
Connect and Compare, 255

Fluency Practice, 226K

Writing

Daily Writing What event in your life could be turned into a legend? Describe that event.

Conferencing, 257B

Grammar Daily Language Activities, 257G
Plurals and Possessives, 257H
Grammar Practice Book, 50

Weekly Assessment, 257II–257JJ

Differentiated Instruction

What do I do in small groups?

Teacher-Led Small Groups

Independent Activities

Focus on Skills

IF... students need additional instruction, practice, or extension based on your **Quick Check** observations for the following priority skills:

✔ **Phonics/Word Study**
Suffixes

✔ **Vocabulary Words**
sores, loosened, mysterious, amazement, midst, responsibility
Strategy: Homophones

✔ **Comprehension**
Strategy: Analyze Story Structure
Skill: Sequence

✔ **Fluency**

THEN...
Approaching **ELL**	Preteach and Reteach Skills
On Level	Practice
Beyond	Enrich and Accelerate Learning

LOG ON ▶ **Suggested Small Group Lesson Plan**

CD-ROM TeacherWorks *Plus*
All-In-One Planner and Resource Center

	DAY 1	DAY 2
Approaching Level **Tier 2** • **Preteach/Reteach** **Tier 2 Instruction**	• Prepare to Read, 257I • Academic Language, 257I • Preteach Vocabulary, 257K	• Comprehension, 257M Analyze Story Structure/Sequence **ELL** • Leveled Reader Lesson 1, 257N
On Level • **Practice**	• Vocabulary, 257S • Phonics, 257S Suffixes **ELL**	• Leveled Reader Lesson 1, 257U
Beyond Level • **Extend/Accelerate** **Gifted and Talented**	• Leveled Reader Lesson 1, 257Y • Analyze Information, 257Y	• Leveled Reader Lesson 2, 257Z • Synthesize Information, 257Z
ELL • **Build English Language Proficiency** • See **ELL** in other levels.	• Prepare to Read, 257AA • Academic Language, 257AA • Preteach Vocabulary, 257BB	• Vocabulary, 257BB • Preteach Main Selection, 257CC

Small Group

Focus on Leveled Readers

Leveled Reader Library

Levels O–T

Caddo Legends
by Guadalupe V. Lopez
illustrated by Yevgenia Nayberg
Approaching

QUILEUTE LEGENDS
BY YOKO MIA HIRANO
ILLUSTRATED BY ARVIS STEWART
On Level

Navajo Legends
by Yoko Mia Hirano
illustrated by Stephen Daigle
Beyond

THREE LEGENDS
BY YOKO MIA HIRANO
ILLUSTRATED BY ARVIS STEWART
ELL

Additional Leveled Readers

LOG ON ▶ **Leveled Reader Database**
www.macmillanmh.com

Search by

• Comprehension Skill	• Guided Reading Level
• Content Area	• Reading Recovery Level
• Genre	• Lexile Score
• Text Feature	• Benchmark Level

Subscription also available.

Manipulatives

Sound-Spelling WorkBoards

Sound-Spelling Cards

about
today
High-Frequency Word Cards

VISUAL VOCABULARY RESOURCES
Visual Vocabulary Resources

DAY 3

- Phonics Maintenance, 257J
  Suffixes **ELL**
- Leveled Reader Lesson 2, 257O

- Leveled Reader Lesson 2, 257V

- Phonics, 257W
  Suffixes **ELL**

- Vocabulary, 257BB
- Grammar, 257EE

DAY 4

- Reteach Phonics Skill, 257J
  Suffixes **ELL**
- Review Vocabulary, 257L
- Leveled Reader Lesson 3, 257P

- Fluency, 257T

- Vocabulary, 257W
- Author Study, 257W
- Fluency, 257X

- Vocabulary, 257BB
- Writing/Spelling, 257FF
- Preteach Paired Selection, 257CC
- Fluency, 257DD
- Leveled Reader, 257GG

DAY 5

- High-Frequency Words, 257L
- Fluency, 257Q
- Self-Selected Independent Reading, 257R
- Book Talk, 257P

- Self-Selected Independent Reading, 257T
- Book Talk, 257V

- Self-Selected Independent Reading, 257X
- Evaluate Information, 257X
- Book Talk, 257Z

- Vocabulary, 257BB
- Leveled Reader, 257GG
- Self-Selected Independent Reading, 257DD
- Book Talk, 257HH

Managing the Class

What do I do with the rest of my class?

- **Practice Book and Reproducibles**
- **ELL Practice Book**
- **Leveled Reader Activities**
- **Literacy Workstations**
- **Online Activities**

Classroom Management Tools

Weekly Contract

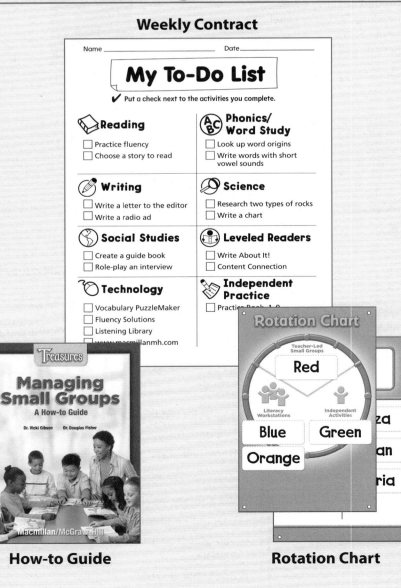

Name _____ Date _____

My To-Do List

✓ Put a check next to the activities you complete.

📖 Reading
- ☐ Practice fluency
- ☐ Choose a story to read

🔤 Phonics/Word Study
- ☐ Look up word origins
- ☐ Write words with short vowel sounds

✏️ Writing
- ☐ Write a letter to the editor
- ☐ Write a radio ad

🔬 Science
- ☐ Research two types of rocks
- ☐ Write a chart

🌐 Social Studies
- ☐ Create a guide book
- ☐ Role-play an interview

📖 Leveled Readers
- ☐ Write About It!
- ☐ Content Connection

🖱 Technology
- ☐ Vocabulary PuzzleMaker
- ☐ Fluency Solutions
- ☐ Listening Library
- ☐ www.macmillanmh.com

🎨 Independent Practice
- ☐ Practice Book, 1–8

Rotation Chart

Teacher-Led Small Groups

Red

Literacy Workstations

Independent Activities

Blue   Green

Orange

...za

...an

...ria

Treasures
Managing Small Groups
A How-to Guide
Dr. Vicki Gibson   Dr. Douglas Fisher

Macmillan/McGraw-Hill

How-to Guide

Rotation Chart

Digital Learning

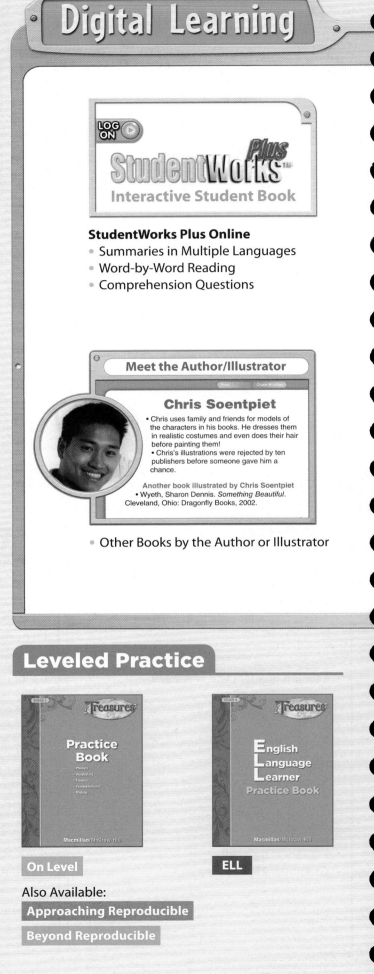

LOG ON ▶
StudentWorks Plus
Interactive Student Book

StudentWorks Plus Online
- Summaries in Multiple Languages
- Word-by-Word Reading
- Comprehension Questions

Meet the Author/Illustrator

Print   Close Window

Chris Soentpiet
- Chris uses family and friends for models of the characters in his books. He dresses them in realistic costumes and even does their hair before painting them!
- Chris's illustrations were rejected by ten publishers before someone gave him a chance.

Another book illustrated by Chris Soentpiet
- Wyeth, Sharon Dennis. *Something Beautiful.* Cleveland, Ohio: Dragonfly Books, 2002.

- Other Books by the Author or Illustrator

Leveled Practice

Treasures
Practice Book
- Phonics
- Vocabulary
- Fluency
- Comprehension
- Writing

Macmillan/McGraw-Hill

On Level

Treasures
English Language Learner Practice Book

Macmillan/McGraw-Hill

ELL

Also Available:
Approaching Reproducible
Beyond Reproducible

Independent Activities

LOG ON ▶ ONLINE INSTRUCTION www.macmillanmh.com

Oral Language Activities

- Focus on Vocabulary and Concepts
- English Language Learner Support

Vocabulary/Spelling Activities

Grade 4, Unit 2
Selection 3, Vocabulary   ⊙ How to Play ▶ Play Again ⊙ Close

preserve

Look to the sky to find the Answer

to keep from being lost, damaged, or decayed; protect

Answers Found

Macmillan
McGraw-Hill

- Differentiated Lists and Activities

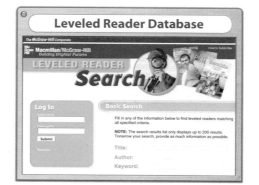

Leveled Reader Database

The McGraw-Hill Companies
Macmillan/McGraw-Hill
Building Brighter Futures   How to Subscribe

LEVELED READER
Search

Log In   Basic Search
Username: Fill in any of the information below to find leveled readers matching
                       all specified criteria.
Password: NOTE: The search results list only displays up to 200 results.
Submit   Tomorrow your search, provide as much information as possible.
Register   Title:
                       Author:
                       Keyword:

- Leveled Reader Database
- Search titles by level, skill, content area, and more

Research Toolkit

Research Roadmap

Step 2. Research

Research answers for the questions you were asked in Step 1. Visit these Web sites. Take notes about them on this page, too!

Kratts' Creatures
Click Creature World on the sign post. You will be on your way to learning about all sorts of animals. Or, check out the Creature of the Week, or the Creature Clubhouse. This excellent site is part of PBS Kids.

Take Notes:

- Research Roadmap
- Research and Presentation Tools
- Theme Launcher Video
- Links to Science and Social Studies

Available on CD

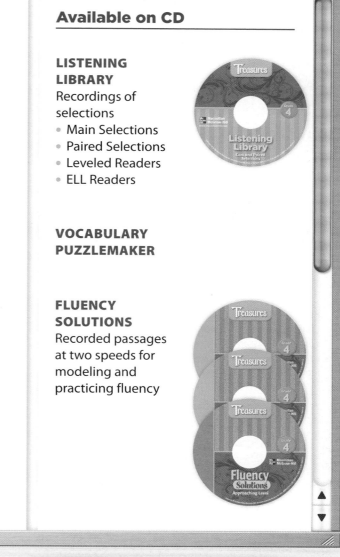

LISTENING LIBRARY
Recordings of selections
- Main Selections
- Paired Selections
- Leveled Readers
- ELL Readers

VOCABULARY PUZZLEMAKER

FLUENCY SOLUTIONS
Recorded passages at two speeds for modeling and practicing fluency

Leveled Reader Activities

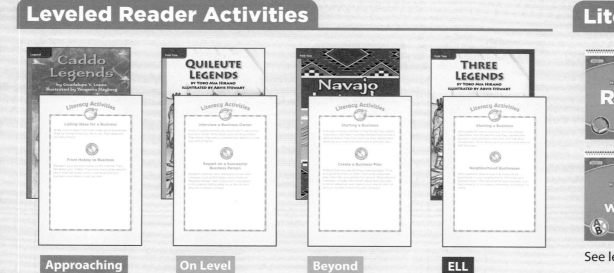

Approaching   On Level   Beyond   ELL

See inside cover of all Leveled Readers.

Literacy Workstations

Reading   Writing

Phonics/   Science/
Word Study   Social Studies

See lessons on pages 226K–226L.

Managing the Class

What do I do with the rest of my class?

Reading

Objectives

- Develop fluency through partner-reading
- Read independently for a sustained period of time; use **Practice Book** page 90 for Reading Strategies and Reading Log

---

Reading — Fluency — 20 Minutes

- Select a paragraph from the Fluency passage on page 95 of your Practice Book.
- With a partner, take turns reading the sentences aloud with expression.

Extension

- Read the paragraph three times, varying your pitch each time. Ask your partner how changing the pitch of your voice helped him or her understand the paragraph.
- Listen to the Audio CD.

> **Things you need:**
> - Practice Book

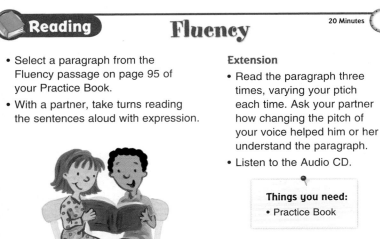

Fluency Solutions
Listening Library

19

Reading — Independent Reading — 20 Minutes

- Read a legend from another culture.
- Remember to check your understanding as you read. Use what you have learned about rereading to help you understand the story.
- Make a list of the main actions or events in the legend.

Extension

- Number the events in the order in which they happened.
- Share your list of events with a partner. Ask your partner to write a summary of the legend using your list.

> **Things you need:**
> - book of legends
> - pen and paper

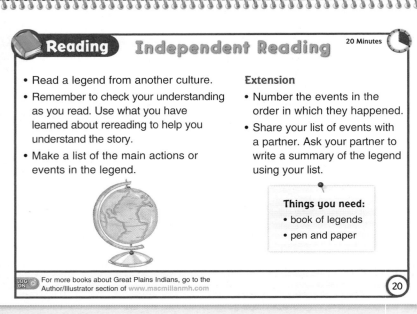

For more books about Great Plains Indians, go to the Author/Illustrator section of www.macmillanmh.com

20

Phonics/Word Study

Objectives

- Use a dictionary to look up the definition of *homophone*
- Write sentences using homophones
- Identify root words and suffixes

Phonics/Word Study — Homophones — 20 Minutes

- Use a dictionary to write the definition of the word *homophone*.
- Then look up the homophones *sore* and *soar*, *beet* and *beat*, *ring* and *wring*, and *ore* and *oar*.
- Write a sentence using each word.

Extension

- For each new sentence, draw a picture that explains the meaning of the word.

> **Things you need:**
> - pen and paper
> - colored pencils
> - dictionary

For additional vocabulary and spelling games, go to www.macmillanmh.com

Vocabulary PuzzleMaker

19

Phonics/Word Study — Suffixes — 20 Minutes

- Create a Two-Tab Foldable®.
- On the top tabs, write *Base Word*, *Suffix*.
- On the first inside tab, write the base words for *flexible, banker, collector* and *comical*.
- On the second inside tab, write the suffixes for these words.
- Guess the meaning of the words, using the meaning of the base word and suffix as clues. Use a dictionary to check meanings.

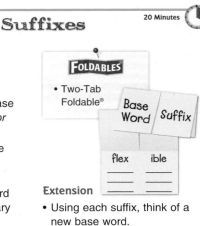

FOLDABLES

- Two-Tab Foldable®

| Base Word | Suffix |
| flex | ible |

Extension

- Using each suffix, think of a new base word.

For additional vocabulary and spelling games, go to www.macmillanmh.com

FOLDABLES®

20

Literacy Workstations

Reading | **Phonics/ Word Study** | **Writing** | **Science/ Social Studies**

Literacy Workstation Flip Charts

Writing

Objectives

- Write a play about a funny event
- Practice writing dialogue and stage directions
- Research the history of tipis

Content Literacy

Objectives

- Research the history of Native American celebrations
- Compare two different tribes' celebrations
- Research and write about the telegraph

Writing — WRITE A PLAY
20 Minutes

- Write a short play about a boy or girl who saves the day.
- Write dialogue that the characters would say.
- Add stage directions that tell the actors how to say the words or where to move.

Extension

- Have your classmates read aloud your play. Revise dialogue as needed, so that it expresses the characters' feelings.

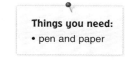

> **Things you need:**
> - pen and paper

19

Science — The Telegraph
20 Minutes

- Use an encyclopedia or the Internet to research the telegraph. Who invented the telegraph? How are messages sent using a telegraph?
- Write about the telegraph using the information you found.

Extension

- Talk with a partner about how the telegraph changed the way we communicate.

> **Things you need:**
> - encyclopedia or online resources
> - pen and paper

19

Writing — Describe a Tipi
20 Minutes

- Use an online encyclopedia or other reference materials to find out how tipis were used in the past, what materials were used to make them, and what the different symbols or designs on them may have meant.
- Take notes.

Extension

- Draw an outline of a tipi on a lined sheet of writing paper.
- Use your notes to write a paragraph that describes your tipi in the outline. Decorate the edges.

> **Things you need:**
> - online encyclopedia or reference materials
> - pen and paper
> - colored pencils

20

Social Studies — Native American Celebrations
20 Minutes

- Research the types of celebrations Native Americans had long ago.
- Use the Internet or history books to help you find information.
- Choose two different Native American groups and take notes about their different celebrations.

Extension

- Using your notes, create a Venn diagram to compare and contrast the two groups.
- Share with a partner.

> **Things you need:**
> - online resources and history books
> - pen and paper

LOG ON ▶ Internet Research and Inquiry Activity
Students can find more facts at www.macmillanmh.com

20

226

Prepare

WHOLE GROUP

ORAL LANGUAGE
- Build Background
- Connect to Theme
- Read Aloud

✔ **PHONICS/WORD STUDY**
- Suffixes

✔ **VOCABULARY**
- Homophones
- Teach Words

✔ **COMPREHENSION**
- Strategy: Analyze Story Structure
- Skill: Sequence

SMALL GROUP

- Differentiated Instruction, pp. 257I–257HH

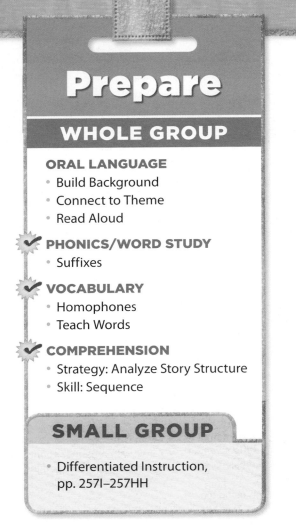

Oral Language

Build Background

ACCESS PRIOR KNOWLEDGE

Share the following information: This photo shows men riding in wagons and on a horse through the water. The wagon with the top on it is called a *covered wagon*. Before cars were invented, people who traveled to and explored new places used horses. There were no moving trucks then, so they loaded their belongings onto wagons.

Write the following words on the board, and briefly define each, using the **Define/Example/Ask** routine: **courage** (the strength to overcome fear), **pioneers** (early settlers of unknown places), **wagons** (sturdy vehicles with wheels, which were usually pulled by horses).

FOCUS QUESTION Have students read "Talk About It" on **Student Book** page 227 and describe the photo. Ask:

- If you were a pioneer, or settler, looking to move into a new area, would you make a ride like this? Why or why not?

- Think about the pioneers' courage. What dangers may they have faced?

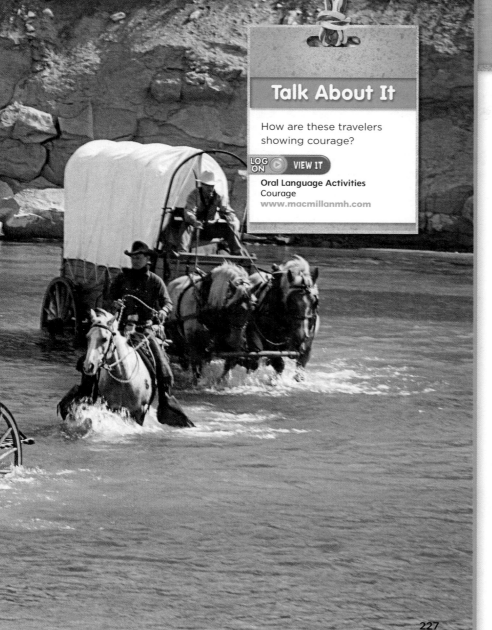

Talk About It

How are these travelers showing courage?

LOG ON ▶ VIEW IT

Oral Language Activities
Courage
www.macmillanmh.com

227

Use the Picture Prompt

BUILD WRITING FLUENCY

Ask students to write in their Writer's Notebooks what they know about pioneers or wagon trains. Students should write for eight minutes without stopping. Meet with individuals during Writing Conference time to provide feedback and revision assignments. Students should self-correct any errors they notice prior to the conference.

Connect to the Unit Theme

DISCUSS THE BIG IDEA

Young people may show surprising courage when facing a difficult situation. As a result, they may improve the lives of others around them.

Ask students what they have learned in this unit about people who took risks.

- What courageous people have we read about so far? How do they help other people by being brave?

- Who are some other people whose courage led to change?

USE THEME FOLDABLES

Write the **Big Idea** statement on the board. Ask students to copy it on their Unit Theme Foldables. Remind them to add details as they complete this week's readings.

Dinah Zike's
FOLDABLES®
Study Organizer

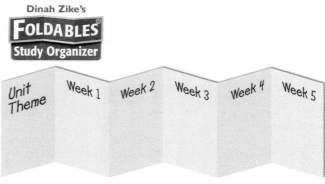

Unit Theme | Week 1 | Week 2 | Week 3 | Week 4 | Week 5

Accordion Book

ELL ENGLISH LANGUAGE LEARNERS

Beginning	Intermediate	Advanced
Use Visuals Tell students about the photograph. *The men are traveling by wagons. Before cars were invented, people used horses to travel.* Ask students to tell you what the men in the photograph are doing. If the answer is correct, repeat it in a louder and slower voice so the rest of the class may hear.	**Describe** Ask students to tell what the men in the photograph are doing. *What do they use to travel? How do people travel now?* Repeat students' responses, correcting grammar and pronunciation as needed.	**Explain** Ask students to discuss what it might be like to travel by horse or wagon. *Is this an easy way to travel? Why or why not?* Elaborate on students' responses.

Objectives

- Identify the characteristics of poetry
- Develop vocabulary
- Read sentences fluently, focusing on phrasing and expression

Materials

- Read-Aloud Anthology, pp. 59-61

Read Aloud

Read "Old Crow Warriors"

Read Aloud

GENRE: Literary Text/Poetry

Share with students the following key characteristics of a **poem**:

- Poems are written in **lines**. Distinct groups of lines are called **stanzas**.

- Poems may or may not have a **rhyme scheme** or a regular **meter,** or rhythm.

- Poems may use **imagery**, **figurative language**, and **symbolism**.

FOCUS ON VOCABULARY

Introduce the following words, using the **Define/Example/Ask** routine. Tell students that knowing these words will help them understand and appreciate the poem.

Vocabulary Routine

Use the routine below to discuss the meaning of both words.

Define: **Swaying** means moving from side to side.
Example: The frail trees were swaying in the harsh winter wind.
Ask: How is swaying different from shaking?

Define: When something is **crisp**, it is fresh and invigorating.
Example: The crisp green apple crunched as I bit into it.
Ask: How is the way an apple is crisp different from the way the wind is crisp?

LISTENING FOR A PURPOSE

Ask students to listen carefully as you read "Old Crow Warriors" on **Read-Aloud Anthology** pages 59–61. Use the Think Alouds and genre study prompts provided.

ELL **Interactive Reading** Build students' oral language by engaging them in talk about the poem's basic meaning.

- Point to the picture of the trees, name them, and ask how they are moving. (The trees are swaying.) Have students repeat chorally.

- After the first stanza, say: *Turn to your partner and discuss what you see and feel based on what you read.*

- After the second stanza, ask: *What season is it? How do you know?*

- After the last stanza, say: *Tell your partner what the voices are saying. Are they real voices? How do you know?*

Think/Pair/Share Use **Copying Master 1**, "I wonder ...," to help students generate questions about the symbolism in this poem. When completed, have students turn to a partner and orally summarize and generate questions about the poem.

RESPOND TO THE POEM

Ask students the Think and Respond questions on page 61. Then have students make a list of other subjects the poet could have included in this poem. Have them share their lists. Then have students choose three subjects and continue writing the poem.

Model Fluency

Reread the poem. Tell students that this time you want them to focus on two aspects of how you read the poem—your **expression**, or how you stress and express words, and your **phrasing**.

Point out that you pause after each stanza. Explain that you also pause after each line that ends with punctuation. However, you do not pause after line breaks without end punctuation. When a sound is repeated, you stress it for drama. Model an example.

Think Aloud Listen as I read the first stanza. I make sure I give "crisp, cold air" appropriate expression, and I pause at all punctuation, even if it comes in the middle of a line, as in, "Take a breath. Can you feel?" Now you try. Repeat each line after me, using the same expression and phrasing as I do.

Establish Fluency Focus Remind students that you will be listening for these same qualities in their reading throughout the week. You will help them improve their reading by adjusting their phrasing to add drama and using expression to convey emotion.

Objective
- Decode multisyllabic words with suffixes

Materials
- Practice Book, p. 82
- Word-Building Cards
- Transparency 10
- Teacher's Resource Book, p. 129

ELL

Transfer Skills Some Spanish suffixes are similar to English suffixes. For example, suffixes -*tion* and -*able* in English are similar to -*cion*, -*sion*, -*ible*, and -*able* in Spanish. If appropriate, point out the similarities to Spanish speakers. Ask them to identify the meanings of words with suffixes. Correct the meaning as needed. See language transfers on pages T16–T31.

HOMEWORK **Practice Book,** page 82

The suffixes -*y*, -*ly*, -*ful*, -*less*, and -*ness* can be added to the end of a root or base word to change its meaning. Sometimes spelling changes are necessary:
penny − y + i + less = penniless
sun + n + y = sunny

Add the suffix to the end of each word. Remember to make any necessary spelling changes. Write the new word. Then use the word in a sentence. **Possible responses provided.**
1. happy + ly = ___happily___
   Pedro happily volunteered to help clean up the beach.
2. thought + ful = ___thoughtful___
   Gina was thoughtful when she helped her neighbor rake the leaves.
3. care + less = ___careless___
   It is careless to litter.
4. kind + ness = ___kindness___
   Carla showed kindness when she sat with the new student at lunch.
5. fun + y = ___funny___
   The funny clown used his talent to make people laugh.
6. cheer + ful + ly = ___cheerfully___
   Chen whistled cheerfully on her way to school.
7. grace + ful + ness = ___gracefulness___
   Dancers are known for their gracefulness.
8. hope + less + ly = ___hopelessly___
   Shawn stared hopelessly out the window at the rain.

Approaching Reproducible, page 82
Beyond Reproducible, page 82

Morphology

✓ Suffixes

EXPLAIN/MODEL

Explain that a suffix is a letter or group of letters added to the end of a base word. A suffix changes the meaning of the base word. It can also change the word's part of speech. Introduce these common suffixes. Write each suffix and sample word on the board. Read and define the suffix. Then use the suffix's meaning to model how to determine the meaning of the sample words.

- **-er, -or** "a person connected with"; makes the base word a noun
  A <u>sweeper</u> got all the dust away.
  My <u>advisor</u> kept a sharp eye on me.
- **-ion, -tion, -ation, -ition** "act, process"; makes the base word a noun
  The new baby was a happy <u>addition</u> to the family.
- **-ible, -able** "can be done"; makes the base word an adjective
  Handing my work in late turned out to be <u>acceptable</u>.
  We used the <u>convertible</u> sofa bed for the sleepover.
- **-al, -ial** "having characteristics of"; makes the base word an adjective
  She was so fake as to seem <u>artificial</u>.
  She preferred <u>classical</u> music to pop.

Think Aloud Look at the first word: *sweeper*. I see the word *sweep*. The end, or suffix, of the word is -*er*. I put the two parts together to get *sweeper,* or someone who sweeps.

PRACTICE/APPLY

Read the Words Display **Transparency 10**. Help students underline the suffix, define it, then use its meaning to determine the meaning of the whole word.

civilization	banker	probable	comical
mansion	actor	possible	recital
rejection	visitor	irresistible	nonessential

Phonics Transparency 10

Throughout the discussion, point out other common word parts, such as the prefixes *ir-* and *non-*. Also discuss some nonexamples of suffixes, as in the words *super, lion,* and *redial.*

Read Multisyllabic Words

TRANSITION TO LONGER WORDS Display the suffixes and words below. Have students chorally read the suffix in the first column. Then tell students to underline the suffix in the longer word in the second column. Model how to read the word and determine its meaning. When they are finished, have students chorally read the words. Point out each word in random order and at varying speeds.

er	helper	or	debtor
ition	addition	ion	action
able	laughable	ible	convertible
ible	permissible	able	fixable
al	disposal	al	formal
ial	editorial	ial	memorial

Phonics Transparency 10

BUILD WORDS Display **Word-Building Cards** *al, ion, ible, aud, magic, adopt, react, attract, classic, comic, nation*. Have students use the word parts to build as many multisyllabic words with suffixes as possible. These and other words can be formed: *magical, adoption, reaction, attraction, classical, comical, national*.

APPLY DECODING STRATEGY Guide students to use the Decoding Strategy to decode *jogger, collector, consolation, suggestion, financial, musical,* and *immovable*. Write each word. Remind students to look for prefixes and suffixes in steps 1 and 2 of the Decoding Strategy procedure. Point out the consonant doubling in *jogger*.

Build Fluency

SPEED DRILL Distribute copies of **Suffixes Speed Drill** on **Teacher's Resource Book** page 129. Use the Speed Drill routine to help students become fluent reading words with these suffixes.

Quick Check

Can students read words with suffixes?

During **Small Group Instruction**

Tier 2

If No → **Approaching Level** Reteach the skill using the lesson on p. 257J.

If Yes → **On Level** Consolidate the learning using p. 257S.

Beyond Level Extend the learning using p. 257W.

Decoding Strategy

Decoding Strategy Chart

Step 1	Look for word parts (prefixes) at the beginning of the word.
Step 2	Look for word parts (suffixes) at the end of the word.
Step 3	In the base word, look for familiar spelling patterns. Think about the six syllable-spelling patterns you have learned.
Step 4	Sound out and blend together the word parts.
Step 5	Say the word parts fast. Adjust your pronunciation as needed. Ask yourself: "Is this a word I have heard before?" Then read the word in the sentence and ask: "Does it make sense in this sentence?"

Vocabulary

STRATEGY
DICTIONARY

Homophones Explain that sometimes two or more words sound alike but are spelled differently and have different meanings. These words are called *homophones.* Remind students to use a dictionary or other reference source to check the meanings of unfamiliar words or familiar words used in unfamiliar ways.

Have students read "Homophones" on the bookmark on **Student Book** page 228. Write *sores* and *soars.*

Think Aloud These two words sound exactly the same, so it is easy to confuse them. From looking them up, I know that *s-o-r-e-s* means "places where the skin has been broken and hurts" and *s-o-a-r-s* means "flies high." If I can't remember which spelling means which, I will need to check a dictionary.

Write *main* and *mane.* Have students use their dictionaries to find the meaning of each word. Then have students write a sentence using each word correctly. Review the multiple meanings of *main* as needed.

Read "History at Your Feet"

As you read "History at Your Feet" with students, have them identify clues that reveal the meanings of the highlighted words. Tell students they will read these words again in *Mystic Horse.*

Vocabulary

sores	amazement
loosened	midst
mysterious	responsibility

Dictionary

Homophones are words that sound the same but have different spellings and meanings. *Sores* and *soars* are homophones. Can you think of other homophones?

HISTORY AT YOUR FEET

by André Melillo

"Do I have to go?" Sam asked. "I've got **sores** on my feet from walking so much."

Sam, his sister Kim, and their family were on their way to the Pawnee Indian Village Museum.

Mom gave Sam some bandages to put on his blisters and said, "You'll enjoy learning about the Pawnee nation."

After that, Sam let out a sigh and **loosened** his tight sandal straps. He then dragged himself toward the museum.

Who Were the Pawnee?

The origins of the Pawnee nation are **mysterious** and unknown. In the early 1800s, there were 10,000–30,000 Pawnee living in four separate bands.

"This museum is located where one band of Pawnee settled back in 1820," explained Mom when they got there.

Anikarus Rushing of the Pawnee nation. The Pawnee mostly lived in the area now known as Nebraska.

228

Quick Check

Can students identify word meanings?

During **Small Group Instruction**

Tier 2

If No → | **Approaching Level** Reteach the words using the Vocabulary lesson, pp. 257K–257L.

If Yes → | **On Level** Consolidate the learning using p. 257S.

Gifted Talented

Beyond Level Extend the learning using p. 257W.

"And now we're standing exactly where the Pawnee lived!" exclaimed Kim in **amazement**.

"That's right," said Dad. "Here's part of the original floor," he said, pointing. "You can see some burned timbers from the fire that destroyed the village."

What Was Life Like?

Sam had to admit that being in the **midst** of all that history was exciting. "What was it like to live back then?" he wondered aloud.

A museum guide spoke up. "It happens to be my job and **responsibility** to tell you just that. The Pawnee hunted mostly buffalo and used every part of the animals they killed for food or clothing. They let nothing go to waste."

Then Kim said, "Clothing? Buffalo aren't shaped like any clothing I've ever seen."

Everyone chuckled. "They'd sew a patchwork of pieces into warm winter robes and pants," explained the guide.

A battle between the Pawnee and the Konza was painted on this bison hide.

Reread for **Comprehension**

Analyze Story Structure

Sequence is the order in which events take place. Time-order words such as *then*, *before*, and *after* are clues to a story's sequence of events. Putting the story's main events in sequence can help you summarize the **plot** and understand the story's structure. Reread the selection. Use your Sequence Chart to help you put events in order.

Event
↓
↓
↓

LOG ON ▶ **LEARN IT** Comprehension
www.macmillanmh.com

229

ELL

Preteach Vocabulary See pages 257BB and 257K to preteach the vocabulary words to **ELL** and **Approaching Level** students. Use the **Visual Vocabulary Resources** to demonstrate and discuss each word. To further reinforce concepts, have students complete page 110 in the **ELL Resource Book**.

HOMEWORK **Practice Book,** page 83

| mysterious | responsibility | midst |
| loosened | amazement | sores |

A. Choose the correct vocabulary word from the list to complete the sentence. Write the words on the lines.

David had a dog. He knew it was his 1. **responsibility** to take care of Spot. Of course, they had fun together. They played and ran and explored. Then one day, in the 2. **midst** of having fun, Spot ran through some poison ivy. He soon was covered with painful 3. **sores**. David took his dog home and washed Spot as best he could. He wrapped Spot up in a quilt and sat with him on the porch. At first, Spot tried to scratch. Then a 4. **mysterious** thing began to happen. Spot stopped wriggling and trying to scratch. David 5. **loosened** the quilt and looked at Spot's legs in 6. **amazement**. They were still red and swollen. Somehow, having his owner take care of him had calmed him down.

B. Add two sentences to the passage.

7. **Answers will vary. Possible response: David was glad that Spot felt better.**

8. **He gave Spot a treat.**

Approaching Reproducible, page 83
Beyond Reproducible, page 83

Vocabulary

✓ TEACH WORDS

Introduce each word using the **Define/Example/Ask** routine. Model reading each word using the syllable-scoop technique.

Vocabulary Routine

Define: If someone has **sores** on his body, he has places on his skin that are broken and painful.

Example: We cleaned the dog's sores and put bandages on them.

Ask: What types of things might cause sores? PRIOR KNOWLEDGE

- If you **loosened** something, you made it less tight. *Dad loosened his tie when he left work.* What kinds of things can be loosened? EXAMPLE

- If something is **mysterious**, it is hard to understand or explain. *The woods seemed dark and mysterious in the moonlight.* What is an antonym for *mysterious*? ANTONYM

- When something creates **amazement**, it causes surprise and wonder. *We stared in amazement at the acrobats far above us.* Tell about a time when you felt amazement. DESCRIPTION

- If you are in the **midst** of something, you are in the middle of it. *In the midst of our social studies lesson, the fire drill began.* What is a synonym for *midst*? SYNONYM

- Having a **responsibility** means having a job or duty to perform. *Clearing the table after supper is my responsibility.* How is a responsibility similar to and different from a job? COMPARE AND CONTRAST

Objectives

- Analyze story structure
- Sequence the events of a story's plot
- Use academic language: *story structure, sequence, chronological*

Materials

- Transparencies 10, 10a, 10b
- Practice Book, p. 84

Skills Trace

Sequence	
Introduce	107A–107B
Practice/ Apply	108–121; Practice Book, 39–40
Reteach/ Review	125M–125Z, 229A–229B, 230–251, 257M–257Z; Practice Book, 84–85
Assess	Weekly Tests; Units 1, 2, 5 Tests
Maintain	155B, 285B, 641A–641B, 642–659, 663M–663Z, 697B

ELL

Academic Language
Preteach the following academic language words to **ELL** and **Approaching Level** students during Small Group time: *story structure, sequence, chronological*. See pages 257AA and 257I.

Reread for Comprehension

✔ **STRATEGY**
ANALYZE STORY STRUCTURE

What Is It? **Story structure** refers to the way an author has organized the events of the plot, using story elements such as character and setting.

Why Is It Important? Understanding how the events of a story are organized can help readers recognize how these events affect the characters, including their relationships and the changes they undergo. It can also help readers to identify and summarize the main events of the plot.

✔ **SKILL**
SEQUENCE

What Is It? Explain that **sequence** refers to the order in which events take place in a story or in which information is given in nonfiction.

Why Is It Important? Putting the story's main events in sequence can help readers summarize the plot and remember key events and the order in which the events occurred. It can also help readers to understand how an event in a story can influence future events.

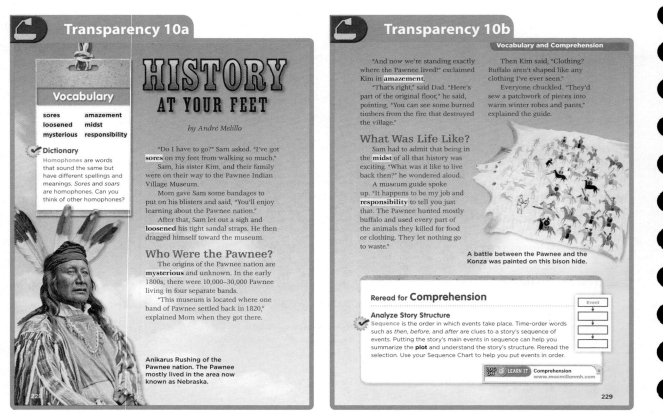

Student Book pages 228–229 available on Comprehension Transparencies 10a and 10b

- To identify sequence as they read, students should look for time-order words and phrases, such as *first, next, then,* and *finally.*

- Events in a story usually occur in **chronological**, or time, order. That is, the earliest events are presented first and continue until the last events occur at the end. Sometimes, however, the events are told out of order. When that happens, the author usually gives clues that help readers recognize the sequence.

MODEL

How Do I Use It? Read the first four paragraphs of "History at Your Feet" on **Student Book** page 228. Display **Transparency 10** and explain that you will use the Sequence Chart to identify and sequence the main events of the story.

Think Aloud It seems as if Sam's family has been sightseeing on foot as the story begins, because Sam complains about having walked too much. The first event is the family's discussion about going to their next destination: the Pawnee Indian Village Museum. I can place that information on my chart.

GUIDED PRACTICE

- Have students read the next section of the story, "Who Were the Pawnee?" Then help them put the events in sequential order. (Mom explains where the museum is. Then Kim expresses her excitement. Finally, Dad points out the original floor and the burned timbers.)

- Help students summarize their answers to fill in the second box of their Sequence Charts.

APPLY

Have students reread the remainder of "History at Your Feet" and complete the Sequence Chart. Ask them to explain how sequencing the plot's main events helped them understand the selection.

Quick Check

Can students sequence the main events of the story's plot?

During **Small Group Instruction**

Tier 2

If No → **Approaching Level** Reteach the skill using the Comprehension lesson, pp. 257M–257P.

If Yes → **On Level** Consolidate the learning using pp. 257U–257V.

Beyond Level Extend the learning using pp. 257Y–257Z.

Transparency 10

Sequence Chart

> The family discusses their next destination.
>
> ↓
>
> At the museum, the family begins to learn.
>
> ↓
>
> Sam admits he is interested.
>
> ↓
>
> The museum guide explains about the Pawnee way of life.

Graphic Organizer Transparency 10

HOMEWORK **Practice Book,** page 84

Recognizing the **sequence**, or order, in which things happen in a story helps you better understand what you read.

A. Read the passage below. Then number the sentences below to show the sequence of events.

The Plains Indians lived in North America before the Europeans came. Since they had no horses, the Plains Indians traveled on foot. To hunt buffalo, they would surround a herd and shoot the buffalo with bows and arrows.

This changed when Spanish explorers came to North America and brought horses with them. Now the Plains Indians hunters were able to ride horses and follow buffalo over long distances. They carried tipis with them and set up camps. The hunters could kill buffalo and pull them back to camp using their horses.

Later, guns again changed the way that Plains Indians hunted.

1. __2__ Spanish explorers brought horses to North America.

2. __3__ The Plains Indians used horses and traveled long distances to hunt buffalo.

3. __1__ The Plains Indians hunted buffalo on foot before the Europeans came to North America.

4. __4__ The Plains Indians used guns to hunt buffalo.

B. Add an event to the paragraphs and tell where it belongs in the sequence of events. Possible response:

Later, the Plains Indians had to settle and live in

reservations. This comes at the end.

Approaching Reproducible, page 84
Beyond Reproducible, page 84

Read

WHOLE GROUP

★ MAIN SELECTION
- *Mystic Horse*
- Skill: Sequence

★ PAIRED SELECTION
- "The Pony Express"
- Text Feature: Charts

SMALL GROUP

- Differentiated Instruction, pp. 257I–257HH

Main Selection

GENRE: Fiction/Legend

Have a student read the definition of a legend on **Student Book** page 230. Students should look for a traditional story about a hero that is based on fact and is connected to a particular person, time, or place in history.

★ STRATEGY
ANALYZE STORY STRUCTURE

Remind students that to analyze a story's structure means to look at the way an author organizes a plot by using story elements such as character and setting.

★ SKILL
SEQUENCE

Explain to students that **sequence** is the chronological order of events in a story. Understanding the sequence can help a reader to summarize the plot's main events and explain their influence on future events.

Comprehension

Genre

A **Legend** is a story that has been handed down by people for many years, and that often has some basis in fact.

Analyze Story Structure

★ Sequence As you read, fill in your Sequence Chart.

Read to Find Out

What gift does the mystic horse give to the boy and his tribe?

230

Vocabulary

Vocabulary Words Review the tested words while reading: **responsibility, sores, midst, loosened, amazement,** and **mysterious.**

Additional Selection Words Students may be unfamiliar with these words. Pronounce the words, give student-friendly explanations as needed, and help students use the previously taught vocabulary strategies: using a dictionary, word parts, context clues.

tipis (p. 233): cone-shaped tents made from wooden poles and animal skins by Native Americans

discarded (p. 234): thrown away

bays (p. 249): reddish-brown horses

chestnuts (p. 249): grayish- or reddish-brown horses

paints (p. 249): pintos; horses with irregular spots or markings

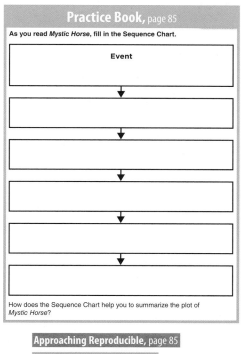

Award Winning Author

Mystic Horse
written and illustrated by PAUL GOBLE

231

Read the Main Selection

Preteach	Read Together	Read Independently
Have Approaching Level students and English Language Learners listen to the selection on **StudentWorks Plus**, the interactive e-Book, before reading with the class.	Use the prompts to guide comprehension and model how to complete the graphic organizer. Have students use **Think/Pair/Share** to discuss the selection.	If students can read the selection independently, have them read and complete the graphic organizer. Suggest that they use their purposes to choose their reading strategies.

LOG ON StudentWorks Plus
Interactive Student Book

Preview and Predict

QUICK WRITE Ask students to read the title, preview the illustrations, think about the genre, and make predictions about the story. Students should also include what they already know about legends.

Set Purposes

FOCUS QUESTION Discuss the "Read to Find Out" question on **Student Book** page 230. Remind students to look for the answer as they read.

Point out the Sequence Chart in the Student Book and on **Practice Book** page 85. Explain that students will use the chart to summarize the story.

Read *Mystic Horse*

Use the questions and Think Alouds to support instruction about the comprehension strategy and skill.

Practice Book, page 85

As you read *Mystic Horse*, fill in the Sequence Chart.

Event

How does the Sequence Chart help you to summarize the plot of *Mystic Horse*?

Approaching Reproducible, page 85
Beyond Reproducible, page 85

Develop Comprehension

1 **GENRE:** Fiction/Legend

What clues can you find in the first paragraph that tell you this is a **legend**, or traditional story? (It takes place in "long ago days." The author talks about the Pawnee people's way of life as if it had been going on in the same way for a very long time.)

2 **SKILL**
SEQUENCE

In what **sequence** did tribe members complete tasks in their village? (First, they pitched tipis. Then they guarded the camp.)

232

Monitor Comprehension

Monitor and Clarify: *Self-Correct*

Explain Students may need to pause at times to check their inferences about what they are reading. To correct inaccurate ideas they may have formed, they can ask themselves literal, interpretive, and evaluative questions such as *Why? How?* or *What if?*

Discuss Have students brainstorm questions to ask themselves, such as *Why do the Pawnee people have to watch over their village?* (Other people may want to take over their land and homes.)

Apply As they read the selection, have students ask and answer a series of *Why?* and *How?* questions and note their answers when they find them.

IN THOSE LONG AGO DAYS, when the Pawnee people had harvested their crops of corn and squash, they would leave their earth-lodge villages and travel out on the Great Plains to hunt buffalo. They had horses to ride and to carry their tipis and belongings when they went great distances in search of the wandering herds.

1

When they were not traveling, and the tipis were pitched, it was the **responsibility** of the older boys, the young men, to look after the herds of horses, and to guard the village. They would stay with the horses at pasture throughout the day, often far away from the camp. All the while they would keep a good lookout for enemies.

2

3

233

Develop Comprehension

3 **STRATEGY**
ANALYZE STORY STRUCTURE

✓ **Teacher Think Aloud** I see that the author has included a lot of information on this first page. To be sure that I understand it all, I can **analyze story structure** as I read. This page includes details about the Pawnee people. I think that they are going to be important characters in this story. The author uses the phrase "in those long ago days." This tells me that the setting, or where and when the story takes place, is in the past. I also read that the Pawnee lived on the Great Plains, which is another detail about the setting. I wonder if the enemies they are on the lookout for will be a major plot conflict later in the story.

PHONICS/WORD STUDY

APPLY DECODING SKILLS While reading, point out words with the sound/ spelling patterns, syllable types, and word parts students have recently learned. Help students blend these words. You may wish to focus on selection words with suffixes, such as *sickly, terribly, fastest, carefully, wonderful, hesitation, loudly, softly,* and *excitedly.*

ELL   ENGLISH LANGUAGE LEARNERS

Beginning	**Intermediate**	**Advanced**
Access Content Preteach story content build language, and develop meaning using the Interactive Question-Response Guide in the **ELL Resource Book**, pages 98–107. Give ample time for students to respond. They may point or use words or short phrases to respond.	**Elaborate** Preteach story content, build language , and develop meaning using the Interactive Question-Response Guide in the **ELL Resource Book**, pages 98–107. Have students respond in complete sentences. Repeat their responses, correcting pronunciation or grammar as needed.	**Restate** Complete the Intermediate task with students. Elicit details to support their responses.

Develop Comprehension

4 DRAW CONCLUSIONS

How did the other people at the camping place feel about the old woman and her grandson? Tell what text evidence you used to reach your **conclusion**. (The narrator says that nobody took much notice of them, so nobody wished them ill. On the other hand, the woman and her grandson had to look for leftover food and clothing, so the others obviously did not make a point of helping these poor people.)

Traveling with the people were an old woman and her grandson. They were poor, living alone without any relatives at the edge of the village. Their only shelter was made of sticks and a patchwork of pieces of old tipi covers which people had thrown away. Nobody took much notice of them.

When the people moved from one camping place to another, the old woman and her grandson would stay behind to look for scraps of food, and to pick up discarded clothes. They had no horse. They walked, and what their dogs could not carry, they packed on their **4** own backs. Their life was hard, but they were happy.

234

Develop Comprehension

5 MAKE INFERENCES

What **inferences** can you make about the kind of life the old woman and her grandson were living? Find details in the illustration on these two pages that give you clues. (The sky is gray and there are diagonal streaks in the air, so it is either raining or snowing. The flames on the open fire lean in one direction, so it must be windy. There are no trees in sight, so the old woman probably had to walk far to find wood. The dog seems happy to be inside the warm tent, but the old woman and her grandson have to be out in the cold to prepare a meal. They had a hard life.)

235

Develop Comprehension

6 STRATEGY
DICTIONARY

The words *sores* and *soars* are **homophones** because they sound the same but are spelled differently and have different meanings. Homophones are easily confused. What does the word *sores* mean here? (The word *sores* refers to places on the horse that are broken and painful.)

One day, as they followed far behind the village, they came upon a sad and sickly worn-out horse standing in the trail. He was terribly thin, with **sores** on his back.

"Grandmother," the boy said, "nobody wants this poor old horse. If we are kind and look after him, he will get well again. He will help us carry our packs! Then I will be able to join the buffalo hunt, and we will have meat, and fresh skins as well!"

236

And so they led the old horse, limping along behind them. People laughed: "You've got yourself a great warhorse, boy! How will we keep up with you now?" But the boy loved his horse, and looked after him well.

7

> **Sequence**
> What is the first thing the boy does when he finds the horse?

8

237

Develop Comprehension

7 AUTHOR'S PURPOSE

What is the **author's purpose** for including the remarks that people make about the boy's horse? (The author lets the reader experience more vividly the way the people made fun of the boy. We are more involved in the story, because we can better understand what the boy was going through.)

8 SKILL
SEQUENCE

What is the first thing the boy does when he finds the horse? (He decides that he and his grandmother should keep the horse and look after him until he is well again.) **Add this information to your Sequence Chart. How might this event influence future events in the story?** (The boy loves his horse and looks after him. If the horse gets well, it could change his and his grandmother's lives.)

> The boy found a sick horse and decided to look after it.

Comprehension

Point of View: *Third-Person Omniscient*

Explain Review the concepts of *point of view* and *narrator*. Remind students that the narrator in a story told from the first-person point of view is a character in the story. When a narrator is not a character in the story, the point of view is called *third person*. Have students identify if this story has a first- or third-person narrator. Explain that if the narrator is not a character but knows the thoughts of all the characters, the point of view is called *third-person omniscient*.

Discuss Read a definition of *omniscient*. Ask what advantages this point of view might have. (We can learn how all the characters feel.)

Apply Have student partners identify passages in which the narrator of this story tells the thoughts of more than one character.

Develop Comprehension

9 **CAUSE AND EFFECT**

Why did the boy attempt to join the warriors? (Now that he finally had a horse of his own, the boy wanted to show that he too had courage and was willing to fight the enemy.)

238

After some days had passed, the boys who were out on the hills looking after the horses spotted enemies approaching on horseback. They quickly drove the herds back to the safety of the camp. The men grabbed their weapons, mounted their fastest horses, and rode out to meet the enemy.

The boy, riding the poor old horse, followed shyly at a distance. But the men pointed at the horse and laughed: "Look! Here's the one who'll leave us all behind! Boy, that's an old good-for-nothing half-starved horse. You'll be killed. Go back home!" **9** **10**

The boy was ashamed, and rode off to one side where he could not hear their unkind remarks. The horse turned his head and spoke to the boy: "Listen to me! Take me down to the river and cover me with mud." The boy was alarmed to hear him speak, but without hesitation he rode to the river and daubed mud all over his horse. **11**

239

Develop Comprehension

10 **AUTHOR'S CRAFT: WORD CHOICE**

The author uses the word *shyly* to describe how the boy follows behind the others. What does the author's **word choice** tell you about how the boy was feeling? (The word *shyly* tells us that the boy did not yet feel completely sure of himself.)

11 **SKILL**
    SEQUENCE

What important event took place after the boy was turned away by the warriors? (The horse talked to the boy and asked him to put mud on his back. The boy did what the horse asked him to do.) Record this event in your Sequence Chart.

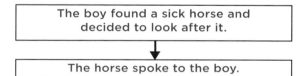

| The boy found a sick horse and decided to look after it. |

↓

| The horse spoke to the boy. |

Develop Comprehension

12 FIGURATIVE LANGUAGE

The author says that the horse "flew like a hawk" and that the arrows were "flying past him like angry wasps." What effect do these **similes** have on your understanding of the action? (The similes create vivid pictures. The phrase "flew like a hawk" makes the boy's ride sound exciting and fast. Comparing the arrows to angry wasps adds suspense to the scene.)

13 SKILL
SEQUENCE

Summarize the horse's instructions using time-order words. (First, leave your bow and arrows behind. Second, cut a long willow stick. Next, ride me to the enemy and hit their leader with the stick. After that, ride back again. Finally, do this four times, but no more than four.) Add this information to your Sequence Chart.

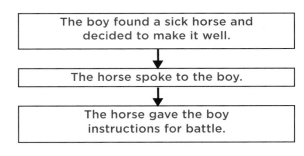

The boy found a sick horse and decided to make it well.

↓

The horse spoke to the boy.

↓

The horse gave the boy instructions for battle.

Then the horse spoke again: "Don't take your bow and arrows. Cut a long willow stick instead. Then ride me, as hard as you can, right into the enemy's **midst** and strike their leader with the stick, and ride back again. Do it four times, and the enemy will be afraid; but do not do it more than four times!"

While the horse was speaking, he was tossing his head, stamping and prancing this way and that, until the boy could hardly hold him back. He **loosened** the reins, and the horse galloped toward the enemy. He was no longer an old sickly worn-out horse! He flew like a hawk, right to where the enemy riders were formed up in line of battle. The boy struck their leader with his willow stick, turned, and rode back to his people with arrows flying past him **12** like angry wasps.

He turned again without stopping, and the horse carried him back to strike another enemy rider. By then his people were cheering loudly. Four times the boy charged back and forth, and each time he hit one of the enemy, just as his horse had told him.

13
14

Sequence
Summarize the horse's instructions using time-order words.

240

ELL ENGLISH LANGUAGE LEARNERS

STRATEGIES FOR EXTRA SUPPORT

Question 12 FIGURATIVE LANGUAGE
Write on the board and say: *An arrow is like a wasp.* Show pictures of an arrow and a wasp. Explain that a wasp flies fast and can sting someone. Ask: *How can an arrow be like a wasp?* Discuss how the arrow and a wasp are similar. Point to the word *like*. Explain that when an author uses the words *like* or *as* in the comparison, it is called a *simile*. Ask students to find similes on page 240, and have them describe what is being compared. Correct the meaning of students' responses as needed.

241

Develop Comprehension

14 | **STRATEGY**
ANALYZE STORY STRUCTURE

Teacher Think Aloud To make sure I am following the story, I will identify the major events that have occurred. The boy found a sick horse. This is the first main event. The horse was able to talk, and it helped the boy scare his tribe's enemies. I have also learned about the boy's character. How would you describe him?

PARTNERS Prompt students to apply the strategy in a Think Aloud by analyzing the main character.

Student Think Aloud The boy is kind. I can tell that because he takes care of the horse even though others make fun of him. He also obeys the horse when he tells him to cover him with mud. The boy is startled by the talking horse, but he follows his directions anyway.

15 **SELF-SELECTED STRATEGY USE**

What **strategies** have you used so far to help you understand the selection? Where did you use them? Why?

RETURN TO PREDICTIONS AND PURPOSES

Have students respond to the story by confirming or revising their predictions and purposes for reading. Encourage them to revise or write additional questions to help focus their attention as they continue to read the selection.

Stop here if you wish to read this selection over two days.

Extra Support

Sequence

Help students review the sequence of major events in the story thus far. As you ask the following questions, emphasize the signal words: What is the *first* main event in the story? (The boy found the horse.) What is the *next* main event of the story? (The horse talked to the boy. The boy was told to cover the horse in mud, and he did this.) What main event happens *after* that? (The boy rode the horse toward the enemy four times.) Encourage students to continue using signal words as they summarize and review the sequence of events.

Develop Comprehension

16 CAUSE AND EFFECT

How did the boy's actions affect the outcome of the battle? (The Pawnee men were encouraged to follow the boy's lead by riding toward the enemy. They were able to drive the enemy away.)

242

Text Evidence

Sequence

Remind students that authors sometimes use clue words to alert readers to the sequence of events in a selection. Then ask, *What words do authors often use to signal the order of events?* (Answers will include *then, after, before, finally, next.*) *Where do authors often place these clue words—at the beginning, middle, or end of a sentence?* (They are almost always found at the beginning of a sentence.) *Find the clue words that indicate the order of events when the boy attacks the Pawnee's enemies. Where are they located in the text?* (Students will note that the clue words *he turned again*, *by then*, and *four times* are found in the last paragraph on page 240.) Then ask, *What can you do if the author does not include clue words to help you place events in sequence?* (Insert your own clue or signal words to see if the events take place in chronological order and make sense.)

The men watched the boy with **amazement**. Now they, too, felt brave enough to follow his example, and they drove the enemy in full retreat from the village. It was like chasing buffalo.

16

The boy was eager to join the chase. He said to himself: "I have struck four times, and I have not been hurt. I will do it once more." And so, again, he rode after the retreating enemy riders. He whipped another with his stick, but at that very instant his horse was pierced by an arrow, and fell. The horse tried to stand, but he could not.

17

18

243

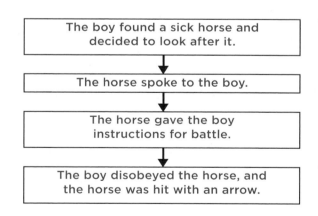

Develop Comprehension

17 CHARACTER

Which of the boy's **character** traits motivated him to ride toward the enemy a fifth time? (The narrator says that the boy was eager to join the chase. It sounds as if he still wanted to prove himself or to be accepted by the others. He was so caught up in the excitement that he seemed to ignore the horse's instructions on purpose.)

18 SKILL
SEQUENCE

What happened after the boy rode into battle again? (The boy neglected to follow the horse's instructions. Because he rode into battle again, the horse was hit with an arrow.) Record this event in your Sequence Chart.

The boy found a sick horse and decided to look after it.

↓

The horse spoke to the boy.

↓

The horse gave the boy instructions for battle.

↓

The boy disobeyed the horse, and the horse was hit with an arrow.

Develop Comprehension

19 COMPARE AND CONTRAST

Compare and contrast the way the Pawnee warriors felt about the boy before and after the battle. (Before the battle, the warriors had ignored him and made fun of his horse. After seeing how bravely he rode against the enemy, the warriors seemed to have gained respect for the boy. The leader even gave him the title of Boy Chief.)

When the enemy had fled, the men returned and gathered round the boy. His horse was dead. They wanted to touch the horse, for they knew he had been no ordinary one, but a horse with mystic powers.

The leader spoke: "Today this boy has shown that he is braver than all of us. From now on we will call him Piraski Resaru, Boy Chief."

19

But the boy cried. He was sad for his horse, and angry with himself that he had not done what the **mysterious** horse had told him. He untied the lariat, pulled out the arrow, and carefully wiped away the blood.

20

244

245

Develop Comprehension

20 CHARACTER, SETTING, PLOT

Think about how the boy's feelings have changed. What new **character** traits did the boy show as he wept over the dead horse? (He was angry with himself and recognized that he was responsible for the horse's death. He understood that his decisions and actions affect those around him.)

ELL ENGLISH LANGUAGE LEARNERS

STRATEGIES FOR EXTRA SUPPORT

Question 20 CHARACTER, SETTING, PLOT
Help students understand how the events of the battle affected the boy and when his feelings changed. Ask: *How did the boy feel before the battle? How did the boy feel when the horse told him to ride to the enemy? How did the boy feel when he rode a fifth time? How did he feel after he rode? Explain the change in his feelings.* If students' responses are correct, repeat them slowly and clearly for the class to hear. Elicit details from students to support their responses.

Develop Comprehension

21 **MONITOR AND CLARIFY: SELF-CORRECT**

The author includes many details in the first two paragraphs of page 246. What can you do to **monitor** and **self-correct** your comprehension? (To monitor and self-correct as I read, I can ask myself questions such as, "Is the author using *he* to refer to the boy or to the horse?" Doing this will help me understand the sequence of events.)

22 **SKILL**
SEQUENCE

Use signal words to **sequence** the events on page 246. (First, the boy climbed the hill to mourn. While he was crying, a thunderstorm began. Then, the boy saw the horse move. After the horse stood up, the boy ran down the hill and put his arms around the horse. Next, the horse said that he came back because the boy had been forgiven. Finally, the horse gave the boy new instructions.) Add the final step in this sequence to your Sequence Chart.

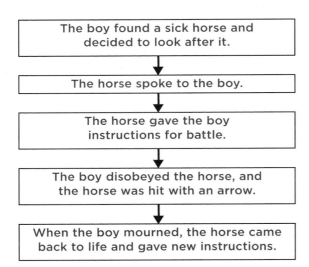

The boy found a sick horse and decided to look after it.

↓

The horse spoke to the boy.

↓

The horse gave the boy instructions for battle.

↓

The boy disobeyed the horse, and the horse was hit with an arrow.

↓

When the boy mourned, the horse came back to life and gave new instructions.

He climbed to the top of a nearby hill to mourn. He sat on a rock and pulled his blanket over his head. While he sat there crying, fearsome dark clouds closed across the sky, and it grew dark as if night was falling. Lightning flashed! Thunder shook the hilltop, and it rained with a terrific downpour.

Looking through the downpour, he imagined he saw the dead horse move his legs a little, and that he even tried to lift his head. He wondered if something strange and wonderful was happening. And then he knew it was **21** true: the horse slowly stretched out his front legs, and then stood up!

The boy was a little afraid, but he ran down from the hilltop and clasped his arms round the horse's neck, crying with joy that he was alive again.

The horse spoke softly to him: "Tirawahat, Our Father Above, is good! He has forgiven you. He has let me come back to you."

The storm passed; the rain stopped. All was still and fresh, and the sun shone brilliantly on his beautiful **22** living horse. "Now take me up into the hills, far away from people," the horse told him. "Leave me there for **23** four days, and then come for me."

246

Tell students that Paul Goble carefully studied the art of Plains Indians so that his illustrations reflect the culture of those peoples. Have students research Plains Indian symbols, such as diamonds, arrows, thunderbirds, and stars, and what each stands for. Remind students to use multiple sources and to credit the sources properly.

When their research is complete, have students make oral presentations explaining step by step how to create art that uses Plains Indian symbols. They should organize the information using a logical structure with an effective introduction and conclusion. Students should make their instructions as precise as possible. Have listeners restate the sequence of actions that form the instructions.

24

247

Develop Comprehension

23 MAKE INFERENCES

Why do you think the horse gave the boy another set of instructions? Explain your **inference**. (The instructions may have been a test to see if the boy learned his lesson and would do as he was told.)

24 GENRE: Fiction/Legend

What details in the story and in the illustrations let you know that this **legend** comes from a Native American culture? (The setting is the Great Plains, and the Pawnee people described in the story live in earth lodges and tipis, which is typical of some Native American cultures. The people ride horses and use bows and arrows to hunt buffalo. The author even uses Pawnee words, such as *Tirawahat*. The illustrations show the colorful designs that the Pawnee people used on their clothing, blankets, and shields.)

Develop Comprehension

25 SKILL
SEQUENCE

What happened when the boy followed the horse's new instructions? (He was rewarded with a herd of horses, which he will use to take care of others.) Record this **sequence** of events.

The boy found a sick horse and decided to make it well.

↓

The horse spoke to the boy.

↓

The horse gave the boy instructions for battle.

↓

The boy disobeyed the horse, and the horse was hit with an arrow.

↓

When the boy mourned, the horse came back to life and gave new instructions.

↓

When he followed instructions, the boy received a herd of horses, which he will use to help others.

26 STRATEGY
ANALYZE STORY STRUCTURE

Student Think Aloud This is a good place in the story to stop and analyze the **story structure**. A major plot conflict that took place in the story is that the horse died because the boy disobeyed him. After the horse died, the boy felt guilty and sad. The boy was given a second chance, and this time he followed his orders. Because he obeyed the horse, he was given a herd of horses that will help many people.

248

Vocabulary

Multiple-Meaning Words

Explain/Model Explain that some words in this legend, such as *bays, chestnuts,* and *paints,* are multiple-meaning words; that is, they are spelled and pronounced the same as their counterparts but have different meanings that can be determined from context. Here, these words refer to specific types of horses. In other contexts they have different meanings.

Think Aloud I see the word *chestnuts* in the story. From context clues I can tell that here it refers to a horse, but this word can also refer to a type of nut that people often eat during the winter.

Practice/Apply Display the words *paints* and *bays.* Have students determine their alternate meanings. (liquid you apply to color a wall; distinct areas of the water that are defined by the shoreline)

When the four days had passed, Boy Chief left the village and climbed into the pine tree hills.

A horse neighed, and the mysterious horse appeared, followed by a herd of spirited horses. They surrounded Boy Chief, snorting and stamping excitedly, horses of every color—beautiful bays, chestnuts, shiny blacks, whites, grays, and paints. **25**

Mounted on his mysterious horse, Boy Chief drove the horses round and round the village. He stopped in front of his grandmother's shelter.

"Grandmother," he said, "now you will always have horses! You need never walk again! Choose the ones you want, and give the rest to those who need them most." And so it was done.

After that, the boy and his grandmother rode whenever they moved camp. They lived in a tipi and were not poor any longer. And, just as his grandmother had looked after him when he was young, so he, too, always took good care of her for all her years. **26**

249

Develop Comprehension

RETURN TO PREDICTIONS AND PURPOSES

Review students' predictions and purposes. Were their predictions correct? What gift does the mystic horse give the boy and his tribe? (a herd of horses)

REVIEW READING STRATEGIES

- **Analyze Story Structure** In what ways did analyzing the story structure help you to understand the selection?

- **Monitor and Clarify: Self-Correct** Do you understand the strategy of self-correcting when you check your comprehension? When might you use it again?

- **Decoding** What difficult words did you encounter? How did the Reading Multisyllabic Words Strategy help you sound out these words?

- **Self-Selected Strategy Use** What strategies did you use to make sense of what you read? Where? How were these strategies helpful?

PERSONAL RESPONSE

Ask students to discuss and write about what might happen to the boy next. Prompt them to use words indicating sequence as they write and to support their predictions with text evidence.

Quick Check

Can students analyze the story structure?

During **Small Group Instruction**

If No → **Approaching Level** Reteach the skill and have students apply it to a simpler text. Use Leveled Reader lessons, pp. 257N–257P.

If Yes → **On Level** Have students apply the skill to a new text to consolidate learning. Use Leveled Reader lessons, pp. 257U–257V.

Gifted & Talented **Beyond Level** Have students apply the skill to a more complex text to extend learning. Use Leveled Reader lessons, pp. 257Y–257Z.

Author and Illustrator

MEET PAUL GOBLE

Have students read the biography of the author and illustrator. Ask:

- What is unusual about Goble's interest in Native Americans?

- How does Goble show the connection between people and nature through his illustrations?

WRITE ABOUT IT

Author's Craft: Contrast

Discuss what happened when Boy Chief listened to the horse. Have students write a personal narrative about an incident in which they followed directions. Then have them contrast their experience with the boy's experience.

Author's Purpose

Remind students that the genre of a story can often be a clue to the author's purpose. Review the definition of a legend on page 230. Have students summarize the story to find clues about Paul Goble's purpose for writing *Mystic Horse.*

Meet **Paul Goble**

Paul Goble first became interested in Native Americans when he was a boy growing up in England. He thought their beliefs, art, and tales were wonderful. When Paul grew up, he moved to the western United States to live and learn among the Native Americans. Paul began to write and illustrate books that retold traditional tales. Before writing each book, he carefully researches Native American customs and clothing. He also likes his books to show how people and nature are connected.

Other books by Paul Goble

LOG ON ▶ FIND OUT
Author Paul Goble
www.macmillanmh.com

✔ **Author's Purpose**
Legends often have some basis in fact. Why did Paul Goble write *Mystic Horse*? Use details from the story in your answer.

250

Author's Craft

Contrast

When writers contrast two or more things, they show how the things are different. In this selection, Paul Goble contrasted the boy and his grandmother with the rest of the Pawnee.

- For example: "They were poor, living alone without any relatives at the edge of the village ... Nobody took much notice of them." (page 234)

- Have students skim the story to find and discuss examples of Goble's use of contrast, such as, "The men grabbed their weapons, mounted their fastest horses, and rode out to meet the enemy. The boy, riding the poor old horse, followed shyly at a distance." (page 239)

Comprehension Check

Summarize

To summarize *Mystic Horse* use the most important details from the selection. Information from your Sequence Chart may help you.

Event
↓
↓
↓

Think and Compare

1. What did the boy find that helped to change his life? Plot

2. Describe the **mysterious** changes that happened to the horse after the boy covered it with mud. Use story details to support your answer. Analyze Story Structure: Sequence

3. Why did the boy ignore the horse's directions? Explain using story details. Make Inferences

4. Is the narrator of this story first or third person? Why did the author choose this point of view? Author's Purpose

5. Read "Who Were the Pawnee?" on pages 228–229 and pages 233–234 of *Mystic Horse*. What do both selections teach the reader about Pawnee life? Reading/Writing Across Texts

251

Make Connections

Text-to-Self Have students respond to the following question to make connections to their own lives. Use the Think Aloud to model a response. *Suppose you lost a friendship because you made a foolish mistake. How would you correct your mistake and repair the friendship?*

Think Aloud: If I lost a friend, I would apologize and promise to never make the same mistake again. I would also try to do nice things for my friend, to demonstrate that I really care.

Text-to-World Have students respond to this question to make connections to the world. Use the Think Aloud to model a response. *How could you explain the boy's actions in battle?*

Think Aloud: The boy was brave. He followed the horse's directions, riding up to the enemy four times. I think that his success made him over-confident. When his people began fighting he wanted to join and disobeyed the horse.

Comprehension Check

SUMMARIZE

Have partners summarize the events that take place in *Mystic Horse* in their own words. Remind students to use their Sequence Chart to help them organize their ideas.

THINK AND COMPARE
Text Evidence

1. **Plot** <u>Answer stated in text</u> The boy found a sad, sick horse as he was walking with his grandmother. LOCATE

2. **Sequence** <u>Answer stated in text</u> After the boy covered the horse with mud, it was no longer an old, sickly, and worn-out horse, but a strong, fast horse that was able to drive the enemy away. COMBINE

3. **Make Inferences** <u>Answer</u> The boy ignored the horse's directions because he wanted to continue fighting the enemy. <u>Evidence</u> He wanted to join the warriors who were chasing the enemy away and felt certain that he would succeed in battle again. CONNECT

4. **Author's Purpose** <u>Answer</u> The narrator is third person. The author chose to write in third person so that he could share the thoughts and feelings of all the characters. <u>Evidence</u> The narrator is not a character in the story. Through the narration, we learn what other characters think and feel. ANALYZE

5. **Text-to-Text** Both tell that the Pawnee hunted buffalo. In *Mystic Horse,* the author describes their crops and villages. "Who Were the Pawnee?" gives specific dates and details about the Pawnee. COMPARE

Objectives

- Read fluently with good expression and phrasing
- Rate: 84–104 WCPM

Materials

- Transparency 10
- Practice Book, p. 86
- Fluency Solutions Audio CD

ELL

Develop Comprehension
Explain the text paragraph by paragraph. To help students visualize the scene, demonstrate the sounds and actions: *neighed, stamping, surrounded,* and *drove.* Then read the phrases with expression and have students echo-read after you. Then ask students to identify the main idea of the passage in phrases or sentences, based on their levels.

Practice Book, page 86

As I read, I will pay attention to my expression and phrasing.

	But there came a time when many days of heavy rain
11	made the Quillayute River overflow. The houses washed
19	away. Then the Quileute moved to the prairies.
27	Not long after, the weather grew cold. The rain turned
37	into hail and sleet. The fishermen could not break through
47	the ice in the rivers to go fishing. Falling hailstones were
58	so big that people were killed. The people grew afraid to
69	go outside. They were running out of food. Men, women,
79	and children were becoming weak and sick.
86	At this time, the Great Chief of the Quileute called a
97	meeting of all the people in the tribe. He stood before them
109	in a patchwork shawl made up of buffalo skins stitched
119	together. The people begged the chief to do something. The
129	**responsibility** of watching over his people weighed heavily
137	upon him. "We will ask the Great Spirit who soars above
148	Earth for help," said the chief. 154

Comprehension Check
1. What were the events that caused the Great Chief of the Quileute to call a meeting? Name the events in the order in which they occurred. **Sequence** There was a flood, and a freeze, and people started to run out of food.
2. What is the purpose of a legend such as this? **Author's Purpose** Legends teach the history of a people. This one teaches the history of the Quileute people.

	Words Read	–	Number of Errors	=	Words Correct Score
First Read		–		=	
Second Read		–		=	

Approaching Reproducible, page 86

Beyond Reproducible, page 86

Fluency

Repeated Reading: Expression and Phrasing

EXPLAIN/MODEL Explain that the text on **Transparency 10** has been marked with slashes that indicate pauses and stops, or **phrasing**. A single slash indicates a pause, usually between phrases. In this passage, a single slash also indicates a slightly longer pause at a dash. A double slash indicates a stop, usually between sentences. Have the class listen carefully to your pauses and also for your **expression**, such as how your intonation changes for exclamations.

> ### Transparency 10
>
> A horse neighed,/ and the mysterious horse appeared,/ followed by a herd of spirited horses.// They surrounded Boy Chief,/ snorting and stamping excitedly,/ horses of every color/—beautiful bays,/ chestnuts,/ shiny blacks,/ whites,/ grays,/ and paints.//
>
> Mounted on his mysterious horse,/ Boy Chief drove the horses round and round the village.// He stopped in front of his grandmother's shelter.//
>
> "Grandmother,"/ he said,/ "now you will always have horses!// You need never walk again!"//

Fluency (from *Mystic Horse,* p. 249)

PRACTICE Reread the first two sentences with students. Then divide them into two groups. Have groups alternate reading sentences. Remind students to pay attention to the pauses and stops as indicated by the slash marks.

DAILY FLUENCY Students will practice fluency using **Practice Book** page 86 or the **Fluency Solutions Audio CD**. The passage is recorded at a slow practice speed and a faster fluent speed.

Quick Check

Can students read fluently with good expression and phrasing?

During **Small Group Instruction**

If No → **Approaching Level** Use the Fluency lesson and model, p. 257Q.

If Yes → **On Level** See Fluency, p. 257T.

Beyond Level See Fluency, p. 257X.

SPIRAL REVIEW

Comprehension

REVIEW SKILL
CAUSE AND EFFECT

EXPLAIN/MODEL

- Remind students that the events in a story often are linked by **cause-and-effect** relationships. One action or event will influence, or cause, another event, producing an effect or result.

- As they read, students should look for main events in the story that cause or influence the events that follow. They might ask themselves "What happens because of that event?" or "What brought about that action?"

- Remind students that cause-and-effect relationships can either be explicit or implicit. Explicit relationships are stated directly, while implicit relationships are implied, or hinted at but not stated.

- Students should look for words and phrases that signal cause and effect, such as *because, due to, as a result, since,* and *therefore.*

Briefly discuss "History at Your Feet" with students and help them identify cause-and-effect relationships. Ask: *Why does the guide tell Sam and his family what life was like for the Pawnee in the early 1800s?*

PRACTICE/APPLY

PARTNERS

Have students work in literature circles to discuss causes and effects in *Mystic Horse.* One student can act as recorder as the others answer these questions.

- What influences the Pawnee to ignore the old woman and her grandson? (The boy and his grandmother are poor.)

- How do the other characters treat the boy—or what is the effect—when he rides the poor old horse? (The effect of the boy riding the poor old horse is that the other Pawnee laugh at the boy.)

- What event results from the boy's obeying the horse the first time? (When the boy obeys the horse by covering him with mud, the horse turns into a strong, healthy horse.)

- What causes Tirawahat to forgive the boy? (Tirawahat forgives the boy because he sees that the boy is truly sorry for his actions.)

- How may the story's events influence the Pawnee's future actions? (The Pawnee may look beyond people's appearance more often.)

PRACTICE BOOK See **Practice Book** page 87 for Characters in Traditional Literature.

Objectives

- Identify cause-and-effect relationships in a story
- Explain the influence of the plot's main events on future events

Skills Trace

Cause and Effect	
Introduce	203A–203B
Practice/ Apply	204–219; Practice Book, 75–76
Reteach/ Review	225M–225Z, 707A–B, 708–723, 729M–729Z; Practice Book, 237–238
Assess	Weekly Tests; Units 2, 6 Tests
Maintain	251B, 333B, 737B

TEST PREP

Test Practice

Answering Questions

To apply **answering questions strategies** to content-area reading, see pages 78–84 in *Time For Kids.*

Paired Selection

GENRE: Informational Text/Expository

Have students read the bookmark on **Student Book** page 252. Explain that almanacs are a special type of informational text. They are expository reference books that

- come out every year and provide current information about people, places, events, or things;

- usually contain tables, charts, diagrams, or other visual information, such as photographs with captions;

- contain headings and subheadings that organize the text.

Text Feature: Charts

EXPLAIN Point out the chart on page 254. Explain that charts usually have columns and rows and show figures and facts about any of a wide array of topics. This chart shows the lengths and locations of some of the most historic trails in the United States.

APPLY Have students identify the different categories of this chart. (Name, Location, and Total Mileage) How many trails are represented? (five)

Ask students how the chart adds to the information in the article. (The chart lists specific facts about the Pony Express and lets you know about other trails.) Ask: *How do the headings help organize the chart?* (They separate topics and let you know what information will appear in each column.)

Social Studies

Genre

Expository texts, such as **almanacs**, have information, facts, and figures about many different subjects.

Text Feature

Charts present a large amount of information, such as names, places, and numbers, in a compact way.

Content Vocabulary

relays	**frontier**
intervals	**telegraph**

THE Pony Express

by Beatriz Santiago

The Pony Express used riders on horseback to deliver mail. Although the Pony Express lasted only a short time, it was one of the most colorful and exciting parts of American history.

A Need for Speed

Many people went west in the late 1800s to seek their fortune. Some of the travelers decided to stay and make their homes there. These new settlers needed a faster way to communicate across the country for both business and pleasure. At this time, the quickest way to move mail west was on John Butterfield's stagecoach line. Butterfield's stagecoaches went west from Missouri, south to El Paso, Texas, then west to San Diego, and north to San Francisco. This route took about 25 days to complete.

The most famous Pony Express rider was Bill Cody, later known as Buffalo Bill.

252

Content Vocabulary

Explain these words using the **Define/Example/Ask** routine. Definitions are provided below.

- **Relays** are a series of people relieving each other or taking turns. Why do relays require teamwork?

- **Intervals** are the chunks of time or space between things. What is an example of an interval that is used in sports?

- A **frontier** is the part of a country or land where people are just beginning to settle. Why did building railroads help push the American frontier westward?

- A **telegraph** is a machine or system that sends messages by wire over long distances. How is a telegraph different from e-mail?

Ads for Pony Express riders called for young, skinny, expert riders under the age of 18, who were willing to risk death on a daily basis.

A Mail Solution

William Hepburn Russell came up with an idea for a faster way to deliver mail. He believed that young men riding fast horses across the center of the country on **relays** could make the journey in just ten days! Relay stations would provide fresh horses every ten miles. The rider would switch to a fresh horse, taking only his *mochila*, or mail bag. The riders would also switch every 50 to 100 miles.

Russell and his partners mapped out a trail from St. Joseph, Missouri, to Sacramento, California. The route would take riders through Kansas, Nebraska, Colorado, Wyoming, Utah, and Nevada. The founders built 190 stations along the trail at ten-mile **intervals**. They bought over 400 horses and hired about 80 young men as riders.

1

2

253

Connect to Content

Pony Express Interviews

Have students imagine that they need to hire Pony Express riders. Ask students to create a list of questions, such as, *Why do you want to be a rider? What are your qualifications?* Working in pairs, students should take turns interviewing each other for the job of Pony Express rider. When they are finished, discuss who would have been hired and why.

Paired Selection

Read "The Pony Express"

As students read, remind them to apply what they have learned about reading almanacs and using charts. Also have them identify clues to the meanings of the highlighted words.

1 SEQUENCE

According to William Russell, how would the mail be delivered from Missouri to Northern California? (First, young men would ride across the middle of the country on relays, giving them fresh horses every ten miles. Then the rider would switch horses and continue riding for another 40 to 90 miles. Next, a new rider would take over. Once the mail got to Sacramento, California, a steamship would bring it to San Francisco.)

2 CONTENT VOCABULARY

Look at the word *intervals* on page 253. What context clue helps you understand the word's meaning? (The words *ten-mile* are a context clue. *Intervals* here means the space between locations. Since *ten-mile* gives an exact space, it is an example of an interval.)

Use the Interactive Question-Response Guide in the **ELL Resource Book**, pages 108–109, to help students gain access to the paired selection content.

Paired Selection

3 **TEXT FEATURE: CHART**

What is the difference in miles between the Lewis and Clark trail and the Pony Express trail? (1,900 miles)

4 **GENRE:** Informational Text/Expository

In what ways is an almanac entry different from a magazine article? (An almanac entry might be updated every year. It is usually broken up into more sections and includes more dates and figures than a magazine article, and it is more likely to have a chart.)

National Historic Trails

Reading a Chart

Almanacs often have tables and charts that list facts and other information. Use this chart to find the lengths and locations of some of the United States' most famous historic trails.

Name	Location (by state)	Total Mileage
Lewis and Clark	Iowa, Idaho, Illinois, Kansas, Missouri, Montana, Nebraska, North Dakota, Oregon, South Dakota, Washington	3,700
Old Spanish Trail	Arizona, California, Colorado, Nevada, New Mexico, Utah	2,700
Trail of Tears	Alabama, Arkansas, Georgia, Illinois, Kentucky, Missouri, North Carolina, Oklahoma, Tennessee	2,200
Pony Express	California, Colorado, Kansas, Missouri, Nebraska, Nevada, Utah, Wyoming	1,800
El Camino Real de Tierra Adentro	New Mexico, Texas	404

3

The Pony Express Riders

The average age of the riders was 22. They received a salary of $25.00 a week, which was a lot of money in those days. Pony riders faced many hardships and dangers, such as snowstorms, hot deserts, and flooded rivers. They always rode alone.

Because their job was so dangerous, riders were very much admired. Newspapers published stories about them. People wrote poems and songs about their courage. They became heroes of the **frontier**. Some of the earliest riders were James Randall, Johnny Fry, and Billy Hamilton.

254

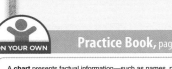

ON YOUR OWN **Practice Book,** page 88

A **chart** presents factual information—such as names, places, and numbers—in a compact form.

Look at the chart from a sports almanac. Then use the chart to answer the questions that follow.

The Top Five Pitchers in Baseball History

Name	Career Length	Games Won	Games Lost
Walter Johnson	21 years	417	279
Christy Matthewson	17 years	373	188
Sandy Koufax	12 years	165	87
Lefty Grove	17 years	300	141
Cy Young	22 years	511	316

1. What does this chart tell you about these pitchers? It tells you how long their careers were and how many games they won and lost.
2. Which of the pitchers had the shortest career? Sandy Koufax
3. Which pitcher won the most games? Cy Young
4. Which pitcher lost the fewest number of games? Sandy Koufax
5. Which pitchers had careers that lasted the same number of years? Christy Matthewson and Lefty Grove
6. Who has the highest numbers in all three categories? Cy Young

Develop Vocabulary Have students discuss the picture on page 253. Explain that the man is a rider for the Pony Express. Read aloud and explain the headings in "The Pony Express." For example, explain the meaning of *solution*. Say: *A solution is an answer to a problem.* Have students restate the meaning. Repeat students' responses, correcting for grammar and pronunciation as needed.

Approaching Reproducible, page 88
Beyond Reproducible, page 88

Mail Service in Ten Days

On April 3, 1860, a large crowd gathered in St. Joseph, Missouri. They cheered as the first rider galloped off with the mail pouch that would arrive in California just ten days later. Another mail carrier headed east from Sacramento at the same time.

From the beginning, the Pony Express did exactly what it promised—it delivered the mail in just ten days!

The End of the Pony Express

When the transcontinental **telegraph** lines were completed on October 24, 1861, it marked the end of the Pony Express. The telegraph could send messages across the country in seconds. Even so, people in the west felt sad. The Pony Express connected the young country in newer, faster ways and showed how Americans could work together. It will always be remembered as an important part of our country's past. **4**

Connect and Compare

1. Look at the chart of National Historic Trails on page 254. Which historic trail is shorter than the Pony Express? How long is that trail, and what is its location? **Reading a Chart**

2. Describe how the author organized the information in the article. **Apply**

3. Think about this article and *Mystic Horse*. How were Pony Express riders similar to the grandson in *Mystic Horse*? Use details to support your answer. **Reading/Writing Across Texts**

Social Studies Activity

Use reference books or the Internet to research and find one of the poems written about Pony Express riders. Use it as a model to create your own poem about a figure from the Old West.

LOG ON ▶ FIND·OUT **Social Studies** Pony Express
www.macmillanmh.com

255

Connect to Content

RESEARCH AND INQUIRY

Pony Express and U.S. Mail Before the Internet, mail was the most important communication resource in the world. Even after the telegraph was invented, most people still relied on mail.

Have three groups research the growth of the U.S. mail system from the Pony Express until 1880, giving each a different span of years (1860–1866, 1867–1873, 1874–1880). When their research is complete, students should present their findings. As a class, create a chart to compare the information from each group. Discuss this question: *How did the Pony Express have a lasting effect on the U.S. mail system?*

Paired Selection

Connect and Compare

1. El Camino Real de Tierra Adentro is shorter. It is 404 miles and runs through New Mexico and Texas. **READING A CHART**

2. The author organized the information in sequence, or chronological order. First, the author writes about how people wanted a faster way to deliver mail. Next, the Pony Express is described. Finally, the author writes about the end of the Pony Express. Each section begins with a subheading. **APPLY**

3. **FOCUS QUESTION** The Pony Express riders were like the grandson in *Mystic Horse* in that they tried new things in uncharted territory, taking great risks. Both ended up helping other people: the boy helped his family and tribe, and the Pony Express riders helped the settlers of the West. **READING/WRITING ACROSS TEXTS**

Social Studies Activity

Ask students to present their Pony Express poems to the class. Then create a class booklet, and have students make a table of contents and a cover for the booklet.

☑ **WRITING WORKSHOP**
- Developing Procedural Writing
- Trait: Word Choice
- Strong Verbs and Descriptive Details

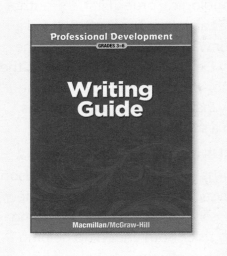

Professional Development
GRADES 3–6

Writing Guide

Macmillan/McGraw-Hill

Trait: Word Choice

Strong Paragraphs: Strong Verbs and Descriptive Details

TEACH/MODEL Remind students that a strong verb is a vivid, specific action word. A descriptive detail describes a person, a thing, or an action. Writers use strong verbs and descriptive details to show readers what is happening. These words help readers create mental pictures of the actions.

Tell students that writing sentences using strong verbs and descriptive details will help them build **strong paragraphs** that create interest and give readers additional information. Write the following paragraph on the board, and read it aloud:

> *Everyone is going everywhere in our room! Alex goes. Allie goes. Peter goes, too. Finally it is my turn. Here I go!*

Point out that readers do not get a strong image from this paragraph because the writer does not use strong verbs or descriptive details. Readers do not know where people go or how they go there. Write the following paragraph, and read it aloud:

> *Everyone is on the move in our room. First, Alex tiptoes quietly to the window. Next, Allie pretends she is a horse. She gallops to the door and then back to her seat. Then Peter hops on one foot all the way across the room. Finally, it is my turn. Here I go! I skip in a circle and clap my hands.*

Help students identify the strong verbs that were substituted for *goes*. Point out that the strong verbs help students visualize how the people move. Then help students identify the descriptive details. Point out that adding descriptive details also gives students a clear image of how and where the people go. As you reread the paragraph, have students use the strong verbs and details to act out the scene. Discuss how the strong verbs and descriptive details helped the students know how to act.

Teacher Write Aloud

PRACTICE/APPLY Further explore with students the use of strong verbs and descriptive details to make their writing specific and more interesting. Write the paragraph on the board and read it aloud. Then complete the Teacher Think Aloud.

> Victor went home. Spot, Victor's dog, was at the door. Victor got the leash. He put the leash on Spot. Victor and Spot went for a walk.

Teacher Think Aloud This paragraph tells me what Victor did, but I can't imagine how he did each action. That's because the writer did not use strong verbs and descriptive details to show me what Victor did. We can write a stronger paragraph by using strong verbs and adding descriptive details, such as when, where, and how Victor acted. This will help readers create a mental image of what is happening.

Ask students to brainstorm strong verbs to replace the ordinary verbs in the paragraph. Have them suggest descriptive details that will help readers create a vivid picture of the scene, such as colors, objects, and setting. List the verbs and details on the board. To complete the Think Aloud, use the verbs and details to write a strong paragraph like the one below. Stop after each sentence to discuss how the verbs and details help students create mental images.

> Victor raced straight home after school. Spot, Victor's dog, waited excitedly at the front door. Victor grabbed Spot's orange leash from the hook. He attached the leash to Spot's orange-and-yellow-striped collar. Victor and Spot headed out the door for their daily stroll around the park.

 Draft Display the Writing Prompt on **Writing Transparency 29**. Tell students to show what they do and how they do it by using strong verbs and descriptive details. Circulate and provide Over-the-Shoulder Conferences as students work.

Objective

- Write a paragraph using strong verbs and descriptive details

Materials

- Writer's Notebooks
- Writing Transparency 29

Daily Journal Prompts

Focus on Strong Verbs and Descriptive Details

Use these and other prompts for independent daily journal writing.

- Write about a moment when you were excited.
- Write about a moment when you were late for school.
- Write about a moment when you were doing a chore or task.
- Write about a moment when you were fixing a meal.

 **Transparency 29**

Focus on a moment from your evening routine (eating, dinner, playing basketball, doing homework). Try to include some strong verbs and descriptive details!

Writing Transparency

Reading and Writing Connection

✔ Trait: Word Choice

STRONG VERBS AND DESCRIPTIVE DETAILS

Remind students that strong verbs and descriptive details help readers create images in their minds. Point out that good writers use strong verbs and descriptive details to write strong paragraphs.

Read the Passage

Use the example from *Mystic Horse* as a model of the author's skilled use of strong verbs and descriptive details.

- Have students read the bookmark. Remind them that strong verbs and descriptive details help readers visualize actions, or create pictures of the actions in their minds.

- **Ask:** *When did you move very quickly? What strong verbs or details describe how you moved?*

- Have students chorally read the excerpt from *Mystic Horse*. Direct their attention to the callout. Have students discuss the strong verbs and descriptive details that helped them see the action.

- **Ask:** *Which verbs could you imagine well enough to act out? Did the author use any verbs that surprised or confused you?*

Writing

✔ **Trait: Word Choice**
Writers include **strong verbs and descriptive details** to help readers visualize actions.

Reading and Writing Connection

Read the passage below. Notice how the author Paul Goble uses strong verbs and descriptive details in his story.

> An excerpt from
> *Mystic Horse*

The author uses strong verbs and details to help us see the action. They help us picture exactly how the boy and the horse looked and moved.

While the horse was speaking, he was tossing his head, stamping and prancing this way and that, until the boy could hardly hold him back. He loosened the reins, and the horse galloped toward the enemy. He was no longer an old sickly worn-out horse! He flew like a hawk, right to where the enemy riders were formed up in line of battle. The boy struck their leader with his willow stick, turned, and rode back to his people with arrows flying past him like angry wasps.

Mystic Horse
written and illustrated by PAUL GOBLE

256

Respond to the Selection

Have students write a response to the selection.

- ☑ **Engagement** Help students deepen their connection to the text and discover their own perspective on it. *Focus on a moment when you spent time with an animal.*

- ☑ **Response** Help students explore more deeply their reactions to particular passages in the reading. *Focus on a moment in the story when a verb made a picture in your head that surprised you. Use text evidence in your writing.*

- ☑ **Literary Analysis** Help students deepen their connection to the text and discover their own perspective on it. *Focus on a place in the story where you thought the author used an especially good strong verb. Use text evidence in your writing.*

Read and Find

Read Darryl's writing below. How did he use strong verbs and descriptive details to help you picture the moment? Use the checklist below to help you.

Read about Darryl's creepy crawler.

Watching a Spider
by Darryl D.

As I lay in bed last night, I saw a spider creeping across my wall. It scurried forward a few inches at a time, froze, then scrambled on a little farther. When it arrived at my desk, it hopped down and began to spin a web. It seemed to slide down an invisible pole as it dropped to the ground.

Writer's Checklist

✓ Does the writer choose **strong verbs** that describe specific actions?

✓ Does the writer use **descriptive details** in his writing to help the reader see what is happening?

☐ Do you get a clear image of the action as Darryl experienced it?

257

Read the Student Model

Have students chorally read the student model at the top of **Student Book** page 257. Discuss what strong verbs and descriptive details this student writer used. Use the Writer's Checklist.

Journal Prompt

Draft Write the following prompt on the board. Have students write a response to the prompt.

> *Focus on a moment when you watched an animal do something. Write a paragraph about that moment. Use strong verbs and descriptive details.*

Tell students that you will be reading and commenting on their writing during Writing Conference time.

Model how to use the Writer's Checklist so students can write and revise their work. Then ask:

- *What moment did you choose?*
- *What strong words and descriptive details did you use to show that moment? Will readers be able to clearly picture the moment? If not, what strong verbs and details could you add?*

ELL ENGLISH LANGUAGE LEARNERS

Beginning	Intermediate	Advanced
Write Sentences Provide model sentences based on the Journal Prompt: *The duck ___ across the grass. It ___ loudly the whole time. Finally, the duck ___.* Help students add strong verbs to complete the sentences. Guide them in including details that show what happened in the moment.	**Describe** Ask students to write three sentences based on the Journal Prompt. Have them describe what happened in the moment, using strong verbs and details. Provide a model if necessary. As you read their sentences, correct grammar and spelling as needed.	**Narrate** Ask students to respond to the Journal Prompt. Have them use strong verbs and descriptive details to create pictures in readers' minds.

Objectives

- Write sentences with strong verbs and descriptive details
- Write strong paragraphs

Materials

- Writer's Notebooks
- Teacher's Resource Book, p. 187

ELL

Develop Meaning Read each verb and discuss its meaning. Have students act out the verb. Then brainstorm other verbs that mean almost the same thing.

HOMEWORK **Teacher's Resource Book,** page 187

After each verb below, please write one strong verb with a similar meaning. Then write a sentence that uses the strong verb and descriptive details.

Example: run <u>gallop</u> <u>Sleek, black horses gallop across the windy plains.</u>

cry ___ _____

eat ___ _____

hit ___ _____

fall ___ _____

need ___ _____

go ___ _____

look ___ _____

Minilessons

Minilesson 1 | Word Choice/Strong Verbs and Descriptive Details

TEACH/MODEL

Remind students that they have been focusing on strong verbs and descriptive details to help readers picture actions. Today they will practice that again. Have students use **Teacher's Resource Book** page 187. Ask them to read the example and identify the strong verb and descriptive details in the sentence.

PRACTICE/APPLY

Have students work independently. Ask students to share their completed work during Sharing Circle. Discuss the strong verbs and descriptive details they used.

Minilesson 2 | Sentence Fluency/Combine Sentences

TEACH/MODEL

Tell students that writers use both simple and compound sentences to make their writing more interesting and easier to understand. Explain that when they write, they can combine some short sentences into compound sentences. Write the following paragraph on the board. Read it aloud. Have students point out simple and compound sentences. Point to a compound sentence that combines two steps for clarity. Point out that if a compound sentence is unclear, it can be broken into two simple sentences.

> Let's make a sand castle. First, grab a pail. Scoop up some sand, and plop it into the pail. Keep scooping and plopping until the pail is full. Pat the sand down. Then turn over the pail, and tap the bottom. Remove the pail, and there is your castle. Decorate it with sand, seaweed, and shells.

PRACTICE/APPLY

Write the following paragraph on the board. Read it aloud. Point out that the writer uses only short, simple sentences. In their Writer's Notebooks, have students rewrite the paragraph so it has simple and compound sentences.

> Lie down in the snow. Stretch your arms out to the side. Slide your arms up. Slide them down. Get up carefully. Look at it.

Conferencing Routine

Dynamic Feedback System

Step 1 Read and appreciate the writing.

Step 2 Notice how the student uses the targeted skill (for example, strong verbs and descriptive details: Ask: *What strong verbs and descriptive details did the writer use?*).

Step 3 Write comments that show how the writing has an impact on you. Direct your comments to those places in the piece where the student has used the targeted skill.

Step 4 Meet with and give the student a revision assignment.

Write Effective Comments

Word Choice At least one of your comments should highlight the way the student includes **strong verbs** and **descriptive details**. Here are some sample comments.

- Your use of strong verbs and descriptive details really helps me understand this step in the process.

- I'm not sure what I would do next to (make a snowman). Could you add some descriptive details to this step?

- You really showed me how to (make pudding) by using strong verbs and descriptive details.

Revision Assignments

Word Choice Here are some examples of effective revision assignments for strong verbs and descriptive details.

- Revise — ■ *Reread your entry.* Find three sentences where you used the same verb and rewrite them with different verbs.

- Revise — ■ **[Underline a section.]** Mark a specific section of a student's writing and then ask the student to revise it in a specific way.

- Revise — ■ **[Underline a section.]** *I underlined a section in your entry that I wished I could picture better. Write three sentences to add more descriptive details about what you did in that moment.*

Teacher-to-Teacher

Over-the-Shoulder Conferences

Use these quick, focused opportunities to comment while students are writing.

- **Step 1** Quietly move close enough to a student that you can read the journal entry he or she is writing.

- **Step 2** Read part of what you see. You don't need to start from the beginning or read the entire piece.

- **Step 3** Show the student a spot in the writing where he or she is using a particular skill or describing something that piques your interest.

- **Step 4** Whisper a sentence or two about why you noticed that spot in the writing, and ask a question that will nudge the student to add a strong verb or a descriptive detail.

- **Step 5** Move on to the next student. Select students strategically. You should see 12–15 students in a 15-minute period.

Research Proven Writing Approach

The Writers' Express
Immediate Impact. Lasting Transformation.   wex.org

Connect Language Arts

WHOLE GROUP

✔ **VOCABULARY**
- Tested Words

✔ **SPELLING**
- Suffixes

✔ **GRAMMAR**
- Plurals and Possessives

SMALL GROUP

- Differentiated Instruction, pp. 257I–257HH

ON YOUR OWN

Practice Book, page 89

Homophones are pairs of words that are pronounced the same but have different spellings and meanings. You can use a dictionary to check the meanings of homophones.

here / hear	needed / kneaded	plains / planes
there / their	seen / scene	buries / berries
rain / rein	four / for	road / rode
blue / blew	through / threw	

Read the passage. Write *correct* **on the lines below if the right homophone is used. If the wrong homophone is used, write the correct word on the line. Use a dictionary to check the meanings of unfamiliar words.**

Some Native Americans lived on the <u>planes</u> in the middle of our country.
                                        1
The land <u>their</u> is beautiful. The sky is <u>blue</u>, and tall grass seems to go on
              2   3
forever. Even today, the miles of grass are a beautiful <u>scene</u>. The Native
                                                              4
Americans <u>road</u> their horses <u>threw</u> the <u>plains</u> hunting buffalo <u>four</u> food.
             5   6   7   8
They also ate <u>berries</u> and nuts to add to <u>there</u> diet. It was a hard life but the
                 9   10
Native Americans were proud of the life they lived.

1.	plains	6.	through
2.	there	7.	correct
3.	correct	8.	for
4.	correct	9.	correct
5.	rode	10.	their

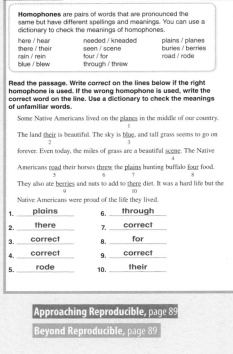

Approaching Reproducible, page 89

Beyond Reproducible, page 89

Build Robust Vocabulary

Day 1 — Teach/Practice

CONNECT TO WORDS

- Practice this week's vocabulary words using the following prompts:

1. Would you be more likely to help a dog with *sores* on its back or one who was snarling? Why?

2. What piece of clothing might be *loosened* after work by a man who was dressed up?

3. Why is a book with a *mysterious* plot suspenseful?

4. Would you react with more *amazement* to a surprise party or to a phone call from a friend?

5. How is being in the *midst* of a project NOT like being at the beginning of one?

6. Whose *responsibility* is it to wash the dishes in your household?

ACADEMIC VOCABULARY

- Review the important academic vocabulary words for the week. These words include: *analyze, story structure, sequence, cause and effect, legend*.

- Write each word on the board. Define each using student-friendly language, and ask students to select the word you are defining. Then point to words in random order for students to define.

Day 2 — Review

CONNECT TO WORDS

- Review the definitions of this week's vocabulary words using **Student Book** pages 228–229. Then discuss each word using these prompts:

1. Where would you get *sores* if your sandals were too tight?

2. When might a tire be *loosened* from a car?

3. Would a *mysterious* person be someone you would trust? Why?

4. When have you reacted with *amazement* to something?

5. If you are in the *midst* of a good book, what might you want to do?

6. Would you be more likely to fulfill a *responsibility* if you were tired or rested? Why?

-  Have students write their own context-rich sentences for this week's words in their Writer's Notebooks. Model an example first.

HOMOPHONES

- Remind students that homophones are words that sound the same but have different meanings and spellings. Review how commonly used homophones are spelled, such as *there, they're, their* and *two, too, to*.

- Display **Transparency 19**. Read the first sentence, and model how to identify homophones for the italicized word *reins*. Discuss the meaning of each homophone.

- Have students identify and define homophones for the other italicized words.

Day 3 Reinforce

CONNECT TO WORDS

- Ask students to create Word Squares for each word in their Writer's Notebooks.
- In the first square, students write the word. (Example: *mysterious*)
- In the second square, students write their own definition of the word and any related words, such as synonyms. (Example: *secret, unexplained, hidden, unpredictable*)
- In the third square, students draw a simple illustration that will help them remember the word. (Example: a drawing of a girl reading a book with a big question mark on it)
- In the fourth square, students write nonexamples, including antonyms for the word. (Example: *obvious, dull, predictable, straightforward*)

RELATED WORDS

- Help students generate words related to *amazement*. Classifying synonyms and antonyms can help improve students' vocabularies.
- Explain that the word *maze* comes from the Old English *maes,* meaning "labyrinth" or "maze."
- Have students use a thesaurus or dictionary to come up with some "shades of meaning" words for *amazement* (*bewilderment, trickiness, confusion, labyrinthine*) as well as some antonyms and nonexamples (*boredom, expectation, routine, no reaction*). Help students create or complete analogies using the words.

Day 4 Extend

CONNECT TO WORDS

- Review this week's vocabulary using the following sentence stems. Have students orally complete each one.

1. I got sores on my feet because ___.
2. My brother loosened ____ to ____.
3. The mysterious ____ made me ____.
4. I was in amazement when ____.
5. The teacher was in the midst of ___ when ____.
6. It was my responsibility to ____.

MORPHOLOGY

- Use the content vocabulary word *telegraph* as a springboard to analyzing the meanings of other words with the root *-graph*. Learning about Greek roots can help raise students' word consciousness.
- Write *telegraph.* Underline *-graph* and explain that it comes from the Greek *graphikos,* meaning "something written." Explain that *tele-* comes from the Greek word meaning "far off." *Telegraph* literally means "something written from far off."
- Write *photograph, autograph,* and *biography* on the board.
- Use the word parts to analyze each word literally: "written picture"; "self-written"; "writing about life." Have students link the literal root meanings to everyday meanings.

Day 5 Assess and Reteach

POSTTEST

- Display **Transparency 20**. Have students complete the cloze sentences using one of this week's vocabulary words.
- Note how quickly and accurately students can complete this task. Work with students who make errors or require too much time to complete this task during Small Group time.

CONNECT TO WRITING

- Have students write sentences in their Writer's Notebooks using this week's vocabulary. Tell students to write sentences that provide information they learned from this week's readings.
- **ELL** Provide the Day 4 sentence stems for students needing extra support.

PERIODIC REVIEW

- Check students' mastery of all the words from Unit 2. Use the Day 1 prompts from each week. Continue to use these words during classroom discussions to reinforce their meanings and usage.

5-Day Spelling

Go to pages T14–T15 for **Differentiated Spelling Lists**.

✔ Suffixes

Spelling Words

sickly	graceful	spotless
hardly	spoonful	painless
quickly	darkness	weakness
slowly	shapeless	darkest
carefully	ageless	clearest
wonderful	illness	thoughtful
beautiful	goodness	

Review door, smart, argue
Challenge brilliantly, straightest

Dictation Sentences

1. The **sickly** boy missed school.
2. There were **hardly** any pears left.
3. Let's run **quickly** to the bus.
4. Walk **slowly** on the ice.
5. He wrapped his foot **carefully**.
6. The parade is a **wonderful** event.
7. The poem was **beautiful**.
8. The athlete was very graceful.
9. A spoonful of sugar is sweet.
10. The darkness hid him from view.
11. The loose dress made her look shapeless.
12. The actress looked ageless.
13. An illness can last a long time.
14. His goodness knew no bounds.
15. The spotless couch was new.
16. The haircut was painless.
17. Cookies were her weakness.
18. The darkest blue looks black.
19. The moon is clearest at dusk.
20. The thoughtful mother was thanked.

Review/Challenge Words

1. The old door was built of stone.
2. You seem smart.
3. Don't argue with your dad.
4. I answered the question **brilliantly**.
5. She walked the straightest line.

Words in **bold** are from this week's selections.

Day 1 — Pretest

ASSESS PRIOR KNOWLEDGE

- Model for students how to spell the word *carefully*. Segment the word syllable by syllable, then attach a spelling to each syllable. Point out that *-ly* is a suffix that means "in a certain way" and makes the word an adverb.

- Use the Dictation Sentences. Say the underlined word, read the sentence, and repeat the word. Have students write the words.

- Have students self-correct their tests. Point out that suffixes always end a word.

- Have students cut apart the **Spelling Word Cards BLM** on **Teacher's Resource Book** page 53 and figure out a way to sort them. Have them save the cards for use throughout the week.

Day 2 — Word Sorts and Review

SPIRAL REVIEW

- Review the *r*-controlled vowel sounds in *door, smart,* and *argue*. Have students find words in this week's readings with the same sounds.

WORD SORTS

- Have students take turns sorting the spelling words and explaining how they sorted them. When students have finished, discuss any words that have any unexpected nuances.

- Review the spelling words, pointing out the suffixes. Use the cards on the Spelling Word Cards BLM. Write the key words *possibly, happily, fearless, hurtful,* and *happiness* on the board. Model how to sort words by suffix type. Place one or two cards beneath the correct key words.

ON YOUR OWN — Phonics/Spelling, pages 55–56

Fold back the paper along the dotted line. Use the blanks to write each word as it is read aloud. When you finish the test, unfold the paper. Use the list at the right to correct any spelling mistakes.

1. _____	1. sickly
2. _____	2. hardly
3. _____	3. quickly
4. _____	4. slowly
5. _____	5. carefully
6. _____	6. wonderful
7. _____	7. beautiful
8. _____	8. graceful
9. _____	9. spoonful
10. _____	10. darkness
11. _____	11. shapeless
12. _____	12. ageless
13. _____	13. illness
14. _____	14. goodness
15. _____	15. spotless
16. _____	16. painless
17. _____	17. weakness
18. _____	18. darkest
19. _____	19. clearest
20. _____	20. thoughtful
Review Words 21. _____	21. door
22. _____	22. smart
Challenge Words 23. _____	23. argue
24. _____	24. brilliantly
25. _____	25. straightest

HOMEWORK — Phonics/Spelling page 57

sickly	darkest	beautiful	carefully	clearest
thoughtful	goodness	spotless	darkness	spoonful
illness	wonderful	slowly	shapeless	ageless
hardly	painless	weakness	graceful	quickly

Suffix Power
Write the spelling words that contain the suffixes below.

-ly
1. sickly
2. hardly
3. quickly
4. slowly
5. carefully

-ful
6. carefully
7. wonderful
8. beautiful
9. graceful
10. spoonful
11. thoughtful

-est
12. darkest
13. clearest

-ness
14. darkness
15. illness
16. goodness
17. weakness

-less
18. shapeless
19. ageless
20. spotless
21. painless

Day 3 Word Meanings

CONTEXT CLUES

Have students copy the three sentences below into their Writer's Notebooks. Say the sentences aloud and ask students to fill in the blanks with a spelling word.

1. The white table cloth was _____. (*spotless*)

2. The _____ woman always felt worse after being in a car. (*sickly*)

3. Did you notice that the plant _____ grew in winter? (*hardly*)

Challenge students to come up with other sentences for spelling words, review words, or challenge words.

Have students do a word hunt for the words in the weekly reading or other materials. They should define the spelling word being used in context.

Day 4 Proofread

PROOFREAD AND WRITE

Write these sentences on the board. Have students circle and correct each misspelled word.

1. I heartly had time to give the cleeress directions. (*hardly, clearest*)

2. The agless woman had carfuly applied her make-up. (*ageless, carefully*)

3. Our dance teacher was graysful as she did her beautyful turns. (*graceful, beautiful*)

4. I can qwikly scare my brother in the darkess part of the night. (*quickly, darkest*)

Error Correction Remind students to watch for spelling changes when they add a suffix to a word ending in *y,* such as *happy.* Give examples of words with suffixes after a *y* where the spelling does *not* change, such as *enjoyment.*

Day 5 Assess and Reteach

POSTTEST

Use the Dictation Sentences on page 257E for the Posttest.

If students have difficulty with any words in the lesson, have them place the words on a list called *Spelling Words I Want to Remember* in their Writer's Notebooks. Look for students' use of these words in their writings.

Challenge student partners to find words for each suffix on the list.

EXTEND

Explain that adding a suffix can cause pronunciation changes as well as spelling changes in base words. Review examples such as *create/creation, magic/magician,* and *tense/tension.* Have students identify the final consonant sound in each base word and notice how the sound becomes /sh/ when the suffix is added.

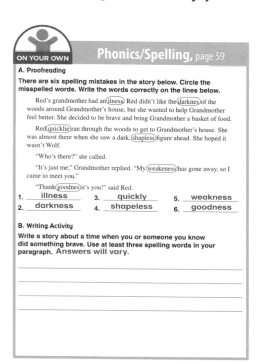

5-Day Grammar

✔ Plurals and Possessives

 Day 1 Introduce the Concept

 Day 2 Teach the Concept

Daily Language Activities

Write the sentences on the board.

DAY 1

We found my sisters dog on my families vacation. it was hiding in some grass. It had to sleep in a box at first (1: sister's; 2: family's; 3: It; 4: first.)

DAY 2

My friends book was a big help. There was a copy in the childrens' section of the library I love reading book's. (1: friend's; 2: children's; 3: library. I; 4: books)

DAY 3

Two boy's came over to see my new fish. They really liked my fishes tank. (1: boys; 2: fish's)

DAY 4

My mothers friend came to visit us. When she saw me she gave me a hug (1: mother's; 2: me,; 3: hug.)

DAY 5

I read a magazine article called Snakes Chere You Up. It was about the writers own snakes. Dr Green's snakes were named Ed and Mo. (1: "Snakes Cheer You Up."; 2: writer's; 3: Dr.)

INTRODUCE PLURALS AND SINGULAR POSSESSIVES

■ Most nouns are made **plural** by adding -s or -es: *horses, boxes, families*.

■ Some irregular nouns have a special spelling in the plural form. Other irregular nouns have the same spelling for both the singular and plural forms: *mouse, mice; deer, deer*.

■ The singular **possessive** form of a noun always ends in an apostrophe and an *s*: *horse's* tail, *box's* shape, *family's* car.

REVIEW PLURALS AND SINGULAR POSSESSIVES

Review with students how to recognize plurals and possessives. Review irregular plural nouns, including how they are spelled.

PLURALS AND PLURAL POSSESSIVES

■ The possessive of a plural noun is formed by adding either an apostrophe or an apostrophe and an *s*.

■ If a plural noun ends in *s*, the possessive is formed by adding an apostrophe only: *students' grades*.

■ If a plural noun does not end in *s*, the possessive is formed by adding an apostrophe and an *s*: *children's shoes*.

See Grammar Transparency 46 for modeling and guided practice.

See Grammar Transparency 47 for modeling and guided practice.

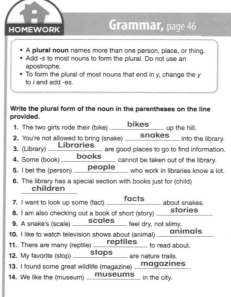

HOMEWORK **Grammar,** page 46

- A **plural noun** names more than one person, place, or thing.
- Add -s to most nouns to form the plural. Do not use an apostrophe.
- To form the plural of most nouns that end in *y*, change the *y* to *i* and add -es.

Write the plural form of the noun in the parentheses on the line provided.

1. The two girls rode their (bike) __bikes__ up the hill.
2. You're not allowed to bring (snake) __snakes__ into the library.
3. (Library) __Libraries__ are good places to go to find information.
4. Some (book) __books__ cannot be taken out of the library.
5. I bet the (person) __people__ who work in libraries know a lot.
6. The library has a special section with books just for (child) __children__
7. I want to look up some (fact) __facts__ about snakes.
8. I am also checking out a book of short (story) __stories__
9. A snake's (scale) __scales__ feel dry, not slimy.
10. I like to watch television shows about (animal) __animals__
11. There are many (reptile) __reptiles__ to read about.
12. My favorite (stop) __stops__ are nature trails.
13. I found some great wildlife (magazine) __magazines__
14. We like the (museum) __museums__ in the city.

ON YOUR OWN **Grammar,** page 47

- A **plural noun** names more than one person, place, or thing.
- Add **-s** to most nouns to form the plural. Do not use an apostrophe.
- A **possessive noun** shows who or what owns or has something.
- Add an apostrophe (') and **-s** to a singular noun to make it possessive.

Write a plural noun or a possessive noun to complete each sentence. Use the singular nouns in the box to help you.

| box | picture | snake | rattle | skin | prairie | book |

1. She carried the noisy __rattles__ from several snakes.
2. When he saw the rattlesnake, he was scared by the __rattle's__ sound.
3. I want to find some __books__ about animals in the library.
4. This book has words but no __pictures__
5. This __book's__ photographs are very interesting.
6. Snakes shed their __skins__ when they grow.
7. Will you help me open those __boxes__ to see what's inside?
8. A __snake's__ bite may or may not contain poison.
9. Oh no, that __box's__ lid is moving!
10. Some types of snakes live in fields and __prairies__

Day 3 — Review and Practice

REVIEW PLURALS AND PLURAL POSSESSIVES

Review how to identify plural and possessive noun forms.

MECHANICS AND USAGE: PUNCTUATION IN LETTERS

- Begin the abbreviation for a person's title, such as *Dr., Mr.,* or *Ms.,* with a capital letter.

- Use a period after an abbreviation in a person's title.

- Use a comma between the day of the month and the year.

- Do not place a period after the two-letter state abbreviation in a United States address.

- Use a comma in the salutation of a friendly letter and a colon in the salutation of a business letter. Use a comma in the closing of a letter.

 See Grammar Transparency 48 for modeling and guided practice.

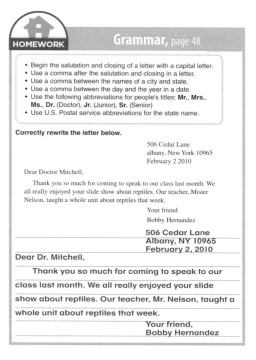

HOMEWORK — **Grammar,** page 48

- Begin the salutation and closing of a letter with a capital letter.
- Use a comma after the salutation and closing in a letter.
- Use a comma between the names of a city and state.
- Use a comma between the day and the year in a date.
- Use the following abbreviations for people's titles: **Mr., Mrs., Ms., Dr.** (Doctor), **Jr.** (Junior), **Sr.** (Senior)
- Use U.S. Postal service abbreviations for the state name.

Correctly rewrite the letter below.

506 Cedar Lane
albany, New York 10965
February 2 2010

Dear Doctor Mitchell,

Thank you so much for coming to speak to our class last month. We all really enjoyed your slide show about reptiles. Our teacher, Mister Nelson, taught a whole unit about reptiles that week.

Your friend
Bobby Hernandez

**506 Cedar Lane
Albany, NY 10965
February 2, 2010**

Dear Dr. Mitchell,

Thank you so much for coming to speak to our class last month. We all really enjoyed your slide show about reptiles. Our teacher, Mr. Nelson, taught a whole unit about reptiles that week.

**Your friend,
Bobby Hernandez**

Day 4 — Review and Proofread

REVIEW PLURAL AND PLURAL POSSESSIVE NOUNS

Have students explain the differences among the *s* endings for possessives and plurals. Review letter punctuation.

PROOFREAD

Have students correct errors in the following letter. First review the conventions of letter form as needed.

1. July 17 2007 (July 17,)

2. Ms Maria Gonzalez (Ms.)

   500 W. Sixth Street

   Los Angeles, CA. 90014
   (CA 90014)

3. Dear Ms. Gonzalez:
   Thank you for the map's you gave to our school. (maps)

4. Sincerely. (,)
   Janice Robeson

 See Grammar Transparency 49 for modeling and guided practice.

ON YOUR OWN — **Grammar,** page 49

- A **plural noun** names more than one person, place, or thing.
- A **possessive noun** shows who or what owns or has something.

Correctly rewrite the letter below.

December 9, 2010

Ms Margaret Wilson
Atlanta Public library
101 Reading Road
Atlanta, GA 33560

Dear ms Wilson:

I am writing to complain about the poor service in the childrens section of your library. Last saturday, I wanted to check out the North American Snake Guide by Doctor david Howard. I waited for more than 30 minute's before anyone came to help me. No ones should have to wait that long.

Yours truly,
Kevin Andrews, Junior

December 9, 2010

**Ms. Margaret Wilson
Atlanta Public Library
101 Reading Road
Atlanta, GA 33560**

Dear Ms. Wilson:

I am writing to complain about the poor service in the children's section of your library. Last Saturday, I wanted to check out the North American Snake Guide by Dr. David Howard. I waited for more than 30 minutes before anyone came to help me. No one should have to wait that long.

**Yours truly,
Kevin Andrews, Jr.**

Day 5 — Assess and Reteach

ASSESS

Use the Daily Language Activity and **Grammar Practice Book** page 50 for assessment.

RETEACH

Use Grammar Practice Book page 50 and selected pages from the **Grammar and Writing Handbook** for additional reteaching. Remind students that it is important to use plurals and possessives correctly as they speak and write.

Check students' writing for use of the skill and listen for it in their speaking. Assign Grammar Revision Assignments in their Writer's Notebooks as needed.

See Grammar Transparency 50 for modeling and guided practice.

HOMEWORK — **Grammar,** page 50

A. Decide whether each underlined word is a plural noun or a possessive noun. Then write *plural* or *possessive* on the line provided.

1. This snake's bite is not poisonous. __possessive__
2. Sidewinders leave J-shaped tracks in the sand. __plural__
3. The teacher's science lesson was very interesting. __possessive__
4. Some reptiles change color to match their surroundings. __plural__
5. We went to see the museum's display. __possessive__
6. I decided to write down some notes. __plural__
7. The facts are very important. __plural__
8. That reptile's skin is shiny. __possessive__

B. Choose the plural or possessive noun that best completes each sentence. Write it on the line provided.

9. (Sharks, Shark's) kill fewer people than snakes do. __Sharks__
10. She checked out books from two (libraries, librarie's). __libraries__
11. The (farmers, farmer's) crops were harmed by the insects. __farmer's__
12. The (colors, color's) of the snakeskin were red, black, and gold. __colors__
13. The (magazines, magazine's) articles were very helpful. __magazine's__
14. Don't touch those (animals, animals') skeletons! __animals'__
15. Several (people, people's) stopped by the exhibit. __people__

Daily Planner

DAY 1	• Prepare to Read • Academic Language • Vocabulary (Preteach)
DAY 2	• Comprehension • Leveled Reader Lesson 1
DAY 3	• Phonics/Decoding • Leveled Reader Lesson 2
DAY 4	• Phonics/Decoding • Vocabulary (Review) • Leveled Reader Lesson 3
DAY 5	• High-Frequency Words • Fluency • Self-Selected Reading

Interactive Student Book

If you wish to preteach the main selection, use StudentWorks Plus for:

• Vocabulary Preteaching
• Word-by-Word Highlighting
• Think Aloud Prompts

Academic Language

Academic words include those harder Tier 2 words that appear in much of students' reading materials as well as the language of instruction. The words chosen for instruction were selected from the **Living Word Vocabulary** list and Avril Coxhead's list of **High-Incidence Academic Words**.

Approaching Level

Prepare to Read

Objective   Preview *Mystic Horse*
Materials   • **StudentWorks Plus**   • self-stick notes

PREVIEW THE MAIN SELECTION

- Have students preview *Mystic Horse* using **StudentWorks Plus**. This version of the Student Book contains oral summaries in multiple languages, story recording, word-by-word highlighting, Think Aloud prompts, and comprehension-monitoring questions.

- Remind students that listening carefully to and following along with the word-by-word reading will help them prepare for the reading of the selection with the class. Ask students to place self-stick notes on any challenging words or places that confuse them. Discuss the confusing items with students prior to the reading of the selection with the rest of the class.

- Ask students to write three or four sentences in their Writer's Notebooks describing their favorite part of the legend.

Academic Language

Objective   Teach academic language
Materials   • none

PRETEACH LANGUAGE OF INSTRUCTION

Tell students that there are many important lesson words you will be using this week. You want them to become familiar with these words *before* the lessons. These words also appear in the directions of the tests they will be taking this year.

Preteach the following academic words: *legend, analyze, story structure, sequence, cause and effect, homophones, suffixes,* and *nonfiction.*

- Define each word using student-friendly language. Tell students that *homophones* are words that sound the same but have different spellings and meanings, such as *soars* and *sores*. Divide the word into its two parts: *homo* and *phones*. Explain that the Greek root *homo* means "same" and the Greek root *phone* means *sound*. Write *same sounds* over the word parts to help students.

- Relate each word to known words. Connect, for example, *sequence* to *time order, cause and effect* to *what happens* and *why,* and *suffixes* to *word endings*.

- Highlight these words when used throughout the week, and reinforce their meanings.

Approaching Level

Phonics/Decoding

Objective Decode words with suffixes

Materials
- **Approaching Reproducible,** p. 82
- **Sound-Spelling WorkBoards** • **Sound-Spelling Cards**
- **Word-Building Cards**

Tier 2

Sound-Spelling WorkBoard

PHONICS MAINTENANCE

- Distribute a **WorkBoard** to each student. Say a sound previously taught, such as /är/, /ôr/, and digraphs. Have students find the **Sound-Spelling Card** on the board for each sound.

- Review the spellings for words with these sounds by providing a sample word containing each spelling. Model how to segment the word and write the spelling for each sound, as needed. In addition, review prefixes and suffixes by writing sample words on the board such as *rewrite, unchanged, forceful,* and *heartless.* Have students identify the prefixes and suffixes and tell what each word means.

- Dictate the following words for students to spell: *recharge, cheerful, thankful, shortest, shop, chart, restart.* Write each word on the board, and have students self-correct their work.

RETEACH SKILL

Suffixes Display the **Word-Building Cards** for the suffixes *-ful, -less, -al, -ion, -able,* and *-ible.* Write *pain* on the board. Say: *If the doctor gives you a shot and it causes you pain, we say the shot is _____.* Place the card *ful* next to *pain,* and have students say *painful.* Then say: *If getting the shot does not cause you pain, we say it is _____.* Place the card *less* next to *pain,* and have students say *painless.* Use a similar process to form the words *hopeful/hopeless* and *careful/careless.*

- Write the words below on the board. Model how to decode the first word in each row, then guide students as they decode the remaining words. For these multisyllabic words, divide the words into syllables using the syllable-scoop technique to help students read one syllable at a time.

- When completed, point to the words in random order for students to chorally read. Repeat several times.

fearful	helpful	joyful	thankful	restful	mouthful
fearless	helpless	joyless	thankless	restless	spotless
medical	physical	refusal	rehearsal	critical	tropical
division	tension	emotion	devotion	vacation	relation
divisible	flexible	sensible	reliable	movable	allowable

Approaching Reproducible, page 82

The suffixes **-y, -ly, -ful, -less,** and **-ness** can be added to the end of a root or base word to change its meaning.

If a word ends in **y,** change the **y** to **i** before adding the suffix.

penny - y + i + less = penniless

If a one-syllable word has a single vowel and ends in a single consonant, double the consonant before adding a suffix that begins with a vowel or with y.

sun + n + y = sunny

A. Complete each word problem to write a word with a suffix.

1. cheery - y + i + ly = **cheerily**
2. care + ful = **careful**
3. thought + less = **thoughtless**
4. kind + ness = **kindness**
5. fur + r + y = **furry**

B. Choose the word from the box that best completes each sentence.

thoughtless	angry	quickly	shyness	beautiful

6. Jonah felt **angry** when he saw people littering the park.
7. He wished people would not be so **thoughtless**
8. He made signs that said "Clean up! Keep our park **beautiful**
9. Jonah even forgot his **shyness** and spoke at the town meeting.
10. Thanks to Jonah, the park **quickly** became cleaner.

Approaching Level

Vocabulary

Objective Preteach selection vocabulary

Materials
- **Visual Vocabulary Resources**
- **Approaching Reproducible,** p. 83
- **Vocabulary Cards**

PRETEACH KEY VOCABULARY

Tier 2

Introduce the Words Display the **Visual Vocabulary Resources** to preteach the key selection words *sores, loosened, mysterious, amazement, midst,* and *responsibility*. Use the following routine, which appears in detail on the cards.

- Define the word in English, and provide the example given.
- Define the word in Spanish, if appropriate, and indicate if the word is a cognate.
- Display the picture, and explain how it illustrates or demonstrates the word.
- Engage students in structured partner-talk about the image, using the key word.
- Ask students to say the word chorally three times.
- Point out any known sound-spellings or focus on a key aspect of phonemic awareness related to the word.
- You may wish also to distribute copies of the Vocabulary Glossary in the **ELL Resource Book**.

REVIEW PREVIOUSLY TAUGHT VOCABULARY

Display the **Vocabulary Cards** from the previous four weeks. Say the meanings of each word, one by one, and have students identify them. Then point to words in random order for students to provide definitions and related words they know.

Context Clues Remind students that context clues are clues within a text that help a reader figure out what a word means. Have students write a context-rich sentence for each vocabulary word. For example, *The scientists were excited to visit the* habitat *that was home to so many rare plants and animals.*

Approaching Reproducible, page 83

| mysterious | responsibility | midst |
| loosened | amazement | sores |

A. Write each vocabulary word next to its definition.

1. in the middle	midst
2. painful spots on the body	sores
3. made something less tight	loosened
4. hard to explain or understand	mysterious
5. having to take care of something	responsibility
6. a feeling of being very surprised	amazement

B. Write a sentence using one of the vocabulary words. Answers will vary.

7. Sample answer: It's my responsibility to take our dog for a walk in the morning.

Approaching Level

Vocabulary

Objectives Review vocabulary and high-frequency words
Materials • **Vocabulary Cards** • **High-Frequency Word Cards**

✔ REVIEW VOCABULARY

Review Words Display the **Vocabulary Cards** for *sores, loosened, mysterious, amazement, midst,* and *responsibility*. Point to each word, read it aloud, and have students chorally repeat.

Then provide the following Yes/No questions. Ask students to answer each question, justifying their answer. Allow other students to respond. Use the discussions to determine each student's depth of word knowledge.

- Would you be concerned about having *sores* on your feet?

- If you *loosened* the lid of a jar, would it be easier to open?

- Is a *mysterious* event easy to understand?

- If you feel *amazement,* are you bored?

- If you were in the *midst* of a dangerous situation, would you be involved in it?

- Does a doctor have a lot of *responsibility*?

HIGH-FREQUENCY WORDS

Top 250 Words The ability to read accurately and effortlessly the most frequently used words in written English will help students develop reading fluency. Display **High-Frequency Word Cards** 41–80. Then do the following:

- Display one card at a time, and ask students chorally to state each word.

- Have students spell each word aloud.

- Ask students to write each word in their Writer's Notebooks as they state each letter aloud. Then have them read the word again.

- When completed, quickly flip through the word card set as students chorally read the words.

- Provide opportunities for students to use the words in speaking and writing. For example, provide sentence starters, such as *I hate to <u>clean</u> because* _____, for oral and written practice. Or point to a word card and ask a question, such as *What is the opposite of different?*

- Continue the routine throughout the week.

ELL

Practice Vocabulary Pair students of different proficiency. Orally model the vocabulary in sentences. For example: *I have the responsibility of keeping my room clean.* On the board, provide sentence frames for pairs to copy and complete using the vocabulary. For example: *We watched the circus performers in* _____. (amazement)

Word Webs

Have students create word webs in their Writer's Notebooks for each vocabulary word. Write the related words provided, and ask students to add other words, phrases, and illustrations.

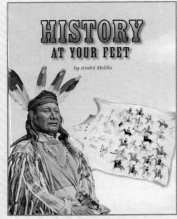

Student Book

Approaching Level

Comprehension

Objective Reteach summarize and sequence

Materials • **Student Book:** "History at Your Feet"

✓ RETEACH STRATEGY: ANALYZE STORY STRUCTURE

Tier 2

- **Define** Tell students that story structure refers to the way an author organizes a plot. Analyzing the story structure by paying close attention to details about the setting, characters, and plot will help a reader to better understand a story.

- **Relate to Real Life** Ask students to imagine that they are writing a biography of someone they admire. Discuss the different ways they could organize the book. What characters, events, and locations would they include? Point out that an author answers these questions when deciding on a story structure.

- **Set Purposes** Remind students that good readers stop and analyze the story's structure as they read. If the reader understands how the story is organized, he or she can proceed. If not, he or she must go back and reread.

✓ RETEACH SKILL: SEQUENCE

- **Define** Tell students that sequence means the order in which events happen. Sequence is also called chronological order or time order. Writers may use clue words such as *first, next, after, while, then,* and *finally* to help readers follow the sequence of events.

- **Relate to Real Life** Cut up the panels of a comic strip that shows a sequence of events, and display the panels out of order. Have a student help you arrange the panels in the correct sequence, or time order.

- **Set Purposes** Remind students that good readers look for clue words to help them follow the sequence of events. Understanding the sequence of events will help them understand what happens in a story and why it happens. It will also help them summarize.

- **Apply** Work with students to identify the sequence of events in "History at Your Feet." Then use the sequence of events to help students summarize the story. Include signal words, such as *first, then, next,* and *after* in your summary. Have students restate the summary in their own words. Students will apply this strategy and skill to a simpler text as they read *Caddo Tales*.

Corrective Feedback

On the board, write the words *First, Next, Then,* and *Finally* in a column, leaving room to write a sentence after each word. Read the first four paragraphs with students. Ask: *What happens first in the story?* Write the event after the word *First.* Then ask what happens next, and record it after *Next.* Continue in this way to complete the chart. Remind students that sequence words such as *first, next, then,* and *finally* help tell the sequence, or order, of events.

Approaching Level

Leveled Reader Lesson 1

Objective   Read to apply skills and strategies

Materials   • **Leveled Reader:** *Caddo Legends*

Leveled Reader

BEFORE READING

Preview and Predict   Have students read the title and preview *Caddo Legends*. Ask students to make predictions about the sequence of events in each legend. Students should note any questions they have before they read.

 Review Vocabulary Words   Have students read the vocabulary words on the inside front cover. Briefly define each and ask students to state related words they have learned.

Set a Purpose for Reading   *Let's read to find out the sequence of events in these legends.*

DURING READING

 **STRATEGY**

ANALYZE STORY STRUCTURE

Remind students that story structure includes the way an author organizes the plot, characters, and setting of a story.

SKILL

SEQUENCE

Remind students to think about the sequence, or time order, of story events as they read. Read the first legend with students. Have students identify events to write in the Sequence Chart.

As you read, help students decode unknown words. In addition, ask open-ended questions to facilitate rich discussion, such as *What is the author telling us about Native American legends? What do these legends reveal about the Caddo people?* Build on students' responses to help them develop a deeper understanding of the text.

After every two pages have students summarize the sequence of events to check their understanding. If they struggle, help students reread the difficult passages and model identifying the sequence.

AFTER READING

Help students compare and contrast the two legends. Have students describe how the actions of the Great Spirit and the Coyote are alike and different. Ask students to compare and contrast how the Caddo people responded to the different situations. Discuss what these legends say about the Caddo.

Leveled Reader

Approaching Level

Leveled Reader Lesson 2

Objective — Reread to apply skills and strategies and develop fluency

Materials
- **Leveled Reader:** *Caddo Legends*
- **Approaching Reproducible,** p. 86

BEFORE READING

 Review the Strategy and Skill Review students' completed Sequence Charts from the first read. Remind students that the sequence of events is the time order in which important events happen. A summary includes all the important events of the story in correct sequence.

Review Vocabulary Words Have students search the book for each vocabulary word. Ask students to read aloud the sentence containing the word and state the word's definition or provide related words. Point out any homophones.

Set a Purpose for Reading *Let's reread to check our understanding of the sequence of events in these legends and to work on our reading fluency.*

DURING READING

Reread *Caddo Legends* with students. Have them read silently two pages at a time, or read aloud to a partner. Stop and have students summarize before they read the next two pages. Model oral summaries as needed.

AFTER READING

Check Comprehension Have partners complete the Comprehension Check on page 16. Review students' answers. Help students find evidence for their answers in the text.

MODEL FLUENCY

Model reading the fluency passage on **Approaching Reproducible** page 86. Tell students to pay close attention to your expression and phrasing as you read. Then read one sentence at a time, and have students echo-read the sentences, copying your expression and phrasing.

During independent reading time, have students work with a partner using the fluency passage. One student reads aloud while the other repeats each sentence back. If students need additional support, have them listen to the "practice speed" version of the passage on the **Fluency Solutions Audio CD**.

Approaching Level

Leveled Reader Lesson 3

Objective Build fluency

Materials
- **Leveled Reader:** *Caddo Legends*
- **Approaching Reproducible,** p. 86

✔ FOCUS ON FLUENCY

Timed Reading Tell students that they will be doing a final timed reading of the fluency passage on **Approaching Reproducible** page 86 that they have been practicing. With each student, follow these directions:

- Place the passage facedown.
- When you say "Go," the student begins reading the passage aloud.
- When you say "Stop," the student stops reading the passage.

As they read, note words students mispronounce and their overall expression and phrasing. Stop after one minute. Help students record and graph the number of words they read correctly.

REREAD PREVIOUSLY READ BOOKS

- Distribute copies of the past six **Leveled Readers**. Have students select two to reread. Tell students that rereading these books will help them develop their skills. The more times they read the same words, the quicker they will learn these words. This will make the reading of other books easier.

- Circulate and listen in as students read. Stop students periodically and ask them how they are figuring out difficult words and how they are monitoring their comprehension. Note students who need additional work with specific decoding or comprehension skills.

- Encourage students to read other previously read Leveled Readers during independent reading time or for homework.

Meet Grade-Level Expectations

As an alternative to this day's lesson, guide students through a reading of the On Level Leveled Reader. See page 257U. Since both books contain the same vocabulary, phonics, and comprehension skills, the scaffolding you provided will help most students gain access to this more challenging text.

Book Talk

Bringing Groups Together Students will work with peers of various language and reading abilities to discuss this week's Leveled Readers. Refer to page 158 in the **Teacher's Resource Book** for more about how to conduct a Book Talk.

Student Book

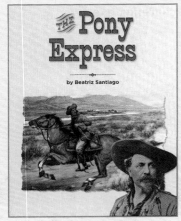

Student Book

Approaching Level

Fluency

Objectives Reread selections to develop fluency; develop speaking skills
Materials • **Student Book:** *Mystic Horse*, "The Pony Express"

✓ REREAD FOR FLUENCY

- Have students reread a portion of *Mystic Horse*. Suggest that they focus on two to four of their favorite pages from the selection. Work with students to read the pages with the appropriate expression and phrasing.

- Provide time for students to read their sections of text to you. Comment on their expression and phrasing, and provide corrective feedback by modeling proper fluency.

DEVELOP SPEAKING/LISTENING SKILLS

- Have a small group of students work together to prepare an oral summary of "The Pony Express."

- Assign each student to read one or two paragraphs of the selection. Have the student identify the main idea of each paragraph and one or two important details.

- Provide time for students to practice orally presenting their paragraph summaries in sequence to the group. Ask listeners to suggest ways for the speaker to improve the volume, phrasing, and expression of the oral presentation.

- Have each group present their oral summaries of "The Pony Express" in correct sequence for the class.

Decodable Text

Use the decodable stories in the **Teacher's Resource Book** to help students build fluency with basic decoding patterns.

Approaching Level

Self-Selected Reading

Objectives Read independently to identify sequence of events and summarize

Materials   • **Leveled Classroom Library**   • other legends

APPLY SKILLS AND STRATEGIES TO INDEPENDENT READING

- **Read Independently** For sustained silent reading, have students choose a legend or read one of the biographies from the **Leveled Classroom Library**. (See the **Theme Bibliography** on pages T8–T9 for book suggestions.) Remind students that the sequence of events is the time order in which events happen in a story. Have students read their books and identify, sequence, and record the most important events on a Sequence Chart.

- **Show Evidence of Reading** While reading, students may generate a reading log or journal. After reading, ask students to use their Sequence Chart to write or orally state a summary of the story, maintaining meaning and logical order. Provide time for students to share their summaries and comments on the book while participating in Book Talks. Ask: *Did any of the events in this story surprise you? Why or why not?*

Approaching

Leveled Classroom Library
See Leveled Classroom
Library lessons on pages T2–T7.

Daily Planner

DAY 1	• Vocabulary • Phonics
DAY 2	• Leveled Reader Lesson 1
DAY 3	• Leveled Reader Lesson 2
DAY 4	• Fluency
DAY 5	• Self-Selected Reading

ELL

Practice Vocabulary Pair ELL students with native speakers. On the board, provide sentence frames for pairs to copy and complete using the vocabulary and additional words when necessary. For example: *As the captain of the math team, it is my _____ to _____.* (responsibility; organize team practices)

On Level

Vocabulary

Objective Review vocabulary
Materials • **Vocabulary Cards**

REVIEW PREVIOUSLY TAUGHT WORDS

Review the Words Display the **Vocabulary Cards** *sores, loosened, mysterious, amazement, midst,* and *responsibility*. Point to each word, read it aloud, and have students chorally repeat.

Then ask the following questions. Have students answer each question and justify their answers. Allow other students to respond. Use the discussions to determine students' depth of knowledge.

- Are *sores* painful or enjoyable?
- If you *loosened* a belt, would you probably feel more comfortable or less comfortable?
- Is a *mysterious* sound more likely to be ordinary or spooky?
- When you feel *amazement*, do you look sad or surprised?
- If you are in the *midst* of a crowd, are you on the outside or in the middle?
- Is a *responsibility* a thing you must do or a thing you wish you could do?

Phonics/Word Study

Objective Decode multisyllabic words with suffixes
Materials • **Word-Building Cards**

RETEACH SKILL

- **Suffixes** Display the **Word-Building Cards** *-ful, -less, -ion, -ible, -able,* and *-al*. Review how to use the suffixes to form words such as *careful, careless, reaction, responsible, avoidable,* and *critical*.
- Write the words below on the board. If necessary, divide the words into syllables using the syllable-scoop technique to help students read one syllable at a time. When completed, point to the words in random order for students to chorally read.

helpful	hopeful	hopeless	shameless	clinical
disposal	creation	reliable	drinkable	incredible
dismissal	national	believable	responsible	wonderful

- **Spelling** Dictate the following words for students to spell: *playful, painless, subtraction, impossible, laughable,* and *formal*. Model how to segment words, such as spelling a word syllable by syllable.

On Level

Fluency

Objectives Reread selections to develop fluency; develop speaking skills

Materials • **Student Book:** *Mystic Horse,* "The Pony Express"

✔ REREAD FOR FLUENCY

- Have students reread *Mystic Horse.* Work with students to read with the appropriate phrasing and expression. Model as needed.

- Provide time for students to read a section of text to you. Comment on their phrasing and expression, and provide corrective feedback.

DEVELOP SPEAKING/LISTENING SKILLS

- Have pairs of students work together to prepare an oral summary of "The Pony Express" to be delivered like a news report.

- Tell each student to read half of the selection. Have them identify two important details in each paragraph and infer the main idea.

- Provide time for students to practice orally presenting their summaries in sequence to their partner. Ask the listener to suggest ways for the speaker to improve their phrasing and expression. Tell students to speak clearly and in a serious tone, like a news reporter, and to use gestures to enhance meaning. They should modulate their voices to avoid sounding flat.

- Have each pair present their oral summaries to the class.

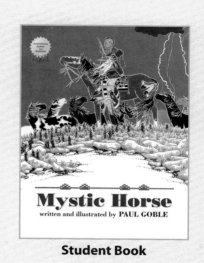

Student Book

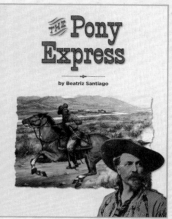

Student Book

Self-Selected Reading

Objective Read independently to sequence and summarize the plot's main events

Materials • **Leveled Classroom Library** • other legends

APPLY SKILLS AND STRATEGIES TO INDEPENDENT READING

- **Read Independently** Have students choose a legend for sustained silent reading. (See the **Theme Bibliography** on pages T8–T9 for book suggestions.) Have students sequence the plot's main events on a Sequence Chart.

- **Show Evidence of Reading** While reading, students may generate a reading log or journal. After reading, ask students to use their Sequence Charts to write a summary of the story, maintaining meaning and logical order. Provide time for students to share their summaries and reactions while participating in Book Talks. Ask: *Did any of the events in this story surprise you? Would you recommend this book? Why or why not?*

On Level

Leveled Classroom Library
See Leveled Classroom
Library lessons on pages T2–T7.

Leveled Reader

On Level

Leveled Reader Lesson 1

Objective Read to apply strategies and skills

Materials • **Leveled Reader:** *Quileute Legends*

BEFORE READING

Preview and Predict Have students read the title and preview the book by reading the legend titles and looking at the illustrations. Ask students to predict what these legends might show them about the Quileute people and their experiences.

 Review Vocabulary Words Have students read the vocabulary words on the inside front cover. Ask students to state related words they have learned. Review definitions, as needed.

Set a Purpose for Reading *Let's read to find out the sequence of events that occurs in each legend.*

DURING READING

 **STRATEGY**
ANALYZE STORY STRUCTURE

Remind students that story structure is the way an author organizes the characters, setting, and plot of a story.

SKILL
SEQUENCE

Remind students that the sequence of events in a story is the order in which events occur. Time-order signal words such as *first, then, next, later*, and *after* offer clues to the sequence of events.

Read the Introduction and "The Creation of the Quileute" with students. Ask open-ended questions to facilitate rich discussion, such as *What is the author trying to show you about the beliefs of the Quileute people?* Build on students' responses to help them develop a deeper understanding of the text. Have students fill in a Sequence Chart for this legend, then continue reading.

Homophones As they read, have students point out this week's new vocabulary words and any homophones they find in the text.

AFTER READING

Ask students to discuss what they learned about the Quileute people by reading their legends. What values, or moral qualities, were most important to them?

On Level

Leveled Reader Lesson 2

Objective   Reread to apply skills and strategies and develop fluency

Materials
- **Leveled Reader:** *Quileute Legends*
- **Practice Book**, p. 86

Leveled Reader

BEFORE READING

✔ **Review the Strategy and Skill**   Review students' completed Sequence Charts from the first read. Remind students that the sequence is the order in which events take place in a story.

A summary includes the most important events of a story in correct sequence. If students' summaries are incomplete, provide a model summary or use a student summary and revise it as a group. Have students copy the revised summary in their Writer's Notebooks.

Set a Purpose for Reading   *Let's reread to check our understanding of the sequence of events in these legends and to work on our reading fluency.*

DURING READING

Reread *Quileute Legends* with students. Have them read silently two pages at a time, or read aloud to a partner. Stop and have students summarize before they read the next two pages. Model oral summaries, as needed.

AFTER READING

Check Comprehension   Have partners complete the Comprehension Check on page 20. Review students' answers. Help students find evidence for their answers in the text.

MODEL FLUENCY

Model reading the fluency passage on **Practice Book** page 86. Tell students to pay close attention to your expression and phrasing as you read. Then read one sentence at a time, and have students echo-read the sentences, copying your expression and phrasing.

During independent reading time, have students work with a partner using the fluency passage. One student reads aloud while the other repeats each sentence back. If students need additional support, have them listen to the "practice speed" version of the passage on the **Fluency Solutions Audio CD**.

Book Talk

Bringing Groups Together Students will work with peers of various language and reading abilities to discuss this week's Leveled Readers. Refer to page 158 in the **Teacher's Resource Book** for more about how to conduct a Book Talk.

Practice Book, page 86

As I read, I will pay attention to my expression and phrasing.

	But there came a time when many days of heavy rain
11	made the Quillayute River overflow. The houses washed
19	away. Then the Quileute moved to the prairies.
27	Not long after, the weather grew cold. The rain turned
37	into hail and sleet. The fishermen could not break through
47	the ice in the rivers to go fishing. Falling hailstones were
58	so big that people were killed. The people grew afraid to
69	go outside. They were running out of food. Men, women,
79	and children were becoming weak and sick.
86	At this time, the Great Chief of the Quileute called a
97	meeting of all the people in the tribe. He stood before them
109	in a patchwork shawl made up of buffalo skins stitched
119	together. The people begged the chief to do something. The
129	**responsibility** of watching over his people weighed heavily
137	upon him. "We will ask the Great Spirit who soars above
148	Earth for help," said the chief. 154

Comprehension Check
1. What were the events that caused the Great Chief of the Quileute to call a meeting? Name the events in the order in which they occurred. **Sequence** There was a flood, and a freeze, and people started to run out of food.
2. What is the purpose of a legend such as this? **Author's Purpose** Legends teach the history of a people. This one teaches the history of the Quileute people.

	Words Read	−	Number of Errors	=	Words Correct Score
First Read		−		=	
Second Read		−		=	

Daily Planner

DAY 1	• Leveled Reader Lesson 1
DAY 2	• Leveled Reader Lesson 2
DAY 3	• Phonics
DAY 4	• Vocabulary • Fluency
DAY 5	• Self-Selected Reading

ELL

Self-Monitor Vocabulary
Have student pairs of different proficiency identify and define unfamiliar words from the main selection using a dictionary. Challenge students to use the new words in sentences. Monitor students as they complete the activity.

Beyond Level

Phonics/Word Study

Objective Decode multisyllabic words with suffixes
Materials • none

EXTEND/ACCELERATE

■ **Read Multisyllabic Words with Suffixes** Write the words below on the board. Challenge students to read the words, using known word parts. When completed, point to the words in random order for students to chorally read.

forgetful	forgetfulness	regretful	regretfully
incapable	gracefully	motionless	undeniable
residual	residually	substantial	substantially
understandably	reprehensible	divisible	evaporation

■ **Define Words** Ask students to use their knowledge of word parts to figure out the meanings of the above words. Then have partners find the words in a dictionary and confirm or revise the meanings. Challenge students to use these words in this week's writing assignments.

■ **Spell Words with Suffixes** Dictate the following words for students to spell: *wonderfully, needlessly, carelessness, political, unstoppable, international, indivisible*. Write the words for students to self-correct.

Vocabulary

Objectives Review sequence; write a story
Materials • none

ENRICH VOCABULARY

■ **Review Sequence** Remind students that the author of *Mystic Horse* told the events of the story in sequence, or chronological order. He used clue words such as *when, while, then, after that, after some days had passed, one day, while, at that very instant*, and *from now on* to help readers follow the sequence of events.

■ **Author Study** Have students read other books by Paul Goble. They should look for themes that recur in his works and compare and contrast the settings, characters, and plots. Then have students write their own story or legend and explain how they have incorporated elements they found in Goble's work. Remind students to use clue words to make the sequence of events clear and to use as many vocabulary words as they can.

Gifted & Talented

Beyond Level

Fluency

Objectives Reread selections to develop fluency; develop speaking skills
Materials • **Student Book:** *Mystic Horse,* "The Pony Express"

REREAD FOR FLUENCY

- Have students reread *Mystic Horse.* Work with students to read the selection with the appropriate expression and phrasing.

- Provide time for students to read a section of text to you. Comment on their expression and phrasing and provide feedback.

DEVELOP SPEAKING/LISTENING SKILLS

- Have students prepare an oral summary of "The Pony Express." They can role-play a Pony Express rider as they give the summary.

- Have students reread the selection. Ask them to determine the main idea and two important details in each paragraph.

- Provide time for students to practice orally presenting their summaries to a partner. Ask the partner to suggest ways for the speaker to improve the volume, phrasing, and pacing of the oral presentation. Students should try to use gestures and modulate their voices in ways that a Pony Express rider might have.

Self-Selected Reading

Objective Read independently to identify the sequence of events and summarize
Materials • **Leveled Classroom Library** • other legends

APPLY SKILLS AND STRATEGIES TO INDEPENDENT READING

- **Read Independently** Have students choose a legend for sustained silent reading. (See the **Theme Bibliography** on pages T8–T9 for book suggestions.) Have students read their books and make a list sequencing the events in the story.

- **Show Evidence of Reading** While reading, students may generate a reading log or journal. After reading, ask students to use their sequence of events list to write a summary of the story, maintaining meaning and logical order. Provide time for students to share their summaries while participating in Book Talks. Ask: *Did any of the events in this story surprise you? Why or why not? Why do readers tend to like surprises?*

- **Evaluate** Have students compare *Mystic Horse* to another legend they know. Have them create a list of similarities and differences, including details related to setting, plot, and characters. Students should share their completed lists with a partner.

Student Book

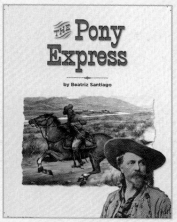

Student Book

Beyond

Leveled Classroom Library
See Leveled Classroom
Library lessons on pages T2–T7.

Leveled Reader

Beyond Level

 ## Leveled Reader Lesson 1

Objective   Read to apply strategies and skills
Materials   • **Leveled Reader:** *Navajo Legends*

BEFORE READING

Preview and Predict Have students preview the book by reading the book title and legend titles and by looking at the illustrations. Ask students to predict what this book is about and the types of events that will occur in the legends.

 Review Vocabulary Words Have students read the vocabulary words on the inside front cover. Ask students to state each definition and any related words they have learned.

Set a Purpose for Reading *Let's read to find out the sequence of events in these legends.*

DURING READING

 **STRATEGY**
ANALYZE STORY STRUCTURE

Remind students that to analyze a story's structure, they should look at how the plot, characters, and setting are interconnected.

SKILL
SEQUENCE

Tell students to define the term *sequence*. If necessary, remind them that the sequence is the order in which events take place in a story.

Read the book with students. Ask open-ended questions to facilitate rich discussion, such as *What beliefs and customs of the Navajo did you find most interesting? Why?* Build on students' responses to help them develop a deeper understanding of the text. Have students fill in Sequence Charts independently as they read.

AFTER READING

Develop Questions Have students discuss what they learned about the customs and values of the Navajo people by reading these legends. Prompt them to develop questions about the Navajo that they would like to research on the Internet during independent time.

Analyze Discuss with students the major events in the plot of *Mystic Horse.* Ask students to imagine that one event happened differently. Ask: *What if the horse did not die? How would that change the story?* Have students write a scene where they change a major plot conflict in *Mystic Horse* and show how that affects the story.

Gifted Talented

Beyond Level

Leveled Reader Lesson 2

Objectives Reread to apply skills and strategies and develop fluency

Materials
- **Leveled Reader:** *Navajo Legends*
- **Beyond Reproducible,** p. 86

Leveled Reader

BEFORE READING

✓ **Review the Strategy and Skill** Review students' completed Sequence Charts from the first read.

Remind students that a summary includes only the most important events of a story and should follow the correct sequence. If students' summaries are incomplete, provide a model summary or use a student summary and revise it as a group. Have students copy the revised summary in their Writer's Notebooks.

Set a Purpose for Reading *Let's reread to check our understanding of the sequence of events in these legends and to work on our reading fluency.*

DURING READING

Have students reread *Navajo Legends* silently or with a partner. If reading in pairs, prompt students to stop every two pages and summarize or ask their partner probing questions.

AFTER READING

Check Comprehension Have students independently complete the Comprehension Check on page 20. Review students' answers. Help students find evidence for their answers in the text.

Synthesize Have students imagine that they are interviewing a character in a legend. Students should create both the questions and the answers. When they are finished, students can act out their interviews with a partner.

Gifted & Talented

MODEL FLUENCY

Model reading the fluency passage on **Beyond Reproducible** page 86. Tell students to pay close attention to your expression and phrasing as you read. Then read one sentence at a time, and have students echo-read, copying your expression and phrasing.

During independent reading time, have students work with a partner using the fluency passage. One student reads aloud while the other repeats each sentence back. Students can check their fluency by reading along with the "expert speed" version of the passage on the **Fluency Solutions Audio CD**.

Book Talk

Bringing Groups Together Students will work with peers of various language and reading abilities to discuss this week's Leveled Readers. Refer to page 158 in the **Teacher's Resource Book** for more about how to conduct a Book Talk.

Beyond Reproducible, page 86

As I read, I will pay attention to my expression and phrasing.

The Navajo are the largest tribe of Native Americans in North
11 America. The ancestors of the Navajo lived in northwestern Canada
21 and Alaska. More than 1,000 years ago, the Navajo began moving
32 south. They settled in the southwestern part of the United States where
44 the present-day states of Colorado, Utah, New Mexico, and Arizona
55 meet. The land is made up of plains, wind-swept cliffs, and high
68 mountains.
69 Spider Rock, the world's tallest natural spire, is located here in
80 Canyon de Chelly (da SHAY) National Park in Arizona. This amazing
89 red sandstone spire, which soars over 800 feet high, has an important
101 place in Navajo mythology. It is the home of Spider Woman, the
113 Navajo "fairy godmother."
116 The Navajo lived in homes called hogans. These houses were made
127 of wooden poles, mud, and tree bark. The Navajo also lived in caves
140 they built in the cliff walls of canyons. These caves were usually high
153 enough over the floor of the canyon so that the people would be safe
167 from enemies and dangerous floods. 172

Comprehension Check
1. What is the author's purpose in writing this selection? **Author's Purpose** The author is providing information about the history and culture of the Navajo.
2. Why did the Navajo live in caves in the cliff walls? **Cause and Effect** The people were safe from enemies and floods in these caves.

	Words Read	−	Number of Errors	=	Words Correct Score
First Read		−		=	
Second Read		−		=	

ELL ENGLISH LANGUAGE LEARNERS

Daily Planner

DAY 1	• Build Background Knowledge • Vocabulary
DAY 2	• Vocabulary • Access to Core Content *Mystic Horse*
DAY 3	• Vocabulary • Grammar • Access to Core Content *Mystic Horse*
DAY 4	• Vocabulary • Writing/Spelling • Access to Core Content "The Pony Express" • Leveled Reader *Three Legends*
DAY 5	• Vocabulary • Leveled Reader *Three Legends* • Self-Selected Reading

LOG ON StudentWorks™ Plus
Interactive Student Book

Use StudentWorks Plus for:
- Vocabulary Preteaching
- Word-by-Word Highlighting
- Think Aloud Prompts

Cognates

Help students identify similarities and differences in pronunciation and spelling between English and Spanish cognates.

pioneers	*pioneros*
mysterious	*misterioso*
responsibility	*responsabilidad*
sequence	*secuencia*
order	*orden*
homophone	*homófono*
plural	*plural*
possessive	*posesivo*

Prepare to Read

Content Objective Learn about a boy and a horse who showed bravery
Language Objective Use key words to discuss a boy and horse who showed bravery
Materials • StudentWorks Plus

BUILD BACKGROUND KNOWLEDGE

All Language Levels

- Have students preview *Mystic Horse* using **StudentWorks Plus**, which contains oral summaries in multiple languages, online multilingual glossaries, word-by-word highlighting, and questions that assess and build comprehension.

- Students can build their word-reading fluency by reading along as the text is read or by listening during the first reading and, at the end of each paragraph, returning to the beginning of the paragraph and reading along.

- Students can build their comprehension by reviewing the definitions of key words in the online glossary and by answering the comprehension questions. When appropriate, the text required to answer the question is highlighted to provide students with additional support and scaffolding.

- After reading, ask students to respond to these questions: *Have you ever done anything that took great courage? How did you feel when you did that?*

Academic Language

Language Objective Use academic language in classroom conversations

All Language Levels

- This week's academic words are **boldfaced** throughout the lesson. Define the word in context, and provide a clear example from the selection. Then ask students to generate an example or a word with a similar meaning.

Academic Language Used in Whole Group Instruction

Theme Words	Key Selection Words	Strategy and Skill Words
courage **pioneers** **wagons**	**sores** **loosened** **mysterious** **amazement** **midst** **responsibility**	**story structure** **sequence** **chronological** **homophones** **plurals** **possessives**

ELL ENGLISH LANGUAGE LEARNERS

Vocabulary

Language Objective Demonstrate understanding and use of key words by talking about courage

Materials • **Visual Vocabulary Resources**
  • **ELL Resource Book**

PRETEACH KEY VOCABULARY

Use the **Visual Vocabulary Resources** to preteach the key selection words *sores, loosened, mysterious, amazement, midst,* and *responsibility*. Focus on two words per day. The following routine that appears in detail on the cards.

Beginning/Intermediate

- Point out any known sound-spellings, or focus on a key aspect of phonemic awareness related to the word.

All Language Levels

- Define the word in English, and provide the example given.
- Define the word in Spanish, if appropriate, and indicate if the word is a cognate.
- Display the picture, and explain how it demonstrates the word. Engage students in a structured activity about the image.
- Ask students to chorally say the word three times.
- Distribute copies of the Vocabulary Glossary, **ELL Resource Book**, page 110.

PRETEACH FUNCTION WORDS AND PHRASES

All Language Levels

Use the Visual Vocabulary Resources to preteach the function words and phrases *stay behind, worn-out, good-for-nothing,* and *night is falling*. Focus on one word per day. Use the detailed routine on the cards.

- Define the word in English and, if appropriate, in Spanish. Point out if the word is a cognate.
- Refer to the picture and engage students in talk about the word. For example, students will partner-talk using sentence frames.
- Ask students to chorally repeat the word three times.

TEACH BASIC WORDS

Beginning/Intermediate

Use the Visual Vocabulary Resources to teach the basic words *harvest, tipi, buffalo, lodge, camp,* and *village*. Teach these "Native Americans of the Great Plains" words using the routine provided on the card.

Visual Vocabulary Resources

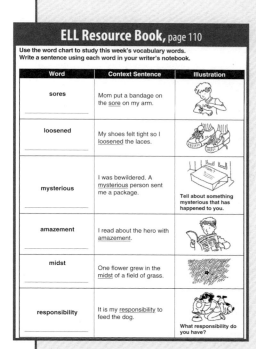

ELL Resource Book, page 110

Use the word chart to study this week's vocabulary words.
Write a sentence using each word in your writer's notebook.

Word	Context Sentence	Illustration
sores	Mom put a bandage on the sore on my arm.	
loosened	My shoes felt tight so I loosened the laces.	
mysterious	I was bewildered. A mysterious person sent me a package.	Tell about something mysterious that has happened to you.
amazement	I read about the hero with amazement.	
midst	One flower grew in the midst of a field of grass.	
responsibility	It is my responsibility to feed the dog.	What responsibility do you have?

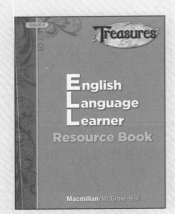

ELL Resource Book

ELL ENGLISH LANGUAGE LEARNERS

Access to Core Content

Content Objective Read grade-level text

Language Objective Discuss text using key words and sentence frames

Materials • **ELL Resource Book,** pp. 98–109

PRETEACH MAIN SELECTION (PAGES 230–249)

All Language Levels

Use the Interactive Question-Response Guide on **ELL Resource Book**, pages 98–107 to introduce students to *Mystic Horse*. Preteach half of the selection on **Day 2** and half on **Day 3**.

- Use the prompts provided in the guide to develop meaning and vocabulary. Use the partner-talk and whole-class responses to engage students and increase student talk.

- When completed, have partners reread the story.

PRETEACH PAIRED SELECTION (PAGES 252–255)

All Language Levels

Use the Interactive Question-Response Guide on ELL Resource Book, pages 108–109 to preview the paired selection "The Pony Express." Preteach the selection on **Day 4**.

Beginning	Intermediate	Advanced
Use Visuals During the Interactive Reading, select several illustrations that show sequence of events. Describe the events in sequence and have students retell the events in order.	**Summarize** During the Interactive Reading, select a few lines of text that include sequence of events. After you have read and explained it, have students summarize the events in sequence, based on the text.	**Summarize** During the Interactive Reading, select a passage that include sequence of events. After you have read and explain it, have students summarize the events in sequence, based on the passage.

ELL ENGLISH LANGUAGE LEARNERS

Fluency

Content Objectives Reread selections to develop fluency; develop speaking skills

Language Objective Tell a partner what a selection is about

Materials • **Student Book:** *Mystic Horse,* "The Pony Express"
• **Teacher's Resource Book**

REREAD FOR FLUENCY

> **Beginning**

■ Have students read the decodable passages in the **Teacher's Resource Book**, page 15.

> **Intermediate/Advanced**

■ Have students reread two to four pages from of *Mystic Horse,* based on their level. Help students read the pages with the appropriate intonation and pacing. For example, read each sentence on the first page and have students echo. Then have students chorally reread additional paragraphs. Tell them to pause briefly at ending marks, such as periods.

■ Provide time for students to read the sections. Comment on their intonation and pacing, and provide corrective feedback by modeling proper fluency.

DEVELOP SPEAKING/LISTENING SKILLS

> **All Language Levels**

■ Have students practice reading "The Pony Express." Work with students to read with the appropriate intonation and pacing.

■ Provide time for students to read the article to a partner. Ask students to share one fact they learned about the Pony Express. Provide the sentence frame: *In the article, I learned that _____.*

Self-Selected Reading

Content Objective Read independently

Language Objective Orally retell information learned

Materials • **Leveled Classroom Library** • other legends

APPLY SKILLS AND STRATEGIES TO INDEPENDENT READING

> **All Language Levels**

■ Have students choose a legend for silent independent reading. (See the **Theme Bibliography** on pages T8–T9 for suggestions.)

■ After reading, ask students to orally summarize the book. Provide time for students to share their reactions with classmates. Ask: *Would you recommend this book to a classmate? Why or why not?*

Student Book

Leveled Classroom Library
See Leveled Classroom
Library lessons on pages T2–T7.

Transfer Skills

Plurals and Possessives In Hmong and Khmer, nouns do not change form to show the plural. Display objects and write on the board the singular and plural forms of regular nouns (*book/books, chair/chairs*) to illustrate the different forms. Help students form plural forms. Spanish, Hmong, and Khmer avoid the use of apostrophe *-s* (*the man's earmuffs*) to show possession. Speakers of these languages commonly use a prepositional phrase (*the earmuffs of the man*) to show possession. Model how to form possessives and have students repeat after you. Point out the use of apostrophe *-s* and *s-* apostrophe in text. See language transfers on pages T16–T31.

Corrective Feedback

During Whole Group grammar lessons, follow the routine on the **Grammar Transparencies** to provide students with extra support. This routine includes completing the items with English Language Learners while other students work independently, having students reread the sentences with partners to build fluency, and providing a generative task, such as writing a new sentence using the skill.

Grammar

Content Objective Identify plural and possessive nouns
Language Objective Speak in complete sentences, using sentence frames

PLURALS AND POSSESSIVES

Beginning/Intermediate

■ Review plural and possessive nouns. Write the following on the board: *All bikes have tires. My bike's tires are flat.* Underline the *-s* in *bikes* and the apostrophe *-s* in *bike's*. Tell students that when a noun ends in *-s* or *-es*, it shows "more than one." When a noun ends in apostrophe *-s* or *s-* apostrophe, it shows ownership, or possession.

All Language Levels

■ Review plural and possessive nouns. Write sentences on the board, such as those provided below. Have students tell whether the underlined noun in each sentence is a plural noun or a possessive noun. Have them say: ＿＿ *is a [plural/possessive] noun.*

   Some legends tell of people who lived long ago.

   Many legends' characters show great bravery.

   A herd of spirited horses appeared.

   The boy's grandmother took good care of him.

PEER DISCUSSION STARTERS

All Language Levels

■ Write the following sentences on the board:

   Before the battle, the boy felt ＿＿.
   The boy chief learned that ＿＿.

■ Pair students and have them complete each sentence frame. Ask them to expand on their sentences by providing as many details as they can from this week's readings. Circulate, listen in, and take note of each student's language use and proficiency.

Beginning	Intermediate	Advanced
Use Visuals Describe the illustrations in *Mystic Horse* to students, using plurals and possessives. Ask: *What do you see?* Help them point and name things using plurals and possessive nouns.	**Describe** Ask students to describe the illustrations in *Mystic Horse,* using plurals or possessives. Have students use complete sentences.	**Describe** Have students describe the illustrations in *Mystic Horse,* using plurals and possessives. Challenge them to add descriptive details in their responses.

ELL ENGLISH LANGUAGE LEARNERS

Sound-Spelling WorkBoard

Writing/Spelling

Content Objective Spell words correctly

Language Objective Write in complete sentences, using sentence frames

All Language Levels

- Write the key vocabulary words on the board: *sores, loosened, mysterious, amazement, midst, responsibility*. Have students copy each word on their **WorkBoards**. Help them say each word and then write a sentence for it. Provide sentence starters, such as:

  Sores on your skin feel ____.

  I loosened my belt because ____.

  The letter I got in the mail was mysterious because ____.

  To my amazement, my friend once ____.

  Being in the midst of a crowd is ____.

  At home it is my responsibility to ____.

Beginning/Intermediate

- Help students spell words using their growing knowledge of English sound-spelling relationships. Model how to segment the word students are trying to spell, and attach a spelling to each sound (or spellings to each syllable if a multisyllabic word). Use the **Sound-Spelling Cards** to reinforce the spellings for each English sound.

Advanced

- Dictate the following words for students to spell: *playful, slowest, bravely, kindness, careful, restless, sickly, coldest, fearless, goodness*. Use the Sound-Spelling Cards to guide students as they spell each word.

- When completed, review the meanings of words that can be easily demonstrated or explained. Use actions, gestures, and available pictures.

Phonics/Word Study

For English Language Learners who need more practice with this week's phonics/spelling skill, see the Approaching Level lesson on page 257J. Focus on minimal contrasts, articulation, and those sounds that do not transfer from the student's first language to English. See language transfers on pages T16–T31.

Leveled Reader

Leveled Reader

Content Objective Read to apply skills and strategies

Language Objective Retell information, using complete sentences

Materials • **Leveled Reader:** *Three Legends*
• **ELL Resource Book,** p. 111
• **Visual Vocabulary Resource,** pp. 409–412

✔ BEFORE READING

All Language Levels

■ **Preview** Read the title *Three Legends*. Ask: *What's the title? Say it again.* Repeat with the author's name. Then page through the book. Use simple language to tell about each page. Immediately follow up with questions, such as *This bird is Thunderbird. Is Thunderbird a real bird? Have you ever seen a bird that looks like this?*

■ **Review Skills** Use the inside front cover to review the comprehension skill and vocabulary words.

■ **Set a Purpose** Say: *Let's read to find out about the three legends and how they are told.*

DURING READING

All Language Levels

■ Have students read each page aloud using the differentiated suggestions. Provide corrective feedback, such as modeling how to blend a decodable word or clarifying meaning by using techniques from the Interactive Question-Response Guide.

■ **Retell** After every two pages, ask students to state the main ideas they have learned so far. Help them to complete the Sequence Chart. Restate students' comments when they have difficulty using story-specific words. Provide differentiated sentence frames to support students' responses and engage students in partner-talk where appropriate.

Vocabulary

Preteach Vocabulary Use the routine in the **Visual Vocabulary Resources,** pages 409–412, to preteach the ELL Vocabulary listed in the inside front cover of the **Leveled Reader**.

Beginning	Intermediate	Advanced
Echo-Read Have students echo-read after you.	**Choral-Read** Have students chorally read with you.	**Choral-Read** Have students chorally read.
Check Comprehension Point to pictures and ask questions, such as *Do you see the great chief on this page? Point to him.*	**Check Comprehension** Ask questions/prompts, such as *What do you see in this picture? Explain why Thunderbird brought the whale.*	**Check Comprehension** Ask: *How is the legend "The Fight" similar to* Mystic Horse? *Read sentences that show similarities.*

ELL ENGLISH LANGUAGE LEARNERS

AFTER READING

Use the chart below and **Think and Compare** questions in the Leveled Reader to determine students' progress.

ELL Resource Book

Think and Compare	Beginning	Intermediate	Advanced
1 Reread page 5. What happened after the woman put the wolf down with other wolves? When did this probably happen? *(Sequence)*	Possible responses: Nonverbal response. A boy. Night.	Possible responses: Next, he became a boy. It was night.	Possible responses: After the woman put the wolf down, he became a young boy. It was probably night.
2 Think about a time when you were amazed by someone or something. What amazed you? How did you react? *(Apply)*	Possible responses: Nonverbal response. Animal. Shout.	Possible responses: I saw a dinosaur. It was very big. I shouted.	Possible responses: I was amazed by a dinosaur at the museum because it was very large. I shouted in surprise.
3 In "The Legend of Thunderbird," the Great Chief had the responsibility of keeping his people safe. What can people do today to keep other people safe? *(Evaluate)*	Possible responses: Nonverbal response. Help. Work together.	Possible responses: People can help each other. We can work together.	Possible responses: People can keep other people safe by helping each other and working together.

BOOK TALK

Develop Listening and Speaking Skills Distribute copies of **ELL Resource Book**, page 111, and form small groups. Help students determine the leader for the discussion of the Book Talk questions. Tell students to remember the following while engaged in the activity:

- Use high-frequency English words to describe people, places, and objects.

- Narrate, describe, and explain with specificity and detail. Ask: *Where did the story take place? Can you describe the setting? What else did you notice?*

- Share information in cooperative learning interactions. Remind students to work with their partners to retell the story and complete any activities. Ask: *What happened next in the story?*

Book Talk

Bringing Groups Together Students will work with peers of varying language abilities to discuss the Book Talk questions. Form groups so that students who read the Beyond, On Level, Approaching, and ELL Leveled Readers are in the same group for the activity.

Progress Monitoring

Weekly Assessment

ASSESSED SKILLS

- Vocabulary: Vocabulary Words, Homophones
- Comprehension: Sequence
- Grammar: Plurals and Possessives
- Phonics/Spelling: Suffixes

Selection Test for **Mystic Horse** *Also Available*

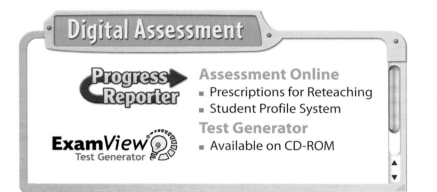

Assessment Online
- Prescriptions for Reteaching
- Student Profile System

Test Generator
- Available on CD-ROM

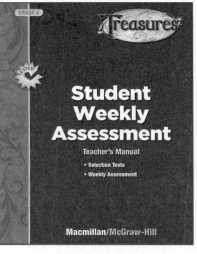

Weekly Assessment
Unit 2 Week 5

Fluency Assessment

Assess fluency for one group of students per week.
Use the Oral Fluency Record Sheet to track the number of
words read correctly. Fluency goal for all students:
84–104 words correct per minute (WCPM).

Approaching Level	Weeks 1, 3, 5
On Level	Weeks 2, 4
Beyond Level	Week 6

Fluency Assessment

Diagnose		Prescribe
Review the assessment answers with students. Have them correct their errors. Then provide additional instruction as needed.		
	IF...	**THEN...**
VOCABULARY WORDS VOCABULARY STRATEGY Homophones	0–2 items correct ...	See **Vocabulary Intervention Teacher's Edition.** **LOG ON ▶** Online Practice: Go to www.macmillanmh.com. **CD-ROM** Vocabulary PuzzleMaker
COMPREHENSION Skill: Sequence	0–3 items correct ...	See **Comprehension Intervention Teacher's Edition.** **SPIRAL REVIEW** See Sequence lesson in Unit 3 Week 1, page 285B.
GRAMMAR Plurals and Possessives	0–1 items correct ...	See **Writing and Grammar Intervention Teacher's Edition.**
PHONICS AND SPELLING Suffixes	0–1 items correct ...	**LOG ON ▶** Online Practice: Go to www.macmillanmh.com. See **Phonics Intervention Teacher's Edition.**
FLUENCY	79–83 WCPM	**AUDIO CD** Fluency Solutions Audio CD
	0–78 WCPM	See **Fluency Intervention Teacher's Edition.**

Response to Intervention

To place students in Tier 2 or Tier 3 Intervention use the *Diagnostic Assessment*.

- Phonics
- Vocabulary
- Comprehension
- Fluency
- Writing and Grammar

Week 6 ★ At a Glance

Review and Assess

✔ Writing Project
- **How-To Article**
- **Writer's Resources:** Use Spell Check

✔ Show What You Know
- **Test Practice**
- **Literacy Activities:** Comprehension, Word Study, Drama, Genre Study

✔ Theme Project
- **Community Projects**
- **Research Strategy:** Using Technology
- **Listening/Speaking**

✔ Computer Literacy
- **Word Processing**

✔ Media Literacy
- **Truth in Advertising**

✔ Assessment
- **Unit Assessment**

Key

✔ Tested in program

Digital Learning

Digital solutions to help plan and implement instructions

☑ Teacher Resources

LOG ON ▶

ONLINE www.macmillanmh.com

▶ **Teacher's Edition**
- Lesson Planner and Resources also on CD-ROM

TeacherWorks™ *Plus*

▶ **Formative Assessment**
- ExamView® on CD-ROM also available

Progress Reporter

▶ **Instructional Resources**
- Unit Videos
- Classroom Presentation Toolkit

VIDEO

▶ **Professional Development**
- Video Library

Professional Development

☑ Student Resources

LOG ON ▶

ONLINE www.macmillanmh.com

▶ **Interactive Student Book**

StudentWorks™ *Plus*

▶ **Leveled Reader Database**

▶ **Activities**
- Research Toolkit
- Oral Language Activities
- Vocabulary/Spelling Activities

Listening Library
- Recordings of Student Books and Leveled Readers

Fluency Solutions
- Fluency Modeling and Practice

Show What You Know

Spiral Review

Show What You Know provides a spiral review of reading comprehension and vocabulary skills and strategies previously taught. After reading fiction and nonfiction selections, students will answer questions that assess reading comprehension and vocabulary.

Have students turn to page 258 in the **Student Book** and read "Reading for Mister Paredo" independently. Distribute pages 5–6 from **Show What You Know**. Have students complete the questions.

Share Your Thinking

After students have completed the questions, model your own thinking on how to arrive at correct answers.

Question 1 Sequence
What happens before Benito opens the door to Mr. Paredo's room?

Tell students that they must **combine** information from different parts of the story to find the **stated** answer. He first knocks quietly and the nurse tells him to knock louder. (B) THINK AND SEARCH

Question 2 Prefixes and Suffixes
In paragraph 1, the word quietly *means —*
Students should *connect* the clues in the word to the *unstated* answer. The suffix *-ly* means "in a certain way." This changes the meaning of the word *quiet*. (H) AUTHOR AND ME

Show What You Know

Review

Cause and Effect
Sequence
Main Idea and Details
Prefixes and Suffixes
Chart

READING FOR MISTER PAREDO

258

Benito knocked quietly on the door to Mr. Paredo's room. There was no answer.

"Fantastic," thought Benito. "I can just go home." When he turned to leave, a nurse caught his eye.

"You better knock louder than that," she said. "Mr. Paredo has a difficult time hearing."

Benito sighed and knocked again. A gruff voice shouted, "What is it?"

He opened the door. An old man lay in the bed. He looked feeble and exhausted, but his deep blue eyes were still dynamic. "What do you want?" he asked.

"Um, I'm the reader," Benito began. "The school sent me to help you, um, read."

Mr. Paredo didn't say anything for a long time. He just stared. At last he muttered, "Well, what are you going to read?"

Benito took a step closer to the bed. He took off his backpack and started rummaging through it. "I didn't know what you would like," he said. "So I brought a bunch of stuff. I have today's newspaper—"

Genre

Fiction

Fiction is a story that comes from imagination and not from fact.

Setting: The time and place where the story takes place

Characters: The people or animals in the story

Plot: The structure of the story; how the events are arranged in a story

Theme: The central lesson or message of the story

"I hate the news," said Mr. Paredo. "It's always unpleasant."

"I also have a sports magazine."

"No. My team always loses."

As Benito was taking the books out of his backpack, a magazine fell out. It landed on the bed, hitting Mr. Paredo right on the leg. He flinched and his blue eyes looked furious. "What was that?" he asked.

"I'm sorry," said Benito as he hurried to put it away.

"Wait," said Mr. Paredo, grabbing Benito's wrist before he could take the magazine. "Is that a comic book?"

"I'm sorry," repeated Benito. "It's mine. I just got it. I didn't mean to hit you with it."

"I love comics," said Mr. Paredo, smiling for the first time. He held the cover very close to his face so he could read the title. "I used to read them all the time. Now my eyes won't let me."

"You like comics?" asked Benito. "If you want, I can read it to you." Mr. Paredo was silent. "Don't worry. I'll describe the pictures so you can almost see them."

"Okay," said Mr. Paredo.

At first, Benito felt unprepared. It was hard to read the words and describe the pictures at the same time. Mr. Paredo would interrupt with so many questions. He wanted to know every detail, from the color of someone's hair to the shape of the speech balloons. But soon Benito became an expert. His descriptions grew longer and more elaborate. When he finished, Benito felt like he had never read one of his comic books more thoroughly.

"I can come back on Saturday if you want. I have more comics," he said.

"Great!" said Mr. Paredo. He smiled as Benito left.

259

Question 3 **Sequence** *What makes Mr. Paredo smile for the first time?*

Students must **combine** information from different parts of the story to find the **stated** answer. Mr. Paredo smiles when he sees Benito's comic book. (B) THINK AND SEARCH

Question 4 **Prefixes and Suffixes** *What does the word <u>unprepared</u> mean?*

Students should **connect** the clues in the word to find the **unstated** answer. The prefix *un-* means *not*, which changes the meaning of the word *prepared*. (H) AUTHOR AND ME

Question 5 **Sequence** *What happens after Benito finishes reading? Explain your answer and support it with evidence from the story.* THINK AND SEARCH

Possible response: Benito offers to come back on Saturday and says he has more comics. Mr. Paredo smiles and says that would be great.

Use the Short-Answer Reading Rubric on page 170 in the Teacher's Resource Book to score students' written responses.

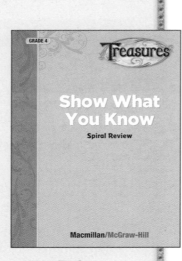

GRADE 4

Treasures

Show What You Know

Spiral Review

Macmillan/McGraw-Hill

pages 5–6

Have students turn to page 260 in the **Student Book** and read "Protect Our Valuable Oceans" independently. Distribute pages 7–8 from **Show What You Know**. Have students complete the questions.

Share Your Thinking

After students have completed the questions, model your own thinking on how to arrive at correct answers.

Question 1 Cause and Effect

Look at the web of information from the article. Which information belongs in the empty oval?

Point out to students that this is a web in which they must fill in the causes of water pollution. Two of the causes are listed, so the students must **locate** the **stated** answer in the article. The first paragraph on page 261 states that cruise ships dump waste into oceans. (A) RIGHT THERE

Question 2 Main Idea and Details

What is the main idea of the article?

Remind students that they must reread and **connect** the clues from the story to find the **unstated** answer, or main idea. The article tells us about how we use the ocean and ways we should protect it. (H) AUTHOR AND ME

Protect Our Valuable OCEANS

WHEN ASTRONAUTS look down at Earth from space, they see a beautiful blue world. Oceans cover more than 70% of our planet. Earth has five oceans. They are the Pacific, Atlantic, Indian, Arctic, and Southern oceans. These oceans are important to us and our planet.

People depend on oceans for survival. Fish, seaweed, and shellfish all come from the ocean. They are the main source of food for more than 3.5 billion people. Some of our salt, fertilizers, and minerals come from the ocean. A great deal of the world's oil and natural gas supply is drilled offshore, which means the oil comes from the ocean, beneath the ocean floor.

Oceans also provide us with transportation. Many cities have ferries, which people use to get to work every morning. Freight and fuel also travel by boat. Oil tankers transport 60% of the oil used by the world. Ships also carry clothes, toys, and other goods you see in stores.

About 21 million barrels of oil run into the oceans each year from street runoff, factory waste, and ships flushing their tanks.

260

Genre

Nonfiction

A nonfiction article tells about a real event, person, or place.

Introduction: Tells what the selection is about

Body: The main text of the selection; gives more detail about the topic

Conclusion: Gives the author's ideas about what is most important to the lesson

Text Features: Elements in addition to the main text that give more information, such as photos and captions, tables, charts, headings, and diagrams

Chart of Ocean Facts

Oceans	Area	Length of Coastline	Elevation Lowest Point
Atlantic Ocean	76.762 million sq km	111,866 km	-8,605 m
Pacific Ocean	155.557 million sq km	135,663 km	-10,924 m
Indian Ocean	68.556 million sq km	66,526 km	-7,258 m
Arctic Ocean	14.056 million sq km	45,389 km	-4,665 m
Southern Ocean	20.327 million sq km	17,968 km	-7,235 m

Use this chart to find facts about the different sizes of oceans and their coastlines.

Even though our oceans do so much for us, we have not been taking care of them. Water pollution is a big problem because it kills many kinds of sea creatures. Some of this pollution results from things people dump into the ocean. For example, cruise ships and cargo ships dump waste into the ocean every day. Other pollution comes from factories and power plants dumping their waste into rivers. The rivers carry this waste to the oceans.

It is not just the dumping of waste into oceans that harms them. For example, nitrogen, a chemical in fertilizers, is carried to the oceans as runoff. As water "runs off" the ground, it flows into our streams and rivers, which carry it to the sea.

Pollutants, such as nitrogen, can cause problems in the ocean and serious imbalances in nature. Nitrogen reduces the amount of oxygen in the ocean; less oxygen can kill some sea animals or cause diseases. Too much nitrogen can produce large amounts of algae, tiny plants that grow in the water, which can hurt other plants and animals.

Luckily there are things we can do to protect oceans. A good start is to learn about them. Another thing we can do is get rid of waste properly. Finally, we can ask our government to get involved by passing more laws to help stop pollution. Oceans are an important part of our world, and we have to take care of them.

261

GRADE 4

Treasures

Show What You Know

Spiral Review

Macmillan/McGraw-Hill

pages 7–8

Question 3 Chart
Look at the chart on page 261. Which ocean has the largest area?

Tell students to look at the chart on page 261. They must **combine** information on the chart to determine the **stated** answer. The area of the Pacific Ocean is 155.557 million sq km. This is the largest. (B) THINK AND SEARCH

Question 4 Cause and Effect
Water pollution is a big problem in the ocean because it —

Have students restate the question and **locate** the **stated** answer in the text. The article says that water pollution is a problem because it kills seas creatures. (F) RIGHT THERE

Question 5 Main Idea and Details
In what way do people depend on the oceans for survival? Explain your answer and support it with evidence from the article. AUTHOR AND ME

Possible response: The oceans are a main source of food, such as fish, seaweed, and shellfish. We get salt, fertilizers, and minerals from the oceans. We get oil and natural gas from beneath the ocean floor.

Use the Short-Answer Reading Rubric on page 170 in the Teacher's Resource Book to score students' written responses.

Show What You Know

SPIRAL REVIEW Spiral Review

Show What You Know Unit Review provides a spiral review of the core skill taught in this unit. Students will review by answering questions and completing short, targeted activities.

Have students turn to pages 262 and 263 of the **Student Book**. Have students note their responses on a separate sheet of paper.

Share Your Thinking

Read the questions for each activity in the Student Book with students. If additional review is needed, go back to the lessons in the **Teacher's Edition**.

Comprehension: Stated or Implied Purpose Discuss with students the difference between making a statement and implying something. Say: *I am going to buy those red shoes.* Then say: *What great red shoes. I really like them. I'm going to see if they have my size.* Guide students to see that the first example states your purpose (to buy the shoes). The second example implies your purpose. Remind students that writers can either state or imply their purpose. Read the activity on page 262 of the Student Book. Have students work in small groups to complete the activity. **To review, see lesson on page 195B of the Teacher's Edition**.

★ Show What You Know

📕 Comprehension

Stated or Implied Purpose

- In expository selections, such as magazine articles, an author states or implies his or her purpose.

- Stated purpose: The author states his or her reason for writing the article. You will be able to find a sentence that ties all the ideas of the article together.

- Implied purpose: You will find ideas in the text and see how they are all connected. You will not find a sentence in the text that ties all of these ideas together.

- Read a magazine article. Explain if the purpose is stated or implied. Use details from the article to support your answer.

📙 Genre

Persuasive Writing

- Persuasive writing states the author's point of view. It uses language to influence, or convince, people to think a certain way about something.

- With a partner, reread "The Ride of His Life" on page 191. What is the author's opinion of Alejandro Abor and the handcycles that he builds?

- Identify the persuasive language the author uses to talk about Alejandro Abor. Explain how these words and phrases influence the reader to think a certain way.

262

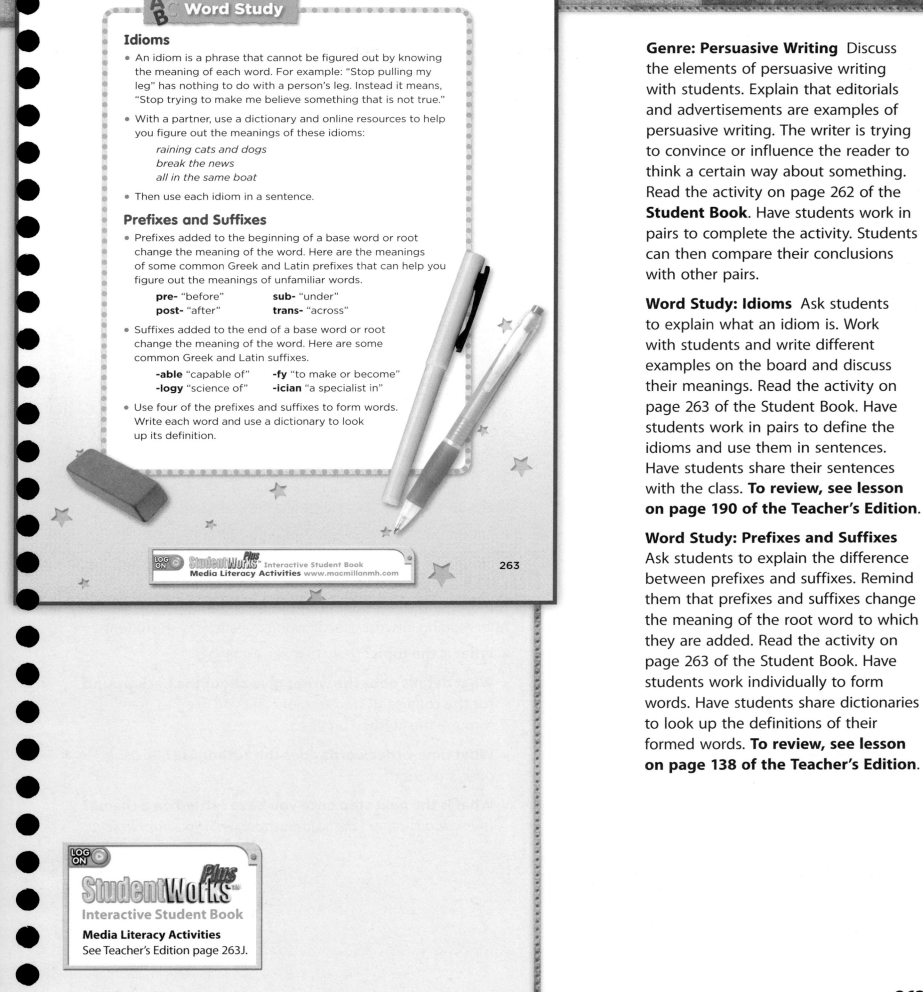

Word Study

Idioms

- An idiom is a phrase that cannot be figured out by knowing the meaning of each word. For example: "Stop pulling my leg" has nothing to do with a person's leg. Instead it means, "Stop trying to make me believe something that is not true."

- With a partner, use a dictionary and online resources to help you figure out the meanings of these idioms:

  raining cats and dogs
  break the news
  all in the same boat

- Then use each idiom in a sentence.

Prefixes and Suffixes

- Prefixes added to the beginning of a base word or root change the meaning of the word. Here are the meanings of some common Greek and Latin prefixes that can help you figure out the meanings of unfamiliar words.

  pre- "before"   **sub-** "under"
  post- "after"   **trans-** "across"

- Suffixes added to the end of a base word or root change the meaning of the word. Here are some common Greek and Latin suffixes.

  -able "capable of"   **-fy** "to make or become"
  -logy "science of"   **-ician** "a specialist in"

- Use four of the prefixes and suffixes to form words. Write each word and use a dictionary to look up its definition.

LOG ON **StudentWorks** *Plus* Interactive Student Book
Media Literacy Activities www.macmillanmh.com

263

LOG ON **StudentWorks** *Plus*
Interactive Student Book
Media Literacy Activities
See Teacher's Edition page 263J.

Genre: Persuasive Writing Discuss the elements of persuasive writing with students. Explain that editorials and advertisements are examples of persuasive writing. The writer is trying to convince or influence the reader to think a certain way about something. Read the activity on page 262 of the **Student Book**. Have students work in pairs to complete the activity. Students can then compare their conclusions with other pairs.

Word Study: Idioms Ask students to explain what an idiom is. Work with students and write different examples on the board and discuss their meanings. Read the activity on page 263 of the Student Book. Have students work in pairs to define the idioms and use them in sentences. Have students share their sentences with the class. **To review, see lesson on page 190 of the Teacher's Edition**.

Word Study: Prefixes and Suffixes Ask students to explain the difference between prefixes and suffixes. Remind them that prefixes and suffixes change the meaning of the root word to which they are added. Read the activity on page 263 of the Student Book. Have students work individually to form words. Have students share dictionaries to look up the definitions of their formed words. **To review, see lesson on page 138 of the Teacher's Edition**.

Objectives

- Identify features of a how-to article
- Plan and organize ideas using a graphic organizer to prewrite
- Draft and revise a how-to article
- Proofread, publish, and present a how-to article

Materials

- Writing Transparencies 30–35
- Teacher's Resource Book, pp. 171, 210, 265

Features of a How-to Article

- It **explains**, or shows, how to do something.
- It begins with an introduction that identifies the **topic**, or task that will be explained.
- It contains **step-by-step directions**
- It has specific **details** that show how to complete the steps.
- It uses **time-order words**. and **spatial words** to make the steps clear.

ELL

Use Illustrations to Construct Meaning To help students understand the process explained in the excerpt, invite a student with good visual abilities to draw or act out the steps as you read. Then ask other students to take turns retelling the steps in their own words as they look at the illustration.

How-to Article

Read Like a Writer

Tell students that you will read an excerpt from a how-to article called "Making a Collage." Ask students to listen for

- the **topic** named in the introduction;
- specific **details** in the **step-by-step directions**;
- **time-order** and **spatial words**.

Making a Collage

Making a collage is fun and easy. It's a great way to decorate!

To begin your project, pick a story or theme for your collage. Once you've settled on the theme, think about images you can use in your collage to illustrate what you want to say.

Start by deciding whether or not it's important to put the images in any particular order. If it is, you can lay them out to get an idea of how they will look together.

Next, paint or color the background on your paper or board. Use colors you want to peek through in the finished picture.

Discuss the Features

After reading, discuss the following questions with students.

- **What is the topic?** (how to make a collage)
- **What details does the writer give about the background for the collage?** (Choose colors that you want to peek through the finished picture.)
- **What time-order words does the author use?** (*to begin, once, start, next*)
- **What is the next step once you have settled on a theme?** (*think about images that will illustrate what you want to say*)

✔ Prewrite

Set a Purpose Remind students that the purpose of a how-to article is to explain how to do something.

Know the Audience Explain that students should focus on the audience, or people who will read the how-to article. Have them consider how to explain the process so the audience will understand what to do.

Choose a Topic Tell students that they will each write a how-to article. Have students brainstorm ideas for their articles. Use the following questions to help generate ideas: *What do you like to make? Think about foods you make, games you play, or projects you've done. Can you explain the process in a few steps?*

Remind students that when they plan, they should focus on a topic, organize the steps in time order, and think about the descriptive details that will help readers understand what to do.

| Minilesson | **Organization** |

Display **Writing Transparency 30**. Explain that this is an example of a Sequence Chart that Diana used to develop ideas for her how-to article. Read the Sequence Chart aloud. Point out the following:

- Diana lists **step-by-step directions**.

- The steps are in **sequential order**.

- The steps **explain** how to make and use a code wheel.

Organize Ideas After discussing Diana's Sequence Chart, have students create their own Sequence Charts to plan their how-to articles. Use Writing Transparency 30 to guide students in organizing their ideas.

Peer Review

Think, Pair, Share Have students discuss their sequence charts with partners and identify details about each step that could be explained better. Ask students to note these details on their charts.

Flexible Pairing Option Pair students with similar topics so the students can share ideas.

Writing Prompt

Write a how-to article about a task or a project that you know how to do.

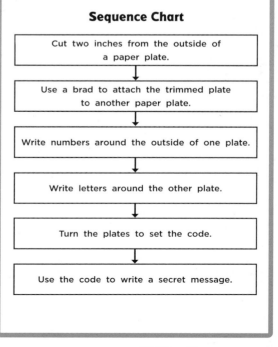

Transparency 30

Sequence Chart

Cut two inches from the outside of a paper plate.
↓
Use a brad to attach the trimmed plate to another paper plate.
↓
Write numbers around the outside of one plate.
↓
Write letters around the other plate.
↓
Turn the plates to set the code.
↓
Use the code to write a secret message.

Writing Transparency

Transparency 31

How to Make a Code Wheel
by Diana J.

It's fun to send secret messages. Here's how you can create a code wheel to write a coded message.

First, cut about two inchs from the outside edge of a paper plate. Trim all the way around the plate. Use the tip of a pencil or pen to make a whole in the center of each plate. Be careful not to poke yourself! Put the Brad through the wholes to connect the plates. Place the small plate over the large one and line up the wholes.

Use the ruler to divide the rim of the large wheel into 26 equal space's. In each space, write a letter of the alphabet. Go from A to Z. Divide the small wheel in the same way. This time write a number from 1 to 26 in each space.

You're ready to use your code wheel. Turn the small wheel so that a number is right under the letter A. Let's say you lined up the letter A with the number 10. Write A=10 on a scrap of paper. This is the key to your code. Look at the code wheel to tell what number to write for each letter. As you write, put a dash between numbers to show that each stands for one letter. I've made three code wheels.

Finally, have some fun! Send your secret message to some friend. Share the key with them if they need help.

Writing Transparency

✔ Draft

Minilesson **Step-by-Step Directions**

Display **Writing Transparency 31** and read it with students. Use the sample as a model for writing a draft. Point out the following features of the writing sample.

■ Her introduction gives the **topic**, or what she will **explain**.

■ She gives **step-by-step** directions. She explains each step in its own paragraph and uses descriptive **details** and strong verbs to show each action.

■ She uses **time-order words** and **spatial words** to provide smooth transitions and make her steps clear.

Note that Diana will revise and proofread her draft in later stages.

Review Your Sequence Chart Have students review their Sequence Charts and the suggestions partners brainstormed during Peer Review time.

Write the Draft Remind students that the purpose of a first draft is to get their ideas on paper. Tell students that it is important that they write as many details about the steps as they can. Share the following tips:

■ Gain your audience's attention from the start. Use different sentence types, like questions, to introduce the **topic**.

■ Picture yourself doing the task. Then write the **steps** you follow in order.

■ Use descriptive **details** and strong verbs to create a picture in your readers' minds.

■ Use **time-order** and **spatial words** to help the reader know exactly when and what to do.

Writer's Resources

Use Spell Check Tell students that when they write drafts on a computer, the computer's spell-checker can be a useful tool for catching spelling errors. Emphasize, however, that a computer's spell-checker will not catch all errors. For example, the spell-checker might not tell when a writer is using the wrong homophone, as in this sentence: *My parents drove* there *car to the beach*. It might also not indicate if a writer typed *form* instead of *from*. Writers still need to proofread carefully.

⭐ Revise

Minilesson Focus

Display **Writing Transparency 32** and point out ways that Diana revises a good how-to article to make it better.

- She organizes a list of supplies in the first paragraph. (Development of Ideas)

- She adds more time-order words and rearranges steps to clarify the procedure. (Organization)

- She replaces the ordinary verbs *make* and *put* with the strong verbs *punch* and *push*. (Word Choice)

- She adds a detail about how to write the secret message and deletes a detail that is not necessary. (Focus and Coherence)

Point out that Diana focused on her ideas while revising. In the next step, she will fix errors in spelling, punctuation, and capitalization.

Guide students to think about the following writing elements as they evaluate and revise the draft of their how-to article:

Focus and Coherence Do you focus on your topic? Do you explain how to do something? Do all your steps relate to the topic?

Organization Are your steps in the correct order? Do you use time-order words to organize your ideas?

Development of Ideas/Word Choice Have you used strong verbs and descriptive details to show the actions and to paint a precise picture of the process?

Conventions/Sentence Fluency Did you use complete sentences that have subjects and predicates? Did you combine shorter sentences into compound sentences?

Peer Review

Think, Pair, Share Have partners take turns reading their drafts aloud. Ask listeners to restate the directions. Have students revise steps that listeners had difficulty restating or found confusing. Then have students share how their partners helped.

Flexible Pairing Option Consider pairing students who are unfamiliar with each other's topics.

ELL

Extend Vocabulary On the board, draw a two-column chart with the following labels: *Time-Order Words, Spatial Words*. List words such as *first, then, next, now, after, finally, under, behind, through, above, right,* and *left*. Have students repeat each word, write it under the correct label, and say a sentence using it.

Transparency 32

How to Make a Code Wheel
by Diana J.

It's fun to send secret messages. Here's how you
~You need two paper plates, a scissors, a ruler, a pencil or pen, a paper fastener
can create a code wheel to write a coded message. ~
(also called a brad), and a sheet of paper
First, cut about two inchs from the outside edge
of a paper plate. Trim all the way around the plate. ~Next,
Use the tip of a pencil or pen to make a whole in the
                                    ^punch
center of each plate. Be careful not to poke yourself!
^Push
Put the Brad through the wholes to connect the plates.
Place the small plate over the large one and line up the
wholes. ∧
        Then
∧Use the ruler to divide the rim of the large wheel
into 26 equal space's. In each space, write a letter of
the alphabet. Go from A to Z. Divide the small wheel in
the same way. This time write a number from 1 to 26 in
each space.
        Now
∧You're ready to use your code wheel. Turn the small
wheel so that a number is right under the letter A.
Let's say you lined up the letter A with the number 10.
Write A=10 on a scrap of paper. This is the key to your
code. Look at the code wheel to tell what number to
write for each letter. As you write, put a dash between
                                    Leave a space between words.
numbers to show that each stands for one letter. I've
made three code wheels.

Finally, have some fun! Send your secret message to
some friend. Share the key with them if they need help.

Writing Transparency

Speaking and Listening

Have students read their how-to articles aloud and present their visuals. Share these strategies.

SPEAKING STRATEGIES

- Speak in a loud, clear voice.
- Watch the audience. Slow down or repeat steps if people look confused.
- Use eye contact effectively.

LISTENING STRATEGIES

- Listen attentively, without interruption.
- Wait until the reader is done to make pertinent comments and ask thoughtful questions.

Transparency 33

How to Make a Code Wheel
by Diana J.

It's fun to send secret messages. Here's how you can create a code wheel to write a coded message. You need two paper plates, a scissors, a ruler, a pencil or pen, a paper fastener (also called a brad), and a sheet of paper.

First, cut about two inchs from the outside edge of a paper plate. Trim all the way around the plate. Next, Use the tip of a pencil or pen to make a whole *(punch)* *(hole)* in the center of each plate. Be careful not to poke yourself! Push the Brad through the wholes *(holes)* to connect the plates. Place the small plate over the large one and line up the wholes *(holes)*.

Then, Use the ruler to divide the rim of the large wheel into 26 equal spaces. In each space, write a letter of the alphabet. Go from A to Z. Divide the small wheel in the same way. This time write a number from 1 to 26 in each space.

Now, You're ready to use your code wheel. Turn the small wheel so that a number is right under the letter A. Let's say you lined up the letter A with the number 10. Write A=10 on a scrap of paper. This is the key to your code. Look at the code wheel to tell what number to write for each letter. As you write, put a dash between numbers to show that each stands for one letter. *Leave a space between words.* I've made three code wheels.

Finally, have some fun! Send your secret message to some friend. Share the key with them if they need help.

Writing Transparency

✔ Proofread/Edit

Minilesson Conventions

Display **Writing Transparency 33** to point out Diana's corrections.

- She made one noun plural, corrected the spelling of a plural, and changed an incorrect possessive to a plural.
- She changed incorrect homophones to *hole* and *holes*.
- She corrected the capitalization of a common noun.

Have students read and reread their how-to articles to correct mistakes in grammar, spelling, and punctuation. Suggest that they proofread for one kind of error, such as using possessives correctly. Review proofreading marks on **Teacher's Resource Book** page 171. Have students apply them as they proofread.

Peer Review

Think, Pair, Share Have partners proofread one another's edited drafts. Ask them to look for errors in plural and possessive nouns. Have students share some of their partners' corrections.

TEACHER CONFERENCE

Use the rubric on page 263G to evaluate student writing and help you formulate questions to foster self-assessment.

- In what way did you inform your audience?
- Could a reader perform the process based on your explanation?
- Do you tell readers more than they need to know?

Publish and Share

Have students write fluidly in cursive or joined italic or type a final copy of their how-to article. Remind them to correctly form letters and check their spacing between words, sentences, and paragraphs. Ask them to use standard margins. Have students compile a classroom how-to book that includes the articles.

PRESENTATION Ask students to use their how-to articles to teach classmates how to do something new. Have students give how-to demonstrations that include props and supplies. Have students follow and act out a partner's directions for the class.

Using Rubrics

READ AND SCORE

Display **Writing Transparency 34**. Tell students to follow along as a volunteer reads the how-to article aloud. Then have students use the student rubric on page 210 of the **Teacher's Resource Book** to assess the writing sample. Guide students to understand that this how-to article is only a fair writing sample, which would score a 2, and that they will work together to improve it.

RAISE THE SCORE

Point out the following shortfalls in the writing sample:

Focus and Coherence Gabe has given step-by-step directions for making a puzzle card, but some information is missing. Some details are incomplete or hard to follow.

Organization Gabe introduces the topic in the first paragraph, but the beginning isn't very engaging. The article could use more transitions to link steps and details.

Development of Ideas/Word Choice Gabe could use more time-order words and spatial words. Some of the verbs are ordinary, so they do not clearly show the action.

Have students work in small groups to revise the how-to article. Remind them to refer to the student rubric.

SHARE AND COMPARE

Ask groups to share and discuss their revised versions of Gabe's how-to article and explain how they improved the writing. Then display **Writing Transparency 35** to show the same article written at an excellent level. Have each group compare its revised version with the transparency. Remind students to review their own how-to articles.

Objective

- Revise a how-to article to raise the writing score from a 2 to a 4

CREATE A RUBRIC

Teacher-Developed Rubric
You might want to copy, enlarge, and then distribute the blank rubric form on page 216 in the Teacher's Resource Book. Remind students that the rubric should assess whether the how-to article focuses on the topic, is logically organized, includes steps that have strong verbs and descriptive details, and demonstrates a strong command of language and conventions.

Transparency 35

How to Make a Puzzle Card
by Gabe M.

Do you need a new idea for a get-well card or birthday card? Make a puzzle card for someone special. You need crayons or markers, two sheets of paper, paper towels, scissors, and two heavy books.

Start by drawing a design or picture on the top of a sheet of paper. Fill the paper with a pattern or color all the way to the edge. Next write your message on the bottom of the page. Make your message stand out. Don't forget to sign your name.

Then squeeze some glue onto the second sheet of paper. Place your drawing over the glued paper. If glue comes out, wipe it up with a paper towel. Put the card under the books to keep it flat.

Wait about an hour before removing the books. Then draw jigsaw puzzle shapes on the back of the card. Follow the lines to cut the card into puzzle pieces.

Finally address an envelope, drop the pieces inside, mail the card, and wait for your friend to tell you how great it is!

Writing Transparency

4-Point Procedural Writing Rubric

Use this four-point rubric to assess student writing.

4-POINT SCORING RUBRIC			
4 Excellent	**3 Good**	**2 Fair**	**1 Unsatisfactory**
Focus and Coherence Sustained focus shows how ideas are related. Introduction and conclusion add depth and sense of completeness.	**Focus and Coherence** Focus generally shows clear relationship between ideas. Introduction and conclusion add some depth and sense of completeness.	**Focus and Coherence** Somewhat focused paragraphs may shift quickly among related ideas. Introduction and conclusion may be superficial, but composition has some sense of completeness.	**Focus and Coherence** Weak connection to prompt and abrupt shifts among ideas show lack of focus. Composition lacks completeness, with minimal, if any, introduction and conclusion.
Organization Logical and controlled progression of thought, with meaningful transitions. Organizational strategy enhances presentation of ideas.	**Organization** Generally logical and controlled progression of thought, with mostly meaningful transitions. Generally effective organizational strategy is not affected by minor wordiness or repetition.	**Organization** Progression of thought may not be logical and needs more meaningful transitions. Organizational strategy is not effective, with some wordiness or repetition.	**Organization** Progression of thought is not logical, and transitions are minimal or lacking. No evidence of organizational strategy, with random, wordy, or repetitive ideas.
Development of Ideas/ Word Choice Thorough, insightful development of ideas creates depth of thought. Shows interesting connections between ideas and willingness to take compositional risks. Precise word choice enhances quality of content.	**Development of Ideas/ Word Choice** Development of ideas reflects some depth of thought. Presentation of some ideas may be thoughtful but shows little evidence of willingness to take compositional risks. Word choice suits purpose.	**Development of Ideas/ Word Choice** Superficial development of ideas, using lists or brief explanations, is general, inconsistent, or contrived and shows little evidence of depth of thinking. Word choice does not suit purpose.	**Development of Ideas/ Word Choice** General or vague development of ideas. Omits words or uses chosen words incorrectly.
Voice Authentic and original writing expresses unique perspective and sustains connection with reader.	**Voice** Mostly authentic and original writing generally expresses unique perspective and generally sustains connection with reader.	**Voice** Somewhat authentic or original but shows little unique perspective and fails to sustain connection with reader.	**Voice** Shows little or no sense of individual voice and no connection with reader.
Conventions/Sentence Fluency Demonstrates consistent command of spelling, capitalization, punctuation, grammar, usage, and sentence structure. Words, phrases, and sentence structure enhance overall effectiveness of communication.	**Conventions/Sentence Fluency** Demonstrates good command of spelling, capitalization, punctuation, grammar, usage, and sentence structure. Generally appropriate words, phrases, and sentence structure contribute to overall effectiveness of communication.	**Conventions/Sentence Fluency** Demonstrates limited command of spelling, capitalization, punctuation, grammar, usage, and sentence structure. Simple or inaccurate words or phrases and some awkward sentences limit overall effectiveness of communication.	**Conventions/Sentence Fluency** Demonstrates little or no command of spelling, capitalization, punctuation, grammar, usage, and sentence structure. May be difficult to read. Misused, omitted, or awkward words, phrases, or sentences interfere with communication.
Presentation Handwriting or typing is neat, consistent, and error free.	**Presentation** Margins are mostly even. Font is appropriate or handwriting is neat and mostly consistent.	**Presentation** Margins are inconsistent. Font is inappropriate or handwriting is difficult to read.	**Presentation** Spacing is uneven. Format is confusing or absent or handwriting is illegible in parts.

Portfolio

Invite students to place their finished how-to articles in their portfolios. Remind students that portfolios should include more than just finished work. Encourage students to review and evaluate their personal collection of work to determine progress and set goals for improvement. They can also discuss their work with teachers and parents/caregivers. Have them jot down ideas for future writing assignments or tell what they learned about writing how-to articles to include in their portfolios.

Anchor Papers

Use these Anchor Papers in the **Teacher's Resource Book** to evaluate students' writing.

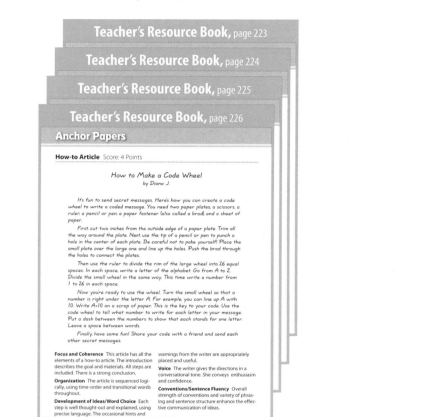

Teacher's Resource Book, page 223
Teacher's Resource Book, page 224
Teacher's Resource Book, page 225
Teacher's Resource Book, page 226

Anchor Papers

How-to Article Score: 4 Points

How to Make a Code Wheel
by Diana J.

It's fun to send secret messages. Here's how you can create a code wheel to write a coded message. You need two paper plates, a scissors, a ruler, a pencil or pen, a paper fastener (also called a brad) and a sheet of paper.

First, cut two inches from the outside edge of a paper plate. Trim all the way around the plate. Next, use the tip of a pencil or pen to punch a hole in the center of each plate. Be careful not to poke yourself! Place the small plate over the large one and line up the holes. Push the brad through the holes to connect the plates.

Then use the ruler to divide the rim of the large wheel into 26 equal spaces. In each space, write a letter of the alphabet. Go from A to Z. Divide the small wheel in the same way. This time write a number from 1 to 26 in each space.

Now you're ready to use the wheel. Turn the small wheel so that a number is right under the letter A. For example, you can line up A with 10. Write A=10 on a scrap of paper. This is the key to your code. Use the code wheel to tell what number to write for each letter in your message. Put a dash between the numbers to show that each stands for one letter. Leave a space between words.

Finally, have some fun! Share your code with a friend and send each other secret messages.

Focus and Coherence This article has all the elements of a how-to article. The introduction describes the goal and materials. All steps are included. There is a strong conclusion.

Organization The article is sequenced logically, using time-order and transitional words throughout.

Development of Ideas/Word Choice Each step is well thought-out and explained, using precise language. The occasional hints and warnings from the writer are appropriately placed and useful.

Voice The writer gives the directions in a conversational tone. She conveys enthusiasm and confidence.

Conventions/Sentence Fluency Overall strength of conventions and variety of phrasing and sentence structure enhance the effective communication of ideas.

Short-Answer Response Rubric

Use the Short-Answer Reading Rubric to score students' short-answer responses to the weekly Comprehension Check questions and the short-answer questions on weekly and unit assessments.

SHORT-ANSWER READING RUBRIC			
3 Excellent	**2** Good	**1** Fair	**0** Unsatisfactory
An **exemplary** response must • be thoughtful and insightful; • be strongly supported with accurate/relevant textual evidence; • show depth of understanding and ability to effectively connect textual evidence to the idea, analysis, or evaluation.	A **sufficient** response must • be reasonable; • be supported with accurate/relevant textual evidence; • be clear and specific.	A **partially sufficient** response may • be reasonable; • be supported by general, incomplete, partially accurate/relevant textual evidence, if any; • weakly connect textual evidence to the idea, analysis, or evaluation; • be somewhat unclear or vague.	An **insufficient** response may • be too general or vague to determine whether it is reasonable or unreasonable; • not address the question or answer a different question than the one asked; • not be based on the selection; • incorrectly analyze or evaluate the text; • offer only incomplete or irrelevant textual evidence, if any; • lack clarity.

Evidence may consist of a direct quotation, a paraphrase, or a specific synopsis.

Objectives

- Use technology in the writing process
- Review word processing skills
- Edit a word processing document

Materials

- www.macmillanmh.com
- word processing application

Vocabulary

word processor a computer program designed for creating and editing text documents

thesaurus a software feature used to find synonyms and antonyms of words

spell check a computer program that identifies words that are spelled wrong in a text file and offers their correct spelling

---

LOG ON ▶ **LEARN IT**

Computer Literacy
Focus on Keyboard and Internet Skills and Media Literacy
www.macmillanmh.com

Safety Alert

Remind students to use the Save As and Save commands to save their files frequently. This helps prevent them from losing their work.

Word Processing
Tools and Features

ACCESS PRIOR KNOWLEDGE

Discuss with students:

- How does a computer make it easier to write an essay, letter, presentation, or report? (Word processors offer different features that make it easy to quickly edit a document.)

- What aspects of writing are easier to do with pen and paper? What aspects of writing are easier with a computer?

EXPLAIN

Introduce the lesson vocabulary by writing each word on the board and asking for a definition.

- Tell students that **word processors** feature different tools that can be used to edit and improve a written document.

- In a word processing document, text can easily be deleted, copied, cut, pasted, and made bigger or smaller.

MODEL

- Show students how to open a word processor program and access a document.

- Then show how to change font style and size and how to delete text.

- Show how to cut or copy and then paste text in a document.

Technology Makes a Difference

Thesaurus and Spell Check

▶ The **thesaurus** can be used to improve the vocabulary and word choices used in a document.

▶ The **spell check** can be used to correct the spelling in a document but it is not always accurate, though, especially with proper nouns. Students must still read through their documents.

Media Literacy

Truth In Advertising

ACCESS PRIOR KNOWLEDGE

■ Show students a cereal box covered with brown paper. The only thing visible should be the word *cereal*. Ask: *Would you buy this box of cereal?*

■ Next, show students a cereal box that is targeted toward children. Ask: *Would you be more likely to buy this box of cereal, or the first box you saw? Why or why not?*

EXPLAIN

■ Some advertisements use **loaded words**. Ads use words such as *best-selling, tastes great,* and *world-famous* to persuade us that we need to buy the product.

■ Advertisements that use the **bandwagon** technique tell us we should buy a product because everyone loves it.

■ Print advertisements depend on a mixture of words and images. Television and online advertising can use words, **images**, **graphics**, animation and **sound** to sell a product.

■ Ask: *Why do you think it is important to understand the techniques that are used in advertising? Why is it important to be an educated consumer?*

MODEL

■ Distribute empty cereal boxes that are targeted to children.

■ Encourage students to identify the different design features of the box: the size and style of the type, the color of the box, the images and graphics used on the box, any promotional offers advertised, and any characters featured.

■ Instruct students to examine the nutritional information on the cereal box. Provide students with the FDA's recommended daily value for different nutritional categories.

■ With students, discuss whether the cereal is nutritious. Ask them if the nutritional information is prominently featured on the cereal box or if it is difficult to find. Why might the information be difficult to find?

■ Have students work together in groups to analyze the advertisement techniques used on the cereal boxes and present their findings to the class.

Objectives

- Identify types of advertising techniques
- Explore the positive and negative impacts of advertising techniques

Materials

- Empty children's breakfast cereal boxes
- FDA nutritional information

LOG ON

StudentWorks *Plus*
Interactive Student Book

Media Literacy Activities
Lessons that have the students explore the effects of advertisement techniques and media influence.

Theme Project Wrap-Up
Research/Organizing and Presenting Ideas

After students complete Step 1, Step 2, Step 3, and Step 4 of their projects, have them work on the following:

 Step 5 **Create the Presentation** Have students give an oral report about the community project they researched. Before the presentation, have students make note cards to aid them in speaking. Remind them to create a bibliography of their sources. Students should include visuals and an effective conclusion in their presentation.

 Step 6 **Review and Evaluate** Use these checklists to help you and your students evaluate their research and presentation. Afterward, discuss how the media might bring more attention to these projects and people.

Teacher's Checklist

Assess the Research Process

Plan the Project
✔ Discussed how people make a difference in their communities, using examples.
✔ Identified multiple resources.

Do the Project
✔ Collected information from experts.
✔ Cited and quoted all sources.

Assess the Presentation

Speaking
✔ Spoke distinctly and loud enough for others to hear.
✔ Stressed key points and backed up opinions with facts and information.

Representing
✔ Showed illustrations that added interest and enhanced meaning.
✔ Delivered information with a clear beginning, middle, and end.

Assess the Listener

✔ Listened quietly and formed an opinion.
✔ Asked questions after the speaker had finished.

Student's Checklist

Research Process
✔ Did you consult expert sources, such as librarians?
✔ Did you use several sources?
✔ Did you credit your sources?

Presenting
Speaking
✔ Did you practice your presentation?
✔ Did your presentation have a beginning, middle, and end?
✔ Did you cite your sources?

Representing
✔ Did you use visuals to help listeners understand your ideas?

SCORING RUBRIC FOR THEME PROJECT

4 Excellent	**3** Good	**2** Fair	**1** Unsatisfactory
The student • presents the information in a clear and interesting way; • uses visuals that effectively present important information; • includes an effective introduction and conclusion.	The student • presents the information in a fairly clear way; • uses visuals that present relevant information; • includes an introduction and conclusion.	The student • struggles to present the information clearly; • may use few, adequate visuals; • includes either an introduction or conclusion.	The student • may not grasp the task;. • may present sketchy information in a disorganized way; • does not have an introduction or conclusion.

 Home-School Connection

Invite family members, adult friends, members of the community, and other students to the presentation of the projects.

■ Introduce each guest by name and, if relevant, offer a brief biographical sketch.

■ Videotape the presentations for family members to borrow or to show at the parent/teacher conferences.

■ As part of your character-building feature, have students present their project to residents of a nursing home or at a senior center.

Big Question Wrap-Up

Review the Big Question with students. Tell them to use their organizers and what they learned to help them respond to the following questions: *What are some ways that people can make a difference? What was most interesting about this project? What community service might you be interested in pursuing?*

Monitoring Progress

Administer the Test

UNIT 2 TEST

TESTED SKILLS AND STRATEGIES

COMPREHENSION STRATEGIES AND SKILLS

- Strategies: Monitor comprehension; analyze text structure; analyze story structure
- Skills: Author's purpose; main idea and details; cause and effect; sequence

VOCABULARY STRATEGIES

- Prefixes and suffixes
- Context clues
- Idioms
- Homophones

TEXT FEATURES AND STUDY SKILLS

- Survey
- Parts of a book
- Chart

LITERARY ELEMENTS

- Hyperbole
- Metaphor
- Stanzas, line breaks
- Rhyme, meter

GRAMMAR, MECHANICS, USAGE

- Nouns (common and proper, singular and plural, irregular plural, possessive)
- Capitalizing proper nouns
- Using commas in a series
- Correct plural forms
- Titles
- Punctuation in letters

WRITING

- Procedural

Use Multiple Assessments for Instructional Planning

To create instructional profiles for your students, look for patterns in the results from any of the following assessments.

Fluency Assessment

Plan appropriate fluency-building activities and practice to help all students achieve the following goal: **84–104 WCPM**.

Running Records

Use the instructional reading level determined by the Running Record calculations for regrouping decisions.

Benchmark Assessment

Administer tests four times a year as an additional measure of both student progress and the effectiveness of the instructional program.

Digital Assessment

Progress Reporter

Assessment Online
- Prescriptions for Reteaching
- Student Profile System

ExamView Test Generator

Test Generator
- Available on CD-ROM

Analyze the Data

Use information from a variety of informal and formal assessments, as well as your own judgment, to assist in your instructional planning. Students who consistently score at the lowest end of each range should be evaluated for Intervention. Use the **Diagnostic Assessment** for guidelines for decision making.

Diagnose		Prescribe
ASSESSMENTS	**IF...**	**THEN...**
UNIT TEST	0–21 questions correct	Reteach tested skills using the **Intervention Teacher's Editions**.
FLUENCY ASSESSMENT		
Oral Reading Fluency	79–83 WCPM 0–78 WCPM	Fluency Solutions Reteach using the **Fluency Intervention Teacher's Edition**.
RUNNING RECORDS	Level 28 or below	Reteach Comprehension skills using the **Comprehension Intervention Teacher's Edition**. Provide additional Fluency activities.

Response to Intervention

To place students in Tier 2 or Tier 3 Intervention use the *Diagnostic Assessment*.

• Phonics
• Vocabulary
• Comprehension
• Fluency
• Writing and Grammar

Glossary

Introduce students to the Glossary by reading through the introduction and looking over the pages with them. Ask the class to talk about what they see.

Words in a glossary, like words in a dictionary, are listed in **alphabetical order**. Point out the **guide words** at the top of each page that tell the first and last words appearing on that page.

ENTRIES

Point out examples of **main entries**, or entry words, and entries. Read through a sample entry with the class, identifying each part. Have students note the order in which information is given: entry word(s), syllable division, pronunciation respelling, part of speech, definition(s), example sentence(s).

Note if more than one definition is given for a word, the definitions are numbered. Note the format used for a word that is more than one part of speech.

Review the **parts of speech** by identifying each in a sentence:

Inter.	*article*	*n.*	*conj.*	*adj.*	*n.*
Wow!	A	dictionary	and	useful	glossary

v.	*adv.*	*pron.*	*prep.*	*n.*
tell	almost	everything	about	words!

HOMOGRAPHS/HOMOPHONES/HOMONYMS

Point out that some entries are for multiple-meaning words called **homographs**. Homographs have the same spellings but have different origins and meanings, and, in some cases, different pronunciations.

Explain that students should not confuse homographs with **homophones** or **homonyms**. Homophones are words that have the same pronunciation but have different spellings and meanings. Homonyms are words that have the same pronunciation and spelling but have different meanings. Provide students with examples.

PRONUNCIATION KEY

Explain the use of the pronunciation key (either the short key, at the bottom of every other page, or the long key, at the beginning of the Glossary). Demonstrate the difference between primary stress and secondary stress by pronouncing a word with both. Pronounce the words both correctly and incorrectly to give students a clearer understanding of the proper pronunciations.

WORD HISTORY

The Word History feature explains the **etymology** of select words. Explain that etymology is the history of a word from its origin to its present form. A word's etymology explains which language it comes from and what changes have occurred in its spelling and/or meaning. Many English words are derivatives of words from other languages, such as Latin or Greek. Derivatives are formed from base or root words.

Glossary

What Is a Glossary?

A glossary can help you find the **meanings** of words in this book that you may not know. The words in the glossary are listed in **alphabetical order**. **Guide words** at the top of each page tell you the first and last words on the page.

Each word is divided into syllables. The way to pronounce the word is given next. You can understand the pronunciation respelling by using the **pronunciation key**. A shorter key appears at the bottom of every other page. When a word has more than one syllable, a dark accent mark (′) shows which syllable is stressed. In some words, a light accent mark (′) shows which syllable has a less heavy stress. Sometimes an entry includes a second meaning for the word.

prehistoric

reptiles

Guide Words
First word on the page   Last word on the page

Sample Entry

Pronunciation   Part of speech

Main entry & Syllable division

sketch•es (skech′əz) *plural noun.* Simple drawings that are done quickly. *I made several **sketches** before finally painting the tree.*

Example sentence

Definition

Pronunciation Key

Phonetic Spelling	Examples	Phonetic Spelling	Examples
a	at, bad, plaid, laugh	d	dear, soda, bad
ā	ape, pain, day, break	f	five, defend, leaf, off, cough, elephant
ä	father, calm		
âr	care, pair, bear, their, where	g	game, ago, fog, egg
e	end, pet, said, heaven, friend	h	hat, ahead
ē	equal, me, feet, team, piece, key	hw	white, whether, which
i	it, big, give, hymn	j	joke, enjoy, gem, page, edge
ī	ice, fine, lie, my	k	kite, bakery, seek, tack, cat
îr	ear, deer, here, pierce	l	lid, sailor, feel, ball, allow
o	odd, hot, watch	m	man, family, dream
ō	old, oat, toe, low	n	not, final, pan, knife, gnaw
ô	coffee, all, taught, law, fought	ng	long, singer
ôr	order, fork, horse, story, pour	p	pail, repair, soap, happy
oi	oil, toy	r	ride, parent, wear, more, marry
ou	out, now, bough	s	sit, aside, pets, cent, pass
u	up, mud, love, double	sh	shoe, washer, fish, mission, nation
ū	use, mule, cue, feud, few	t	tag, pretend, fat, dressed
ü	rule, true, food, fruit	th	thin, panther, both
ů	put, wood, should, look	th	these, mother, smooth
ûr	burn, hurry, term, bird, word, courage	v	very, favor, wave
ə	about, taken, pencil, lemon, circus	w	wet, weather, reward
b	bat, above, job	y	yes, onion
ch	chin, such, match	z	zoo, lazy, jazz, rose, dogs, houses
		zh	vision, treasure, seizure

808

809

Aa

ab•sorbed (ab zôrbd′) *verb.* Soaked up something such as a liquid or the sun's rays. *It was a hot day, so the plant **absorbed** the water immediately.*

a•chieved (ə chēvd′) *verb.* To have done or carried out successfully. *She studied hard and **achieved** the grade she wanted.*

ac•quaint•ance (ə kwān′təns) *noun.* A person one knows, but who is not a close friend. *Carole is an **acquaintance** from camp.*

ac•tive (ak′tiv) *adjective.* Lively, busy. *Carlos is always **active**; he hardly ever sits still.*

ad•vanced (ad vanst′) *adjective.* Beyond the beginning level; not elementary. *As a singer, Sheila was really **advanced** for her age.*

ag•ile (aj′əl) *adjective.* Able to move and react quickly and easily. *Bonita is an **agile** softball player.*

al•loy (al′oi) *noun.* A metal formed by fusing two or more metals. *Brass is an **alloy** of copper and zinc.*

a•maze•ment (ə māz′mənt) *noun.* Great surprise or wonder. *To the **amazement** of the audience, the children played some difficult music perfectly.*

am•bu•lance (am′byə ləns) *noun.* A special vehicle that is used to carry sick or injured people to a hospital. *My neighbor once had to call an **ambulance** to take him to the hospital.*

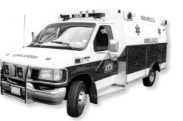

an•ces•tors (an′ses tərz) *plural noun.* People in the past from whom one comes. *Your great-grandparents are some of your **ancestors**.*

an•noyed (ə noid′) *adjective.* Bothered or disturbed. *Kevin looked **annoyed** when his little sister came out to join the game.*

an•nu•al (an′yü əl) *adjective.* Measured by the year. *The **annual** rainfall in our hometown is close to 20 inches.*

an•tic•i•pa•tion (an tis′ə pā′shən) *noun.* A feeling of excited expectation. *Tim was full of eager **anticipation** as he got on the roller coaster.*

a•pol•o•gize (ə pol′ə jīz′) *verb.* To say one is sorry or embarrassed; make an apology. *Aaron said, "I'd like to **apologize** for being late."*

ap•plaud•ed (ə plôd′əd) *verb.* Showed approval for or enjoyment of something by the clapping of hands. *The crowd **applauded** the soldiers as they came off the ship.*

ap•pre•ci•at•ed (ə prē′shē āt′əd) *verb.* Understood the value of; was grateful for something. *The boss **appreciated** how much his workers did for the company.*

as•sem•bled (ə sem′bəld) *verb.* To have put or fit together. *Anita and Grace **assembled** their wagon in just three hours.*

as•sured (ə shůrd′) *verb.* Made certain or sure. *Our hard work **assured** the success of the festival.*

a•void•ed (ə void′əd) *verb.* Stayed away from. *Butch **avoided** doing hard work.*

a•ware (ə wâr′) *adjective.* Knowing or realizing. *I don't wear headphones when I run, so I am **aware** of what is around me.*

awk•ward (ôk′wərd) *adjective.* Lacking grace in movement or behavior; clumsy or uncomfortable. *Until Julio learned the steps, his dancing was **awkward**.*

Bb

bar•be•cue (bär′bi kū) *noun.* A meal, usually meat, cooked outdoors over an open fire. *We had a great **barbecue** in the park.*

at; āpe; fär; câre; end; mē; it; īce; pîerce; hot; ōld; sông; fôrk; oil; out; up; ūse; rüle; půll; tûrn; chin; sing; shop; thin; this; hw in white; zh in treasure.

The symbol ə stands for the unstressed vowel sound in about, taken, pencil, lemon, and circus.

810

811

bar•gained (bär'gind) *verb.* To have talked over the terms of an agreement or sale. *My dad* **bargained** *with the salesperson to get a deal on our new car.*

bid•ding (bid'ing) *noun.* A period in which bids, offers of payments, are made or received. *The auction house started the* **bidding** *for the antiques.*

bor•der (bôr'dər) *noun.* A line between one country, state, county, or town and another. *A river runs along the* **border** *between the two states.*

boy•cotts (boi'kots) *plural noun.* Protests in which people refuse to buy from or work for a person, nation, or business. *The* **boycotts** *against the unfair company were very successful.*

Word History

Boycotts comes from Charles Boycott, who was shunned by Irish farmers for his harsh actions against them.

brit•tle (brit'əl) *adjective.* Likely to break or snap. *Susan's fingernails became* **brittle** *and started to break.*

Cc

cam•ou•flage (kam'ə fläzh') *verb.* To hide or conceal by using shapes or colors that blend with the surroundings. *The chameleon is able to* **camouflage** *itself by changing the color of its skin.*

car•at (kar'ət) *noun.* A unit of weight equal to 1/5 of a gram, usually used to measure gems. *The ring had a three* **carat** *diamond in the center.*

chal•leng•es (chal'ənj ez) *plural noun.* Those things that call for work, effort, and the use of one's talents. *Ted's greatest* **challenges** *are in Art and Spanish.*

char•i•ty (char'i tē) *noun.* The giving of help to the poor or needy. *After the flood, some of the families refused to accept any* **charity.**

cir•cu•lar (sûr'kyə lər) *adjective.* Having or making the shape of a circle. *The referee's arm made a* **circular** *motion as he blew the whistle.*

cit•i•zen (sit'ə zən) *noun.* A person who was born in a country or who chooses to live in and become a member of that country. *Carmine is an Italian* **citizen** *but often visits the United States.*

civ•il•i•za•tions (siv'əl ə zā'shənz) *plural noun.* Human societies in which agriculture, trade, government, art, and science are highly developed. *Charles studies the ancient* **civilizations** *of Asia.*

cli•mate (klī'mit) *noun.* The average weather conditions of a place or region through the year. *Most deserts have a hot, dry* **climate.**

clus•tered (klus'tərd) *verb.* To have grown, or grouped together, things of the same kind. *The grapes were* **clustered** *in a bunch.*

col•lage (kə läzh') *noun.* A picture made by pasting paper, cloth, metal, and other things in an arrangement on a surface. *Once I made a* **collage** *of my day's activities by using clippings from magazines.*

Word History

Collage comes from the French word *collage,* from *colle,* meaning "glue" or "paste."

col•o•ny (kol'ə nē) *noun.* A group of animals or plants of the same kind that live together. *I found a* **colony** *of ants in my yard.*

com•mo•tion (kə mō'shən) *noun.* A noisy disturbance; confusion. *We ran into the hall to see what was causing the* **commotion.**

com•mu•ni•ca•tion (kə mūni kā'shən) *noun.* An exchange or sharing of feelings, thoughts, or information. *Music is one form of* **communication** *that does not require speech.*

com•ple•ted (kəm plēt'əd) *verb.* Finished; did. *I had to wait until I* **completed** *my homework before I could go to the movies.*

con•ceived (kən sēvd') *verb.* To have formed an idea; thought up. *The plan was* **conceived** *after everyone had gone to bed.*

con•densed (kən densd') *verb.* To have made thicker or more compact; to have reduced the volume of. *The chef* **condensed** *the sauce by boiling it for 20 minutes.*

con•di•tions (kən dish'ənz) *plural noun.* The state something is in. *Because of the* **conditions** *at the playground, we weren't allowed to play there.*

at; āpe; fär; câre; end; mē; it; īce; pîerce; hot; ōld; sông; fôrk; oil; out; up; ūse; rūle; pull; tûrn; chin; sing; shop; thin; <u>th</u>is; hw in white; zh in treasure.

The symbol ə stands for the unstressed vowel sound in about, taken, pencil, lemon, and circus.

con•duc•ted (kən dukt'tid) *verb.* To have directed, led, guided, or transmitted. *When Susie lost her sneaker, she* **conducted** *a search of the entire locker room.*

con•sist•ed (kən sis'təd) *verb.* Contained; was made up. *The batter* **consisted** *of a cup of flour, one egg, and a cup of milk.*

con•vinced (kən vinst') *verb.* To have caused a person to do or believe something. *Raj finally* **convinced** *his father he was old enough to go on the trip.*

crank•y (krang'kē) *adjective.* To be cross or in a bad temper; grouchy. *Roni is always* **cranky** *before she's had breakfast.*

cur•i•ous (kyür'ē əs) *adjective.* Eager to learn new, strange, or interesting things. *We were all* **curious** *to know who our new teacher might be.*

cur•rent (kûr'ənt) *noun.* A portion of a body of water or of air flowing continuously in a definite direction. *The* **current** *took the raft far out to sea.*

Dd

dec•ades (dek'ādz) *plural noun.* Periods of ten years. *Our family has lived in the same city for nearly six* **decades.**

Word History

Decades comes from the Greek *deka,* meaning "ten."

de•cayed (dē kād') *adjective.* Having undergone the process of decomposition; rotted. *We walked in the woods past* **decayed** *stumps of trees.*

de•fend (di fend') *verb.* Guard against attack or harm. *The rabbit could not* **defend** *itself against the snake, so it ran away.*

def•i•ni•tion (def'ə nish'ən) *noun.* An explanation of what a word or phrase means. *Our teacher Mr. Mitchell asked us what the* **definition** *of "like" is.*

de•mon•stra•ted (de'mən strā'təd) *verb.* Showed by actions or experiment. *The performer* **demonstrated** *great skill with both the piano and the drums.*

de•scen•dants (di send'ənts) *plural noun.* People who come from a particular ancestor. *My neighbors are* **descendants** *of a French explorer.*

de•signed (di zīnd') *verb.* To have made a plan, drawing, or outline of something. *Penelope's sister* **designed** *the perfect sundress for her.*

des•per•ate (des'par it) *adjective.* Very bad or hopeless. *I needed money, but the situation was not* **desperate.**

di•ges•ted (di jes'tid) *verb.* To have broken down food in the mouth, stomach, and intestines. *After my dog had* **digested** *his dinner he was hungry again.*

dis•ap•point•ment (dis'ə point'mənt) *noun.* A feeling of being disappointed or let down. *Losing the match was a* **disappointment***, but I still like tennis.*

dis•miss (dis mis') *verb.* To discard or reject. *John was able to* **dismiss** *the story he heard as a rumor.*

dis•play (di splā') *noun.* A show or exhibit. *The children's artwork is the main* **display** *on the family refrigerator.*

dis•rupt (dis rupt') *verb.* To throw into disorder or confusion. *An argument might* **disrupt** *the meeting.*

diz•zy (diz'ē) *adjective.* Having the feeling of spinning and being about to fall. *I was* **dizzy** *when I got off the Ferris wheel.*

dove (dōv) *verb.* Plunged head first into water. *We watched as the woman* **dove** *perfectly off the board and into the deep pool.*

dove (duv) *noun.* A medium-size bird of the pigeon family. *The* **dove** *cooed quietly on the window ledge.*

draw•backs (drô'bäks) *plural noun.* Things that make something more difficult or unpleasant. *One of the* **drawbacks** *of his job is the long hours.*

drought (drout) *noun.* A period of time in which there is little or no rainfall. *The terrible August* **drought** *affected the wheat crop.*

at; āpe; fär; câre; end; mē; it; īce; pîerce; hot; ōld; sông; fôrk; oil; out; up; ūse; rūle; pull; tûrn; chin; sing; shop; thin; <u>th</u>is; hw in white; zh in treasure.

The symbol ə stands for the unstressed vowel sound in about, taken, pencil, lemon, and circus.

Dust Bowl (dust bŏl) *noun.* The region in the central United States that suffered from the great dust storms of the 1930s. *Oklahoma was part of the* **Dust Bowl**.

Ee

eaves•drop•ping (ēvz'drop'ing) *noun.* Listening to other people talking without letting them know you are listening. *He was* **eavesdropping** *on her neighbors.*

ech•o•lo•ca•tion (ek'ō lō kā'shən) *noun.* A way to find out where objects are by making sounds and interpreting the echo that returns. *Bats rely on* **echolocation** *when they hunt for insects.*

ee•rie (ir'ē) *adjective.* Strange in a scary way. *We heard an owl's* **eerie** *hooting as we walked home in the dark.*

e•lec•tri•cal (i lek'tri kəl) *adjective.* Relating to the form of energy carried in wires for use to drive motors or as light or heat. *Dad carefully connected the* **electrical** *cables to the new DVD player in the den.*

e•merge (i mûrj') *verb.* To come into view or become known. *After months in hibernation, the bears* **emerge**.

en•coun•ter (en koun'tər) *verb.* To meet or face, usually unexpectedly. *Katie listens to the traffic report so she does not* **encounter** *any delays.*

en•cour•aged (en kûr'ijd) *verb.* To have inspired with courage, hope, or confidence. *The bright sunlight* **encouraged** *us to continue our hike.*

end•less (end'lis) *adjective.* Having no limit or end. *The line of people for the show seemed* **endless**.

en•dured (en dûrd' or en dyûrd') *verb.* Survived or put up with. *The workers* **endured** *the hot sun all day.*

e•nor•mous (i nôr'məs) *adjective.* Much greater than the usual size, amount, or degree; extremely large. *The* **enormous** *pumpkin weighed over 300 pounds.*

en•ter•pri•sing (en'tər prī'zing) *adjective.* Showing energy and initiative; willing or inclined to take risks. *Brian, an* **enterprising** *young man, ran for class president and won.*

e•sta•blished (i stab'lishd) *verb.* To have begun, created, or set up. *We* **established** *a scholarship in memory of my mother.*

e•va•po•rate (i vap'ə rāt') *verb.* To change from a liquid or solid into a gas. *Heat makes water* **evaporate**.

> **Word History**
> **Evaporate** comes from the Latin *evaporatus,* "dispersed in vapor," from *ex,* "out," and *vapor,* "exhalation."

e•ven•tu•al•ly (i ven'chū ə lē) *adverb.* In the end; finally. *We* **eventually** *got a DVD player because the good movies were not being shown on television.*

ex•as•per•at•ed (eg zas'pər ăt'əd) *verb.* Annoyed greatly; made angry. *Helping me with my math so* **exasperated** *my dad that my mom took over.*

ex•po•sure (ek spō'zhər) *noun.* The condition of being presented to view. *After each* **exposure** *to the new toy, the dog began to recognize it and would pick it up without being asked.*

Ff

fam•ished (fam'isht) *adjective.* Very hungry; starving. *After a long day of running and swimming, the children were* **famished** *and wanted to eat as soon as possible.*

flinched (flincht) *verb.* Drew back or away, as from something painful or unpleasant; winced. *When the door suddenly slammed, Myra* **flinched**.

fool•ish•ness (fū'lish nəs) *noun.* The act of not showing good sense. *I wanted to race across the street, but my mom will not allow that* **foolishness**.

frag•ile (fraj'əl) *adjective.* Easily broken; delicate. *My toothpick ship is too* **fragile** *to take to show-and-tell.*

freeze-dried (frēz'drī'd) *verb.* To dry while frozen under high vacuum for preservation. *On the camping trip, John mixed a cup of boiling water with a teaspoon of* **freeze-dried** *coffee.*

fre•quent•ly (frē'kwənt lē) *adverb.* Happening often. *I* **frequently** *eat cereal for breakfast.*

fron•tier (frun tir') *noun.* The far edge of a country, where people are just beginning to settle. *Many Americans moved to the* **frontier** *in covered wagons.*

fu•els (fū'əlz) *plural noun.* Substances burned as a source of heat and power, such as coal, wood, or oil. *When the world runs out of fossil* **fuels**, *we will be forced to use alternate energy sources.*

at; āpe; fär; câre; end; mē; it; īce; pîerce; hot; ōld; sông; fôrk; oil; out; up; ūse; rūle; pùll; tûrn; chin; sing; shop; thin; this; hw in white; zh in treasure.

The symbol ə stands for the unstressed vowel sound in about, taken, pencil, lemon, and circus.

816

817

Gg

gaped (gāpt) *verb.* Stared with the mouth open, as in wonder or surprise. *The audience* **gaped** *at the acrobats.*

gen•u•ine (jen'ū in) *adjective.* Sincere; honest. *My friends and I made a* **genuine** *effort to help all the kids that were new to the school.*

glanced (glansd) *verb.* To take a brief or hurried look. *He* **glanced** *at the magazines on the table.*

glis•tened (glis'ənd) *verb.* To shine with reflected light. *The snow on the fir trees* **glistened** *in the sun.*

globe (glōb) *noun.* Earth (as a shape). *Our* **globe** *is the home of billions of people.*

glo•ri•ous (glor'ē əs) *adjective.* Having or deserving praise or honor; magnificent. *The colors of the maple leaves in autumn are* **glorious**.

Great De•pres•sion (grāt'dē presh'ən) *noun.* A worldwide economic downturn that began in 1928. *My grandparents tell stories about how difficult it was to find a job during the* **Great Depression**.

guard•i•an (gär'dē ən) *noun.* A person or thing that guards or watches over. *My older brother sometimes acts like he is my* **guardian**.

Hh

hab•i•tat (hab'i tat') *noun.* The place where an animal or plant naturally lives and grows. *A swamp is a common* **habitat** *for many creatures.*

han•dy (han'dē) *adjective.* Within reach, nearby; easy to use. To **come in handy** is to be useful. *It's amazing how many times a dictionary can* **come in handy**.

harm•less (härm'les) *adjective.* Not able to do damage or hurt. *My dog looks mean, but really she is* **harmless**.

head•lines (hed'līnz) *plural noun.* Words printed at the top of a newspaper or magazine article. *The most important news has the biggest* **headlines**.

hi•ber•nate (hī'bər nāt') *verb.* To sleep or stay inactive during the winter. *Bears eat a lot to get ready to* **hibernate**.

hi•lar•i•ous (hi lâr'ē əs) *adjective.* Very funny. *Keisha tells* **hilarious** *jokes that make everyone laugh.*

hoist•ing (hoist'ing) *verb.* Lifting or pulling up. **Hoisting** *logs out of the water, the men soon grew tired.*

Ii

i•den•ti•fied (ī den'tə fīd') *verb.* Proved that someone or something is a particular person or thing. *The fingerprints on the gold watch* **identified** *the butler as the thief.*

im•pres•sive (im pres'iv) *adjective.* Deserving admiration; making a strong impression. *The track team won five races, which was its most* **impressive** *result all year.*

in•ci•dent (in'si dənt) *noun.* An event or act. *After the pep rally, there was a funny* **incident** *involving bales of hay and the school mascot.*

in•de•pen•dence (in'di pen'dəns) *noun.* Freedom from the control of another or others. *America gained its* **independence** *from Great Britain.*

in•jus•tice (in jus'tis) *noun.* Lack of justice; unfairness. *The workers felt it was an* **injustice** *that they could not vote on the issue.*

in•sec•ti•cides (in sek'ti sīdz') *plural noun.* Chemicals for killing insects. *Our family room was sprayed with* **insecticides**.

at; āpe; fär; câre; end; mē; it; īce; pîerce; hot; ōld; sông; fôrk; oil; out; up; ūse; rūle; pùll; tûrn; chin; sing; shop; thin; this; hw in white; zh in treasure.

The symbol ə stands for the unstressed vowel sound in about, taken, pencil, lemon, and circus.

818

819

Glossary

Making a Difference

263R

Glossary

in·spire (in spīr') *verb.* To stir the mind, feelings, or imagination. *Nature can **inspire** some people to write poetry.*

in·sult (in'sult) *noun.* A remark or action that hurts someone's feelings or pride. *It would be an **insult** not to invite Marta to the party.*

in·tel·li·gent (in tel'i jənt) *adjective.* Able to understand and to think especially well. *An **intelligent** person was needed to solve the difficult puzzle.*

in·ter·act (in'tər akt') *verb.* To act together, toward, or with others. *My teacher and our class **interact** on a daily basis.*

in·ter·fere (in'tər fir') *verb.* To take part in the affairs of others when not asked; to meddle. *My mom hates to **interfere** with my business, but she often gives me good advice.*

in·ter·vals (in'tər vəlz) *plural noun.* The spaces or time between two things. *There are **intervals** of 50 miles between each rest stop on the highway.*

in·ves·ti·gates (in ves'ti gāts') *verb.* Looks at something carefully in order to gather information. *Every morning, our dog Lulu **investigates** our yard for cats.*

Word History

Investigates comes from the Latin *investigare,* meaning "to track."

is·sues (ish'üz) *plural noun.* 1. Subject matters under discussion. 2. Individual copies of a magazine. *1. My brother and I disagree on certain **issues**. 2. All the **issues** of my favorite comic book were stacked on the shelf.*

i·tems (ī'təmz) *noun.* Things in a group or list. *Christine always makes a list of the **items** she needs from the grocery store.*

Jj

jour·ney (jûr'nē) *noun.* A trip, especially one over a considerable distance or taking considerable time. *Ping made a **journey** to China to meet his grandparents and uncles.*

jum·ble (jum'bəl) *noun.* A confused mixture or condition; mess. *My messy room is a **jumble** of toys and books.*

Ll

la·bor (lā'bər) *noun.* 1. Hard work. 2. People who work at jobs that require physical strength. *1. We all needed naps after a day of **labor** in the yard. 2. The **labor** unions asked for better pay.*

leg·a·cy (leg'ə sē) *noun.* Something handed down from the past; heritage. *The medical research foundation she founded will be her **legacy**.*

leg·en·dary (lej'ən der'ē) *adjective.* Relating to a legend, or a story that has been handed down for many years and has some basis in fact. *Johnny Appleseed's efforts to spread the apple tree have become **legendary**.*

log·i·cal (loj'i kəl) *adjective.* Sensible; being the action or result one expects. *When it rains, I do the **logical** thing and put my bicycle in the garage.*

loos·ened (lü'sənd) *verb.* Made looser; set free or released. *Brad **loosened** his necktie when the ceremony was over.*

lum·ber·ing (lum'bər ing) *adjective.* Moving in a slow, clumsy way. *Put a **lumbering** hippo in the water, and it becomes a graceful swimmer.*

lurk (lûrk) *verb.* To lie hidden. *Many animals **lurk** in their dens so they can surprise their prey when it walks by.*

Mm

mag·ni·fy (mag'nə fī') *verb.* To make something look bigger than it really is. *Devices such as microscopes help to **magnify** small things.*

mas·sive (mas'iv) *adjective.* Of great size or extent; large and solid. *The sumo wrestler had a **massive** chest.*

at; āpe; fär; câre; end; mē; it; īce; pîerce; hot; ōld; sông; fôrk; oil; out; up; ūse; rüle; pùll; tûrn; chin; sing; shop; thin; this; hw in white; zh in treasure. | The symbol ə stands for the unstressed vowel sound in about, taken, pencil, lemon, and circus.

midst (midst) *noun.* A position in the middle of a group of people or things. *"There is a poet in our **midst**," said the principal, "and we need to clap for her."*

mi·grant work·ers (mī'grənt wûr'kərz) *plural noun.* Persons who move from place to place for work. *The **migrant workers** traveled from farm to farm.*

mis·chief (mis'chif) *noun.* Conduct that may seem playful but causes harm or trouble. *The kittens were always getting into **mischief** when we weren't home.*

mis·un·der·stood (mis'un dər stúd') *verb.* Understood someone incorrectly; got the wrong idea. *I **misunderstood** the directions my teacher gave and did the wrong page for homework.*

mo·ti·vate (mō'tə vāt') *verb.* To provide with a move to action. *The thought of a college scholarship will always **motivate** me to study hard.*

mut·tered (mut'ərd) *verb.* Spoke in a low, unclear way with the mouth closed. *I could tell he was mad by the way he **muttered** to himself.*

mys·te·ri·ous (mi stîr'ē əs) *adjective.* Very hard or impossible to understand; full of mystery. *The fact that the cookies were missing was **mysterious**.*

Nn

nat·u·ral (nach'ər əl) *adjective.* 1. Unchanged by people. 2. Expected or normal. *1. We hiked through **natural** surroundings of woods, streams, and meadows. 2. The **natural** home of the dolphin is the open ocean.*

ne·glec·ted (ni glekt'əd) *verb.* Failed to give proper attention or care to; failed to do. *I **neglected** to finish my science project and could not present it at the fair.*

now·a·days (nou'ə dāz') *adverb.* In the present time. *People hardly ever write with typewriters **nowadays**.*

nu·mer·ous (nü'mər əs or nū'mər əs) *adjective.* Forming a large number; many. *The mountain climbers faced **numerous** problems, but they still had fun.*

nu·tri·ents (nü'trē ənts or nū'trē ənts) *plural noun.* Substances needed by the bodies of people, animals, or plants to live and grow. *Sometimes we get ill because we are not getting the proper **nutrients**.*

Oo

o·be·di·ence (ō bē'dē əns) *noun.* The willingness to obey, or to carry out orders, wishes, or instructions. *It is important to show **obedience** to safety rules.*

Word History

Obedience comes from the Latin word *obedire,* meaning "to hearken, yield, or serve."

o·pin·ions (ə pin'yənz) *plural noun.* Beliefs or conclusions based on a person's judgment rather than on what is proven or known to be true. *I want to find out what my classmates' **opinions** are about recycling.*

op·por·tu·ni·ties (op'ər tü'ni tēz) *plural noun.* Good chances or favorable times. *School offers students many **opportunities** to join clubs and organizations.*

or·a·to·ry (ôr'ə tôr'ē) *noun.* Eloquence and skill in public speaking. *The President was a master of campaign **oratory**.*

out·stretched (out'strechtd') *adjective.* Stretched out; extended. *His **outstretched** palm held the quarter I had dropped.*

o·ver·flow·ing (ō'vər flō'ing) *verb.* To be so full that the contents flow over. *The trunk was **overflowing** with old toys.*

at; āpe; fär; câre; end; mē; it; īce; pîerce; hot; ōld; sông; fôrk; oil; out; up; ūse; rüle; pùll; tûrn; chin; sing; shop; thin; this; hw in white; zh in treasure. | The symbol ə stands for the unstressed vowel sound in about, taken, pencil, lemon, and circus.

Unit 2

Pp

par•a•lyzed (par'ə lizd') *adjective.*
1. Having lost movement or sensation in a part of the body. 2. Powerless or helpless. *Sue was **paralyzed** by stage fright.*

part•ner•ship (pärt'nər ship') *noun.* A kind of business in which two or more people share the work and profits. *Janell, Pat, and Erik formed a gardening **partnership**.*

pe•cul•iar (pi kūl'yər) *adjective.* Strange; not usual. *I had the **peculiar** feeling that I was being watched.*

per•sis•tence (pər sis'təns) *noun.* The ability to keep trying in spite of difficulties or obstacles. *In order to run a business, a person must have a lot of **persistence**.*

phras•es (frāz'iz) *plural noun.* Groups of words expressing a single thought but not containing both a subject and predicate. *When I proofread my report, I made **phrases** into complete sentences.*

pol•i•cy (pol'i sē) *noun.* A guiding plan that people use to help make decisions. *The school has a strict "no t-shirt" **policy**.*

pos•i•tive (poz'i tiv) *adjective.* Certain; sure. *I am **positive** I left my backpack right here on the counter.*

pre•his•tor•ic (prē'his tôr'ik) *adjective.* Belonging to a time before people started recording history. *Explorers found **prehistoric** drawings along the cave walls.*

pro•claimed (prə klāmd' or prō klāmd') *verb.* Announced publicly. *The principal **proclaimed** May 20 as the day for our class trips.*

prop•er•ties (prop'ər tēz) *plural noun.* Characteristics of matter that can be observed. *Scientists measured the **properties** of gold in their lab.*

pro•tes•ted (prō test'əd) *verb.* Complained against something. *When the workers lost their jobs in the factory, they **protested**.*

pur•chased (pûr'chəsd) *verb.* Got by paying money; got by sacrifice or hardship. *Sally **purchased** the chess board using what she saved from her monthly allowance.*

Rr

ranged (rānjd) *verb.* To go between certain limits. *The prices for a music player **ranged** from fifty to two hundred dollars.*

re•al•is•tic (rē'əlis'tik) *adjective.* Seeing things as they are; practical. *I dream of being a famous rock star, but I should also be **realistic** and stay in school.*

reef (rēf) *noun.* A ridge of sand, rock, or coral at or near the surface of the ocean. *Boaters have to be careful not to scrape against the **reef** below.*

ref•er•ence (ref'ər əns or ref'rens) *noun.* A statement that calls or directs attention to something. *The speech makes a **reference** to a play written by William Shakespeare.*

re•form (ri fôrm') *noun.* A change for the better. *She worked for a **reform** of the political system.*

reg•is•ter (rej'i stər) *noun.* 1. A formal record or list. 2. The range of a voice or instrument. *verb.* To enroll. *Every college student must **register** before attending class.*

re•lays (rē'lāz) *plural noun.* Fresh sets, teams, or supplies that replace or relieve another. *Post office workers work in **relays** in order to get your letters from one place to another quickly.*

at; āpe; fär; câre; end; mē; it; īce; pîerce; hot; ōld; sông; fôrk; oil; out; up; ūse; rūle; pu̇ll; tûrn; chin; sing; shop; thin; this; hw in white; zh in treasure.

The symbol ə stands for the unstressed vowel sound in about, taken, pencil, lemon, and circus.

824

825

re•leased (ri lēsd') *verb.* To have set free or loose. *The girl opened the gate to the pen and **released** the pigs.*

re•lo•cat•ed (rē lō'kā tid) *verb.* To have moved to a different location. *The store **relocated** down the block from the park.*

rep•tiles (rep'tilz) *plural noun.* Cold-blooded vertebrates of the group Reptilia, which includes lizards, snakes, alligators, crocodiles, and turtles. *Most **reptiles** lay eggs, although some give birth to live young.*

res•i•dent (rez'i dənt) *noun.* A person who lives in a particular place. *The new **resident** shocked neighbors by planting the entire front yard with sunflowers.*

re•spon•si•bil•i•ty (ri spon'sə bil'i tē) *noun.* The quality or condition of having a job, duty, or concern. *Taking care of the dog was my **responsibility**.*

roamed (rōmd) *verb.* Moved around in a large area. *The grizzly bear **roamed** over the valley and the nearby mountains.*

route (rūt or rout) *noun.* A road or course used for traveling. *Trucks must follow a special **route**.*

rum•bling (rum'bling) *noun.* A heavy, deep, rolling sound. *The **rumbling** of thunder woke me up.*

Ss

sanc•tu•ar•y (sangk'chū er'ē) *noun.* A protected place for wildlife where predators are controlled and hunting is not allowed. *My friend runs a **sanctuary** for injured hawks and owls.*

scorn•ful•ly (skôrn'fəl ē) *adverb.* In a way that shows that something or someone is looked down upon and considered bad or worthless. *The critic was unhappy with the new artist's paintings so he spoke **scornfully** about them.*

seg•re•ga•tion (seg'ri gā'shən) *noun.* The practice of setting one racial group apart from another. *The Civil Rights movement fought against **segregation**.*

se•lec•ting (si lek'ting) *verb.* Picking out among many; choosing. *I spent a long time **selecting** the right gift.*

self•ish (sel'fish) *adjective.* Thinking only of oneself; putting one's own interests and desires before those of others. *A second piece of cake sounded good, but I didn't want to be **selfish**.*

sen•si•ble (sen'sə bəl) *adjective.* Having or showing sound judgment; wise. *If you make a mistake, the **sensible** thing to do is apologize.*

sev•e•ral (sev'ə rəl or sev'rəl) *adjective.* More than two, but not many. *Louisa slept for **several** hours.*

shim•mer (shim'ər) *verb.* To shine with a faint, wavering light; glimmer. *The lake began to **shimmer** in the rays of the setting sun.*

silk•en (sil'kən) *adjective.* 1. Made of silk. 2. Like silk in appearance. *1. The queen's **silken** robe was exquisite. 2. Antonio wrote a poem about the girl's long **silken** hair.*

Silk Road (silk rōd) *noun.* A trade route that connected China with the Roman Empire. *The **Silk Road** was about 4,000 miles long.*

sim•il•ar (sim'əl ər) *adjective.* Having many but not all qualities alike. *Zack and Nick have **similar** haircuts.*

sky•scrap•ers (skī'skrā'pərz) *plural noun.* Very tall buildings. *The city has many **skyscrapers**, and some of them are 50 stories tall!*

slen•der (slen'dər) *adjective.* Thin, especially in an attractive or graceful way. *The swan stretched its long **slender** neck and flapped its wings.*

slith•ered (slith'ərd) *verb.* Slid or glided like a snake. *When the snakes **slithered** across the ground, they moved quickly and hardly made a sound.*

snick•er•ing (snik'ər ing) *verb.* Laughing in a mean or disrespectful manner. *The children stopped **snickering** when their mother told them to be kinder.*

at; āpe; fär; câre; end; mē; it; īce; pîerce; hot; ōld; sông; fôrk; oil; out; up; ūse; rūle; pu̇ll; tûrn; chin; sing; shop; thin; this; hw in white; zh in treasure.

The symbol ə stands for the unstressed vowel sound in about, taken, pencil, lemon, and circus.

826

827

soft·ware (sôft′wâr′) *noun.* Written or printed programs of information that are used on a computer. *The artist used a new design* **software** *to help plan her latest sculpture.*

sol·i·tar·y (sol′i ter′ē) *adjective.* Living, being, or going alone. *After everyone else quit, Jim was the* **solitary** *player left in the game.*

Word History

Solitary comes from the Latin *solitarius,* meaning "alone, lonely."

sores (sôrz) *plural noun.* Places where the skin has been broken and hurts. *My hands had* **sores** *after raking leaves all morning with no gloves on.*

spe·cial·ized (spesh′ə līzd′) *verb.* To have concentrated on a particular product, activity, branch of a profession, or field of study. *When she went to cooking school, she* **specialized** *in bread baking.*

spe·cial·ty (spesh′əl tē) *noun.* A special thing that a person knows a great deal about or can make very well. *Making quilts is my aunt Lisa's* **specialty**.

spin·off (spin′ôf′) *noun.* A product derived from another field. *This new plastic used in eyeglass frames is a* **spinoff** *from the aerospace industry.*

strikes (strīks) *plural noun.* 1. The stopping of work to protest something. 2. Pitched balls in the strike zone or that a batter swings at and misses. *1. The workers threatened* **strikes** *if conditions did not improve. 2. One rule of baseball is three* **strikes** *and you're out.*

strut·ting (strut′ing) *verb.* Walking in a self-important way. *When Marilyn returned from her trip to Europe, she came* **strutting** *in showing off her new Italian boots.*

stur·dy (stûr′dē) *adjective.* Having strength; hardy. *The bookshelf we built was* **sturdy** *enough to hold our entire collection of books.*

sub·urbs (sub′ûrbz) *plural noun.* The areas around a city where people live. *Many people commute from the* **suburbs** *to the city using public transportation.*

Word History

Suburbs comes from the Latin *suburbium*—from *sub-* "under" and *urbs,* meaning "city."

sul·tan (sul′tən) *noun.* The king or ruler in certain Muslim countries. *Modern-day Turkey was ruled by a* **sultan** *at one time.*

swarms (swôrmz) *plural noun.* Large groups of insects flying or moving together. *When the hive fell,* **swarms** *of angry bees flew out.*

Tt

tan·gles (tang′gəlz) *plural noun.* Knotted, twisted, confused masses. *The garden hose had not been rolled back up and was full of* **tangles**.

tech·nique (tek nēk′) *noun.* A method or way of bringing about a desired result in a science, an art, a sport, or a profession. *Part of Orli's* **technique***, when she is running, is to breathe in and out through her mouth.*

Word History

Technique comes from the Greek word *teknikos,* meaning "relating to an art or a craft."

tech·nol·o·gy (tek nol′ə jē) *noun.* Electronic products and systems that have various uses. **Technology** *has changed the ways that artists create their work.*

tel·e·graph (tel′i graf′) *noun.* A system or equipment used to send messages by wire over a long distance. *Before the telephone, a* **telegraph** *may have been used to relay a message.*

tem·po·rar·y (tem′pə rer′ē) *adjective.* Lasting or used for a short time only. *We recorded a* **temporary** *message for the answering machine.*

at; āpe; fär; câre; end; mē; it; īce; pîerce; hot; ōld; sông; fôrk; oil; out; up; ūse; rūle; púll; tûrn; chin; sing; shop; thin; this; hw in white; zh in treasure. | The symbol ə stands for the unstressed vowel sound in about, taken, pencil, lemon, and circus.

---

ter·ri·to·ry (ter′i tôr′ē) *noun.* Any large area of land; region. *My brother's* **territory** *for selling medical office supplies is North Carolina.*

threat·ened (thret′ənd) *adjective.* Having a sense of harm or danger. **Threatened** *by the hawk circling above, the mouse escaped under a log.*

trans·form (trans fôrm′) *verb.* To change in form, appearance, or structure. *To* **transform** *a barn into a modern home, you need to invest a lot of time and expense.*

Word History

Transform comes from the Latin *transformare,* meaning "to change in shape."

trans·la·tion (trans lā′shən) *noun.* A changing of a speech or piece of writing into another language. *Maria's grandmother spoke only Spanish, so Maria needed a* **translation** *of the letter from her.*

Uu

un·fair (un fâr′) *adjective.* Not fair or just. *Punishing all of us for the actions of my little sister seemed* **unfair**.

un·ions (ūn′yənz) *plural noun.* Groups of workers joined together to protect their jobs and improve working conditions. *Some labor* **unions** *stage strikes to get workers the safety equipment they need.*

u·nique (ū nēk′) *adjective.* Having no equal; the only one of its kind. *The Everglades is* **unique** *in that there is no other place on Earth like it.*

un·sta·ble (un stā′bəl) *adjective.* Not settled or steady; easily moved or put off balance. *Although the raft looked* **unstable***, it floated very well.*

Vv

var·ied (vâr′ēd) *adjective.* Consisting of many different kinds. *The organisms in this coral reef are* **varied**.

ven·ture (ven′chər) *noun.* A business or some other undertaking that involves risk. *Rea's new* **venture** *was a carpet-cleaning service.*

vi·o·lat·ed (vī′ə lā′tid) *verb.* To have failed to obey; to have broken. *Mel was yelled at because she* **violated** *the "no talking during a test" rule.*

vis·i·bly (viz′ə blē) *adverb.* Plainly seen. *The firemen were* **visibly** *fatigued.*

vol·un·teer (vol′ən tîr′) *noun.* A person who offers to help or does something by choice and usually without pay. *I am a* **volunteer** *at the nursing home.*

W

week·days (wēk′dāz′) *plural noun.* The days of the week except Saturday and Sunday. *We go to school only on* **weekdays**.

at; āpe; fär; câre; end; mē; it; īce; pîerce; hot; ōld; sông; fôrk; oil; out; up; ūse; rūle; púll; tûrn; chin; sing; shop; thin; this; hw in white; zh in treasure. | The symbol ə stands for the unstressed vowel sound in about, taken, pencil, lemon, and circus.

Additional Resources

Contents

Instructional Routines

Professional Development

- Read the routine prior to using *Treasures*. Use the Routine QuickNotes as a reminder of key routine steps throughout Unit 2, or as needed.

- View the online classroom video clip through **TeacherWorks Plus**. Watch master teachers use these routines.

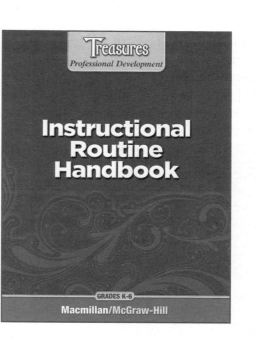

1. **Phonological Awareness/ Phonemic Awareness**
   Rhyme
   Oddity Tasks
   Sound Categorization
   Oral Blending
   Oral Segmentation
   Manipulation

2. **Phonics**
   Blending
   Introducing Sound-Spelling Cards
   Letter Recognition
   Building Words
   Building Fluency
   Reading Decodables
   Multisyllabic Words Routine

3. **Fluency**
   Strategies

4. **Vocabulary**
   Define/Example/Ask Routine
   Strategies

5. **High-Frequency Words**
   Read/Spell/Write Routine
   Reading Pre-decodables

6. **Spelling**
   Dictation

7. **Comprehension**
   Strategies
   Skills
   Reading Big Books
   Reading Student Book

8. **Writing**
   Conferences
   Revision Assignments
   Writing Process
   Using Rubrics
   Using Anchor Papers
   Writers' Express Sequence

9. **Research Process**
   Big Question Board

10. **Classroom Management**
    Workstation Flip Charts
    Contracts
    Centers
    Small Groups

11. **Listening/Speaking/Viewing**

12. **Assessment**

Objectives

- Analyze text structure
- Monitor and adjust comprehension
- Identify cause and effect relationships
- Share self-selected texts from a variety of genres

Genre Literary Nonfiction/Biography

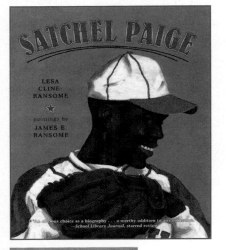

Approaching Level

Summary

This book describes the life of Satchel Paige, a famous African American baseball player, from his early years in Mobile, Alabama, to his historic induction into the Baseball Hall of Fame.

FYI for your information

Andrew "Rube" Foster formed the first successful Negro League in 1920. The Negro Leagues operated for several decades but began to decline as the major and minor leagues recruited the most talented African American players, luring them away from the Negro Leagues. Historians mark the early 1950s as the end of Negro League baseball.

Satchel Paige

by Lesa Cline-Ransome

Before Reading

BUILD BACKGROUND

Explain that in the past, African Americans were not allowed to play major-league baseball. African Americans created their own leagues and called them the Negro Leagues. Brainstorm a list of famous baseball players of the past with students. Ask students:

- *Have you seen a baseball game in person or played baseball?*
- *What do you know about baseball today?*

PREVIEW AND SET PURPOSES

Tell students to look at the illustrations throughout the book. Have them formulate questions based on the images they see. Invite students to set a purpose for reading, such as to find answers to one or more of their questions.

During Reading

APPLY COMPREHENSION SKILLS AND STRATEGIES

The following are suggestions for dividing the reading into manageable sections. For each section, Think Alouds and discussion questions are provided. Use these to review comprehension strategies and skills taught in this unit.

Pages 1–10

STRATEGY
ANALYZE TEXT STRUCTURE

Teacher Think Aloud I know that a text structure is the way an author organizes and presents information. Some kinds of text structures include sequence, compare and contrast, problem and solution, and cause and effect. After reading the first pages of this book, I think the author will use a sequential text structure, presenting information in time order. I see the author uses phrases that are related to time, such as "when Mrs. Lula Paige first held…" and "By the time…" and uses dates to put events in Satchel Paige's life in correct time order.

Cause and Effect What causes Satchel to go to reform school? What effect does this have on him? (Satchel's family is poor, so Satchel steals and is sent to reform school. There, he learns to become a better baseball player.)

STRATEGY
MONITOR COMPREHENSION

Teacher Think Aloud When I pause to monitor my
understanding, I realize that I'm confused about why Satchel
returned to baseball soon after getting married. I thought
that Satchel wanted a more settled life. If I use what I know
about sports, though, I can figure out that he might have
missed something about baseball, maybe the excitement and
challenge. The text also says baseball was his true love. Now
I understand more clearly why he returned to the game.

Cause and Effect How did Satchel's ability as a baseball player
affect his family? (He was able to bring money to his family by
playing baseball. He was paid to play for the Mobile Tigers, and
he won bets with his pitching feats. Later, he earned money by
playing in the Negro Leagues.)

STRATEGY
MONITOR COMPREHENSION

Teacher Think Aloud When I reread a passage aloud to
monitor my comprehension, I sometimes notice details I
missed the first time. The words the author uses to describe
Satchel's teammates help me understand how talented
they were. For example, she says Bell ran so fast that "if you
blinked you'd swear he never left home plate."

Author's Purpose The author says that Satchel's teammates
loved the game so much that they became players "better than
anyone could ever dream." What was the author's purpose in
writing this? (She helps the reader understand their greatness.)

After Reading

LITERATURE CIRCLES
Use page 253 in the **Teacher's Resource Book** to review
Listening and Speaking guidelines for a discussion. Use these
questions to guide a discussion of the book in small groups:

- *What was your favorite part of the book?*
- *How did the illustrations help you understand more about
  Satchel Paige?*
- *Why is Satchel Paige one of baseball's greatest players?*

Write About It
Explain that in Satchel Paige's day, baseball games were
broadcast on the radio. Pretend Satchel Paige is coming to
your town. Have students use details from the book to write
radio ads that convince fans to buy tickets to the game. Remind
students to capitalize proper nouns, such as names of people.

Social Studies
Connect to Content

SPORTS TEAMS

With the class, make a list of
Texas sports teams. Discuss with
the class how some team names
are tied to the region a team is
from or the state's history. Give
as examples the Houston Astros
and the Dallas Cowboys. Discuss
what these and other team
names reflect about economic
and cultural aspects of life in
Texas, past and present.

Classroom Library

Objectives

- Monitor and adjust comprehension
- Identify author's purpose
- Analyze text structure
- Analyze cause and effect relationships

Genre Literary Nonfiction/Biography

On Level

Summary

Hokusai was an artist who lived in Japan from 1760 to 1849. He was born into poverty, taught himself to draw, became the pupil of a famous Japanese master, and moved on to develop his own approach. He became one of the most influential artists in the world. His masterpiece is *Thirty-Six Views of Mount Fuji,* which was completed when he was over 70 years old.

FYI for your information

Haiku are perhaps the best-known Japanese art form. Haiku are very short poems, usually three lines long, with fewer than twenty syllables. A haiku focuses on a detail of nature or everyday life and is a personal reflection of the poet. Often a word that symbolizes the season is included. Other Japanese art forms include woodblock engraving, Noh and Kabuki drama, and calligraphy.

Hokusai, The Man Who Painted a Mountain

by Deborah Kogan Ray

Before Reading

BUILD BACKGROUND

Point out Japan on a world map. Explain that Japan is an archipelago, or a collection of islands. Tell students that Mount Fuji is an important symbol to the Japanese. Brainstorm a list of other things that students know about Japan. Ask students:

- *What symbols mean a lot to you?*
- *What physical feature do you think represents your state or country? What do you think this symbol means to other people?*

PREVIEW AND SET PURPOSES

Have students look at the illustration on the cover, read the title, and think about its meaning. Then have them set a purpose for reading, such as to find out why someone painted a mountain.

During Reading

APPLY COMPREHENSION SKILLS AND STRATEGIES

Following are suggestions for dividing the reading into manageable sections. For each section, Think Alouds and discussion questions are provided. Use these to review comprehension strategies and skills taught in this unit.

Pages 1–6

STRATEGY
MONITOR COMPREHENSION

Teacher Think Aloud After reading the story's beginning, I think the author's purpose is to inform, but the author could have more than one purpose. As I read, I will pause at regular intervals to monitor and, if necessary, adjust my understanding of the author's purpose.

Author's Purpose One purpose the author has is trying to convince us that Hokusai was both dreamy and observant. What details does she use to support this idea? (He was always looking at Mount Fuji or the pictures on the backs of the mirrors.)

Pages 7–12

STRATEGY
ANALYZE TEXT STRUCTURE

Teacher Think Aloud In this biography, the author seems to be using a sequential text structure. As I read, I will look for time-order phrases and dates as well as signal words that indicate the time order of events.

Sequence How did Hokusai go from polishing mirrors to being an engraver? (Hokusai discovered a library and went to live and work there. He copied the illustrations from the books so well that he was offered a job in a print shop as a woodblock engraver.)

Pages 13–18

STRATEGY
ANALYZE TEXT STRUCTURE

Teacher Think Aloud On the first page of this section, I see the signal phrase *When Hokusai was eighteen years old.* Phrases like these help me to put important events in Hokusai's life in the correct time order.

Cause and Effect Shunsho invites Hokusai to become his pupil. What effect does this have on the rest of his life? (Hokusai trains under Shunsho and becomes an artist. He earns money as an artist and has his own studio and patrons.)

Pages 19–end

STRATEGY
ANALYZE TEXT STRUCTURE

Teacher Think Aloud As I read the last part of the book, I learn about the last part of Hokusai's life. It's interesting that as he gets older, he goes back to some of his early interests—a pilgrimage to Mount Fuji and the many pictures he had promised to make for his mother.

Sequence How does Hokusai sum up the events of his own life for the scholars? (Starting at the age of five, he needed to sketch. By 70, he had not really done anything notable. At 72, he "finally understood something." Then he thinks about what might come next if he continues to learn.)

After Reading

LITERATURE CIRCLES
Use page 253 in the **Teacher's Resource Book** to review Listening and Speaking guidelines for a discussion. Use these questions to guide a discussion of the book in small groups:

- *What was your favorite part of the book?*
- *What did the mountain mean to Hokusai?*
- *Look at the woodcut from* Thirty-Six Views of Mount Fuji *near the end of the book. Tell what you like about it. What do you think some of the other views might show?*

Write About It
Have students imagine a conversation between Hokusai and one of the masters who does not like his new work. Tell students to write a conversation between the two people as they discuss Hokusai's art. Remind students to use the correct forms of plural and possessive nouns.

Listening/Speaking

HAIKU
Remind students that a haiku is a poem about nature—usually one detail of nature. Provide simple directions: Line 1, five syllables; line 2, seven syllables; line 3, five syllables. Have students write and illustrate their own haiku. Display their work, and have students recite the poems. Remind them to speak clearly, with an appropriate rate.

Objectives

- Monitor and adjust comprehension
- Identify author's purpose
- Identify sequence

Genre Literary Nonfiction/Biography

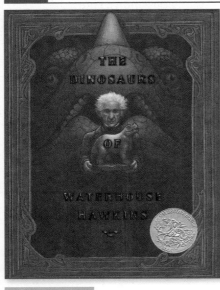

Beyond Level

Summary

Waterhouse Hawkins spent his career working to bring dinosaurs to life once again. He was the first person to create full-size models of dinosaurs.

FYI for your information

The fanciful illustrations will give readers insight into how Waterhouse Hawkins's mind worked as he sketched dinosaurs and made life-size models. Many of the illustrations are based on original sketches made by Hawkins.

The Dinosaurs of Waterhouse Hawkins

by Barbara Kerley

Before Reading

BUILD BACKGROUND

Remind students that dinosaurs lived on Earth millions of years ago but scientists didn't start to study their fossils until a few hundred years ago. Brainstorm a word web around the word *dinosaur*. Ask students:

- *Where have you seen dinosaur sketches, skeletons, or models? What do they show us about these creatures?*
- *Why do you think people today are excited about dinosaur discoveries?*

PREVIEW AND SET PURPOSES

Have students preview the cover and the illustration on the first two pages. Ask students when and where they think this story might take place. Then have students set a purpose for reading, such as to find out who Waterhouse Hawkins was.

During Reading

APPLY COMPREHENSION SKILLS AND STRATEGIES

The following are suggestions for dividing the reading into manageable sections. For each section, Think Alouds and discussion questions are provided. Use these to review comprehension strategies and skills taught in this unit.

Pages 1–20

STRATEGY
MONITOR COMPREHENSION

Teacher Think Aloud As I read these pages, I want to be sure I understand the information. I will reread the text and look at the illustrations to understand the steps Waterhouse Hawkins took to build life-sized replicas of dinosaurs. With the help of scientist Richard Owen, he designed the creatures and made small clay models. He then built life-sized clay figures, and created the molds for them. Next he built iron skeletons and brick foundations, which he covered with cement casts from the dinosaur molds.

Author's Purpose What does the author's purpose seem to be in writing this biography? What clues in the text show you this? (The author seems to be writing to inform readers of Waterhouse Hawkins's work. Upon the Queen's visit to his studio, Waterhouse explains his process for building the dinosaur models.)

Pages
21–34

STRATEGY
MONITOR COMPREHENSION

Teacher Think Aloud Waterhouse Hawkins is thrilled that he was invited to build his dinosaurs in New York. Unfortunately, his dream was shattered. I'll reread these pages and ask myself questions to clarify who Boss Tweed was and why Waterhouse's work was vandalized.

Sequence What was the sequence of events leading up to the destruction of Hawkins's workshop? How does this help you understand why the workshop may have been broken into? (Hawkins sets to work to build the Paleozoic Museum. The work is then halted by Boss Tweed. Hawkins speaks out against Boss Tweed. Then his workshop is broken into. This leads me to infer that Boss Tweed has something to do with the break-in.)

Pages
35–43

STRATEGY
MONITOR COMPREHENSION

Teacher Think Aloud After having his work destroyed, I wonder if Waterhouse will give up and return home. I'll read ahead to find out. I see that he leaves New York to work in Princeton, New Jersey and Washington, D.C. Then he returns home to learn of the discovery of dinosaur skeletons.

Author's Purpose No major events happen in the last section of the book. Why did the author include it? (She wanted to tell readers that even though new things were learned about dinosaurs, people still respected Hawkins's work.)

After Reading

LITERATURE CIRCLES

Use page 253 in the **Teacher's Resource Book** to review Listening and Speaking guidelines for a discussion. Use these questions to guide a discussion of the book in small groups:

- *What part of the book did you find most interesting? Why?*
- *How would you describe Waterhouse Hawkins?*
- *Do you think Waterhouse Hawkins had an interesting job? Why or why not?*

Write About It

Tell each student to pretend to be Waterhouse Hawkins as he plans his dinner party. Have them write a persuasive letter to include with the invitations to the famous scientists. The letter should convince the scientists to attend the party. Tell students to consider their audience and use appropriate voice. Remind them to punctuate the letter properly.

Science
Connect to Content

DINOSAUR MODELS

With the class, brainstorm a list of movies that show life-like dinosaurs. Have students look up the dates of the movies and add this to the list. Note the special effects that were used to make these dinosaurs seem life-like, such as sounds, texture, and size. How are these models different than Waterhouse Hawkins's models? Discuss with the class how models have changed due to changing movie and special effects technology.

Classroom Library

Additional Readings

30 MINUTES DAILY

By the Authors and Illustrators

For additional information on authors, illustrators, and selection content, go to www.macmillanmh.com.

Farris, Christine King. *Martin Luther King, Jr.: His Life and Dream.* **Silver Burdett and Ginn, 1986.** Tells how the life, leadership, and works of Dr. King significantly affected the civil rights movement.
ON LEVEL

Moss, Marisa. *Brave Harriet.* **Silver Whistle, 2001.** The first American woman to have received a pilot's license describes her 1912 solo flight across the English Channel, the first such flight by any woman.
ON LEVEL

Related to the Theme
(spans 3+ grade levels)

Use these and other classroom or library resources to ensure students are reading at least 30 minutes a day outside of class. Enlist the help of your school librarian to teach students how to use library resources, such as card catalogs and electronic search engines, to find other books related to the unit theme.

Adler, David A. *A Picture Book of Jackie Robinson.* **Holiday House, 1994.** A good introduction to Robinson's life that touches on his accomplishments as well as the bigotry and prejudice he faced.
APPROACHING

Bruchac, Joseph. *A Boy Called Slow: The True Story of Sitting Bull.* **Philomel, 1994.** This book recounts the life of the Lakota Sioux hero using a subtle portrayal of Plains Indian life.
APPROACHING

Fritz, Jean. *Where Do You Think You're Going, Christopher Columbus?* **Putnam, 1980.** In this account of Columbus's voyages, the author captures the explorer's vision as well as his stubbornness.
ON LEVEL

Lester, Julius. *Black Cowboy, Wild Horses.* **Dial Books, 1998.** An African American cowboy is accepted by a herd of wild mustangs, and they trust him enough to take them to the corral.
ON LEVEL

Atkins, Jeannine. *Wings and Rockets: The Story of Women in Air and Space.* **Farrar, Straus and Giroux, 2003.** Tells the stories of courageous women who have challenged the status quo in order to fly.
BEYOND

Brill, Marlene Targ. *The Trail of Tears: The Cherokee Journey From Home.* **Millbrook Press, 1995.** A dramatic retelling of the removal of the Cherokee people to Oklahoma and an account of their loss of their lands in the Southeast.
BEYOND

Library Resources

Reference Sources

Have students choose a theme-related topic to read more about. Using library reference materials such as encyclopedias or online search engines, have students research the subject. As needed, review how to find information in reference texts using organizational features such as prefaces and appendixes.

After students complete their research, they should write a summary of the information, highlighting the main ideas and most significant details. Remind them to compare and contrast information they find on the same topic in different sources.

Soentpiet, Chris. *Around Town.* **Lothrop, Lee & Shepard, 1994.** An exuberant tour of New York City with detailed watercolors that capture the fun of the city.
APPROACHING

Peterson, Cris. *Amazing Grazing.* **Boyds Mills, 2002.** This describes how three contemporary ranchers protect the environment by using innovative means to raise their cattle.
ON LEVEL

Goble, Paul. *The Girl Who Loved Wild Horses.* **Atheneum, 2001.** A girl is truly happy living among the wild horses.
APPROACHING

Hill, Elizabeth Starr. *Bird Boy.* **Farrar, Straus and Giroux, 1999.** Chang cannot talk, but he can help with his father's fishing cormorants. This story tells how Chang feels when he raises a young bird.
APPROACHING

Jeffrey, Laura S. *Christa McAuliffe: A Space Biography.* **Enslow, 1998.** A biography of the teacher who became an astronaut, but whose life tragically ended when the space shuttle Challenger exploded.
APPROACHING

Rumford, James. *Traveling Man: the Journey of Ibn Battuta, 1325–1354.* **Houghton Mifflin, 2001.** The reader follows Ibn Battuta's incredible journey from Morocco to China during the fourteenth century.
APPROACHING

Stone, Tanya Lee. *Ilan Ramon, Israel's First Astronaut.* **Millbrook, 2003.** A biography of the Israeli astronaut who died in the explosion of the space shuttle Columbia on February 1, 2003.
ON LEVEL

Turner, Pamela S. *Gorilla Doctors: Saving Endangered Great Apes.* **Houghton, 2005.** The story of the Mountain Gorilla Veterinary Project, a group formed by scientists working to save the mountain gorilla.
ON LEVEL

Wells, Rosemary. *Mary On Horseback: Three Mountain Stories.* **Dial, 1998.** Moving narratives based on a nurse who changed the lives of the people in Appalachia during the 1920s.
ON LEVEL

Green, Michelle Y. *A Strong Right Arm: The Story of Mamie "Peanut" Johnson.* **Dial Books, 2002.** The story of Mamie Johnson's triumphs in baseball despite the bias against female athletes and African Americans.
BEYOND

Hesse, Karen. *The Cats in Krasinski Square.* **Scholastic Press, 2004.** A brave girl from the Warsaw ghetto outwits German soldiers in this inspiring, fact-based story of World War II.
BEYOND

Naidoo, Beverley. *Out of Bounds: Seven Stories of Conflict and Hope.* **HarperCollins, 2003.** A portrayal of young South Africans who lived under apartheid and how they worked against it.
BEYOND

Selection Honors, Prizes, and Awards

My Brother Martin

Unit 2, p. 140
by **Christine King Ferris**
Illustrated by **Chris Soentpiet**
NAACP Image Award (2004)

Illustrator: Chris Soentpiet, winner of the Society of Illustrators Gold Medal; Parents' Choice Gold Award (2001), ALA Notable Children's Book (2002), and IRA Children's Book Award (2002) for *Coolies*

Mighty Jackie: The Strike-out Queen

Unit 2, p. 166
by **Marissa Moss**
Illustrated by **C. F. Payne**
Texas Bluebonnet Award (2004)

Author: Marissa Moss, winner of the Children's Choice Award (2002) for *Oh Boy, Amelia!;* American Booksellers Association "Pick of the Lists" (1997) for *Amelia's Notebook;* Children's Literature Choice List (1999) for *Rachel's Journey: The Story of a Pioneer Girl*

Wild Horses: Black Hills Sanctuary

Unit 2, p. 204
by **Cris Peterson**
Illustrated by **Alvis Upitis**
Book Critics Society Ten Best (2003)

Author: Cris Peterson, winner of American Women in Agriculture "Woman of the Year" (2002); Wisconsin Farm Bureau Book of the Year (2000) and Ohio Farm Bureau Women's Award for Children's Literature (2000) for *Century Farm: One Hundred Years on a Family Farm;* Ohio Farm Bureau Women's Award for Children's Literature (1996) for *Harvest Year* and (1995) for *Extra Cheese, Please!*

Mystic Horse

Unit 2, p. 230
by **Paul Goble**

Author/Illustrator: Paul Goble, winner of the Caldecott Medal (1979) for *The Girl Who Loved Wild Horses;* ALA Notable Children's Book (1984) for *Buffalo Woman;* Aesop Prize (1993) from the American Folklore Society for *Love Flute*

Resources

Audio Bookshelf
44 Ocean View Drive
Middletown, RI 02842
800-234-1713
www.audiobookshelf.com

Discovery Education
One Discovery Place
Silver Spring, MD 20910
800-323-9084
http://discoveryeducation.com

Dorling Kindersley
375 Hudson Street
New York, NY 10014
Tel: 800-631-8571
Fax: 201-256-0000
http://us.dk.com

GPN Educational Media
1407 Fleet Street
Baltimore, MD 21231
800-228-4630
http://shopgpn.com

Innovative Educators
P.O. Box 520
Montezuma, GA 31063
888-252-KIDS (5437)
Fax: 888-536-8553
www.innovative-educators.com

Library Video Co.
P.O. Box 580
Wynnewood, PA 19096
800-843-3620
www.libraryvideo.com

Listening Library
400 Hahn Road
Westminster, MD 21157
800-733-3000
http://randomhouse.biz/educators/

Live Oak Media
P.O. Box 652
Pine Plains, NY 12567
800-788-1121
www.liveoakmedia.com

Macmillan/McGraw-Hill
220 East Danieldale Road
DeSoto, TX 75115-9960
Tel: 800-442-9685
Fax: 972-228-1982
www.macmillanmh.com

Microsoft Corp.
One Microsoft Way
Redmond, WA 98052
800-642-7676
www.microsoft.com

National Geographic Society
1145 17th Street N.W.
Washington, DC 20036
800-647-5463
www.nationalgeographic.com

Recorded Books
270 Skipjack Road
Prince Frederick, MD 20678
800-638-1304
www.recordedbooks.com

Sunburst Communications
Sunburst Technology
1550 Executive Drive
Elgin, IL 60123
888-321-7511 ext.3337
www.sunburst.com

Tom Snyder Productions
100 Talcott Avenue
Watertown, MA 02472
800-342-0236
www.tomsnyder.com

Weston Woods
143 Main Street
Norwalk, CT 06851
800-243-5020
www.teacher.scholastic.com/products/
westonwoods/

Web Sites

Go to www.macmillanmh.com.
Use the zip code finder to locate other resources in your area.

The Academy of Natural Sciences
http://www.ansp.org/

Acadia National Park
http://www.nps.gov/acad

Agriculture in the Classroom
http://www.agclassroom.org/

Arches National Park
http://www.nps.gov/arch

Asian American History Resources Online - CET
http://www.cetel.org/res.html

Association of Zoos and Aquariums
http://www.aza.org/

Bronx Zoo
http://www.bronxzoo.com/

Cincinnati Zoo
http://www.cincinnatizoo.org/

Colonial Williamsburg
http://www.history.org/

Denali National Park and Preserve
http://www.nps.gov/dena

Ellis Island
http://www.ellisisland.org/

Glacier National Park
http://www.nps.gov/glac

Grand Canyon National Park
http://www.nps.gov/grca

Grand Teton National Park
http://www.nps.gov/grte

High Museum of Art, Atlanta
http://www.high.org/

International Civil Rights Center and Museum
http://www.sitinmovement.org/

Japanese American National Museum
http://www.janm.org/

K12Station – Library of K–12 Education Links
http://www.k12station.com/k12link_library.html

Kids.gov
http://www.kids.gov/

KidsHealth in the Classroom
http://classroom.kidshealth.org/

Meteorology
http://www.wxdude.com/

The Metropolitan Museum of Art, New York
http://www.metmuseum.org/

Minneapolis Institute of Arts
http://www.artsmia.org/

Minnesota Zoo
http://www.mnzoo.com/

MoMA | The Museum of Modern Art
http://www.moma.org/

Monterey Bay Aquarium
www.montereybayaquarium.org

Mount Rushmore National Memorial
http://www.nps.gov/moru

Museum of Fine Arts, Boston
http://www.mfa.org/

Museum of Science, Boston
http://www.mos.org/

Museum of Science and Industry, Chicago
http://www.msichicago.org/

NASA
http://www.nasa.gov/

NASA Kids' Club
http://www.nasa.gov/audience/forkids/kidsclub/flash/index.html

National Air and Space Museum
http://www.nasm.si.edu/

National Civil Rights Museum
http://www.civilrightsmuseum.org/home.htm

National Museum of African American History and Culture
http://nmaahc.si.edu/

National Museum of American History
http://americanhistory.si.edu/

National Museum of the American Indian
http://www.nmai.si.edu/

National Museum of Women in the Arts
http://www.nmwa.org/

National Music Museum
http://www.usd.edu/smm/

National Park Service
http://www.nps.gov/

National Weather Service Education Resources
http://www.nws.noaa.gov/om/edures.shtml

National Women's History Museum
http://www.nwhm.org/

National Zoo
http://nationalzoo.si.edu/

Native American Facts for Kids: Resources on American Indians for Children and Teachers
http://www.native-languages.org/kids.htm

New England Aquarium
http://www.neaq.org/index.php

New York Aquarium
http://www.nyaquarium.com/

Newseum
http://www.newseum.org/

Omaha's Henry Doorly Zoo
http://www.omahazoo.com/

Philadelphia Museum of Art
http://www.philamuseum.org/

Philadelphia Zoo
http://www2.philadelphiazoo.org/

Plimoth Plantation
http://www.plimoth.org/

Redwood National and State Parks
http://www.nps.gov/redw

Rocky Mountain National Park
http://www.nps.gov/romo

Saint Louis Art Museum
http://www.slam.org/

San Diego Zoo
http://www.sandiegozoo.com/

San Francisco Museum of Modern Art
http://www.sfmoma.org/

Shedd Aquarium
http://www.sheddaquarium.org/

Smithsonian Education
http://www.smithsonianeducation.org/

Smithsonian: Science and Technology
http://www.si.edu/Encyclopedia_SI/science_and_technology/

Space Center Houston
http://www.spacecenter.org/

Tennessee Aquarium
http://www.tennis.org/

United States Holocaust Memorial Museum
http://www.ushmm.org/

University of California Museum of Paleontology
http://www.ucmp.berkeley.edu/

The White House Historical Association
http://www.whitehousehistory.org/

Yellowstone National Park
http://www.nps.gov/yell

Yosemite National Park
http://www.nps.gov/yose

Zion National Park
http://www.nps.gov/zion

Word List

Week	Vocabulary	Differentiated Spelling
1 **My Brother Martin**	unfair ancestors numerous segregation avoided injustice	**APPROACHING** unblock, unborn, unchain, unload, unlock, recall, repay, resell, rewash, rewind, retie, indirect, incorrect, illegal, overact, overheat, subway, premix, preplan, superheat **ON LEVEL** unblock, **unborn**, unchain, unload, unlock, recall, relearn, resell, rewash, **rewind**, imperfect, indirect, incorrect, illegal, overact, overheat, subway, **premix**, preplan, supersize **BEYOND** unblock, unborn, unchained, unloaded, unlocked, recalled, relearned, reselling, rewashed, rewind, imperfect, indirectly, incorrectly, illegally, overacting, overheat, submarine, preseason, preplan, superpower
2 **Mighty Jackie**	legendary muttered gaped snickering insult flinched	**APPROACHING** choose, kitchen, touch, chance, march, ketchup, branch, couch, patch, chef, rush, north, thanks, graph, photo, whole, fifth, shed, whirl, think **ON LEVEL** choose, kitchen, **touch**, **chance**, sketched, ketchup, snatch, stretching, **pitcher**, chef, rush, thirty, northern, graph, photo, whole, fifth, headphone, whirl, width **BEYOND** choose, kitchen, character, touchdown, sketched, ketchup, flinched, duchess, cherish, chef, marshal, photograph, physical, phrase, bathtub, whole, nowhere, finished, whirl, width
3 **Making a Splash**	similar challenges designed achieved varied	**APPROACHING** shred, through, sprout, spring, split, throb, throat, shrink, screw, shrimp, screech, straight, sprang, shrunk, splash, straps, strand, script, thrill, throne **ON LEVEL** shred, **through**, sprout, sprawl, split, throb, throat, shrink, screw, shrimp, screech, straighten, sprang, shriek, **splashing**, straps, strand, script, thrill, throne **BEYOND** shredding, throughout, sprout, sprawl, split, throb, throttle, shrink, scrawny, shrugged, screech, straighten, sprang, shriek, splashing, stringy, strand, script, thrillingly, throne

T14 Unit 2 | **Key** Spelling words in bold appear in the selection. | **LOG ON** For additional spelling activities, go to www.macmillanmh.com.

Unit 2 (continued)

Week	Vocabulary	Differentiated Spelling
4 **Wild Horses**	descendants sanctuary threatened fragile habitat emerge	**APPROACHING** door, dart, fort, floor, carpet, ford, core, cord, spark, yard, smart, large, worn, far, stormy, bore, bark, warp, tar, backyard **ON LEVEL** **door**, dart, fort, morning, carpet, ford, core, cord, spark, award, smart, **charge**, worn, argue, stormy, bore, guard, ward, warp, **backyard** **BEYOND** aboard, seminar, force, morning, carpet, scorch, uproar, predator, spark, award, guitar, charge, afford, argue, Oregon, guard, enlarge, barnyard, charcoal, forecast
5 **Mystic Horse**	sores loosened mysterious amazement midst responsibility	**APPROACHING** sickly, hardly, quickly, slowly, carefully, wonderful, thankful, graceful, spoonful, darkness, shapeless, ageless, illness, goodness, spotless, painless, weakness, darkest, clearest, oldest **ON LEVEL** **sickly**, **hardly**, **quickly**, **slowly**, **carefully**, **wonderful**, **beautiful**, graceful, spoonful, darkness, shapeless, ageless, illness, goodness, spotless, painless, weakness, darkest, clearest, thoughtful **BEYOND** acrobatic, gymnastic, fantastic, allergic, carefully, wonderful, beautifully, graceful, spoonful, darkness, shapeless, ageless, illness, goodness, spotless, painless, weakness, darkest, clearest, thoughtful

Word List

Key Spelling words in bold appear in the selection.

 LOG ON For additional spelling activities, go to **www.macmillanmh.com**.

Language Transfers:

The Interaction Between English and Students' Primary Languages

Dr. Jana Echevarria
California State University, Long Beach

Dr. Donald Bear
University of Nevada, Reno

It is important for teachers to understand why English Language Learners (ELLs) use alternative pronunciations for some English words. Many English sounds do not exist or transfer to other languages, so English Language Learners may lack the auditory acuity to "hear" these English sounds and have difficulty pronouncing them. These students are not accustomed to positioning their mouth in a way the sound requires. The charts that appear on the following pages show that there is variation among languages, with some languages having more sounds in common and thus greater transfer to English than others.

For example, an English speaker may be able to pronounce the /r/ in the Spanish word *pero* ("but"), but not the /rr/ trill in *perro* ("dog"). The English speaker may also lack the auditory acuity to detect and the ability to replicate the tonal sounds of some Chinese words. Similarly, a Vietnamese speaker may have difficulty pronouncing /th/ in words such as *thin* or *thanks*.

Further, English Language Learners make grammatical errors due to interference from their native languages. In Spanish, the adjective follows the noun, so often English Language Learners say "the girl pretty" instead of "the pretty girl." While English changes the verb form with a change of subject (*I walk. She walks.*), some Asian languages keep the verb form constant across subjects. Adding /s/ to the third person may be difficult for some English Language Learners. Students may know the grammatical rule, but applying it consistently may be difficult, especially in spoken English.

When working with English Language Learners, you should also be aware of sociocultural factors that affect pronunciation. Students may retain an accent because it marks their social identity. Speakers of other languages may feel at a social distance from members of the dominant English-speaking culture.

English Language Learners improve their pronunciation in a non-threatening atmosphere in which participation is encouraged. Opportunities to interact with native English speakers provide easy access to language models and give English Language Learners practice using English. However, students should not be forced to participate. Pressure to perform—or to perform in a certain way—can inhibit participation. In any classroom, teacher sensitivity to pronunciation differences contributes to a more productive learning environment.

Phonics, word recognition, and spelling are influenced by what students know about the sounds, word structure, and spelling in their primary languages. For example, beginning readers who speak Spanish and are familiar with its spelling will often spell short *o* with an *a*, a letter that in Spanish makes the short *o* sound. Similarly, English Language Learners who are unaccustomed to English consonant digraphs and blends (e.g., /ch/ and *s*-blends) spell /ch/ as *sh* because /sh/ is the sound they know that is closest to /ch/. Students learn about the way pronunciation influences their reading and spelling, beginning with large contrasts among sounds, then they study the finer discriminations. As vocabulary advances, the meaning of words leads students to the sound contrasts. For example, *shoe* and *chew* may sound alike initially, but meaning indicates otherwise. Students' reading and discussions of what they read advances their word knowledge as well as their knowledge in all language and literacy systems, including phonics, pronunciation, grammar, and vocabulary.

Phonics Transfers:
Sound Transfers

This chart indicates areas where a positive transfer of sounds and symbols occurs for English Language Learners from their native languages into English. This symbol (✔) identifies a positive transfer. "Approximate" indicates that the sound is similar.

Sound Transfers	Spanish	Cantonese	Vietnamese	Hmong	Korean	Khmer
Consonants						
/b/ as in bat	✔	approximate	approximate	approximate	approximate	✔
/k/ as in cake, kitten, peck	✔	✔	✔	✔	✔	✔
/d/ as in dog	✔	approximate	approximate	✔	approximate	✔
/f/ as in farm	✔	✔	✔	✔		
/g/ as in girl	✔	approximate	✔	approximate	approximate	
/h/ as in ham	✔	✔	✔	✔	✔	approximate
/j/ as in jet, page, ledge		approximate	approximate		approximate	
/l/ as in lion	✔	✔	✔	✔	✔	
/m/ as in mat	✔	✔	✔	✔	✔	✔
/n/ as in night	✔	✔	✔	✔	✔	✔
/p/ as in pen	✔	✔	✔	approximate	✔	✔
/kw/ as in queen	✔	approximate	✔		✔	✔
/r/ as in rope	approximate					✔
/s/ as in sink, city	✔	✔	✔	✔	✔	approximate
/t/ as in ton	✔	✔	approximate	approximate	✔	✔
/v/ as in vine	✔		✔	✔		
/w/ as in wind	✔	✔			✔	✔
/ks/ as in six	✔				✔	✔
/y/ as in yak	✔	✔		✔	✔	✔
/z/ as in zebra			✔			
Digraphs						
/ch/ as in cheek, patch	✔	approximate		✔	✔	✔
/sh/ as in shadow			✔	✔	✔	
/hw/ as in whistle					✔	✔
/th/ as in path	approximate		approximate			
/TH/ as in that	approximate					
/ng/ as in sting	✔	✔	✔	✔	✔	approximate

Sound Transfers	Spanish	Cantonese	Vietnamese	Hmong	Korean	Khmer
Short Vowels						
/a/ as in cat	approximate		approximate	✔	✔	
/e/ as in net	✔	approximate	approximate		✔	
/i/ as in kid	approximate	approximate			✔	
/o/ as in spot	approximate	approximate	approximate	approximate	approximate	✔
/u/ as in cup	approximate	approximate	✔		✔	✔
Long Vowels						
/ā/ as in lake, nail, bay	✔	approximate	approximate	approximate	✔	✔
/ē/ as in bee, meat, cranky	✔	approximate	✔	✔	✔	✔
/ī/ as in kite, tie, light, dry	✔	approximate	✔	✔	✔	✔
/ō/ as in home, road, row	✔	approximate	approximate		✔	
/ū/ as in dune, fruit, blue	✔	approximate	✔	✔	✔	✔
/yü/ as in mule, cue	✔	approximate			✔	
r-Controlled Vowels						
/är/ as in far	approximate	approximate				
/ôr/ as in corn	approximate	approximate				
/ûr/ as in stern, bird, suburb	approximate	approximate				
/âr/ as in air, bear						
/îr/ as in deer, ear						
Variant Vowels						
/oi/ as in boil, toy	✔	approximate	approximate		✔	✔
/ou/ as in loud, down	✔	approximate	✔	approximate	✔	✔
/ô/ as in law	approximate	✔	✔	approximate	approximate	✔
/ò/ as in laundry	approximate	approximate	✔	approximate	approximate	✔
/ôl/ as in salt, call	approximate	approximate			approximate	✔
/ü/ as in moon, drew	✔	approximate	approximate	✔	✔	✔
/ù/ as in look		approximate	approximate		approximate	✔
/ə/ as in askew			approximate		✔	

Phonics Transfers:
Sound-Symbol Match

Sound-Symbol Match	Spanish	Cantonese	Vietnamese	Hmong	Korean	Khmer
Consonants						
/b/ as in bat	✔		✔			
/k/ as in cake	✔		✔			
/k/ as in kitten	✔		✔	✔		
/k/ as in peck						
/d/ as in dog	✔		✔	✔		
/f/ as in farm	✔			✔		
/g/ as in girl	✔		✔			
/h/ as in ham			✔	✔		
/j/ as in jet, page, ledge						
/l/ as in lion	✔		✔	✔		
/m/ as in mat	✔		✔	✔		
/n/ as in night	✔		✔	✔		
/p/ as in pen	✔		✔	✔		
/kw/ as in queen			✔			
/r/ as in rope	approximate					
/s/ as in sink, city	✔		✔			
/t/ as in ton	✔		✔	✔		
/v/ as in vine	✔		✔	✔		
/w/ as in wind	✔					
/ks/ as in six	✔					
/y/ as in yak	✔			✔		
/z/ as in zebra						
Digraphs						
/ch/ as in cheek, patch	✔					
/sh/ as in shadow						
/hw/ as in whistle						
/th/ as in path			✔			
/TH/ as in that						
/ng/ as in sting	✔		✔			
Short Vowels						
/a/ as in cat			✔	✔		
/e/ as in net	✔		✔			
/i/ as in kid						
/o/ as in spot			✔	✔		
/u/ as in cup						

Sound-Symbol Match	Spanish	Cantonese	Vietnamese	Hmong	Korean	Khmer
Long Vowels						
/ā/ as in lake						
/ā/ as in nail						
/ā/ as in bay						
/ē/ as in bee						
/ē/ as in meat						
/ē/ as in cranky						
/ī/ as in kite, tie, light, dry						
/ō/ as in home, road, row						
/ū/ as in dune			✔	✔		
/ū/ as in fruit, blue						
/yü/ as in mule, cue						
r-Controlled Vowels						
/är/ as in far	✔					
/ôr/ as in corn	✔					
/ûr/ as in stern	✔					
/ûr/ as in bird, suburb						
/âr/ as in air, bear						
/îr/ as in deer, ear						
Variant Vowels						
/oi/ as in boil	✔		✔			
/oi/ as in toy	✔					
/ou/ as in loud						
/ou/ as in down						
/ô/ as in law						
/ô/ as in laundry						
/ôl/ as in salt	✔					
/ôl/ as in call						
/ü/ as in moon, drew						
/ù/ as in look						
/ə/ as in askew						

How to Use the Phonics Transfer Charts

To read and speak fluently in English, English Language Learners need to master a wide range of phonemic awareness, phonics, and word study skills. The Phonics Transfer Charts are designed to help you anticipate and understand possible student errors in pronouncing or perceiving English sounds.

1. Highlight Transferrable Skills If the phonics skill transfers from the student's primary language to English, state that during the lesson. In most lessons an English Language Learner feature will indicate which sounds do and do not transfer in specific languages.

2. Preteach Non-Transferrable Skills Prior to teaching a phonics lesson, check the chart to determine if the sound and/or spelling transfers from the student's primary language into English. If it does not, preteach the sound and spelling during Small Group time. Focus on articulation, using the backs of the small **Sound-Spelling Cards**, and the minimal contrast activities provided.

3. Provide Additional Practice and Time If the skill does NOT transfer from the student's primary language into English, the student will require more time and practice mastering the sound and spellings. Continue to review the phonics skill during Small Group time in upcoming weeks until the student has mastered it. Use the additional resources, such as the extra decodable stories in the **Teacher's Resource Book**, to provide oral and silent reading practice.

Teaching Supports for Students Transitioning from Spanish to English

The **Sound-Spelling Cards** have been created to assist you in working with English Language Learners. For example:

1. The dotted border on many of the cards indicates that the sound transfers from Spanish to English. On these cards, the same image is used in both English and Spanish (e.g., *camel/camello*). Therefore, students learning the sound in Spanish can easily transfer that knowledge to English.

2. Students whose primary language is not English will need additional articulation support to pronounce and perceive non-transferrable English sounds. Use the articulation photos on the backs of the Sound-Spelling Cards and the student-friendly descriptions of how to form these sounds during phonics lessons.

Sound-Spelling Cards

Transfer Skill Support

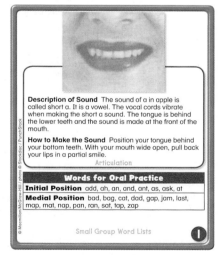

Description of Sound The sound of *a* in apple is called short *a*. It is a vowel. The vocal cords vibrate when making the short *a* sound. The tongue is behind the lower teeth and the sound is made at the front of the mouth.

How to Make the Sound Position your tongue behind your bottom teeth. With your mouth wide open, pull back your lips in a partial smile.

Articulation

Words for Oral Practice	
Initial Position	add, ah, an, and, ant, as, ask, at
Medial Position	bad, bag, cat, dad, gap, jam, last, map, mat, nap, pan, ran, sat, tap, zap

Small Group Word Lists

Articulation Support

Grammar Transfers:
Grammatical Form

This chart can be used to address common mistakes that some English Language Learners make when they transfer grammatical forms from their native languages into English.

Grammatical Form	Transfer Mistakes in English	Native Language	Cause of Difficulty
Nouns			
Plural Marker -s	**Forgets plural marker -s** *I have 3 sister.*	Cantonese, Haitian Creole, Hmong, Korean, Vietnamese, Khmer	Native language does not use a plural marker.
Countable and Uncountable Nouns	**Confuses countable and uncountable nouns** *the homeworks* or *the informations*	Haitian Creole, Spanish	Countable and uncountable nouns are different in English and native language.
Possessives	**Uses prepositions to describe possessives** *the book of my brother* as opposed to *my brother's book*	Haitian Creole, Hmong, Spanish, Vietnamese	Possession is often described using a prepositional phrase.
	Avoids using 's *dog my father* as opposed to *my father's dog*	Haitian Creole, Vietnamese, Khmer	A noun follows the object in the native language.
Articles			
	Consistently omits articles *He has book. They want dog not cat.*	Cantonese, Haitian Creole, Hmong, Korean, Vietnamese, Khmer	There is no article in the native language or no difference between *the* and *a*.
	Overuses articles *The English is difficult. The soccer is popular in the Europe.*	Haitian Creole, Hmong, Spanish	Some languages use articles that are omitted in English.
a/an	**Mistakes *one* for *a/an*** *She is one nurse.*	Haitian Creole, Hmong, Vietnamese	The native language either does not use articles or uses articles differently.
Pronouns			
Gender-Specific Pronouns	**Uses pronouns with the inappropriate gender** *He is my sister.*	Cantonese, Haitian Creole, Hmong, Korean, Spanish, Khmer	The third person pronoun in the native language is gender free, or the personal pronoun is omitted.
	Uses inappropriate gender, particularly with neutral nouns *The day is sunny. She is beautiful.*	Spanish	Nouns have feminine or masculine gender in the native language, and the gender may be carried over into English.

Grammatical Form	Transfer Mistakes in English	Native Language	Cause of Difficulty
Pronouns			
Object Pronouns	**Confuses subject and object pronouns** *Her talks to me.*	Cantonese, Hmong, Khmer	The same pronoun form is used for subject and object in the native language.
	Omits object pronouns *That girl is very rude, so nobody likes.*	Korean, Vietnamese	The native language does not use direct objects.
Pronoun and Number Agreement	**Uses the wrong number for pronouns** *I saw many red birds. It was pretty.*	Cantonese, Korean	The native language does not require number agreement.
Subject Pronouns	**Omits subject pronouns** *Mom isn't home. Is at work.*	Korean, Spanish	Subject pronouns may be dropped because in the native language the verb ending gives information about the number and/or gender.
Pronouns in Clauses	**Omits pronouns in clauses** *If don't do homework, they will not learn.*	Cantonese, Vietnamese	The native language does not need a subject in the subordinate clause.
Pronouns and Nouns	**Overuses pronouns with nouns** *This school, it very good.*	Hmong, Vietnamese	This is popular in speech in some languages. The speaker mentions a topic, then makes a comment about it.
	Avoids pronouns and repeats nouns *Carla visits her sister every Sunday, and Carla makes a meal.*	Korean, Vietnamese	In the native language, the speaker repeats nouns and does not use pronouns.
Pronoun *one*	**Omits the pronoun *one*** *I saw two dogs, and I like the small.*	Spanish	Adjectives can stand alone in the native language, but English requires a noun or *one*.
Possessive Forms	**Confuses possessive forms** *The book is my.*	Cantonese, Hmong, Vietnamese	Cantonese and Hmong speakers tend to omit the final *n* sound, which may create confusion between *my* and *mine*.

Grammar Transfers:
Grammatical Form

Grammatical Form	Transfer Mistakes in English	Native Language	Cause of Difficulty
Verbs			
Present Tense	**Omits -s in present tense, third person agreement** *He like pizza.*	Cantonese, Haitian Creole, Hmong, Korean, Vietnamese, Khmer	Subject-verb agreement is not used in the native language.
Irregular Verbs	**Has problems with irregular subject-verb agreement** *Tom and Sue has a new car.*	Cantonese, Hmong, Korean, Khmer	Verbs' forms do not change to show the number of the subject in the native language.
Inflectional Endings	**Omits tense markers** *I study English yesterday.*	Cantonese, Haitian Creole, Hmong, Korean, Vietnamese, Khmer	The native language does not use inflectional endings to change verb tense.
Present and Future Tenses	**Incorrectly uses the present tense for the future tense** *I go next week.*	Cantonese, Korean	The native language may use the present tense to imply the future tense.
Negative Statements	**Omits helping verbs in negative statements** *Sue no coming to school.*	Cantonese, Korean, Spanish	The native language does not use helping verbs in negative statements.
Present-Perfect Tense	**Avoids the present-perfect tense** *Marcos live here for three months.*	Haitian Creole, Vietnamese	The native language does not use the present-perfect verb form.
Past-Continuous Tense	**Uses the past-continuous tense for recurring action in the past** *When I was young, I was talking a lot.*	Korean, Spanish	In the native language, the past-continuous tense is used but in English the expression *used to* or the simple past tense is used.
Main Verb	**Omits the main verb** *Talk in class not good.*	Cantonese	Cantonese does not require an infinitive marker when using a verb as a noun. Speakers may confuse the infinitive for the main verb.
Main Verbs in Clauses	**Uses two or more main verbs in one clause without any connectors** *I took a book went studied at the library.*	Hmong	In Hmong, verbs can be used consecutively without conjunctions or punctuation.
Linking Verbs	**Omits the linking verb** *He hungry.*	Cantonese, Haitian Creole, Hmong, Vietnamese, Khmer	In some languages, *be* is implied in the adjective form. In other languages, the concept is expressed with a verb.
Helping Verb in Passive Voice	**Omits the helping verb in the passive voice** *The homework done.*	Cantonese, Vietnamese	In Cantonese and Vietnamese, the passive voice does not require a helping verb.

Grammatical Form	Transfer Mistakes in English	Native Language	Cause of Difficulty
Verbs			
Passive Voice	**Avoids the passive voice** *They speak English here.* *One speaks English here.* *English is spoken here.*	Haitian Creole	The passive voice does not exist in the native language.
Transitive Verbs	**Confuses transitive and intransitive verbs** *The child broke.* *The child broke the plate.*	Cantonese, Korean, Spanish	Verbs that require a direct object differ between English and the native language.
Phrasal Verbs	**Confuses related phrasal verbs** *I ate at the apple.* *I ate up the apple.*	Korean, Spanish	Phrasal verbs are not used in the native language, and there is often confusion over their meaning.
Have and *be*	**Uses *have* instead of *be*** *I have thirst.* *He has right.*	Spanish	Spanish and English have different uses for *have* and *be*.
Adjectives			
Word Order	**Places adjectives after nouns** *I saw a car red.*	Haitian Creole, Hmong, Spanish, Vietnamese, Khmer	Nouns often precede adjectives in the native language.
	Consistently places adjectives after nouns *This is a lesson new.*	Cantonese, Korean	Adjectives always follow nouns in the native language.
-er and *-est* Endings	**Avoids *-er* and *-est* endings** *I am more old than you.*	Hmong, Korean, Spanish, Khmer	The native language shows comparative and superlative forms with separate words.
-ing and *-ed* Endings	**Confuses *-ing* and *-ed* forms** *Math is bored.*	Cantonese, Korean, Spanish, Khmer	Adjectives in the native language do not have active and passive meanings.
Adverbs			
Adjectives and Adverbs	**Uses an adjective where an adverb is needed** *Talk quiet.*	Haitian Creole, Hmong, Khmer	Adjectives and adverb forms are interchangeable in the native language.
Word Order	**Places adverbs before verbs** *He quickly ran.* *He ran quickly.*	Cantonese, Korean	Adverbs usually come before verbs in the native language, and this tendency is carried over into English.
Prepositions			
	Omits prepositions *I like come school.*	Cantonese	Cantonese does not use prepositions the way that English does.

How to Use the Grammar Transfer Charts

The grammar of many languages differs widely from English. For example, a student's primary language may use a different word order than English, may not use parts of speech in the same way, or may use different verb tenses. The Grammar Transfer Charts are designed to help you anticipate and understand possible student errors in speaking and writing standard English. With all grammar exercises, the emphasis is on oral communication, both as a speaker and listener.

1. Highlight Transferrable Skills If the grammar skill transfers from the student's primary language to English, state that during the lesson. In many lessons an English Language Learner feature will indicate which skills do and do not transfer.

2. Preteach Non-Transferrable Skills Prior to teaching a grammar lesson, check the chart to determine if the skill transfers from the student's primary language into English. If it does not, preteach the skill during Small Group time. Provide sentence frames and ample structured opportunities to use the skill in spoken English. Students need to talk, talk, and talk some more to master these skills.

3. Provide Additional Practice and Time If the skill does NOT transfer from the student's primary language into English, the student will require more time and practice mastering it. Continue to review the skill during Small Group time. Use the additional resources, such as the grammar lessons in the **Intervention Kit** (K–3) or review lessons, in upcoming weeks.

4. Use Contrastive Analysis Tell students when a skill does not transfer and include contrastive analysis work to make the student aware of how to correct their speaking and writing for standard English. For example, when a student uses an incorrect grammatical form, write the student sentence on a **WorkBoard**. Then write the correct English form underneath. Explain the difference between the student's primary language and English. Have the student correct several other sentences using this skill, such as sentences in their Writer's Notebooks.

5. Increase Writing and Speaking Opportunities Increase the amount of structured writing and speaking opportunities for students needing work on specific grammatical forms. Sentence starters and paragraph frames, such as those found in the lessons, are ideal for both written and oral exercises.

6. Focus on Meaning Always focus on the meanings of sentences in all exercises. As they improve and fine-tune their English speaking and writing skills, work with students on basic comprehension of spoken and written English.

To help students move to the next level of language acquisition and master English grammatical forms, recast their responses during classroom discussions or provide additional language for them to use as they respond further. Provide leveled-language sentence frames orally or in writing for students to use as they respond to questions and prompts. Below are samples.

English Language Learner Response Chart

Beginning (will respond by pointing or saying one word answers)	**Sample Frames** (simple, short sentences) *I see a _____. This is a _____. I like the _____.*
Early Intermediate (will respond with phrases or simple sentences)	**Sample Frames** (simple sentences with adjectives and adverbs added, and compound subjects or predicates) *I see a _____ _____. The _____ animal is _____. There are _____ and _____.*
Intermediate (will respond with simple sentences and limited academic language)	**Sample Frames** (harder sentences with simple phrases in consistent patterns; some academic language included) *The animal's prey is _____ because _____. The main idea is _____ because _____. He roamed the park so that _____.*
Early Advanced (will begin to use more sophisticated sentences and some academic language)	**Sample Frames** (complex sentences with increased academic language, beginning phrases and clauses, and multiple-meaning words) *When the violent storm hit, _____. As a result of the revolution, the army_____. Since most endangered animals are _____, they _____.*
Advanced (will have mastered some more complex sentence structures and is increasing the amount of academic language used)	Use the questions and prompts provided in the lessons for the whole group. Provide additional support learning and using academic language. These words are boldfaced throughout the lessons and sentence starters are often provided.

Cognates

Cognates are words in two languages that look alike and have the same or similar meaning (e.g., *school/escuela*, *telephone/teléfono*) and can be helpful resources for English Language Learners. This list identifies some Spanish cognates for the academic language used during the lessons.

Students must also be aware of false cognates—words that look similar in two languages, but have different meanings, such as *soap* in English and *sopa* (meaning *soup*) in Spanish.

accent	*acento*	**context**	*contexto*
action	*acción*	**contrast**	*contrastar*
action verb	*verbo de acción*	**definition**	*definición*
adjective	*adjetivo*	**demonstrative**	*demostrativo*
adverb	*adverbio*	**denotation**	*denotación*
alphabetical order	*orden alfabético*	**description**	*descripción*
analogy	*analogía*	**dialogue**	*diálogo*
analyze	*analizar*	**dictionary**	*diccionario*
antecedent	*antecedente*	**direct**	*directo*
antonym	*antónimo*	**effect**	*efecto*
apostrophe	*apóstrofe*	**evaluate**	*evaluar*
article	*artículo*	**event**	*evento*
author	*autor*	**example**	*ejemplo*
cause	*causa*	**exclamation**	*exclamación*
classify	*clasificar*	**family**	*familia*
combine	*combinar*	**fantasy**	*fantasía*
compare	*comparar*	**figurative**	*figurativo*
complex	*complejo*	**fragment**	*fragmento*
comprehension	*comprensión*	**future**	*futuro*
conclusion	*conclusión*	**generalization**	*generalización*
confirm	*confirmar*	**generalize**	*generalizar*
conjunction	*conjunción*	**glossary**	*glosario*
connotation	*connotación*	**Greek**	*Griego*
consonant	*consonante*	**homophone**	*homófono*

idea	*idea*	**prefix**	*prefijo*
identify	*identificar*	**preposition**	*preposición*
illustration	*ilustración*	**prepositional**	*preposicional*
indirect	*indirecto*	**present**	*presente*
introduction	*introducción*	**problem**	*problema*
irregular	*irregular*	**pronunciation**	*pronunciación*
language	*lenguaje*	**punctuation**	*puntuación*
Latin	*Latín*	**reality**	*realidad*
myth	*mito*	**relationship**	*relación*
negative	*negativo*	**sequence**	*secuencia*
object	*objeto*	**singular**	*singular*
opinion	*opinión*	**solution**	*solución*
order	*orden*	**structure**	*estructura*
origin	*orígen*	**subject**	*sujeto*
paragraph	*párrafo*	**suffix**	*sufijo*
part	*parte*	**syllable**	*sílaba*
perspective	*perspectiva*	**synonym**	*sinónimo*
persuasion	*persuación*	**technique**	*técnica*
phrase	*frase*	**text**	*texto*
plural	*plural*	**theme**	*tema*
possessive adjective	*adjetivo posesivo*	**verb**	*verbo*
predicate	*predicado*	**visualize**	*visualizar*
prediction	*predicción*	**vowel**	*vocal*

ELL ENGLISH LANGUAGE LEARNERS

The **English Language Learners** in your classroom have a variety of backgrounds. An increasing proportion of English Language Learners are born in the United States. Some of these students are just starting school in the primary grades; others are long-term English Language Learners, with underdeveloped academic skills. Some students come from their native countries with a strong educational foundation. The academic skills of these newly arrived students are well developed and parallel the skills of their native English-speaking peers. Other English Learners immigrate to the United States with little academic experience.

These English Learners are not "blank slates." Their oral language proficiency and literacy in their first languages can be used to facilitate literacy development in English. Systematic, explicit, and appropriately scaffolded instruction and sufficient time help English Learners attain English proficiency and meet high standards in core academic subjects.

Beginning

This level of language proficiency is often referred to as the "silent" stage, in which students' receptive skills are engaged. It is important that teachers and peers respect a language learner's initial silence or allow the student to respond in his or her native language. It is often difficult for teachers to identify the level of cognitive development at this stage, due to the limited proficiency in the second language. It is important to realize that these beginning students have a wide range of abilities in their first language. They are able to transfer knowledge and skills from their first language as they develop English and learn grade-level content. Beginning students include those with limited formal schooling: young students just starting school, as well as older students. Other beginning students have had schooling in their native language and are academically parallel to nativeEnglish-speaking peers.

The Beginning Student...

- recognizes English phonemes that correspond to phonemes produced in primary language;
- is able to apply transferable grammar concepts and skills from the primary language;
- initially demonstrates more receptive than productive English skills;
- produces English vocabulary to communicate basic needs in social and academic settings;
- responds by pointing to, nodding, gesturing, acting out, and manipulating objects/pictures;
- speaks in one-or two-word responses as language develops;
- draws pictures and writes letters and sounds being learned.

Early Intermediate

At this level, students are considered more advanced beginning English Learners. They are developing early production skills, but their receptive skills are much more advanced than their speaking ability. At this stage it is critical that the students continue to listen to model speakers.

The Early Intermediate Student...

- recognizes English phonemes that correspond to phonemes produced in primary language;
- is able to apply transferable grammar concepts and skills from the primary language;
- understands more spoken English than the beginning student;
- speaks in one- or two-word utterances;
- may respond with phrases or sentences;
- produces English vocabulary words and phrases to communicate basic needs in social and academic settings;
- begins to ask questions, role-play, and retell;
- begins to use routine expressions;
- demonstrates an internalization of English grammar and usage by recognizing and correcting some errors when speaking and reading aloud;
- increases correct usage of written and oral language conventions.

Intermediate

Students at this level begin to tailor their English language skills to meet communication and learning demands with increasing accuracy. They possess vocabulary and knowledge of grammatical structures that allow them to more fully participate in classroom activities and discussions. They are generally more comfortable producing both spoken and written language.

The Intermediate Student...

- pronounces most English phonemes correctly while reading aloud;
- can identify more details of information that has been presented orally or in writing;
- uses more complex vocabulary and sentences to communicate needs and express ideas;
- uses specific vocabulary learned, including academic language;
- participates more fully in discussions with peers and adults;
- reads and comprehends a wider range of reading materials;
- writes brief narratives and expository texts;
- demonstrates an internalization of English grammar and usage by recognizing and correcting errors when speaking and reading aloud.

English Language Learners

Early Advanced

Students at this language proficiency level possess vocabulary and grammar structures that approach those of an English-proficient speaker. These students demonstrate consistent general comprehension of grade-level content that is presented.

The Early Advanced Student...

- applies knowledge of common English morphemes in oral and silent reading;
- understands increasingly more nonliteral social and academic language;
- responds using extensive vocabulary;
- participates in and initiates more extended social conversations with peers and adults;
- communicates orally and in writing with fewer grammatical errors;
- reads with good comprehension a wide range of narrative and expository texts;
- writes using more standard forms of English on various content-area topics;
- becomes more creative and analytical when writing.

Advanced

The student at this language proficiency level communicates effectively with peers and adults in both social and academic situations. Students can understand grade-level text but still need some English language development support, such as preteaching concepts and skills. While the English language proficiency of these students is advanced, some linguistic support for accessing content is still necessary.

The Advanced Student...

- understands increasingly more nonliteral social and academic language;
- responds using extensive vocabulary;
- communicates orally and in writing with infrequent errors;
- creates more complex narratives and expository writing in all content areas.

English Language Learner Profiles
Facilitating Language Growth

Beginning

Student's Behaviors	Teacher's Behaviors	Questioning Techniques
▪ Points to or provides other nonverbal responses ▪ Actively listens ▪ Responds to commands ▪ Understands more than he or she can produce	▪ Gestures ▪ Focuses on conveying meanings and vocabulary development ▪ Does not force students to speak ▪ Shows visuals and real objects ▪ Writes words for students to see ▪ Pairs students with more proficient learners ▪ Provides speaking and writing frames and models	▪ Point to the _____. ▪ Find the _____. ▪ Put the _____ next to the _____. ▪ Do you have the _____? ▪ Is this the _____? ▪ Who wants the _____?

Early Intermediate

Student's Behaviors	Teacher's Behaviors	Questioning Techniques
▪ Speaks in one- or two-word utterances ▪ Uses short phrases and simple sentences ▪ Listens with greater understanding	▪ Asks questions that can be answered by yes/no ▪ Asks either/or questions ▪ Asks higher-order questions with one-word answers ▪ Models correct responses ▪ Ensures supportive, low-anxiety environment ▪ Does not overtly call attention to grammar errors ▪ Asks short "wh" questions	▪ Yes/no (Did you like the story?) ▪ Either/or (Is this a pencil or a crayon?) ▪ One-word responses (Why did the dog hide?) ▪ General questions that encourage lists of words (What did you see in the book bag?) ▪ Two-word responses (Where did I put the pen?)

Intermediate

Student's Behaviors	Teacher's Behaviors	Questioning Techniques
▪ Demonstrates comprehension in a variety of ways ▪ Speaks in short phrases or sentences ▪ Begins to use language more freely	▪ Provides frequent comprehension checks ▪ Asks open-ended questions that stimulate language production	▪ Why? ▪ How? ▪ How is this like that? ▪ Tell me about _____. ▪ Talk about _____. ▪ Describe _____. ▪ What is in your book bag?

Early Advanced

Student's Behaviors	Teacher's Behaviors	Questioning Techniques
▪ Participates in reading and writing activities to acquire information ▪ Demonstrates increased levels of accuracy and correctness and is able to express thoughts and feelings ▪ Produces language with varied grammatical structures and academic language ▪ May experience difficulties in abstract, cognitively demanding subjects	▪ Fosters conceptual development and expanded literacy through content ▪ Continues to make lessons comprehensible and interactive ▪ Teaches thinking and study skills ▪ Continues to be alert to individual differences in language and culture	▪ What would you recommend/why? ▪ How do you think this story will end? ▪ What is this story about? ▪ What is your favorite part of the story? ▪ Describe/compare _____. How are these similar/different? ▪ What would happen if _____? ▪ Why do you think that? Yes, tell me more about _____.

Fostering Classroom Discussions

Strategies for English Language Learners

One of the most effective ways in which to increase the oral language proficiency of your English Language Learners is to give students many opportunities to do a lot of talking in the classroom. Providing the opportunities and welcoming all levels of participation will motivate students to take part in the class discussions. You can employ a few basic teaching strategies that will encourage the participation of all language proficiency levels of English Language Learners in whole class and small group discussions.

☑ WAIT/DIFFERENT RESPONSES

- Be sure to give students enough time to answer the question.
- Let students know that they can respond in different ways depending on their levels of proficiency. Students can
  - answer in their native language;
  - ask a more proficient ELL speaker to repeat the answer in English;
  - answer with nonverbal cues (pointing to related objects, drawing, or acting out).

> **Teacher:** Where is Charlotte?
>
> **ELL Response:** (Student points to the web in the corner of the barn.)
>
> **Teacher:** Yes. Charlotte is sitting in her web. Let's all point to Charlotte.

☑ REPEAT

- Give positive confirmation to the answers that each English Language Learner offers. If the response is correct, repeat what the student has said in a clear, loud voice and at a slower pace. This validation will motivate other ELLs to participate.

> **Teacher:** How would you describe the faces of the bobcats?
>
> **ELL Response:** They look scared.
>
> **Teacher:** That's right, Silvia. They are scared. Everyone show me your scared face.

☑ REVISE FOR FORM

- Repeating an answer allows you to model the proper form for a response. You can model how to answer in full sentences and use academic language.
- When you repeat the answer, correct any grammar or pronunciation errors.

> **Teacher:** Who are the main characters in the story *Zathura*?
>
> **ELL Response:** Danny and Walter is.
>
> **Teacher:** Yes. Danny and Walter <u>are</u> the main characters. Remember to use the verb <u>are</u> when you are telling about more than one person. Let's repeat the sentence.
>
> **All:** Danny and Walter <u>are</u> the main characters.

☑ REVISE FOR MEANING

■ Repeating an answer offers an opportunity to clarify the meaning of a response.

> **Teacher:** Where did the golden feather come from?
>
> **ELL Response:** The bird.
>
> **Teacher:** That's right. The golden feather came from the Firebird.

☑ ELABORATE

■ If students give a one-word answer or a nonverbal cue, elaborate on the answer to model fluent speaking and grammatical patterns.

■ Provide more examples or repeat the answer using proper academic language.

> **Teacher:** Why is the girls' mother standing with her hands on her hips?
>
> **ELL Response:** She is mad.
>
> **Teacher:** Can you tell me more? Why is she mad?
>
> **ELL Response:** Because the girls are late.
>
> **Teacher:** Ok. What do you think the girls will do?
>
> **ELL Response:** They will promise not to be late again.
>
> **Teacher:** Anyone else have an idea?

☑ ELICIT

■ Prompt students to give a more comprehensive response by asking additional questions or guiding them to get to an answer.

> **Teacher:** Listen as I read the caption under the photograph. What information does the caption tell us?
>
> **ELL Response:** It tells about the butterfly.
>
> **Teacher:** What did you find out about the butterfly?
>
> **ELL Response:** It drinks nectar.
>
> **Teacher:** Yes. The butterfly drinks nectar from the flower.

Making the Most of Classroom Conversations

Use all the speaking and listening opportunities in your classroom to observe students' oral language proficiency.

■ Response to oral presentations

■ Responding to text aloud

■ Following directions

■ Group projects

■ Small Group work

■ Informal, social peer discussions

■ One-on-one conferences

The **English Language Learner Resource Book** provides Speaking and Listening Checklists to help you monitor students' oral language proficiency growth.

Support for Students with Dyslexia

Characteristics of Dyslexia

A student with dyslexia is a student who continually struggles with reading and spelling but displays an ability to learn when there are no print materials involved. Even though the student receives the same classroom instruction as most other students, he continues to have difficulties with reading and spelling.

Students identified with dyslexia often have difficulties in the following areas

- reading words in isolation
- decoding nonsense words accurately
- oral reading (slow and inaccurate)
- learning to spell

The difficulties in these areas are usually the result of student's struggles with:

- phonological awareness: segmenting, blending, and manipulating words
- naming letters and pronouncing their sounds.
- phonological memory
- rapid naming of the letters of the alphabet or familiar objects

Effective Instruction

To address the needs of a student with dyslexia, instruction should be delivered in small groups. The instruction should be explicit, intensive, employ multisensory methods, as needed, and be individualized. It should include instruction on:

- phonemic awareness that has students detect, segment, blend and manipulate sounds
- phonics, emphasizing the sound/symbol relationships for decoding and encoding words
- morphology, semantics and syntax
- fluency with patterns of language
- strategies for decoding, encoding, word recognition, fluency and comprehension

Resources:
The International Dyslexia Association Website: www.interdys.org
The Dyslexia Handbook: Procedures Concerning Dyslexia and Related Disorders (Revised 2007) Texas Education Agency, Austin, TX, Publication Number: GE8721001

Treasures Reading and Language Arts Program

Treasures is a scientifically-based core program that offers sequential, explicit, and effective instruction in phonological awareness, phonics, morphology, fluency, vocabulary, and reading comprehension. Students are given many opportunities to practice and review these skills to help prevent reading difficulties before they begin.

Tier 2 INTERVENTION

Weekly Small Group Lessons
Intervention Teacher's Editions

Tier 2 Instruction is provided in weekly small group lessons in the *Treasures* **Teacher's Editions**. These lessons provide targeted instruction in priority skills taught in the week. *Tier 2 Intervention* **Teacher's Editions** provide additional instruction for struggling students in the areas of phonemic awareness, phonics, vocabulary, fluency, and comprehension, grammar and writing.

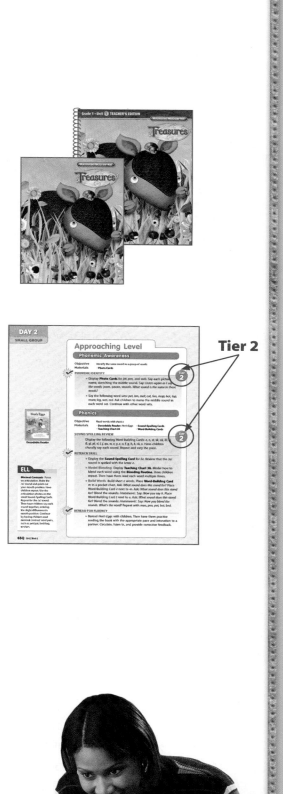

Tier 3 INTERVENTION

Reading Triumphs
Intervention Program

Reading Triumphs provides intensive instruction. Explicit, sequential lessons delivered through clear instructional routines for all the key components of reading are embedded in the program. The "no assumption instruction" allows for both teacher and student success.

B

C

Key 2 = Unit 2

D

E

Grammar

See also under **Approaching Level Options; Beyond Level Options; English Language Learners; On Level Options.**

Index

S

T

V

W

Photography

All photos by Ken Karp or Ken Cavanagh for MacMillan/McGraw-Hill except the following:

iv: (tl, tcl, tcr, ccl, bl, br) Macmillan/McGraw-Hill; (tr) Deborah Attoinese Photography; (ccr, cr) Anthony Colella/Richter-Colella Studios; (cl) Photography by Monet. v: (br) Macmillan/McGraw-Hill; (tl) Doug Martin; (tr) Ferguson & Katzman Photography. xii: (br) Thomas Kitchin & Victoria Hurst/Getty Images. xiii: (br) Macmillan/McGraw-Hill. 136A–B: Photodisc/Fotosearch. 136C:(l, cl, r) Bettmann/Corbis ; (bcl) Bettmann/Corbis; (bkgd) Macmillan McGraw-Hill. 136I: Courtesy Chris Soentpiet www.soentpiet.com. 161B: (b) Gabe Palmer/Corbis. 162A–B: Radius Images/Alamy. 162C: (cl) Bernard Hoffman/Getty; (l) Bettmann/Corbis. 162I: Courtesy Chris Soentpiet www.soentpiet.com. 188A–B: Digital Vision/Fotosearch. 188I: Courtesy Chris Soentpiet www.soentpiet.com. 200A–B: Digital Vision/PunchStock. 200C: (l) AP Images/Scott Neville. 200I: Courtesy Chris Soentpiet www.soentpiet.com. 225B: (b) Jim Cummings/Corbis. 226A–B: John Anderson/Alamy. 226C: (l) Corel Stock Photo Library TiConUno s.r.l./Alamy; (cl) Macmillan/McGraw-Hill; (cr) Getty Images; (r) Getty Images; (bkgd) Photographers Choice RF/SuperStock. 226I: Courtesy Chris Soentpiet www.soentpiet.com. 258A–B: Brad Perks Lightscapes/Alamy. 263B–F: (b) Macmillan McGraw-Hill . 263H: (br) Royalty Free/Corbis. 263L: (br) Digital Vision Photography/Veer. Teacher's Notes: (marker) Royalty Free/Corbis; (sharpeners) Pixtal/PunchStock.

Acknowledgments

The publisher gratefully acknowledges permission to reprint the following copyrighted material:

"Adelina's Whales" text and photographs by Richard Sobol. Text and photographs copyright © 2003 by Richard Sobol. Reprinted by permission of Dutton Children's Books, a division of Penguin Books USA Inc.

"The Adventures of Ali Baba Bernstein" by Johanna Hurwitz. Copyright © 1985 by Johanna Hurwitz. Reprinted by permission of William Morrow and Company.

"The Ant and the Grasshopper" retold and illustrated by Amy Lowry Poole. Copyright © 2000 by Amy Lowry Poole. Reprinted by permission of Holiday House.

"The Astronaut and the Onion" by Ann Cameron from GLORIA RISING. Text copyright © 2002 by Ann Cameron. Reprinted by permission of Frances Foster Books, an imprint of Farrar, Straus and Giroux.

"At Home in the Coral Reef" by Katy Muzik, illustrated by Katherine Brown-Wing. Text and illustrations copyright © 1992 by Charlesbridge Publishing. Reprinted by permission.

"Because of Winn-Dixie" by Kate DiCamillo from BECAUSE OF WINN-DIXIE. Copyright © 2000 by Kate DiCamillo. Reprinted by permission of Candlewick Press.

"Brave New Heights" by Monica Kulling from MORE SPICE THAN SUGAR: POEMS ABOUT FEISTY FEMALES compiled by Lillian Morrison. Compilation copyright © 2001 by Lillian Morrison. Reprinted by permission of Marian Reiner from the author.

"The Cricket in Times Square" by George Selden, illustrated by Garth Williams from THE CRICKET IN TIMES SQUARE. Copyright © 1960 by George Selden Thompson and Garth Williams. Reprinted by permission of Farrar, Straus and Giroux. [McGraw-Hill acknowledges the use of a trademark due to illustrator restrictions.]

"Dear Mrs. LaRue" written and illustrated by Mark Teague. Copyright © 2002 by Mark Teague. Reprinted by permission of Scholastic Press, a division of Scholastic, Inc.

"How Ben Franklin Stole the Lightning" by Rosalyn Schanzer. Copyright © 2003 by Rosalyn Schanzer. Reprinted by permission of HarperCollins Publishers.

"I Love the Look of Words" by Maya Angelou from SOUL LOOKS BACK IN WONDER. Copyright © 1993 by Tom Feelings. Reprinted by permission of Dial Books, a division of Penguin Books USA Inc.

"Ima and The Great Texas Ostrich Race" by Margaret Olivia McManis, illustrated by Bruce Dupree. Text copyright © 2002 by Margaret McManis. Illustrations copyright © 2002 by Bruce Dupree. Reprinted by permission of Eakin Press/A Division of Sunbelt Media, Inc.

"Leah's Pony" by Elizabeth Friedrich, illustrated by Michael Garland. Text copyright © 1996 by Elizabeth Friedrich. Illustrations © 1996 by Michael Garland. Reprinted by permission of Boyds Mills Press.

"The Life and Times of the Ant" by Charles Micucci from THE LIFE AND TIMES OF THE ANT. Copyright © 2003 by Charles Micucci. Reprinted by permission of Houghton Mifflin Company.

"Light Bulb" and "Lightning Bolt" by Joan Bransfield Graham from FLICKER FLASH. Text copyright © 1999 by Joan Bransfield Graham. Reprinted by permission of Houghton Mifflin Company.

"Me and Uncle Romie" by Claire Hartfield, paintings by Jerome Lagarrigue. Text copyright © 2002 by Claire Hartfield, paintings copyright © 2002 by Jerome Lagarrigue. Reprinted by permission of Dial Books, a division of Penguin Books USA Inc.

"Mighty Jackie: The Strike-Out Queen" by Marissa Moss, illustrated by C. F. Payne. Text copyright © 2004 by Marissa Moss, illustrations copyright © 2004 by C. F. Payne. Reprinted by permission of Simon & Schuster Books for Young Readers.

"Mountains and plains" and "No sky at all" from AN INTRODUCTION TO HAIKU: AN ANTHOLOGY OF POEMS AND POETS FROM BASHŌ TO SHIKI. Copyright © 1958 by Harold G. Henderson. Reprinted by permission of Doubleday Anchor Books, a Division of Doubleday & Company, Inc.

"My Brother Martin: A Sister Remembers, Growing Up with the Rev. Dr. Martin Luther King, Jr." by Christine King Farris, illustrated by Chris Soentpiet. Text copyright © 2003 by Christine King Farris, illustrations copyright © 2003 by Chris Soentpiet. Reprinted by permission of Simon & Schuster Books for Young Readers.

"My Brothers' Flying Machine" by Jane Yolen, paintings by Jim Burke. Text copyright © 2003 by Jane Yolen, illustrations copyright © 2003 by Jim Burke. Reprinted by permission of Little, Brown and Company.

"My Diary from Here to There" story by Amada Irma Pérez, illustrations by Maya Christina Gonzalez from MY DIARY FROM HERE TO THERE. Story copyright © 2002 by Amada Irma Pérez, illustrations copyright © 2002 by Maya Christina Gonzalez. Reprinted by permission of Children's Book Press.

"Mystic Horse" by Paul Goble. Copyright © 2003 by Paul Goble. Reprinted by permission of HarperCollins Publishers.

"The New Kid" from AT THE CRACK OF THE BAT: Baseball Poems compiled by Lillian Morrison, illustrated by Steve Cieslawski. Text copyright © 1992 by Lillian Morrison. Illustrations copyright © 1992 by Steve Cieslawski. Reprinted by permission of Hyperion Books for Children.

"Roadrunner's Dance" by Rudolfo Anaya, pictures by David Diaz. Text copyright © 2000 by Rudolfo Anaya, illustrations copyright © 2000 by David Diaz. Reprinted by permission of Hyperion Books for Children.

"Snowflake Bentley" by Jacqueline Briggs Martin, illustrated by Mary Azarian. Text copyright © 1998 by Jacqueline Briggs Martin, illustrations copyright © 1998 by Mary Azarian. Reprinted by permission of Houghton Mifflin Company.

"The snow is melting" and " Winter solitude" from THE ESSENTIAL HAIKU: VERSIONS OF BASHŌ, BUSON, AND ISSA. Introduction and selection copyright © 1994 by Robert Hass. Unless otherwise noted, all translations copyright © 1994 by Robert Hass. Reprinted by permission of The Ecco Press.

Excerpt from "So Long, It's Been Good to Know Yuh." Words and music by Woody Guthrie. www.woodyguthrie.org Copyright © 1940 (Renewed), 1950 (Renewed), 1951 (Renewed) by TRO-Folk. Reprinted by permission of The Richmond Organization (TRO).

"A Walk in the Desert" by Rebecca L. Johnson with illustrations by Phyllis V. Saroff from A WALK IN THE DESERT. Text copyright © 2001 by Rebecca L. Johnson, illustrations copyright © 2001 by Phyllis V. Saroff. Reprinted by permission of Carolrhoda Books, Inc.

"When I Went to the Library" by Ken Roberts from WHEN I WENT TO THE LIBRARY edited by Debora Pearson. Copyright © 2001 by Ken Roberts. Reprinted by permission of Groundwood Books/Douglas & McIntyre.

"Wild Horses: Black Hills Sanctuary" by Cris Peterson, photographs by Alvis Upitis. Text copyright © 2003 by Cris Peterson, photographs copyright © 2003 by Alvis Upitis. Reprinted by permission of Boyds Mills Press, Inc.

ILLUSTRATIONS
Cover Illustration: Gloria Domingo Manuel.

10–31: Maya Christina Gonzalez. 40–41: Ginger Nielson. 42–59: Brian Biggs. 60–63: Olwyn Whelan. 65: Ken Bowser. 80: Kim Johnson. 82–97: Anna Rich. 120–121: Robert Casilla. 125: Viviana Diaz. 140–155: Chris Soentpiet. 166–183: C.F. Payne. 184–185: Steve Cieslawski. 220–223: Ande Cook. 230–251: Paul Goble. 258–259: Darryl Ligasan. 270: Ann Boyajian. 272–285: Nicole Wong. 296–319: Mark Teague. 330: Dean Macadam. 340–341: David LaFleur. 342–361: Renato Alarcão. 362: Wendy Born Hollander. 363: (tr)(ml) Renato Alarcão; (bl)(cr) Wendy Born Hollander. 364: (t) Renato Alarcão; (tr)(bl) Wendy Born Hollander. 365: (bkgd) Renato Alarcão; (insets) Wendy Born Hollander. 372–391: Jerome Lagarrigue. 396–397: Susan Swan. 408–409: Loretta Krupinski. 410–429: Garth Williams. 433: Argosy. 440–455: Charles Micucci. 456–459: Amy Lowry Poole. 465: Bridget Starr Taylor. 476–477: James Bentley. 478–497: Bruce Dupree. 508–525: Jim Burke. 527: Jim Burke. 528–529: Bandelin-Dacey Studios. 532–533: Bill Cigliano. 534–535: Argosy. 548: Laura Westlund. 550–559: Phyllis V. Saroff. 574–595: David Diaz. 614–631: Katherine Brown-Wing. 632–635: David Groff. 658: Richard Sobol. 660–661: Jesse Reisch. 664–665: Fabricio Vandenbroeck. 666–667: Marion Eldrige. 676–677: Stacey Schuett. 678–697: Michael Garland. 706–707: Greg Shed. 708–723: Ying-Hwa Hu & Cornelius Van

Wright. 746–769: Mary Azarian. 770–771: Tina Fong. 778–797: Rosalyn Schanzer. 802–803: Stacey Schuett. 804: Paul Mirocha.

PHOTOGRAPHY

iv: Purestock/SuperStock. v: (t) Jeff Greenberg/PhotoEdit; (b) © 2005 Twentieth Century Fox. All rights reserved. vi: Kayte M. Deioma/PhotoEdit. vii: (t) Brian Bahr/Getty Images. viii: Masterfile. ix: Masterfile. x: Bob Daemmrich/PhotoEdit. xi: Bill Heinsohn/Alamy. xii: (tl) Lon Lauber/OSF/Animal Animals/Earth Scenes; (cl) Martin J. Miller/Visuals Unlimited; (cl-bkgd) Tom Bean. xiii: William Smithey Jr/Getty Images. xiv: Comstock/SuperStock. xv: AP Images/Neil Eliot. 2-3: Purestock/SuperStock. 4: Veronique Krieger/Getty Images. 4-5: Ryan McVay/Getty Images. 5: Bettmann/Corbis. 6-7: Jose Luis Pelaez/Corbis. 8: Rusty Hill/FoodPix/Jupiter Images. 9: David Hiser/Getty Images. 30: (tl, c) Children's Book Press. 32: (bl) Ted Streshinsky/Corbis. 33: (c) Morton Beebe/Corbis; (br) Najlah Feanny/Corbis. 34: (bl) Arthur Schatz/Time Life Pictures/Getty Images; (tr) PunchStock. 35: Walter P. Reuther Library/Wayne State University. 37: Myrleen Ferguson Cate/PhotoEdit. 38-39: Tom & Dee Ann McCarthy/Corbis. 58: (bl) Brian Biggs; (tr) Ben Hurwitz. 65: Photodisc/Getty Images. 66–67: Jeff Greenberg/PhotoEdit. 68: (t) Getty Images; (cr) Russel Illig/Photodisc/PunchStock; (br) C Squared Studios/Getty. 70-71: (all) Mi Won Kim /Time For Kids. 72: (t) Esta Shapiro/Time For Kids; (bl) Courtesy David Hsu. 73: Courtesy David Hsu. 74: Lewis Wickes Hines/Corbis. 77: (tcr) Brand X Pictures/PunchStock; (cr) PhotoLink/Getty Images. 78-79: Mitch Tobias/Masterfile. 81: Stock Trek/Getty. 96: (tl) Das Anuda/Courtesy Farrar, Straus and Giroux; (cr) Courtesy Anna Rich. 98: NASA Johnson Space Center Collection. 98-99: (bkgd) NASA/CORBIS. 99: (br) PatitucciPhoto/Aurora Photos; (r) NASA Johnson Space Center Collection. 100: (tr) GustoImages/Artemi Kyriacou/Jupiter Images. 100-101: (bkgd) BigStockPhoto. 101: (tr) NASA/Roger Ressmeyer/Corbis; (br) NASA/Corbis. 103: Dan Bigelow/Getty Images. 104-105: Don Mason/Blend Images/Jupiter Images. 106:Steven Weinrebe/Index Stock Imagery. 107: Don Smetzer/Stone/Getty Images. 108-114: © 2005 Twentieth Century Fox. All rights reserved. 116-117: (bkgd) Wetzel & Company. 117: © 2005 Twentieth Century Fox. All rights reserved. 120: (tr) Courtesy Candlewick Press; (bl) © 2005 Twentieth Century Fox. All rights reserved. 121: © 2005 Twentieth Century Fox. All rights reserved. 124: © 2005 Twentieth Century Fox. All rights reserved. 125: Ryan McVay/Getty Images. 126: Brand X Pictures/PunchStock. 128: Michael Okoniewski/AP-Wide World Photos. 129: (br) Michael Okoniewski/AP-Wide World Photos; (bl) Hemera Technologies/Alamy. 131: (cr) Nic Hamilton/Alamy; (tr) Ryan McVay/Getty Images; (br) Pixtal/PunchStock. 132-133: Kayte M. Deioma/PhotoEdit. 134: Digital Vision Photography/Veer. 134-135: Ingram Publishing/AGEfotostock. 135: Owen Franken/Corbis. 136-137: Corbis. 138: Bettmann/Corbis. 139: (cl,cr) Bettmann/Corbis. 154: (c) Courtesy Chris Soentpiet/www.soentpiet.com. 156: Bettmann/Corbis. 156-159: Macmillan/McGraw-Hill. 157: AP Photo. 158: Jack Balletri/Bettmann/Corbis. 161: Michael Newman/PhotoEdit. 162-163: Lori Adamski Peek/Getty Images. 164: Bettmann/Corbis. 165: Bernard Hoffman/Getty. 182: (cr) Courtesy C.F. Payne. 187: Royalty-Free/Corbis. 188-189: Brian Bahr/Getty Images. 190: (t) Brian Nicholson/AP Photo; (b) Bryn Lennon/Getty Images. 191: (tr) Al Grillo/AP Photo; (br) Phil Cole/Getty Images. 192: Brian Bahr/Getty Images. 193: (tr) Todd Warshaw/Pool/Getty Images; (bl) Petros Giannakouris/AP Photos. 194: Nadia Borowski Scott/Zuma Press/Newscom. 195: (tr) STR/AFP/Getty Images; (bl) Petros Giannakouris/AP Photo. 196:Tamara Reynolds. 199: (bl) Photodisc/PunchStock; (bc) Ana de Sousa/Shutterstock; (r) Stockdisc/PunchStock. 200-201: Steve Bloom Images/Alamy. 202: Scott Neville/AP Photos. 204-217: (all) Alvis Upitis. 218: (t) Boydsmills Press; (cr) Alvis Upitis. 218-219: Alvis Upitis. 225: Kevin Peterson/Getty Images. 226-227: Carson Ganci/Design Pics Inc./Alamy. 228: TiConUno s.r.l./Alamy. 228-229: (bkgd) Photographers Choice RF/SuperStock. 229: Macmillan/McGraw-Hill. 250: Courtesy Paul Goble. 252: (br) Getty Images; (bkgd) Wetzel & Company. 253: Getty Images. 253-255: (bkgd) Wetzel & Company. 257: Robert Llewellyn/Alamy. 260: (br) Michael St. Maur Sheil/Corbis; (t) Jerry Driendl/Getty Images. 260-261: Jerry Driendl/Getty Images. 263: (tr) Stockbyte/PunchStock; (cr) Royalty-Free/Corbis; (bl) McVay/Getty Images. 264-265: Masterfile. 266: Dennis MacDonald/AGEfotostock America. 266-267: Gary He/Macmillan/McGraw-Hill. 267: Charles Krupa/AP Images. 268-269: Whit Preston/Stone/Getty Images. 271: (tl) Daryl Balfour/Getty Images; (cr) Stephen Cooper/Getty Images. 284: (tl) Courtesy Groundwood Books; (cr) Courtesy Nicole Wong. 286: John Cancalosi/DRK. 287: Michael & Patricia Fogden/Minden. 288: (tl) Michael Fogden/Animal Animals; (bl) Bruce Coleman, Inc/Alamy. 291: Tipp Howell/Getty Images. 292-293: Masterfile Royalty-Free. 294: (bl) Ulrike Schanz/Animal Animals; (b) Royalty-Free/Corbis. 295: Mary Grace Long/Asia Images/Getty Images. 318: Courtesy Scholastic. 320: Okapia/Hund/Kramer/Photo Researchers.

321-323: Manuela Hartling/Reuters/Corbis. 325: Royalty-Free/Corbis. 326-327: Masterfile. 328: Time & Life Pictures/Getty Images. 329: (tl) Time & Life Pictures/Getty Images; (tr) Corbis. 331: Marc Longwood. 332: Eric L. Stewart/Lyon College. 333: Warner Brothers/Everett Collection. 337: (tcr, br) Brand X Pictures/PunchStock; (cr) Siede Preis/Getty Images; (bl) PhotoLink/Getty Images; (bc) Ana de Sousa/Shutterstock; (b) Michael Scott/Macmillan/McGraw-Hill. 338: Group 4/Image Source Black/Alamy. 360: (tl) Courtesy Peachtree Publishers; (br) Courtesy Renato Alarcão. 367: Amos Morgan/Getty Images. 368-369: Jeff Greenberg/Alamy. 370: (bl) Chris Steele-Perkins/Magnum; (bc) Getty Images; (br) Comstock Images/Getty Images. 371: Photodisc/Getty Images. 390: (cl) Courtesy of Penguin Group; (tr) Photo by Jessica Tampas. Courtesy Claire Hartfield. 392: Frank Chmura/Alamy. 395: Alan Levenson/AGEfotostock America. 398: Time & Life Pictures/Getty Images. 399: Danita Delimonte/Alamy. 401: (bl) Pixtal/PunchStock; (cr) Stockdisc/PunchStock. 402-403: Bob Daemmrich/Photo Edit. 404: Marta Lavandier/AP Images. 404-405: (bkgd wooden blocks) Dynamic Graphics/Jupiter Images; (bkgd wood texture) Dynamic Graphics/PunchStock; (bkgd close-up of wood grain) Ryan McVay/Getty Images. 405: The Granger Collection, New York. 406-407: Gabe Palmer/Corbis. 428: (tl) Marcia Johnston. Courtesy Farrar, Straus & Giroux; (cr) Courtesy Estate of Garth Williams c/o Frost National Bank. 430: (tr) B. G. Thomson/Photo Researchers; (cr) Karen Marks/Bat Conservation International/Photo Researchers. 430-431: Steve Kaufman/Corbis. 431: Pat Little/AP Images. 432: Jeff Lepore/Photo Researchers. 432-433: Tim Flach/Stone/Getty Images. 435: Dan Bigelow/Getty Images. 436-437: Michael & Patricia Fogden/Corbis. 438: Masterfile. 439: Steve Hopkin/Ardea. 454: Anita Lambrinos/Courtesy Charles Micucci. 461: Amos Morgan/Getty Images. 462-463: Bill Heinsohn/Alamy. 464: Bob Stefko/Getty Images. 465: (tr) Bettmann/Corbis; (tl) Christopher and Sally Gable/Getty Images. 466: Stephen Pingry/AP Photo. 467: AGEfotostock/SuperStock. 468: Doug Mazell/Jupiter Images. 469: Mary Altaffer/AP Photo. 470: OJPhotos/Alamy. 473: (cr) Ryan McVay/Getty Images; (bl) PhotoLink/Getty Images; (bc) Ana de Sousa/Shutterstock; (br) Photodisc/PunchStock. 474-475: Troy Wayrynen. 496: (tl) Justin A. Woods; (br) Donna Freeman courtesy of Pelican Publishing Company. 498: Richard Hutchings. 499: North Wind Picture Archives/Alamy. 500: (tl) The Ima Hogg Papers/The Center for American History/The University of Texas at Austin; (b) Travelwide/Alamy. 501: Thais Llorca/epa/Corbis. 503: Rubberball Productions/Getty Images. 504-505: Library of Congress/Getty Images. 506-507: Bettmann/Corbis. 507: Science Museum, London/Topham-HIP/Image Works. 526: (tr) Jason Stemple/Curtis Brown Limited; (bcl) Courtesy Jim Burke. 531: Frank Siteman/AGEfotostock America, Inc. 537: (l) Brand X Pictures/PunchStock; (tr) Ken Cavanagh/Macmillan/McGraw-Hill; (br) Stockbyte/PunchStock. 538-539: Lon Lauber/OSF/Animal Animals/Earth Scenes. 540: George H. H. Huey/Corbis. 540-541: Brand X Pictures/PunchStock. 541: Jeff Foott/Getty Images. 542-543: Stephen Krasemann/NHPA. 544: Jack Barrie/Bruce Coleman. 545: Dave Tipling/Alamy. 546-547: Bruce Clendenning/Visuals Unlimited. 547: Martin J Miller/Visuals Unlimited. 549: (tr) Steve Warble; (b) Brian Vikander. 550: Barbara Gerlach/Visuals Unlimited. 551: (t) Richard Day/Daybreak Imagery; (b) Tom Bean. 552: (tr) Bayard A. Brattstrom/Visuals Unlimited; (b) Rob Simpson/Visuals Unlimited. 553: John Cunningham/Visuals Unlimited. 554: (t) LINK/Visuals Unlimited; (b) John and Barbara Gerlach/Visuals Unlimited. 555: Hal Beral/Visuals Unlimited. 556: Malowski/Visuals Unlimited. 557: John Gerlach/Visuals Unlimited. 558: (tr) Barbara Gerlach/Visuals Unlimited; (b) Joe McDonald/Visuals Unlimited. 559: Tom J. Ulrich/Visuals Unlimited. 560-561: Bruce Clendenning/Visuals Unlimited. 562: (tr) Courtesy Lerner Publishing Group; (b) Martin J Miller/Visuals Unlimited. 562-563: Bruce Clendenning/Visuals Unlimited. 563: (bl) Barbara Gerlach/Visuals Unlimited; (bc) Rob Simpson/Visuals Unlimited; (br) Steve Warble. 564: Mitsuaki Iwago/Minden Pictures. 565: (tl) Steve Kazlowski/Danita Delimont.com; (br) Robert W. Ginn/Alamy. 566: (tl) Inside OutPix/PunchStock; (cl) Renee Morris/Alamy; (bc) blickwinkel/Alamy; (br) Andrew Harrington/Alamy. 567: Royalty-Free/Corbis. 569: Jim Jordan/Getty Images. 570-571: Joel Sartore/National Geographic Image Collection. 572-573: John Cancalosi/Ardea. 573: ZSSD/SuperStock. 590: (tl) Photo by Mimi. Courtesy Rudolfo Anaya; (cr) Courtesy of David Diaz. 597: BananaStock/Alamy. 598-599: William Smithey Jr/Getty Images. 600: Frank Staub/Index Stock Imagery. 601: Corey Rich/Aurora Photos. 602-603: Ken Wilson/Wildfaces. 605: William Campbell/Corbis Sygma. 606: Galen Rowell/Corbis. 609: (cr) PhotoLink/Getty Images; (bc) Ana de Sousa/Shutterstock; (br) Stockbyte/PunchStock. 610-611: Jupiter Images/Comstock/Alamy. 612: (t) Boden/Ledingham/Masterfile; (bl) Brandon Cole Marine Photography/Alamy. 612-613: Boden/Ledingham/Masterfile. 613: Brandon Cole/Visuals Unlimited. 616-629: (bkgd) Wetzel & Company/Janice McDonald. 630: Yuusuke Itagaki, Courtesy Charlesbridge Publishers. 630-631: (bkgd) Wetzel & Company/

Acknowledgments

Janice McDonald. 637: BananaStock/AGEfotostock. 638-639: (bkgd) James Watt/Animal Animals/Earth Scenes. 640: (tr) Amos Nachoum/Corbis; (br) Roger Tidman/Corbis. 640-641: (bkgd) Stephen Frink Collection/Alamy. 642-657: Richard Sobol. 658: (author) Courtesy Robert Sobol. 658-659: Richard Sobol. 663: (cr) Rubberball Productions/Getty Images. 669: (cr) Stockdisc/PunchStock; (br) Tracy Montana/PhotoLink/Getty Images. 670-671: Comstock/SuperStock. 672: Comstock/SuperStock. 673: Underwood & Underwood/Corbis. 672-673: Digital Vision/Getty Images. 674-675: Corbis. 696: Alice Garland. 698-699: Corbis. 699: Dorothea Lange/Stringer/2005 Getty Images. 700: (t) John Springer Collection/Corbis; (c) Bettmann/Corbis. 703: Comstock Images/Alamy. 704-705: The Granger Collection, New York. 722: (tr) Rob Layman; (cl) Courtesy Cornelius Van Wright and Ying-Hwa Hu. 724: James L. Amos/Corbis. 724-725: Joe Ginsberg/Getty Images. 725: (t) Pat Roque/Associated Press; (b) Joe Ginsberg/Getty Images. 726: (t) Victoria & Albert Museum, London/Art Resource, NY. 726-727: Joe Ginsberg/Getty Images. 727: ImageDJ/Jupiter Images. 729: Tipp Howell/Getty Images. 730-731: Damian Dovarganes/AP Photo. 732: Brian Harkin/Getty Images. 733: (all) Taro Yamasaki. 734: Ric Francis/AP Photo. 735 (all) Arthur Schatz/Time Life Pictures/Getty Images. 736-

737: Aurelia Ventura/La Opinion Photos/Newscom. 738: Staples, Inc. 741: (br) Royalty-Free/Corbis; (bc) Ana de Sousa/Shutterstock. 742-743: Randy Olson/National Geographic/Getty Images. 744: Gary Buss/Getty Images. 745: Richard Hutchings/Corbis. 768: (tl) Sharron L. McElmeel/McBookwords LLC; (cr) Courtesy Mary Azarian. 773: ImageState/Alamy. 774-775: Justin Sullivan/Getty Images. 776: (tr) Schenectady Museum; Hall of Electrical History Foundation/Corbis; (bl) W. Dickson/Corbis. 777: Bettmann/Corbis. 796: Courtesy Roz Schanzer. 801: Michael Newman/PhotoEdit. 804-805: Chris Howes/Wild Places Photography/Alamy. 807: (tr) Stockdisc/PunchStock; (br) Photodisc/PunchStock. 808: (l) Digital Vision Ltd./Getty Images; (r) Ingram Publishing/Alamy. 810: Comstock/Alamy. 811: Photodisc Collection/Getty Images. 814: Creatas/SuperStock. 815: Adam Jones/Visuals Unlimited. 818: Jeremy Woodhouse/Getty Images. 819: Charles George/Visuals Unlimited. 821: Mel Curtis/Getty Images. 822: Jeff Foott/Discovery Images/Getty Images. 825: Digital Vision Ltd./Getty Images. 826: (r) S. Solum/PhotoLink/Getty Images; (l) Ingram Publishing/Alamy. 829: Digital Vision Ltd. 830: Peter Yates/Corbis. 831: Robert Harding World Imagery/Getty Images.

834

Use this page to record lessons that work well or need to be adapted for future reference.

Lessons that work well

Lessons that need adjustments

Use this page to record lessons that work well or need to be adapted for future reference.

Lessons that work well

Lessons that need adjustments

Use this page to record lessons that work well or need to be adapted for future reference.

Lessons that work well

Lessons that need adjustments

Use this page to record lessons that work well or need to be adapted for future reference.

Lessons that work well

Lessons that need adjustments

Use this page to record lessons that work well or need to be adapted for future reference.

Lessons that work well

Lessons that need adjustments

Use this page to record lessons that work well or need to be adapted for future reference.

Lessons that work well

Lessons that need adjustments